The Edible South

The Edible

The Edible South

The Power of Food and the Making of an American Region

MARCIE COHEN FERRIS

THE UNIVERSITY OF NORTH CAROLINA PRESS
Chapel Hill

This book was published with the assistance of the Fred W. Morrison Fund for Southern Studies of the University of North Carolina Press.

Manufactured in the United States of America

Designed by
Richard Hendel
Set in Miller, Didot, and Sentinel types by Tseng Information Systems, Inc.

The paper in this book meets the guidelines for permanence and durability of the Committee on Production Guidelines for Book Longevity of the Council on Library Resources.

The University of North Carolina Press has been a member of the Green Press Initiative since 2003.

Complete cataloging information for this title is available from the Library of Congress.
ISBN 978-1-4696-1768-8 (cloth: alk. paper)
ISBN 978-1-4696-1769-5 (ebook)

18 17 16 15 14 5 4 3 2 1

Contents

Preface

I LOOK FOR FOOD IN EVERYTHING

Food catches my attention. I can scan a page of a book or an old letter and find food as though it's highlighted in fluorescent yellow marker. It jumps out at me—snippets of *biscuits*, *cornbread*, *cake*, *preserves*, *elderberry wine*—and pulls me in. My brother-in-law, writer Jim Magnuson, says that when I scan the horizon, the food grid rises up above everything else. When I was a child, my parents, Huddy and Jerry Cohen, asked familiar questions—how was school? the field trip? summer camp? I reported back with detailed descriptions of friends' distinctively southern bag lunches (how come no one else ate my suspiciously Jewish egg-and-olive sandwiches?), the fancy bakery cookies purchased at Goldsmith's downtown department store in Memphis, reports of taboo road food, and platters of fried chicken at Camp Wah-Kon-Dah in Rocky Mount, Missouri. My mother sighed, "What happened *besides* the food?!" We began to see a pattern. For me, food *was* what happened.

Why does food have this magnetic appeal to me, while others seldom note food or, worse, wonder what's the fuss? For the non–food seers, food is banal, so ordinary that it is virtually invisible. For food seekers, it is the boldface headline of life. In the most basic way, food catches my attention because I know what it feels like to eat something delicious, to be hungry, to dislike the taste or texture of a food, to both struggle with food and be enchanted by food. If only for a sentence or a scene, a description of food enriches my understanding. It is a sensual experience, because, in food, an emotional world comes into view—a place of color, imagined tastes, interaction, and memory. Food helps me understand the world around me, but it is also my entry to the past.

Food is the center of our holidays at the farm where my husband, Bill Ferris, was raised in Mississippi. On Christmas Day, the family gathers around the dining room table. The ritual surrounding the preparation for this southern meal is elaborate. Activity begins months in advance as casseroles and desserts are prepared and frozen by Liz Martin, an expert cook and housekeeper. She has worked in culinary tandem with Bill's mother, Shelby Flowers Ferris, for over thirty years. In the last twenty-four hours before the meal, work reaches a crescendo. Bill's three sisters, and now the next generation of grandchildren and nieces and nephews, divide up chores, polishing silver, setting tables, and arranging bowls of camellias. The other meals surrounding Christmas Day are just as important, such as the traditional gumbo we enjoy for supper on Christmas Eve. Eating this meal reminds us of the family's deep ties to New Orleans, the Creole city that has seduced each generation of Ferrises.

Throughout the holiday, we gather daily for breakfast, a hearty noontime dinner, and a light supper in the evening. Mrs. Ferris sits at the head of the table. She is the center of life at the farm. Now in her mid-nineties, she still plans the menus and coordinates our meals. It is difficult to rise before her, at five A.M. each morning. There are fresh grapefruits cut and ready for each of us at our places at the table, designated by napkin rings personalized with our names. These rituals reinforce our southern family and Shelby's love.

Between meals at the farm in Mississippi, we go our separate ways, some to write and read, others to work outside or tend to children. Shelby and her daughters chat and work as they move through the day. In the kitchen, these women, divided now by place and time and their own families, become the family of their childhood once again. When we gather to eat, there is a joy that overlays a quiet sense of grief. The family has suffered many losses, including the death of Bill's brother Grey, his wife, Jann, and their daughter Shelby. Grey's strength and quiet wisdom, Jann's breathtaking beauty and joyful spirit, and Shelby's wit and energy are painfully absent. There is a huge void in the difficult years that follow. Mealtime helps to ease the silent pain we all feel.

In the summer of 2008, we returned to Vicksburg to be with family and to attend Grey's funeral. As everyone gathered, food arrived in an elaborate display of community support and love. Emily Compton and her daughter Dannie arrived with homemade Vicksburg tomato sandwiches, stuffed eggs, tomato aspic, and a beautiful congealed salad of brandied peaches and ginger that glistened like amber. (When my own beloved father died during the summer of 2013, Dannie Weatherly wrote, wishing she could send tomato sandwiches to comfort us in Chapel Hill.) Bobby Ferguson, a talented carpenter and friend of the Ferris family, delivered a casserole prepared by his wife, Elaine, who told us, "I just made what my family loves." There were stiff drinks of bourbon enjoyed with cheese straws, platters of fried chicken and pulled pork, and delicacies brought from New Orleans by Jann's mother, Mittie Terral, whose weekly visits from Louisiana revived the family with gumbos and étouffée. Dr. Eddie Lipscomb, a veterinarian from nearby Port Gibson, brought a pecan-smoked brisket he lovingly prepared for the family. There were strawberry cakes, blueberry pound cakes, caramel cakes, and double fudge brownies baked by Mary Bell Gibbs, whose mother was famous for her brownies, too.

While we attended Grey's funeral in town, Story Stamm Ebersole, a talented Vicksburg caterer, laid out supper for the family—platters of Mrs. Compton's tomato sandwiches and big bowls of chicken salad. Food never tasted as good as that meal. We ate and drank in small groups and later gathered in a large circle around Shelby Ferris, telling family stories until late in the night. Throughout those trying days, food poignantly symbolized the foundations of southern family, community, memory, and tradition. A central purpose of *The Edible South: The Power of Food and the Making of an American Region* is to explore the meaning and influence of food in southern history, extending my analysis beyond one family to that of the larger historical southern family, a people as diverse and as complicated as the region itself.

It is with deep gratitude that I recognize the friends, colleagues, and institutions that made this work possible. I begin with the resilient librarians and archivists who embraced my research. Special thanks are due to Harlan Greene and Dale Rosengarten, Special Collections at the Marlene and Nathan Addlestone Library, College of Charleston; Avery Institute of Afro-American History and Culture, College of Charleston; Christopher Harter and Andrew Salinas, Amistad Research Center, Tulane University; John Dann, Barbara DeWolfe, Clayton Lewis, and Jan Longone, William L. Clements Library, University of Michigan; Georgia Historical Society, Savannah, Georgia; Historic New Orleans Collection; Cynthia Harris and Ashley Stark, Hale Library, Kansas State University; Beverly Brannan, Prints and Photographs Division, Library of Congress; Elizabeth Sherwood and Greg Lambousy, Louisiana History Center; Angela Stewart, Margaret Walker Center, Jackson State University; Clinton Bagley, Hank Holmes, Alanna Patrick, Anne Webster, and Chrissy Wilson, Mississippi Department of Archives and History; Victor Jones Jr., New Bern–Craven County Public Library, New Bern, North Carolina; Susan Tucker, Newcomb Center for Research on Women, Tulane University; W. Troy Valos, Norfolk Public Library, Norfolk, Virginia; Ann Wright, Special Collections, Pack Memorial Library, Asheville, North Carolina; Sarah Hutcheon, Schlesinger Library, Harvard University; Beth Bilderback and Henry Fulmer, South Caroliniana Library, University of South Carolina; South Carolina Historical Society; Amy Evans, Southern Foodways Alliance Oral History Collection, University of Mississippi; Leon Miller, Kenneth Owen, and Eira Tansey, Howard-Tilton Memorial Special Collections, Tulane University; Jerry Ball, Biltmore Industries Collection, and Helen Wykle of the D. H. Ramsey Special Collections Library, University of North Carolina at Asheville. I am also profoundly grateful to Athena Angelos for her thorough research in the Farm Security Administration/Office of War Information Collection, Prints and Photographs Division, Library of Congress. At the High Hampton Inn in Cashiers, North Carolina, Ann Austin and Will McKee graciously granted me access to the High Hampton Inn's papers on site.

I am especially appreciative of the dedicated librarians at the University of North Carolina at Chapel Hill: Jacqueline Solis of Davis Library, who fielded hundreds of my research queries with good humor and the investigative skills of a detective; Laura Clark Brown, Holly Smith, Matt Turi, and former curator Tim West of the Southern Historical Collection; Steve Weiss and Aaron Smithers of the Southern Folklife Collection; Diane Steinhaus of the Music Library; the staff of the Southern Oral History Collection; and the talented graduate students in folklore, history, and library science, including Sam Crisp, Virginia Ferris, Anne Skilton, Helen Thomas, Tim Williams, and Marwa Yousif, who located materials in the Southern Historical Collection for me.

Elizabeth Engelhardt and other scholars offered a close reading of my book manuscript, and their insightful, productive criticism helped my writing and research immeasurably. Robert Allen, Warren Belasco, Fitz Brundage, Bob Cantwell, Rayna Green, Jacqueline Hall, Bernie Herman, Glenn Hinson, Woody Holton, Jim Horton, John Kasson, Joy Kasson, Jim Leloudis, John McGowan, Kathy Roberts, Ann Romines, Ted Rosengarten, Patricia Sawin, Laurel Sneed, Charlie Thompson, Rachel Willis, and Charles Reagan Wilson read numerous fellowship applications and supported my effort, for which I am eternally grateful. Research leaves funded by the University of North Carolina's W. N. Reynolds Grant, the University Research Council, and the Department of American Studies gave me important time to complete my book manuscript. The friendship of colleagues in American studies–folklore and Jewish studies at the university has provided motivation and encouragement. Former American studies administrator Debbie Simmons-Cahan was unwavering in her steadfast support and good cheer. The passion of my students for the narratives that lie within southern food inspired this book. Special thanks to Sara Camp Arnold, Sara Bell, Whitney Brown, Nina Bryce, Laura Fieselman, Tema Larter Flanagan, Chris Fowler, Emily Hilliard, Daniel L. Pollitt, Sarah McNulty Turner, and Emily Wallace for their contributions to this project and to southern food studies.

William Andrews, David Auerbach, Ira Berlin, Hodding Carter III,

Angela Jill Cooley, Josh Davis, Jinny Turman Deal, Walt Edgar, Eli Evans, Rien Fertel, Darryl Gless, Susan Glisson, Kay Goldstein, Mike Green, Minrose Gwin, Hank Haines, Tom Hanchett, Jessica Harris, Reg Hildebrand, Alan and Karen Jabbour, Wilma King, Nick Kotz, Alan Kraut, Lucy Long, Malinda Maynor Lowery, Bobbie Malone, Jere Nash, Jocelyn Neal, Moreton Neal, Frederick Douglass Opie, David Orlansky, Ted Ownby, Dan Patterson, Sharon Paynter, Theda Perdue, Barry Popkin, Larry Powell, Jedediah Purdy, Stuart Rockoff, Leonard Rogoff, Ann Romines, Jamie Simpson Ross, Ruth Salvaggio, David Shields, Vin Steponaitis, Julia Stern, Ann Stewart, Carrie Streeter, John Martin Taylor, John Vlach, Harry Watson, Anne Mitchell Whisnant, Heather Williams, Psyche Williams-Forson, Ashley Young, and Kenneth Zogry all generously responded to my questions and shared their knowledge and experience. The collegiality of Karen Cox and Rebecca Sharpless has been a special gift.

For the opportunity to publish parts of this work during my research and writing, I thank David Davis, John T. Edge, Elizabeth Engelhardt, Ted Ownby, and Tara Powell. Special appreciation is due to Ayse Erginer and Dave Shaw of *Southern Cultures* for creating a standing special issue devoted to food.

As the field of food studies evolves, one of the great pleasures has been to work with local faculty and students in founding the Triangle University Food Studies (TUFS) group. I am especially grateful for TUFS's interest in my work and, most important, for the friendship of the founders of TUFS, Alice Ammerman, Anna Childs, Sharon Holland, Randall Kenan, and Charlie Thompson. There could be no better partners for fostering excellence in food studies than Inger Brodey, Jim Ferguson, and Bernie Herman at the University of North Carolina and Kelly Alexander at Duke University's Center for Documentary Studies (CDS). Much appreciation is also due to Tom Rankin at CDS, Dean Laurie Patton (Duke University), and Dean Karen Gil, Senior Associate Dean Terry Rhodes, and Dean Barbara Rimer (UNC-CH) for their strong support of food studies.

The folks at the Southern Foodways Alliance are "my people," and they provide a warm home where I return annually for excellent food studies scholarship and enduring friendships. It has been my privilege to speak at their conferences and to publish work in their series, *Cornbread Nation: The Best of Southern Food Writing.* Special thanks to SFA director John T. Edge and SFA staff Sara Camp Arnold, Amy C. Evans, Melissa Booth Hall, Mary Beth Lasseter, and Joe York and SFA friends Ann and Dale Abadie, Lex and Ann Alexander, Brett Anderson, Jean Anderson, Jim Auchmutey, Ben and Karen Barker, Scott Barton, Sarah Blacklin, Scott Blackwell and Ann Marshall, Roy Blount Jr., Ann Cashion, Sheri Castle, David Cecelski, Ashley Christensen, Langdon Clay, Maude Schuyler Clay, Nancy Carter Crump, John Currence, Susan Dosier, Crescent Dragonwagon, Nathalie Dupree, Lolis Eric Elie, Belinda Ellis, Barbara Fant, Randy Fertel, John Fleer, Donna Florio, John Folse, Martha and Paul Fogleman, Martha Foose, Sara Foster, Damon Lee Fowler, Sarah Fritschner, Lynn Gammill, Cynthia Gerlach, Peter Hairston, Alex and Betsy Hitt, Blair Hobbs, Linton and Gina Hopkins, Pableaux Johnson, Joyce Emerson King, Phoebe Lawless, Matt Lee, Ted Lee, Jane Lear, Carroll Leggett, Judy Long, Ronni Lundy, Dean McCord, Nancie McDermott, April McGreger and Phil Blank, Kate Medley, Adrian Miller, Debbie Moose, Angie Mosier, Joan Nathan, Sheila and Matt Neal, Davia Nelson, Sandy Oliver, Mollie O'Neill, Louis and Marlene Osteen, Donna Pierce, Carol Puckett, Susan Puckett, Kathleen Purvis, Dale Volberg Reed, John Shelton Reed, Julia Reed, Andrea Reusing, Mike Riley, Sara Roahen, Glenn Roberts, Miriam Rubin, Fred and Jill Sauceman, Kim Severson, Pope and Peggy Shuford, Nikki Silva, Elizabeth Sims, Bill Smith, Leni Sorensen, Pat Stevens, Frank and Pardis Stitt, Marion Sullivan, Fred Thompson, Toni Tipton-Martin, Amy Tornquist, Natasha Trethewey, Michael Twitty, Rob Walsh, Andrea Weigl, Ari Weinzweig, Jay Wiener, Liz Williams, Thomas Williams, Virginia Willis, and Alex Young. The devastating loss of John Egerton, who died in the fall of 2013, was a poignant reminder of the core mission of the Southern Foodways Alliance, which John founded. As the moral anchor of this institution, John urged us to never forget the healing power of food by honoring southern working people and their core culinary heritage. I was blessed to know John's wisdom, humor, kindness, and generosity of spirit.

When Nancie McDermott founded the Culinary Historians of Piedmont North Carolina in Chapel Hill in 2011, she created a gathering place where our community and invited guests can share their food-related passions and talents. I am grateful to Nancie, Claire Cusick, Jill Warren Lucas, Colleen Minton, and Jamie Fiocco and the staff of Flyleaf Books for fostering this intellectual salon. Keebe Fitch, Sandra Gutierrez, Deborah Miller, and Katherine Walton have been so supportive of my work.

At the University of North Carolina Press, I am privileged to work with its devoted, talented team. My editor, Elaine Maisner, patiently nurtured this book from development to completion. Her wise counsel was invaluable. Special thanks are also due to Dorothea Anderson, Kay Banning, Dino Battista, Ivis Bohlen, Kim Bryant, Ellen Bush, Mary Caviness, Robbie Dircks, Michael Donatelli, Chuck Grench, Laura Gribbin, Jennifer Hergenroeder, Gina Mahalek, Ron Maner, Joanna Ruth Marsland, Joe Parsons, Heidi Perov, former editor-in-chief David Perry, Alison Shay, John Sherer, Mark Simpson-Vos, former director Kate Torrey, Paula Wald, and Vicky Wells. On the press's Board of Governors, heartfelt appreciation is due to chair Jack Evans and board member Eric Muller. Rich Hendel designed this book, and I am profoundly thankful for both his friendship and his artistry.

I am deeply grateful to William Eggleston, to his family Rosa, Winston, Andra, and Bill, and to the Eggleston Artistic Trust for permission to use the photograph, *Sumner, Mississippi*, on the cover of my book. William Eggleston's pioneering color photography evokes timeless narratives of the American South. Many thanks to John Hill for sharing his beautiful photograph of Edna Lewis.

Emma Patterson, my literary agent at Brandt & Hochman, lovingly oversaw this project after the loss of our dear friend and agent Wendy Weil in September 2012. Emily Wallace and Gail Goers did extensive work in preparing the manuscript for publication. Emily edited text and finalized footnotes and bibliography, while Gail served as illustration editor, coordinating the herculean task of securing images and permissions. Their combined expertise, talent, and good humor allowed me to deliver my manuscript on schedule. Bob Rudolph, my dear friend and technology guru for over fifteen years, thoughtfully addressed computer issues that ranged from daily maintenance to firestorms, and I am indebted to him for his great skill, fortitude, and calm demeanor. Many thanks are also due to Peter Renfro for his mastery of shipping and scanning.

Friends, family, and dogs sustained me while researching and writing this book. Daily conversations with Meredith Elkins provided encouragement and laughter, as did visits with Kaye Anne Aikins, Sandy Armentrout (of blessed memory), Dick Barnes, Amy Bauman, Denise Broussard, Bill Cox and Judy Rosenfeld-Cox, Elaine Eff, Lyn Gagnon, Sally Greene, Martha Hauptman, John and Sharon Hays, Ryan Hipp, Richard and Lisa Howorth, Bob and Cecelia Jolls, Frank and Harriet Livingston, Scott and Kody Magnes, Bobbie and Bill Malone, James and Susan Moeser, Ellen O'Brien, Susan Harbage Page, Sandi Prentis, Carol and George Retsch-Bogart and the Chapel Hill Sukkot Group, Penny Rich, Lesley Silver, Holly Wagner, Lydia Wegman, Janie Weinberg, Genie and Gilles Wicker, and Shelly Zegart. Special thanks are due to Jack Bass and Nathalie Dupree, Linda and Stephen Bingler, Cathy and Andy Burka, Ernest and Diane Gaines, Kay and Buck Goldstein, Nancy and Ferris Hall, Becky and Bernie Herman, Mary Hartwell and Beckett Howorth, Dorothy and Tom Howorth, Herman and

Nancy Kohlmeyer Jr., Gary and Joan Levy, Etta Pisano and Jan Kylstra, and Bonny Wolf and Michael Levy, who were generous hosts during research trips.

No words can adequately express the appreciation and love I feel for my husband, Bill, and my stepdaughter, Virginia, who weathered the highs and lows of this project. (They also did the grocery shopping and cheerfully ate the same meal for approximately five years as they completed books [Bill] and a master's degree in library science [Virginia].) Bill listened and edited ad infinitum. I am deeply grateful for their support, and for that, too, of our exuberant Labrador retriever, Roper Ferris. I am indebted to Shelby Flowers Ferris, Martha Ferris and Kos Kostmayer, Hester and Jim Magnuson, Shelby and Peter Fitzpatrick, Gene and Joyce Ferris, and the extended Ferris family for their love and constant encouragement, and to my "little" family—my sister, Jamie Cohen, my former brother-in-law, John August, and my mother, Huddy Cohen, as together we endured the loss of my father, Jerry Cohen. This work is dedicated to his memory.

The Edible South

Introduction

To understand a culture, past or present, we should endeavor to understand how a society feeds itself. It is the ubiquity and everydayness of eating that makes understanding it historically so important.
— Gerard Fitzgerald and Gabriella Petrick, "In Good Taste: Rethinking American History with Our Palates"

Throughout southern history, the politics of power and place has established a complex regional cuisine of both privilege and deprivation that continues to impact the daily food patterns of southerners today. Whites, blacks, and Native Americans struggled for control of their bodies and minds, nourishment, livelihood, land, and citizenship. In food lies the harsh dynamics of racism, sexism, class struggle, and ecological exploitation that have long defined the South; yet there, too, resides family, a strong connection to place, conviviality, creativity, and flavor. A constant tension underlies southern history, and that same tension resides in southern foodways, a cuisine largely shaped by the divisive racial history of the region. Contradiction is a central theme in the history of southern food, where the grim reality of slavery, Jim Crow segregation, extreme hunger, and disfranchisement contrast with the pleasure and inventiveness of the region's cuisine. The South cannot claim culinary exceptionalism in the United States or the world. Yet the DNA of our region—its mix of racial and ethnic populations, its politics of colonization, and its abundant food resources—created an extraordinarily rich and dynamic cuisine. Examining the historical arc of food in the American South uncovers the tangled interactions of its people over time, a world of relationships fraught with conflict, yet bound by blood and land.

For decades, scholars of the American South have pondered and interpreted the historical manuscript and print collections of the South, but few have paid close attention to the edible history that lies within these pages. While southern collections of letters, diaries, and journals are filled with food descriptions of the early South, finding them—and interpreting their meanings—remains a challenge. Until recently, food was not included in finding aids and catalog descriptions, except under categories such as "cookery" or "remedies and recipes." Southern historian Anne Firor Scott recalls similar problems locating women in manuscript collections in the 1960s. A former director of the University of North Carolina's Southern Historical Collection often asked her, "Well, Mrs. Scott, have you found any women today?"[1] The turbulent social activism of the 1960s and 1970s spawned a generation of scholars who rejected a vision of the past that ignored ordinary Americans, including women. With their new focus on the "everyday and everydayness," social historians and folklorists embraced the study of material culture, including foodways.

The historic interactions between southerners and food tell us much about this distinctive region. Food reflects both our national and our regional culture as surely as do art, literature, music, politics, and religion. In 1992, literary scholar Peggy Whitman Prenshaw edited a special issue of the *Southern Quarterly* titled "The Texts of Southern Food," in which she described the "complex cultural legacy" of regional foodways.[2] Prenshaw's introduction includes a thoughtful historiography of southern food, which references three classic studies of southern foodways—Sam Bowers Hilliard's *Hog Meat and Hoecake: Food Supply in the Old South, 1840–1860* (1972), Joe Gray Taylor's *Eating, Drinking, and Visiting in the South: An Informal History* (1982), and John Egerton's *Southern Food: At Home, on the Road, in History* (1987).[3] Sam Hilliard, a historical geographer, argued that the South has one of the strongest and most pervasive food cultures in the country, in large part due to the region's poverty, isolation, and historically small number of immigrants. He explored the foodways patterns of both black and white southerners and the ways in which these worlds overlapped and separated. Hilliard used food to define the South as a cultural region and to mark its social boundaries.[4] In his iconic text, historian Joe Gray Taylor created an engaging introduction to southern food history, drawing from a rich canon of the region's primary documents and historical scholarship. Journalist John Egerton, known for his insightful political analysis of the modern South, sought "fresh insights" on race and class by turning to southern foodways.[5] These important works by Hilliard, Taylor, and Egerton marked a turning point in the evolution of southern food history.

Today, food is increasingly recognized as an important tool of analysis in southern cultural and economic history, as well as in the social sciences, yet the challenge of food studies remains food itself. Even now, in the "enlightened" post–women's movement era, cooking and the food-related labor of women are often devalued by some scholars who believe these subjects belong outside the academy, and by contemporary enthusiasts who solely associate food and labor with masculinity, male celebrity, and bravado. Women's voices demand and deserve recognition because they are central to the culinary culture of our nation and to southern foodways.

Food foregrounds the once-silenced voices of those whose hands and minds have so deeply shaped southern cuisine—women in particular—among enslaved cooks, house slaves, and field hands of the antebellum South, the white and black working poor of the post–Civil War South, and food workers of the contemporary industrial South. Historian David Shields notes: "Cuisine implies much more than cooking; it represents a complex expression of community that emerges in a distinct locale and is dependent on soil, agriculture, preparation, and rites of consumption."[6] The detail, the texture of everyday life—pigs smoked, oysters shucked, tamales shaped, cakes baked, chicken fried, bourbon imbibed, corn milled, seeds saved, the *foods shared at a common table and those denied*—enables us to more clearly understand the American South. Southerners know who we are, in part, by the foods we eat and those we don't, a series of complex culinary decisions and patterns shaped by five centuries of historical interaction.

Shifting Southern Borders of Food

In the past, to discuss southern food we would *first* define the borders of the South and theorize about what makes the South distinctive, including its food. The "old" map of the South traditionally referred to the eleven states of the former Confederacy, but today these rigid borders are more fluid. The South "is found wherever southern culture is found," existing "as a state of mind both within and beyond its geographical boundaries."[7] Beyond the question of what constitutes the South's borders, a new vision of Southern Studies challenges conventional tropes of southern identity, including what belongs in the canon of southern food and its bona fide artifacts. The "new Southern Studies" considers landmarks of southern identity *other* than the Civil War, Reconstruction, and barbecue. Rather than the old white-and-black South, the "new Southern Studies" recognizes the diverse cultures and ethnicities of the South, whose global influences shape the region and its foodways.

Southern food is also a barometer of the contemporary South, where a return to local food and small-scale heritage agriculture exists alongside industrial farming. The challenges of our regional food systems—environmental degradation, sustainable agriculture, food access, and food-related disease—are especially acute in the American South, and have been throughout its history. Here again, power is critical to the control of land, mind, bodies, and food. To understand these challenges, we look to the southern past to observe the same factors at play—

exhaustion of cotton and tobacco fields from the colonial era to the Depression, Jeffersonian-inspired models of small subsistence farms, African American land loss, and the early twentieth-century grip of pellagra and hookworm that plagued white and black working poor. We must consider how this history impacts current institutional policy and individual action.

Encountering the Edible South

To approach the unwieldy, vast history of southern foodways, this work highlights selected historical moments, places, and people in the complex narrative of the region's culinary cultures. Rather than being an encyclopedic overview of cuisine, *The Edible South* steps beyond the iconic dishes and recipes of southern food to examine a cultural conversation found in the historical interactions of southerners across time. A comprehensive study of southern foodways is found in the growing canon of southern foodways scholarship. In the pages that follow, I examine an assemblage of evocative voices as they have spoken, written, eaten, celebrated, reformed, and fought for food across the centuries of southern history.

Part 1, "Early South—Plantation South," analyzes the racial and gendered codes of food in the eighteenth- and nineteenth-century South in travel and promotional literature, the diaries of literate white native-born southerners and outsiders who came south for work, the autobiographies and narratives of former slaves, the observations of white missionaries and activists in southern Freedmen's Bureaus and schools for newly freed African Americans, and popular regional cookbooks by white and black southern authors.

Part 2, "New South," considers the early twentieth-century South through a discussion of regional food issues—from the transformation of plantation agriculture to sharecropping and tenant farming's impact on the southern diet. Central institutions in this food-related history include the South's African American educational institutions and white settlement schools and the region's first cooperative extension, home economics, and sociology programs. Progressive-Era social science research and documentary projects also grappled with entrenched racism, poverty, and hunger. This section concludes with a look at twentieth-century efforts to promote and sell the South and its racial mores to both tourists and locals through constructed memories of southern food from the plantation to the mountain South.

Part 3, "Modern South," examines the food landscapes of the region from the segregation of the 1950s to the passage of historic civil rights legislation in the 1960s. Because of caste and the threat of sexual familiarity between the races, whites-only barbecue cafés, bus station restaurants, and dime store lunch counters became battlegrounds during the civil rights movement. Throughout the South, in national parks, in school lunchrooms, and in community fund-raising dinners in mill towns, white and black southerners struggled against racial injustice and labor exploitation often expressed at the table. Part 3 concludes with southern voices from the counterculture food co-ops and farmers' markets of the post–civil rights era, to the birth of "nouvelle/new southern cuisine" and the renaissance of small-scale farming and local food economies in the contemporary South.

Together these worlds speak of an evolutionary South, a place continually pulled back by the past and at the same time wrenched forward into a changing present. Southern food provides access to this place of contradictions, where a cuisine of memory, the region's volatile racial past, and its transformative future lies waiting to be tasted.

I

Early South—Plantation South

From the first exploratory expeditions to the Carolina coast by Europeans in the late sixteenth century to the temporary settlements of the seventeenth-century Chesapeake and the sturdier farmhouses and plantations of the colonial and antebellum South, European and American travelers and naturalists wrote about food they observed and consumed in the American South. Other writers overlooked food in their southern travels because of its ordinariness. Food was *there*, of course, but was not the literary device a particular writer might choose for telling his or her story or remembering particular moments in travels. For writers who *saw* food, descriptions of foods shared by southeastern Indian tribes, the paltry rations of enslaved Africans, and the lavish dining of well-to-do white planters made a story more colorful and more relatable to their readers.

In the chapters in Part 1, we explore culinary conversations in the early South through the end of the plantation era, a world defined by its extremes of wealth and poverty, abundance and hunger, power and impotence. In these narratives lie a series of complex historical interactions centered on the production and consumption of food, as well as *access* to food. In Chapter 1, a variety of literary genres reveal the abundant food landscape of the early South and the core ingredients and methods of southern foodways. In Chapter 2, the negotiation of food production and food service uncovers the culinary dynamics of the slaveholding plantation household. In Chapter 3, the experiences of northern-born teachers and nannies disclose their encounters with the food cultures of the antebellum South. In Chapter 4, the devastating hunger and impoverishment wrought by the Civil War brings to light the food-related tragedies and strategies of this turning point in southern history. In Chapter 5, the food-related politics of Reconstruction-era white southerners speak of both the denial and the gradual acceptance of a South without slavery. In Chapter 6, African Americans resist the inhumanity of slavery in southern kitchens and use food as a tool of empowerment during emancipation and Reconstruction. Finally, in Chapter 7, the canon of nineteenth-century southern cookbooks written by black and white authors proffer a coded grammar of culinary instructions that veiled the monumental changes of the century. By analyzing these voices, we uncover an expressive language of food that expands our understanding of the intersection of race and region in the American South.

I

Outsiders

TRAVELERS AND NEWCOMERS ENCOUNTER THE EARLY SOUTH

The story of food in the South begins at least 13,000 years ago, with the arrival of the First People (rather than the first Europeans) to the American continent. The earliest southerners were nomadic tribes, small groups of people who foraged for food, gathered native plants, hunted wild game, and fished. This subsistent diet marked a level of sustainability unsurpassed by future agriculturists in the South. Native people left bits of their tools behind, such as spear points and scrapers. This artifactual evidence reveals a very different South. Imagine Ice Age bison, ground sloths, and mastodons. Biscuits and fried chicken came *many* millennia later.

Archaeologist Vin Steponaitis argues that by the time Europeans arrived, southeastern Indians of the Mississippian Period, 1000–1500 CE, "had a way of life that was recognizably different from that of the Northern and Western tribes."[1] In Cherokee mythology of the southern Appalachians, the ancestral mother, Selu, bestowed the gift of corn on all Indian people in this era, and her name remains the tribal word for corn.[2] Because a woman goddess gave birth to corn in native tradition, female tribe members continued this gendered labor and became the South's first intensive farmers.[3] According to Steponaitis, just the "sheer quantity" of available food—gathered and cultivated—in the Lower Mississippi Valley "was unsurpassed anywhere on the continent . . . providing the ideal setting for political centralization."[4]

Yet the introduction of agriculture did not begin a wholly progressive arc in the American South. Native people faced health challenges tied to dependence on corn—malnourishment, periodic food shortages, and increased infectious diseases as a result of larger, more permanent settlements.[5] Beyond its long-term impact upon health, scientist Jared Diamond argues that the rise in farming also created deep class divisions and sexual inequality, as those with power seized food, and women were burdened with frequent pregnancies and farm labor.[6] These scenarios occurred not only in the early South, but also in eras to come. A reliance on corn was nutritionally devastating for sharecroppers of the New South and inhabitants of the contemporary industrial South. The intersection of climate, geography, and human society determined the patterns of southern agriculture and foodways across the South for the generations of Native, African, and European Americans who followed. Cultural negotiation and exchange, both peaceful and embattled, created the South's core cuisine.

In 1584, Sir Walter Raleigh commissioned a reconnaissance party to find an appropriate site for a British colony in the New World. It made landfall in the Outer Banks of North Carolina, just above Roanoke Island, and in mid-July began to explore the region. Reports sent to Raleigh suggest the region's wealth of food resources. In *A Briefe and True Report of the New Found Land of Virginia* (1590), Thomas Hariot gave a detailed account of the second journey commissioned by Raleigh. Food was of such significance that Hariot dedicated one section of his report to the foods eaten and grown by the Algonquians, as well as the region's edible natural resources. Hariot's *Report* was illustrated with Theodor De Bry's engravings, based upon the evocative watercolors of John White, who captured the daily activities of the coastal eastern tribe. Six of White's twenty-three watercolors recorded Algonquian foodways.

Native people and European explorers initiated their process of mutual discovery as they cooked, ate together, and shared unfamiliar foods.[7] Communication with and ultimately conquest of the region by Europeans *began* with food. English settlers established the first permanent community in Jamestown on May 14, 1607, at the southern end of Chesapeake Bay, and colonists hoped that forced trade with the Indians for food and the marketing of natural resources would bring a good profit. The central problem for colonists was not finding the imagined cache of gold and other riches, but getting enough food, especially after the Indians withdrew and left the English to manage on their own.

Now remembered for its "starving time," the colony experienced several years of drought, exacerbated by strained relations with the Indians, intense summer heat, and late supply ships. One Jamestown colonist described the "world of miseries" that ensued in the summer of 1609: "Now all of us at James Towne begin to feel the sharp prick of hunger which no man [can] truly describe but he which hathe Tasted the bitterness thereof."[8] Colonists turned to their own dogs, cats, and horses for food, and some did "those things which seem incredible," including digging up corpses out of graves to eat them. One man, so desperate and mad, murdered his pregnant wife and "salted her for his food."[9] A 2012 archaeology discovery in Jamestown confirms this gruesome archival evidence. The remains of a fourteen-year-old English girl were uncov-

Theodor de Bry, "Their Sitting at Meate," engraving based on watercolor illustrations by John White. From Thomas Hariot, *A Briefe and True Report of the New Found Land of Virginia* (1590). "Picturing the New World: The Hand-Colored De Bry Engravings of 1590," North Carolina Collection, Wilson Library Special Collections, University of North Carolina at Chapel Hill.

ered in an early garbage pit. Cut marks on her skull and skeleton suggest that starving colonists resorted to cannibalism, removing the girl's brain and flesh, "presumably to be eaten."[10] By September 1609, more than half the colonists had died of typhoid, dysentery, and, possibly, salt poisoning from tainted drinking water. With Jamestown's mythic place in the American narrative—there are those who lionize it as the first English settlement and those who note its racism and exploitation of Native people and the land—food is crucial to its history, no matter the contested viewpoints about this time.

How could one best describe the exotic South to families living an ocean away, to overseas investors and stockholders backing early exploratory voyages, and to individuals considering making the journey themselves? Thick descriptions of climate, topography, rivers, plants, and animals interested readers, but accounts of how and what people ate were particularly compelling. Detailed reports and illustrations of southern food bridged foreign cultures and distant worlds. Understanding both the foods available in the early South and the shared experience of mealtime were crucial steps in tolerating strangers in a strange land. Other literary expressions in the early South, including the documentary works penned by European-born naturalists, travelers' accounts, and promotional materials written to encourage Old World investors and settlers, delineated the core foods of southern cuisine—cornmeal, greens, cane sugar/molasses, peanuts, field peas, pork, rice, and sweet potatoes—foods that remain on the southern table today. Slavery's rigid control of people and food stands out in these narratives, where racial power established a divided and contradictory southern cuisine of privilege, utility, and deprivation.

A Southern Core Cuisine

Mark Catesby, the early eighteenth-century British naturalist distinguished by his careful observations and evocative illustrations of the flora and fauna of the colonial southeast coast and the West Indies, provided early descriptions of "Frumentum Indicum, Maiz Dictum: Indian Corn." Catesby noted that everyone—both enslaved African Americans and white settlers in Virginia and Carolina—ate corn. They prepared it in many ways, but "three principally," which sound familiar to native southerners, even today. The first was pone, "heavy, though very sweet and pleasant, while it is new." The second was corn mush, "in the manner of hasty-pudding," eaten by "Negroes with cider, hog's-lard, or molasses." The third method was hominy, in which kernels of corn were boiled until tender. Milk or butter was added, creating a dish "generally more in esteem than any other preparation of this grain."[11] Cooking the hominy with "a mixture of bonavis," a type of kidney bean, is similar to the Lowcountry dish "hoppin' John," a West African–derived mixture of field peas and rice, seasoned with a bit of fat meat and salt and pepper. Catesby recorded that "phaseoli," or kidney beans, were "of great use for feeding Negroes, being a strong hearty food."[12] Slave owners favored economical foods for enslaved workers that were easily acquired and grown and that also provided the necessary calories and nutrition to sustain their "property."

Catesby's list of "common European culinary plants" and fruits that grew well in the Carolina climate—carrots, parsnips, turnips, peas, beans, cabbage, "colliflowers," apples, blackberries, figs, peaches, pears, thyme, savory, and "all aromatik herbs"—suggest the flow of plant materials between England and the American South.[13] An early eighteenth-century letter from Elizabeth Hyrne, who came with her husband and young family to South Carolina's rice country, is filled with requests for goods from England, including desperately needed pots and pans, seeds and seedlings. She reminded her brother in Lincolnshire to "writ upon every paper of seeds what they be. . . . Any one thath hath a garden will give you seeds or plants if they have to spair."[14] Hyrne closed her letter with a request for a crucial object to a young mother attempting to replicate the proper culinary routines of English family life in the American South. She wrote, "Send my son a high cane chair with a table to it."[15]

The non-heading, leafy greens that Europeans referred to as "coleworts"—a term that evolved into "collards"—also came with early settlers to the southern colonies, where different varieties—collards, mustard, turnip, kale—thrived across the region.[16] Usually planted in August, the plants mature in just over two months, providing a steady supply of nutritious greens throughout the winter. Leafy greens persevered in the American South's "collard belt" from eastern North Carolina to Mississippi, while cabbage, which could be shipped more successfully, eventually replaced greens as a market crop in England.[17] Enslaved cooks embraced southern-grown greens as they had in West Africa, where similar plants were a critical part of local foodways. For generations, cooks valued the "cut and come again" ability of the plant to regenerate as leaves were picked for eating throughout the winter, a traditional time of food scarcity.

Pigs arrived with the earliest European explorers, including Christopher Columbus in 1493 and Hernando de Soto in 1539, who brought livestock to the Caribbean and the early South, respectively. From early on, southerners chose pork over beef, given the region's focus on staple money crops rather than grazing lands for livestock. Pork was easily salted and smoked in a manner that southerners preferred, but not so with beef, which was difficult to keep any length of time.[18] Most beef was eaten quickly, while the meat was fresh. Pigs were easier and cheaper to raise in the South, as the animals could find winter forage in the woods. The exceptional taste of southern pork was also attributed to the rich mast—the acorns and nuts—that pigs encountered in the southern forest.

One promotional tract, a "True Relation of South Carolina, an English Plantation, or Colony in America," published in 1712, posed a conversation between "James Freeman, a Carolina Planter," and "Simon Question, a West-Country Farmer."[19] Freeman described southern planters who "raised great stocks" of hogs because of their profitability. Pigs grazed freely during the day and then each evening were called home, "at the lowd sound of a horn," tempted by surplus rations of "corn, pease, pompeons, potatoes, peaches, or whatever else is allow'd to cause them to remember their home."[20] In the heat of a southern summer, pigs, like people, enjoyed watermelons, too. "They are a fine cooling pleasant sort of fruit in the hottest months," noted Freeman, "and the overplus, or offel, we throw to our hogs, and plant the more of them for that use."[21]

John Martin Bolzius, a German minister who came to coastal Georgia with a group of his co-religionists in 1734, sent information on the colony's foodstuffs and the dietary preferences of the locals to his colleagues in Europe.[22] His writings were a primer on the core foods of the southern Lowcountry, including the region's ubiquitous peanuts, rice, and sweet potatoes. "Peanuts and potatoes are not the same thing," wrote Bolzius.[23] One might confuse them, both growing underground, but he explained that "the peanuts have a shell, a little harder than an eggshell, and if fried in ashes or in the baking oven they taste as good as hazelnuts."[24] He recommended potatoes as a tasty, quickly prepared, nutritious food, particularly good for "heavy workers," referring to enslaved field hands.[25] "The best and most profitable crop is rice," he wrote, "which is planted to great advantage by those who have Negroes."[26] Excess rice, Indian corn, beans, potatoes, beef, and pork grown in the colony were traded for West Indian sugarcane brandy, syrup, brown sugar, and Madeira.[27] Bolzius dismissed the opinions of local whites, who argued that slaves were "stupid and not inclined to learn."[28] He criticized white slaveholders for their inhumane treatment of enslaved people and for failing to "keep them in a Christian way regarding *food*, clothing, work, and marriage."[29]

Just as Bolzius and Catesby introduced their readers to the highly regulated food codes of plantation slavery, including which foods were favored as "hearty" rations for enslaved workers, traveler Janet Schaw described the heady worlds of the white plantation elite in the Caribbean, including the elaborate food, wine, and hospitality that slavery made possible. In these privileged southern worlds, Schaw alluded to the African American cooks, who would forever shape the core cuisine of the American South with the flavors and cooking methods of their West African homelands.

A self-described "Lady of Quality," Schaw kept a journal of her travels with a small party of friends and family who sailed from their native Scotland to the West Indies, North Carolina, and Portugal in 1774.[30] She recounted the perilous journey at sea, losing much of the ship's stores of food during a terrible storm, and, upon their safe arrival in the Caribbean, enjoying Scottish friends' island hospitality. After settling into their lodgings on Antigua, a servant brought Schaw a refreshing glass of *sangarie*—brandy or wine mixed with spices and water.[31] They enjoyed a sumptuous "family dinner" at the sugar plantation of a

"Mr. Halliday," which Schaw noted in detail for "her *eating* friends" back home in Scotland.[32]

The elaborate ritual and number of courses served at the Antigua plantation table demonstrate the great wealth that slavery made possible on the brutal sugar plantations of the West Indies, as well as the melding of Afro-Caribbean and Anglo-European foods and manners. The dining table was laid with three rows of dishes, six dishes in a row in the high-style manner of "courtly" eating influenced by Continental manners.[33] The "courtly" style of the elite required more elaborate cooking equipment, better quality foodstuffs, and imported spices, sugar, nuts, and wines as compared to the simple food preparations of middling English women, who largely boiled meat or roasted it on a spit.[34]

Schaw and the other dinner guests encountered an abundant dinner table laid with a tureen of turtle soup dramatically displayed at the head of a middle row of fish, including local varieties such as "king fish," grouper, mullet, and snapper.[35] On the table's side rows were dishes of "guinea fowl," a West African favorite and precursor of southern fried chicken; turkey; mutton; beef, salted and brought by the barrel from New England; "fricassees" of vegetables; and pickles.[36] The second course of pastry, puddings, jellies, and preserved fruit included a dish of "palmetto cabbage," a delicacy made from a species of local palm tree.[37] Dessert was "thirty two different fruits," such as citrus, pineapples, pears, guava, and grapes.[38] This lavish meal, including multiple courses of soup, fish, several meats, vegetable side dishes, pickled items, and many desserts, suggests the culinary contours of well-to-do white landowners in the plantation South.

The host's performance of position and power at his Caribbean dining table gave Schaw pause, comparing the elaborate meal to that of a lord mayor or duke in England. She did not seem to take into account the human cost of such excess: "Why should we blame these people for their luxury? since nature holds out her lap, filled with every thing that is in her power to bestow, it were sinful in them not to be luxurious."[39] Although Schaw did not mention the enslaved West African cooks who prepared the meal, their presence—and the worlds they and their families had been forced to leave behind—was experienced in every dish on the table, including the red pepper–flavored sauce served with the fish and "a little [pepper] pod laid by every plate."[40] A typical West African meal as the enslaved cooks would have known it in their countries of origin included a starch (rice, millet, or manioc) or a fish dish, served with a vegetable-based sauce or relish, much like the peppered-flavored sauce served to Schaw and her party.[41]

Europeans and Visitors from the North

"The Grand Tour"

Drawn by both professional interests and a desire to observe the plantation South and the institution of slavery, the number of European travelers grew to its apogee in the antebellum era.[42] They were Europeans, both anonymous travelers and well-known chroniclers such as Harriet Martineau (England), Alexis de Tocqueville (France), and Fredrika Bremer (Sweden), as well as Americans, including the most recognized documentarian of antebellum life, Frederick Law Olmsted (Connecticut).[43] They came to the South on horseback, by train, and by steamboats down the Ohio and Mississippi Rivers, following a route, or "grand tour," which was popular by the 1830s.[44] Southern cuisine wove in and out of their accounts of travel. Slavery historian John Blassingame explains: "Much of what the traveler saw was new to him. Consequently, he was much more likely to comment on things which resident whites accepted as commonplace."[45] And what was more commonplace than food? Travelers described savory—and unsavory meals—at roadside taverns and urban "hotels," refreshments taken in the modest homes of farmers, elegant feasts hosted by wealthy planters, the quality and quantity of slave rations, and participation in festive barbecues and holiday celebrations.

Davis Thacher, a young man seeking adventure and employment as a tutor in the South, left his home in Apponganset, a small bayside town in southeastern Massachusetts, in 1816.[46] His brothers accompanied him to nearby New Bedford, where he took a sloop to New York City and continued by boat to Charleston, South Carolina. After failing to find a job in Charleston, Thacher attended a January 1817 court session, "having no better business" to fill his time. He described a case in which food featured prominently. "Yesterday and today attended the trial of the cook and cabin boy of the Sch.[ooner] Maria, Capt. Lathan, who were indicted for poisoning the crew and passengers while off the capes of Virginia."[47] Although he was "frequently with the cook, and was seen to smile when he was told the mate was sick," the cabin boy was found not guilty.[48] The young man "promised to return to his parents and quit the seas forever."[49] The cook, a free black man from New York, was tried next. A passenger had offended him before they left New York, and the cook threatened to "pepper their soup."[50] The cook was found guilty and sentenced to hang on February 21, 1817. "I think he would have been cleared had he had a white face," wrote Thacher.[51] This persistent trope of an African American cook who poisoned or tainted food to avenge abuse by whites was a constant in period narratives, post–Civil

War memoirs, and segregation stories of the Jim Crow South, and it still endures in popular books and film and in other media.

Thacher eventually found work as a tutor for a doctor and his family on a nearby plantation in Christ Church Parish. He described fishing one night with a companion, "by the light of torch," and returning just before sunrise. "I caught 62 sea crabs, twelve stone crabs, and 7 cooters. . . . The stone crabs have claws as large as our largest lobsters—the cooters are a species of sea turtle . . . esteemed by the natives—make excellent soup."[52] Writers like Thacher recorded what we would refer to today as *terroir*, the sense of place embodied in everyday life. As folklorist Bernie Herman explains, "More than the taste of place . . . [*terroir*] defines the particular attributes of place embodied in cuisine and narrated through words, actions, and objects. It captures a consciousness of association and belonging."[53] Thacher's nocturnal fishing adventure in the Carolina Lowcountry was an initiation—a food-centered ritual of place—that made him feel a part of the South.

John Boynton was twenty-six years old when he left New England to seek a teaching position in the South in 1836. His letters to family describing his travels south from Massachusetts to New York, to the Chesapeake, and eventually to Mississippi, reveal a contradictory mix of racism and public disavowal of slavery and southern culture. Looking at enslaved laborers in a Maryland tobacco field, Boynton was reminded "of what I have witnessed at home—a platter of baked beans with a large quantity of black ones among them. No reflections on baked beans by the way."[54] Boynton's food metaphor suggests a common attitude of whites—northern and southern—who casually disregarded the humanity of enslaved workers.

Boynton was overwhelmed by the worlds he encountered in rural Mississippi. He wrote his father, "It would take more than 19 full letters to tell you the half of what I've seen in one week."[55] He hunted wild turkey, deer, and a strange animal to him, "opossums by scores. Had one for dinner today—first rate."[56] Boynton tired of the constant conversation of "Land and Negroes—Land and Negroes."[57] Clearly, white wealth was represented by investment in both property and people. Enslaved women were not "worth so much [as men]," Boynton noted, yet "a good cook, however, is worth $2000."[58] Local cooking appeared to be done "entirely by the slaves."[59] Boynton described his own "comfortable situation," and how an enslaved boy saw to his every need. Yet he assured his father, "Slavery is slavery, still any way you can fix it. . . . I trust to give my views in full on this subject, but I cannot do it while I am an inhabitant of this southern clime."[60]

Another New Englander, Jeremiah Evarts, who later became a Christian missionary and activist for Cherokee rights, traveled through the South in the 1820s.[61] There he experienced the untold wealth and privilege of the Sea Island cotton plantations. After a long day on horseback in coastal Georgia in March 1822, Evarts was invited to dine with a physician at his Savannah table. He was assured the meal would be "plain . . . without company and without ceremony."[62] "Dinner was best drumb fish, with appropriate dressings," wrote Evarts, "ducks, and southern bacon, oysters cooked in two ways, Irish potatoes in two ways, beets, onions, bread, and boiled rice."[63] (Drum fish are found along the Atlantic and Gulf coasts and have remained an important food source from the colonial period until the present. The fish makes a distinctive "drumming" sound by popping its air bladder.)[64] After the main course, "then came cherry-pye, cranberry-pye, quince, orange and other preserves, with salad, cheese, butter, and cream (beat to a foam with a flavor from juice of pine-apple) . . . then came oranges, plaintains, raisins, and walnuts with several sorts of cordials and wine."[65] Evarts criticized the luxury of the so-called plain meal and the extravagance of his hosts. "Yet this was a dinner made for invalids. . . . O that men would spend their money as cheerfully in the service of their Maker, as they do for their own gratification."[66]

After visiting a nearby plantation on the Sea Island of Daufuskie, where the food was also "abundant and of great variety," Evarts noted, "How all these things could be cooked would puzzle a northern man."[67] This display of excess was at the core of southern cuisine and pointed to the enslaved labor behind the production and preparation of plantation meals. The state of slaves, he wrote, "is abject beyond my powers of description."[68] Evarts pointed out the irony that those who prepared such abundance for the master had "rarely tasted flesh."[69] Their daily fare was "coarse and scanty."[70] As an outsider, Jeremy Evarts, like John Boynton and Davis Thacher, witnessed dizzying southern worlds in which even the simple act of eating uncovered a society in constant opposition—labor versus indolence, privilege versus hardship, freedom versus enslavement, abundance versus scarcity, and civility versus inhumanity.

Southern Hospitality

The "big eating" frequently included in the descriptions of southern meals was a central aspect of the social practices of white southerners referred to as "southern hospitality." Historian Edmund Morgan noted this culinary sociability among white elites in colonial Virginia, where he described dining as "a fine art."[71] Yet the dining table, the "ritual center of Virginia hospitality," was not accessed with ease.[72] Architectural historian Dell Upton counted numerous "social barriers"—from formal parks, driveways, and raised terraces to doorways, loggias, and entry halls—that a visitor passed through to reach John Tayloe's dining room at Mount Airy in Richmond County, Virginia.[73] Each boundary emphasized the master's power.[74] In 1828, a Maryland traveler referred to the white citizens of Natchez, Mississippi, as "peculiarly hospitable."[75] "It seems to be their chief delight to entertain strangers," he wrote, "and the greatest harmony and social intercourse exists among them."[76] Rogene "Genie" Scott, a young teacher from Vermont, came to the South to work for a number of slaveholding families in the late 1850s. Soon after her arrival, she determined that southerners "justly deserve the appellation of 'hospitable'" and reflected on their ability to make one feel at ease in their homes, "which is not always the case in my own loved New England."[77] Scott's assessment reflects historian David Hackett Fisher's quip that "Virginias dined," while "New Englanders merely ate."[78] As months passed and Scott observed the daily injustices of slavery, her comments about the hospitality of her hosts ceased. In Norfolk, Virginia, British architect Benjamin Latrobe dined with welcoming locals but had no kind words for the particular mix of dishes served at one time. After the meal, he observed, "If there is morality in cooking, this must be culinary adultery."[79]

Susan Dabney Smedes tied the hospitality of her father's Virginia family to English ancestry in her late nineteenth-century nostalgic account of plantation life. She spoke of "sons of noble houses" who brought the customs and manners of the Old World to the South.[80] Associating white southerners with British nobility was a familiar narrative of the "Cavalier Myth," which emerged in the mid-1830s and continued to inspire white southerners even up to the early twentieth century. Smedes considered the tidewater region of Virginia as "truly English," where "everybody kept open house; entertaining was a matter of course, anything and everything was made the occasion of a dinner-party."[81] Aspiring and well-to-do white women of the South expressed this longing for gentility through the hierarchy and ritual of domestic hospitality. Hosts displayed their largesse, which guests enjoyed, but "at the cost of independence" and indebtedness.[82]

Swedish travel writer Fredrika Bremer found the performance of southern hospitality overbearing and tedious at the table of her Macon, Georgia, hosts in May 1850. In Sweden, guests paid more attention to conversation than the display of manners she observed at the table of elite white southerners. She was annoyed that guests could not help themselves and instead depended on other guests and servants. "You seldom get just what you wish for, or as much or as little as you want, and not on the part of the plate where you wish to have it."[83] Bremer described a scene of pickle persecution. A guest is offered and declines pickles. Another guest observes that her neighbor's plate is pickle-less. Pickles are offered again, and once more refused. Just when the guest is "waiting for some reply interesting to you," a servant appears, "and with horror you behold pickles ready to be put upon your place. . . . Thus goes on the meal—one incessant bustle of serving, which takes away all enjoyment of the food.[84] As an outsider, Bremer saw irony in southern hospitality where guests were held "hostage" at the table, beholden to the master and mistress of the household.

Another inversion of southern hospitality—the inhumane practice of denying enslaved people sufficient fresh food for rations, as well as the sadistic use of food by slaveholders as a means of control and punishment—was noted by travelers like Jeremiah Evarts and Fredrika Bremer, who were astonished at the discordant scenes of plenty and starvation they witnessed. Bremer discussed the "deeds of cruelty" suffered by house slaves in South Carolina: "Some of the very blackest of these deeds have been perpetuated by women; by women in the higher class of Charleston society! . . . Ah! the curse of slavery . . . has fallen not merely on the black, but perhaps at this moment still more upon the white."[85] Reality constantly shifted as outsiders assessed what lay beneath the fine dining and good manners of affluent white southerners.

Two diary entries set in Charleston almost fifty years apart reflect the stunned reactions of newcomers to the South as they confronted the complicated racial "etiquette" of white elites at the table. In 1785, Timothy Ford, a graduate of Princeton, moved to Charleston, South Carolina, to pursue his law career at the age of twenty-three. Visitors like Ford were enthralled by the architecture and beauty of Charleston, but they also noted the city's enslaved labor force—the great numbers of slaves and their living conditions and how slavery impacted slaveholders and daily life.[86] "The most obvious division of the inhabitants of Charleston is into *Black* & *White*," noted Ford, "the former being to the latter as 5 to one."[87] The number of servants that attended slaveholding white Charlestonians at mealtime took Ford aback. "They surround the table like a cohort of black guards."[88]

Mary Reed Eastman, a young white woman from Massachusetts on a "wedding journey" with her minister husband, Ornan Eastman, in 1832, arrived in Charleston by ship, where they enjoyed the hospitality of New England friends, "Dr. and Mrs. Porter."[89] South Carolina was just one stop in the more than 5,000 miles they traveled from Massachusetts down the East Coast to Augusta, Georgia, then west to New Orleans and back home via the Mississippi and Ohio Rivers. Like Timothy Ford, Mary Eastman was intrigued by the rituals of race and service at the Porters' home, where she observed a similar "cohort" of enslaved staff attending the dinner table. What extravagant place was this where the white hostess ruled with such studied effortlessness and black servants wore gold watches? "There were 12 at the table, and 4 slaves in attendance, who were constant in offering to us all the table afforded, with hardly a look from the mistress—one black man who seemed the head of the department, was handsomely dressed and had his gold watch chain and seal."[90] Through their enslaved labor and the world of material goods displayed in their home and at the dining table, the Porters demonstrated their wealth and status in Charleston society.

The formal and working courtyards behind the home also fascinated Mary Eastman, who observed "trees and shrubs—cows and poultry, attached to most of the houses—the kitchen is in a separate building, a small two story house in the yard."[91] These were the worlds of Charleston's back lots, of "unseen Charleston," where enslaved laborers worked and lived in outbuildings or in rented rooms.[92] Controlling enslaved African Americans in private workspaces, as well as in public arenas such as the city's market halls, became a matter of great concern to white Charlestonians after the Denmark Vesey slave insurrection in 1822.[93]

Eastman was aware of the tightened regulations and surveillance of enslaved workers and free blacks as she walked through the newly built marketplace in Charleston. "The bells of the City ring at ¼ before 9 [at night]. At 9 the drums beat and the colored people all retire. A watch is set over the City, and any black, who is in the street after 9 without a passport from his master, is taken and confined."[94] White slaveholders could not pretend that participants in the Vesey uprising were radical outsiders; confessions from slaves revealed a plot in which house servants planned to kill their masters with the domestic tools they had at hand.[95] The supposed innocence of the kitchen and the loyalty of enslaved cooks was called into question as knives for chopping vegetables and scaling fish were imagined as implements of murder.[96] Increasingly, kitchens were positioned so slaveholders could better observe their workers, and servants' presence in the family home was limited as much as possible.[97]

From here, we enter the interior of the plantation household, guided by members of the white plantocracy, whose diaries and writings are filled with narratives of the daily power dynamics entwined in food preparation, service, and eating. Like the authors of travel literature in the early

South and antebellum period, white southern-born diarists and correspondents used the expressive power of food to describe their lives, and in doing so, they revealed details about both the planter's table and the rations in the slave quarters. Centuries later, these historic culinary encounters add color, nuance, and texture to our understanding of the complex negotiations of slave society and the plantation economy.

2

Insiders

CULINARY CODES OF THE PLANTATION HOUSEHOLD

Contradictory dominions of food caught the attention of explorers, documentarians, and travelers as they experienced the early South, but a critical hearth of southern culinary cultures—the plantation household—is most clearly seen in the writings of southern-born diarists and correspondents in the antebellum period. White mistresses and masters of the plantocracy were central players in the intricate interplay of power and palate. Knowing one's place in the hierarchy of the plantation household was paramount. White slaveholding wives fell in step below their husbands, with daughters below sons, but the mistress also recognized her authority as overseer of the household—the central location of production and reproduction in the antebellum South.[1] Food was at the center of this domestic economy. Planters' wives presided over enslaved laborers, who tended vegetable gardens and small livestock, maintained dairy operations, preserved food, cooked daily meals, and waited on white families at table. As household administrators, mistresses controlled the distribution of foodstuffs. With keys to locked larders in hand—the symbol of their authority—white slaveholding women both excelled and chafed at the responsibility of feeding their "families," black and white.[2] A complex dynamic ensued as planters' wives and enslaved cooks negotiated influence in these culinary spaces. The knowledge of experienced black cooks served as a currency of gendered power bound by the limits of slavery.

The one-dimensional stereotype of the plantation mistress as a delicate and cultured lady of leisure was toppled by a generation of women social historians in the 1970s and 1980s.[3] Their exhaustive analysis of white slaveholding women's diaries, journals, and correspondence revealed a more accurate picture of the plantation mistress and her responsibilities.[4] Some had superior skills in housekeeping and managing enslaved workers, while others had none. Feelings about their duties ranged from joy and satisfaction to frustration, anger, and deep despair. Regardless of their success or failure in the culinary arts and the domestic worlds they ruled, white slaveholding women wrote about food, the table, and the garden, assuming different voices as dutiful and neglectful mothers, as accomplished and awkward hostesses, as skillful and frustrated housekeepers, and as willing and resentful managers of slaves. Many white slaveholding men were also avid diarists and record keepers, keeping detailed accounts of plantation food and crop yields and slave work assignments, including sicknesses, births, and deaths of slaves as well as descriptions of special plantation occasions, hunting and fishing expeditions, and fashionable meals and fetes in their urban townhouses. Decoding the culinary narratives in these descriptions of plantation society makes audible the constant undercurrent of power maintained and resisted within an irreconcilable society of "haves" and "have-nots" in the antebellum South.

The Lowcountry White Elite

In Conversation with Food

Among the thousands of diaries, journals, and letters that document the white aristocracy of the southern plantation household, iconic voices reveal the inner workings of the region's cuisine and how it was shaped by human innovation, an abundant natural food system, and slavery. One of the earliest of these southerners was planter Eliza Lucas Pinckney of the South Carolina Lowcountry. A figure of the Enlightenment, Pinckney was known for her intellectual curiosity and deep interest in science and reason. Her lifetime conversation with food, captured in letters and diaries, is enlivened by the extensive food-related writings of the plantation elite—two of her children, Harriott Pinckney Horry and Charles Cotesworth Pinckney, and a cousin, Mary Motte Alston Pringle. Inside these social rings of the Lowcountry, we encounter John Berkley Grimball, a wealthy planter, Fanny Kemble, an English-born actress-turned–plantation mistress, and Judah P. Benjamin, the Jewish attorney who rose to become a distinguished leader of the Confederacy. Their voices communicate daily dramas and relationships of racial and gendered power in the details of food preparation and service. These food-related narratives conclude with the domestic voice of a Lowcountry wife and mother, Mary Elizabeth Pearson Boyce, whose quiet diary entries of the 1850s belie the oncoming Civil War.

Eliza Lucas was just seventeen years old when she was left in charge of her family's three South Carolina plantations after her father returned to Antigua in the British West Indies. She managed over 5,000 acres and the hundreds of enslaved people who worked the land. Lucas was well known for her experimentation with edible plants, seeds, and crops new to South Carolina in the 1730s. In a 1742 letter to her brother, she described her large fig orchard and her plans to export its dried fruit. After carefully figuring her expenses and profits, Lucas concluded, "I love the vegitable world extremely."[5] In 1744, Eliza Lucas married a nearby planter, Charles Pinckney, with whom she had three children.

Harriott Pinckney Horry, Eliza Lucas Pinckney's daughter, inherited her mother's passion for agriculture and botany, taking on the management of her husband's Lowcountry plantations after his death, where she, too, experimented with plants and developed new technologies for rice cultivation. Rather than assuming the roles of "deputy husbands and daughters" by *temporarily* taking over the business responsibilities of absent husbands and father, Eliza Lucas Pinckney and Harriott Pinckney Horry remained active managers and businesswomen, as well as wives and mothers, throughout their adult lives. Historian Constance Schulz argues that both women "transcended the 'separate spheres' to which their gender might have confined them."[6] In the spring of 1791, George Washington stopped for noon dinner at the Horrys' Hampton Plantation to express his gratitude for the family's service during the Revolutionary War. Harriott Horry and her mother greeted Washington, as did Pinckney's granddaughters, who were bedecked in sashes with the president's likeness.[7]

In 1815, Horry traveled to New England and recorded observations about the places she experienced, including the food. Horry's party stopped in Richmond, Virginia, where they stayed in the lodgings of Mary Randolph, well known for her hospitality and culinary fare. In 1824, Randolph published the first regional American cookbook, *The Virginia House-Wife, or Methodical Cook*. This work is also recognized as the earliest southern cookbook published in the region. Horry began a journal of her favorite recipes in 1770, as her mother had done twenty years earlier.[8] A compilation of dishes from her mother, friends, and printed sources, Horry's recipe journal reflects the melding of American, African, Caribbean, English, French, and Native American flavors and cooking methods, seen in recipes for "curing Bacon in Virginia," rice bread, charlottes (a layered dessert of fruit, custard, and sponge cake), Shrewsbury Cakes (a buttery sugar cookie), and sausages mixed with West Indian spices.[9]

As an "absentee proprietor" who lived in Charleston, Horry's brother, Charles Cotesworth Pinckney, kept a diary concerning his Sea Island plantation in South Carolina's "old Beaufort District."[10] The seasonality of the southern table is captured in Pinckney's descriptions of springtime foods and planting. Cows gave milk, chickens laid eggs, and cool weather crops of cauliflower and broccoli were harvested from the garden. Cured hams, hog shoulders, and sides prepared the previous fall were taken from the storeroom to eat, while freshly butchered cuts of hog meat were hung in the smokehouse. Enslaved field hands completed the spring planting of Pinckney's cotton, sweet potatoes, Irish potatoes, corn, and oats.[11]

Pinckney's records of drum fishing in April 1818 suggest the scale of this activity and how the catch was distributed to plantation slaves, who depended on the food to supplement their seasonal rations: "April 6th. Left Charleston in the Steamboat with my daughters at 6 o'clock this morning. April 7th. Arrived at the Island about nine o'clock this morning. Sent the Boat a Drum fishing and caught 7 Drum. Gave a Drum to each of the overseers and one among the fishermen."[12] Master and slaves worked multiple fishing lines from a boat and on a good day could bring in a haul of twenty fish, which weighed between thirty and eighty-five pounds apiece.[13] The large, active drum fish were valued for both sport and food. Pinckney counted a total of 219 drum fish caught in the 1818 spring season, which lasted just over five weeks.

While the drum fish were running, Pinckney divided the catch among his overseers and slaves. Overseers received whole fish, while the slaves at Pinckney's plantation received "14 heads, 19 backbones, and 37 sides of Drum fish."[14] Although a "side of drum" was a choice food, giving slaves the less desirable parts of an animal, such as the fish head and backbone, or the hog's tail, brain, gizzard, and chitterlings, was typical on most southern plantations. Enslaved cooks improvised cooking methods that transformed tougher cuts, as well as offal—the entrails and internal organs of a butchered animal—into tasty dishes.[15]

The Pinckneys' cousin, Mary Motte Alston Pringle, was the mistress of the Miles Brewton home in Charleston, a large household in which twenty-two slaves cared for the twelve white members of the Pringle household in 1850.[16] By 1860, thirty-two slaves served the six Pringles living in the Brewton home.[17] Mary Pringle, like her cousin Harriott and her great-aunt Eliza Lucas Pinckney, kept a journal of recipes and household remedies, which included typical Lowcountry recipes for "rice cakes for breakfast," oyster soup, "shrimps in vinegar," the "Baltimore method for cooking terrapin," and, in a home full of finely crafted furniture, important directions for how "to polish mahogany."[18] More revealing of the complicated domestic relationships of power, status, and race is Pringle's "Household Inventory Book," which she kept between 1834 and 1865. Mary Pringle oversaw her household with "an almost scientific precision," as seen in her daily and annual accounts of domestic artifacts, ranging from those of great value—the family silver—to those of little note—the weekly piece of soap and "osnaburgs" or linen towels dispensed to the household slaves.[19] From her locked storeroom, Pringle gave the cook daily cooking supplies of "1½ quarts of whole rice,

Kitchen, Miles Brewton House (west end, south side), 27 King Street, Charleston, South Carolina. Historic American Buildings Survey, HABS SC, 10-CHAR, 5B-3. Prints and Photographs Division, Library of Congress, Washington, D.C.

1 pint corn grist, 1 pint rice flour, a spoonful of lard," and, for the washing of household linen, "1 quart of rice *every Monday* for starch."[20] Mary Pringle, or a slave in her stead, purchased fruits, vegetables, poultry, meat, and fish each day at Charleston's Market Hall.[21]

John Berkley Grimball's 1832 diary reveals the gendered significance of a "proper" table in Charleston, where elegant food and service reflected not only on a mistress's domestic skills, but also on the master's masculinity, wealth, and power. Grimball was as concerned with his family's class position and status among the wealthy white elite of Charleston as Charles Pinckney was in charting drum fish and crop yields and Mary Pringle was in keeping accounts of her tea towels and "kitchen things." Both John Berkley Grimball and his wife, Margaret Ann "Meta" Morris Grimball, kept extensive diaries written from their Charleston, South Carolina, home and their rice plantation located in the Colleton District in the southeast region of the state.[22] Like the Pinckneys and other white Lowcountry planters, they spent the summer months in the city away from the malarial conditions of their Lowcountry plantation.

Writing almost thirty years before the Civil War, Mr. Grimball, thirty-two years old, described the active social scene of Charleston in the summer and fall of 1832, before he returned to Grove Plantation. Art historian Maurie McInnis notes how Grimball carefully recorded the details of the small, all-male dinner parties he attended "to guide him in the performance of his own," including his drawings of the dinner table and placement of dishes so that he could re-create a similar style and aesthetic when he returned the hospitality of his hosts.[23] Grimball wrote, "I put down these dinners because they are given by men of acknowledged Taste—and will afford hints, should I undertake to give one myself."[24] The weekly round of dinners hosted by a group of white gentlemen friends began around three or four o'clock in the afternoon and continued until nine or ten in the evening—an elaborate production of dining, status, business, politics, and enslaved service.[25]

When Grimball entertained eight friends in his Charleston home on November 30, 1832, several courses were served with appropriate pairings of wine and champagne. Grimball's ambition to be seen as a man of substance among his circle of elite colleagues was reflected in the food and beverages they ate and drank that evening—"a Tureen of Turtle soup at each end of the table—A ham in the centre," roast turkey, a "haunch of venison," turtle steaks, a "macaroni pie," "Floating Island," English cheeses, cakes, and tropical fruits. Grimball's enslaved cook had not made the turtle soup in some time. Like any host "afraid to risk a trial" on his guests, Grimball took the turtle—"soup and steaks and fins"—and the soup pot to a local coffeehouse to be prepared by an experienced cook. "The soup was excellent and abundant—and the Steaks and fins also. . . . I paid Mr. Stewart—$5 and to Daniel the cook, who also came and dished it up, I gave $1."[26] A successful evening staged with stylish food and drink reinforced Grimball's standing among Charleston's white aristocracy.

English-born Fanny Kemble was one of the most illustrious diarists of the antebellum Lowcountry. Born into a noted family of British actors, Kemble met her southern husband-to-be, Pierce Mease Butler, while she was touring in Philadelphia in 1832. The couple married in 1834.

In 1838, Butler, with hesitation, took his wife—who had strong antislavery beliefs—and his two young daughters to visit the Georgia cotton and rice plantations he had inherited from his grandfather. Kemble viewed Pierce Butler's plantations with the eyes of an outsider-turned-insider multiplied by three identities—those of an Englishwoman, a nonsoutherner, and an abolitionist. As a new slaveholder and reluctant plantation mistress, she paid close attention to the substandard conditions that enslaved African Americans endured.

Kemble's observations frequently included descriptions of the enslaved community's food and rations. "They go to the fields at daybreak, carrying with them their allowance of food for the day, which toward noon, and *not till then*, they eat, cooking it over a fire, which they kindle as best they can, where they are working. Their second meal in the day is at night, after their labor is over, having worked, at the *very least*, six hours without intermission of rest or refreshment since their noonday meal (properly so called, for it is meal, and nothing else)."[27] Kemble imagined how well an English farmer would survive a day of hard physical labor fueled by only two meals of "Indian corn or hominy." She noted the absence of proper chairs, tables, dishware, and utensils in slave quarters. They ate from "cedar tubs or an iron pot, some few with broken iron spoons, more with pieces of wood, and all the children with their fingers."[28]

Kemble's accounts of slave rations closely resemble those of other travelers to the South, who noted a range of practices regarding the quantity and quality of food allotted by masters to enslaved laborers. In Virginia, Frederick Olmsted, an inveterate traveler and social critic, observed that "the general allowance of food was thought to be a peck and a half of meal, and three pounds of bacon a week. . . . It is distributed to them on Saturday nights."[29] Kemble was horrified by the inadequate rations, but Olmsted and Fredrika Bremer found the rations to be sufficient, or even generous.[30] But there is no question that food supplied to slaves throughout the plantation South was grossly inadequate. "The lack of food was egregious," explains historical archaeologist Anne Yentsch, "the inhumanity staggering."[31]

The basic diet of enslaved African Americans in the South included a weekly subsistence ration of cornmeal (usually a peck—about eight quarts a week for each slave) and two to five pounds of pork, most often fatback, which varied depending upon the position of the slave; his or her work, age, and gender; and the regional location of the plantation.[32] On occasion, molasses, sweet potatoes, seasonal vegetables and fruits, salt, and coffee might be added to this ration.[33] Enslaved people supplemented this diet, as best they could, by growing a few vegetables, raising small livestock, hunting and fishing, gathering wild foods, and petty theft, when needed.[34]

Kemble could not understand the absence of a "decent kitchen or flower garden" on Butler's plantations.[35] Pierce Butler made light of his wife's criticism. Kemble noted, "He laughed, and said rice and cotton crops were the ornamental gardening principally admired by planters."[36] When Kemble enjoyed early spring peas at nearby Hamilton Plantation, where the mistress, Anne Couper Fraser, had a garden, she sarcastically considered the bargain one might make for this precious food: "At dinner we had some delicious green peas. . . . Don't you think one might accept the rattlesnakes, or perhaps indeed the slavery, for the sake of the green peas? It is a world of compensations—a life of compromises, you know."[37]

John and Anne Fraser frequently sent the Butlers gifts of food from their plantation on St. Simon's Island, including the largest drum fish Kemble had ever seen.[38] "Abraham," the Kembles' enslaved cook, cleaned the fish and took the offal for the slaves. Kemble could not fathom that slaves willingly ate the fish entrails—an example of how they carefully negotiated the privation of slavery. The cook explained to a surprised Kemble, "We colored people eat it, missis." "Why do you say we colored people?" asked Kemble. "Because missis, white people won't touch what we too glad of."[39]

Kemble was undone by the skills and forethought required of a slaveholding plantation mistress, as well as the alienation she experienced in this prescribed role. Returning home famished after a long morning ride on horseback, she found nothing to eat for the noon meal. "Abraham" replied to his mistress, "Being that you order none, missis, I not know."[40] Kemble wrote, "Wouldn't a Yankee have said: 'Wal, now, you went off so uncommon quick, I kinder guessed you forgot all about dinner,' and have had it all ready for me? But my slaves durst not, and so I fasted till some tea could be got for me."[41] When Kemble made a misstep in her domestic duties, the enslaved cook took no action to correct his mistress. Kemble was initiated into the racial codes of the plantation kitchen, where her failure to communicate dinner instructions revealed the delineated roles of whites and blacks in slavery, as well as a subtle statement of enslaved resistance. Offered no special treatment from his mistress, the cook in turn offered no "pass" for his forgetful owner. Kemble described "Abraham" as "quite a tolerable cook," noting, "I believe this is a natural gift with them, as with Frenchmen."[42] Ultimately, Kemble was unable to accept her role as a southern wife and plantation mistress. Her marriage to Pierce Butler ended in divorce in

1849. In 1863, Kemble published her antislavery account of her former husband's estates, *Journal of a Residence on a Georgia Plantation*.[43]

Negotiating Insider Status in the Plantocracy

Many Lowcountry residents had ties to the West Indies, as did Judah Benjamin, born on the island of Saint Croix in 1811. He came from a family of English merchants and Sephardic Jews that moved to Charleston in 1821.[44] Although Jews encountered Charleston's white Gentile aristocracy in their small businesses, and in service professions as attorneys, teachers, and booksellers, few ever crossed into the social worlds of the slave- and landholding elite like the Pringle, Grimball, and Butler families. A telling food-related anecdote in Judah Benjamin's correspondence suggests the power of embracing regional customs—including what the locals ate and drank—to confirm one's identity and acceptance in the racially and ethnically divided South.

Twenty-one-year-old Judah Benjamin made his way to New Orleans in the early 1830s, as did many other ambitious white southerners who followed the westward movement of the cotton economy into the interior South. Benjamin became a practicing attorney in the city, and in February 1833, he married the daughter of a well-to-do Catholic family. Later that spring, Benjamin sent a New York business friend detailed instructions for preparing the strong Creole-style coffee beloved by New Orleanians. "Poor untaught savages of New York!" Benjamin wrote. "How I pity you—yet I will make an exception in your favor. . . . For a small family, say four persons, take mocha and java grains in the proportion of about 1/3 of former to 2/3 of latter. Roast them brown, not black . . . then put into your biggin [coffee pot with a strainer]."[45] He explains how to pour the water onto the ground coffee in terms a financier would understand—"furnish it by installments in the brokers terms, till you have poured on the whole quantity."[46] Once the water drained through the grounds, Benjamin advised his friend, he should take the resulting coffee "nectar" and place two or three tablespoons in a cup, "which is then to be filled with boiling milk."[47]

Benjamin's praise of New Orleans–style coffee and his "expert" knowledge after so short a time in the city suggest how quickly he embraced his new life in Louisiana, Creole cuisine, and his elevated social status. Although New Orleans was known for its religious tolerance, as evidenced by acceptance of Catholics, there was strong pressure to conform to the manners, foodways, and racial codes of middle- and upper-class white Creole society. By 1853, Benjamin was a sugar planter, a U.S. senator from Louisiana, and, after secession in December 1860, a high-ranking official in the Confederacy. Members of the exclusive social organization the Boston Club honored their newly elected senator, "the Honorable J. P. Benjamin," and one of their few Jewish members, with a dinner at New Orleans's St. Charles Hotel, on November 21, 1853.[48] Benjamin's memories of his Jewish family's futile attempts at acceptance in Charleston's closed society receded as he became a member of Louisiana's slave-owning elite.

The Quiet and the Storm

While news of the tenuous political situation between the free and the slave states swirled throughout the South in the decade before the Civil War, diary entries contrast the era's political turbulence with the daily rhythm of life on southern plantations and farms. This sense of calm before a storm ended with the first shots at Fort Sumter on April 12, 1861. Mary Elizabeth Pearson Boyce captured the prewar patterns of a slaveholding family in her diary of 1854–55, written on the family's cotton plantation, Fonti Flora, in Blair, South Carolina, north of Columbia. "Thursday Sept 28th 1854. Mr. B[oyce] had a day of it, hunting birds, etc. they returned this evening with two rice birds, two partridges and a dove. . . . Daughter made some muscadine preserves to day, they are very nice. Minnie cooked three meals for her dolls in her tiny pot, skillet, etc. etc."[49] Just over a year later, Mary Boyce noted the seventeenth anniversary of her marriage in her diary and commented, "We have been spared in great mercy to each other. . . . We had a nice ripe watermelon this evening."[50]

Boyce's short entries, one year apart, speak of the family's entitlement and ease, of the seasonal activities of fall bird hunts in rice fields, of the gendered responsibilities of plantation life, the intimacy of marriage, and the evocative taste of a ripe watermelon on an Indian summer evening. One imagines the tiny cast-iron pot and skillet used by Boyce's young daughter, Minnie, to cook "three meals for her dolls." Her play foreshadowed responsibilities she would later have as a grown woman. By the time she married in 1864, the South was deeply entrenched in a war that drastically changed the life her mother had imagined for her privileged daughter.[51]

Perhaps no diaries and letters of the antebellum South reveal the region's racial pathologies and culinary pleasures more clearly than those of young, northern-born, working-class, white women employed as governesses and teachers by white slaveholding families. They were liminal figures in the plantocracy—part professional, part hired help, part servant, part trusted family member—and always dispensable. If the situation was not considered "agreeable" to the family, it ended as abruptly as it began. As household slaves knew, and white nannies quickly learned, these roles changed as quickly and maddeningly as shifting sand. In the following chapter, we examine the voices of three New England–born governesses who came to the South as the region roiled toward Civil War. They draw us inside the southern household, revealing the daily dramas that unfolded in kitchens and at dining tables as the explosive political tensions of wartime enveloped southerners and nonsoutherners alike.

3

I Will Eat Some for You

FOOD VOICES OF NORTHERN-BORN GOVERNESSES IN THE PLANTATION SOUTH

Located at the heart of the plantation household, white governesses from the North were privy to an intimate portrait of family life in the interstices between slaveholders and the enslaved. Descriptions of food—the distinct tastes of southern cuisine; the rituals of daily meals, special occasions, and holidays; the challenges of food supply and preparation in the southern heat; and, most important, the racial codes of slavery in the domestic sphere—were central to the observed worlds of governesses. In the strange and alien worlds of the plantation South, governesses kept careful records of the ways of the locals in letters and diaries, including what and how they ate. As correspondents, the young women "pondered" their new experiences, kept loneliness at bay, and shared their life-changing adventures with distant friends and family. "Catherine W. B.," a young female teacher who came south, captured the comforting power of the pen in a letter sent back home. "It is among my chief sources of pleasure to be able to communicate with my absent friends," she wrote. "Often have I thanked Heaven for the blessings which the pen affords."[1]

Historian Wilma King said of eighteen-year-old Tryphena Holder (born in 1834 in Massachusetts), a teacher and nanny who came to Vicksburg, Mississippi, in 1852 to work for wealthy cotton planters: "She fought rural isolation with approved weapons: ink, pen, and paper."[2] The same year Holder arrived in Mississippi, Ruth Hastings (born in 1831 in Massachusetts), age twenty-one, accepted a position as a governess at Colonel John Nicholas Williams's plantation home in Society Hill, South Carolina. She was paid $300 a year, plus room and board, a typical financial arrangement for southern governesses.[3] Her father, John Hastings Jr., lost his job and the family home soon after his daughter began her education, and she was forced to take a leave from school. Anxious to help, Ruth Hastings wrote her parents once she was working in South Carolina, "I know I can do you more *real* good here than there [at school], because I can earn money to help to get us a *home of our own.*"[4] In 1859, nineteen-year-old Rogene Scott (born in 1840 in Vermont) began work as a tutor on the Tanner family's sugar plantation in Cheneyville, Louisiana.[5]

Hastings and Holder were recent graduates of female academies in the Northeast, Hastings from Emma Willard's Troy Female Seminary in Troy, New York, and Holder from the Maplewood Young Ladies' Institute in Pittsfield, Massachusetts.[6] Scott attended a music school in Burlington, Vermont, where she trained as a teacher. The progressive curriculums at female academies emphasized women's intellectual development and "self-support," as well as traditional notions of motherhood, home, and family.[7] Young graduates brought these lessons with them to the slaveholding South and quickly learned that their real educations had only begun.

The northern-born governesses and teachers slowly transformed from outsiders to insiders and observers to participants in the rural South, and the narratives of food in their correspondence and diaries chart this evolution. They began as travel writers, describing the excitement and travails of making the journey south in a bone-tiring combination of steamboats, trains, and carriages. Once they settled into their southern homes, the young women became ethnographers of a sort, documenting and critiquing southern society, manners, food, and institutions, including slavery. Many young women prepared for their journeys south by reading memoirs of teachers, such as Emily Burke's *Reminiscences of Georgia*. Burke described her New England readers—women like Holder, Hastings, and Scott: "In anticipation of being engaged in teaching at the South, [they] were desirous to collect as much information as possible relative to those customs by which their future comfort and happiness might be greatly enhanced or diminished."[8]

Descriptive accounts of food in the northern-born teachers' letters and diaries became virtual "souvenirs," as described by historian Eric Plaag, allowing friends and family back home to vicariously experience their culinary adventures in the South.[9] In July 1852, Ruth Hastings mailed a taste of South Carolina to her family back home in Massachusetts. The mistress of the plantation, "Mrs. Williams," suggested she send dried peaches, which Hastings carefully packaged in a box, accompanied by written instructions: "You can make some like them, I think. They are boiled a very little, half cooked, with ½ weight of sugar, and then rolled in sugar, and dried very quickly in the hot sun. . . . They chop the peaches here very fine, with a knife, and eat sugar and milk or cream on them. They are delicious. Do try them."[10] Typically, spoilage and expense prevented shipping food by mail, so, more often, written narratives of taste captured the young women's experiences and delineated the essential southernness of their worlds.[11] "Here's Amy with an immense slice of watermelon," wrote Ruth Hastings to her sister Mary. "Do you have them yet? I will eat some for you."[12] "Amy" was an enslaved girl owned by Colonel Williams and his wife, Sarah Cantey Witherspoon Williams. Ruth Hastings speaks of her frequently in her letters, describing chores she completed for Hastings, or food "Amy" brought her, such as "pindars" (peanuts) and a "bunch of violets."[13]

As delighted as they were by the abundance and variety of southern foods, the transplanted northern women grew homesick for the tastes of New England. Surrounded by the budding green of a Tennessee spring, Rogene Scott missed the seasonal tastes of Vermont: "I suppose your Maple Sugar is all made," wrote Scott. "I wish I had some."[14] Tryphena Holder Fox, who married a local doctor in 1856, longed for her mother's home cooking in the summer of 1859. "I wish you could send me one of your famous apple pies," she wrote. "You do not know how often I eat one in my imagination."[15]

The mid-nineteenth-century experiences of governesses Holder, Hastings, and Scott in Louisiana, Mississippi, and South Carolina vary in the arc of their life paths, yet together their letters reveal the complex contours of the South's culinary cultures. Reading along, as their families did back in New England, we see their first observations of slavery, the culinary extravagance of white elites, the physical landscape of detached southern kitchens, food storerooms, and outbuildings, the racial and gendered hierarchy of food preparation and service, and the core cuisine of the plantation table and slave quarters. Hastings and Scott returned to the North before the outbreak of the Civil War, but Tryphena Holder Fox remained in the South, where she, along with thousands of white middle-class and elite southern women, was caught in the maelstrom of an embattled region.

Observing Slavery

The three young northern governesses entered the southern plantocracy, falling into the worlds of slavery like Alice, Lewis Carroll's 1865 fictional character, who slipped into the fantastical rabbit hole of *Alice's Adventures in Wonderland*. Once inside these privileged worlds of enslaved service and hospitality, how did one get out? As teachers, Hastings and Scott constantly grappled with the immorality of slavery, while Tryphena Holder Fox soon embraced the institution as a wife and slave owner. As young women whose duties focused on raising and educating children, their initiation into slavery was closely tied to southern food, as enslaved laborers grew, prepared, and served meals to white masters and their families.

The views of southern slavery of Ruth Hastings, a tutor to the young daughters of Colonel John Nicholas Williams and Sarah Cantey Witherspoon Williams, were largely shaped at the dining table and in the family's South Carolina mansion, the Factory, named for the large cotton mill that stood nearby.[16] Colonel Williams inherited one of the largest cotton plantations and fortunes in Darlington County, South Carolina. His wealth was reinforced by political and family connections to the states' slaveholding elite, including James Chesnut and his wife, the famous diarist of the Civil War–era South, Mary Boykin Chesnut. Mealtime practices at the Williams table reinforced Ruth Hastings's sense of alienation from the foreign world of the elite white southerners. "You can't imagine how strange it looks to me to see the children and Serena give the negroes about the house a biscuit or a wafer, or piece of gingerbread half eaten or a piece of melon from which all that I call good had been eaten," wrote Hastings. "They give the [slave] children Amy, Ellen, and even to Nelly, bones half picked and bits of meat or anything they happen to eat at lunch. I haven't learned yet how to give my leavings with a good grace. I am trying to learn."[17]

Ruth Hastings had just arrived in Society Hill when she wrote her family and described the disparate landscape of the plantation South she viewed from her room—a bucolic scene of birds singing and a "profusion of flowers" in the garden and greenhouse, contrasted to the busy working kitchen in the yard "swarming with the servants of the house."[18] In 1850, the Williams family owned over 400 slaves, who were dispersed across the family's cotton plantations in the South Carolina midlands near the Pee Dee River.[19] During the late summer, Hastings went to see the cotton crop at several of the Williams plantations. She described the unbelievable heat, broken by the cooling properties of South Carolina's favorite fruit: "It was a cloudy day, or we should have melted I'm sure. . . . We stopped at one place and had some peaches at the overseers house."[20] Ultimately, Hastings was deeply troubled by the inhumanity of slavery and could not shed her feelings of being a northern outsider, all of which affected her stomach. She had frequent headaches and nausea during her stay with the Williams family. When a letter arrived from her family, the Williamses hid it from their governess until she had eaten breakfast, "lest it should take away all my appetite, as letters do sometimes."[21]

Young teachers were advised to keep their opinions on slavery to themselves while they were working for, and living in the homes of, white slaveholding southerners. In Kentucky, the young governess Rogene Scott received a letter from her friend Emma Holcombe, who encouraged her to take a lucrative teaching position working for the Tanner family in Cheneyville, Louisiana, but warned her friend about her "Abolition principles." She wrote Scott, "Have you learned self control enough to keep *utterly silent* on the subject, to indicate your views by no word, look or sign, nay to bear teasing and bantering with patience and good humor? . . . Remember that whether the whole South be wrong or not, you single handed, a young and inexperienced girl are not going to set them right."[22] Scott heeded her advice, but the Louisiana family clearly knew her antislavery feelings. Peter Tanner, the master of the plantation, enjoyed teasing Scott about her opinions. "Nearly every evening we get out the checker board and try our skill," wrote Scott. "He calls me 'the North'—I call him 'the South'—so we 'the North' and 'the South' engage in a miniature battle and sometimes he whips the Abolitionist soundly and sometimes *vice versa*."[23]

Tryphena Holder Fox left teaching to marry into white, slaveholding, southern society. She never questioned the morality of slavery in her writings and quickly adopted the racial attitudes of her former employers, her husband, and the neighboring plantation families in Louisiana. Defensive in regard to northern attitudes toward slaveholders, Fox proudly described the new room added to the detached kitchen in which her slave "Mary" slept. "It stands two feet from the ground and is large, airy and comfortable. Mary occupies it at present and some of the abolitionists ought to take a peep at the poor slaves quarters."[24]

The constant attention required of slaves to their masters was a powerful initiation for Ruth Hastings into the pampered lifestyle of elite white planters. "They live in so much more *style* than I am quite at home with yet," she wrote.[25] "The servants are all very obliging. Cannot do enough for me. Old Mammy, the nurse, was in my room yesterday while I was dressing, and talked all the time. Said I must make myself at home. She would see I had everything I wanted. I should grow fat and healthy here."[26] That morning, before Hastings came downstairs for breakfast, "Old Mammy" brought a bowl of fresh berries to the young teacher, who had arrived frail and thin from New England.[27]

Northern teachers' reports of caring, solicitous black servants dedicated to the welfare of their white masters and guests were illustrated in frequent descriptions of fortifying meals and treats. These writings foreshadowed a genre of popular, post–Civil War memoirs and novels of the "Lost Cause." This movement, led by white southerners in the half century after the war, enshrined the memory of the Confederacy. Texts such as Joseph Holt Ingraham's *The Sunny South, or, The Southerner at Home: Embracing Five Years' Experience of a Northern Governess in the Land of the Sugar and the Cotton* (1880) provided rich but sentimentalized accounts of a mythic "golden age" of the plantation table and enslaved service. Ingraham (1809–60), born in Maine, spent his life as a writer and minister in Mississippi and wrote *The Sunny South* as a pro-southern, defensive response to Harriet Beecher Stowe's *Uncle Tom's Cabin* (1852). Written in the form of letters by a northern-born governess, "Kate Conyngham," Ingraham's novel was a mix of local color and a celebration of the mythic Old South and its imagined world of benevolent planters and loyal slaves.

Although much of Ingraham's account of the plantation table is accurate, the exaggeration of slaves' utter devotion to white service is extreme, such as the description of Kate's morning rituals in the verdant, paradisiacal plantation household. She was awakened "by the soft footstep of my pretty negress Eda," who brought "a laver of cool fresh water from the spring, and snowy napkins."[28] For the first mornings after her arrival, "Eda" offered a wine mint julep to the governess. Not tempted, she was given "coffee, black, and clear, and fragrant enough for a Turkish Sultana."[29] Called to the table by a silver bell, Kate was served breakfast in a cool piazza "adorned" with caged mockingbirds and canaries, which sang throughout the meal. "Four or five varieties of warm bread load the table, with succotash, and hominy, and ham always. Two men and two negresses, all well dressed and in white aprons, wait on table, and anticipate every wish."[30] Passages such as this may have evoked a past era of racial entitlement for postwar white readers in the South, but they only confirmed northerners' perceptions of the region as a degenerate and exotic land.

"We Just Live Here & That Is All—It Is the Same Unvarying Round of Eating & Sleeping, Day after Day & Month after Month"[31]

Tryphena Holder Fox had been wed just over a month and was setting up housekeeping in Louisiana when she explained the chief responsibilities of a "southern lady" in a letter to her mother. In 1856, the young governess married David Raymond Fox, a Vicksburg native and physician, and the couple left Mississippi for the Louisiana community of Jesuit's Bend in Plaquemines Parish.[32] They began their family as Fox established a medical practice serving the sugar plantations thirty miles south of New Orleans. "In this country," wrote Fox, "all provisions are kept under lock and key and one of the principal duties of a southern lady's housekeeping is to carry the key and give out the proper quantities of groceries for each meal, otherwise the cook would waste twice as much as was needed and pilfer as much more."[33] Fox most likely emulated Sophia Messenger, her former employer and the mistress of Baconham Plantation in Warren County, Mississippi.[34] With the help of servants, "a Southern lady does not do much manual labor," noted Fox, but "she had head-work enough to keep her busy."[35] By "head-work," Fox meant the management of her household. It was Tryphena Fox's responsibility to oversee meals for her family and the slave rations, supply clothing for both white and black families, tend vegetable and flower gardens, care for small livestock, nurse the sick, dispense medicines, and supervise the daily work of domestic staff.[36]

Tryphena Fox's accounts of food held additional importance since she was a new and unsure wife and mother. She wrote her mother, Anna Rose Cleveland Holder, recounting her successes and failures in the kitchen, including frustrating attempts to teach her house slaves "proper" housekeeping skills and recipes prepared in the manner that Holder remembered from childhood. "[Mary] is a very good servant and cooks almost everything in good order, excepting light bread. I have let her try *twice* & she has brought me in both times heavy sour bread, not fit to be eaten in any way."[37] With no local bakery nearby, Fox relied on her own skills and those of her enslaved cooks. By the 1880s, bread baking was one of the first cooking tasks relegated to both bakeries and savvy home bakers, who sold their wares at curb markets and door-to-door.[38] Historian Rebecca Sharpless notes that "the greatest test, and the greatest headache" in the southern kitchen was the production of consistent, high-quality, yeast-raised wheat bread or "light bread," which had a finer, lighter crumb than cornbread and biscuits.[39] Outdated stoves, inaccurate recipes, and a lack of kitchen skills on the part of the mistress challenged black cooks.[40] Fox admitted as much to her mother: "I am so sorry I do not know more about housekeeping or rather cooking for, if I showed her [Mary] once, it would be enough."[41]

Two months later, the baking scene in Tryphena Fox's kitchen was much improved: "I have learned Mary to make very nice soda biscuits and from a new cook-book which Dr R. gave me, have taught myself how to make *light bread*, and I am as proud of my first light loaf in the safe [cupboard] as a girl is of her first beau."[42] The soda biscuits Fox refers to became the favorite quick bread of the southern table, particularly after commercial leavenings like baking powder (baking soda plus cream of tartar) and supplies of wheat flour from the Midwest were increasingly available after the Civil War.[43]

Despite occasional triumphs, Tryphena Fox was exasperated by the challenges and tensions of managing enslaved people in her home. Like most young white women of her class and position, she was trained in household skills but lacked the authority and experience to control enslaved workers.[44] Fox's New England mother had passed on no skills in managing servants.[45] In 1858, the Foxes purchased an enslaved cook,

Kitchen, Refuge Plantation, Satilla River, Woodbine, Camden County, Georgia. Photograph by L. D. Andrew, from an old photograph in possession of B.C. Heyward, Historic American Buildings Survey, HABS GA, 20-WOBI.V, 1-3. Prints and Photographs Division, Library of Congress, Washington, D.C.

"Susan," who arrived pregnant and accompanied by a young daughter. Fox wrote: "I find her a good washer & ironer and pastry cook & able to cook plain, every day meals. . . . How much trouble she will give me, I don't know, but I think I can get along with her, passably well any how."[46] Two years later, Fox criticized the cook as "impudent & lazy & *filthy*."[47] She described the tensions in the household, in which the fiction of female civility and friendship was impossible to maintain in the daily swirl of labor. "Perhaps I do not treat her right—probably I do not for I do not like her & never did, & *never shall*," wrote Fox. "It is not pleasant to live on the same place & in as close proximity as one is obliged to do with the cook & be all the time at enmity with her & feel angry, whether I say anything or not."[48]

Enslaved women responded in kind, viewing their mistresses as "handmaidens" of slavery, who foisted their work onto slaves.[49] In the spring of 1861, while "Susan" recovered from childbirth, Fox trained another enslaved woman, "Maria," to take her place in the kitchen. Unsatisfied with her work, Fox punished the servant for leaving "dirty dishes standing untouched" in the kitchen.[50] When Tryphena Fox looked for "Maria" the next morning, she had escaped.[51] Fox regretted the lost time and training she had invested in the runaway slave: "I had taught her after a great deal of pains & many an hour's hard work on my part to sweep & dust & arrange a room nicely, to wash & iron fine clothes, particularly shirts, to cook cakes & custards & jellies."[52] Enslaved women and mistresses worked at odds and in tandem, reflective of the "explosive intimacy" of the plantation household and its unpredictable mix of praise and punishment, trust and distrust, affection and animosity.[53]

The Southern Culinary Landscape

When Ruth Hastings described the view from her window, she referred to one of the most distinctive features of the plantation landscape—a separate kitchen removed from the main house.[54] Locating the kitchen in a work yard moved the heat, smell, vermin, and risk of fire, as well as the enslaved cook and her assistants, away from the master's house, but not so far that the mistress could not keep an eye on the meal-in-progress and other food-related chores. Until the late seventeenth century, slaves and masters in the Chesapeake Region lived and worked close by, which reinforced their identity as a plantation "family." As racial codes tightened in the antebellum South, there was more physical separation between slaves and masters. "The detached kitchen," writes folklorist John Vlach, "was an important emblem of hardening social boundaries and the evolving society created by slaveholders that increasingly demanded clearer definitions of status, position, and authority."[55]

Tryphena Fox noted the location of her Louisiana kitchen at Hygiene, "about twenty yards to the west, and from the house to the storeroom, about thirty yards to the south."[56] She wrote her brother, "You know our Southern kitchens are built very open—much like a barn."[57] The Fox's detached kitchen was of simple frame construction, a single room with a fireplace and chimney at one end. This one-room plan was found on many southern plantations.[58] Another typical kitchen form was a two-room structure with fireplaces located in the middle or at the gable ends of the building. One of the two rooms was often used for slave quarters.

Smokehouse (west front, south side), Walthall House, State Route 61, Newbern, Hale County, Alabama. Photograph by W. N. Manning, September 25, 1935, Historic American Buildings Survey, HABS ALA, 33-NEWB, 1-7. Prints and Photographs Division, Library of Congress, Washington, D.C.

In her autobiography, *The Making of a Southerner* (1946), Katharine Du Pre Lumpkin wove descriptions of her great-grandfather's Georgia plantation kitchen into a narrative that confronted her family's racist past and the racial justice she sought as a young woman growing up in the New South. Lumpkin imagined the kitchen as it would have operated during slavery, including the slave cook, "Aunt Sarah," as she prepared waffles in the "big house" for white guests. The kitchen was "a separate building, some thirty feet removed from the house, connected with it by a firm walk fashioned of oak trees split and set solidly in the ground, flat side up."[59] On "very special occasions," "Aunt Sarah" donned a starched white apron and walked to the dining room of the plantation house, "accompanied by a small slave boy carrying a great bowl of batter."[60] She made waffles over the large fireplace and served them directly to the table in a carefully orchestrated performance of food and power. "It was said she did this only for those whom she delighted to honor."[61]

As the keeper of the key to the locked storeroom, Tryphena Fox frequently walked the domestic triangle between the house, the kitchen, and the storeroom to get food supplies.[62] Fox noted the constant "back and forth" with enslaved workers: "I have to go to the store-house with Henry or Phillis twice a day and sometimes get my feet wet."[63] In Cheneyville, Louisiana, Rogene Scott was temporarily placed in charge and made the "keeper of the key" to the storehouse when her employer and the mistress of the plantation went to the city for the day. She chafed at the responsibility and was glad to return the keys to Mrs. Tanner when she returned. "It was quite a task even if I had none of the *work* to do myself," wrote Scott. "I had to run at the call of everybody for a little milk or a little sugar or a little of almost everything else, for all these things are kept under lock and key, and all these steps took *up time* even if they did not *tire one*, and time is a precious commodity with me."[64]

The Plantation Table

Curious about what his daughter was eating in South Carolina, Ruth Hastings's northern father asked if she lived on "hog and hominy."[65] Hastings responded with a description of a typical day of eating at the Factory, which mirrored the culinary patterns of white elite families in the antebellum South—a core cuisine of pork, cornmeal, and local vegetables and fruits expanded and enriched by a planter's money and slave labor. The Williams family, like other wealthy, white slaveholding families, had their own hogs, poultry, dairy cows for butter and milk, cattle for beef, rice from the nearby Lowcountry, corn, sweet potatoes, and other vegetables grown in the plantation gardens and fields, orchards, and store-bought food stuffs, such as wheat flour, sugar, coffee, and spices.[66] Most meals included many dishes. At breakfast, cold meats from the previous evening meal were often served with hot breads, such as biscuits or "hot cakes."

Hastings worried that the bountiful diet of the southern planter's table was too rich for her delicate constitution. The tempting varieties of "hot breads" were particularly difficult to pass up. Domestic reformers of the era, Harriet Beecher Stowe and Catharine Beecher, expressed concerns about indulging in such foods and recommended "cold, sliced yeast bread" as a healthier practice.[67] Ruth tried to resist but failed.

"There are so many nice things to eat and make oneself sick with that I find it difficult sometimes to eat cold bread instead of hot cakes, every variety you can imagine, made of rice, sweet potatoes, corn, wheat, everything that ever was cooked I do believe, and so very good, too, that I am afraid I shall get to be a real epicure. If I had nothing else but eating to attend to I should surely."[68] One imagines that back home in Troy, New York, the Hastings family ate character-building bowls of porridge for breakfast rather than warm, sweet potato waffles drizzled with fresh butter and cane syrup. Hastings slowly began to put on some needed weight. "I weighed 95, now I weigh 101, so don't feel bad any more about my being so thin. I expect I should grow so fat you won't know me, eating hominy and clabber."[69] Clabber—naturally curdled milk—was Colonel Williams's favorite dish. Ruth wrote, "I hope it won't make me quite as fat as he is."[70] Williams weighed over 350 pounds.[71]

After completing morning school lessons with the Williams children, Hastings stopped at noon, ate a cold biscuit for a snack, and rested until the family ate dinner at two o'clock, or sometimes as late as half past three in the afternoon. The bells of the nearby cotton mill kept Hastings on schedule and woke her in time to "dress for dinner." Hastings described the midday meal to her sister Mary: "For dinner, always first some kind of soup, then two or three kinds of meat, always some fresh meat. Today chicken pie, ham, new potatoes, beets, onions, peas, rice, which they eat with meat as we do potatoes, often sweet potatoes, lettuce, then for dessert today what Mrs. W[illiams] called a Cherry Charlotte."[72]

Ruth Hastings was so taken by Mrs. Williams's Cherry Charlotte that she asked for the recipe to share with her mother. "If you have cherries do try it. You must stew the cherries and make them quite sweet. Then line a pan with slices of bread, buttered, and put a layer of bread, and another of cherries till you have as much as you want or the dish is full. The juice must go in too. It soaks into the bread, and makes it very delicious."[73] Hastings explained that "tea," served usually in the early evening, "is much the same as breakfast, only no meat, sometimes a kind of gingercake."[74] After an evening of reading or a quiet game, Hastings and the Williams children ate a light supper before bedtime, such as sponge cake and clabber.[75]

Ruth Hastings knew her revived appetite would surprise her mother: "You will think I am learning cookery. I wish I could learn some of the dishes peculiar to the south. Rice for instance. They never have [it] watery and sticking together as we do, but the kernels separate and dry."[76] By late August of her first summer, Hastings had grown tired of hominy and "almost tired of clabber, too."[77] Hastings was not the only close observer in the family. The Williamses also observed Hastings's eating habits. "Mrs. W says I am not learning very fast to eat *southern* food."[78]

The rice that Hastings described was prepared in the preferred method of the Carolina plantation kitchen, shaped by the culinary practices of enslaved African American cooks. A proper plate of rice appeared "white, dry, and every grain separate."[79] Historian Judith Carney compares this to the West African method of preparing rice, which involved "steaming and absorption, boiling rice first for 10–15 minutes, draining off excess water, removing the pan from direct heat so grains can absorb the moisture and leaving the pot covered for at least an hour before eating. Often the product was encased in a thick residue of crust on the inner edges of the pot."[80] In the center of the browned ring of rice that adhered to the side of the pot were the "snow-white grains" of properly cooked rice.[81]

In Kentucky, Rogene Scott similarly described the abundant table of her southern employers in letters to her family. Overwhelmed by the unfamiliar worlds of the South, she noted her physical reaction to the experience. "I am beginning to have stys on my eyes and very severe ones too owing I think to the change of diet, climate and so forth. Bacon and hot rolls are the *staff of life* in KY."[82] Like Hastings, Scott wrote that the midday table was "loaded" with several kinds of meat, vegetable side dishes, and desserts.[83]

In Louisiana, Rogene Scott enjoyed the French- and African American–influenced dishes of Rapides Parish, which lies to the west of the Atchafalaya River. Today this culturally rich region is known for its Cajun cuisine, shaped by displaced eighteenth-century French-speaking Catholics, who made their way from Canada to the ethnically and racially diverse worlds of southern Louisiana. The rustic cuisine reflects how settlers incorporated the local fish and critters of the bayous, marshes, and rice fields into the food traditions they brought from Acadia.[84] "Oh let me tell you what a fine dish I partook of the other day," wrote Scott. "It was a mess of bullfrog. I could not have distinguished it from chicken if I had tried. Turtle soup I have also become very fond of, eels also. This Bayou Boeuf produces the very finest fish I ever saw and many a nice meal have I eaten from its contents. These southern creeks are very prolific, for they produce everything from Alligator, Garfish etc. down to the smallest *minnow*."[85]

Scott noted that though the Tanners' home and school were not grand—not unlike "our very old houses at home"—the family lived well, given her observations of their daily food and clothing. She wrote: "The

Southerner feels differently; if he has a plenty to eat and drink and wear he scarcely thinks of anything else; I have fallen greatly in love with my style of living because it is so simple and wholesome and I so perfectly satisfied with it."[86] Scott's assessment is a particularly apt description of cultural values in Cajun Louisiana, where local people have long valued the bountiful natural resources of the region and celebrated family, hospitality, and good food above material wealth.

Negotiating Wartime

By the time the first shots of the Civil War were fired at Fort Sumter in April 1861, Rogene Scott had moved from Louisiana to a teaching position in Nashville, Tennessee. She eventually returned to Vermont, where she married and continued to teach. Ruth Hastings went home to New England in 1853 and observed the war from a distance as a young bride after her marriage in 1860. Tryphena Fox was caught in the thick of the war. To avoid active conflict, she and her husband left Louisiana after the fall of New Orleans in late April 1862 to live with her in-laws on their plantation near Vicksburg.[87]

From the letters of Fox, Hastings, and Scott—three young, northern-born women whose firsthand accounts documented the contested culinary landscapes of the plantation South—we now turn to the war that slavery wrought. On the home front and the battlefront, southerners captured their experiences during the Civil War through personal diaries, letters to family, and memoirs published after the war. From 1861 through 1865, food was central to these stories, as shortages plagued the South and its Confederate troops. We will meet Tryphena Holder Fox again, as she struggles to provide for her family during the war, and afterward as she and thousands of southerners begin the slow process of rebuilding their homes in a world transformed by emancipation and Reconstruction.

4

An Embattled Table

THE LANGUAGE OF FOOD IN THE CIVIL WAR SOUTH

On December 15, 1860, Margaret Ann "Meta" Morris Grimball, the wife of South Carolina rice planter John Berkley Grimball, wrote in her diary, "It seems strange that we should be in the midst of a revolution so quiet, and plentiful, & corn for table up here. Everything goes on as usual, the planting, the negroes, all just the same; & a great Empire tumbling to pieces about us."[1] Spanning 1860 to 1866, Grimball's diary reveals an elite, white, southern woman's experience in the months preceding the outbreak of the Civil War and its duration. Her entry of December 15 anticipated the historic secession of South Carolina from the Union just days later on December 20. As Grimball "hoped for a peaceful settlement of this separation," nearby planters continued to entertain lavishly in the first days of the war.[2] Less than a month after secession, Grimball noted a gathering hosted by a neighbor in early January 1861 to formally "introduce his daughter" into society. A festive afternoon of horseback riding, driving, and rowing on the river was followed by a "handsome" seated dinner for thirty guests. The revelers danced until five o'clock in the morning. Grimball wrote, "They then went to their rooms, and after resting 3 hours had breakfast, hot cakes, omelet, sausages, spare ribs, which B. said were not spare at all."[3] This description of white excess and wealth made possible by enslaved labor suggests the aristocratic bubble in which planters and their families lived, and a shared mentality that never questioned the morality of their rarified circumstances.

From the opulent meals enjoyed by white elites like the Grimballs in the early days of the Civil War to the region-wide shortages of comestibles and supplies that particularly impacted the urban South and Confederate troops, food serves as a powerful lens to the wartime South. Although there was dramatic variation in southerners' access to food during the war, all shared the experience of want, whether a famished soldier on the battlefront, a family seeking refuge in the city, or planters and Confederate officers paying exorbitant prices to obtain scarce luxury items. Food was a universal language that all understood despite differences in race, class, gender, religion, and region. These food narratives expressed the bravado of white southerners, the starvation of blacks and whites alike, the cruelty of mercenary overseers, and planters' desperate attempts to save their landholdings. As the war continued, frustration and deep resentment over losing household enslaved labor—especially cooks—was a frequent theme in Confederate women's correspondence as their families ate burned biscuits and sodden loaves of unrisen bread. Thousands of Civil War letters, journals, drawings of camp life, and notes scribbled into military field guides describe the food-related struggles of men at battle and their families on the home front.

Hannah Crasson, a former slave on a North Carolina plantation, shared a parable-like story about the Civil War in a slave narrative collected by the Federal Writers' Project of the New Deal–sponsored Works Progress Administration in the late 1930s. (The language here—misspellings, colloquial phrases, incorrect grammar—is verbatim from the published transcriptions and reflects the racial politics of the era. I discuss this contested practice in more detail in Chapter 5, which explores food and black voice in slave narratives and memoirs.) At the start of the war, a white planter in North Carolina predicted the Confederacy's quick and efficient defeat of the Union army. "Marster Joe Walton" told his slaves what they should expect: "There is a war commenced between the North and the South. If the North whups, you will be as free a man as I is. If the South whups, you will be a slave all your days."[4] Before leaving for the war, Walton bragged he would "whup the North" and be back in time for dinner. "He went away," recalled Crasson, "and it wuz four long years before he cum back to dinner. De table wuz shore set a long time for him. A lot of de white folks [s]aid dey wouldn't be much war, dey could whup dem so easy. Many of dem never did come back to dinner."[5]

The "four long years" of the Civil War, followed by Reconstruction—a difficult "crossing" that slowly moved the region from slavery to freedom—is explored through the prism of food in this chapter. We begin with the strategic blockades of the South by Union forces that effectively starved Confederate soldiers, as well as the region's most vulnerable residents and livestock. The food shortages that followed take us to both "high" and "low" worlds in the South where soldiers, enslaved laborers, well-to-do planters, and the poor and working-class people of the urban South negotiated the daily struggles of the wartime table. Resistance and accommodation marked the food interactions of white and black southerners as they experienced hunger on the battlefield, brutal food riots, slave insurrection, the destruction of southern food supplies, the difficulties of travel in a besieged region, and the trials of living in Union-occupied cities and towns.

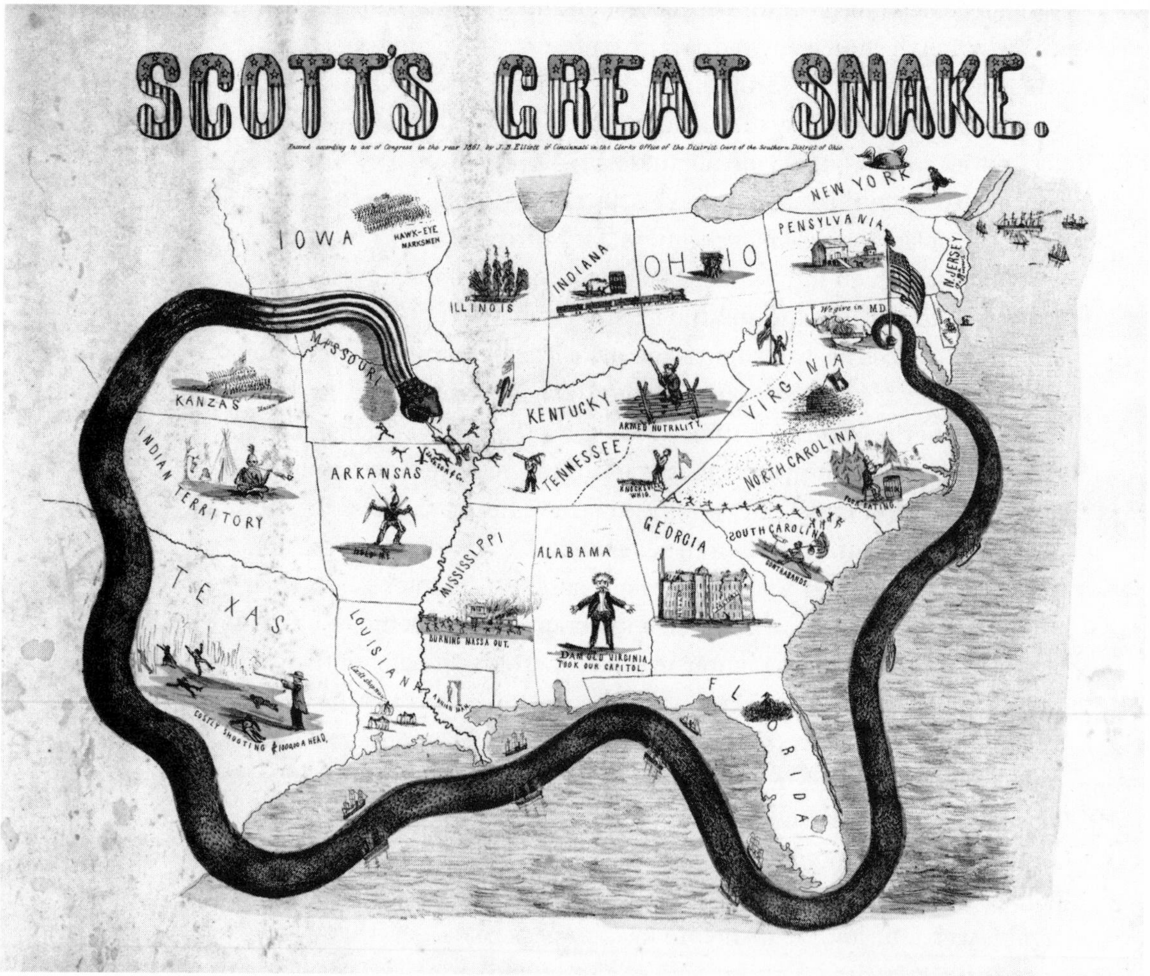

"Scott's Great Snake," published by J. B. Elliott of Cincinnati, Ohio, 1861. This cartoon map illustrates General Winfield Scott's plan to crush the South through a blockade of southern ports and control of the Mississippi River. Geography and Map Division, Library of Congress, Washington, D.C.

Starving the South **Planters Feel the Pinch**

President Lincoln's April 1861 proclamation of a blockade of all southern ports produced food shortages throughout the Confederacy by mid-1862. The blockade escalated the collapse of a fragile food supply increasingly compromised by the Union army's destructive occupation of southern cities and food-growing areas, the damage to vital transportation arteries, and the loss of free and enslaved male labor for local food production. Food historian Andrew Smith argues that northern military strategists fully recognized the power of "starving the South" and from the first days of the war instituted campaigns to effectively cut off the South's food supply and force southern states to return to the Union.[6] The intent of the "anaconda" strategy of the North was to strangle the

South by cutting it off from needed goods and split the Confederacy in half when the Union army took control of the Mississippi River.[7]

Before the war, planters and small farmers in the South produced food crops—largely vegetables and corn—to support their own families and slaves and livestock, but the majority of acreage was dedicated to the region's profitable cash crops of cotton, sugar, rice, and tobacco. Except for rice and sugar and corn grown for animals, the South used no surplus food crops for export nor stockpiled food for its own use. Acreage was devoted to money, not food. Cotton planters like Benjamin L. C. Wailes, in Warren County, Mississippi, purchased great quantities of corn and pork from Ohio and Missouri farmers, who shipped the crops in barrels via Mississippi River flatboats.[8] Dry goods merchants sold southerners commercially produced staples such as imported coffee, tea, spices, and luxury items from Europe and the Caribbean, flour and pork from the Midwest, and fruits, vegetables, and dairy products from New England.[9]

In the first months of the war, twenty-year-old diarist Kate Stone recalled the springtime planting of more food crops than usual at her family's northeastern Louisiana cotton plantation, Brokenburn. Stone's widowed yet "resourceful" mother, Amanda Stone, purchased the plantation after her husband's death, and it was her charge to see that the family and slaves had enough food to eat. "We must save all sorts of seeds, as we will get no more from the North. Mama is having quantities of peas, potatoes, and all things eatable planted, as our only chance for anything from this time until the close of the war will be to raise it ourselves," wrote Stone. "Strict economy is the order of the day."[10]

Confederate families learned to live on a "strict war footing," as Stone described, "cornbread and home-raised meal, milk and butter, tea once a day, and coffee never."[11] When the family expected company, Kate Stone could not imagine having no "boug[h]ten delicacies" to serve them. "A year ago we would have considered it impossible to get on for a day without the things that we have been doing without for months."[12] The situation changed rapidly when Union troops moved closer to northeast Louisiana. The Stones were forced to burn $20,000 worth of cotton at the demand of Union officers, and by early 1863 federal forces confiscated food supplies and animals at Brokenburn.[13]

Parthenia Antoinette Hague's postwar Lost Cause memoir, *A Blockaded Family: Life in Southern Alabama during the Civil War* (1888), recounts her experience as a young plantation teacher during the Union blockade and how food production was altered given their restricted access: "When the blockade had inclosed the South, our planters set about in earnest to grow wheat, rye, rice, oats, corn, peas, pumpkin, and ground peas. . . . Rarely grown before the war, [ground peas] were generally called 'goobers.'"[14] Reserved largely for feed for livestock, peanuts—also known as ground peas, goobers, and pindars—were generally eaten by the lowest social classes. As food scarcities increased during the war, the peanut broke class barriers and was valued by all southerners as a nutritious food and as a substitute for lard and as fuel oil for lamps and a lubricant for machinery.[15]

Although smuggling of goods was rampant and some legitimate trade by permit was allowed, the Union blockade halted the flow of cash crops out of the South and prevented needed food provisions produced in the North and the Midwest from flowing back into the region. On December 17, 1862, Union general Ulysses S. Grant issued General Order #11 as an attempt to stop the smuggling of goods, including food, across enemy lines.[16] In an overtly anti-Semitic action, Grant singled out southern Jewish merchants and traders for breaking the trade blockade. The order stated, "The Jews, as a class, violating every regulation of trade established by the Treasury Department, and also Department orders, are hereby expelled from the Department."[17] After great outrage from the Jewish community, President Lincoln rescinded Grant's order.

By 1863, southern supplies of wheat and flour had dwindled to such an extent that a Confederate broadside was sent to planters requesting "any quantity of wheat and flour for the use of our army in Virginia."[18] Thomas Ruffin, a prominent planter in the North Carolina Piedmont and innovator in scientific agriculture, received a broadside signed by William H. Oliver: "By instructions just received it is important that a large quantity of wheat and flour should be collected immediately. I therefore appeal to every man who has wheat or flour on hand, to sell it to me for the use of our soldiers."[19]

Culinary Insurrection

Wartime only increased slaveholders' worry about slave uprisings and crimes against whites—the same fears seen in antebellum Charleston following the Denmark Vesey insurrection. Most horrific for slaveholders were incidents in which the apparent safety of their domestic worlds, even the food they ate, was used against them by their slaves. These fears played out in a narrative of domestic insurgence in South Carolina when local officials determined that Elizabeth "Betsy" Witherspoon had been murdered by her house slaves. A wealthy widow, Witherspoon was found dead in her Society Hill, South Carolina, bed in September 1861. The Witherspoon family figured prominently in the world of Ruth Hastings, the young nanny who worked for the Williams family at their cotton plantation from 1852 to 1853. Betsy Witherspoon was the mother of Ruth's employer, Sarah Cantey Witherspoon Williams. Mary Chesnut, a cousin of the victim, recounted the details of the bizarre murder that centered on purportedly "indulged" slaves who took advantage of the widow, essentially enslaving her in her own household.[20]

Actions preceding Mrs. Witherspoon's murder reveal the motivation for the crime. Witherspoon's slaves, "William" and "Rhody," had "given a ball" some distance from Society Hill while their mistress was away.[21] The slaves took a selection of Mrs. Witherspoon's tableware for their meal and outing. In nineteenth-century slaveholding society, dining was an intimate, genteel activity, shared with one's family or trusted colleagues and friends of the same status, position, and, most important, race. Racial codes forbade blacks from eating or drinking with whites or tainting objects associated with the slaveholder's table. This "etiquette" reflected the underlying white fear of defilement from interracial intimacy.[22] Only when performing an act of service could blacks cross this culinary line, which enabled enslaved workers to prepare food for whites, carry it to them on dishware, wash and fold their linens, and polish their silver.

When Betsy Witherspoon's son John discovered that her slaves had taken his mother's cherished belongings, he promised to punish them. As a ploy to distract him from his threats, the slaves allegedly murdered Mrs. Witherspoon in such a manner as to appear she died of natural causes while asleep. That night, slaves entered the house with a key Mrs. Witherspoon had given "Rhody" to let herself in each morning, a privilege that no "proper" mistress bestowed on a slave. What was a good mistress, if not the sole keeper of the keys? To add insult to injury, after the slaves entered the house at midnight to kill Witherspoon, they first enjoyed "a rale fine supper and a heap of laughing at the way dey's all look tomorrow."[23] They *ate* their mistress's food before they killed her. Witherspoon's murder horrified white slaveholders, but the slaves' bold use of her *personal tableware and food* was unthinkable. These antics, explains historian Julia Stern, were also an expression of slave resistance in which they "lampooned" the white family by mocking their social pretensions with their own belongings.[24] By flaunting Mrs. Witherspoon's china, linens, and silverware, the slaves asserted that they, too, were human beings—not animals or mere property—and that they, too, could *dine*.

Mary Chesnut described the anxiety of her mother-in-law, Mary Cox Chesnut, a week or so after Witherspoon's murder.[25] Restricted to her bed because of arthritis, the elder Mrs. Chesnut usually ate her meals in her room but instead surprised her son and daughter-in-law by coming into the dining room to give them an urgent message: "I warn you. Don't touch that soup. It is bitter. There is something wrong about it."[26] She believed the cook had poisoned the soup, inspired by the slave murder of Mrs. Witherspoon. Here again is the trope of black culinary skills inverted to be life threatening rather than life enhancing. The Chesnuts attempted to calm her: "Go back, mama, the soup is very nice—don't worry yourself—&c&c." Slaves serving the meal heard this exchange, but as was custom, remained poised, "without change of face."[27] The elder Mrs. Chesnut had lived in South Carolina and comfortably accepted the institution of slavery for more than sixty years when she expressed her fears about the soup. But these were different times. The enslaved cooks in the kitchen now had her attention as individuals capable of thinking, and even plotting, especially as the true meaning of the Civil War became a reality.

Similar motifs of wartime domestic insurrection were echoed in Kate Stone's diary entries in early spring 1863. After a violent confrontation instigated by "Jane," an enslaved cook owned by Amanda Stone's sister, in which Stone's head house servant was harmed, the cook was brought in to speak to Amanda Stone. "Jane" "came with a big carving knife in her hand and fire in her eyes," wrote Kate Stone, who observed her mother's conversation with the intimidating cook.[28] The same night, "Jane" left the plantation, taking her two children with her. Later in the month, Kate Stone heard that "Jane" and her two children had drowned during their escape attempt and noted in her diary, "a short freedom for them."[29]

As confrontations with their slaves and Union soldiers increased, the Stone family finally left Brokenburn for Texas. After stopping near Monroe, Louisiana, Amanda Stone sent her son James with a Confederate officer and five soldiers back to Brokenburn to get her household slaves who remained at the plantation. Kate Stone wrote, "All our and Aunt Laura's house servants, the most valuable we own, were left."[30] The search party crept up to the slave quarters and observed the Stones' housekeeper "Lucy" sitting "before a most comfortable fire drinking the most fragrant coffee" and, like Mrs. Witherspoon's slaves, mocking her mistress.[31] "They were abusing Mamma, calling her 'that Woman' and talking exultantly of capering around in her clothes and taking her place as mistress and heaping scorn on her."[32] At daylight, soldiers surrounded the quarters and "captured" the slaves. Stone explained the risk of such an act: "The penalty for removing anything from the property confiscated by the government was hanging."[33]

The Confederate officer regretted not being able to stay at Brokenburn and enjoy "one good breakfast with the Negroes," who claimed the plantation's foodstuffs for themselves and purchased other provisions from nearby Union troops.[34] Stone recounted the soldier's description of "jars of delicious pinkish cream, roll after roll of creamy yellow butter, a yard alive with poultry, and hams and fresh meat just killed."[35] This particular story, like that of Betsy Witherspoon, had a powerful twist because of its domestic setting and the slaves' "violation" of both food meant for white bodies and the intimate spaces and objects reserved for whites at mealtime. Stone did not fail to contrast this scene with her family's limited wartime rations: "The fare is coarse and commonly served. . . . I am nearly starved."[36]

Not all plantations were "flowing with milk and honey," as Kate Stone's politicized remembrance of Brokenburn suggests, nor did the majority of slaves experience the largesse of these worlds before and during the war. Slaves suffered from insufficient food at plantations located near enemy lines. Pauline Grice, a former slave from Georgia, recalled the terrible hunger as both Confederate and Union soldiers pilfered food the year before surrender: "Dey done took all de rations and us couldn't eat de cotton."[37] Many slaves fled plantations and joined the Union army, not because they were anxious to fight but to fill their hungry stomachs. An ex-slave was asked why he took up with the Union army. Was it because of the Emancipation Proclamation? He declared, "No, missus, we never hear nothing like it. We's starving, and we come to get somfin' to eat. Dat's what we come for."[38] As the threat of Union occupation became a reality, many planters moved their slaves to safer locations nearby or, like the Stone family in Louisiana, headed west with their slaves to Texas. Former slave Van Moore remembered his Virginia master's enticing description of Texas, with "lakes full of syrup and covered with batter cakes, and dey won't have to work so hard."[39]

Surrounded Cities

Urban Southerners Respond to the Union Blockade

Southern cities were particularly hard hit by the blockade, given their dependence on local markets, grocers, and food entrepreneurs, who could not restock empty shelves, procure flour to bake bread, or secure fresh meat for butchers. Large numbers of refugees seeking the basic necessities of life exacerbated already grim conditions in the South's urban centers. New Orleans was the largest city and commercial center in the Confederacy affected by the blockade, which prevented any river traffic from reaching the city or continuing on to the Gulf of Mexico for trade with the eastern states, Europe, and the Caribbean.[40] At the time, nearly a third of the nation's exports—2.2 million bales of cotton, rice, timber, sugar, and other commodities—was shipped out of New Orleans.[41] This trade was crippled by the blockade.

Confederate families also suffered food losses when Union forces commandeered available food supplies for their troops. Sixteen-year-old Clara Solomon of New Orleans kept a diary during the blockade, in which she spoke of Benjamin "Beast" Butler, the "Gen. commanding the Department of the Gulf" in 1862.[42] Butler, the notorious commander of the Union occupation forces, assumed his position in New Orleans that spring. "He promises protection to our unprotected & starving population," wrote Clara. She quoted from Butler's bulletin to the citizens of New Orleans: "Ready only for war, we had not prepared ourselves to feed the hungry & relieve the distressed with provisions. But to the extent possible within the power of the Com. Gen. it *shall be done*."[43] Local whites hated Butler with a passion for the martial law he imposed upon their city but acknowledged improvements in sanitation and reduced crime because of his effective leadership.[44] Solomon complained of the inflated price of flour sold at "Old But.'s Shop," a Union-operated commissary, nicknamed by the locals in honor of General Butler.[45] "Ma has an idea of making an investment there. I do not countenance it, for indirectly we will have to be fed from their hands."[46]

The Assault on Southern Salt

The most severe food shortages began in 1863 and 1864 when the South's salt supply was destroyed by Union attacks on important salt mines in southwestern Virginia, Louisiana, coastal North Carolina, and other locations in the region.[47] Without salt, the diet and health of southerners was seriously compromised. Salt was needed to disinfect wounds and was also an important ingredient in the food of draft animals.[48] Southern cooks depended on salt to preserve meat, particularly the copious quantities of pork favored in the region. After pigs were slaughtered in the fall, the hindquarters were salted and cured in smokehouses for several months to create hams and bacon. For southern-style pork barbecue, whole hogs and shoulders were seasoned with salt and other spices, slow-cooked over hardwood coals, and swabbed with a sauce or dip. Pork belly was packed in salt or a salty brine to create salt pork for seasoning meat and slave rations. Vegetables could not be preserved properly without salt, a key ingredient in pickling brines. To add insult to injury, food tasted bland without salt. Charley Roberts, an ex-slave, recalled the salt shortage on the Hogg Plantation near Allendale, South Carolina, and this unusual means of acquiring it during the war: "We went to the smokehouse where there were clean boards on the floor where the salt and grease drippings would fall from the smoked hams hanging from the rafters. The boards would be soft and soaked with salt and grease. Well, we took those boards and cooked the salt and fat out of them, cooked the boards right in the bean soup. That way we got salt and the soup was good."[49]

"This Is All That Is Left of Me"

The Richmond Bread Riot

As the war waged on for years rather than the months that southerners anticipated, coping with food shortages, and in many cases starvation, led to anger, rebellion, and even riots among working-class Confederate women who could not provide for their families, particularly in urban areas. In 1863, food riots broke out across the South as women protested food shortages and rising prices caused by speculation and hoarding, military impressment of food, and the inflation of Confederate currency.[50]

The largest and most brutal food riot took place in the Confederate capital of Richmond, Virginia, on April 2, 1863.[51] Richmond symbolized the growing problems of the embattled Confederacy. As southerners fled rural areas for refuge, the infrastructure of cities failed. Urban populations doubled and tripled during the war, as did crime rates and the needs of the working poor. Food prices escalated as the salaries of government workers and laborers and the level of support for widows remained unchanged.[52] Denied a meeting with Virginia governor John Letcher to discuss their grievances, a group of working-class women protesters took to the streets. They stormed into shops and warehouses, shouting, "Bread! Bread! Our children are starving while the rich roll in wealth."[53]

Sara Agnes Rice Pryor, the wife of a Confederate officer, witnessed the riots. She recalled an encounter with a young female protester, not more than eighteen years old. When the girl raised her arm to remove her sunbonnet, her sleeve slipped, revealing "a mere skeleton of an arm."[54] Seeing Pryor's shocked expression, she replied, "This is all that's left of me! . . . We are starving. As soon as enough of us get together we are going to the bakeries and each of us will take a loaf of bread. That is little enough for the government to give us after it has taken all our men."[55] Hal Tutwiler, a Confederate soldier, described the scene in a letter to his sister: "We found that a large number of women had broken into two or three large grocery establishments, & were helping themselves to hams, middlings, butter, and in fact every thing eatable they could find. Almost every one of them were armed."[56]

Troops were deployed, and officers threatened to fire upon the crowd of thousands gathered in Richmond's Capital Square. After Jefferson Davis pleaded with the angry mob to disperse, the riot slowly drew to a close. More than sixty men and women were arrested and tried for their participation in the tumult. In the aftermath of the riot, city officials and members of a women's benevolent society provided limited food aid to the working poor of Richmond.[57] Ironically, there was enough food to feed the city's residents, but inflated prices and the disorganized distribution of food by the Confederacy and its commissary officers kept it out of reach of Richmond's poorest citizens.

Historian Drew Gilpin Faust argues that the food riots revealed a new spirit of self-assertion as Confederate women increasingly rejected "the ideology of sacrifice."[58] Women wrote to army officials, begging to keep their sons at home, and by the end of the war, women were encouraging their husbands to desert their units and return home to help plant and harvest food crops. Without protection of their physical safety and food for their families, the social "contract" that had once guaranteed women's loyalty and support to husbands and the Confederacy was now bankrupt.

Starvation Parties and Other Merriments

The Wartime Tables of the White Southern Elite

Obtaining food was a far different experience for those who had money and access to power during the Civil War. Choice foods and even luxury items such as wine and champagne were available to those well-to-do southerners who could afford expensive goods brought in by blockade-runners. Sarah Hillhouse Lawton, the Georgia-born wife of Confederate brigadier general Alexander Lawton, complained about the high prices of food in Richmond in 1864 but still had the means to pay the inflated sums. As quartermaster general, her husband oversaw the distribution of noncomestible supplies for the army, such as clothing and equipment. While refugees from other southern cities streamed into Richmond, Sarah Lawton wrote of the ingenuity required of a wife and mother during wartime, although money trumped creativity: "Household matters still fill up my daily life, as in peace times[,] and the struggle to live comfortably, requires considerable effort and forethought. We contrive to have all our wants supplied. I send to market every morning and get fresh vegetables. We have fresh meat in small quantities, some two or three times a week. The rest of the time, ham."[59] Lawton attached her market expenses for a week in June 1864: "Wednesday—5 ½ lbs of veal, $33. 1 peck green peas, $12. Thursday—Lettuce, $1.50, cherries, 2 qts for $3.00. Friday—Squash, 1 doz for $6. Asparagus $3.00. Saturday—snap beans $4 . gooseberries $2. Butter 4 lbs for $48.00 Sunday and Monday—nothing. Tuesday—Lettuce $1.50, Beans $4. Raspberries $20."[60] Six months earlier, a barrel of flour cost $115 in the streets of Richmond.[61] Some of the city's Confederate elite made do with a "starvation party," which emphasized music and dancing but "not a cent for a morsel to eat."[62]

Mary Chesnut and her women friends were members of an exclusive social circle that included the wives of planters and Confederate officers, such as her Richmond neighbor and confidante, Varina Davis, first lady of the Confederacy. For most of the war years, they ate and entertained in a style that most southerners could not imagine. Chesnut hosted an elaborate luncheon for her friends in mid-January 1864, a time of such desperation that most southerners were hard-pressed to find basic food staples. Given the "wartimes," Chesnut was disappointed by the variety of foods she could offer her guests, but she settled upon terrapin stew, gumbo, fish, oysters, game, eggs, ham, homemade bread and butter, chocolate, and jelly cake—an unthinkable feast for the majority of war-weary southerners.[63]

Early in the war, Chesnut noted her enslaved cook's exasperated requests for foods she had once prepared for her master and mistress at Mulberry Plantation in South Carolina. After the war began, slaves were scattered between nearby plantations or hired out to the hotel in nearby Camden. When Chesnut returned to Mulberry after accompanying her husband on military business, she asked her cook if she lacked anything.[64] "Lack anything?" the cook replied. "I lack everything. What is cornmeal and bacon, milk and molasses? Would that be all you wanted?"[65] Chesnut could pretend that slaves were easily satisfied with less and needed no more than basic rations. The cook assured her this was not the case. By arguing she deserved the same quality of food her mistress ate, the cook demanded that Chesnut recognize her humanity and equality.

Want, even hunger, eventually touched the worlds of the Chesnuts and their friends by the final months of the war and its aftermath. On March 5, 1865, Mary Chesnut described a far different Columbia, South Carolina, than the gracious city she had experienced in 1862: "Columbia is but dust and ashes—burned to the ground. Men, women, and children left there, houseless, homeless, without one particle of food—picking up the corn left by Sherman's horses in their picket ground and parching it to stay their hunger."[66] Although Union forces did not occupy the city until February 17–18, 1865, Columbia was devastated by fire after General William Tecumseh Sherman's destructive "March to the Sea" between Atlanta and Savannah.

The Chesnuts spent the last three months of the war in temporary quarters in Lincolnton, North Carolina, and Chester, South Carolina, where locals would not accept their Confederate money as payment for foodstuffs. Chesnut made light of giving up her clothing instead: "I am bodily comfortable, if somewhat dingily lodged, and I daily part with my raiment for food. We find no one who will exchange eatables for Confederate money. So we are devouring our clothes."[67] With her larder empty, a gift of food from a local woman, "Mrs. McDonald," was a "godsend." A servant carried in a tray filled with "fowls ready for roasting, sausages, butter, bread, eggs, preserves."[68] Chesnut thanked her profusely for the gift from her mistress, but Chesnut's servant "Ellen" replied, "Missis, you oughtn't to let her see how glad you was—it was a letting of yourself down."[69] Chiding her mistress for being overly solicitous to a woman of a lesser class reflected a southern code of honor so ingrained it was taken on by slaves. If Chesnut's position was diminished, so was her slave's. In the end, "Ellen" admitted that hunger trumped propriety when the family was near their "last mouthful."[70]

Susan Matilda Middleton wrote her friend Mary Chesnut in April 1865, describing a similar lack of food supplies and the generosity of South Carolina neighbors. She noted a "new device" that helped her family cope with a less-than-satisfactory supper. "We keep a cookery book on the mantelpiece, and when our dinner is deficient, we just read a pudding or a crème. It does not entirely satisfy the appetite, this dessert in imagination, but perhaps it is as good for the digestion."[71]

Hunger Takes the Battlefield

Given the blockades and destruction of crucial transportation routes, Confederate officials could not effectively deliver available food supplies to its citizens, soldiers, and animals. Food rotted in railcars and in fields. Draft animals and livestock starved from lack of feed. Weakened soldiers marched for days without rations, foraging for what food they could find from farmers and villagers who had little or none to spare. Mary Chesnut described Lucius Bellinger Northrop, the incompetent commissary general, as the "most cussed and vilified man in the Confederacy. He is held accountable for everything that goes wrong in the army. I hear that alluded to oftenest of his many crimes. They say [P. G. T.] Beauregard [Confederate commander of the forces in the western theater] writes that his army is upon the verge of starvation."[72]

When rations for Confederate soldiers were available in the first months of the war, the food was meager at best—dry cornbread, hardtack biscuits, bacon, a bit of beef, a portion of bean or cabbage soup, molasses or sorghum, occasional provisions of rice, hominy, potatoes, and field peas.[73] E. S. Hammond, a Confederate soldier from Lynchburg, Virginia, carried a copy of John Curry's *Volunteers' Camp and Field Book* (1862) throughout his military service.[74] Besides basic military skills, the book included recipes for dishes that could be prepared with the typical soldier's rations, such as bread, biscuits, "slap jacks," coffee, rice pudding, and "a simple soup."[75] Isaac Levy and his brother Zeke prepared such a soup in camp near Adam's Run, South Carolina, in April 1864. The Orthodox Jewish brothers observed the spring holiday of Passover by making do with a kosher-style "seder stew" prepared with onions, parsley, carrots, turnips, a "young cauliflower," and a bit of beef.[76] Robert Caldwell, a Confederate private in North Carolina, wrote his wife, "Mag," on June 3, 1864, describing his modest comforts in camp near Wilmington—a blanket that also served as his bed, "cornbread, black coffee, and Nassau [foodstuffs run through the Union blockade via the Caribbean] meat to eat."[77] A quart of buttermilk cost a dollar.

As the war continued and food shortages increased, Confederate forces were sickened by the lack of nutritious food and maladies resulting from contaminated water and rotten meat. Dysentery, scurvy, typhoid, and pneumonia were the "principal killer diseases of the war," as well as malaria and yellow fever spread by mosquitoes in the summer heat.[78] Some of the worst scenes of starvation and disease existed in Confederate prisons, such as the dreaded Andersonville Prison in Georgia, where 29 percent of the 33,000 prisoners died.[79] On bad days, prisoners received no food at all, and on good days, they received less than a pound of substandard food.

Sergeant John Bodamer of the 24th New York Cavalry was captured during the Virginia campaigns and incarcerated in Confederate prisons in Salisbury, North Carolina; Danville, Virginia; and Belle Isle in Richmond.[80] In each prison, thousands of Union soldiers died from exposure and disease, exacerbated by starvation. Bodamer kept a diary of the miserable conditions and the paltry daily rations at Danville, including the inflated costs of items prisoners could purchase. A dozen biscuits cost five dollars; a dozen apples, three dollars; a gallon of molasses, forty-five dollars; a blanket, one hundred dollars.[81] On October 12, 1864, he wrote: "Starvation stares us in the face." October 14, 1864: "Several men died of cold and exposure." October 31: "Today we received corn bread mix with a little wheat flour and that was sour. Not fit for a hog to eat." November 1: "Today no meat in the soup[;] there was . . . lung and guts of the critter and also dung in the guts. Now this is outrageous to be treated in this manner by the so called Southern Confederacy."[82]

Surviving letters from the Finch family of Prince William County, Virginia, reveal a family divided by the Civil War and the daily challenges of living in a war zone where food supplies were meager. In the early 1850s, the Finches moved from the snow belt west of Albany, New York, to a farm in Maple Valley, Virginia. Staunch Unionists, but unable to leave their property and return north, the family was soon caught between two worlds. Three sons enlisted in the New York cavalry. One son, Madison, was drafted into the Virginia cavalry. The first battle of Manassas at Bull Run in July 1861 was fought nearby. Over 1,000 soldiers were en-

"Housewife Looted by Soldiers," sketch by Trooper Edgar H. Klemroth of the 6th Pennsylvania Cavalry. Klemroth enlisted at age nineteen and was mustered into service on August 20, 1861, as a corporal in company A. He was present at the Battle of Gettysburg as a sergeant major and was discharged from military service on December 31, 1864. William L. Clements Library, University of Michigan.

camped a half mile from their farm, where Thirza Finch, a twenty-nine-year-old daughter, remained. Correspondence from the Finch brothers to their sister speaks of the contrast in the quality of rations of Union and Confederate troops, as well as the young woman's many tense food-related encounters with defecting soldiers near the battlefront.

In October 1861, Madison Finch (born in 1835) asked his sister to send bread and butter to his camp near Sangster's Station, Virginia: "Am not very well and our bread does not agree with me. You can boil another beef tongue if you have time."[83] The twenty-six-year-old soldier also requested socks and some red pepper—the socks to warm his feet, the pepper to warm his insides and enliven his rations. Edwin Finch (born in 1846), a private in the 15th New York Cavalry, was stationed in Hart Island, a small island in New York City, located at the western end of Long Island sound, which served as a Confederate prison for several months in 1865. The barracks were tidy, with straw ticks and blankets to sleep on, and good rations of coffee, "fresh and salt beef," and "bakers bread." By March 1865, Edwin was in New Kent County, Virginia. Living in a tent with six soldiers, he described decent rations compared to those of most Confederate soldiers at the time. "We buy meal and condensed milk and desolve it and have mush and supper and fried mush for breakfast and corn dodgers for dinner, you must know we live high, for a days rations we draw six small hard tack and a small piece of meat and a cup of soup and one of coffee."[84]

Thirza Finch described the growing fear she felt as soldiers and men deserting their units came seeking food, medical care, and shelter. She worried the family's pro-Union stance would be discovered. On May 27, 1862, Thirza was staying with her neighbor, Mrs. Manchester. Union soldiers asking for food awakened the two women. They believed the soldiers might be Confederates, who had come to take Thirza's father and "Mr. M." The soldiers asked "Mrs. Manchester if she puts powdered glass in her bread, [and] try hard to find out if we are secesh."[85] In the following days, Thirza nursed sick soldiers worn from battle. She prepared rice and fish and baked pancakes for their supper: "Another soldier drops in all bruised up, looks as though he had been fighting, asks for supper, pays me a silver quarter for it, they go out on the porch, father not come, fear he will not."[86] Frightened and alone, she slipped out the back door and walked to her neighbor's home.

Almost four months after the Confederate surrender, Thirza Finch reported the sudden appearance of Confederate colonel John Mosby and his "Raiders," made infamous by their guerrilla tactics and surprise raids on Union supplies during the war. On this occasion, Mosby's crew staged a more benign maneuver in which the aim of the mission was to steal a dance and dessert. "Mosby and 25 of his men came suddenly on some ladies and gents being at Falls Church. Told them not to be afraid. Danced a set with the ladies. Went to the wagon, devoured the [ice] cream and eatables they had for the occasion."[87]

"Don't Mussel the Ox That Treads Out the Corn"

African Americans soldiers who fought for the Union army suffered from hunger and disease while fighting the Confederacy and endured even worse conditions because of racism in the Union forces.[88] Black soldiers received less pay than white soldiers, fewer benefits, and inferior food.[89] Congress passed legislation in June 1864 to equalize pay, but black soldiers were still not given the "same rights and recognitions as whites."[90] A member of the 20th U.S. Colored Troops from New York State complained to a military official about insufficient rations for black soldiers in a New Orleans military camp during August 1864. "Soldiers 24 hours on Guard" were given very little bread and sometimes no meat for days.[91] Their daily soup was so insubstantial, they called it "meat

"City Point, Va. African American army cook at work," photograph from the siege of Petersburg, Virginia, June 1864–April 1865, glass, stereograph, and wet collodion. LC-B811-2597, Prints and Photographs Division, Library of Congress, Washington, D.C.

tea."[92] "It is spoken Don't mussel the ox that treads out the corn. Remember we are men standing in Readiness to face thos[e] vile traitors an[d] Rebels who are trying to Bring your Peaceable homes to Destruction. And how can we stand them in A weak and starving condition?"[93]

Joseph Miller, a slave who served with Union Company I, 124th U.S. Colored Troops, described the desperate condition of his wife and children, who were forced to leave a nearby contraband camp near Miller's bivouac in Kentucky on a bitter cold night in 1864: "At night I went in search of my family," testified Miller. He found them, "cold and famished," crowded into a "colored" meetinghouse by soldiers.[94] "They had not received a morsel of food during the whole day. My boy was dead. . . . I had to return to camp that night so I left my family in the meeting house and walked back. I had walked there. I travelled in all twelve miles. Next morning I walked to Nicholasville. I dug a grave myself and buried my own child."[95]

As conditions deteriorated, so too did the performance and morale of troops, Confederate ones in particular, given their overall weakened physical condition and lack of food supplies.[96] In October 1863, infantryman James Graham wrote his father in Hillsborough, North Carolina, and asked him for a "box of eatables and some lard," as their only provisions were beef and flour.[97] They could buy nothing near their camp in Virginia, because "it has been completely overrun by the Yankees." It was impossible for the debilitated southern troops to compete against stronger Union soldiers, whose daily rations were more steady and substantial and frequently included tins of calorie-rich condensed milk and processed meat.[98] Canning technology and manufacture came to the industrial North much sooner than the South, and Union troops benefited from the tinned foods included in their rations.[99] The demand for processed foods created during the Civil War helped launch the canning industry and manufacturers such as Borden's.[100] General Ulysses S. Grant recognized the Achilles' heel of the southern troops. His "starvation policy" targeted Confederate supply lines.[101] No episode in the Civil War represented the deadly consequences of this food-related policy more so than the siege of Vicksburg in the summer of 1863.

Vicksburg, 1863

During the forty-seven-day siege of Vicksburg, Mississippi, in the spring and early summer of 1863, food supplies were quickly depleted by the more than 30,000 Confederate troops who defended the city—home to 4,500 citizens before the war.[102] On May 24, 1863, Vicksburg resident Emma Balfour wrote: "I realized that we are a besieged people yesterday when I saw several hundred mules in the morning & eight or nine hundred in the evening, driven beyond our lines—given to the Yankees or to starvation, because we have not the food to feed them—or, are afraid to use it for that purpose. No corn is issued for horses, except those of officers in the field."[103]

Forced to take refuge in earthen caves dug into Vicksburg's 200-foot-high bluffs above the river, citizens endured a daily barrage of shelling, so heavy it reminded them of hail.[104] Families moved furniture and cooking supplies into the caves to make the rough quarters livable. Mary Loughborough, the wife of a Confederate officer, had only recently arrived in Vicksburg when she and her two-year-old daughter moved into one of the excavated caves. Even in these compromised circumstances, the racial etiquette of slavery remained unchanged, as black cooks and servants continued to care for white families in the bluffs. "Our dining, breakfasting, and supper hours were quite irregular," wrote Loughborough. "When the shells were falling fast, the servants came in for safety, and our meals waited for completion some little time; again they would fall slowly, with the lapse of many minutes between, and out would start the cooks to their work."[105] Many refugee families avoided cooking, surviving on bread and milk, "provided their cows were not killed from one milking time to another."[106] Before long, "fruits and vegetables were not to be procured at any price. . . . Every one felt the foreboding of a more serious trouble, the great fear of starvation that stared all in the face."[107] Sanitation and clean drinking water soon became a critical issue in the city.

Confederate supplies of grain, produce, and livestock from the nearby Yazoo Delta were blocked by Union forces, which replenished their own reserves with daily steamship deliveries of potatoes, pickles, kraut, fresh ham, dried apples, peaches, biscuits, and butter.[108] The only food available in good quantities for both civilians and soldiers was field peas, which were ground into flour and baked into a hardtack-like biscuit.[109] By mid-June 1863, soldiers' rations were cut by half, then to a quarter, providing at most a handful of peas and rice each day.[110]

Out of desperation, Confederate soldiers and citizens ate mule meat while it lasted. Skinned rats appeared in the city markets, while dogs and cats "disappeared mysteriously."[111] A writer in the *Chicago Tribune* ridiculed the desperate Confederates' situation with a faux bill of fare for an invented "Hotel de Vicksburg," proprietors, "Jeff. Davis & Co."[112] The menu included mule tail soup, boiled mule bacon and poke greens, mule sirloin, "mule bump stuffed with rice," mule ears "fricasseed a la got'ch," mule spare ribs, mule tongue "cold a la Bray," mule hoof "soused," and "mule foot jelly."[113] For dessert, there were "cottonwood berry pies" and "chinaberry tarts," served with white oak acorns, beechnuts, and "Mississippi Water, vintage of 1492, superior, $3."[114] The menu noted, "Gentlemen to wait on themselves. Any inattention on the part of servants to be promptly reported at the office."[115]

On June 28, 1863, Lieutenant General John Pemberton received an angry note from Confederate soldiers in the trenches in Vicksburg, warning of desertion because of their hunger: "If you can't feed us, then you had better surrender us, horrible as the idea is, than suffer this noble army to disgrace themselves by desertion. I tell you plainly, men are not going to lie here and perish, [even] if they love their country terribly. You had better heed a warning voice, though it is only the voice of a private soldier."[116] Less than a week later, Pemberton surrendered to Grant, on July 4, 1863.[117] Given Grant's strategy to abandon assault and let the surrounded city slowly starve, Jefferson Davis blamed the Confederate force's defeat on a "want of provisions inside and a General outside who wouldn't fight."[118] Known as the "Gibraltar of the Confederacy" because of its strategic, protected position above the Mississippi, when Vicksburg fell the course of the war changed for the South.

Two days before the surrender, J. M. Swords, editor of the *Vicksburg Daily Citizen*, satirized the upcoming event as Grant's version of a celebratory rabbit hunt and dinner: "The great Ulysses—the Yankee Generalissimo, surnamed Grant—has expressed his intention of dining in Vicksburg on Saturday next, and celebrating the 4th of July by a grand dinner and so forth."[119] Union forces occupied the city on July 4 and, after commandeering the newspaper's press, issued a final edition of the paper printed on the only available material—the blank side of bolts of wallpaper—with the following response to Sword's satirical column: "Two days bring about great changes, The banner of the Union floats over Vicksburg, Gen Grant has . . . dined in Vicksburg, and he did bring his dinner with him."[120]

As Union troops marched into the city, they shared their rations with Confederate soldiers. They threw food at the feet of the defeated men, yelling, "Here rebs, help yourselves, you are naked and starving and need them."[121] One Union soldier recalled Confederate soldiers staying the night with them as stories of the siege were recounted and food shared: "It was a night long to be remembered, for some of these men actually cried as they ate of the bounty spread before them, and were surprised to know that we had lived just as well during the entire siege. We had built bakeries and served them with fresh meat, broiled—no butter—and light, hot bread."[122] By the last year of the conflict, soldiers deserted the Confederacy in large numbers as much because of severe hunger as the need to help their own families.

Embattled Kitchens

In Mississippi, Tryphena Holder Fox faced the same plight of other white and black southern wives and mothers, as they attempted to provide for their families despite food shortages and raids from Union soldiers, who confiscated livestock, crops, and food supplies. Writing to her mother on July 3, 1863, the day before the fall of Vicksburg, Fox described the tense conditions in occupied territory: "How are these nine children to be fed then—they are all under six years of age. Older people can get along with a piece of dry corn bread, but the little ones will soon suffer from diarrhea & dysentery. Oh! Mother! You northern people know nothing of the horrors of war & may you be spared what I have suffered during the last year."[123]

Many planters abandoned their plantations, and the Foxes were one of only four white families who remained in the area.[124] Union troops had controlled the region surrounding her in-law's plantation since mid-May, following the battle of the Big Black River. Soldiers set up camp in the yard, and several were stationed around the plantation as pickets to watch for Confederate activity. Unlike some areas of the South where women seldom encountered Union soldiers, this was not the case on the borders of the Confederacy, such as Mississippi, where troops were sent to conquer and then occupy Confederate territory.[125] In October 1863, Samuel Agnew, a white minister and farmer in northeast Mississippi, noted the arrival of Union soldiers, who limited their looting mainly to the dining room and larder. After Mrs. Agnew gave the soldiers food she had prepared for the noon meal, they stole more, took "fine knives and forks, all her butter and every egg," and "drank up all the milk they could find."[126] The soldiers encouraged the family slaves to leave with them and, in the final injurious act, ate up "Mothers pound cake with gusto[,] all her preserves . . . all the jellies in the safe." In the ultimate insult, they broke the emptied glass canning jars after devouring their contents.[127]

Confederate women were active participants in the war as boundaries between the home front and the battlefield blurred, and food was central to their actions.[128] After the fall of Vicksburg in July 1863, the Union army consolidated the occupation of the western border of the Confederacy. White women in these occupied territories became the "domestic line of supply" for Confederate soldiers, providing food, clothing, shelter, information, and emotional support.[129] The Union army eventually classified Confederate women as "combatants," because of their support of guerrilla activity.[130] Yet as slaveholding women increasingly suffered food shortages, buried loved ones, and experienced financial devastation, their belief in the Confederate cause deteriorated.[131] By refusing to accept the economic deprivation continued military struggle would have required, women directly subverted the South's military and economic effectiveness, as well as civilian morale.[132]

The July 1863 defeat of southern forces at both Gettysburg and Vicksburg ultimately led to the Confederacy's defeat. In the spring of 1865, General Robert E. Lee attempted to rally the embattled Army of Northern Virginia against Grant's Army of the Potomac. Again, the lack of food proved fatal for the Confederacy. Although Confederate rations had been stockpiled in Richmond, the needed food supplies were prevented from reaching southern troops.[133] Lee expected a delivery of rations at the Amelia Court House, west of Richmond, and instead received ammunition. Munitions were "the last thing they needed," writes historian James McPherson. "The worn-out horses could scarcely pull the ordnance the army was carrying."[134] Lee paused to allow his starving troops to forage for food. As Union forces intercepted other supply trains, Lee reluctantly agreed to Grant's terms of surrender, on April 9, 1865, at Appomattox Court House.

Going Home for Supper **Southerners after Surrender**

Smith Kitchin, a sergeant in the 17th South Carolina Infantry Regiment, Company A, fought in the bloody battles at Manassas in 1862 and at Petersburg and Sayler's Creek, Virginia, in the last days before the Confederate surrender. On April 6, 1865, at Sayler's Creek, Union forces captured 6,000 of Lee's army. Upon hearing this news, a stunned Lee said, "My God! Has the army been dissolved?"[135] On July 3, 1865, Kitchin and three other soldiers requested two days of rations from the commissary to sustain thirteen of their comrades during their travels back home. They received salt beef, "hard bread," sugar, and coffee. The weary soldiers left Charlotte, North Carolina, by train. They stopped at the Catawba River later that morning, unable to continue because Union forces had destroyed the bridge. After crossing the river by a rough pontoon bridge and a rowboat, the soldiers waited for another train to continue their journeys. By noon that day, Kitchin arrived at "Lewises Turnout," where he started home on foot. Kitchin described his homecoming: "My folks had heard nothing from me from the time of the evacuation of Petersburg and Richmond and they had almost come to the conclusion that I had been killed or was dead[,] for the last letter they had got from me was wrote while I was in hospital. . . . They had some presentiment that I would be at home that day, after they ate their dinner, they said they would sit down and watch the gate until I would come. I came into the yard in a opposite direction of the gate, and caught them sitting watching for me at the gate. And the surprise can be easier imagined than described."[136]

The same summer after the war ended, Eliza Clifford Gordon Stiles made arrangements to move her family back to their plantation, Etowah Cliffs, in northern Georgia. Eliza's husband, William Henry Stiles Jr., left earlier to survey the house and urged his wife to get there soon, "if we ever expect to claim the place again."[137] Her father stayed to oversee the harvest of corn, sugarcane, peas, and sweet potatoes at their farm near Dawson, Georgia, in Terrell County—"all important to feed us on next winter up in Bartow [County]." The more than 200-mile journey from Dawson to Etowah Cliffs was challenging, at best. Eliza Stiles's letter to her brother William reveals the logistics of the difficult two-week journey, including feeding the assembled group of family, newly emancipated ex-slaves, and livestock on the road. "So you see we are going to travel in true country style—camping every night and cooking enough to last us for the next day. I shall only carry 3 servants for myself, a cook and washer, nurse and little girls to wait on table, and Henry will carry 3 men and their wives—for as we have to carry the corn and meal for us to eat—we have to make our force very small."[138]

Stiles discussed the demeanor of the former slaves who cared for the family during their journey upcountry: "Our negroes so far, behave exactly the same as usual and have given us no trouble though we know that they hear at Dawson and all about all that is going on in the country. They are perfectly obedient, respectful and talk in the most natural manner . . . as if there were no such thing possible of leaving us. How long things will go on so we cannot tell, but Henry supposes after January he will have to pay them wages if they are still with us."[139] Stiles's assessment reflects the instability of black labor and racial politics following the war. If one maintained a semblance of order, including blacks waiting on their white employers at mealtime, it was possible to pretend that little had changed, even in the aftermath of war.

White and black southerners alike were dazed by what the long Civil War had wrought—the end of the Confederacy and slavery. With these institutions, so too went a "southern way of life" that depended on enslaved labor for its economic livelihood. Once-prosperous white households swirled in domestic turmoil as the loss of slave labor profoundly impacted their worlds, including food preparation and service. Nothing would be the same, even mealtime. African American voices take us back to this tumultuous era to examine the food-related politics of slavery, emancipation, and freedom in their own words of testimony and memoir and in the narratives of ex-slaves.

5

Culinary Testimony

AFRICAN AMERICANS AND THE COLLECTIVE MEMORY OF A NINETEENTH-CENTURY SOUTH

In March 1873, Nancy Johnson, a former slave in Georgia, sought reimbursement for her family's property stolen by General Sherman's troops as they moved toward the coast in late 1864.[1] The same soldiers freed Johnson and her husband but stole their food, crops, and livestock over a period of two days. They ignored the couple's pleas that the property belonged to them, not their master. "I swore to the men so, but they wouldn't believe I could have such things," said Nancy Johnson.[2] She managed to reclaim her oven, which had been taken by the soldiers. Johnson then "put a pot on and made a pie & they took it to carry out to the head men [officers]." The soldiers stripped the farm bare. "They found our meat, it was hid under the house. . . . They took the bacon under the house, the corn was taken out of the crib, & the rice & the lard. Some of the chickens they shot & some they run down; they shot the hogs. . . . They carried it to their camps; they had lots of wagons there. They took it to eat, bless you! I saw them eating it right there in my house. They were nearly starved."[3]

Reconstruction-era testimonies like the Johnsons' vividly recall how Union forces confiscated both black and white southerners' food supplies throughout the war. The reports also confirm that Union soldiers, too—not just Confederates—suffered from hunger and difficult conditions on the battlefield and in camp. The Johnsons, like thousands of enslaved people in the South, engaged in a marginal economy, selling and trading home-raised goods to slowly accumulate personal property. After their farm was ransacked, they submitted a claim for $514.50 and were awarded $155 for the seized property.[4] Although free, they faced the end of the war economically worse off than they had been before the conflict began, devastated by their Yankee "protectors."[5]

The food narratives embedded in the chronicles of former slaves like the Johnsons claiming "their due" after the Civil War belong to an essential genre of African American literature and history—the slave narratives, memoirs, and autobiographies written by fugitive slaves before the

Civil War and by former slaves in the postbellum era.[6] Before the publication of these texts, African American voices were silenced in a world and time dominated by the words and legacy of white slaveholding southerners. Mining these texts for food-related stories and themes reveals a complex world of African American "consciousness"—historian Larry Levine's term to understand the minds of enslaved people in the plantation South—and the concurrent experiences of survival, accommodation, and resistance as blacks negotiated the movement from slavery to freedom. To explore the historical landscapes, experiences, and cultural mind-sets that food reveals in these worlds, we begin with the iconic voices of Frederick Douglass and Harriet Jacobs, black southerners and ex-slaves who documented their journeys to freedom, followed by the penetrating food motifs of the Works Project Administration (WPA) slave narratives, and ending with the food-entwined observations of white activists in southern Freedmen's Bureaus and schools for newly freed African Americans.

Slave Autobiographies

Iconic slave narratives, such as Frederick Douglass's *Narrative of the Life of Frederick Douglass, an American Slave, Written by Himself* (1845) and Harriet Jacobs's *Incidents in the Life of a Slave Girl* (1861), frequently used stories of food to underscore the depravity of slavery and the underside of "southern hospitality."[7] In these slave narratives, Douglass and Jacobs destroyed the trope of uncivilized blacks and civilized whites by exposing the brutality of their own slaveholders.[8] The supposed gentility and mannered world of the plantation table, supported by a benevolent master and moral mistress and loyal slave cooks and servants, was unmasked as a white-controlled gulag that terrorized the enslaved. Power and the racial control of food, not only what was served on the master's table but every bite a slave consumed, was a key aspect of slavery's authority and psychosis.

Frederick Douglass's description of mealtime for slave children at a tobacco plantation on the Eastern Shore of Maryland is unforgettable. Coarse boiled cornmeal, or "mush," was poured into a large wooden trough on the ground. Then, "like so many pigs they would come and devour the mush; some with oyster-shells, others with pieces of shingle, some with naked hands, and none with spoons. He that ate fastest got most; he that was strongest secured the best place; and few left the trough satisfied."[9] Feeding enslaved children as though they were animals reinforced slaveholders' disconnect from the human lives before them. Lyrics from a slave song in Douglass's memoir capture the reality of plantation food production and of what remained for enslaved workers: "We raise de wheat, Dey gib us de corn; We bake de bread, Dey gib us de crust; We sif' de meal, Dey gib us de huss [husks]; We peel de meat, Dey gib us de skin; And dat's de way Dey take us in."[10] The creativity of enslaved cooks to turn these "seconds" into nourishment that sustained their families is central to the power and persistence of African American cuisine in southern culture.

In his second autobiography, *My Bondage and My Freedom* (1855), Frederick Douglass contrasted the substandard rations of slaves with the "blood-bought luxuries" of the master's table. He flipped the traditional notion of plantation hospitality upon itself through descriptions of slaveholders' gluttony, such as that of his own master, Colonel Lloyd: "Here, appetite, not food, is the great desideratum. Fish, flesh and fowl, are here in profusion. . . . The teeming riches of the Chesapeake bay. . . . The dairy, too, probably the finest on the Eastern Shore of Maryland. . . . All conspired to swell the tide of high life, where pride and indolence rolled and lounged in magnificence and satiety."[11]

In *Incidents in the Life of a Slave Girl*, Harriet Jacobs described her Edenton, North Carolina, slave owners and the horrors she experienced because of her master's sexual predation and her mistress's jealousy and hatred. Dr. James Norcom and his wife, Mary Matilda Norcom—the Flints in Jacobs's narrative—expressed their particular form of sadism at the dinner table. If Sunday dinner was not served on time, Mrs. Flint waited in the kitchen until the meal was "dished" and then "spit in all the kettles and pans that had been used for cooking" to prevent the slave cook and her children from eating after the white family was served.[12] In this scenario, Jacobs reversed another racial convention of the time, depicting the white mistress, rather than the slave cook, as uncivilized and "dirty," polluting the food with her own saliva.[13] Mrs. Flint's behavior, explains literature scholar Minrose Gwin, became a form of "madness" in Jacobs's descriptions of two of the central women in her narrative—the mistress, Mrs. Flint, "a scorned white woman," and Linda Brent (pen name for Harriet Jacobs), "the beleaguered slave girl," both victims of slavery.[14] Food also distinguished the important character of Aunt Martha, Brent's pious, enslaved grandmother and protector. As a young slave, she became a cook at Horniblow's Tavern in Edenton and established a successful baking business.[15] Her popular preserves, cakes, crackers, and biscuits, as well as her tidy, ordered kitchen and tea shop, symbolize Aunt Martha's civility, again contrasted to the debauchery of the white slaveholders.

Household slaves, like the cook in Jacobs's narrative, often suffered worse exploitation than other slaves because they were so closely observed by white slaveholders. Jacobs noted Mrs. Flint's acute eye in the kitchen: "The slaves could get nothing to eat except what she chose to give them. Provisions were weighed out by the pound and ounce, three times a day."[16] The mistress knew exactly how many biscuits could be prepared from a quart of flour and "what size they ought to be."[17] Women slave owners frequently accused cooks and household servants of any number of misdemeanors, from surreptitiously eating a biscuit, to purposely ruining a recipe out of spite or inattention, to stealing silverware and other valuables. Masters were equally hard on domestic slaves. Dr. Flint, a vindictive "epicure," intimidated the slave cook at every meal.[18] "If there happened to be a dish not to his liking, he would either order her to be whipped, or compel her to eat every mouthful of it in his presence."[19] As punishment, the master also locked up the cook, removing her for hours from her nursing baby. Food, including the cook's breast milk, was Flint's chosen tool of torture to terrify and abuse his slave. By preventing the mother from feeding her child with her own breasts, Flint denied her womanhood.

Harriet Jacobs described the ultimate perversion of southern cooking as a pillar of the "gracious" plantation. "A 'favorite' punishment," writes Jacobs, "was to tie a rope around a man's body, and suspend him from the ground. A fire was kindled over him, from which was suspended a piece of fat pork. As this cooked, the scalding drops of fat continually fell on the bare flesh."[20] In this gruesome torture, the slave, again, is equated with an animal and literally "cooked."[21]

Booker T. Washington, the post-Reconstruction, Progressive-Era educator, was a child of former slaves and the first principal of Tuskegee Institute (founded in 1881) in Alabama. In his autobiography, *Up from Slavery* (1901), Washington remembered how a simple baked sweet became a symbol of his powerful drive for freedom. As a young child, Washington helped his mother, a slave cook, with her never-ending work on a plantation in Virginia. Washington observed the young white daughters of the house and their female friends as they stood in the yard outside the "big house" eating ginger cakes. "At that time those cakes seemed to me to be absolutely the most tempting and desirable things that I had ever seen," wrote Washington. "I then and there resolved that, if I ever got free, the height of my ambition would be reached if I could get to the point where I could secure and eat ginger-cakes in the way that I saw those ladies doing."[22]

WPA Slave Narratives

In the late 1930s, employees of the Federal Writers' Project (FWP), a New Deal agency, collected over 2,000 oral narratives of slavery from older, largely rural, black southerners. Remembered experiences of mealtime, slave rations, dishes prepared for the plantation household, and the seasonal cycles of food production, as well as food-related abuse by slave masters and near starvation, are recurrent topics in the slave narratives.

The interviews with ex-slaves were conducted at the height of segregation and racial terrorism against African Americans. Southern white interviewers attempted to capture black vernacular speech through misspellings, idiomatic phrases, and incorrect grammar.[23] The racial practice of manipulating language this way, considered a benign means of preserving regional "color" at the time, effectively disempowered poor blacks as uneducated, "innocent," or childlike. Others claim interviewers used exaggerated dialect to reflect the "vitality" of black language.[24] As head of the FWP's Office of Negro Affairs, Sterling Brown argued loudly against the popular misrepresentation of African Americans in the New Deal documentary projects.[25] In Florida, FWP editor Stetson Kennedy criticized excessive "artistic" license regarding black language, much preferring the "directness of the ex-slave speech."[26] Stetson recommended that interviewers' racist terms and patronizing expressions be deleted from edited narratives.[27] Selections from the slave narratives included here are printed as they appeared at publication in the 1930s and 1940s. Ultimately, ex-slave interviewees maintained their power by preserving their collective memories of resistance and survival for posterity—including hundreds of personal foodways narratives—and also choosing how they conveyed these stories to interviewers. John Blassingame described the slave narratives as "the single most important thing that was ever done" for nineteenth-century scholarship.[28]

During the FWP interviews, black men and women behaved as was expected of them before and after slavery by attempting to please the white interviewer and convey deference and good humor. As a means to protect themselves from possible repercussions for speaking negatively of their former masters and their descendants, ex-slaves often recalled benevolent masters who provided abundant food for their "white and black families."[29] At the same time, they routinely described other slaves' experiences as far worse than their own.[30] Historian C. Vann Woodward argued that interviewees' nostalgia for slavery was also shaped by their struggles during the Great Depression, including hunger as bad or worse than conditions former slaves had experienced in the plantation South. He stated, "For many the memory of slavery that often returned was that of eating and eating regularly."[31]

George Fleming, a former slave from Laurens, South Carolina, remembered ample food provided for plantation-era field hands, which he contrasted to the Depression and the minimal government pension

"Ex-slave on a farm near Greensboro, Alabama." Photograph by Jack Delano, May 1941. LC-USF33-020949-M2 (b&w film nitrate neg.), U.S. Farm Security Administration/Office of War Information Black & White Photographs, Prints and Photographs Division, Library of Congress, Washington, D.C.

he received in the late 1930s. "Dar was no want of food fer de hands. Marse knw'd if dey worked dey had to eat. Dey had collards, turnips and other good vegetables wid cornbread[.] Chunks of meat was wed [with] de greens, too, and us had lots of buttermilk. . . . I been a long time gitting dis pension, and it ain't much when you gits it. Back in slavery times we didn't have nor worries 'bout rent or something-to-eat."[32] Woodward recalled the words of a former enslaved man from North Carolina, whose experience was typical of the majority of slaves whose families experienced hunger on a daily basis: "It's all hard, slavery and freedom, both bad when you can't eat."[33]

The food stories in slave narratives can be read as tales within tales, in which food anecdotes and descriptions, like fables, reveal a deeper meaning, a lesson of survival, or a precautionary message. For example, ex-slave Alex McCinney's story of a discarded biscuit on a Mississippi plantation veils a story of hunger and hierarchy: "I recollect seein' one biscuit crust, one mornin'. Dey throwed it out to de dogs, an' I beat de dog to it."[34] Often a food narrative was told with a rhetorical purpose, such as describing hard work or difficult times or emphasizing the strength of family bonds. An interviewee shaped the moral "flavor" of the narrative, as did the white interviewer-editor who crafted the final transcription. Survival skills reside in ex-slave Stephen McCray's story of whether a full stomach was worth the degrading behavior required of a slave by his master. He explained this quandary from the perspectives of a raccoon and a dog. He preferred to be a hungry "coon" (offensive slang for a black person) than a fat dog, subjected to his master's constant abuse. "The coon said to the dog: 'Why is it you're so fat and I am so poor, and we is both animals?' The dog said: 'I lay round Master's house and let him kick me and he gives me a piece of bread right on.' Said the coon to the dog: 'Better then that I stay poor.' Them's my sentiment. I'm lak the coon. I don't believe in [a]'buse."[35]

Although slave narratives vary dramatically regarding the quantity and quality of rations and the treatment of enslaved laborers related to food, this vast memory bank is an important window on to the core foodways of slavery, as well as the diet of white southerners. Another story from George Fleming of South Carolina reveals this culinary landscape, yet must be read as his own memory "portrait" rather than an accurate account of plantation life: "Everybody have plenty to eat. Lots of times we had fish, rabbits, possums and stuff like dat; lots of fishing and hunting in dem days. Some slaves have lil' gardens of deir own, but most de vegetables come frum de big garden. Missus was in charge de big garden, but co[ur]se she didn't have to do no work. . . . Even de poor white trash had plenty to eat back in dem times. Marse have a hundred head of hogs in de smokehouse at one time."[36] Fleming's memories of slavery as a time "when everybody have plenty to eat" may have reflected the "fat" rather than the "lean" days of his own experience. The majority of enslaved people knew only deprivation and hunger in the plantation system. Despite his expansive memory, Fleming *did* accurately reflect central aspects of antebellum food systems in the plantation South. Most southerners, free and enslaved, lived on small farms and plantations where they grew much of what they ate, pork was the meat of choice, slaves were resourceful provisioners, white mistresses oversaw vegetable and flower gardens but did little physical labor, and even poor whites could eat relatively well if they had access to land.

Anna Wright, a child of enslaved parents, grew up on the James Ellis Plantation in Scotland County, North Carolina.[37] Born in 1865, she had memories of the plantation South that were largely based on the stories of her mother, who described trying times after the Civil War when white and black alike did not have enough to eat. Wright recalled a largely vegetable diet eaten by blacks, supplemented with small game that men hunted, including squirrels, rabbits, possums, and raccoons.[38] As times improved for the plantation owner, "Master James," so too did the food, including iconic dishes of the southern culinary canon—fried chicken and catfish, cornbread "dressing," seasonal fruit cobblers, and cakes. Wright discussed each dish in detail. After it was seasoned and floured, the chicken was simmered in ham gravy in a lidded heavy pot until tender, then uncovered and "fried a golden brown as quick as possible."[39] Chicken dressing was made from soft cornbread mixed with bacon grease, onions, and boiled eggs and seasoned with black pepper.[40] Fish was dipped in meal and fried. Catfish was stewed with onions. "Sweets" were cobblers made with summer blackberries and cooked in a large pan with two crusts. Cakes were "mostly plain or had jelly fillin', 'cept fer special company."[41]

More typical of the daily slave diet were dishes like "kush," griddle cakes, baked onions, cornmeal dumplings, greens, and "pot liquor"—the liquid in which vegetables were cooked, seasoned with a piece of salt pork. Anna Wright explained kush—a cornmeal-based dish—as cornbread cooked in a griddle and "mashed up with raw onions an' ham gravy poured over hit."[42] "Ashe cakes" were made of either wheat flour or cornmeal, wrapped in a damp cloth, and cooked in hot ashes on the hearth. Onions were prepared similarly. "Cornmeal dumplin's wus biled in de turnip greens, collards, cabbages. . . . At supper de pot licker wus eat wid de dumplin's. Dat's why de folks wus so healthy."[43]

Anna Wright's sense that this diet was wholesome contrasts sharply with contemporary perceptions of southern food as fried, fattening, and unhealthy. Yet she described a diet centered on local, seasonally grown vegetables and fruits, fresh fish and game, homemade condiments, minimal amounts of meat used mainly for seasoning, molasses and sorghum for sweetening, and poultry on special occasions. The biggest challenge of this diet was getting enough of it. Hardworking laborers needed all the calories they could get, and pork fat—minimally processed, unlike commercial pork products today—was an essential ingredient.

Ex-slaves described the great divide between the culinary abundance enjoyed by white slaveholders and the hunger and meager rations they experienced as slaves. Recurrent motifs in these narratives of racial disparity involved slaves' daily acts of food-related resistance and the slaveholder's punishment that followed. Louisa Adams recalled her North Carolina master who "worked us hard and gave us nuthin. . . . We were so hungry we were bound to steal or perish."[44] A combination of malnourishment, temptation, and tenacity prompted house slaves to take food by a variety of means. Slave narratives describe food eaten furtively as enslaved cooks and servants carried dishes from outdoor kitchens to the master's dining room. Julia Brown, a former slave in Georgia, recalled bringing a platter of waffles, "golden brown and pipin' hot," to the master's table. Not allowed such foods, she took one while out of sight, but swallowed it with difficulty: "I jest couldn't get rid of that waffle 'cause my conscience whipped me so."[45] Brown had so internalized the scripted punishments for the slightest infraction that her own conscience "whipped" her for taking the forbidden food. Other narratives, such as the one that follows, describe terrible violence inflicted upon slaves because of food-related incidents. These narratives served as powerful morality tales that emphasized the evils of slavery, an institution so dangerous it turned slaveholders into monsters.

Henrietta King, an ex-slave in Virginia, was disfigured for life when, as a young girl, she could not resist a piece of candy on her mistress's washstand. King emptied the chamber pots in the white household each morning. The hungry child saw the peppermint stick but knew to not touch it. One morning, she could not stop herself. "Ain't had a father workin' in de fiel' like some of de chillum to bring me eats—had jes' little pieces of scrapback each mornin' throwed at me from de kitchen. . . . I went straight in dere an' grab dat stick of candy an' stuffed it in my mouf an' chew it down quick so ole Missus never fin' me wid it."[46] The mistress confronted King the next morning and beat her severely. Unable to restrain the squirming girl on her lap, she positioned King's head under her rocking chair, crushing the child's facial bones. King was never able to chew solid food again. "Been eatin' liquid, stews, an' soup ever since dat day, an' dat was eighty-six years ago."[47] Years later when news came that "ole Missus had died," Henrietta King recalled her torturer, the "she-debbil what's burnin' an' twistin' in hell. . . . Didn't make me drap [drop] no tears."[48] Besides maiming her for life, the mistress destroyed a central aspect of Henrietta King's humanity—her ability to eat and enjoy food.

Scholars have long struggled to understand the cultural mentality of white slaveholders that could lead to such perverse displays of cruelty and warped "affection" in their own households, often directed at "beloved" slaves who were intimately tied to white families as cooks, house servants, and wet nurses who breast-fed planters' children. Ike Simpson, an ex-slave from Texas, described the white female slaveholder's "love" for him as a child, like that of a master for his favorite dog. "She kept me right wid her most of de time, an' when mealtime come she put me under de table and I ate out ob her hand. She'd put a piece ob meat into a biscuit an' hand it down to me."[49] Fear, insecurity, paranoia, stress, and plain meanness were exacerbated as slaveholding women attempted to maintain their black and white "families" and command authority at home, including their primacy as sexual partners to husbands.[50] The issue of racial purity persists in these remembered narratives, expressed in the rage of slave owners should blacks touch or consume foods meant for white bodies, and done so covertly beyond the legitimate boundaries of the kitchen. Ironically, white fears regarding the racial defilement of food existed side by side with interracial sex, forced by white masters upon enslaved women.

Food and Freedom

The food stories of survival, accommodation, and resistance interwoven in the FWP's slave narratives bring voice to generations of African Americans in the South as they fought to maintain their humanity, belief systems and culture, dignity, livelihood, and families on the journey from slavery to freedom. As the nineteenth century came to a close, African Americans in the South looked back upon a tumultuous era shaped by the institutionalization of slavery in the antebellum plantation South and the liberation of enslaved people after President Lincoln's Emancipation Proclamation of January 1863. Following the Civil War, Freedmen's Bureaus, missionary-sponsored programs, the experience of free labor, the right to vote, and the creation of African American schools were crucial way stations in the transformative journey that moved enfranchised black citizens into the new century and a "New South."

Inverting the racial hierarchy of paternalism that existed during slavery, a former slave came to a Freedmen's Bureau in South Carolina to seek help not for himself, but for former slaveholders, who were unable to provide food for themselves and their children. "They's might bad off. He's in bed, sick—ha'n't been able to git about this six weeks—and his chil'n's begging food of my chil'n. They used to own three or four thous'n acres. . . . It's no use tellin' them kind to work; they don't know how to work, and can't work; somebody's got to help 'em, Sir."[51] Like the slave autobiographies of Frederick Douglass and Harriet Jacobs, this narrative contrasts the ex-slave's fortitude and civility with the slaveholder's physical and emotional collapse after the war. The narrative also suggests a common motif in African American animal trickster tales, where a weaker character uses his wit and savvy to prevail over a stronger figure. Larry Levine describes these tales as narratives of "social protest or psychological release."[52] The ex-slave who sought aid from the Freedmen's Bureau for the traumatized slaveholder was like B'rer Rabbit, a survivor in his own prickly brier patch of slavery. Despite the inhumanity and daily traumas of plantation slavery, African Americans persevered and provided for their hungry families, a motif played out in slave narratives against the collapse of the plantocracy.

In 1868, Joseph Burt Holt and his wife, Julia Rollins Holt, traveled from Maine to Mississippi as white agents for the Freedmen's Bureau, where they provided relief and educational activities for freed blacks and refugees after the Civil War.[53] The stories of food interwoven in the Holts' observations reflect the postwar experiences of African Americans as they established independent lives and communities during Reconstruction and introduced "foreigners" in their midst to the tastes and culture of their southern home. Jackson, Mississippi, was flooded with large numbers of freedmen and their families, who sought both the protection of federal authorities in urban areas and opportunities to work outside the plantation.[54] Tensions were high as white and black southerners confronted the meaning of freedom.

Jackson's white community avoided the Holts because of their association with the Freedmen's Bureau, but the African American community embraced them. Julia Holt noted, "Not one friendly acquaintance to come in to see us except in a business way. . . . But we are fully occupied with our work for the colored people."[55] She described the slow but steady progress she observed among black families: "Many of the people are getting comfortable homes, keep a cow, and have nice gardens, look as comfortable in the house as of the white people we used to visit in Tenn."[56] African American neighbors brought a continual supply of homegrown vegetables and fruits to the Holts: "We've had vegetables enough brought in by our col'd friends today to last a week—sweet potatoes, lima beans, okra, and large squash called here kershaw [cushaw] and cantaloupe."[57] The Holts bought other food staples such as coffee and sugar at the military commissary in Jackson. Tins of canned lobster, cranberry sauce, and oysters listed on the Holts' commissary receipts suggest the New Englanders' longing for the tastes of their northern home.

On July 4, 1868, the ringing of a bell suspended around a mule's neck awakened the Holts. One can imagine the solemnity of the lone Freedmen's Bureau band marching through the streets of Jackson that morning. The white citizens of Jackson expressed their distaste for the federal holiday through their complete and utter silence. "No other bell was rung, no gun was fired, not even a firecracker," wrote Joseph Holt to his daughter.[58] A picnic for the Freedmen's Bureau children, given by their parents, was organized at the African American schoolhouse and grove surrounding it. "They formed in procession headed by the Marshall of the day (Colored). Then your Mother and the Colored teacher followed by the schools with many other Colored people making a procession of well dressed, well behaved children."[59] After the day of inspirational remarks and singing, Julia Holt noted how the children's speeches particularly moved the black community. She recalled, "My cook listened in wonder exclaiming, 'I never 'spected to live to see this day.'"[60] The nexus of black institutional life, which centered on family and church during slavery, expanded and flourished after the war and, most important, was "liberated" from the supervision of whites, such as the military officers and bureau agents like the Holts.[61] Blacks took control of their schools, churches, and benevolent societies. From this institutional base, states historian Eric Foner, freed African Americans "laid the foundation for the modern black community, whose roots lay deep in slavery but whose structure and values reflected the consequences of emancipation."[62]

Empty Kitchens

After the war's end, Reconstruction marked the beginning of a long, difficult journey as "slaves stepped into freedom and tried to define its dimensions."[63] The most routine activities, including cooking and housekeeping, became expressions of personhood as newly freed ex-slaves tested their new status. Enslaved cooks, now free, who continued to work for whites as paid servants demonstrated their autonomy in a variety of ways. Some walked away from their former positions at plantations, while others demanded that employers respect their ways of doing things. With so little "hired help" available, whites began to recognize a shift in power as black servants requested fair working conditions as free labor. Many "mammies" transformed from the beloved, docile "pets" of white families into newly empowered laborers.

"Emeline" was a much-admired black cook who disappeared from the kitchen of Pine Hill Plantation in Leon County, Florida, in May 1865. As guests arrived for dinner, the mistress's daughter was sent to find her, with keys to the kitchen storeroom in hand. She found "Emeline" in her house, dressed in her Sunday best, about to go to an emancipation picnic hosted by three regiments of blacks soldiers stationed near the plantation. "Take dem keys back ter yer Mother, an' tell her I don't never 'spects ter cook no more, not while I lives—tell her I'se free, bless de Lord! Tell her if she want any dinner she kin cook it herself."[64]

Even white antislavery activists experienced the strident autonomy of African American cooks. After the war, Charles and Etta Stearns, northern-born abolitionists, moved to Georgia to model a plantation run fairly and efficiently with free labor. At their newly named "Hope

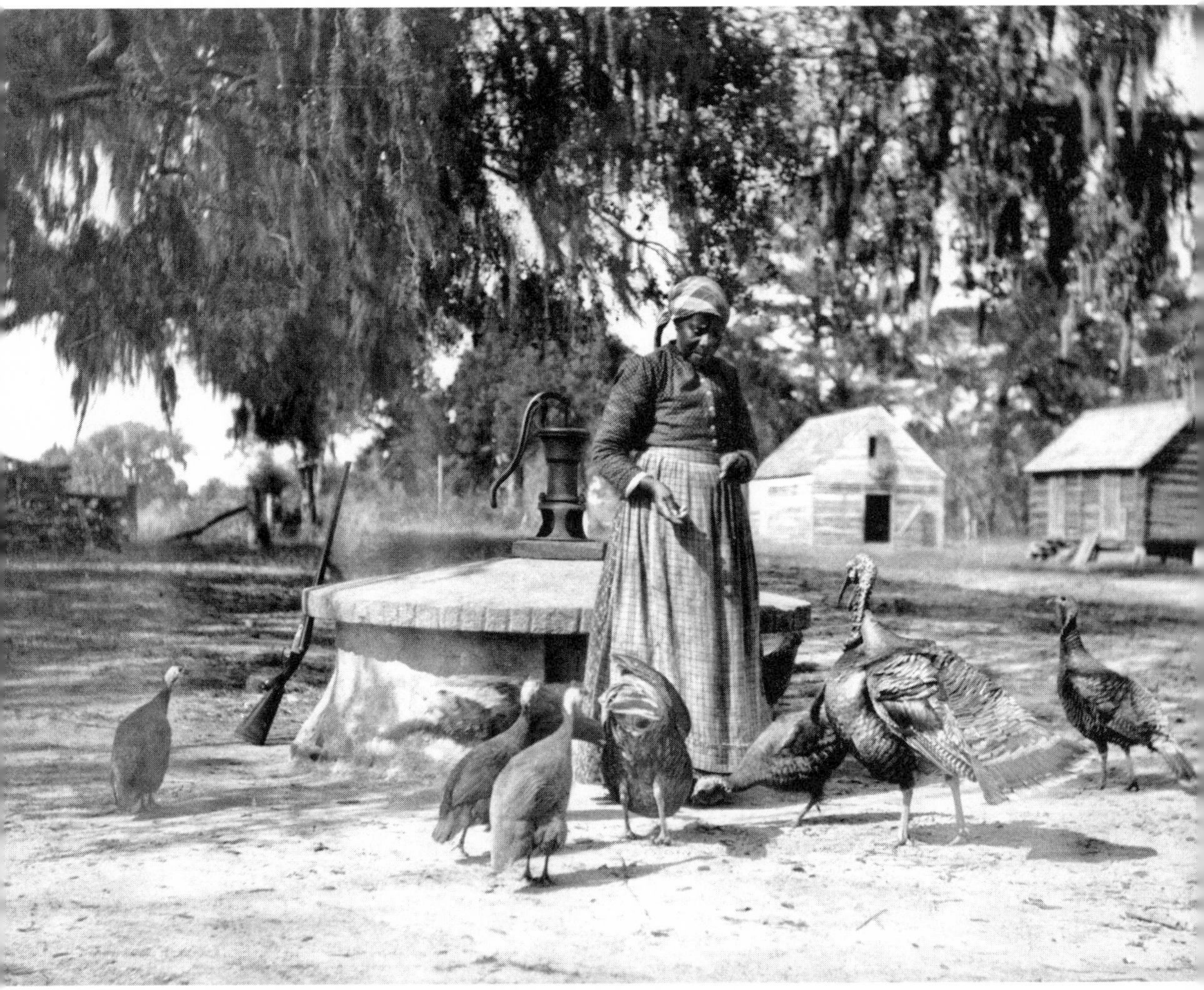

"Patience and Turkeys," Dean Hall Plantation, Berkeley County, South Carolina, built by William A. Carson, ca. 1827. Berkeley County Photograph Collection, Accession no. 1001.35, Folder 1001 Berkeley (23–43), South Caroliniana Library, University of South Carolina, Columbia, S.C.

on Hope Ever Plantation," trouble brewed when Etta Stearns pushed her new rules of domestic efficiency upon the black cook, "Margaret," and directed her to wash the dishes in a new manner. The former enslaved cook explained *her* rules of the house. She was cook of the house and wanted no trouble from another authoritarian, although well-intentioned, white woman: "We done cl[e]aned dishes all our days, long before ye Yankees heard tell of us, and now does ye suppose I gwine to give up all my rights to ye, just cause youse a Yankee white woman?"[65]

White female heads of households reluctantly learned to make due with fewer household servants, particularly cooks, as former slaves left southern plantations. By May 1865, all but two of Ella Gertrude Clanton

Thomas's household slaves had left her Georgia plantation. New servants came and left as quickly as they had arrived, testing their newly won freedom, negotiating for better work situations, and searching for family members from whom they had been separated during the war. A "mulatto woman named Leah" asked about being the cook, and Thomas hired her immediately: "That night and the next morning I ate two biscuits which she baked. . . . At dinner the next day she baked one of the best plum pies I ever tasted."[66] When the new cook stayed less than forty-eight hours, Thomas told her husband, "I do not know but what we are fighting shadows."[67]

Gertrude Thomas was confounded by the behavior of African American laborers after emancipation. Speaking to freed black cooks and house servants was no longer a one-sided conversation in which former slaveholders held the power and control. The sense of mutual obligation that had once existed between slaves and masters was no longer assumed.[68] White slaveholders who believed they knew their former slaves intimately and had trusted them to remain on the plantation as hired workers after the war were repeatedly shocked by the exodus of even the most trusted servant. Thomas complained about her former slaves and hired workers, exasperated by what she interpreted as laziness and disrespect, unable to see the independent spirit and ambition of a newly freed people. Historian Leon Litwack argues that this "legacy of distrust, bitterness, and recrimination" would shape race relations in the South for decades to come.[69] Part 1 of *The Edible South* concludes with the politics of the "reconstructed table" and an overview of the region's nineteenth-century culinary texts authored by white and black southerners. The monumental economic and social changes of the era were interwoven into recipes, domestic advice, and cooking instructions.

6

The Reconstructed Table

Throughout Reconstruction, white women of the former Confederacy struggled to accept the meaning of an emancipated workforce. The era was marked by efforts to restore racial superiority through the political and economic reenslavement of black southerners, including their roles in the kitchen. This massive shift of labor pushed middle- and upper-class whites to fundamentally reconsider the meaning of domesticity in their own lives as they confronted a growing "servant problem." With few options but to do it themselves, they struggled to balance cooking, housework, child care, and the daily responsibilities of wives and mothers in a changing southern landscape. Constant negotiations with domestic workers, new household technology, and an expanding canon of prescriptive cookbooks for the "servantless household" reflect white southern women's frustrations as they pondered the value of a cultivated mind versus the "routine of a domestic drudge."[1]

Power struggles between white employers and black domestic workers continued well into the twentieth century. Desiring to be with their own families, African American women preferred work outside white homes that required "live-in" servants. Historian Jane Turner Censer describes the "bleaching" of the southern white household as its workforce changed in the postwar years.[2] White middle- to upper-class housewives of the era, like Tryphena Holder Fox in Louisiana, sought white domestic servants, as she explained to her mother, "some good Irishman or Dutchman," married, without children.[3] When Gertrude Thomas complained to her husband about her struggles to retain servants at their Georgia home, he told her, "So much for the blessings of freedom."[4] Thomas wrote in her diary, "What I wish now is a sober respectable white woman or coloured who will find it to her interest to take an interest in pleasing me and interesting herself in my children."[5] White southerners attempted to construct lives without enslaved labor, while still maintaining their racial authority. Empty kitchens and less-than-satisfactory meals were visceral reminders that the South they once knew had vanished. Southern cookbooks reveal a region in transition as domestic workers came and went like "birds of passage."[6]

"Coffee after Dinner," Dean Hall Plantation, Berkeley County, South Carolina, built by William A. Carson, ca. 1827. Berkeley County Photograph Collection, Accession no. 1001.27, Folder 1001 Berkeley (23–43), South Caroliniana Library, University of South Carolina, Columbia, S.C.

Cookbooks bridge the era of Reconstruction to the early New South, when these seemingly benign texts became increasingly important in a growing consumer culture and the selling of a remembered South to southerners, outsiders, and tourists. Several "tried and true" southern cookbooks were in print by the 1870s, from Mary Randolph's beloved *The Virginia House-Wife* (1824) to Marion Cabell Tyree's *Housekeeping in Old Virginia* (1879). These works provided a rich cache of iconic recipes from both white and black women authors of the South. Cookbooks served not only as how-to guides for regional cooks, but also as sentimental souvenirs for outsiders that evoked the taste memories of the South's distinctive cuisine.[7] One genre of white-authored southern cookbooks of the nineteenth century presented a bucolic, pre–Civil War South of white elites and loyal black servants who lived in racial harmony—an imagined world northern reformers recognized as bankrupt.

Nineteenth-century southern cookbooks were influenced by earlier works that English women brought with them to the colonies, such as Hannah Glasse's *The Art of Cookery, Made Plain and Easy* (1747) and Gervase Markham's *The English Huswife* (1623). These works reflected the culinary styles of sixteenth- and seventeenth-century England. Eliza Smith's *The Compleat Housewife; Accomplish'd Gentlewoman's Companion* (1742) was the first cookbook published in the colonies, in Williamsburg, Virginia.[8] Another eighty years passed before a new cookbook broke the bonds of English cuisine and expressed a distinctly southern vision of the American table. In 1824, Mary Randolph's *The Virginia House-Wife* was published. Although the "warp" of *The Virginia House-Wife* was "solidly English," writes culinary historian Karen Hess, the larger "tapestry" revealed an eclectic Virginian and southern cuisine influenced by Native American flavors, but most importantly by enslaved cooks and with the culinary imprint of Africa and the Caribbean.[9] Hess writes, "Nothing in the history of early American cookbooks quite prepares us for the sumptuous cuisine presented by Mary Randolph."[10]

The author of *The Virginia House-Wife* evoked a more complex narrative of the antebellum South than only that of a pampered, white, southern mistress.[11] Born into the white slaveholding "first families of Virginia," Mary Randolph and her husband were set to live a life of privilege at their Virginia home, Moldavia, until politics took a different turn and their finances tumbled. Using her business acumen and the culinary skills of enslaved labor, Mary Randolph opened a boardinghouse in Richmond in 1808. In 1820, the Virginia couple sold their successful business and moved to Washington to be near their son. At age fifty-seven, Mary Randolph banked on her reputation as one of the finest hostesses and "cooks" in Richmond to sell cookbooks, and she did.

There is no mistaking the world from which Mary Randolph wrote *The Virginia House-Wife*. Randolph stood firmly in the slave South, as her recipes attest in their scale, ingredients, and techniques. Enslaved black cooks were responsible for the labor and innovation in her kitchen. Careful directions for curing bacons and hams and for preserving seasonal fruits, recipes for boldly seasoned stews such as gumbo and pepper pot, for "barbecue shote" (a young hog), wild duck, roast shad, fried chicken, curried catfish, oyster loaf, biscuits, "cornmeal bread," pound cake, rice pudding, and ice creams, and numerous instructions for vegetables and legumes—from okra and tomatoes to fried eggplant, squash, sweet potatoes, and field peas—clearly speak of a cuisine drawn from Randolph's experience on a Virginia plantation. She directed her work to both experienced slaveholding mistresses and young, newly married women just taking up housekeeping.

Mary Randolph's motto, "Method is the soul of management," suggests the influence of early nineteenth-century "enlightened" thinking upon the author, whose text emphasized order and reason. "The grand arcanum of management lies in three simple rules," wrote Randolph. "Let everything be done at the proper time, keep every thing in its proper place, and put every thing to its proper use."[12] She compared the government of a family to that of a nation, noting, "The contents of the Treasury must be known, and great care taken to keep the expenditures from being equal to the receipts."[13] Randolph clearly accepted the racial and gendered hierarchy of the plantation, but one senses she advocated greater power for women according to their capabilities, for which she was a prime example. A deeper message lay behind her advice to young housekeepers to not waste the day but to rise early, as a "late breakfast deranges the whole business of the day."[14] Seize the day *and* one's power. After nineteen editions, *The Virginia House-Wife*, a literary expression of the contested southern past, is still in print. It represents a high point in southern cuisine and flavor but also rises from the lowest depths of the region's history. Slavery built the southern table of Mary Randolph.

A number of nineteenth-century southern women authors followed in Mary Randolph's footsteps, as they, too, created cookbooks that codified the essential patterns of southern cuisine.[15] Lettice Bryan's *The Kentucky Housewife* (1839) and Sarah Rutledge's *The Carolina Housewife* (1847) pay homage to Randolph's similarly titled work and contain recipes comparable to those of *The Virginia House-Wife*. *The Carolina Housewife* was notable for its "nearly a hundred dishes in which rice or corn form a part of the ingredients"—evidence of the power of the Lowcountry rice kitchen.[16]

Lettice Bryan's *Kentucky Housewife* is one of the only volumes to include the word "slaves" in the text.[17] Her use of the term, and its glaring absence in Randolph's and Rutledge's texts, suggests the growing divide over slavery throughout the nation. Southern cookbook authors—black and white—hoped their works would find audiences outside the South too. Bryan added a brief serving instruction at the end of many of her 1,300 recipes, which would have been particularly helpful to nonsouthern readers. For "Grilled Cat-Fish," she advised her readers to "serve them in a warm dish, put over them two spoonfuls of lemon pickle, two of pepper vinegar, and a good quantity of melted butter and chopped parsley."[18] Bryan clearly spoke loudest to a southern white female audience. "Shun the deleterious practices of idleness, pride, and extravagance," wrote Bryan, "recollecting that neither of them constitutes the lady."[19]

African American voices were central to these culinary worlds, but in print, they lay only *behind* the recipes of nineteenth-century cookbooks by white southerners. Ignoring their intellectual hand in the creation of the distinctive cuisine of the South, particularly on the printed page, was the same denial of African Americans' humanity that whites had honed since slavery's introduction in the southern colonies. Two African American women, Malinda Russell and Abby Fisher, ended the silencing of black women in these domains. Russell's *A Domestic Cook Book* (1866), the first cookbook by an African American, and Fisher's *What Mrs. Fisher Knows about Old Southern Cooking* (1881) are among the most important nineteenth-century voices in the literary canon of southern cuisine.[20] Malinda Russell, a free black woman, was born and raised in east Tennessee. Abby Fisher, born in 1832, was an ex-slave from South Carolina. Her mother was a slave, and her father was a white slaveholder. Earlier professional manuals had been published by African American men: Robert Roberts, from Charleston, South Carolina, author of *The House Servant's Directory* (1827); and Tunis Campbell, a free black from New Jersey who trained as a hotel steward and later wrote *Hotel Keepers, Head Waiters, and Housekeepers' Guide* (1848). Food became a means of economic empowerment and independence for working, freed African American women like Malinda Russell and Abby Fisher.[21]

We can recount the story of Malinda Russell's life, thanks to the sleuthing of culinary historians Janice and Dan Longone, a breathtaking tale of courage, adversity, family tragedy, and fortitude. Russell shared her own narrative in the opening pages of her cookbook. After her plans to leave the slave South for Liberia were thwarted, Russell remained in the Upper South, where she cooked for a living and raised her son. To distance herself from the growing domestic terrorism of the final years of the Civil War, she moved to Michigan. Writing a cookbook was a crucial piece of Russell's economic survival: "This is one reason why I publish my Cook Book, hoping to receive enough from the sale of it to enable me to return home. I know my book will sell well where I have cooked, and am sure those using my receipts will be well satisfied."[22] The many recipes for cakes, pies, fruit preserves, custards, and elegant pastries in *A Domestic Cook Book*, rather than the iconic southern dishes and instructions of plantation cuisine, reflect Russell's professional experience as a skilled baker and a cook in private homes. In

Russell's cookbook, we see an alternative story of black women during and after the Civil War as they, too, claimed the American dream of a home and family.

Abby Fisher's skills provided for her family of eleven in San Francisco, where she and her husband manufactured pickles and preserves. She could not read or write, but with the support and assistance of her white female patrons in California, Fisher published her own cookbook in 1881. The book featured recipes and directions for her award-winning goods but also included "old chestnuts" of plantation cookery. White nostalgia for a mythic Old South became a money-making business after the Civil War. Cookbooks like *What Mrs. Fisher Knows about Old Southern Cooking* served an audience hungry for that "old plantation flavor," especially from a bona fide ex-slave-cook-turned-savvy-businesswoman.

In spite of the racial chasm between their experiences, Malinda Russell and Abby Fisher shared the same ambitions as Mary Randolph. By publishing cookbooks, all three authors hoped to profit from their reputations as talented cooks. Russell understood the power and meaning of authorship and carefully credited those who had influenced her work. "I learned my trade of FANNY STEWARD, a colored cook, of Virginia, and have since learned many new things in the art of Cooking," wrote Russell. In recognition of her white counterpart, Mary Randolph, dead for over thirty years, Russell noted, "I cook after the plan of the 'Virginia Housewife.'"[23]

A number of southern cookbooks—many from northern presses—were published at the same time as Russell's and Fisher's cookbooks in the closing decades of the nineteenth century. These texts sought to inspire and train white southern women readers frustrated by postwar depression, servant problems, and outdated kitchens. In Louisiana, Tryphena Holder Fox called upon Marion Harland's new *Common Sense in the Household: A Manual of Practical Housewifery* (1871). She sent her mother a jar of homemade preserves in late December 1872, possibly made from Harland's recipe for "Preserved Orange Peel" or "Lemon Marmalade."[24] "I made then after a rec[e]ipt in Marion Harland's Common Sense. . . . Mine have a slightly bitter taste though I hope it will not affect their goodness—any how you must take them as I *intended* & not as you may find them."[25] Born and raised in Virginia, Marion Harland (Mary Virginia Terhune) was a popular cookbook author and novelist of the mid-nineteenth century. Her best-selling, step-by-step, "common sense" cookbook included many southern recipes, such as ambrosia, fried chicken, and gumbo, that appealed to both native-born southerners and newcomers like Fox.[26]

Marion Harland dedicated her cookbook to "fellow-house-keepers, North, East, South and West," and she wrote in a sisterly voice that reflected her empathy for white middle-class American housewives without servants.[27] "You are mistress of yourself, though servants leave," she wrote. "Have faith in your abilities. You *will* be a better cook for the mental training you have received at school and from books."[28] These words resonated with southern housewives like Gertrude Thomas, who complained of the erratic work patterns of the freed black and white working-class women she hired after the war. Another popular regional text, *The Dixie Cook-Book* (Atlanta, 1885), directly addressed the challenges faced by southern matrons "since the war."[29] The volume was dedicated to the "Mothers, Wives, and Daughters of the 'Sunny South,' who have so bravely faced the difficulties which *new social conditions* have imposed on them as mistresses of southern homes, and on whose courage and fidelity in good or ill fortune the future of their beloved land must depend."[30]

Another text in this genre of postwar cookbooks was *Mrs. Hill's Southern Practical Cookery and Receipt Book* (1872). Georgian Annabella Hill's culinary and housekeeping instructions were designed for "young and inexperienced Southern housekeepers."[31] With her husband dead and the family plantation sold, Hill needed a means of support. Hill's noted hospitality sustained her during financially insecure times. Culinary historian Damon Fowler describes Hill's New York–published text as an unusual combination of the local and the cosmopolitan, of antebellum cookery and Reconstruction-era advice for servantless white homemakers.[32] In over 1,000 recipes, Hill mixed classic southern dishes and Georgia specialties with wide-ranging references to experts in domestic science—the scientific principles applied to the home-centered worlds of food preparation and kitchen technology.

The Reverend Ebenezer Warren's introduction to Hill's cookbook, written in 1867 for the first edition, is a classic call to white southern women in the "degenerate" postwar years to return to their kitchens and revive the "good housewifery" of the South's "old times."[33] With the war just two years past, Warren was cynical about the excesses of plantation times: "The days for romance have passed, if they ever existed."[34] His vision of an industrious, moral future that awaited white southerners foreshadowed the New South, and central to this vision was white women's labor—not directing the labor of others but doing the work themselves. "As she had performed so gracefully the duties of mistress of the establishment in the past," wrote Warren, "so she will, with a lovelier grace, perform whatever labor duty demands."[35]

Warren added some words of advice for the "sterner sex," too. The plantation era had passed, and with it had gone the enslaved labor force that had cooked, hauled water, cured hams, and stored food in the detached kitchens and outbuildings of work yards. The reverend encouraged white husbands to improve their homes, to make them more efficient and appealing for their wives by not merely updating but by tearing down the domestic landscape of the old plantation. "Look around your premises and see if a reformation is not greatly needed. . . . Your kitchen is set quite a distance in the rear of your dwelling; the smoke-house off in another direction quite as far. . . . If you cannot do otherwise, burn that kitchen and smoke-house where they stand. . . . Unite your kitchen with your dwelling."[36] Reform was slow to come, though, as the majority of poverty-stricken, white and black southerners made do with what little they had after the war. More affluent white southerners who survived the war with some resources gradually renovated homes to accommodate cast-iron cookstoves and indoor plumbing. "Changes began," wrote historian Joe Gray Taylor, "but in the countryside the old ways would remain strong for two generations."[37]

A final cookbook takes us to the dividing line between the Old South and the New South, as white southerners rewrote the region's history in the final decades of the nineteenth century to reconcile the defeat of the Confederacy. Marion Cabell Tyree's *Housekeeping in Old Virginia* (1879) called upon the classic imagery of the "Cavalier Myth" to describe the noble English origins of Virginia's lauded hospitality. Her preface takes the reader back to the days before the American Revolution, when the great sons of Virginia ripped the "glittering arms of King George from their sideboards" and introduced a "new style of living . . . noted for its beautiful and elegant simplicity."[38] A recipe best explains this evolved southern style to Tyree's readers. Combine the "thrifty frugality of New England with the less rigid style of Carolina," she wrote, and you have Virginia hospitality, the "very perfection of domestic art."[39]

Marion Tyree collected over 1,700 southern recipes attributed to the white daughters and wives of the "first families of Virginia." The names of these prominent women, printed in the front pages of the text, established a pedigree for Tyree's book. A publicity quote from the *Chicago-Inter Ocean* quipped, "If two hundred and fifty matrons of Virginia can not teach their sisters in other states something these sisters don't know about housekeeping, then corn bread is a failure, and Lady Martha Washington is a free and independent American myth."[40] First Lady Mrs. Rutherford B. Hayes endorsed the cookbook, as well as the wives of the chief justice of the Supreme Court and the nation's secretary of state, governors, and senators. No one was better positioned to reach such an elite group of American women than Tyree, a native of Lynchburg and the last surviving granddaughter of Virginia's revolutionary legislator Patrick Henry.

Tyree urged her white female readers to persevere in the kitchen—young housewives with little experience in the kitchen arts because of their youth and an older generation that had once depended on skillful cooks now long absent: "Be not daunted by one failure, nor by twenty. Resolve that you will have good bread, and never cease striving after this result till you have effected it. If persons without brains can accomplish this, why cannot you?"[41] And what persons would this be? Certainly, Tyree's unreconstructed slander was aimed at African American cooks and domestic workers. The initials of Tyree's white contributors may follow each recipe, but the invisible hands and skills of African American women remain embedded in the text despite their anonymity.

On the final pages of *Housekeeping in Old Virginia*, advertisements promoted the latest Champion Monitor cast-iron cookstoves, Dr. Scott's "electric corset" with magnetized boning, and new convenience foods, such as "Nestle's Milk Food for Infants and Invalids." The cookbook concluded with instructions for common medicinal remedies and house-cleaning advice. None were more evocative of the post–Civil War South than directions "To Freshen Old Black Silk," "To Restore the Pile of Velvet," and "To Renew Black Crape Veils."[42] White female daughters of the failed Confederacy were pulled between two worlds and two eras. One demanded they look back as ever-vigilant caretakers of the memory of lost fathers, husbands, and sons of the Old South, dressed in the worn velvet, black silks, and crepes of mourning. The other faced forward to a New South, where all southerners would slowly and painfully redefine the meaning of both regional and American citizenship. Food remained an evocative force that tugged both ways, reminding white southerners of the flavors of the plantation table and black southerners of the bitter taste of slavery. The region was irrevocably drawn into a century of unimaginable change as sharecropping replaced plantation agriculture, an industrialized South was born, and an era of progressive reform and consumption influenced the southern table.

II

New South

In the Big Rock Candy Mountains
All the cops have wooden legs,
And the bulldogs all have rubber teeth,
And the hens lay soft boiled eggs.
There the farmer's trees are full of fruit,
And the barns are full of hay,
And I'm bound to go
Where there ain't no snow,
And the rain don't fall,
And the wind don't blow
In the Big Rock Candy Mountains.

In the Big Rock Candy Mountains
You never change your socks,
And the little streams of alcohol
Come a-tricklin' down the rocks.
. . .
There's a lake of stew, . . .
And a gin lake, too,
You can paddle all around 'em
In a big canoe
In the Big Rock Candy Mountains.
—Harry "Haywire Mac" Kirby McClintock (1882–1957),
"The Big Rock Candy Mountains"

In the first decades of the twentieth century, southerners—Confederate veterans and former slaves, newly arrived European immigrants, sharecroppers and landowners, mill workers and businessmen, tenant farmwives and middle-class club women, hobos and drifters—struggled to gain secure footing in the rapidly shifting landscape of the American South. As the old plantocracy crumbled, a mythic Dixie was revived in the post-Reconstruction South. Food provides a window onto monumental changes in this era as southerners struggled to recover from the Civil War and strained to embrace modernity. The pull between the past and a vision of progress in the South is exemplified in pivotal movements between the late nineteenth century and the beginning of World War II in which food signifies the region's identity struggle. Southerners witnessed the birth of the New South, the term popularized in 1886 by Henry Grady, editor of the *Atlanta Constitution*, to describe a coming era of "growing progress and prosperity."[1] Black southerners demanded their rightful place in this changing South despite constant threats of violence and even death.

Native Tennessean Harry "Haywire Mac" McClintock's 1928 recording of "The Big Rock Candy Mountains" sprang from this New South world.[2] The son of railroad men, McClintock was an adventurer/country singer/union activist. His ballad touched a nerve during the Depression years, as thousands of unemployed men left the South and wandered the country "riding the rails" searching for work, food, and shelter. "The Big Rock Candy Mountains" described a land where food was abundant and free for the taking—"a lake of stew, . . . / and a gin lake, too"—a distant fantasy in the pinched times of the American South.

In Part 2, we explore these New South worlds through the lens of regional food politics and practices. Chapter 7 considers the monumental repercussions for regional food production and access as southern agriculture transformed from plantations to sharecropping and industrial farming, impacted by federal relief programs and legislation in the first decades of the twentieth century. In Chapter 8, we examine the reform-minded efforts of home economists and the field of domestic science to address the problems of a deeply malnourished South. Chapter 9 analyzes two southern "dietaries," ethnographic case studies of diet at the turn of the twentieth century that reveal the intransigent racism of the era as manifested in disease and nutritional collapse. Chapter 10 investigates the early twentieth-century settlement schools in both the Lowcountry and the mountain South, where changing the southern diet was at the heart of educational programs. In Chapter 11, we return to the rural South and the homes of poor and working-class southerners, where Progressive-Era reforms and educational interventions deeply shaped southern food and health. In Chapter 12, the daily lives and foodways of working-class and impoverished southerners are examined through the southern university-based social science research and New Deal documentation of the 1930s. To conclude this journey through the New South, Chapters 13 and 14 consider the "selling of the South" to the nation through a new food-centered consumer culture and tourism that promoted branded regional narratives.

7

The Shifting Soil of Southern Agriculture and the Undermining of the Southern Diet

Whether living in the former plantation districts of the Carolinas and Georgia, in the Mississippi Delta, in the Alabama Black Belt, among the rice fields of northeastern Arkansas, amid the sugarcane operations in southwest Louisiana, or on the small hay and grain farms of the Piedmont and the Upcountry South, the majority of southerners at the end of the nineteenth century still encountered a world shaped by agriculture and the seasonal rituals of farming and food production. The springtime preparation of fields for seed, summer cultivation and tilling, and harvest and market in the late summer and fall tied southerners to generations of farm families before them. But beneath these traditional practices, nothing was the same, not the people who worked the fields, not the crops, not the owners of the land, not even the land. Margaret Mitchell's epic novel, *Gone with the Wind* (1936), and the film (1939) were an elegiac commentary on the importance of land to southerners. Planter Gerald O'Hara speaks sharply to his strong-willed daughter, who is distracted by the young men and parties of the Old South: "Do you mean to tell me, Katie Scarlett O'Hara, that Tara, that land doesn't mean anything to you? Why, land is the only thing in the world worth workin' for, worth fightin' for, worth dyin' for, because it's the only thing that lasts."[1]

As the turn of the twentieth century heralded the New South, dramatic changes in southern agriculture significantly impacted the food and health of black and white working-class southerners.[2] How a region of great agricultural wealth and productivity could struggle to feed its people was bound to the seismic shifts in southern farming that altered food availability and access across the South. This era was marked by the disempowerment of thousands of black and white tenant farmers and sharecroppers throughout the South, who soon were in debt, losing farmland, and, in principle, reenslaved to large landowners as former plantations were divided into rental shares. "This was a feudal land," writes John Egerton, with its "ruling nobles"—landowners—and its "peasants"—sharecroppers and tenant farmers.[3] Food was at a premium for working families stripped of control of their land.

Ultimately, these changes forced thousands of white and black families off the land and into cities to seek work in southern textile mills and factories. In these worlds, wages made the promise of three meals a day for children more probable. Thousands more left the South completely, drawn by economic opportunities outside the region—blacks pulled by the Great Migration and the chance to escape Jim Crow racism and poor whites looking for steady employment. Historic agricultural legislation of this era supported important twentieth-century reforms in southern farming and foodways, yet because of racism, it also ensured growing land loss for black farmers. Laws created separate land-grant colleges for southern blacks and whites, home economics programs at southern universities, industrial schools, and settlement schools, as well as the food-related initiatives of agricultural experiment stations, county extension agencies, and "home demonstration" professionals. From here, we examine foundational shifts in southern agriculture that systematically undermined the daily diet of working southerners as the Old South confronted the New South.

Southern Agriculture Transformed, and Not a Bite to Eat

The plantations of the antebellum South, once the source of unimaginable wealth for a white elite minority, were not tenable without slave labor. After planters reclaimed land confiscated by the federal government during the war, they watched sons walk away from their birthright, the next generation as much demoralized by the prospect of rebuilding without money and slaves as they were by the war and its aftermath.[4] Planters became landlords, dividing their estates and large farms into smaller pieces rented to African American freedmen and poor whites to work. This system of farming, which turned thousands of impoverished, landless, white and black southerners into thousands of impoverished sharecroppers and tenant farmers, was tenacious. Because it made money for landowners and creditors, it lasted well into the 1940s, but not without protest. It was the target of a generation of agronomists, documentarians, federal relief workers, home economists, reformers, scholars, and scientists who attempted to push southern farmers out of tenancy, end the region's addiction to cotton, and encourage agricultural diversity and market-oriented farms. Close to two-thirds of southern farmers were sharecroppers or tenants, with an average yearly income of less than $1,000.[5]

Cotton became the crop of choice in the growing cash economy of the

"Sharecropper's cabin surrounded by cotton field ruined by hail. Note absence of garden; sharecropper has two crops, corn and cotton. It is extremely unlikely that another cotton crop may be grown this year." Photograph by Russell Lee, New Madrid County, Missouri, May 1939. LC-USF33-011565-M2 (b&w film nitrate neg.), Prints and Photographs Division, Library of Congress, Washington, D.C.

New South, with tobacco a close second.[6] "Unlike grain or vegetables," explains historian Edward Ayers, southern farmers believed "cotton would always be worth *something*."[7] Yet for all its virtues—it was easy for a family to grow, it required no expensive equipment or special agricultural knowledge or methods, it did not spoil, and it could be quickly turned into credit for the farmer and cash for the merchant—cotton was not edible.[8] Black and white farm families raised cotton, and tobacco, too, to the "detriment of raising food for their own families."[9] A garden required cash to buy seeds, time to tend it, and a patch of soil—and most tenants and sharecroppers had none of these. Store credit was expensive, too, but children had to eat. *The Collapse of Cotton Tenancy*, a 1935 publication from the University of North Carolina Press, examined "How the Tenant Lives" in the South and pointed to the "most meager and ill-balanced diet of any large group in America."[10] Joint authors of the study, Fisk University sociologist Charles Johnson, Edwin Embree of the Rosenwald Fund, and Will W. Alexander, director of the Commission on Interracial Cooperation, noted, "Because the growing of household produce does not fit into the economy of a cash-crop, it is not encouraged by landlords, whose prerogative it is to determine the crops grown."[11]

To raise cotton and tobacco, tenant farmers and sharecroppers needed money to purchase seed and other supplies to get crops into the ground, as well as food for their hungry families.[12] They turned to landlords and the plantation commissary or a local "furnishing" merchant for credit to secure operating supplies and staple foods.[13] A period conversation between a black tenant and her white landlord illustrated the food-related failings of this arrangement for the working poor: "Boss man,—'What's the trouble, Julia, don't you feel well?' I say, 'I'm just hungry, Mr.—.' 'Ain't you got nothing to eat at your house, Julia?' 'I ain't got nothing but fat back and corn bread, and I done eat that so long that I believe I got the pellagacy [pellagra], Mr.—.' His face turns red when I say that, and he said, 'Well, Saturday, I'm gonna give you some flour too. Just come by the office.'"[14] Merchants extended credit to tenant farmers in the form of crop liens—a promissory agreement that guaranteed repayment through money banked on the tenant's pending crop sale. If less money came in from the crop than was expected, the farmer remained in debt to the landlord and merchant. Thus ensued a permanent cycle of poverty and liability, until the merchant called in his debt by foreclosing on the farmer's meager belongings, and for the few small landowners, their homes and land.[15]

Hoping that a better crop year was always on the horizon, poor tenant farmers and sharecroppers continued to buy the cheapest and most filling food they could find for their families at the plantation commissary or a store in town, a monotonous diet dependent on cornmeal, salt pork, field peas or beans, and molasses.[16] Herein lies the *most* significant factor in the degeneration of the early twentieth-century southern diet as daily meals were inextricably shaped by a culture of racism and poverty.[17] This system was so pervasive and deep-rooted that it continues in the contemporary South, where low income and lack of food access limit the working poor to the most substandard food options. The diseases are different today—diabetes and obesity instead of the New South's pellagra and typhoid—but the causes behind these conditions remain the same: poverty and racial disfranchisement of generations of working-class southerners.[18]

Many landlords of the New South forbade their tenants from using rented acreage for anything other than cotton—even a small garden plot—preferring that they buy food supplies from the plantation commissary, where prices were higher than stores in town. In her ethnographic study of African American life in 1930s Indianola, Mississippi, anthropologist Hortense Powdermaker recorded this memory from a black teacher: "Just a few years ago a tenant was compelled to plant cotton up to his doorstep and was not permitted to have his own vegetable patch. Occasionally some cropper would fool the landlord and plant way off where it couldn't be seen. If he was caught, he was punished."[19] With the passage of agricultural reform legislation in the early 1900s, county extension agents and home demonstration educators urged farmers to diversify and plant more food crops for both market and home use. Extension agents often went to landlords to seek permission for their tenants to plant a garden plot and, more frequently than not, were turned down.

Sociologist Rupert Vance described the choke hold of cotton and tobacco on eastern North Carolina in the early 1930s, where he found "the most abject rural poverty in America."[20] Vance contrasted the wealth represented by cash crops and the near absence of food crops to feed hungry tenant farm families: "First in the nation in its combined production of cotton and tobacco, no other area produces cash crops of such value; no area has increased its tenancy so rapidly, and in no area do livestock, milk, and home-grown vegetables play so little part in farming."[21] In a regional dietary survey, Vance confirmed poor southerners' dependence on corn, particularly low-quality cornmeal, which provided little nutrition on its own. Corn constituted 23 percent of the food intake of white Tennessee and Georgia "mountaineers" and 32 percent of the diet of southern black tenant farmers.[22] Corn was less than 2 percent of the diet of northern farmers of the same economic standing.[23] Salt pork made up 40 percent of southern tenant farmers' diet.[24]

Any southerner raised in a cotton-growing town from the 1870s up until as late as the 1970s remembers cotton planted in every available bit of earth. The Works Projects Administration (WPA) publication *Arkansas: A Guide to the State* (1941) confirms how the crop dominated the landscape in cotton-growing regions in the South. In the city of Blytheville, "many of the town's thoroughfares run into cottonfields."[25] A WPA writer described the people of this section of Arkansas and their single-minded focus on cotton: "[They] talk about cotton, they dream about it, they wear it, and like millions of Americans they eat foods made from cottonseed oil."[26] Growing up in Blytheville in the 1960s and 1970s, I stared into the endless expanses of cotton that lay on the other side of the chain-link fences that bordered my friends' backyards on the edge of town. Homes in "the country" were so completely surrounded by cotton

"Negro day laborers brought in truck from nearby towns, waiting to be paid off for cotton picking and buy supplies inside plantation store on Friday night." Marcella Plantation, Mississippi Delta. LC-USF34-052200-D (b&w film nitrate neg.), Prints and Photographs Division, Library of Congress, Washington, D.C.

fields that they looked like ships afloat in a sea of green in the early summer, and by early fall, they were adrift in a swath of white powder puffs.

The Farm Ideal of the Upcountry South Fades

In the first two decades of the twentieth century, family-owned farms prevailed in the Upper South where a decent living could be made in sections of Kentucky, Virginia, and Tennessee.[27] These farms offered a quality and pace of life in the "diversity and diversion" of raising animals and a mix of food crops and fruit trees, rather than the driving, physical labor of growing cotton, which offered little sense of ownership and at the end of the day, nothing to eat.[28] Upcountry farmers prospered from government programs during World War I that supported bigger yields to mitigate European food shortages.[29] Eased regulations and loans allowed farmers to enlarge their operations. The gains were short lived, though, when crop prices dropped after the war and farmers were saddled with higher taxes and expenses.

In the southern mountains, hunting, fishing, raising a few pigs and cattle, tending a patch of corn, vegetables, and fruit trees, plus trade and barter with one's neighbors had once provided a comfortable subsistence for working families.[30] This culture of agrarian self-sufficiency faded as new railroads and extractive industries like timber and coal changed the rural landscape.[31] Forced to sell some or all of their land, small farmers moved to towns and cities, seeking jobs in industry and the growing consumer economy of the early 1900s to the 1920s. Some abandoned agriculture completely, while others maintained a foothold on their farms and worked in the textile mills of the Carolina Piedmont seasonally after their crops were harvested.[32]

The agrarian ideal of the Upcountry South was virtually unachievable by the majority of poor farmers in the less-temperate interior and coastal South, who owned little or no land, with what they did own depleted from overplanting. With so many farmers growing cotton, a surplus of the crop caused prices to drop even further by the end of the 1920s. Dreams of a piece of land, a home, and three "square" meals a day faded as the return on cotton diminished and the South entered the Depression and the lean years that followed. With declining prices for both cotton and tobacco, many small landowners could no longer afford to pay mortgages and feed their families. Tenant farmers and sharecroppers were caught in the same economic trap, but with even less recourse. "Their lives became not only poorer," writes Edward Ayers, "but more barren."[33]

Moving On

Decades of poverty, hunger, racial brutalization, and increasing disfranchisement forced thousands of African Americans to leave the South, beginning an exodus in 1915 during World War I that continued until the 1970s. Over 6 million black southerners left the rural and urban South, including thousands of former landowners, farm laborers, and sharecroppers. They chose one of three central migration routes, which led them to the urban Northeast, to the cities of the Midwest, or to California. News from family and friends already established outside the South, as well as the black-owned newspapers published in northern and midwestern cities, alerted southern blacks to higher wages and good schools for their children.[34] New wartime industries in these regions needed laborers, and black southerners needed decent jobs. White landowners in the Mississippi Delta were loathe to give up the black laborers and tenants who worked their plantations and threatened to take action.[35] Police prevented blacks from purchasing train tickets and even pulled them off trains headed north. Not unlike the covert escapes that Jews devised to get their families safely out of Europe in the 1930s and early 1940s, blacks developed similar plans by traveling at night or walking miles to a distant and less-volatile train station. Black travelers were identifiable by their lunch boxes of cold chicken and soft-boiled eggs and pocketsful of biscuits that sustained them during long journeys.[36] Psyche Williams-Forson discusses the legendary "chicken bone express," the colloquial term for train routes frequented by blacks leaving the South.[37] Chicken bones allegedly tossed from train windows left culinary evidence of the common paths of black migration.[38]

Once they were safely established in northern cities, participants in the Great Migration called upon the rich cultural heritage they carried from the South—the music, dance, language, and food traditions that would powerfully shape the worlds they encountered throughout the nation.[39] In Chicago, Detroit, Los Angeles, New York, and St. Louis, tidy backyard patches of field peas, yellow squash, collards, and snap beans were evidence of displaced African American southerners. Black-owned cafés, street stands, and farm trucks loaded with southern produce and food products on the streets of Harlem, Chicago, Kansas City, Washington, D.C., and other destinations of the Great Migration offered a taste of home for the southern black diaspora.[40] In Ralph Ellison's *Invisible Man* (1953), the nostalgic, powerful pull of food draws the black protagonist in New York City back to the South as he encounters a street vendor in Harlem selling baked yams from a cart: "I stopped as though struck by a shot, deeply inhaling, remembering, my mind surging back, back. At home we'd bake them in the hot coals of the fireplace, had carried them cold to school for lunch; . . . we'd love them candied, or baked in a cobbler, deep-fat fried in a pocket of dough, or roasted with pork and glazed with the well-browned fat. . . . More yams than years ago, though the time seemed endlessly expanded, stretched thin as the spiraling smoke beyond all recall. I moved again. 'Get yo' hot, baked Car'lina yam,' he called."[41]

The 3 R's Relief, Recovery, and Reform

For those who remained in the South, the "boldly modernist" federal relief and farm programs of President Franklin Roosevelt's New

Deal—a string of 1930s economic programs designed to provide "Relief, Recovery, and Reform" from the Depression—represented policies that would forever change the character of southern agriculture from plantations and small family-owned farms to large-scale, industrial agriculture.[42] "Federal policies became the legal basis for agribusiness," states historian Pete Daniel, "part of a new grid that, along with science and technology, would supersede labor-intensive agriculture."[43] These changes in southern farming also brought dramatic reductions in food production and access for the majority of the South's working poor, who accepted government surplus food in desperate times. Mildred Cotton Council grew up in rural Chatham County, North Carolina, and remembered when her father reluctantly received "Roosevelt's WPA food," including cheese, whole wheat flour, yellow cornmeal (they were used to white), and canned meat.[44] Resolute about his family's ability to provide for themselves, Mr. Cotton thanked the government agents and asked them to not bring any more. "It will take me a long time to use all this," he said.[45] The huge commercial chicken and pork operations that dominate southern agribusiness today originated in this period when farmers were encouraged to "get big or get out" of growing food. To do so required more land, chemical fertilizers, and mechanization. The U.S. Department of Agriculture (USDA) helped to make this possible but systematically favored white farmers over black in supporting farm loans and other needs.[46]

The "keystone" of the New Deal's agricultural relief programs was overseen by the Agricultural Adjustment Administration (founded in 1933), which paid landowners—again, largely well-to-do white farmers—to take land out of cotton and tobacco production and thereby reduce the surplus and raise the value of these crops.[47] In principle, landowners were expected to share 50 percent of their payments with their tenant farmers and sharecroppers, who desperately needed the money to feed their hungry families. In most cases, they did not. Landowners used the funds to purchase tractors, combines, and mechanized cotton pickers to accelerate crop production. Tenant farmers and sharecroppers were evicted; small farmers went bankrupt and sold their land to larger landowners.

Protests of tenant evictions were mounted by the Southern Tenant Farmers' Union, founded in 1934 in northeastern Arkansas by farmers, black and white, men and women.[48] Although it grew to over 35,000 members and was a powerful example of early interracial civil rights activism, the organization was undermined by allegations of communism, continued violence against sharecroppers, and divisiveness within the labor movement.[49] The southern sociologists who authored

"Families of evicted SFTU [*sic*] sharecroppers on the Dibble plantation, Parkin (vicinity), Arkansas." LC-USF34-014005 (b&w film nitrate neg.), Prints and Photographs Division, Library of Congress, Washington, D.C.

The Collapse of Cotton Tenancy criticized the New Deal programs that failed tenant farmers and pushed them off the land with little or no resources—including food—for their families.[50] Soon after, President Franklin Roosevelt established the Resettlement Administration to address rural poverty through loans to struggling farmers, commodity adjustments, and resettlement programs that moved farmers from marginal land to more productive regions.[51] Access to food was a critical aspect of these relief efforts.

Industrial Agriculture at the Cost of Food

Although the process was gradual at first, by the 1930s and 1940s thousands of displaced farm laborers had been replaced by a combination of mechanized agriculture, fertilizers, weed-killing chemicals, pesticides, and defoliants.[52] Pesticides and laboratory-developed seed varieties produced food crops suitable for livestock feed but not human consumption. In the 1940s and 1950s, Delta and Pine Land Company—the largest cotton plantation in the Mississippi Delta—gradually phased out its mules and thousands of its sharecroppers in favor of mechanical cotton pickers.[53] After fields were picked mechanically, a small crew of laborers was needed at the end of the harvest season to walk the fields and gather cotton that had been missed by the machines, a process called "scrapping."[54] Landowners and field hands alike risked long-term health complications after continued exposure to the pesticides and defoliants sprayed on the fields, including arsenic and calcium cyanide. By 1956, crop dusters were spraying 1.2 million pounds annually of pesticide on the Delta and Pine Land fields.[55]

Under a banner of progress and efficiency, the USDA, the Agricultural Adjustment Administration, and other government farm programs that supported expansion and mechanization exemplified in corporate plantations such as Delta and Pine Land, represented the "federalization" of American agriculture.[56] The USDA encouraged large farmers to plant not only cotton but also commercial-grade soybeans and rice in the Arkansas, Mississippi, and Louisiana Deltas and corn and peanuts in Georgia and Alabama. Thanks to the "miracle of science," thousands of acres of food offered no edible return for the remaining field workers. Former cotton planters expanded their operations to include livestock, pecan orchards, timber, and hunting preserves with an eye on scale and expansion. By World War II, the USDA had become a "silo that primarily fed substantial farmers."[57]

From the 1930s to the 1960s, this "capitalization" of plantations and farms erased the scattered tenant homes from fields associated with the older notion of small, self-sufficient farms and "forty acres and a mule."[58] To maximize every bit of ground for mechanized farming, a string of identical workers' homes were constructed on a plantation road or highway near tractor sheds and fields. Large numbers painted on the sides of the small homes reminded workers they were "owned" by the landlord and the plantation. Thousands of poor white and black working-class southerners moved to towns and cities, carrying with them the grinding poverty, hunger, and racism reflected in the southern diet.

Enacting Southern Food Reform

From this sweep through the post-Reconstruction transformation of southern farming and the effects of these changes on regional diet, we conclude with a brief overview of historic legislation behind early twentieth-century programs and policies that impacted agriculture, food-related scholarship, and food practices.[59] In May 1862, President Lincoln established the cabinet-level Department of Agriculture. That same summer, Lincoln signed the Morrill Land-Grant Act, which set aside public land in each state to create "land-grant" colleges in which agriculture, the "mechanic arts," domestic science, and nutrition would be taught—the early food studies programs of the second half of the nineteenth century. A second Morrill Act in 1890 required segregated states to create separate land-grant institutions to serve African Americans. The origins of historically black colleges and universities in the South, such as North Carolina Agricultural & Technical College (1891) and Fort Valley State University in Georgia (1895), reside in the second Morrill Act. The Hatch Act (1887) provided federal funding to create agricultural experiment stations dedicated to research in agriculture and food production in each state. With the passage of the Smith-Lever Act (1914), officials at the USDA founded the Cooperative Extension Service. Statewide programs were headquartered at land-grant colleges and universities. An extension of the Smith-Lever Act, the Smith-Hughes Act (1917) promoted vocational education in "agriculture and the trades and industries," including food-focused home economics and home demonstration programs. Despite the "good intentions" of this body of legislation and its many initiatives, white men controlled the USDA.[60] Their legacy would long privilege well-to-do white male farmers over the working-poor minorities, women, and small farmers of the rural South.[61]

Empowered by a missionary impulse and the raft of agricultural legislation at the end of the nineteenth century, a vast network of reform spread across the region in the first decades of the twentieth century. An army of change-minded interventionists brought public health programs, improved food and diet, scientific agriculture, and education to the South. Private and public battles were waged between the "southern way of life" and a vision of a more ordered, cohesive, and modern South.[62] A heritage of privilege and paternalism informed the "coercive reformism" of the largely white, middle-class, urban southerners who committed themselves to the "education and uplift of the common man."[63] Sponsored by religious organizations, volunteer groups, and northern philanthropies, they took on the pressing social issues of their time, with reforming the southern diet high among their concerns. Food was at the core of new domestic science departments, agriculture experiment stations, home and farm extension programs, industrial colleges, and settlement schools. These progressive institutions symbolized a cautiously changing South, but one still unwilling to release the choke hold of race and class that characterized the region from the plantation era to the dawn of the New South and beyond.

8

Home Economics and Domestic Science Come to the Southern Table

High rates of tenancy and sharecropping, unhealthy work environments in southern industries, and relentless poverty made the South a virtual laboratory to examine food, diet, illiteracy, public health issues, and substandard living conditions in rural America. In 1908, President Theodore Roosevelt appointed a national Commission on Country Life to address these problems.[1] The country life movement, a social ideology that promoted improvements in the quality of rural life, agricultural education, research, and farm production, gained momentum in the South in the early 1900s.[2] Concurrently, oil baron John D. Rockefeller Jr. and his educational foundation, the General Education Board, directed millions of dollars toward rural improvements in the South, particularly focused on public education, health, agriculture, and food production. The Rockefeller Sanitary Commission helped to eradicate hookworm in the South by the late 1920s.[3]

Chaired by Cornell University's dean of the College of Agriculture, Liberty Hyde Bailey, the Commission on Country Life recommended the creation of a national extension service to educate thousands of rural Americans. The USDA's Seaman Knapp, a former professor of agriculture at Iowa State University, created the model for this program in Louisiana, where he set up successful demonstration farms to improve rice cultivation, and in Texas, where he worked with cotton farmers to eliminate the boll weevil. In 1904, Knapp was appointed as a "special agent" by the USDA to promote southern agriculture. The USDA and Rockefeller's General Education Board paid extension agents to work with southern farmers, using Knapp's hands-on "home demonstration" methods.[4] At the time of Knapp's death in 1911, over 500 extension agents were at work in the rural South.[5]

In honor of Seaman Knapp's contributions to southern agriculture, the General Education Board funded the Knapp School of Country Life (1913) at the George Peabody College for Teachers (1875) in Nashville, Tennessee. The Peabody curriculum provided graduate-level education for southern teachers focused on improving rural life in the South. Courses were offered in agriculture and economics, health education, rural education, home economics, and industrial arts. Home demonstration agents took seminars in "Canning Club Methods" for the newly popular boys' and girls' canning clubs across the South. These clubs encouraged southern youth—in separate clubs for whites and blacks—to adopt "modern," more efficient and productive methods of scientific agriculture, as well as up-to-date canning technology, as they raised and processed thousands of pounds of corn and tomatoes for profit.[6] By 1919, Peabody College offered a Bachelor of Science degree in home demonstration.[7] The Knapp demonstration farm included a model orchard, a herd of Holstein cows, and row crops, which provided food for the college cafeteria.[8] Opportunities for both black and white southerners to train in food-focused professions grew in the South as agricultural science, home economics, and the study of diet and nutrition became critical tools in fighting deep-seated impoverishment and hunger throughout the region.

Home Economics, Southern-Style

Many of the young white and black women who became home demonstration and extension agents in the early twentieth-century South—where their work was largely focused on food and nutrition—trained in the new profession of home economics. The field originated in the urban Northeast at the turn of the twentieth century with Ellen Richards, a Massachusetts Institute of Technology–trained chemist and the university's first female graduate and faculty member. Inspired by the efficiency and order of an industrializing, *white* America in the Progressive Era, Richards advocated the scientific management of the American household. In a special Woman's Laboratory at MIT, Richards attempted to raise the status of housework by housewives to a "domestic science" through the study of bacteria, household design, food preparation, nutrition, and sanitation. Richards was also concerned about the poor diet of working-class people and immigrant families she observed in Boston.[9] Period theories of "race improvement" informed her ideology.[10] Her work resonated with teachers in rural settlement schools in the South, who modeled Richards's efforts as they attempted to reform the diet of white and black working-class and impoverished southerners.[11]

Ellen Richards's leadership and the support of Liberty Hyde Bailey and Wilbur Atwater, director of the first U.S. Agricultural Experiment Station at Yale University, transformed home economics into an accepted, although contested, academic field of study until interest in the discipline waned in the 1960s.[12] Atwater's visionary work in agriculture and food science would later directly impact the South. Early twentieth-century proponents of home economics regarded it as a legitimate discipline, while others, including the American Association of University Women, considered it a mere "skill set."[13] In 1923, the USDA established the Office of Home Economics. Throughout the country, including the South, young women who were trained in food science became consumer-oriented educators, extension agents, demonstrators of new kitchen appliances for gas and electrical utility companies, and product development consultants and spokespersons for regional and national food manufacturers.

Black and white southern women's clubs were early supporters of home economics and food-related vocational education programs in the New South. They had long recognized women's pivotal role in reforming home life as mothers and in improving community life, described as "municipal housekeeping."[14] By the 1910s and 1920s, southern club women organized for child-labor reform, improved food and diet, education, sanitation, temperance, and other issues perceived as "natural extensions" of women's roles as wives and mothers.[15] The nascent women's movement in the South grew out of these efforts.[16] The success of food-related reform captured the attention of the southern press, inspired by stories of middle-class black and white housewives and mothers waging a battle against poverty and ill health in kitchens across the region. A racial and class subtext also underlay white middle-class women's interest in "scientific" cooking.[17] Food purity and good nutrition was considered essential to supporting white bodies and white superiority.[18]

Northern-educated reformers and educators hoped to improve and update the southern diet by training a generation of young female professionals at regional white institutions such as Peabody College in Nashville and Newcomb College in New Orleans and at black industrial schools such as Hampton Institute in Virginia and Tuskegee Institute in Alabama. Standard courses in cooking and nutrition were offered in southern programs, as well as in specialty areas such as "dinner work," "the school lunch," "household engineering and equipment," "Mother craft," "poultry raising," "chafing dish and fancy cooking," and "table service."[19] Anna Monroe Gilchrist, a Columbia University–trained home economist, came to the University of Tennessee in Knoxville in 1903, where she later developed a degree course in home economics in the College of Liberal Arts.[20] She brought significant attention to the cause when she invited Ellen Richards from MIT to lecture in the university's Summer School of the South in 1904 and 1905.[21] Converse College in

South Carolina offered a combined major in chemistry and home economics in the early 1900s.[22] Georgia State College for Women required its students to take home economics courses.[23] The passage of the Smith-Lever and Smith-Hughes Acts in 1914 and 1917, which funded programs in home demonstration and agriculture, created a demand for home economics teachers, accelerating the growth of degree programs in higher education at both white and black institutions.

"The Practical Side of Life"
Home Economics at Newcomb College

Professor Harriet Amelia Boyer led the home economics program at Newcomb College in New Orleans, a private college for white female students. The new program reflected the educational mission of philanthropist Josephine Louise LeMonnier Newcomb, whose gift in 1886 established the independent women's college at Tulane University as a memorial to her deceased daughter. Newcomb stipulated that the college "shall look to the practical side of life as well as to literary excellence."[24] What could be more practical than a training program for female teachers in "the study of the sanitary, economic, and aesthetic aspects of food, clothing, and shelter?"[25] Female students chose a two-year diploma in home economics or a four-year degree program with courses in domestic science, physical education (the college strongly advocated women's sports, including specific basketball rules for women), chemistry, bacteriology, "household physics," and nutrition.[26]

Harriet Boyer also encouraged home economics students to take courses in the "industrial arts," a program that grew into the Newcomb Arts School, renowned for the work of its student and faculty potters, bookmakers, embroiderers, and jewelers. Sadie Irvine, one of the principal designers and graduates of the program, illustrated Boyer's student text, entitled *Notes and Recipes: Freshman Domestic Science* (1915). Irvine's beautiful drawings—similar to those found on Newcomb pottery—depict local semitropical fruits and vegetables such as the "Bur Artichoke," okra, bananas, and figs. Newcomb artist Mary McNaughton contributed drawings of Gulf seafood such as "Southern Shrimp," "River Crayfish," blue crab, "Florida Red Snapper," and "Horse Mackerel, or Tunny" (tuna). Sadie Irvine's illustration of Louisiana oyster boats, or "luggers," is accompanied by a caption: "The Barataria waters lie west of the Mississippi, near the Gulf Coast. They are the home of great oyster beds and are free from contamination of sewage. The Louisiana oysters are of large size and fine flavor."[27] (These fertile waters were polluted by the disastrous oil spill following the explosion and fire that destroyed the Deep Water Horizon drilling rig in September 2010.)

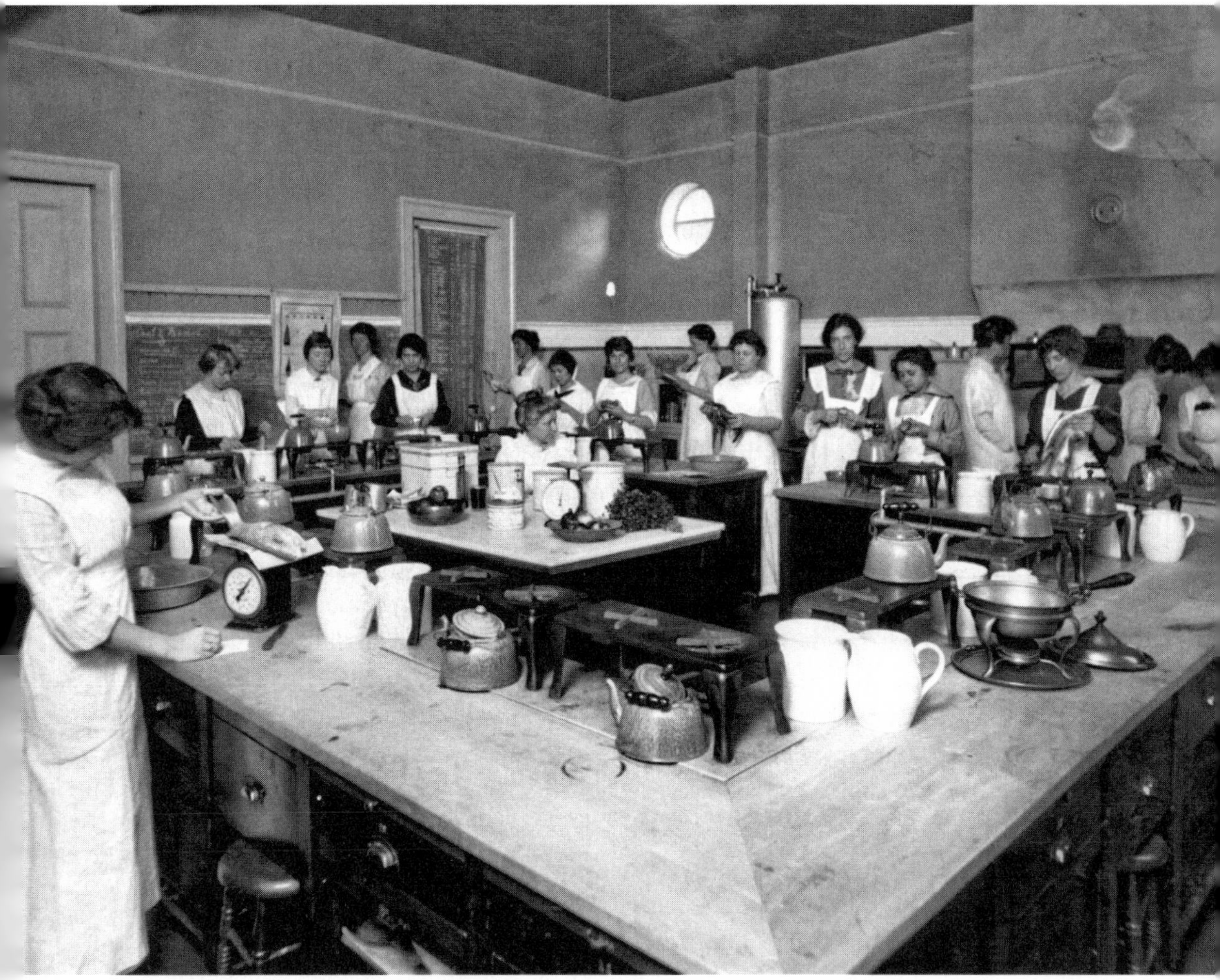

Domestic science students, Washington Avenue Campus, Newcomb College, New Orleans, Louisiana, ca. 1915. NP #551, Newcomb Archives, Newcomb College Institute, Tulane University, New Orleans, Louisiana.

Boyer's *Notes and Recipes* concluded with pages for student notes, including inspirational quotes from home economist Ellen Richards and England's acclaimed Victorian cookbook author Isabel Beeton, author of *Mrs. Beeton's Book of Household Management* (1861). From Richards: "We suffer from disease through ignorance. We escape through knowledge"; and "A large part of the art of cooking consists in making inexpensive food material palatable and attractive."[28] From Beeton: "I have always thought that there is no more fruitful source of family discontent, than badly-cooked dinners and untidy ways."[29]

Inquiries to Harriet Boyer from gas and utility companies in New Orleans, as well as commercial food manufacturers, suggest the influence of home economists in the consumer culture of the early twentieth-century South. An endorsement of a new stove or brand of baking powder was a valuable marketing tool. The New Orleans Railway and Light Company invited Harriet Boyer's 1914 domestic science class to visit its "House Electric" for a demonstration of electric cooking appliances.[30] Rumford Baking Powder representatives were delighted to send Boyer a number of their "1914 souvenirs" as thanks for her praise of their product at a cooking school demonstration in New Orleans. "We feel highly complimented in your use of the goods, and that you use them from the stand point of absolute quality, purity, and wholesomeness."[31] In 1917, Boyer received a special offer from the USDA's Bureau of Plant Industry: "The Department of Agriculture, as you perhaps know, is interested in promoting the culture and the use of the chayote, or as it is called in New Orleans, mirliton, or vegetable pear. . . . If you would like to receive some from the Department of Agriculture, for experimental cooking purposes, we shall be glad to forward some to you a little later in the autumn."[32] This local pear-shaped squash is typically cooked until tender and then baked with a savory stuffing. (Floods from Hurricane Katrina destroyed virtually all of the mirliton vines in New Orleans and coastal parishes in 2005. Since that time, Dr. Lance Hill of Tulane University has single-handedly led efforts to reestablish this beloved local plant from heirloom mirlitons that survived in Broussard, Louisiana.)[33]

Harriet Boyer was elected president of the Southern Home Economics Association at the organization's annual conference in March 1920, hosted by Newcomb College in New Orleans. After daytime sessions at Newcomb, conference participants enjoyed "a typical French banquet" at Antoine's in the French Quarter and a picnic at the "historic Spanish Fort," prepared by the home economics department's senior-class students.[34] Boyer headed the home economics department at Newcomb from 1909 until the early 1920s, when Pierce Butler, dean of the college, ended the program to focus resources on the "liberal arts and sciences."[35] Butler's decision reflected the divide in academia regarding home economics. In 1917, Mary Leal Harkness, a professor of Latin at Newcomb, argued that home economics created mediocrity in both schools and women by "elevating things above thoughts."[36]

Hampton and Tuskegee African American Industrial Schools Confront the Southern Diet

African American industrial schools were the earliest southern institutions dedicated to rural reform and "uplift" through vocational education, agricultural extension activities, and home demonstration work. By the late nineteenth century, food was a key aspect of these reform activities, particularly efforts to improve the diets of black families, to encourage black farmers to plant more food crops for family use, and to diversify crops beyond cotton. Hampton Institute (founded in 1868) and Tuskegee Institute (founded in 1881) were leading post-Reconstruction-era institutions of higher education established for African Americans. Both programs were well known for their model programs in agriculture and domestic science. Support from the Rockefeller Foundation's General Education Board helped fund Hampton's and Tuskegee's agricultural extension programs in the early 1900s.[37] The Anna T. Jeanes Foundation (1907), also administered by the General Education Board, sponsored African American teachers to supervise industrial education in rural black schools throughout the South.

HAMPTON INSTITUTE

Nutritious meal plans and a working farm at Hampton Institute reflected southern inroads into the burgeoning domestic science and home economics movement in New England and the growth of manual and industrial training programs for African Americans. Mary Peake, a free black woman from Norfolk, Virginia, created the first school for black children in the coastal community of Hampton, Virginia, in the fall of 1861. In 1868, Brigadier General Samuel Chapman Armstrong, a white commander of several "colored" regiments during the war, founded the Hampton Normal and Agricultural Institute for African American and Native American students. As a child of the abolitionist generation, Armstrong believed deeply in the moralizing power of the "Christian home," and he incorporated this philosophy into the daily lives of Hampton students.[38] Central to this ideology was the "civilizing" power of mealtime and the professionalization of food service, inspired by the emerging field of home economics. To implement his educational programs, Armstrong hired a dedicated group of young female teachers from the Northeast and Midwest, trained in female academies, many of them, like himself, the children of reformers.

In January 1869, Louise Lane Gilman and Rebecca Bacon came to Hampton to teach. Both young women were raised in Connecticut families devoted to the antislavery movement. Bacon's sister, Alice, joined her at Hampton in 1871. A devotee of the emergent field of folklore, Alice Bacon later established the Hampton Folklore Society, in 1893, one of the first regional organizations to collect examples of black folk culture.[39] Hampton students, faculty, and graduates published their findings in the institute's journal, the *Southern Workman*.

Soon after she arrived at Hampton, Louise Gilman wrote her sister about the working farm at Hampton Institute: "The farm is a level tract lying close to the shore (of Hampton Creek). I have not walked about it yet, but hear of the 60,000 cabbage plants to be transplanted and tasted the canned peaches that were raised on it and today we had a 'farm turkey' for dinner."[40] She noted that Hampton's farmer, Francis Richardson, was a Quaker, a faith known for its condemnation of slavery. The farm reinforced Hampton's commitment to entrepreneurship and to training free, skilled black laborers.[41] Other schools, such as Amherst, Oberlin, Oneida, and Wesleyan, also incorporated work and physical labor as a crucial aspect of their curriculums.[42] Armstrong believed that manual labor built character and would help his students develop important skills as teachers.[43] Students were expected to work two days a week and apply a portion of what they earned toward their education. Farm produce grown at Hampton was used in meals for the boarding facility, as well as fare for students, faculty, and visitors. Asparagus, cabbage, peaches, peas, white and sweet potatoes, and strawberries were shipped and sold to markets in Baltimore, Philadelphia, New York, and Boston.[44] A market wagon from Hampton made weekly runs into town to sell milk, meat, and vegetables to community members.[45]

Louise Gilman described the simple meals at the "teachers' mess," or dining hall, and the cooks who cared for them. "Our breakfasts are generally eggs, or roast oysters (which are very fine, and the largest I ever saw in my life) or sometimes we have a little codfish, or cold meal, perhaps. . . . I think you will see that we do not starve."[46] She thought the food was "quite as good as in many of the country boarding places within forty miles of the York where nice people spend their summers."[47] By "nice people" Louisa referred to the middle- and upper-class whites who vacationed on Chesapeake Bay and the York River during the summers, although middle-class blacks had also established beachside enclaves in the region by the 1890s. In the first years at Hampton, African American cooks prepared a traditional southern diet for students and faculty. By the early years of the twentieth century, more "nutritious" dishes reflected the reform cuisine of home economics and Hampton's domestic science and cooking faculty.[48] A former student at Hampton fondly remembered the Boston baked beans served at "Bean Morning" in the dining hall, a meal prepared by a young Hampton cook sent for training at the famous Boston Cooking School, the Massachusetts bastion of domestic science education.[49]

In the early 1870s, Hampton Institute's dining rooms were segregated, a decision made by Rebecca Bacon, Armstrong's first assistant principal.[50] Armstrong and his staff were accused of "drawing the color line" and becoming "Southernized" by maintaining the racial codes of the segregated South in Hampton's dining facilities.[51] A black teacher and alumna, Sara Peake, opposed being "grouped according to color.

There can be no mistaking that we are 'graduates.' . . . We carry our diplomas on our faces."[52] Peake told Armstrong, "It impresses me as a very peculiar kind of Christianity which enables folks to leave their homes, relatives and friends to come and labor for and with the Negro and yet makes it an impossibility for them to summon up enough respect and unprejudiced friendship to eat at the same table with him."[53]

When Native American students arrived at Hampton Institute in 1878, their food services were similarly segregated. Meals for the students were prepared and served in a separate dining room and kitchen, purportedly to make them more comfortable and to accommodate their dietary needs but clearly a sign of administrators' concerns regarding friction between the Indian and African American students. The Indian students had a difficult time adjusting to the "foreign" southern diet and the humid warm climate of coastal Virginia.[54] Officials recommended a "better supply of beef" in lieu of pork, as well as more fresh fruits and milk.[55] Armstrong hired a physician to review their diet.[56] "Negro and Indian pupils, hitherto eating together," wrote Armstrong, "were separated at meals, because the salt food and pork, which the former delight in, was injurious to the latter."[57] Between 1878 and 1888, 31 of the 427 Indian students died.[58] Plagued by tuberculosis, pneumonia, the unfamiliar diet of white and black southerners, and pure homesickness, another 111 ill students were sent back to their reservations.[59] Despite Armstrong's efforts to desegregate Hampton's dining facilities, his administrators argued that the black and Indian students preferred to socialize with their own race.[60] By 1900, the segregated dining hall for Indian students was replaced by separate tables in the main student dining room.[61] Full integration of Hampton's dining facilities did not occur until the Indian program ended in 1923.

Courses in food chemistry, cooking, nutrition, sanitation, and management of institutional food services became part of the curriculum at Hampton Institute when a building for the program was erected in 1898, administered by home economist Elizabeth Hyde.[62] To fulfill Hampton's work requirement, students served as waitresses in the teachers' dining room and at the Holly Tree Inn, a Hampton boardinghouse and guest quarters.[63] They gained hands-on experience working in the vegetable gardens and the dairy and tending livestock. First-year students lived for three months in Hampton's Abby May Home, a "practice home," where the young women learned by doing, as they prepared meals, "kept house," and shopped for weekly groceries on a strict budget.[64]

Carrie Alberta Lyford directed the newly named Home Economics School at Hampton in the 1920s. The press at Hampton published Lyford's *A Book of Recipes for the Cooking School* (1921), a compilation

"The cheese press screw; students studying agricultural sciences, Hampton Institute, Hampton, Virginia." Photograph by Frances Benjamin Johnston, 1899 or 1900. LC-USZ62-89342, Prints and Photographs Division, Library of Congress, Washington, D.C.

of "carefully tested" recipes for home economics teachers and students that emphasized the science of food preparation.[65] Lyford's spirit of reform was clearly expressed in her recipes for "tried and true" southern dishes, such as collard greens. "In those parts of the country where collards grow readily they are among the most valuable greens and give a much needed variety to the diet. They belong to the cabbage family and are valuable for their bulk and for the mineral matter they contain."[66] Lyford suggested boiling collards—without salt pork—for fifteen to twenty minutes, instead of the long, slow cooking that most southerners preferred, and serving the collards with "white sauce." Made of flour, butter, and milk, white sauce was a favorite dish of Progressive-Era cooking schools.[67] According to its proponents, any dish, including collards, could be made elegant and up-to-date when "dressed" in a blanket of white sauce.

In a July 1911 issue of Hampton's newsletter, the *Southern Workman*, columnist Virginia Church made a strong case for training young black women "to teach others of their race the principles of sanitation, hygiene, and domestic science."[68] Church took offense at outsiders who viewed Hampton as "a sort of factory where cooks, waitresses, and housemaids are turned out *ad infinitum*."[69] She imagined the disappointment of a white Norfolk housewife who thought she could drive up to Hampton and pick one of the "bright-looking, neatly dressed girls" to work as her maid. "She is not to be blamed if, in hasty judgment, she decides that education has made them 'too good to work' and complains in irritation that she supposes she'll have to go to an employment bureau in Norfolk, after all," wrote Church. "The unruffled head of the visitors' office agrees calmly that she supposes she will."[70]

At Hampton, food preparation began in the garden, where young women were taught self-sufficiency by raising their own food and teaching others to do the same. Cooking was "not a matter of boiling eggs, roasting meat, or serving a meal correctly. It goes deeper than that," stated Church.[71] Female students learned to arrange a dining room, set the table, and serve meals. Although bread making, meat cookery, diets for invalids, and the chemistry of cooking, canning, and food preservation were standard courses in the domestic science curriculum, Hampton's mission was not solely to teach a practical craft or a skill. The program taught skills necessary for food independence in the black community. Virginia Church's entreaty to the young African American women of Hampton suggested the almost religious fervor of the program's mission: "With the love of her own race and the desire for their betterment strong within her, let her . . . show these people how to grow wholesome food in their small plots of ground; how to enrich what small area they own and make the most of it; how to can what vegetables or fruit they may produce and save them for future use. Let her . . . show her people how to cook food that shall make for strength; how to shine pans until they reflect faces also shining and clean. . . . When that time comes—and it is not, after all, so far distant—will not the people of both races bless the young disciple of work who has gone into the movement with her whole heart and soul."[72]

TUSKEGEE INSTITUTE

At Tuskegee Institute, Dorothy Hall—the "Girls' Industrial Building"—was dedicated in 1901, marking the beginning of a woman's curriculum that included cooking in the four-year academic program.[73] Tuskegee students took both academic and industrial courses, and all women were required to take cooking lessons—considered both a science and a fundamental skill in everyday life.[74] A model kitchen and two dining rooms served as a laboratory for practicing culinary and housekeeping skills. Tuskegee graduate Mary Dotson directed the domestic science program. Dotson learned to cook beside her mother as a child in Alabama. At Tuskegee, she was introduced to the new field of food science. "I began to study chemistry in the academic department," wrote Dotson, "and when it was applied in my cooking lessons my eyes were opened. I now saw much that I had not dreamed of."[75]

The domestic science programs at Tuskegee and Hampton were inspired by an 1895 survey that assessed the status of African American women's education in the South. Funded by the John F. Slater Fund, a northeastern foundation that supported the industrial education of black southerners, two white female philanthropists from Washington, D.C., traveled to Alabama, Georgia, North Carolina, South Carolina, and Virginia.[76] In each state, they visited schools and met with African American women in their homes. They reported on the "conditions of squalor" in which many families lived and recommended that the foundation fund teachers to instruct "the homely arts of cooking and sewing, of nursing, homemaking, and housekeeping—arts which lie at the base of all real living and progress."[77] Norfolk, Virginia, was chosen as the test location for the program. Sarah Evelyn Breed, a young white graduate of the New York Cooking School, one of the leading domestic science programs in the Northeast, was hired as the first instructor.[78] Breed and an assistant taught basic cooking classes to black schoolchildren and organized meetings to enlist the support of their mothers.

Local whites and blacks were suspicious of the new domestic science program in Norfolk. Whites feared any activity that threatened to change the subordinate status of southern blacks. Blacks resented programs that appeared to push them back into servile positions, although the industrial education program was not seen in this way. Despite these concerns, the program grew from one school to more than thirty, serving over 4,000 students in seven counties.[79] Later adopted by public school systems, the Norfolk program influenced domestic science curricula at nearby Hampton and Tuskegee, where the Slater Fund research team met with Margaret Murray Washington, "Lady Principal" of Tuskegee Institute and wife of Booker T. Washington.[80] Domestic science programs were also established at Spelman Seminary in Atlanta and at smaller black institutions in the South, such as Mt. Meigs Institute in Alabama (1888), Utica Normal and Industrial Institute in central Mississippi (1903), and Voorhees Industrial Institute in South Carolina (1897), founded by Tuskegee graduates Cornelia Bowen, William Holtzclaw, and Elizabeth Evelyn Wright, respectively.

Outside the worlds of academia, African American educator and activist Nannie Helen Burroughs founded the National Training School for Women and Girls, in 1909, in Washington, D.C. Domestic science was an important part of the program. With its focus on teaching and professional careers for young African American women, and unlike Hampton and Tuskegee, Burroughs's "School of Three B's—the Bible, Bath, and Broom"—prepared students to become skilled domestic workers rather than "shiftless" untrained servants.[81]

Across the South, a combination of Progressive-Era efficiency and Jim Crow paternalism shaped white club women's efforts to control the lives of their black domestic workers. In Asheville, North Carolina, Edith Vanderbilt, wife of multimillionaire George W. Vanderbilt, established a School for Domestic Science to train African American housekeepers at the Biltmore Estate in the early 1900s.[82] The young women were taught "plain and fancy cooking," serving, "waiting at table," care of the dining room and bedroom, washing, ironing, and soap making.[83] In 1916, the Atlanta Women's Club—the white boosters behind a series of cooking classes designed to train their African American cooks—hoped to create a permanent vocational school for African American women "who have not had the opportunity to equip themselves for domestic service."[84]

"Cast Down Your Bucket Where You Are"
Booker T. Washington and the Labor of Food

Booker T. Washington, renowned black educator and political leader in southern race relations, directed Tuskegee Institute from its founding until his death in 1915. A graduate of Hampton Institute, Washington touted vocational training, including scientific agriculture, domestic service, and cooking, as the democratization of American education—a path to educate all Americans, not just white elites.[85] In his controversial Atlanta Compromise speech at the opening ceremony of the Cotton States Exposition in Atlanta, on September 18, 1895, Washington exhorted African Americans to accept social segregation and denial of their political and civil rights, if in turn, whites supported the economic advancement of blacks through industrial education.[86] "To those of my race . . . I would say cast down your bucket where you are, cast it down in making friends, in every manly way, of the people of all races by whom we are surrounded," said Washington. "Cast it down in agriculture, in mechanics, in commerce, in domestic service, and in the professions. . . . Our greatest danger is, that, in the great leap from slavery to freedom, we may overlook the fact that the masses of us are to live by the productions of our hands."[87] Despite public criticism that

Washington's commitment to vocational education locked blacks in perpetual service to whites, training programs at Tuskegee offered food-related studies for blacks in areas from scientific agriculture to nutrition and institutional food service.

Booker T. Washington valued African Americans' historic and deep connection to the land and feared educating "our students out of sympathy with agricultural life."[88] With training in agriculture and food production, he hoped Tuskegee students would return to plantation districts, "to put new energy and new ideas into farming, as well as into the intellectual and moral and religious life of the people."[89] In 1896, Washington hired George Washington Carver, a young botanist trained in Iowa, to establish a Department of Agriculture at Tuskegee. For over forty years, Carver excelled as a teacher and scientist at Tuskegee, where his groundbreaking research increased yields of important southern food crops. His work in plant hybridization led to the development of thousands of products from peanuts, sweet potatoes, and other southern plants.

Both Hampton and Tuskegee displayed examples of their students' vocational training at the Cotton States Exposition's Negro Building, including agricultural exhibits. The farm- and food-related displays disappointed Alice Bacon, the assistant principal at Hampton. "While statistics prove that the negro is still mainly an agriculturist," wrote Bacon, "a visit to the Negro Building would lead one to suppose that that was the smallest part of his work."[90]

African American Farmers' Conferences

On February 23, 1892, Booker T. Washington sponsored the first Tuskegee Negro Conference at the institute, an annual event focused on scientific agriculture, food production, land retention, and rural reform.[91] Nearly 500 African American men and women attended the initial conference. By 1898, 2,000 people participated in the two-day program held at the Tuskegee demonstration farm.[92] The yearly farmers' conferences at Tuskegee inspired Hampton Institute and other black colleges in the South to create similar programs. Printed declarations were published at the conclusion of each Tuskegee farmers' conference, emphasizing Washington's goals of agricultural diversification and self-improvement, including the moral appeal "to treat our women better."[93]

Black women homemakers were important participants in Tuskegee's programs for the public.[94] At the 1910 conference, an African American woman described using what she had learned to successfully convince her husband to acquire land *and* improve the cooking arrangements in their one-room wooden cabin, which housed their family of nine: "He had only one room to his house. I told him he had got to get more, and he got them. I have one 'specially for cooking, 'cause I don't propose to have everybody see what I cooks. I have learned a heap here at this meeting today. Let sardines and snuff and candy and red ribbons alone. Get your man to buy land, just one acre at a time, if he can't get any more than that, and then work it. Some of you men jest want to put us women in the white folks' kitchens to work and feed you, while you walk up and down the road."[95]

The annual Tuskegee farmers' conference concluded with a barbecue dinner prepared by institute students. To reinforce lessons in crop diversification and self-sufficiency, participants left with new recipes and packets of vegetable seeds provided by the secretary of the U.S. Department of Agriculture.[96] The conferences became an annual homecoming and reunion for African American farm families in Alabama and throughout the South.[97] The legacy of the first Tuskegee conference continues in the annual farmers' conference at Tuskegee today. A recent conference included sessions on food and nutrition, livestock, and alternative energy sources such as biofuels, as well as an update on the successful settlement of the African American farmers' class-action lawsuit (*Pigford v. Glickman*) in 1999 and 2010, which paid $1.25 billion to black farmers who had been denied federal aid or were underpaid by the government.[98]

As the foot soldiers of a Progressive-Era war on malnutrition and exemplars of the profession of domestic science in the South, a generation of newly trained white and black teachers, agricultural specialists, and home economists spread the gospel of healthy food, nutritional science, and updated farming practices to beleaguered, working-class southerners across the region. Public health physicians and scientists brought the tools of agricultural and nutritional science to the region, where groundbreaking "dietary" field studies in Alabama and Virginia examined the food deficiencies of the South's working poor. In the first decades of the new century, the great researcher of pellagra, Dr. Joseph Goldberger, began his journey to find a cure and cause for the "wasting" disease that ravaged thousands of southern citizens.

9

The Southern "Dietaries"

FOOD FIELD STUDIES IN ALABAMA AND EASTERN VIRGINIA

Tuskegee, Alabama, and eastern Virginia were the sites of the earliest field studies of southern foodways, in the 1890s, overseen by Wilbur Atwater, the Wesleyan agricultural chemist who directed the first U.S. Agricultural Experiment Station.[1] Atwater and his associates conducted dietary fieldwork in communities across the United States in which they collected detailed records of what people ate for a period of one to two weeks.[2] This innovative methodology created a cultural snapshot, using the lens of food to capture a community in a specific moment in time.[3] Field researchers determined the nutrient value of all food consumed by participants in each study—the specific breakdown of carbohydrates, fats, proteins, water, and calories—a method Atwater learned in Germany from leading chemists in the new field of nutritional science.[4] The end products of the field studies were "dietaries," a term used by nutritionists to describe the combination of on-site ethnographic interviews, observation, and collection of nutritional statistics.[5] These important studies provided crucial evidence in the investigation of endemic food-related diseases in the South, including pellagra, which is examined at the conclusion of this chapter. Today, these dietaries point to a powerful academic intersection "where nutrition, anthropology, and history meet."[6]

Tuskegee Dietary Study, 1895–1896

Wilbur Atwater and his collaborator, Charles Woods, chose Tuskegee as the site of the first field study because it was one of the few places in the South where local people were receptive to a scientific study focused on the African American community.[7] H. M. Smith, a chemist and Atwater's principal investigator, was sent to work with staff at Tuskegee, including John Wesslay Hoffman, professor of agricultural chemistry and biology.[8] Professor B. B. Ross, a chemist at the Alabama Experiment Station and on the faculty at the Agricultural and Mechanical College of Alabama in Auburn, conducted the food analysis for the study.[9] Booker T. Washington served as research supervisor for the field study.[10]

The African American farm manager at the Tuskegee Normal and Industrial Institute chose eighteen families, including his own, to participate in Atwater's field study.[11] Some of the families lived and worked in the village of Tuskegee, where their quality of life reflected the influence of the institute. Other participants lived outside of town, where they worked as laborers, sharecroppers, and tenant farmers in what remained of the old plantation system. Researchers visited the homes of field study participants daily, conducting careful measurements of all food consumed.[12] Charts and tables reflected the nutritional analysis of food eaten by the family, caloric intake by gender and age, and costs of foods based on prices at nearby markets.[13] The dietaries also listed family members in each household, as well as livestock, and a brief description of the home with particular attention to the material culture of food preparation and eating was included. The published dietaries presented this primary data, plus the researchers' analysis and recommendations to correct food-related "deficiencies."

"Dietary 100" described the modest kitchen and substandard diet of a family of six that lived in a two-room log cabin several miles outside of Tuskegee. The kitchen included "a pine table, one or two chairs, a small portable cupboard, the usual pot and frying pan, and a few dishes for the table. There was no churn, as the family had no cow. In the cupboard were a piece of salt pork and a jug of molasses, and near by a sack of corn meal."[14] The family purchased basic provisions weekly. By the end of the week, "there was very little left in the house. Fried pork and corn pone, cooked in the fireplace, composed the daily diet."[15] The family of "Dietary 100" was plagued by the chronic problems of sharecroppers—a steep mortgage, the dominance of cotton, no vegetable patch, no source of milk for the children—yet the farmer was "trying to better his condition" after attending the annual farmers' conference at Tuskegee.[16] Booker T. Washington observed similar scenes of malnutrition when he arrived at Tuskegee in June 1881.

As the new director of Tuskegee, Washington spent his first month traveling through the state to educate himself and promote the institute. "I ate and slept with the people," he wrote. "I had the advantage of seeing the real, everyday life of the people."[17] As he joined families for meals, Washington noted that the "common diet of the people" was fat pork and cornbread.[18] They purchased these staples at high prices from a store in town, despite having land around their cabins for a vegetable garden. "Their one object seemed to be to plant nothing but cotton; and in many cases cotton was planted up to the very door of the cabin."[19]

Washington's observations again confirmed that African American families, and poor whites, too, were entrapped by a regional agricultural system that favored large landowners.

Washington was invited to share dinner with an African American family of four during his travels. He soon realized that they seldom, if ever, sat down to eat together.[20] There was only one fork. When the wife rose in the morning, she fried bacon and prepared a large cornmeal hoecake in an iron skillet for the family. When breakfast was ready, the husband took his portion and ate as he walked to the fields. The mother sat in the corner and ate her breakfast, either from a plate or from the frying pan. The children were given their portion and ate in the yard. The experience was not unlike his own as a child of former slaves in Virginia, where his family shared scraps of food and had little or no tableware. "I cannot remember a single instance during my childhood or early boyhood," wrote Washington, "when our entire family sat down to the table together, and God's blessing was asked, and the family ate a meal in a civilized manner."[21]

Southern Hunger

A Season of Cotton and the "Mortgage System"

The Tuskegee study offers a compelling portrait of the annual cycle of work and how the seasonal diet of struggling cotton-farming families was impacted by the "mortgage system."[22] Although the study findings—informed by the racial attitudes of white field researchers—suggested that "improvidence" was in part responsible for black farmers' inability to better support their families, the realities of the crop lien system and the seasonal demands of cotton farming suggest a far different truth.[23] Drawing from the field study observations, we can reconstruct the annual patterns of farmwork and food production for the Tuskegee cotton tenant farmers. These patterns of food and labor, like those discussed earlier in relation to the collapse of the plantocracy, mirror the recurring cycles of hunger and malnutrition central to the crisis in southern agriculture at the turn of the twentieth century. The following section examines the typical food available to farming families in the yearly cotton season in Tuskegee, including the core staples that came to symbolize the South's deepest pathologies of race and class.

In Alabama, the cotton season began in early March when farmers plowed and prepared fields for planting. Credit at the local store or commissary was available to the farmer to purchase seed and supplies to put in the crop, as well as staple foods such as flour, coffee, baking soda, salt, sugar, and canned goods. This "furnish" of supplies—fixed by the landlord or merchant at a few dollars a month—lasted only part of the year.[24] The busy season of planting began in April, followed by "chopping"—the hoeing and thinning of cotton plants. During this time, the farm family planted collards, field peas, and sweet potatoes—*if* they had the seeds, the time, and a plot of soil—to help sustain the family through the fall.

When cotton was ready to pick in mid-August, the entire family worked in the fields from sunrise to sunset until the harvest ended in late November. "At the end of the season if the crop is a failure[,] the debtor has absolutely nothing," wrote the field researchers."[25] Given the high interest rates charged by the landowner or the store merchant who issued credit to the farmer, typically there was little money left, even in a good crop year. The leanest months were late winter into early spring, when the "furnish" ended. Sweet potato supplies diminished, and farm families "got by" on what was left of cornmeal, molasses, and a few store-bought provisions until their credit was exhausted.[26] The gnawing pain of hunger was common in February. If a family owned a cow, they might be forced to sell it for cash, losing their supply of fresh milk, a vital source of protein, just when they needed it most.[27]

The Tuskegee dietary study listed "fat salt pork, corn meal, and molasses" as the "staple foods of the negroes of this region."[28] Professor Hoffman provided more detail of how these foods were prepared. Cornmeal was mixed with water, shaped into cakes, and baked on the flat surface of a hoe or griddle in the fireplace. Cornbread was made into "cracklin bread" by adding crumbled bacon to the basic meal recipe. Thinly sliced salt pork was fried until all the fat was rendered. Molasses was added to the fat, making "sap," eaten with cornbread. Hot water sweetened with molasses was a common drink. Collards and turnips were boiled with bacon to flavor the stewed vegetable mixture. Possum was an occasional treat, "put in a large pot, surrounded with sweet potatoes, seasoned with red pepper, and baked."[29] Hoffman noted, "One characteristic of the cooking is that all meats are fried or otherwise cooked until they are crisp."[30]

In the 1960s, folklorist Henry Glassie described a typical noontime dinner eaten by farmers in the Deep South not unlike those recorded in the Tuskegee dietaries, including field peas cooked with fatback, "pepper sauce," pork, buttermilk biscuits, cornbread, and sugarcane or sorghum syrup.[31] He noted the cultural integration of white and black southerners, symbolized by their shared taste for "heavy suppers of black-eyed peas and turnip greens, cracklin' bread and buttermilk, lemonade and sweet potato cobbler."[32] A brief discussion of the three "m's"—meal, meat, and molasses—eaten by the African American families of Tuskegee suggests why these ingredients became crucial, but nutritionally inadequate, foods of the southern working-class table.[33]

The Three M's

MEAL

Bigger and more efficient flour mills in the Midwest, and even southern mills such as Ballard and Ballard in Louisville, Kentucky, developed an important market in the South for their cheap, bolted (sifted) cornmeal and bleached flour.[34] This development was apparent to the Tuskegee research team, which noted that, "of late, since wheat flour has become so cheap, it has been considerably used."[35] With inexpensive wheat flour available, biscuits became a staple food throughout the South, quickly prepared and served hot, three times a day, even in the most modest of southern homes.[36] While southern farmers grew some corn, which was ground into meal for the family and livestock, the bulk of their cornmeal came in twenty-four-pound bags from the store.[37] Cornmeal was the basis of cornbread, eaten daily in a variety of forms, such as simple "pone"—derived from the Indian term "suppone"—to hoecakes and more elaborate versions prepared with milk, buttermilk, eggs, and shortening.[38] Hominy grits, a dish as commonly seen on southern working-class tables as cornbread, was prepared from ripe corn, which was treated with lye, then dried and broken into bits and cooked into a porridge.[39] The bolted cornmeal from the Midwest lost much of its nutritive value after processing, shipping, and long storage time in warehouses and on store shelves.[40] The "empty" calories of the poor grades of processed flour and meal sold at general stores contributed to the dietary problems of malnourished southerners.

MEAT

Meat on the tables of both white and black southern farm families and laborers was pork, and like the flour and meal eaten by poor southerners in the early twentieth century, it came largely from outside the South from the great meat-processing centers of the Midwest—Chicago, Cincinnati, Des Moines, Indianapolis, and border cities like Louisville.[41] Impoverished southerners could afford only the lowest quality and grade of pork. Researchers observed that the black Tuskegee families ate mostly "fat sides, butchered and salted in the meat-packing houses of Chicago and elsewhere, and brought in large quantities to the Southern market."[42] Few could afford to keep a hog but instead came to the store each Saturday to buy bacon and lard, or if they lived a distance in the country, they received a weekly ration sent out by the merchant

Ballard's Obelisk Flour, Ballard and Ballard Company. Ms2010-032, Special Collections, Virginia Polytechnic Institute and State University, Blacksburg, Va.

or commissary agent. Cheap pork so dominated the local diet that the Tuskegee researchers noted that a farmer speaking of "meat" meant "fat pork."[43] "Some of them knew it by no other name," wrote the field team, "nor did they seem to know much of any other meat except that of opossum and rabbits, which they occasionally hunted, and of chickens which they raised to a limited extent."[44] Researchers noted that local whites in Tuskegee also ate little "fresh meat," or beef, although not for "lack of generous diet, for the tables of white people were bountifully spread."[45] Cotton and pigs, rather than cattle and hay, dominated the "Black Belt," a term referring to the region stretching 300 miles across central Alabama, northeastern Mississippi, and into Tennessee.[46]

MOLASSES

Molasses, and sorghum, too, beat out "meal" and "meat" as the most nutritious member of the infamous three "m's." Historian Frederick Opie explains that just one tablespoon of blackstrap molasses "provides about a fifth of the recommended daily intake (RDI) of iron and copper, over a quarter of the RDI for manganese, and a seventh of the RDI for potassium."[47] A good source of calcium and vitamins, molasses was eaten three times a day by poor southerners and was especially

"Feeding the sorghum cane into the mill to make syrup on property of Wes Chris, a tobacco farm of about 165 acres in a prosperous Negro settlement near Carr, Orange County, North Carolina." Photograph by Marion Post Wolcott, September 1939. LC-USF33-030514-M3 (b&w film nitrate neg.), U.S. Farm Security Administration/Office of War Information, Prints and Photographs Division, Library of Congress, Washington, D.C.

important for growing children, pregnant women, nursing mothers, and women who became iron-deficient during their menstrual cycles.

Cane molasses is made from sugarcane, and sorghum molasses is made from sweetgrass sorghum, both plants that were introduced to the American South from Africa during the Atlantic slave trade.[48] Atwater and Woods described the process of making the sticky syrups. The stalks of the sugarcane and sorghum plants were pressed between rollers to squeeze out the green juice, which was then boiled in an evaporator pan and reduced to sweet syrup. Molasses is the strongly flavored residue that remains when sugar is processed and the refined white sugar is removed.[49] Different grades of molasses were available, from dark blackstrap, which retained more residue, to the more choice, lighter, Louisiana- and Georgia-made ribbon cane syrup.[50] "There are persons who go about from farm to farm with the rollers and make the molasses," the field-workers noted. "Individual farmers who have no conveniences for making syrup carry their cane to other farms where it is worked."[51]

Mules powered the portable roller mills that crushed the sorghum and sugarcane stalks.

Eastern Virginia Dietary Study, 1897–1898

After the completion of the Tuskegee dietary study, Wilbur Atwater and the Office of Experiment Stations continued the "nutrition investigations" with two field studies in African American communities in eastern Virginia.[52] In May 1897, H. B. Frissell, principal of Hampton Institute, and his assistant, W. F. Schultz, oversaw a month-long study of the diet of twelve African American families in and around Franklin, Virginia, in Southampton County—a region that bordered the Great Dismal Swamp, known for its malarial conditions. The families "obtain their living almost entirely from the soil," wrote Frissell, who described the typical southern system of farm tenancy.[53] Since the rent for small tracts of land required most of what they made from cotton, peanuts, and sweet potatoes, families depended heavily on fishing and hunting for their own tables.[54] The soil was depleted after generations of planting tobacco.

Describing a family of four who farmed five acres "on share," Frissell noted that "muskrat, opossum, raccoon, and other game, fish, frogs, turtle, and even snakes in certain seasons, furnished part of the diet. Cash was paid for all food purchased, since the family could obtain no credit. They lived in a two-room house with 1 acre of ground surrounding it. There were no improvements, and the location was very unhealthful."[55] Weekly purchases from the store were limited to necessities such as "3 cents' worth of salt," coffee, tea, and baking powder.[56] Frissell described the homes as crudely constructed, with no "sanitary conveniences."[57] Drinking water was drawn from shallow surface wells and was "as a rule, stagnant and brackish, and often muddy."[58] All cooking was done in the open fireplace, as "cook stoves were unknown."[59] "Ash cakes" made from a mixture of cornmeal, salt, and water were baked in the ashes of the fireplace. Most families ate little or no fresh meat, due to its cost. Instead, they depended on cheap, store-bought bacon, once their own supplies of homegrown pork were depleted in the early spring.[60] "Side bacon," referred to as "white meat" by the locals, was fried in a cast-iron pan.[61] Ham and pork shoulders were boiled in iron pots suspended in the fireplace.[62]

One Franklin family of two, a fifty-one-year-old man and his forty-five-year-old wife, experienced "better circumstances than the majority of those studied," owing to good health, their farming skills, and better-situated farmland.[63] The couple lived in a four-room home and rented thirty acres. One-third of their crop was used for rent money.

Eight acres were planted in corn and three acres in peanuts, and one acre was devoted to "truck garden" produce for the city vegetable market.[64] A good selection of livestock, including a cow and calf and several pigs and chickens, provided eggs, milk, poultry, sausage, and side bacon during the week. The farmwife canned her own pickles and blackberries and prepared seasonal vegetables such as sweet potatoes, string beans, cabbage, and mustard greens, often served with a bit of salted or smoked herring.[65] Researchers tallied that the two individuals each consumed 5,350 calories per day—twice as many as some of the study participants—and in line with the calorie intake of a typical working-class white family.[66]

The second weeklong field study was conducted in May 1898, in and around Hampton, Virginia. Isabel Bevier, a thirty-eight-year-old professor of chemistry and "household science" at Lake Erie College in Ohio and a former student of Wilbur Atwater, oversaw this study of seven families.[67] Bevier had also studied at MIT with chemist/home economist Ellen Richards, who encouraged her to accept Atwater's invitation to conduct the Hampton dietary study.[68] Bevier feared that the warm climate and working "among colored people" would increase the difficulty of completing a dietary study in Hampton. She expressed her concerns to Richards, who replied, "Of course you will do it. You cannot afford professionally to do otherwise, since Professor Atwater has asked you."[69] Once Bevier accepted the assignment, Atwater directed her to stop in Washington, D.C., and meet with Dr. A. C. True, director of the USDA, who would oversee her arrangements in Hampton. Of her experience in Hampton, Bevier wrote, "The Hampton experience was a wonderful new chapter in my life, and I came away from Hampton Institute with great admiration for the work that Dr. Frissell and his staff were doing, and for the way in which the colored people responded to their efforts. Over and over again they said to me, 'Hampton has done so much for us; we must do all we can for it.'"[70]

As in the Tuskegee field study, several of the Hampton families chosen for the dietary study were associated with Hampton Institute, and their foodways reflected an educated, middle-class lifestyle. The remaining families in the Hampton dietary study lived in the country at Butler's Farm. Union general Benjamin Butler established this historic African American settlement after his May 1861 decree that slaves who made it to the Union line were considered "contraband of war" and would not be returned to slavery. The farming families that Isabel Bevier studied in 1898 were likely descendants of freed slaves who arrived at Fort Monroe after Butler's order. They made a living raising sweet potatoes, corn, fruits, and berries for the Washington, D.C., and Baltimore markets.[71]

Many African Americans also worked in the hotels near Fort Monroe and in the shipyards and fishing industries of Newport News.

Although the data collected in the eastern Virginia field studies revealed a diet similar to that of Tuskegee's African American families and their dependence on "hog and hominy," there were significant differences in the Virginia dietaries due to the proximity to Chesapeake Bay and the abundant supply of fish.[72] The Virginia families had more protein in their daily diets—for the families near Franklin, salt herring, and for the families near Hampton, a variety of fresh fish such as bluefish, croaker, eel, flounder, mullet, sturgeon, and also turtle.[73] The research team noted, "Judging solely by the amount of nutrients[,] the negro families in Virginia were on the average more abundantly fed than those studied in Alabama."[74] "More abundantly fed" was relative when one considered the pervasive impoverishment among black farming families in rural Alabama and Virginia.

Other than the middle-class black families who were graduates of Hampton and Tuskegee, the majority of the African American families in the Alabama and Virginia dietary studies suffered from malnourishment due to insufficient food supplies during the late winter and early spring. Most of the families knew frequent hunger. Salt pork, bacon, fatback, and lard filled empty bellies and provided calories, as did biscuits and cornbread "sopped" with molasses, but were deficient in essential vitamins and the lean protein found in better grades of beef and pork. This diet of necessity ultimately had deadly consequences for the working poor of the South, black and white.

The Southern Diet and Pellagra

Almost thirty years after the Alabama and Virginia dietary studies, public health crusader and physician Dr. Joseph Goldberger determined that this substandard southern diet of the three "m's"—meat, meal, and molasses—rather than germ contamination, was the cause of pellagra, a devastating disease that killed thousands in the first decades of the twentieth century.[75] The illness was characterized by the four "d's"—dermatitis, diarrhea, dementia, and death.[76]

Goldberger, the child of Jewish immigrants on New York's Lower East Side, entered the Progressive-Era worlds of science and public health through his education at the College of the City of New York in the early 1890s.[77] His work in epidemiology for the U.S. Public Health Service led to his investigation of pellagra. Earlier he had worked in the South to help combat yellow fever and typhoid epidemics that raged through the Lower Mississippi valley in the late 1890s and early 1900s. When he returned to Mississippi in 1914, Goldberger's challenge was not only to find a cause and cure for pellagra, but to determine why the disease was so prevalent in the South. In 1912, South Carolina alone had 30,000 cases of pellagra—the fatality rate was 40 percent.[78]

Joseph Goldberger and his colleagues conducted dietary studies and eating experiments at southern orphanages, mill villages, and state prisons, where the rural populations were fed as cheaply as possible.[79] Historian Alan Kraut notes that impoverished southerners, but most frequently blacks, were subjects of medical research in the South, including the infamous Tuskegee syphilis experiments (1932–72), conducted without the participants' informed consent.[80] In April 1915, Goldberger began a controversial experiment at the Rankin State Prison Farm near Jackson, Mississippi.[81] Governor Earl Brewer promised pardons for eleven volunteers from among the white prisoners, including several serving life terms for murder, and Goldberger controlled the diets of these eleven to see if he could induce pellagra. Protein-rich foods such as buttermilk, field peas, fresh vegetables, and meat were removed from the usual prison fare. The diet replicated the typical meal plan of southern mill workers, sharecroppers, and tenant farmers.[82]

After six months of eating a daily diet of biscuits, cornbread, brown gravy, cane syrup, collards, sweet potatoes, and grits, six of the volunteers were stricken with the symptoms of pellagra.[83] Goldberger ended the experiment in November, and the ill prisoners received their pardons from Governor Brewer. They were released with a suit of new clothes and five dollars.[84] With medical care and a balanced diet, the newly freed men recovered after a few weeks. Based on the prison study and his other eating experiments, Goldberger argued that pellagra was caused by protein deficiencies and the lack of a balanced diet.[85] To further prove his theory, Goldberger held "filth parties," at which he, his wife, Mary, and his colleagues at the U.S. Pellagra Hospital in Spartanburg, South Carolina, injected themselves with blood samples from patients who had contracted the disease.[86] None developed pellagra. In 1916, Goldberger shared his research with the black men and women gathered at the annual Tuskegee farmers' conference.[87]

In the summer of 1927, Joseph Goldberger and his colleague Edgar Sydenstricker, an economist and statistician for the U.S. Public Health Service, toured the flood-ravaged states of Arkansas, Louisiana, Mississippi, Louisiana, and Tennessee. The record-breaking Mississippi River flood that spring destroyed crops, livestock, and structures. Thousands of residents had little access to fresh food for months. After massive outbreaks of pellagra, Nan Cox, a Red Cross nurse in Cleveland, Mississippi, sought the advice of public health officials.[88] She needed suggestions for canned groceries to help prevent pellagra among the flood refugees.[89] Word reached Goldberger, and he and Sydenstricker traveled south to assist the Red Cross and to continue their study of the disease. Goldberger advised relief agencies to distribute canned salmon, beef, and tomatoes to hungry families.[90] An ounce of brewer's yeast was also effective.[91]

That fall, Goldberger and Sydenstricker published a report on pellagra in the Mississippi River flood area.[92] Aware of the political implications of offending government officials, the two scientists wrote the most cogent analysis to date of the life-threatening health implications of the tenant farm system of cotton production. They explained why pellagra escalated after the flood, and how it would have done so even if no flood had occurred that spring.[93] The true culprit was southern staple-crop agriculture, which impoverished thousands of white and black southerners. Food was at the heart of this perfect storm of economic injustice and the disfranchisement of working-class people. Women were the victims of pellagra more often than men, as were African Americans.[94] "The dietary habits of the tenants, in fact, of the population as a whole in this area," wrote Goldberger and Sydenstricker, "play an extremely important part, we believe, in the endemic prevalence of pellagra."[95] They recommended that government officials consider measures to stabilize the incomes of the most vulnerable southerners by diversifying agriculture in the region, with more food crops and the development of community dairies and vegetable gardens.[96]

A diet enriched with fresh lean meat, field peas, fresh garden vegetables, canned tomatoes, eggs, and buttermilk helped to cure and prevent pellagra.[97] Goldberger and Sydenstricker determined that a combination of high protein and nutrient-filled foods acted as a "Pellagra Preventative Factor," although it was unclear which substance was corrective.[98] Joseph Goldberger died in 1929 before scientists identified a deficiency of tryptophan and niacin (vitamin B3) as the cause of pellagra.[99] Commercial agriculture was to blame for the disappearance of niacin in cornmeal.[100] Native Americans traditionally soaked corn kernels in lime to soften it before grinding, a process which also activated niacin in the plant.[101] With the advent of commercial milling in the late nineteenth century, corn was no longer treated with lime and the niacin remained inactive.[102] Milling also diminished protein in the corn.[103] Beginning in the 1920s, commercially manufactured foods, including bread, milk, flours, and cereals, were increasingly fortified with vitamins.[104]

Pellagra was just one of the critical public health challenges that Progressive-Era educators and benevolent workers confronted at institutions founded in the South in the early twentieth century, including white settlement schools established in the southern mountains and black industrial schools and agricultural colleges in the Lowcountry. Improving the food and diet of working-class and poor southerners became the mission of white and black school directors and teachers across the region. In the next chapter, we travel to these worlds to examine food as a central tool in the political manipulation of regional culture as reformers sought to advance health and education and to address other social needs in the rapidly changing New South.

IO

Reforming the Southern Diet One Student at a Time

THE MOUNTAIN SOUTH AND THE LOWCOUNTRY

By the turn of the twentieth century, the mountain South, contrary to romantic depictions of Appalachia's rural character and hearty, home-grown cooking, was a rapidly industrializing region. Railroads connected the area to both local and global markets, while textile mills and timber and coal companies tapped the region's natural resources and its people for labor. The same forces impacting Appalachia were felt throughout the nation, as industrialization, nativist fears regarding rising European immigration, and a growing sense of economic and social displacement racked America. Reformers, educators, and mission workers turned to the mountain South, seeking a simpler, preindustrial world, including the wholesome cuisine prepared by people descended from the "pure" bloodlines of early Anglo-Saxon settlers. There they grappled with conflicting agendas of preservation and progress, simultaneously providing education and social services, selling the redemptive power of tradition, and promoting the virtues of modernity, particularly at the southern table.[1] In these worlds, food reveals the juxtaposition of southern "old ways" and reform-minded change, poverty and abundance, and, ultimately, a power struggle between natives and outsiders to control regional culture.

The Mountain South Hindman Settlement School

Kentucky natives Katherine Pettit and May Stone founded one of the first educational programs in the southern mountains, Hindman Settlement School, in 1902. The two women met at a meeting of the Kentucky Federation of Women's Clubs, where Reverend J. T. Mitchell of Hazard, a small mountain town in eastern Kentucky, addressed the group. Mitchell asked if the organization could identify an appropriate woman to teach the local "wives, mothers, housekeepers, young ladies and little girls."[2] Mitchell emphasized that if the teacher could make lessons in cooking and homemaking "particularly enthusiastic," the students would find the "intellectual and moral features" of the lessons interesting, too.[3] It took little to convince Pettit and Stone to accept the minister's challenge. Within weeks, they began an adventure that would last a lifetime.

To prepare themselves and train others who would work with them in the mountains, Pettit and Stone traveled to the country's leading "social settlements," where they met with founders Jane Addams at Hull House in Chicago and Lillian Wald at Henry Street Settlement on New York's Lower East Side.[4] In these urban settlement schools, activist reformers and educators took up residence in poor neighborhoods to better the lives of largely immigrant families through educational programs, including cooking classes to "Americanize" ethnic culinary patterns, vocational training, and other community services. Although the residents of eastern Kentucky had needs specific to a rural Appalachian setting, Pettit and Stone modeled their mountain program on the same foundational tenets of residency, reform, and education.

Under the auspices of the Kentucky Federation of Women's Clubs and the Woman's Christian Temperance Union, Pettit and Stone launched a seemingly benign operation to "improve" local Appalachian culture, and diet was a pivotal focus of their work. They observed how the locals ate and found a diet not dissimilar from that of the working poor of Tuskegee and Hampton. "They live on fat bacon, corn bread and a few vegetables, all cooked in the most unwholesome way. Everything is fried in as much grease as they can get."[5]

Travel writer and outdoor enthusiast Horace Kephart recounted similar scenes of the mountain table, but with details guaranteed to shock his middle-class readers and to further label mountain southerners as the uncivilized "other." In his classic study of the mountain South, *Our Southern Highlanders* (1913), Kephart wrote, "In some of these places you will find a 'pet pig' harbored in the house. I know of two cases where the pig was kept in a box directly under that table, so that scraps could be chucked to him without rising from dinner."[6]

For three summers beginning in 1899, Pettit and Stone and a small group of women volunteers made the difficult three-day journey from Louisville and Lexington to Hazard, Kentucky, where they established a temporary camp. Orchestrating change from their traditional role in the domestic sphere gave women reformers unparalleled access to mountain families. Under the general rubric of domestic science, the "lady teachers" initiated cooking classes, instruction in "proper" table manners, and hands-on garden and farm projects. Pettit studied nutrition at W. H. Kellogg's Battle Creek Sanitarium in Michigan—the famous Progressive-Era center known for its unorthodox health therapies, including a grain-based, vegetarian diet.[7] She brought those lessons to eastern Kentucky.

"Bad cooking" was one of Pettit and Stone's chief criticisms of the region and its people: "Without any regard to the laws of health, how can the people be strong, mentally or morally?"[8] In their journals written during the summer of 1899, the teachers set priorities in reforming local food preparation: "To teach them to make good bread, to cook the vegetables in as many ways as possible, and the meat without so much grease; in every way to make the best use of the material they have."[9] By "good bread," Pettit and Stone meant convincing local women to switch from cornbread to light bread (yeast bread, made from wheat flour) and biscuits. In their privileged worlds, cornmeal was associated with malnourishment and illiteracy and wheat flour with the cultivated practices of the educated elite. This culinary intervention was next to impossible when cornbread required so little to prepare—just an iron skillet, a bowl, a spoon, and a source of heat—and wheat flour-based breads called for store-bought ingredients, equipment, and technology that few local women had or wanted.[10]

With the help of community members, the teachers set up makeshift and then permanent dining halls and kitchen facilities for the students at Hindman. Dishes, pots and pans, food supplies, and even a stove, dragged on a slide by a horse, were hauled to the mountain site the teachers called Camp Industrial in the summer of 1900. Pettit and Stone noted, "A number of men worked hard leveling places for the tents, making floors, pitching the tents, putting up boxes for china closets, pantries, chicken coops, making kitchen and kindergarten tables, bookcases, dressing tables, various shelves and dairy."[11] Katherine Christian of Lexington, Kentucky—who also studied "hygienic cooking" at Battle Creek (applying scientific principles to the preparation of food for nourishment and digestion)—took charge of the cooking lessons and taught nearly eighty students that summer.[12] Locals referred to Christian as the "goodest-cooking" of the women teachers, while Pettit was the "up-and-comingest" for her drive and Stone was the "ladyest" for her amiable personality.[13]

Students walked several miles to Hindman each day, toting a food item to contribute to the cooking class.[14] At the end of the summer, Christian created a cookbook for her students and encouraged them to prepare the new dishes at home.[15] Mrs. Simon Stacey, an adult student, learned to make rice pudding, a favorite dessert of the era's cooking schools—particularly those with an Americanization mission—because of its bland flavor and "purity" symbolized by its white hue.[16] When Pettit and Stone visited her, they found Mrs. Stacey's dinner table covered with a clean cloth and set as the teachers had instructed her, including a vase of flowers. "She told us that she had tried to cook everything like we had taught her and that she had learned from the cookbook we sent her. She had a rice pudding with blackberries around it, just as we had served it the day she was with us. She said she had taught her friends our way of cooking and that she had made beaten biscuit for many weddings."[17]

The daily schedule for students at Hindman was rigorous, and mealtime was as regimented as study and work time. Breakfast was served promptly at 6:30 A.M., a ninety-minute lunchtime break was scheduled at midday, and supper was eaten at 5:30 P.M. Lights were out by nine o'clock each night, when the electricity for campus and the town was shut off.[18] Students filed into the dining hall and stood behind their chairs at assigned tables for twelve.[19] Teachers sat with students and reinforced manners and table etiquette, but not all did so happily.[20] Educator John C. Campbell noted the complaints of settlement schoolteachers who criticized monotonous food and insufficient rations.[21] They also protested the lack of a separate teacher's dining table, as was the practice at Wellesley and Vassar in the Northeast and at Tougaloo and Hampton in the South.[22] Many teachers received care packages from their families to supplement their daily diets. In March 1916, Hindman teacher Dorothy Hancock Stiles noted, "My fruit arrived from Louisville this morning, and Good Heavens! Instead of sending half a crate of oranges, grapefruit and lemons mixed, Miss Cobb ordered half a crate of each. . . . Molly is busy thinking up lemon flavored dishes."[23]

At Hindman, food was served family-style in large bowls, and students were expected to try at least three bites of each dish.[24] Albert Stewart, who was just five years old when he came to Hindman, learned to hide his required serving of spinach inside a biscuit.[25] Baked beans, macaroni and cheese, meatloaf, and canned salmon croquettes were typical entrées, dished up with Hindman-grown fruits and vegetables.[26] Cornbread, despite the reservations of Pettit and Stone, was served with pitchers of heated sorghum or molasses.[27] Beaten biscuits—the hands-down favorite food of all students—were eaten hot with homemade butter and jelly.[28] The white, wheat-based dough was prepared in a patented beaten biscuit machine, whose rollers created delicious, flaky layers when the silver dollar–sized biscuits were baked.[29]

Teachers promoted scientific cookery at Hindman, including recipes like Mrs. Stacey's rice pudding and instructions for light bread and quickly cooked vegetables prepared without lard, but the beaten biscuit was a product of another racially motivated domestic trend of the era. American Studies scholar Elizabeth Engelhardt connects Pettit and Stone's fondness for beaten biscuits—which required the labor, time, and skill of servants—to the plantation nostalgia of the early twentieth century.[30] This culinary reintroduction shares much in common with the school's craft enterprises, which looked decidedly to the past and the revival of old ways. Female settlement school leaders, middle-class craft enthusiasts from "away," and wealthy northern philanthropists developed programs to *revive* and sell mountain "handicrafts," from basketry to furniture making and weaving.[31] These popular and successful consumer ventures relied heavily on the myth that regional artists and their crafts—including both outdated practices and some never associated with the region—would soon disappear, if not for dedicated efforts of outsiders. Handmade objects were also seen as a corrective to the ills of an impersonal, industrial world.[32] These tactics of cultural intervention reflected in Appalachian diet and craft—both responses to modernization—suggest larger societal tensions as reformers reacted to rapid change in the mountain South and the nation.

In 1915, two recent graduates of Wellesley College, Dorothy Hancock Stiles and Dorothy "Molly" Gostenhofer, came to Hindman Settlement School to teach. May Stone, who attended Wellesley in the early 1880s, inspired many young women from Wellesley and other northeastern universities to come to eastern Kentucky. Stiles and Gostenhofer—both twenty-two years old—spent two years at Hindman, working with young boys, who nicknamed Stiles "Miss Fashion" and Gostenhofer "Miss Grasshopper." Stiles enjoyed working with her students at Hindman, where they labored in the gardens and on the farm. She was not as positive about the school's food. During one supper, "a bowl of sweet potatoes met my eye—nothing more, nothing less. Later on came a bowl of something like liquid peanut butter, which proved to be sorghum, and of course there were the ever present corn muffins."[33] The same week, Stiles was asked to make the blessing before the noon meal. "The one that occurred to me on the spur of the moment—'For what we are about to receive make us thankful'—I thought would make the teachers laugh, so [I] made up a unique one utterly malapropos and extremely short."[34]

Soon after her arrival, Dorothy Stiles contracted typhoid, a severe bacterial infection that brought on fever, exhaustion, intestinal upset, and weight loss.[35] Typhoid and hookworm spread quickly in rural locations with poor sanitation conditions and were two of the primary epidemics targeted by the Rockefeller Sanitary Commission. Stiles described her diminishing weight as she participated in the "Hindman local sport of having typhoid."[36] "[I] managed to get a glimpse of myself

Dorothy Hancock Stiles and Molly Gostenhofer, Hindman Settlement School, Hindman, Kentucky, 1915. Dorothy Hancock Stiles Papers A/S856, Hollis no: 001817950, Schlesinger Library, Radcliffe Institute for Advanced Study, Harvard University.

in the mirror. Vanitas, vanitas," she wrote. "I don't look much thinner in the face, though my hands and arms are sights. On the whole I have macaroni legs and spaghetti arms."[37] As Stiles convalesced, she was fed small meals throughout the day to rebuild her strength. When finally able to enjoy a piece of toast topped with an egg, Stiles pondered it: "A simple thing is an egg, yet it may be fraught with great joy."[38]

The young teachers' sense of adventure and freedom was thrilling as they explored the mountain trails near Hindman, removed from the watchful eyes of parents and professors back home in New England.[39] This window of independence closed quickly. By the following January, Stiles was married and living in London with her new husband, Laurence Wellington, an attaché to the American Embassy.[40] One imagines the young woman returning to her journals to recall a mountain outing with her Wellesley colleagues in the spring of 1916: "Miss H. led us to a huge flat rock on the very top most pinnacle from which we could see the faint blue line of Pine Mountain 25 miles away. . . . I lay flat on my stomach on the rock and ate oranges over the edge, looking way down at the valley below. We also had sardines, crackers, and the bananas which had reached a soufflé consistency in the saddle bags. . . . Stopping at Jones' store for eggs, Molly rode on home, and Miss H. and I waited to have the saddle bags filled. . . . Rode home sitting on 10 dozen eggs—Rather nerve racking on a feisty horse."[41]

Like the women reformers of Hindman, John C. Campbell devoted his professional life to issues of rural education and the folk and craft revival in the mountain South. Campbell's first wife, Grace Buckingham, followed by his second wife, Olive Arnold Dame, were active partners in this quest. Mountain families carefully observed John and Grace Campbell after they arrived in the mountains in the early 1890s. Mrs. Campbell's cooking and housekeeping were of particular interest to the locals. If she was a dismal failure in the kitchen, her food tasteless or ill prepared, the Campbells' standing among the mountain people plummeted, as did Mrs. Campbell's womanly authority and her ability to reform the food of the locals.

Grace Campbell described a "triumph in the cooking line," when a supper she prepared for two local couples in Joppa, Alabama, was received with enthusiasm. Aware of the reputation of one of the women as a good cook, Campbell did her "level best" to prepare a tasty meal. After serving "pork and beans, fresh bread, baking powder biscuits, coffee, chopped pickle, jelly, apple sauce with sliced lemons in it, and fig cake," she anxiously waited her guests' response.[42] "She [Mrs. Ogletree] kept quite still for quite a while, but finally she said, 'well Mistress Campbell, I shall never know unless I ask, do you make your biscuits with sweet milk or butter-milk?' I said with sweet milk, and she said she and Mrs. Cordell would have to get me to give them some lessons, and Mrs. Cordell, who is very mild and deliberate, said, 'Yes, indeed, they are–the–best–biscuits–I–ever–ate.' 'And I like your light bread, too,' said Mrs. Ogletree."[43] The mountain women's praise of Grace Campbell's biscuits and light bread was a true victory, given local resistance to "uppity" foods associated with outsiders and domestic science.

After receiving a grant from the Russell Sage Foundation to study social and economic conditions in the mountain South in the early 1900s, John C. Campbell reported on the diet of mill families. He pointed out the tenacity of regional foodways as he described how little class affected the core diet of mountain people. "Poor" or "moderately well to do," they ate the same kinds of food.[44] "There seems to have grown up a habit or custom as to kinds of food which the people have come to like," wrote Campbell.[45] He took issue with scholars such as Holland Thompson who argued that the food patterns of mountain people improved after finding work in textile mills. In North Carolina, Thompson suggested, cotton mill workers' food, "though not always well chosen," was "abundant."[46] As the early twentieth-century boom in the textile mills and the timber and coal industries declined by the 1920s and 1930s, many workers returned home to the southern mountains, dispirited by the loss of employment yet grateful for gardens and small farms to feed their families.[47]

In his extensive descriptions of diet in the Highlands, Campbell referred to Goldberger's work linking substandard diet to pellagra but was unsure how extensive the disease was in the mountain South.[48] In fact, pellagra was at epidemic levels in the region by this period.[49] Campbell described the buying habits of locals at country stores in the mountains: "Here one may purchase salt, vinegar, molasses, soda, coffee, sugar, white flour, and usually some kind of canned goods—'salmons,' tomatoes, and peaches."[50] The pellagra-preventative foods that Goldberger recommended to victims of the Mississippi River flood of 1927—canned tomatoes and salmon—were available in the mountain general stores, but at the time their beneficial health properties were little understood by both locals and outside reformers like Campbell.

The Lowcountry Penn School—"In Time the Whole Island Was to Become Our School"

Three hundred miles southeast of her colleagues in the mountains, educator Rossa Belle Cooley confronted similar food-related challenges as she directed the Penn Normal, Industrial, and Agricultural School on the Sea Island of St. Helena, near Beaufort, South Carolina. Under Cooley's leadership, Progressive-Era theories of diet, nutrition, and scientific agriculture became central aspects of the school's curriculum. Founded by Philadelphia missionary Laura Towne in 1862, the Penn School was part of the Civil War–era "Port Royal Experiment," according to which northern abolitionists and missionaries were charged with educating the former plantation slaves of the Union-controlled Sea Islands and leading them into freedom and self-sufficiency. Before her death in 1901, Towne asked Dr. Hollis Burke Frissell, president of Hampton Institute, to help chart the school's future.[51]

As the first chairman of the board of trustees at Penn, Frissell instituted the Hampton vision of "education for life" at the St. Helena Island school, the same blended program of academic and industrial education that he successfully administered at Hampton in Virginia. Abstract knowledge was useless according to Frissell. The Sea Islander needed a practical education, as historian Gerald Robbins explains, "knowledge which he could readily apply to life, knowledge that would improve his living conditions; and, finally, knowledge that would put food on the table."[52] Frissell inspired Hampton graduates and teachers to come to St. Helena, including Penn's principal, Rossa Belle Cooley, and assistant principal, Grace Bigelow House. Through the support of Penn's trustees, northern philanthropists, and foundations such as Phelps-Stokes, Rosenwald, Slater, and Rockefeller's General Education Board, the teachers and other Hampton-trained staff who followed initiated a new educational program integrally tied to the agricultural and fishing worlds of the island. As Cooley wrote, "In time, the whole island was to become our school."[53]

Rather than work against the seasonal labors of the Sea Islanders, Cooley and her teachers took the "school to the farms" and scheduled classes between times of planting, harvest, and oystering. Cooley described "the call of the sweet potatoes" in the early fall, when classes were temporarily halted while the island families participated in the harvest.[54] "The father or big brother plows up the furrows with the family ox, or pony, or mule. The mother and the children follow with their hoes, and the potatoes are dug and placed in piles to be gathered for the storage. Great banks are made of them—layers of earth piled upon layers of potatoes, till sweet-potato pyramids take their place beside the house or barn ready for the winter's demand."[55] Food-themed student and parent organizations proliferated on the island, encouraging healthy competition and excellence in the home and in the field. One imagines enthusiastic islanders, young and old, participating in the Canning Club, the Corn Club, the Garden Club, the Home Acre Club, the Home-Makers' Club, the Peanut Club, the Pig Club, the Progressive Young Farmers' Clubs, and the Tomato Club.

Students and faculty alike practiced improved farming methods on a "home acre" and "teacher acre" of their own. Annual agricultural prizes, farmers' conferences, exhibitions, fairs, and parades sponsored by the Penn School encouraged students to vie for the best tomato, largest corn crop, and tidiest yard. At the annual school parade celebrating the spring term, canning club girls waved their empty canning jars, while other students brandished rakes and hoes and held banners declaring, "Corn Will Win" and "Plant and Protect."[56] At the closing "Exhibition Day," students demonstrated their academic and farm skills to the community. The agricultural class presented a play, "The Soil Builders and the Soil Robbers."[57] Dressed as the farmer, a home demonstration agent, and the local crops of corn, cotton, and sweet potatoes, they acted out the dramatic story of soil exhaustion and proper crop rotation.[58]

Graduates of Hampton Institute were in strong demand at the many African American colleges and industrial schools in the South, where they became farm managers, teachers of agriculture and domestic sci-

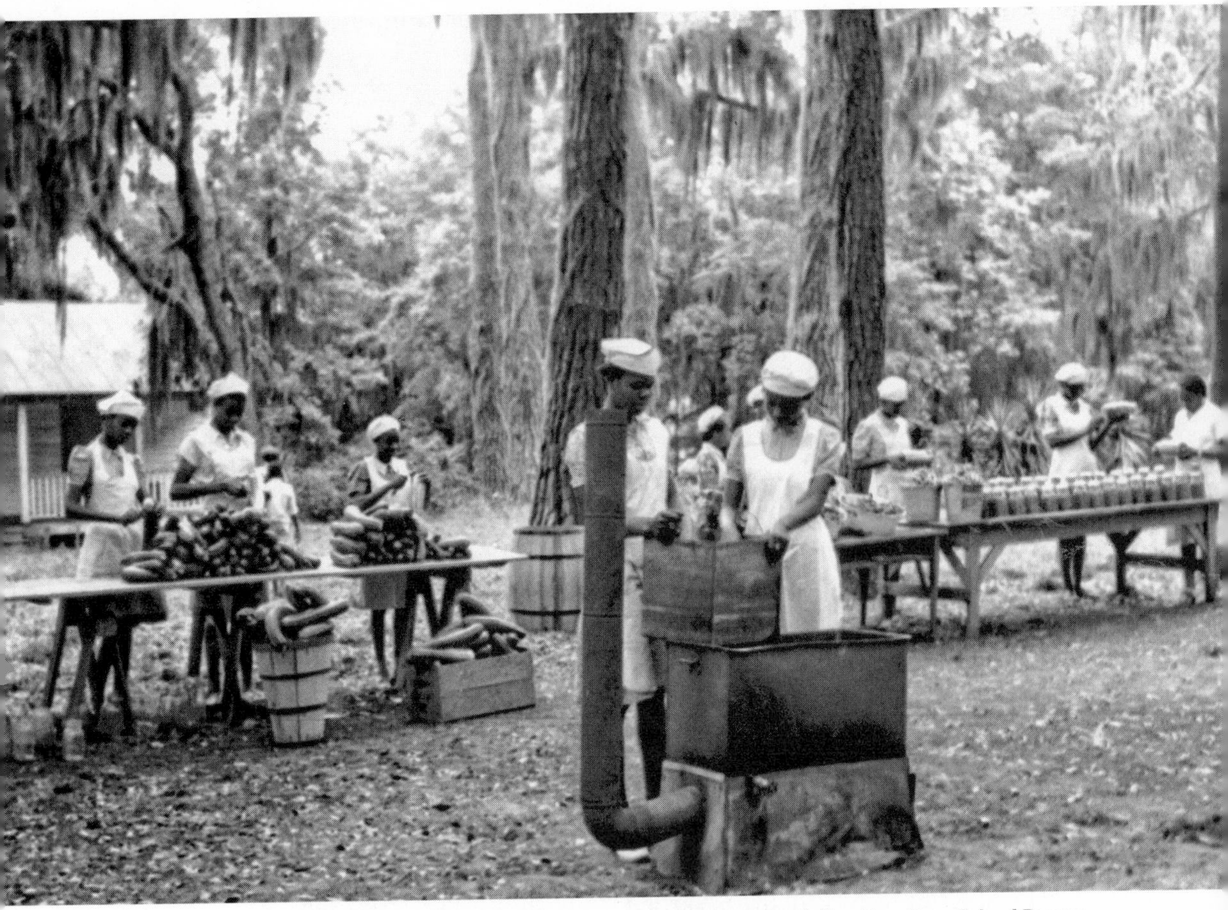

"Canning, circa 1942," Penn School, St. Helena Island, South Carolina. Penn School Papers, P-3615/1455b, Penn School Collection, Wilson Library, University of North Carolina at Chapel Hill, by permission of Penn Center, Inc., St. Helena Island, S.C.

ence, and supervisors of trade programs. A sense of community kept Hampton alumni in close touch and fostered an active network regarding employment. Hampton-trained P. W. Dawkins managed the farm at Penn in the early 1900s and founded the school's annual farmers' conference in 1905. His wife, Emma Jennie Dawkins, was the cooking and sewing instructor at Penn. In a 1903 annual report, Dawkins described the "limited variety of common vegetables known and used" by the islanders.[59] "The people have been educated in eating grits and rice since the days of slavery. . . . The lesson for thousands to learn is what to eat, and a still greater number must be taught how to eat it."[60] Dawkins concluded, "The cooking class is doing much good in this connection."[61] Penn's successful, diversified farm was planted in fifteen acres of corn, two acres of Sea Island cotton, two acres of navy beans, 1,000 strawberry plants, one and one-half acres of peas, and four bushels of potatoes.[62] The Dawkinses eventually left Penn to work at the African Methodist Episcopal Church–founded Kittrell College (established in 1886) in North Carolina.

Teacher Linnie Lumpkins, who graduated from Hampton in 1904, came to Penn in 1905 with Penn principal Rossa Cooley.[63] Lumpkins, fondly known by her students as "Sugar Lump," taught "girls' housekeeping" and cooking classes at Penn.[64] Lumpkins's marriage to Joshua Enoch "J. E." Blanton, who graduated from Hampton in 1905 and then followed Dawkins as the Penn School farm manager, was the first wedding celebrated at the school.[65] The 1909 ceremony took place at Hampton House, the home of Penn's principals, Cooley and Bigelow.[66] Joshua and Linnie Blanton went on to direct the Voorhees Industrial Institute in Denmark, South Carolina, where they remained until 1947.[67] Linnie Blanton continued her studies at Columbia University and also participated in summer sessions at Spelman College in Atlanta. J. E. Blanton was a founder of the famous St. Helena Quartet, known for its performances of African American spirituals.[68]

The Penn curriculum integrated academic subjects with scientific agriculture, domestic science, and manual trades, including bulrush basket making, which Cooley described as the one "native domestic craft" still in practice on the island.[69] (Today, this tradition continues in the vibrant sweetgrass basketry of the Lowcountry.) The domestic science curriculum for Penn's female students reinforced the same values of the larger curriculum—efficiency, order, self-sufficiency, and thrift—but with a home-centered focus on hygiene and nutrition. Teachers like Linnie Blanton taught basic cooking lessons, as well as special classes on canning, dairy, food conservation, fruit and nut trees, gardening, "home beautification," labor-saving devices, meal planning, and poultry breeding.[70] Della Harvey, "Colored Supervisor of Rural Schools" for St. Helena Island and Beaufort County, reported the productive "summer work" of 1918—the results of local women and girls' canning clubs: "canned fruit, 2411 qts., canned vegetables: 3915, fruits preserved: 182, jelly made: 283 glasses." She wrote, "This is the work done by Clubs with my assistance."[71]

After the construction of the new Frissell Community Building in 1925—named in honor of Hampton's Horace Burke Frissell—students in the cooking class prepared and served a daily hot lunch for the school community. "Around the tables sit the boys and girls learning almost unconsciously those lessons in amenities needed in every home," wrote Cooley. "Home-making is learned that can travel from the Community House to the island farms."[72] But scholar and civil rights activist W. E. B. Du Bois argued that such programs essentially reenslaved African American women as domestic drudges in their own households and those of white employers.[73] In 1913, Du Bois published a cartoon that lampooned the homemaking profession with the caption, "The New Education in the South: Domestic Science for Colored Girls Only."[74]

Du Bois would have cringed at Lucretia Kennard's positive "progress" report of an African American industrial school in Denton, Maryland, in 1907. Kennard, an 1892 Hampton graduate, described a meal prepared by the school's female students for a local white school board, who were served beefsteak, mashed white potatoes, sweet potatoes, creamed cabbage, rice pudding, cookies, and coffee. The meal was such a success that the superintendent requested another for visiting school administrators. "The girls did beautifully and the visitors seemed greatly pleased," wrote Kennard. "Nothing of the kind was ever heard of here before, so you see we are trying to do our race some good and be of service in some way."[75] The work Kennard noted—young black women in service to white men as cooks and servants—locked women into industrial education, rather than the higher education based in liberal arts that Du Bois envisioned for African Americans.

From the mainland, other reform initiatives of the era reached the Penn School (and Hampton and Tuskegee, too) in domestic-focused programs such as the Better Homes in America campaign. From the 1920s to the 1940s, this nationwide program sponsored racially segregated competitions to encourage improvements in housing and home ownership.[76] Assistant Principal Grace Bigelow oversaw the Penn School's island-wide efforts to build new model homes and update old homes to the "modern" standards recommended by the competition.[77] The school won a "special" award for a simple two-room cabin, which stood apart from the suburban homes submitted by white contestants. In 1923, a permanent home demonstration center was completed on the grounds of the Penn School and opened to great fanfare.[78] Penn's model home for 1924 became the Girls Practice House, where female students lived for several weeks as they trained in cooking, household management, and "acting as hostess."[79] A Better Homes campaign promotional pamphlet noted that students learned "for the first time what really constitutes a home," a veiled advocacy of the white, middle-class vision of American life promoted by the campaign.[80]

By 1924, Penn administrators had acquired additional land and expanded the school farm to 276 acres.[81] Hampton-trained teachers, extension agents "from Washington," and even Seaman Knapp, "the father of demonstration farming," came to Penn to support the school's agricultural program.[82] Knapp encouraged local farmers to plant more food crops and reduce their cotton cultivation, especially given the growing boll weevil infestation spreading across the South. After his visit to Penn in 1909, Knapp designated the school farm as an official demonstration station.[83] Penn's J. E. Blanton oversaw field experiments with island farmers to increase agricultural productivity.[84] A molasses mill was enlarged. Sea Islanders planted more corn, peanuts, pecans, rice, sugarcane, and sweet potatoes.[85] Blanton wrote: "We are concentrating our efforts this year on food production, in the honest conviction that if the men here produce their food they will have very little trouble in getting money enough to pay taxes and get other home needs. . . . We are working to the end that they may make enough meat, meal, rice, peas, potatoes, etc. . . . to run the family, feed the cows, hogs, horses, etc. and have some to sell."[86]

Penn educators believed that the combination of education, improved agricultural productivity, land security, crop diversification, and income from craft production would increase islanders' economic independence and decrease out-migration to the mainland for employment. With a new bridge planned to connect Beaufort and the Sea Islands, Cooley and others saw the threat commercial development posed to the traditional livelihood of local African Americans. In 1923, members of the St. Helena Cooperative Society asked school trustees to pay local farmers' delinquent taxes and prevent the "tax sale" of their land. "The crisis is here. The Bridge is in sight. White people doubtless are counting on the lands on the St. Helena for truck farming. The whole demonstration in rural Negro Education will be crippled if the Negroes must lose their lands on this Island."[87] The bridge connecting St. Helena to Beaufort opened on July 7, 1927. The dire predictions proved true, not only for the South Carolina Sea Islands, but also for the Core Sound region in coastal North Carolina and the Eastern Shore of Virginia, where small farmers were pushed out by high taxes and the encroachment of commercial truck farming operations.

Hampton, Hindman, Penn, Tuskegee, and the many other settlement and industrial schools throughout the South were central locations of rural and agricultural reform in the South, a movement focused in no small part on rehabilitating the diet of working and impoverished southerners. After the 1914 passage of the Smith-Lever Act, which funded cooperative extension programs at land-grant agricultural colleges and universities throughout the country, the southern home and small farm became the locus of food-related reform in the first decades of the twentieth century. Settlement schools, industrial programs, and agricultural colleges remained important educational resources for area farmers and homemakers, who enthusiastically attended annual school-sponsored farmers' conferences, institutes, and fairs. More significant, though, especially for its impact on the southern table, were the personal visits of trained home demonstration and extension agents who entered the daily lives of rural white and black southerners. Intrepid reformers, they led a quiet revolution to improve the southern diet, foster economic self-sufficiency, and increase regional food production.

11

Agricultural Reform Comes Home

The success of home and farm demonstration work in the South—the hands-on instructional methodology developed by agriculturist Seaman Knapp—was reflected in impressive numbers. In 1912, more than 100,000 southern farmers participated in racially segregated demonstration programs led by 700 extension agents.[1] Food was key to these educational programs, which largely focused on improving southern crop yields by promoting the latest scientific farming methods. To most effectively change entrenched, outdated, and inefficient farming practices in the South, Knapp recognized that the entire family must be involved, not just the farmer, or even just the farmer and his wife.[2] He encouraged the development of rural clubs for white homemakers and their children. By educating children in modern methods of scientific agriculture and domestic science, parents would follow. Although he initially opposed having black extension agents, Knapp was convinced of their value after visiting Tuskegee, where he hired Tom Campbell as the first African American demonstration agent.[3]

Home Demonstration—Mother, Father, and Children, Too

White and black women educators—most of them recent graduates of home economics and domestic science programs—taught southern homemakers to turn homemade pickles, cakes, and jams into much-needed cash for their families. Equally important, female educators emphasized Progressive-Era ideas about nutrition and sanitation and the impact of both on moral character.[4] Engaged in a form of "nostalgic modernism," home economists attempted to alter the eating habits of working-class and impoverished southerners by influencing the heartbeat of the southern home—the grandmothers, mothers, and daughters who struggled daily to feed their families cheaply and efficiently.[5]

At the University of North Carolina (UNC) at Chapel Hill, home economists took to the "rails" to spread the gospel of domestic science at special women's institutes scheduled throughout the state in the early 1900s.[6] A passenger train car provided by the Southern Railway Company was retrofitted into a "demonstration railway car" by removing seats to make way for a full kitchen, with oil stove, icebox, kitchen cabinet, and "fireless cooker."[7] An editorial in support of the women's institutes argued that the "best farms are impossible without the best farm homes. . . . A knowledge of modern domestic science is as important and useful to the woman who is to develop and maintain the ideal farm home of the future as is a knowledge of modern agricultural science to the man who is to build up a model farm."[8] The institutes offered "how-to" classes on planting fruit and vegetable gardens, raising poultry, making butter, baking bread, cooking meat, basic nutrition, and home sanitation. Anxious to support all efforts to build southern agriculture and thus increase its own profits from transporting goods, the Southern Railway Company formed a separate agricultural division to address the needs of both their male and their female farm customers.[9] One of the company's railcars was fitted up as a "model farm dairy."[10]

Tait Butler, director of North Carolina's annual summer farmers' institutes, the educational programs for farmers sponsored by the state's Department of Agriculture, argued that science could improve rural life in the South, including the region's substandard diet, but that the first step was getting inside homes and reaching working-class women: "Owing to our social ideas and customs there is probably no place which has been less influenced by modern discovery and the recent advance in scientific knowledge than has the Southern home."[11] North Carolina was one of the five "pioneer states" in the South to organize programs for women and girls.[12] (Mississippi, South Carolina, Tennessee, and Virginia were the other four states.) Mae Card, a graduate of the domestic science department at Ontario Agricultural College, and Viola Boddie, a North Carolina native and faculty member at the State Normal and Industrial College for Women in Greensboro, spoke to over eighty women who attended twenty-one institutes the first summer of the program.[13] Card lectured on "Home Making and Home Conveniences" and gave cooking demonstrations. Boddie spoke on "Educating the Farmers' Daughters" and "Literature for the Farm Home."[14] Male instructors gave presentations on dairying, poultry, farm gardens, and "the Boys on the Farms."[15]

With trained extension agents as instructors and good-natured competition as a motivator, home demonstration programs brought up-to-date farming techniques, as well as sanitary, efficient, and, most important, profitable methods of home food production, to southern homemakers.[16] Girls' tomato clubs, boys' corn clubs, mothers' home-making clubs, livestock clubs, and canning clubs—the same popular programs seen at the Penn School in the South Carolina Lowcountry—spread throughout the South, funded by state agricultural colleges and

Lee County, South Carolina, booth, South Carolina State Fair, Columbia, South Carolina, 1914. South Caroliniana Library, University of South Carolina, Columbia, S.C., photographs 12258.1 os.

support from Rockefeller's General Education Board.[17] Male extension agents worked with boys' clubs and farmers, promoting scientific agriculture and business practices that emphasized crop diversification and increased yield.[18] Female agents taught women and girls state-of-the-art gardening, food preservation, and marketing skills to sell their home-produced goods.[19] Government campaigns such as the "Live-at-Home" program, which encouraged farm families to grow and conserve more food, were imbued with patriotic fervor during World War I and its aftermath.[20] Beyond lessons to increase home productivity and income, home demonstration agents brought important public health information to their constituencies, including recommended diets to prevent pellagra, advice regarding hygiene, and best practices for prenatal care.[21]

"Egg and Butter Money"

The impact of southern-born, black and white female extension agents on rural women was profound. Their professional stature and ties to the South and, most important, their gender gave them unprecedented access to the public and the private domestic worlds of southern women. As historian Lu Ann Jones explains, female agents could "scrutinize and intervene in the most private aspects of family life—from how a woman prepared meals, preserved food, and arranged her kitchen, to how she dressed, raised her children, and kept flies and rodents out of her house."[22] Safely within the sphere of the southern home and black and white women's accepted roles and responsibilities, female extension agents strengthened their constituents' sense of self-worth by recognizing their contributions to the household economy.

Without women's home production of food, both for their own use and for sale, most rural families could not have survived the volatility of the southern staple-crop market in the first decades of the twentieth century.[23] They sold surplus eggs, butter, and produce to local merchants and peddlers and brought the same to weekly "curb markets" and regular customers in town.[24] In the 1920s, female extension agents organized these markets, providing an established, in-town venue where local farm women could sell homegrown fruits and vegetables and homemade specialty foods, from highly prized layer cakes, pies, and preserves to biscuits, light bread, prepared salads, and fresh meats.[25] On one day in the 1930s, Nettie Shull, the most successful vendor at the Staunton, Virginia, curb market, sold $100 worth of homemade potato chips, fried apple pies, potato salad, and dressed poultry—a substantial addition to the family income, especially during the Depression years between World War I and the onset of World War II.[26]

In 1945, Jane Simpson McKimmon, the retired director of North Carolina's home demonstration programs, reported fifty-five successful "farm woman's markets" in the state.[27] A white middle-class wife and mother in Raleigh, McKimmon at age fifty earned a bachelor's degree from North Carolina State University and a master's degree in 1929.[28] She was assistant director of the North Carolina Agricultural Extension Service from 1924 to 1946. McKimmon's memoir, *When We're Green We Grow*, is both the story of her career and a larger history of the dynamic, women-led, home demonstration movement.[29] "Not for anything would I miss going every Saturday morning to the market in the basement of the city auditorium in my own town, Raleigh," wrote McKimmon. "It is a joy to see all of those eager faces and the well displayed things they are selling, and I can never resist Mrs. Wilkersons's pepper-hot sausage and good spare ribs, Mrs. Tunstall's cakes, Mrs. Sauls' sweet potatoes, or the country butter and water-ground meal."[30]

Producing and selling these goods not only connected rural women to social and economic networks that stretched far beyond their farms but also shifted how they thought about themselves.[31] Women used their "egg and butter" money to buy special treats for themselves and their families and, not infrequently, to pay rents and mortgages and buy needed farm equipment.[32] As resourceful entrepreneurs, rural southern women determined the direction and tone of family life in the struggling farm economy—either backward toward the endless labor of unforgiving cotton crops, or forward toward a more stable income centered on a mix of diversified crops, livestock, and home production.

The unusual success of the federally funded Unified Farm Program—an early 1940s initiative to increase home farm production and improve diet in rural Greene County, Georgia—points to women's crucial role in improving nutrition and income for their families.[33] UNC sociologist Arthur Raper closely studied economic and social conditions in Greene County and observed poor white and black families whose diet seldom, if ever, included meat, poultry, or eggs.[34] Historian Clifford Kuhn notes that few families had extensive vegetable gardens, and thus only a handful of women canned fresh produce for use throughout the year.[35] For those who typically planted collards, sweet potatoes, and rutabagas to supplement a basic diet of cornmeal, "side meat," and molasses, "new" vegetables such as carrots, spinach, rhubarb, English peas, beets, and lettuce were rare "novelty" foods.[36]

To participate in the Unified Farm Program, which granted larger loans, longer leases on farmland, and more supervision, Greene County sharecroppers and tenants agreed to plant gardens, can vegetables, and keep chickens and a milk cow.[37] Farmwives joined home demonstration clubs. Each received a pressure cooker and canning jars.[38] The "precious" cookers—so-called by local families—sped up the canning process *and* gave women a sense of empowerment as they mastered the technology.[39] "The traditional subservience of the woman on the cotton farm" disappeared, according to Arthur Raper, as she became "commander-in-chief" of a more efficient household.[40] One husband who assisted his wife with seasonal canning noted that the new cookers "set women free."[41] By 1941, the Georgia county's home canners had produced thousands of quarts of canned vegetables, fruits, meat, and juice, which provided variety in the monotonous local diet.[42] Families caught the canning spirit. Cooking demonstrations helped women learn to prepare meals from unfamiliar canned goods.[43] A graduate student who worked with Raper described the beauty of shelves lined with glass jars of brightly colored foods.[44] A farmwife explained: "It's the same as having a garden in your house all winter."[45]

Extending the Reach

Southern Farm Bulletins and Nutritional Studies

Beyond the participatory farmers' institutes and curb markets, published bulletins were an important means of communication between farmers, rural families, and agricultural colleges.[46] Eugene B. Ferris, who directed agricultural experiment stations in McNeill and Holly Springs, Mississippi, in the early 1900s, and Dorothy Dickins, the first female scientist associated with the state's experiment stations, in the 1920s, wrote scores of food-related bulletins available to avid readers throughout the state. Ferris examined the cultivation of corn, peanuts, sweet potatoes, satsumas, snap beans, sugarcane, and winter legumes in Mississippi, while Dickins explored dietary reform, including studies on soybeans as a low-cost protein and molasses, collards, mustard greens, and turnip greens as inexpensive sources of iron in the southern diet.[47]

As a child of a physician in the Mississippi Delta, Dorothy Dickins saw the daily hunger and poverty of sharecropping families in the region. She later trained as a social scientist. With advanced degrees in chemistry, nutrition, and family economics from Mississippi State College for Women, Columbia University, and the University of Chicago, Dickins returned to her home state to study the eating habits of poor, rural black and white residents.[48] Historian Ted Ownby positions Dickins as a rare female voice challenging the southern Agrarians, who promoted the value of rural life.[49] Her growing critique of the limits of farming, especially for rural women, reveals a feminist challenge to southern agriculture and the agrarian ideal.[50]

Two of Dorothy Dickins's nutritional studies, from 1927 and 1928, convey the extensive food-related research of the state experiment stations. Similar in style to the Atwater dietary studies conducted in Tuskegee in the 1890s, the reports examined the food habits and health of rural Mississippians by race and region—the first, white farm families in central Mississippi, and the second, African American tenant farmers in the Mississippi Delta.[51] The 1927 study was completed in February and March, just before the devastating levee break in April that flooded millions of acres in the Mississippi River basin. Dickins began her 1928 report with a question meant to provoke her readers—how could there be two Mississippis, represented by an impoverished diet and by a diet of abundance? "Is it true that the poor Mississippi farmer dines daily off of corn-meal, salt pork, and molasses," wrote Dickins, "while his more prosperous neighbor indulges in chicken, candied yams, and corn pone?"[52]

The Mississippi food studies included Dickins's analysis and data collected by local women hired as project supervisors. Sample menus from white and black families were categorized by the quality of their diets. A "better" African American weekday meal plan began with fried eggs, fried potatoes, biscuit, butter, and molasses for breakfast; cabbage, cornbread, peach pie, and milk for noon dinner; and fried eggs, biscuit, butter, molasses, and milk for supper.[53] The "most inadequate" African American meal plan included only rice, cornbread, and coffee for breakfast, a noon "dinner" of peas and cornbread, and no food for supper.[54] In central Mississippi, white families with a "good variety of food" enjoyed an abundant diet of seasonal food, including a source of animal protein, such as a dinner of "fried steak with onions, tomato gravy, baked sweet potatoes, biscuits, butter, and custard."[55] A white family whose food had "little variety"—canned salmon, fried sweet potatoes, and biscuits with molasses and butter for supper—still ate better than most impoverished African Americans.[56]

Although Dickins noted that the diet of African American families in the Delta was "lower in energy value" than that of whites, she argued that both groups suffered from serious nutritional deficiencies and needed to increase their food intake through home production.[57] "The average Mississippi farmer can more easily afford . . . to put labor into raising food than he can to put cash into purchasing food. . . . It behooves him to adopt this motto: 'variety and quantity of food raised at home.'"[58] In her Delta report of the food patterns of African American tenant farmers, Dickins concluded, "It is the school, the agricultural extension department, the public health department, and yes, even the church, that must teach and encourage these people, mothers and fathers, boys and girls to increase their food supply."[59] She advised black families to drink better-quality milk, to raise and preserve more fruits and vegetables, and to increase their yield of eggs for family consumption and for sale. "Evidently," stated Dickins, "the majority have not yet adopted the slogan coined by Negro Extension Workers: 'Take what you have and make what you can out of it.'"[60]

Dickins's racial ideology was central to her scientific theories about the underlying cause of blacks' poor nutrition.[61] Like most white southerners, she believed that flawed character and physiology impeded African American progress.[62] Outside this skewed racial lens, poverty, racial discrimination, and inequitable government programs were clearly the real cause of black hunger. Historian Angela Jill Cooley notes that racial inequalities "were built into the South's labor system and through dietary distinctions built into the very molecules of life and human flesh."[63] Ultimately, as Cooley explains, "differences in the southern diet based on race" justified white racist views of African Americans.[64]

On the Road Again

The Politics of Race, Class, and Food

When Selma Parrish, a white home demonstration agent in Kershaw County, South Carolina, acquired her assigned vehicle for work, the occasion was newsworthy. "Miss Selma Parrish has received her Ford touring car, and is now touring the county. The work of organizing demonstration clubs continues in various sections of the county."[65] In Camden, South Carolina, twenty girls signed up for Parrish's domestic science classes, and as many women signed up for the Camden Demonstration Club.[66] The local newspaper reported that Parrish was in great demand and could use the help of "Camden's best housekeepers" as volunteer teachers.[67] The promotional piece for the extension agent continued: "The Old South was famed for its culinary art, but those who added luster to the antebellum kitchen are fast passing away. Do not let it become a 'lost art,' but learn from those who are willing to teach, and at the same time learn all the up-to-date methods taught by our County Demonstrator, Miss Parrish."[68]

The young African American women who became county extension agents in the 1920s were charged with the same teaching mission as their white colleagues, but, given the racial inequity of the segregated South, they accomplished the same, or even more, with far less resources.[69] Emma McDougald, the first African American home demonstration agent in Wayne County, North Carolina, had no money allotted in her work budget for a car in 1922.[70] She traveled by train and by foot to the home demonstration clubs she founded in eastern North Carolina, as well as to the many farms, schools, clubs, and churches she visited to recruit African American women to participate in extension programs.[71] "I took the work in May," said McDougald, "but the task was so great that if I have done anything at all it has been through the Lord and the good friends he has sent me in Wayne County."[72]

Jane Simpson McKimmon hired McDougald and five other black women as extension agents.[73] In 1933, McKimmon arranged for the new African American agents to attend the annual summer school held for the state's white home demonstration agents.[74] She described the first morning of the joint conference of white and black women workers: "Provision was made for them in the home agent's conference room that summer, and a mutual feeling of respect and appreciation was engendered when each had an opportunity to hear reports of the other's good work."[75] The black agents opened the meeting with a song, "I'll Grow My Home Supplies." Its spirited lyrics inspired the women agents and their "troops": "Yes, I've been farming by old plans, / With little food to eat; / But now my plans for home supplies, / Include my bread and meat. . . . / With gardens, corn and pork and hay, / With poultry and a cow, / We'll bid farewell to mortgages, / And live as Kings know how."[76] Funds from the Anna T. Jeanes Foundation supported additional black teachers for summer home demonstration club work.[77] Trained at Hampton, Tuskegee, and other southern black institutions, the Jeanes teachers developed industrial education programs in black public schools in North Carolina and throughout the region.[78] These teachers, too, struggled to make do with the substandard conditions and lack of educational resources in black schools.

School lunchrooms were an indication of the economic disparities, not only between races in the South but by class among white southerners. Dorothy Dickins observed these divisions as a lunchroom supervisor for city schools in Jackson, Mississippi, a position she held at the beginning of her career.[79] Surveys taken in 1925 and 1926 of twenty-seven white school lunchrooms in Shelby County, Tennessee, documented thirteen with running water and just nineteen with enough storage space and appropriate stoves for the lunch program.[80] Sixteen of the schools had no window screens.[81] A series of photographs from the 1940s documents the entrenched racism of South Carolina's segregated schools. Lunchrooms in the white schools are notable for the floral tie-back curtains at the windows, freshly painted walls, flowers on the tables, fruit, and individual bottles of milk for each student. Few of these amenities exist in the "colored" lunchroom, where children sit on simple benches at crowded, rough-hewn tables.[82] The ability of white and black school administrators to notably improve diet and physical surroundings was challenging, at best, in southern worlds bound by poverty and racism.[83]

Lucille Cook Watson lived between two worlds in this time. She married into the wealthy Watson family, which owned Cross Keys, a cotton and cattle plantation in Tensas Parish, Louisiana. After her husband's death in 1934, Watson managed the plantation. To help keep the operation afloat, Watson worked for the state's Emergency Relief Administration as a caseworker in the 1930s. Despite the difficult times, Watson's social calendar was filled with horseback rides and hunt breakfasts shared with well-off white friends and neighbors. Her job for the relief agency exposed her to the substandard living conditions of the impoverished working people in the area. She processed their daily requests for

Rich Hill School lunchroom, Lancaster, South Carolina, 1946. South Caroliniana Library, University of South Carolina, Columbia, S.C., photographs 12363.14.

Grammar school lunchroom, Blacksburg, South Carolina, 1946. South Caroliniana Library, University of South Carolina, Columbia, S.C., photographs 12363.6.

food aid, such as that of one mother who explained, "My grocerys, as I told you, would only last this week are almost out. I would like to know if you all couldn't help me in some form to-day. Some one said they were issuing flour to-day, if so, I need it. . . . Please try to help me."[84]

Day after day, Watson drove from one plantation to another in the eastern Louisiana parish bounded by the Mississippi River—former estates now divided among sharecroppers and tenant farmers who rented the land. She submitted reports on the eligibility of dozens of families for aid based on her own observations and those of neighbors and landlords. When a husband or son fell ill and could not work, food supplies grew dangerously low. In July 1933, Watson visited a family in their two-room cabin on Ashland Plantation. "The field comes up around the house—and there is very little space for a yard," Watson reported.[85] Drought and illness took a heavy toll on the family, whose circumstances were dire by midsummer: "Family had only enough food in the house to give them a scanty supper. Woman stated she could not obtain credit. . . . Family planted garden in field—they are eating tomatoes—will have some butter beans soon. . . . Visitor feels that this women has made every effort to make a living for her children since the death of her husband in 1932, and that family are now up against it for a bare living."[86] Watson recommended two weeks of work aid for the needy family.

Despite the poverty, Watson emphasized one woman's attempts to keep a nice home and act as a "proper" hostess during an October 1933 inspection. Watson found the husband sick in bed with "chills and a fever," and his wife and children in the fields picking cotton. Stopping her work, the farmwife came to the house to greet Watson and "was very courteous and hospitable." Watson described the four-room tenant quarters: "Every part of the house shows evidence of the efforts that have been made to improve it. . . . There were several pictures placed around the room, but most of them were cut out of magazines and used to best advantage. Mr. Crossgrove was lying on a cot over in the far corner of the front room. . . . They are indeed a relief problem at present."[87] Watson issued a government-paid grocery order for the hungry Crossgrove family. The goods listed suggest the staple diet of a sharecropping family and the slight improvements that aid provided: cornmeal and flour (twenty-four pounds of each), ten pounds of "meat" (most likely pork or cheap cuts of beef), four pounds of lard, five pounds of rice, canned tomatoes (four tins), two pounds of cheese, two pounds of macaroni noodles, two pounds of grits, fifteen cents worth of white potatoes, a soup bone, and a can of molasses.[88] A twenty-five-cent jar of Vicks salve for Crossgrove's sick husband and son completed the order. Later, the Unemployment Bureau received a letter of appreciation from Mrs. Crossgrove: "I want to thank you for the groceries you sent me, and the kindness you have shown me during the illness of my husband and son. I certainly appreciate all this for I was really in need of help. Mr. Crossgrove and William are both improving and I am sure that William will be able to go to working a few days. Yours very truly, Mrs W. C. Crossgrove."[89]

Governor Gardner's "Live-at-Home" Campaign

In North Carolina, the "Live-at-Home" campaign gained force after Governor Max Gardner, sworn into office just days after the stock market crash in 1929, actively promoted the program to address the growing food shortage threatening the rural citizens of his state.[90] With so much of North Carolina's agricultural land planted in nonfood cash crops, there was little space or time allotted to family gardens and food production. As prices for tobacco and cotton plummeted, more and more rural families could not afford even the most basic staples for the table. North Carolinians imported "one of every three pounds of beef, two of five pigs, two of three quarts of milk, and one of two chickens and eggs eaten in the state."[91] In December 1929, Dean I. O. Schaub of North Carolina State College of Agriculture and Engineering launched the "Live-at-Home" campaign in partnership with the state's Department of Agriculture and extension service.[92] Schaub also directed the state Agricultural Extension Service and experiment station. A primary mission of "Live-at-Home" was to improve the living situation of the rural poor and thus slow the migration of low income whites and blacks out of the state to the North.[93] According to the governor, the program encouraged farmers to grow the "food and feed-stuffs and livestock products necessary for family and farm consumption the year round" and encouraged "the city folks of this state to give a preference to the North Carolina farmer in their purchase of the supplies which he grows."[94] To help publicize the program, journalists were invited to a special "Live-at-Home" luncheon at the governor's mansion on December 17, 1929, featuring food and beverages produced in North Carolina.[95]

As director of North Carolina's home demonstration program, Jane Simpson McKimmon mobilized her staff to organize Governor Gardner's feast. The menu rivaled any farm-to-table feast of today's local food movement: "The meal began with cold pressed scuppernong juice from the Coastal Plain Test Farm and was followed by an oyster cocktail from Hyde County or one of shrimp from Southport. The piece de resistance was turkey," followed by country hams with baked yams, turnip salad, corn pone, spinach, "a wealth of other vegetables," and hot rolls.[96] Dessert was ice cream served with a Sandhills peach conserve and a slice of homemade cake. "Pecans, sorghum and peanut candy . . . came from the east, apples and kraut juice from the foothills of the mountains; and sweet milk from the Guernsey breeders' association." "Buttermilk [came] from the creameries."[97] The luncheon concluded with a North Carolina touch of the industrial 1920s—complimentary cigarettes and cigars sent from the "big tobacco companies of North Carolina" and also "a wealth of favors from cotton and woolen mills in the shape of socks, hose, and dress patterns."[98]

From the Depression through World War II, female home demonstration agents and teams of women volunteers conducted "Live-at-Home" training sessions with rural North Carolina homemakers on gardening and food preservation. Fifty-one of the home demonstration counties in the state organized "hot lunch" programs for rural public schools.[99] In conjunction with the program, Works Progress Administration laborers built 140 log cabin–style community clubhouses for the home demonstration programs, complete with stone fireplaces, kitchens, and modern plumbing facilities.[100] Figures for 1933 home production in North Carolina show 140,000 relief gardens, 11.5 million jars of canned food, and thirty curb markets throughout the state.[101] In the Piedmont region of the state, Iredell County alone reported 107,462 quarts canned from individual gardens in 1934.[102] "Live-at-Home" events were organized throughout the state, such as in coastal Onslow County, where a women's group sponsored a lecture and banquet featuring locally grown peaches, oysters, homemade pickles, baked ham, and yaupon tea, made from a native evergreen holly.[103]

Women members of the home demonstration club in Buncombe County, North Carolina, published a fund-raising cookbook, *Good Victuals from the Mountains* (1951). Money raised from cookbook sales funded a Home Demonstration Club House for the twenty-six clubs in the county.[104] Mrs. S. B. Tweed of Fletcher, North Carolina, project chair, shared her recipe for a "North Carolina Sparkler": "2 qts. ginger ale, 2½ cups lemon juice, ½ cup of bruised mint leaves, 2 cups sugar, 1 cup water. Boil sugar and water to a syrup with lemon juice and leaves. Cool and strain. Add ginger ale. Serve over ice with lemon sections or mint leaves."[105]

By 1930 a mandatory "Live-at-Home" curriculum was implemented in all public schools in North Carolina.[106] The program focused on small livestock management, the growing and preserving of food, and scientific agriculture. Students created "Live-at-Home" scrapbooks, including fifth-grader Isador Wade, who illustrated the problems of one-crop agriculture in cut-out pictures of cotton and tobacco fields. His caption stated, "Farmer Johnson planted only cotton and tobacco on his land. When he sold them it took all his money to buy provisions and pay for the fertilizer."[107] Governor Gardner personally presented silver loving cups to Ophelia Holley and Leroy Sossamon, winners of the first "Live-at-Home" student essay contest.[108] His political friends worried that the public would criticize the governor for posing with the young African

Governor O. Max Gardner poses with "Live-at-Home" essay contest winners, Ophelia Holley, Windsor Colored High School, Windsor, North Carolina, and Leroy Sossaman, Bethel High School, Cabarrus County, North Carolina, in front of Aycock Statue on Capitol Square, Raleigh, North Carolina, June 23, 1930. Courtesy of the State Archives of North Carolina.

American girl and white boy in a photograph.[109] "Undaunted, Governor Gardner arranged the black girl on his right and the white boy on his left, ordered the photographer to proceed," and replied, "If I ever get into politics again I'll use this picture for myself."[110]

As North Carolina's white and black extension service and home demonstration agents traveled county to county to preach the gospel of vegetable gardens and diversified, small-scale agriculture in the 1920s and 1930s, a new Department of Sociology was launched at the state's flagship university in Chapel Hill. The program brought rural and agricultural reform throughout the South as its faculty and students confronted the region's social and economic problems, including the deficient diet of working-class southerners. The following chapter explores one "moment" in this historical sweep—the 1920s to 1940s New South era of social science research, documentary work, and New Deal programs that identified "southern diet" and "southern cookery"—two distinctly different views of the region's food—as the South's greatest problem and its most beloved treasure.

12 The Deepest Reality of Life

SOUTHERN SOCIOLOGY, THE WPA, AND FOOD IN THE NEW SOUTH

Thus, the way of the South, as the way of culture,
has also been the way of history and the way of America.
– Howard W. Odum, The Way of the South: Toward the Regional Balance of America

In late February 1920, Columbia University–trained sociologist Howard Odum, a native of Georgia, arrived in Chapel Hill, where he founded the South's first Department of Sociology and School of Public Welfare, at UNC. Odum and his colleagues introduced the discipline of "regional sociology," which brought the tools of social science to bear on the contemporary problems of the South. Diet, or the "food habits" of southerners, was chief among these concerns. Odum joined documentarians, government officials, public health physicians, reformers, scholars, and statisticians, who turned their attention to the Depression-era South and responded to President Franklin Roosevelt's infamous designation of the region as the "Nation's No. 1 economic problem."[1]

Odum's new Institute for Research in Social Science (IRSS), founded in 1924, assembled a diverse group of scholars, including UNC-trained sociologists Rupert Vance and Arthur Raper, and Guy B. Johnson, who studied black folk culture in the South. In his massive ethnography of the South, *Southern Regions of the United States* (1936), Odum addressed diet and folkways as important aspects of regional culture.[2] He described "two contrasting pictures" of the culinary South, a world of plenty and a world of deprivation: "One portrays the excellence of southern cooking with its contributions to the art of living; the other the subsistence diet of the masses of marginal folk, commonly ascribed as a major factor in deficiencies of vitality and health."[3] Odum connected the substandard diet of the "masses" to the South's problems in health, politics, race relations, and leadership.

Taking on the South's culinary cultures was not a task for the faint of heart. A Mississippi columnist's virulent response to Odum's 1937 speech to the American Dietetic Association convention in Richmond suggests the symbolic power of food in the region.[4] Offended at Odum's statistics and "slanderous" remarks regarding southerners' "slow starvation and deterioration" in the "richest land in the world," the writer invited Odum to come visit Mississippi. There he would take him to a "negro cabin in the delta" and "fill your belly" with ham (three kinds—fried, broiled, and baked), sweet potatoes "popping open with sweetness," corn pone, biscuits, flour gravy, molasses, fried chicken, possum, collards, cabbage, turnips, cowpeas, butterbeans, buttermilk, stalks of ribbon cane, and finally, a "slab of pie."[5] He concluded that the country might be better off without "government," the "professorial persons" of the IRSS, and the "Southern Association for the Advancement of Colored People," for whom he imagined an unpleasant ending on a dark and stormy night in the Atlantic Ocean, "without life-rafts or life preservers."[6] Despite the exaggerated unreality of the poor sharecropper's abundant dinner table, sentimental depictions such as this referenced the white South's tight grasp on a mythic past, an imaginary benevolent land of milk and honey, for *all*. Confronting the reality of malnutrition's deep connection to cash crop agriculture was an essential factor in Odum's commitment to regional planning, to ending insularity, and to successfully reintegrating the South into the nation.[7]

Two divergent schools of regionalist thought emerged in southern universities at this time: a regionalism based in research, analysis, and planning, promoted by Howard Odum and Rupert Vance at Chapel Hill, and the pastoral vision of a southern utopia in harmony with nature and "rural virtues" touted by the Agrarians, a group of twelve scholars at Vanderbilt University.[8] The Agrarian manifesto, *I'll Take My Stand* (1930), made a case for preserving southern agricultural heritage and rural values by shielding the region from the invasive forces of industrialization and technology couched in the "positivism" of New South boosters.[9]

Not unlike the journalist's romantic depiction of the food of black sharecroppers in the Mississippi Delta, similar narratives of the homegrown food of hardworking white farmers—and the moral value of their labor—were key to the Agrarian narrative. Consider Andrew Nelson Lytle's description of the "bountiful" dining table of a Tennessee "countryman" before industrialization. Each dish was *personally* resonant because ingredients came from the farmer's land and hard work, intended for his family rather than the larger marketplace: "Bulging-breasted fowls, deep-yellow butter and creamy milk, fat beans and juicy corn, and its potatoes flavored like pecans, fill his dining-room with the satisfaction of well-being, because he has not yet come to look upon his produce at so many cents a pound, or his corn at so much a dozen."[10] The ideal world that Lytle depicts was distinctly white, devoid of any hint of the institution of slavery. The black cook who would have prepared the meal, alongside the white farmwife and her daughters, is invisible in his southern Camelot. Lytle and the Agrarians ignored the enormous changes in southern agriculture in the 1930s, which made self-sufficiency—the ability of a farmer to provide food for his family from a garden and livestock—impossible for white and black tenant farmers bound by crop liens, volatile cotton and tobacco markets, and growing land loss.

Southern Sociologists and the "Geography of Nutrition"

Chapel Hill sociologist Rupert Vance understood the economic and social challenges of the small family farmer and sharecropper in the New South. As a child in rural Arkansas, he contracted polio and lost the use of his legs. Vance later witnessed his father lose his cotton farm to bankruptcy.[11] In 1929, Vance drew upon his recently completed dissertation, "Human Factors in Cotton Culture," which became a classic in southern sociology. He discussed the crippling impact of what he labeled the "cotton culture complex" on struggling farm families, including how they ate: "Among the most obvious of the material culture traits associated with cotton are the food habits of its growers."[12] Vance described the inadequate diet of the white and black working poor bound to cotton, again referencing the infamous three "m's" noted by other social scientists and physicians: "The Negro cropper, the white tenant, and the small cotton farmer live upon a basic diet of salt fat pork, corn bread, and molasses," he wrote. "This forms the 'three M diet,' meat, meal, and molasses. . . . When cotton farmers purchase food, these are the articles of diet they purchase; first, because all three are cheap, and second, because food likes and dislikes come to be matters of habit imposed by culture."[13]

Vance's focus on the relationship between culture and regional diet was groundbreaking and revealed his deep understanding of food, place, and policy. "Somewhere on the outer edge of the uncharted field of human geography," he wrote, "lies an undeveloped sector, the geography of nutrition."[14] Recognizing that the South had become a research site for public health physicians who investigated the "biology" of nutritional diseases such as pellagra and rickets, Vance saw similar possibilities for social scientists who studied "the human geography of diet" in the South.[15] (Pellagra and rickets were caused by severe malnutrition, pellagra linked to niacin/vitamin B3 deficiency, rickets to lack of vitamin D and calcium. Rickets caused bone deformity and fractures, particularly in children.) Like Odum, Vance noted the region's "reputation for deficient diet," despite its abundant plant and animal life.[16] His explanation for this conundrum reads like a contemporary definition of unsustainable foodways: "When a people in the midst of a land capable of variety limit their diet to a few staples they are in the grip of tradition."[17] He turned to the cultural and folk history of the region to document the origins of food patterns in an agricultural system that left large numbers of southerners impoverished, hungry, and sick. "Behind the folk stands a tragic history," wrote Vance. "What we need to know is that, in spite of its tragic history, the mold in which the South is to be fashioned is only now being laid."[18] Layering the region's history with detailed survey information on "food habits" of rural southerners gathered by home demonstration agents across the South, Rupert Vance exposed the impact of race, class, and agribusiness upon "the South's Heritage of Food."[19]

Soon after Vance arrived in North Carolina, William Terry "W. T." Couch, a UNC alumnus, was appointed director of the University of North Carolina Press.[20] Under Couch's leadership, the press's series on social studies flourished and included publications by Vance and Odum, who tirelessly fought for the emphasis on regional social science studies at the press. Couch edited his own volume, *Culture in the South* (1935). This collection of essays examined southern social, economic, and political life and was his response to the work of the Agrarians.[21]

Many of the contributors to *Culture in the South* included ethnographic descriptions of the diet and food habits of southerners in their work. In his essay "The Negro in the South," W. T. Couch mixed economic and social analysis, folk culture, and stereotypical depictions of working-class African Americans. "Jim"—an imaginary sharecropper created by Couch to represent poor black sharecroppers—"doesn't own a cow; for many years he has had no garden and the family has lived on fat back, corn pone, molasses, and 'thickenin' gravy."[22] In her essay "The Industrial Worker," Harriet Herring, a UNC sociologist and labor activist who specialized in the textile industry, described the idyllic vision of the improved diet of a Progressive-Era white mill operative in the South: "The store that supplied him with food was able, because of increasing rapidity of distribution of such products, to tempt him continually with fruits and vegetables, while the community nurse and school teacher were all busy educating him to the need of this sort of food."[23]

J. Wesley Hatcher described "three distinct classes" of Appalachian people in Couch's *Culture in the South* and used food to illustrate their economic and social statuses.[24] Accordingly, educated and "moral" mountain southerners were associated with abundant households, and illiterate, debased Appalachians were associated with impoverishment. Reformers, educators, and local-color writers of the time reinforced these popular images. The industrious "Grandmother Elliot"—"tall, straight, and graceful in every line, [whose] garden is her joy"—was contrasted to an "ill-nourished and scrawny" mountain woman, "ignorant of every method of making food either palatable or wholesome in its preparation."[25] The "best off," like Grandmother Elliot and her kin, lived in the valley, where "there is stewed or fried chicken, or it may be roast turkey, fried ham, fried eggs, mashed Irish potatoes, candied sweet potatoes, beans, corn bread, biscuit, butter, preserves, jellies, honey, pickles, sweet and butter milk, coffee, yellow layer cake, white layer cake, each cake six inches high, loaf cake, stacked apple pie, fried apple pie."[26] The "worst off" were those "shunted to the starvation points, where slopes are steepest, soil is poorest and thinnest . . . easy accessibility impossible."[27] A single "handleless skillet" served as cooking utensil, wash basin, and toilet, and "a corn patch among the 'deadened trees' on the mountain side, perhaps a few Kentucky Wonder beans among the corn and a straggling patch of onions and turnips are the extent of food resources."[28] Sensationalized descriptions of the moral character and lifestyle of working-class white and black southerners, like Hatcher's assessment of the people of Appalachia, remained a part of the social science canon of the era but were later rejected in light of contemporary scholarship and the social realism of New Deal documentation projects.

The New Deal and Southern Food **FSA Photography**

Food leads us to the research of southern social scientists and the federally funded documentary work of photographers and writers in the New Deal programs of the 1930s and 1940s. Roy Stryker, who oversaw the Farm Security Administration (FSA) photo-documentary project in Washington, D.C., approached Howard Odum in Chapel Hill for his assistance.[29] On June 17, 1939, Stryker wrote Odum: "Dorothea Lange is to be in Washington for a couple of weeks—or possibly longer. While she is here, I am anxious to utilize some extra time she has to make some pictures in your sub-region. . . . It occurred to me that one of the most likely things for her to start on would be some of the sharecropper and tenant wives whom Mrs. Hagood has already interviewed."[30] Odum agreed to Stryker's request. (Stryker worried that Lange, a perfectionist in the darkroom, would slow down production in the Washington office.)[31] By the end of the month, Lange was on a train bound for North Carolina.

The FSA photographers were charged with collecting images of

America as the nation came out of the Great Depression, providing "visual arguments" for government-supported rural relief initiatives.[32] Given Odum's regional focus and the infrastructure he created for researchers, the North Carolina Piedmont offered a prime area for documentation. Responding to growing criticism from political conservatives who argued that New Deal programs like the FSA should be discontinued as the nation mobilized for World War II, Stryker sought uplifting photographs to symbolize America's indomitable strength of character.[33] He wrote FSA photographer Jack Delano in 1940, urging him to "emphasize the idea of abundance—the 'horn of plenty' and pour maple syrup over it. I know your damned photographer's soul writhes, but to hell with it. Do you think I give a damn about a photographer's soul with Hitler at our doorstep?"[34]

In a 1942 memo to FSA photographers Russell Lee and Arthur Rothstein, Stryker added "Production of Foods" to his "shooting scripts," which specified topics his team should record with their cameras.[35] He wanted images of "fruit, vegetables, meat, poultry, eggs, milk and milk products. . . . Packaging and processing [of these]; picking, hauling, sorting, preparing, drying, canning, packaging, loading for shipping; field operations—planting; cultivation; spraying; dramatic pictures of fields, show 'pattern of the country'; get feeling of the productive earth, boundless acres; warehouses filled with food, raw and processed, cans, boxes, bags, etc."[36] The memo reflected the growing pressure on Stryker to present an inspirational vision of America, rather than the hundreds of images of haggard and hungry working southerners taken by FSA photographers. He added: "People—*we must have at once*: Pictures of men, women and children who appear as if they really believed in the U.S. Get people with a little spirit. Too many in our file now paint the U.S. as an old person's home and that just about everyone is too old to work and too malnourished to care much what happens."[37]

In North Carolina, Dorothea Lange's work took on a different focus. Instead of solely documenting rural poverty, as she had done for other FSA assignments, Lange worked with Chapel Hill sociologists Margaret Jarman Hagood and Harriet Herring, who had just finished an ethnography of agricultural and industrial life in thirteen counties in the Carolina and Virginia Piedmont.[38] Hagood had also recently published *Mothers of the South* (1939), a study of white tenant farm women that would become a classic text.[39] Drawing on Hagood's fieldwork in North Carolina, the two sociologists hoped to illustrate how photography could be used as a documentary tool in social research.[40] Hagood accompanied Lange and, later that summer, FSA photographer Marion Post (later Wolcott), who continued the project through the fall.[41]

Hagood and Herring assembled notes for Lange, prepared an itinerary, and sought permission from landowners to photograph on their property.[42] In an outline to assist Lange in her shooting, Harriet Herring specified images needed for the study, such as "daily household processes to show kitchens and cooking, dining rooms and family eating" and "family, group and community recreational and community activities: parties, picnics, 'dinner-on-the-grounds,' hunting, fishing (Negro on creek bank, hand seining, fishing for shad with bows etc.)."[43]

Food habits of southern tenant families were a central focus of Hagood's research and of the FSA photographers. Much of a woman's day was taken up with food preparation for large families plus field hands. Cooking began "before light" and did not end until well "after dark," especially in the summer, with the added chores of field work and canning.[44] Hagood noted that "the traditional Southern pattern of overflowing tables with many sorts of meats simply does not exist in this group."[45] The bountiful South was a world away from tenant farmers. Many families ate meals that consisted of only cabbage, sweet potatoes, or field peas.[46] During the tobacco harvest, children ate cold leftovers from breakfast because older daughters and mothers could not leave work in the middle of the day.[47] Dorothea Lange, Marion Post Wolcott, and Jack Delano later captured these food scenes, which ranged from "hard times" to "getting by," depending on a family's income and the vagaries of health, weather, crop blights, and the tobacco market.

Lange had an eye for photographing food—from field to table—because of her experience documenting farms and agricultural laborers throughout the country, as well as a working partnership with her husband, agricultural economist Paul Taylor.[48] She brilliantly communicated "relationships between people and their environments," capturing the hard farm labor of southern men and women, white and black.[49] In her photographs of the Whitfield family, a white tenant family in rural Person County, North Carolina, Lange recorded a woman's constant round of housecleaning, churning, preparing food, nursing and washing the baby, and feeding children. In the North Carolina Piedmont, Lange also photographed the daughter of black sharecroppers as she planted sweet potatoes in Olive Hill. White children of a mill worker ate watermelon on the front porch of their rented log home near Roxboro. A handwritten menu in a store window in downtown Siler City advertised pimento cheese, chicken, baked ham, and deviled egg sandwiches. A black tenant woman fed chickens on a rented farm in Granville County. A straggly corn crop withered in the summer heat in Orange County. In downtown Mebane, a window of the Golden Rule Store was filled with a colorful display of southern-milled flour, including "Carolina's Best,"

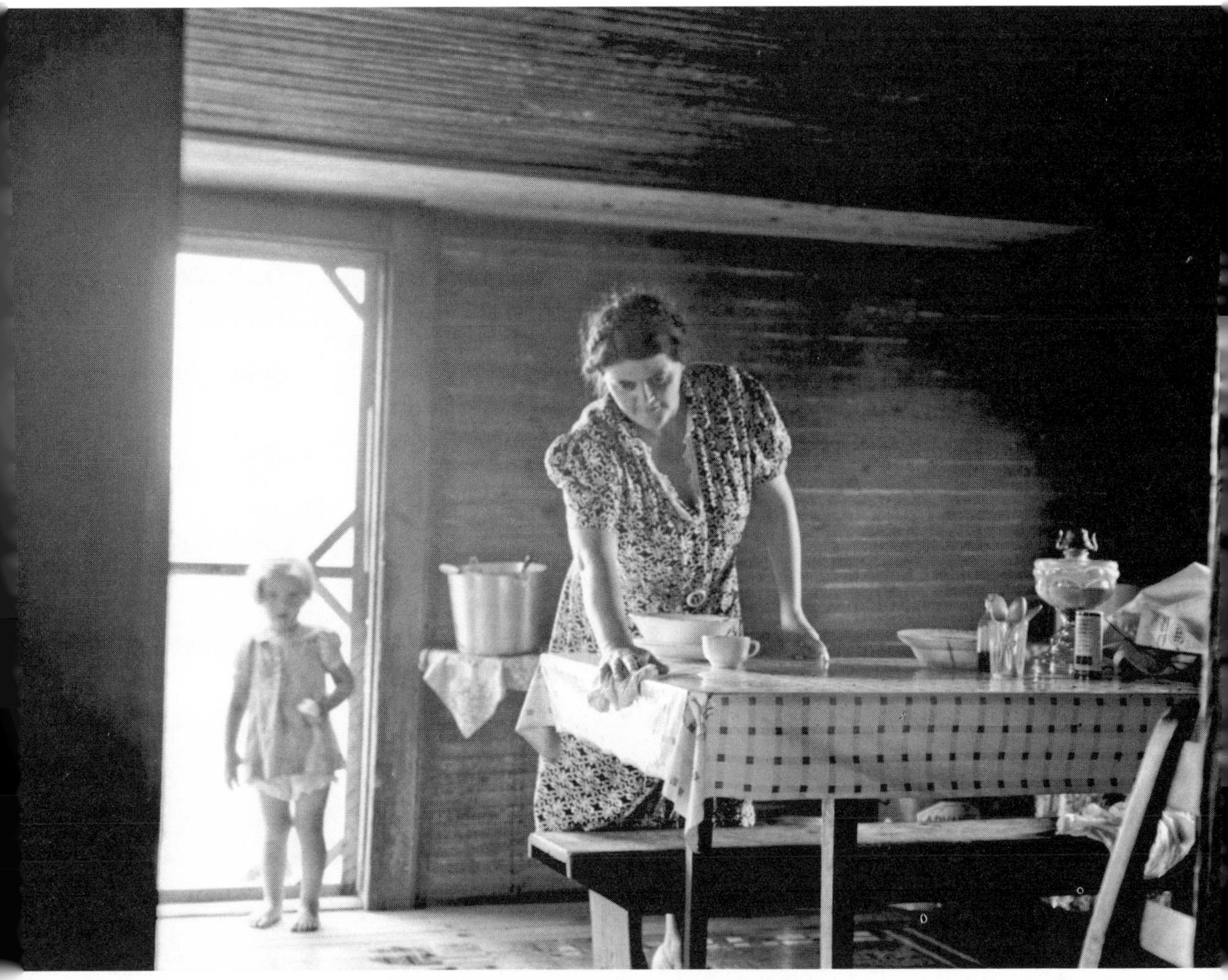

"Wife of tobacco sharecropper in kitchen of home. Person County, North Carolina." Mrs. Whitfield and three-year-old daughter Katie Collen. Photograph by Dorothea Lange, July 1939. LC-DIG-fsa-8b33747 (b&w film nitrate neg.), U.S. Farm Security Administration/Office of War Information, Prints and Photographs Division, Library of Congress, Washington, D.C.

"Red Band," "Rising Star," and "Robert E. Lee Finest Patent Flour." In Gordonton, an advertisement-covered country store and gas station tempted customers to purchase a cold Coca-Cola.

Dorothea Lange wrote extensive captions for most of her photographs, often using language from the memoranda that Herring, Hagood, and other researchers prepared for the photographed sites.[50] In Person County, a black sharecropper posed with his baby daughter outside their rented log cabin, standing beside a slat basket filled with greens. For this image Lange wrote: "In background is a sweet potato patch with a negro man chopping. Could hear the sound of the hoe on the small rocks in the soil. . . . The man was shy of having his photograph

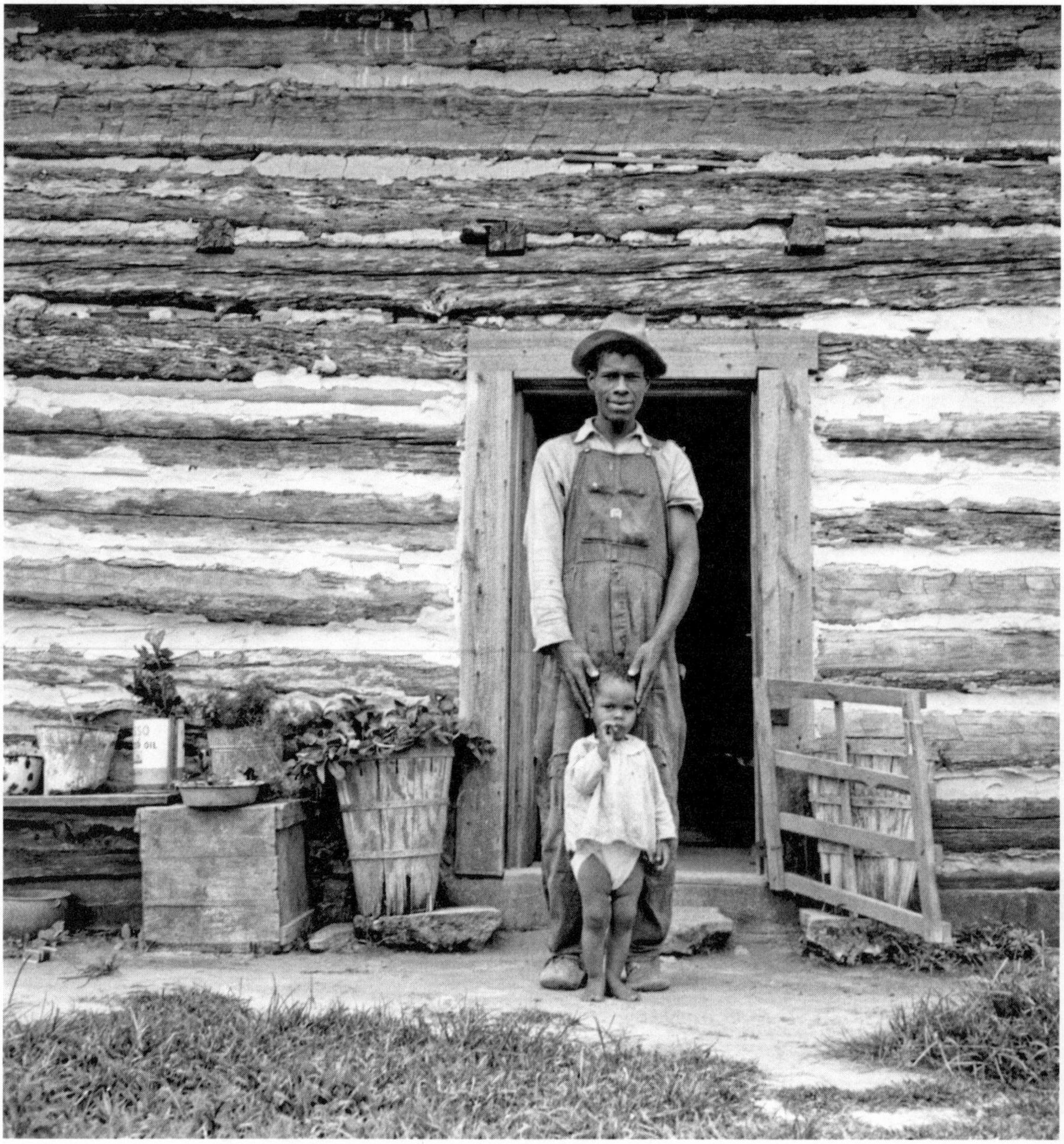

"Young sharecropper and his first child. Hillside Farm. Person County, North Carolina." Photograph by Dorothea Lange, July 1939. LC-USF34-020258-E (b&w film nitrate neg.). U.S. Farm Security Administration/Office of War Information, Prints and Photographs Division, Library of Congress, Washington, D.C.

made but finally held the baby in front of the house for one picture. They have just moved here this year—'They treat us better here than where we did live'; . . . no privy in sight, had to get water from 'the spring' so far away that the man was gone about 20 minutes to get a bucket of water."[51] In Chapel Hill, on a rare day off, Lange photographed the exterior of Harry's Delicatessen, a favorite hang-out of university students and faculty at 175 E. Franklin Street. The city-style delicatessen contrasted sharply with rural country stores she had documented throughout the summer.

Marion Post Wolcott arrived in North Carolina in the fall of 1939 to continue the work that Lange had begun. Traveling with Margaret Jarmon Hagood, she photographed the cotton and tobacco harvest and the seasonal rituals of canning, corn shucking, hog killing, and sorghum making and the storing of fall sweet potatoes. Wolcott documented women preparing hearty meals for farm laborers who brought in the fall crops, recording biscuit making, the passing of plates of layer cake, and the "washing up" after the midday meal. Hagood noted the racial etiquette of the meal at an all-day corn shucking at the Wilkins home in Granville County, North Carolina. "The food was prepared by the wife and her four sisters-in-law and one Negro woman. . . . Two tables were put together in the dining room. All the white men ate first, then the table was cleared and dishes washed and the table re-set for the white women and children. After they ate the dishes were washed and the table reset again for the Negro men."[52]

In October 1939, Marion Post Wolcott came to Durham, North Carolina. Authorities at the Agricultural Adjustment Administration had temporarily closed the tobacco market to control falling prices after farmers rejected acreage controls and produced a bumper crop that fall.[53] Piedmont farmers brought their tobacco to the loose-leaf auctions, where auctioneers sold it to buyers for the large commercial tobacco manufacturers. When the market reopened, Wolcott photographed the city's tobacco warehouses and bars, cafés, and food stands that kept the farmers and auctioneers fed and "watered" late into the night. Many farmers stayed overnight—sometimes several days—waiting for their tobacco to be auctioned. A hot meal of fried eggs and steak at the Farmers Café, the Little Acorn, or the Leaf revived farmers after a long night on the rough wooden pallets and piles of tobacco that served as makeshift beds.[54] Wolcott photographed the Liberty Café in Satterfield and Stone's warehouse on the corner of Rigsbee and Seminary Streets in Durham. The larger cafés had a segregated side for African American customers.[55] Leonard Rapport, who later became a distinguished archivist and historian, was a young interviewer at the time who worked for

"Farmer talking with another farmer who has just purchased a turkey. Outside warehouse where auction sales are being held. Durham, North Carolina." Photograph by Marion Post Wolcott, November 1939. LC-USF33-030733-M1 (b&w film nitrate neg.), U.S. Farm Security Administration/Office of War Information, Prints and Photographs Division, Library of Congress, Washington, D.C.

the WPA's Southern Writers' Project in Durham.[56] Knowing the worlds of the tobacco market well, Rapport agreed to guide Wolcott—only twenty-nine years old herself—through the largely all-male preserve.[57] They worked through the night, which Rapport remembered as "one of the great experiences," spending "the whole night on the tobacco market going over after supper . . . staying until breakfast, and going in all those warehouses, camp warehouses, where the men were sleeping."[58]

Wolcott documented the tobacco auctions, as well as the entrepreneurial worlds that surrounded the warehouses. In Durham, farmers could buy bushel baskets of apples, patent medicines, and even a good hound dog while waiting for their tobacco to come up for auction. Farmers in Mebane, North Carolina, sold pigs and Thanksgiving turkeys to other farmers who came to sell their tobacco. On the opening day of the tobacco market, the white Parent Teacher Association in Mebane sponsored a Brunswick stew dinner to raise money for a new school gymnasium. Wolcott photographed the men and women standing near large cast-iron pots of stew as it cooked outdoors. Hungry patrons enjoyed the hearty dish with crackers and a cold soda pop.

The FSA Comes to the IRSS

In the spring of 1940, Hagood and Herring showcased their research alongside Lange's and Wolcott's photography at Howard Odum's IRSS in Chapel Hill.[59] The IRSS sociologists used the "subregional laboratory"—thirteen counties in North Carolina and Virginia—for research and study.[60] In early May, they hosted a weeklong conference focused on regional planning and development that included discussions on southern diet, food production, and consumption.[61] FSA photographer Edwin Rosskam mounted more than one hundred of Lange's and Wolcott's photographs for the exhibit displayed on panels in the university's Alumni Building on McCorkle Place.[62] Herring and Hagood stipulated exhibit headings such as "The Lay of the Land," "Tobacco for the Market," "Rural People," "Farm Houses," and "Folkways."[63] The caption for a panel entitled "Farm Housekeeping" stated, "For farm women field work varies with the seasons, the burden of childbearing shifts with the time, but housekeeping—cooking, cleaning, washing—goes on forever."[64]

The partnership between the FSA and Howard Odum and the IRSS continued with photographer Jack Delano's time in North Carolina in 1940 and 1941.[65] Delano photographed the lives of migrant agricultural labors and tenant farmers in the Piedmont and eastern North Carolina, capturing their improvised kitchens and makeshift living quarters. In an oral history conducted in 1965, Delano's story of a southern woman and her award-winning canned goods reflected Stryker's layered vision of the FSA's documentary work: "She was a woman, perhaps, who was the daughter of an ex-slave who lived in this county, and this county had a history, and this county had an economy; and everything around this woman, everything that produced this woman with her three hundred cans was important and essential, including the kind of clothes she wore, including the kind of pictures that hung on the wall in her house, including the kind of church she went to, including the kind of school her children went to, and so on and so forth."[66] Delano's description of Stryker's ethnographic-like focus suggests the administrator's strong belief in the communicative power of people and region—particularly the culturally rich South—to tell a story of the American experience that all citizens would embrace. More than half of the images taken by the FSA photographers under Stryker's leadership were "Southern scenes of revelation and timeless poignancy."[67]

Federal Writers' Project

Southern Life Histories and Food

In conjunction with the photography of the FSA, written stories of southern life offered evocative descriptions of food—from the hunger of children during the Depression to raucous political barbecues and church-sponsored "dinner on the grounds." These narratives, told in the white and black "voices of the people," were a facet of the literary-focused New Deal documentary projects, including the "Life Histories" of the FWP, the WPA State Guides, and features on regional food collected for the "America Eats" project.[68] In 1938, W. T. Couch, director of the University of North Carolina Press, became the southeast regional director of the FWP.[69] Couch believed that asking ordinary southerners to tell their own stories strengthened their self-worth and diminished stereotypes of uneducated "hillbillies" and degenerate sharecroppers.[70] He wanted southerners to become active participants in shaping a new future for the South.[71]

Ida Moore, a former high school principal from South Carolina, conducted the first life histories for Couch.[72] Her work became a model for other writers in the southern FWP, who used Moore's interview guidelines.[73] "The purpose of this work," she wrote, "is to secure material which will give an accurate, honest, interesting, and fairly comprehensive view of the kind of life that is lived by the majority of the people in the South."[74] Moore's guidelines included "Diet" as an interview topic. In the reform-minded language of the day, she encouraged interviewers to determine the subject's "1. Knowledge of balanced diet, 2. To what extent knowledge is applied, and 3. To what extent it is possible to have balanced diet on wage earned."[75]

In the late 1930s, folklorist and FWP writer Gertha Couric completed a "life history" for two white women farmers near Richlands, Alabama. Dora Hayes, age sixty-eight, and Annie Fuller, age seventy, "made a success of their farm without the help of a man."[76] Invited to stay for dinner, Couric described a typical southern "groaning board" of platters of turkey, country ham, fried chicken, and sausage, with sides of turnip greens, peas, stewed tomatoes, pickles, brandy peaches, cornbread, and hot biscuits, and, for dessert, buttermilk, coffee, fruitcake, and coconut cake. "Miss Annie" told Couric, "If we had known you was coming we *would* have had something."[77] Fuller discussed the impact of diversifying their crops, reflecting local agricultural reform efforts: "It use to be nothing but cotton; now we raise our own food. As I told you, we don't spend but mighty little on flour and sugar. We don't sell our vegetables. We can them to use in the winter. We still have about three hundred quarts to last us 'til our spring garden comes in."[78]

Interviewer Gertha Couric had the tables turned when another FWP worker in Alabama recorded her story. After her husband's death, Couric opened a tearoom in Eufaula, Alabama, to provide for her daughter. She recalled a telling conversation with an African American cook in the tearoom who hinted at which kitchen-related activities were "proper" for a middle-class, white woman in the segregated South: "'Miss, (they all called me 'Miss'), is you ever cooked a whole meal in your life?' I thought about a minute, a little ashamed to answer. 'No, Liza, I don't think I ever did.' Then she said with much enthusiasm, 'Yes, Ma'am. I knowed your Ma raised your right.'"[79]

In April 1939, FWP worker Sadie Hornsby interviewed Robert and Gladys Walker, African American owners of a popular barbecue stand in Athens, Georgia. Hornsby captured the economic transition of an African American family in the New South from a history of domestic work for whites to building their own business. Mr. Long explained: "We dug our first barbecue pit in our own back yard, and that good old meat was barbecued in the real Southern style. We done so much business that first summer that we decided to keep our stand going through the winter with home barbecued meat. . . . We done business there more'n two years. Our business grew out of that hole in the ground."[80]

In Raleigh, North Carolina, white café waitress Alma Kingsland spoke of her difficult childhood in Harnett County to FWP interviewer Mary Hicks in January 1939. In the 1920s, Kingsland's father lost the family farm and her mother died from pellagra. Kingsland described the family's battle with the disease and the financial realities of attempting to change an impoverished diet: "We eat the same things after the doctor told us to quit for the simple reason that we couldn't afford nothing else. We did eat salmons and tomatoes and a few other cheap things, but we couldn't afford green vegetables."[81]

Food serves as a barometer of southern society in W. T. Couch's edited volume of FWP life histories, *These Are Our Lives* (1939).[82] Planned as the first of what Couch hoped would be several subject-specific works featuring FWP materials, later volumes were abandoned after growing criticism of New Deal initiatives. Couch resigned from the FWP in the fall of 1939. Many of the life histories profiled in Couch's edited volume were of working-class cooks, domestic workers, dairymen, farmers, fishermen, boardinghouse managers, lunchroom workers, peddlers, shrimpers, storekeepers, waitresses, and vegetable sellers, who grew, supplied, prepared, and served food to their neighbors. Their stories provide the texture and taste of the rapidly changing racial and economic landscapes of the New South.

WPA State Guides and "America Eats"

A Southern Tour

Researcher and writer Katherine Kellock, an experienced traveler and tours editor of the FWP, developed the American Guide Series, guidebooks to every state and territory, which included regional food traditions and restaurant listings.[83] The conservative white southerners who contributed to the guidebooks glorified the Old South and its racial hierarchy while also celebrating the fast-paced worlds of a modernizing New South.[84] Food sections of southern WPA guidebooks evoked nostalgic, romanticized images of the plantation South and praised the "magical powers" of African American cooks. Of the dozen or so guides to the southern states, as well as of stand-alone city volumes, the food sections of the Louisiana and North Carolina guides are particularly compelling.

Lyle Saxon, a novelist, journalist, and longtime resident of the French Quarter, became director of the Louisiana FWP in 1935 and supervised a large team of field-workers who conducted thousands of interviews in the state.[85] *The WPA Guide to New Orleans* (1938), edited by Saxon and considered a "model" of the guidebooks, included an extensive section on local restaurants, as well as an introduction to "Creole Cuisine."[86] The serious appreciation of cooking as a cultural art in New Orleans is revealed by the volume's nine pages devoted to recipes for the city's most "famous dishes," such as "Madame Begue's Crayfish Bisque," "Antoine's Bouillabaisse," "Galatoire's Trout Marguery," "Gombo Zhebes (Gumbo of Herbs)," "Pompano En Papillotes," "Red Beans," "Pecan Pralines," and at the bar, a "Ramos Gin Fizz," a "Sazerac Cocktail," a refreshing "Planter's Punch," and the classic "Creole Coffee" to begin and end the day.[87]

The essay on the city's restaurants captures defining features of New Orleans's life: from the strong allegiance to neighborhood as seen in the French Quarter's coffee and beignet cafés, Morning Call and Café Du Monde, and fine dining at Galatoire's, to the vibrant downtown mercantile scene at department stores such as the Rendezvous at Maison Blanche; ethnic restaurants like Kolb's (German) and Manale's (Italian); tearooms such as the elegant Court of the Two Sisters; bars and clubs from Pat O'Brien's to the Absinthe House Bar; dinner and dancing at elegant hotel restaurants like Roosevelt's Fountain Room; and popular cafeterias like Morrison's, patronized by city workers and tourists.[88] Reflective of the period racial codes that outlawed integrated dining establishments, the 1938 guide also included a separate section, "Negro Restaurants," such as the African American–owned and –operated National Lunch Room and the Astoria Hotel on South Rampart Street in the city's "vice district" of Storyville.[89]

Lyle Saxon was largely responsible for the writing and development of the Louisiana Writers' Project's publications, *Gumbo Ya-Ya: A Collection of Louisiana Folk Tales* (1945), which includes a chapter on food-related folklore, and *Louisiana: Guide to the State* (1947), which discusses the key ingredients of Creole cooking and the influence of European, African American, and Native American peoples on this distinctive cuisine.[90] Folklorist Benjamin Botkin included several of Saxon's Louisiana food essays in "Pleasures of the Palate" in his edited volume, *A Treasury of Southern Folklore* (1949).[91]

North Carolina: The WPA Guide to the Old North State (1939), one of the earliest of the guide series, includes an essay titled "Eating and Drinking." The piece is a general history of southern food rather than a collection of recipes and culinary anecdotes as found in other WPA guidebooks. It also highlighted regional foods, such as eastern North Carolina's "fish muddle," Sunday morning breakfasts of broiled salt roe herring and hot biscuits, coastal oyster "brush roasts," sourwood honey and Libertwig apples from the mountain counties, peaches from the Sandhills, Cherokee Indian acorn bread, and Moravian Christmas cookies from Winston-Salem.[92] Also noted is North Carolinians' love of native black walnuts, hickory nuts, and chinquapins (similar to chestnuts), and in the fall, wild grapes and the "luscious 'simmon pudding" made from candy-sweet persimmons.[93]

Katherine Kellock, who conceived the idea for the guidebooks, developed "America Eats," a project similar in format to the guidebooks that documented the role of "American cookery" in national life.[94] Kellock did not want a cookbook or the breezy food writing typical of most women's sections in newspapers.[95] She encouraged writers to find the stories behind American food by talking to both cooks and eaters and to experience regional food events, traditional dishes, and distinctive cooking methods. Southern examples included Kentucky Burgoo and South Carolina chicken bog (slow-cooked stews overseen by male cooks), oyster roasts in North Carolina, cane grinding and candy pullings in Alabama, Coca-Cola parties in Georgia, Maryland crabs, Mississippi hoecake and chitlins, Florida hushpuppies, and the annual banquet of the Polk County Possum Club in Mena, Arkansas.[96]

Dividing the nation into five regions, Kellock used the FWP model to hire local writers and researchers.[97] In the South, Eudora Welty collected "recipes gleaned from ante-bellum homes in various parts of Mississippi," such as stuffed eggs, beaten biscuits, and mint juleps.[98] She assured readers, "Yankees are welcome to make these dishes. Follow the directions and success is assured."[99] Zora Neale Hurston wrote about Florida's "Diddy-Wah-Diddy," an African American imaginary land "of no work and no worry for man and beast," where "the food is even already cooked."[100] In this edible paradise, African Americans experienced unimaginable abundance: "If a traveler gets hungry all he needs do is to sit down on the curbstone and wait and soon he will hear something hollering 'Eat me!' 'Eat me!' 'Eat me!'" A baked chicken comes along with a knife and fork stuck in its sides, followed by a sweet potato pie, "pushing and shoving to get in front of the traveler. . . . Nobody can ever eat it all up."[101] Welty's and Hurston's essays reveal racial subtexts of the era. Welty's romantic reference to "ante-bellum homes" suggests the branding of a mythic plantation South as it was packaged and sold to tourists and a growing consumer class in the early twentieth century. Hurston's retelling of an African American folktale remembers a hungry South, the violent history of enslaved blacks in the plantation South denied humane treatment, and the subsistence food rations.

Lyle Saxon oversaw the southern region for "America Eats," and Kellock gave him the task of editing the collected essays into a final volume.[102] The project came to an abrupt end when the FWP became the Writers' Unit of the War Services in May 1942 and Kellock was dismissed from her position.[103] Saxon left the unfinished project that July.[104] Kellock's papers were placed in the Library of Congress, while many of the essays and articles vanished or were put in state archives and libraries.[105] Pat Willard and Mark Kurlansky recently published collections of "America Eats" essays from each of the five regions, including a large number from the South—the most prolific of the national projects—largely due to Lyle Saxon's drive and editorial acumen.[106]

Ethnography of the Southern Table

The New Deal era brought the faces and words of struggling southerners and their everyday worlds, including vivid descriptions of the tastes and smells of the region's food, to the rest of the nation. George Tindall described Erskine Caldwell and Margaret Bourke-White's *You Have Seen Their Faces* (1937) and Dorothea Lange and Paul Taylor's *An American Exodus* (1939) as "social reportage with photographic illustration."[107] Filmmaker Pare Lorentz examined the environmental exploitation of the Mississippi River and the devastating social impact of its power—as well as the prosperity that modernity promised—for thousands of southerners in his social documentary *The River* (1937). *Let Us Now Praise Famous Men* (1941) combined the poetic, nontraditional literary voice of writer and journalist James Agee with the luminous photography of Walker Evans, who was also one of Roy Stryker's talented FSA documentarians.[108]

Agee and Evans worked together in Hale County, Alabama, during the summer of 1936 to document three white tenant families for *For-*

tune magazine. When their story was not published, they expanded the article into a book-length work that became an iconic American documentary work. Agee wrote, "If I could do it, I'd do no writing at all here. It would be photographs; the rest would be fragments of cloth, bits of cotton, lumps of earth, records of speech, pieces of wood and iron, phials of odors, plates of food and of excrement."[109] At the home of "George Gudger" (Floyd Burroughs—the names of the subjects were changed to protect their identities), Agee described the diet of southern poverty: "The odors of cooking. Among these, most strongly, the odors of fried salt pork and of fried and boiled pork lard, and second, the odor of cooked corn. The odors of sweat in many stages of age and freshness, this sweat being a distillation of pork, lard, corn, woodsmoke, pine, and ammonia."[110] When folklorist William Ferris asked Evans how a photographer enters into a community, he replied, "I would say just get in there, and really get into it and do it, up to the hilt. Thoroughly. Everything. . . . The whole damn business: How they wash their clothes, and how they eat. . . . What we are interested in is people and how they really live. I'm a realist and I'm interested in the deepest reality of life and social life."[111] Evans also adjusted interiors to make a stronger composition, as seen in the careful arrangement of the Burroughs kitchen, which contradicts Agee's descriptions of a cluttered, cramped space.[112]

In 2013, Agee's original *Fortune* manuscript was published, including the real names of the families and a stand-alone chapter entitled "Food" that did not appear in *Let Us Now Praise Famous Men*.[113] This discovery brings to light one of the most evocative period descriptions of the daily food patterns of the white working poor in the American South. In prose that reads like a playwright's staging instructions for actors, Agee notes each family member as he or she appears at the table, capturing what and how they ate. One feels the heat, the cold, the annoying buzz of flies, the begging dogs and cats. Detailed descriptions of breakfast, noontime dinner, and evening supper reflect the cycles of the relatively abundant food supply in the summer contrasted to the food scarcity in the late winter: "There is always coffee: coalblack, crudely bitter, silty, scorching hot. There is nearly always biscuit, fresh-baked and likewise hot, and very heavy. Where there isn't biscuit there is warmed over cornbread."[114] Additional foods reported by Agee were some variation of the "fat" and "lean" diet of southern sharecroppers: eggs, sorghum, buttermilk, salt pork, field peas, beans, molasses, boiled and fried vegetables, "winter greens," an occasional chicken, fish, dried fruits, canned salmon, sweet potato pie, and summer preserves.[115] "Once in a great while there is cake."[116] The three families' situations varied, some "harder off" than others, such as the Tingles, who "raised virtually nothing in their gar-

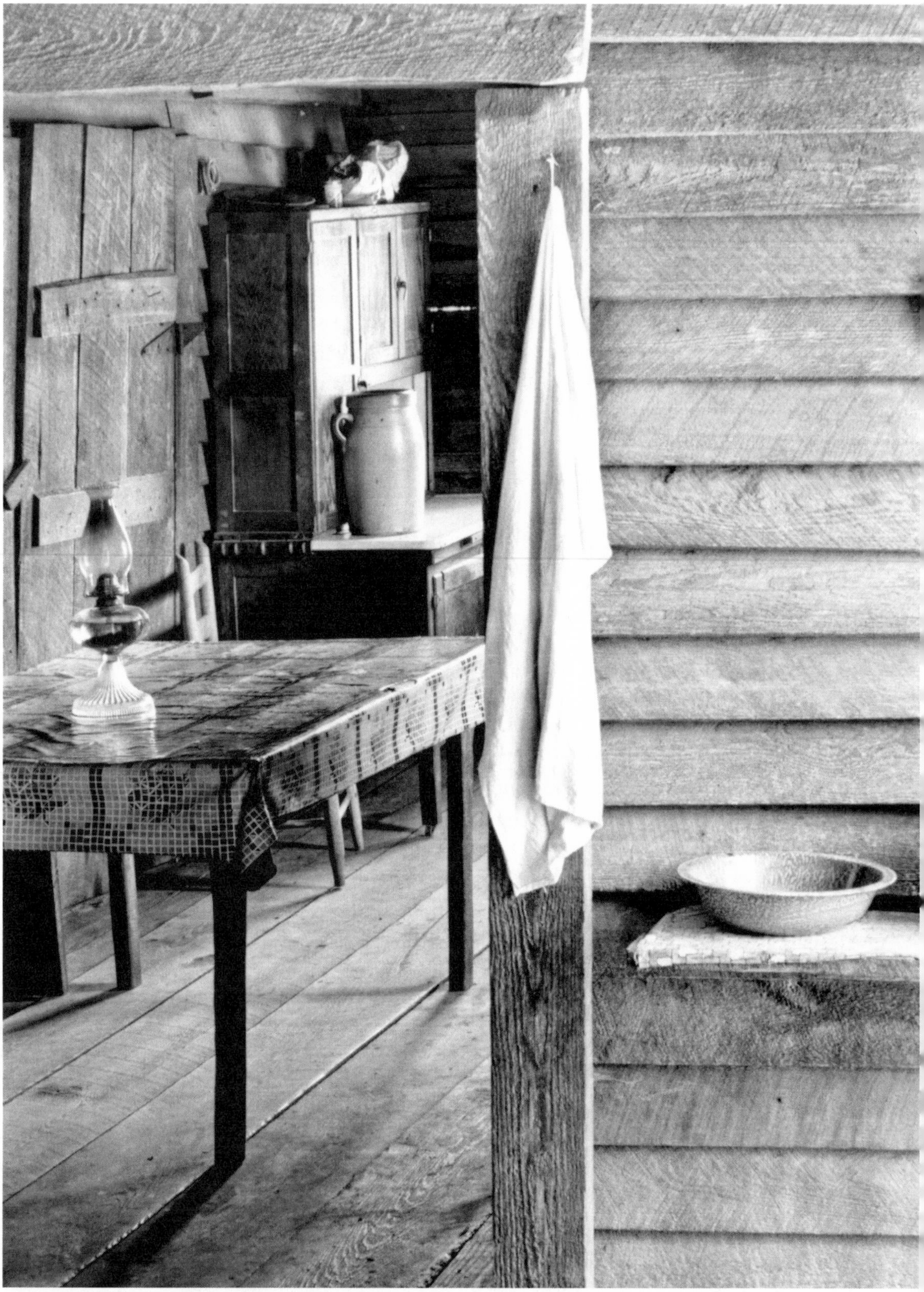

den. . . . Everything, in fact, fried, boiled, or baked, is heavily seasoned with lard, and flows lard from every pore. So, after even a meal or two, do you."[117]

This social realism even touched children's literature, as seen in the poignant books of Newbery Medal award–winning author and illustrator Lois Lenski.[118] Her beloved series of regional novels, including many southern-themed stories—such as *Bayou Suzette* (1943), *Strawberry Girl* (1945), *Blue Ridge Billy* (1946), and *Mama Hattie's Girl* (1953)—introduced the foodways, culture, and family struggles of both white and black Depression-era children to young readers around the world. A favorite is *Cotton in My Sack* (1949), which explores the hardscrabble lives of white sharecroppers set in my birthplace of Mississippi County in northeast Arkansas.[119] Lenski describes the packed lunches of cold biscuits, molasses, and boiled sweet potatoes eaten by impoverished boys and girls, unable to pay fifteen cents for the school-provided hot lunch, as well as the tempting tamale vendor, candy counter, and popcorn and hot dog stands of a Saturday visit "in town." Beginning in 1941 when health issues prevented winters in Connecticut, Lenski and her husband spent time in the South, purchasing a second home in Tarpon Springs, Florida, in the mid-1940s. She noted in her autobiography: "On my trips south I saw the real America for the first time. I saw and learned what the word *region* meant as I witnessed firsthand different ways of life unlike my own. What interested me most was the way children were living."[120] Lenski consulted WPA guidebooks as part of her extensive research, which eventually included lively correspondence and collaboration with local teachers and schoolchildren, as well as residential visits to each community featured in her novels.[121] In Mississippi County, Lenski lived and ate with a farm family for the month of October 1947 as she observed, and even participated in, the fall cotton harvest.[122]

This food-centered era of southern documentary work continued into the 1940s with the works of psychologist and sociologist John Dollard, in *Caste and Class in a Southern Town* (1937), anthropologist Hortense Powdermaker, in *After Freedom* (1939), and the interracial team of social scientists Allison Davis, Burleigh B. Gardner, and Mary R. Gardner, in *Deep South* (1941).[123] Each conducted in-depth fieldwork and research in Mississippi communities that focused on race relations and class divi-

"Washstand in the dog run and kitchen of Floyd Burroughs' cabin. Hale County, Alabama." Photograph by Walker Evans, 1935 or 1936. LC-USF342-T01-008133 (b&w film nitrate neg.), U.S. Farm Security Administration/Office of War Information, Prints and Photographs Division, Library of Congress, Washington, D.C.

sion: Dollard and Powdermaker in Indianola and Davis and the Gardners in Natchez. Analysis of food habits, particularly racial and class taboos that regulated where and how a person should eat, provided important evidence of the "racial etiquette" that shaped daily life in the segregated South.[124]

Dollard noted that "the commonest of these taboos are those against eating at a table with Negroes, having them in the parlor of one's house as guests, sitting with them on the front porch of one's home, and the like."[125] To break these racial taboos, Dollard explained, implied social equality.[126] "The white-caste view on this matter is simple and logically consistent. It is felt that social equality would lead directly to sexual equality."[127] Historian Ed Ayers argues that the issue of sexual control was always central in the South, from plantation-era miscegenation to Jim Crow racial division of public space, and "is actually what segregation was about all along."[128]

Both Powdermaker and the Davis/Gardner team observed the same restrictions on interracial eating. Exceptions were noted for young white and black children who ate together on "special occasions" or, for instance, if a "white man and colored man went fishing, they might grill their fish over an open fire and eat together, in the open."[129] Rules were bent to allow white children to eat with black domestic workers. Powdermaker noted a white informant's "happiest memory of her childhood," which was when she went "Across the Tracks" with the family's African American cook to her home, where "they all sat down at the table and ate turnip greens."[130] Local businesses made special accommodations so they would not lose black customers. In Natchez, a café served both whites and blacks, but blacks were seated at a separate counter.[131] In Indianola, whites and blacks could be served at the same soda fountain, but a separate set of glasses was kept for each race to ensure "cleanliness"— "thick glasses for colored, thinner ones for white people."[132]

Dollard broke an important food-related taboo in Indianola when he disrespected his landlady and hostess by criticizing the food served at her table. As a consequence, she dispensed a punishment in keeping with his ill manners. While he worked in Indianola, Dollard stayed in a boardinghouse operated by Mary Kathleen Craig Claiborne. Her fourteen-year-old son, Craig Claiborne, who became an esteemed southern food writer, journalist, and food editor for the *New York Times*, later recounted a memory of Dollard in his memoir, *A Feast Made for Laughter* (1982): "In the beginning he criticized the cooking of the greens, complaining that there was not a vitamin left in the lot. And as a result of his well-intentioned explanations and at the base encouragement of the other boarders, my mother willingly committed one of the most wicked acts of her life. Dr. Dollard was placed at a bridge table, covered, of course, with linen, and set with sterling, and he was served a mess of raw greens that he ate with considerable and admirable composure and lack of resentment."[133]

Food was often a point of contention and negotiation between white employers and black domestic workers. Powdermaker observed these workplace dynamics in Indianola, where a black cook's day began early and ended late, allowing little time to prepare a meal for her own family. Black domestic workers often took leftover food home to their own families, despite white employers' complaints. Powdermaker connected this practice to the region's plantation past and the master's responsibility to feed his enslaved people.[134] "The cook, if she thinks about the custom at all," wrote Powdermaker, "is more likely to regard it as a supplement to grossly inadequate wages. Many a highly respectable colored woman takes food home to her family with no sense of wrong-doing."[135]

Dollard, Davis, and the Gardners were associated with the distinguished Chicago School of sociology, recognized by the 1920s for its groundbreaking research and survey methods in urban, poverty, immigration, workplace, family, and ethnic and race studies. Hortense Powdermaker was a student of the noted scholar Bronislaw Malinowski at the London School of Economics.[136] In the 1930s, Powdermaker became involved in psychological anthropology at Yale University's Institute of Human Relations, where she was a colleague of John Dollard. Institute director Edward Sapir encouraged Powdermaker to conduct her participant-observer community study in the South.[137]

Research, scholarship, and mentorship created strong ties among the social science programs at Chicago, Columbia, and UNC. After thirteen years at the University of North Carolina Press, W. T. Couch became director of the University of Chicago Press. These scholars brought the texture and patterns of everyday life in the segregated South to light, including the most basic of human activities, eating. By doing so, they exposed a world so deeply imbedded in white supremacy and racial violence that Americans were hard-pressed to recognize their own countrymen at southern lunch counters and cafés. Howard Odum and his colleagues and students at UNC joined hands with photographers, writers, and policy makers of the New Deal, who turned the South into a laboratory to explore the "way of the South" and to identify solutions to move the region and the nation forward. Food in this moment reveals a struggle to release the region from the double bind of impoverishment and racism.

13

Branding the Edible New South

In the first decades of the twentieth century, New South boosters offered a conciliatory olive branch to northerners through a vision of a welcoming South exemplified by new commercial southern food products, fine southern restaurants and down-home cafés, nostalgic cookbooks, and a developing southern market for national food brands. Food symbolized a changing region, as conservative white southerners struggled to retain the racial constructs of the Old South and black and white progressives pushed the South into the modern era. As early as 1870, Frederick Douglass spoke out against white efforts to preserve a mythic southern past—a movement that rapidly expanded in the consumer culture of the early twentieth century. "The South has a past not to be contemplated with pleasure, but with a shudder," wrote Douglass. "She has been selling agony, trading in blood and in the souls of men. If her past has any lesson, it is one of repentance and reformation."[1]

White Confederate memorial organizations, such as the United Daughters of the Confederacy and the United Confederate Veterans, frequently used food to "heal" regional wounds by reviving nostalgic images of an abundant plantation table and the enslaved cooks who created these meals.[2] Food also symbolized a blended Old and New South, as seen in a menu for a special "Georgia Products Dinner" organized by the Georgia Society of New York in 1917. The southern tableaux included Robbin Island oysters, "cassolette of shrimps 'Victoria,'" opossum with sweet potatoes, "corn bread pone," fried chicken "Georgia Style," mashed turnips, field peas, "Irish Potatoes Gaufret," hot biscuits, "Fancy shaped" ice cream, sweet potato pie, and to end the meal, mints, pecans, peanuts, and Pall Mall cigarettes.[3] A black quartet sang "old fashioned Southern songs" during the meal, followed by a "moving picture show" featuring Georgia scenes. These performances and the decidedly mixed menu of elite and down-home southern dishes, combined with the stylish, citified custom of a cigarette to end the meal, reflected the South's identity crisis as it rebranded in the evolving consumer culture of the early twentieth century.

From here, we explore the Old South culinary brand as it evolved in the New South food-centered consumer culture of product advertising, innovative self-service grocery stores, racial trademarks such as "Aunt Jemima," black kitchen "collectibles," the taste of "plantation flavor," commercially published southern cookbooks, and Dixie-themed restaurants and cafés. In this era, an invented tradition of southern food was refined for the American market. Exaggerated in every possible way—sweeter, richer, "mysterious," even comical—this inflated version of southern cuisine stood in sharp contrast to the core foodways born of the region's ecological, political, and cultural foundations.

"A Marketplace of Goods" Food, Race, and Consumer Culture in the American South

From the 1890s until the 1940s, the expansion of consumer culture, including thousands of new food products, pulled the insular South back into the nation as urbanization, industrialization, commercial manufacture, and modern advertising shaped the daily lives of southerners.[4] A rising middle class of merchants and businesspeople and a growing working class of industrial laborers bought food with cash rather than the store credit received by previous generations of tenant farmers and sharecroppers.[5] Black and white working southerners participated in a regional and national consumer culture that brought a "marketplace of goods" to the South.[6] The popularity of new food products, southern brands, modern grocery store chains, and dining venues was located in the "spectacle" they offered and the sights to be seen, a world of difference from the older spoken worlds of the South, where stories and word of mouth shaped ideas and behavior.[7] The "authority of the eye" became a powerful selling tool for northern and southern entrepreneurs as they crafted a narrative of a forward-looking New South tethered to the past by the tastes and romantic images of a delectable, yet mythic, Old South.[8]

Increasing racial balkanization of the South in this era was reinforced by technological innovation that made it possible to cheaply produce visual imagery tied to racist stereotypes.[9] These images, particularly prevalent in food products, were promoted and spread through a national mass market and advertising. White and black southerners, and a growing national market of consumers and tourists throughout the country, simultaneously supported and resisted this "geography of consumption" in which racial difference and black inferiority lay at the heart of its selling power.[10] "The culture of segregation," explains historian Grace Hale, "turned the entire South into a theater of racial difference, a minstrel show writ large upon the land."[11]

The most abhorrent artifacts of racist consumption were reproduction photo-postcards of violent southern lynchings, in which the pho-

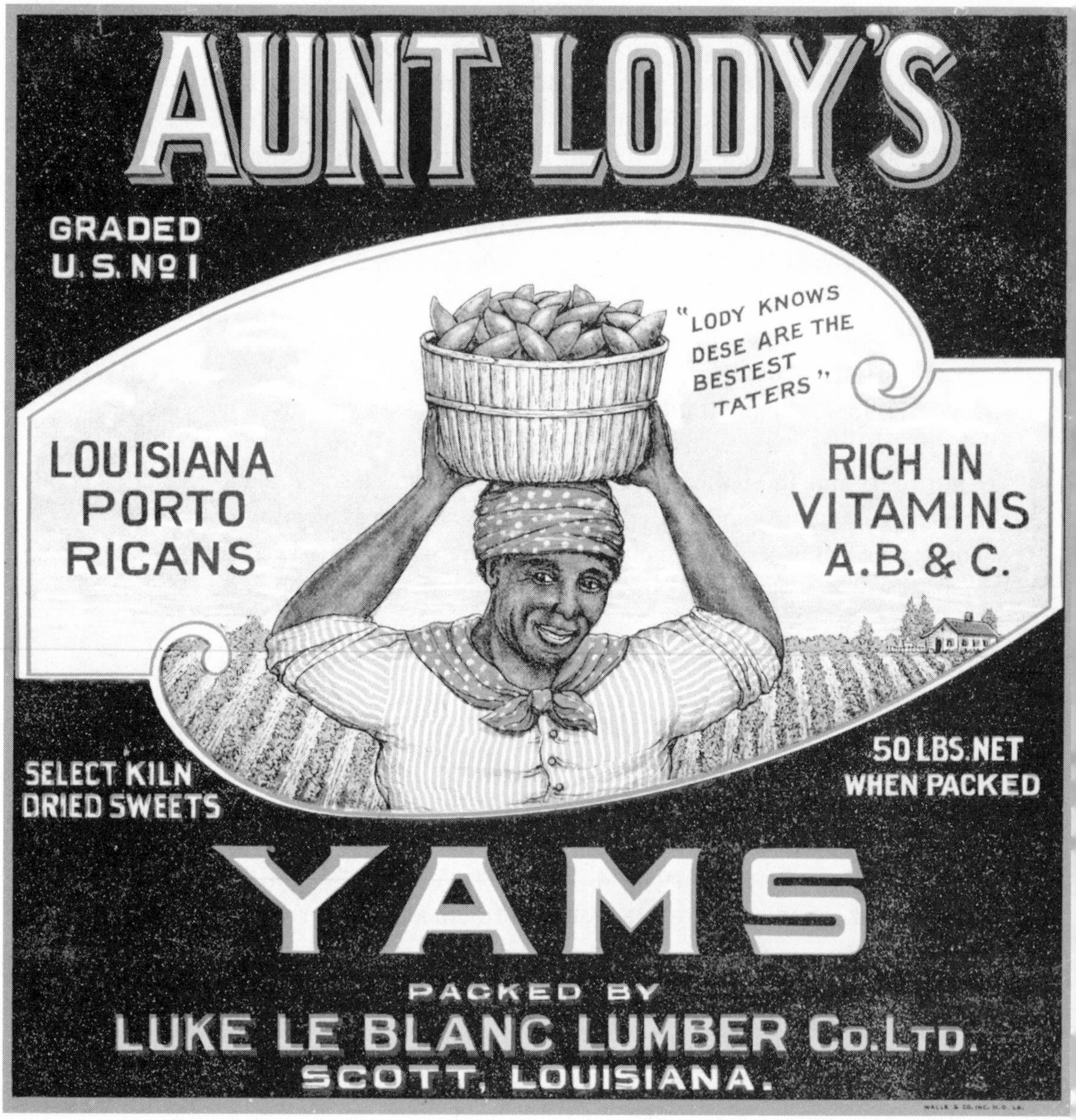

Aunt Lody's Yams, Luke Le Blanc Lumber Co., Ltd., Scott, Louisiana, trade card. 1979.369.59, Historic New Orleans Collection, New Orleans, La.

tographer, the printer, the consumer, and the U.S. Postal Service were complicit.[12] After the May 16, 1916, lynching of Jesse White in Robinson, Texas, a white spectator sent his mother a postcard from the scene, a shocking image of the black victim—hanged and burned—which he surreally conflated with a southern food ritual in his remarks on the back of the card: "This is the barbecue we had last night. My picture is to the left with a cross over it. Your sone [*sic*] Joe."[13] The subtext of this chilling message was the unquestioned authority of southern whites to control a black man, to literally cook him alive, as if he were an animal. Despite the grotesque circumstances, when southerners gathered, they also ate, and lynchings were no exception. White families enjoyed a picnic meal as they waited for the horrific drama to unfold.

More benign, but still culpable, in this racist consumer landscape were the visual worlds that FSA photographers captured in photographs of roadside billboards, advertisement-covered rural stores, and the catalog- and newspaper-lined walls of southern tenant farmers' shacks. Food manufacturer's trade cards, food packaging labels, cookbooks, menus, magazines, newspapers, radio commercials, and flyers and brochures promoting tourist attractions, restaurants, cafés, and vacation train travel were the ephemeral texts of this culinary-focused consumer revolution in the New South.[14] Late nineteenth-century trade cards in New Orleans—the small, brightly colored, promotional cards tucked into packages, handed out, or mailed by retailers—convey a strong sense of place, race, regional imagery, and the branding of a mythic South.[15] McIlhenny Company's Tabasco featured fresh okra and tomatoes; Old Time Syrup, a mule turning a sugarcane mill; Aunt Lody's Yams, a black "mammy" carrying a basket of yams on her head; Colonial Produce Company, a plantation house sitting beside fields of strawberries; Cake Walk Cove Oysters, a black "dandy" and his stylish "missus" stepping out in a "cake walk" strut; Capitol Packing Company's Hominy Grits, the art deco statehouse of Louisiana; and Alligator Brand Pure Louisiana Molasses, an alligator sunning in the grassy reeds while a river steamboat passes in the distance.[16]

Throughout the early twentieth century, the Old South and its cultural trappings—from "Mammy's cooking" to Stephen Foster's melodies to advertisements featuring delicate southern belles, Spanish moss-covered magnolias, and columned mansions—provided a sense of stability for whites in a rapidly changing America.[17] Cuisine was a central pillar of this reinvented version of the southern past, including the plantation legend and the Lost Cause, the post–Civil War efforts by white southerners to make sense of their defeat. This politicized remembrance glorified "the valor of southern soldiers" and imagined a time that never existed—of the "family, black and white," who lived together peacefully in plantations governed by just paternalism.[18] C. Vann Woodward described the creation of the Old South as "one of the most significant inventions of the New South."[19] This New South world, as Ed Ayers explains, "was an anxious place, filled with longing and resentment, for people had been dislodged from older bases of identity and found no new ones ready at hand."[20]

Culinary nostalgia for the Old South was part of a broader national movement led by advertisers and manufacturers to sentimentalize a quickly disappearing rural past.[21] Unmoored by the economic instability of the Depression, American anxiety continued to escalate, with growing industrialism, the rise of an independent black middle-class, and the arrival of thousands of European immigrants.[22] By the 1930s and 1940s, the visual landscape of American culture was awash in tributes to a preindustrial time in the country's history.[23] Iconic characters drawn from the popular literary genre of plantation memoir and Joel Chandler Harris's "B'rer Rabbit" in his popular Uncle Remus folktales (later appropriated for a popular southern brand of molasses) reassured white consumers threatened by modernity yet attracted to the convenience and innovation of the new era.[24] Ironically, the promotion of the Old South in national popular culture would not have existed but for the changing technology of an industrializing America.[25] These same forces also fueled the many New Deal projects that collected and celebrated American folklore and captured early American themes in WPA murals, film, music, and dance.[26]

The white South was caught in a freeze-frame fantasy of the plantation era—reflected in popular culture, from "Dixie's finest" food products, to Tin Pan Alley's musical odes to the region, to "southern colonial-style" architecture. Southern general stores, markets, and, later, independent grocery stores offered a vast selection of new brand-name food products to white and black consumers.[27] Visual emporiums for new advertisements and product labels, these venues "became the central institution in the economic and cultural transformations of the late nineteenth and early twentieth-century South."[28] From here, products entered southern homes and quickly became a part of the culture of everyday life.

Selling the "Dixie Brand"

Clarence Saunders, an innovative businessman and grocer in Memphis, Tennessee, recognized the potential of this expanding marketplace of goods but realized that, to succeed, the selling strategies of old-fashioned grocery stores needed updating. In traditional grocery stores, customers were removed from the actual products, separated by a counter and sales clerk. In 1916, Saunders replaced the old grocery store model with the first-ever self-service system for food shopping. In his reinvented "Piggly Wiggly" markets, customers chose their own products from open shelves and placed them in a personal shopping basket as they walked through the store aisles. Rather than the male head of the house or black housekeepers, who customarily did the shopping for their employers at the turn of the century, Clarence

"Country store on dirt road. . . . Gordonton, North Carolina." Photograph by Dorothea Lange, July 1939. LC-USF34-T01-019911-E (b&w film nitrate neg.), U.S. Farm Security Administration/Office of War Information, Prints and Photographs Division, Library of Congress, Washington, D.C.

Saunders wanted "the High Heel Society" to visit his stores—his moniker for white, middle- and upper-class southern women.[29] His successful campaign emphasized the immaculate Piggly Wiggly interior, a home economist's dream with its bright, efficient, sanitized shopping experience.[30] Advertisements described "The Aristocracy of the Piggly Wiggly Basket," a world of fashionable white women shoppers carrying their market baskets.[31] Historian Lisa Tolbert observes that Saunders also emphasized the independence of his female customers in his advertising campaign: "You take what you please from the shelves—look it over, compare prices—make your own decisions, leisurely."[32]

New products like White Lily flour (Knoxville, Tennessee, 1883), Martha White flour (Nashville, Tennessee, 1899), Coca-Cola (Atlanta,

"C. T. Moore. Up-to-date groceryman. Bennettsville, S.C. We don't have to get what you want, we have it now." Postcard, J. E. Spencer. South Caroliniana Library, University of South Carolina, Columbia, S.C., postcards marl.co.36.

1886), Pepsi (New Bern, North Carolina, 1898), and Duke's Mayonnaise (Greenville, South Carolina, 1917) quickly became beloved New South brands sold in grocery stores like Piggly Wiggly.[33] Eugenia Duke, a white homemaker in the South Carolina Piedmont, used her own mayonnaise on store-bought "sliced-bread" for sandwiches she made and sold from her home to thousands of soldiers at nearby Fort Sevier.[34] C. F. Sauer, a Richmond, Virginia, company, purchased the recipe and the mayonnaise venture of Duke's business in 1929. Grocery store promotions featured impressive pyramids of Duke's Mayonnaise, neatly dressed salesmen, and attractive, middle-class white women posing with bottles of the sandwich spread. These campaigns emphasized taste, convenience, efficiency, and, most important, the "purity" of this always uncooked mayonnaise, just as a woman would prepare it at home. Duke's Mayonnaise appealed not only to stay-at-home mothers, writer Emily Wallace notes, but to working men and women in the textile mills of the Carolinas, who prepared food for their quick lunch breaks or purchased readymade sandwiches from roving "dope carts," which carried snacks, cold drinks ("dope" was a nickname for Coca-Cola, whose "secret recipe" included cocaine until the early 1900s), candy bars, packages of Nabs, and BC "Headache" Powder.[35]

When they chose products off the shelf at Piggly Wiggly, white middle-class women consumers typically reached for the "Dixie brand," a marketing device that historian Karen Cox equates with much more than the physical place of the South.[36] Labeling a food product with a southern touchstone of the white Confederate past was a savvy move for market-conscious manufacturers and advertisers who recognized the monetary value of a good story. These coded symbols appeared in many guises, from a distinctive southern plant or animal to the word "Dixie," from idolized heroes and heroines like Robert E. Lee (whose name and image appeared on a popular brand of southern flour) to the African American mammy who adorned hundreds of southern food products from pancakes to pralines. The "Dixie brand" conveyed southern origins—consumers assumed the product was manufactured in the South, when often it was not—but a much deeper narrative was embedded in a southern label.[37] Dixie connoted the Confederate past, a rural, slower, more innocent South, an era when agriculture reigned rather than industry, a less anxious, more leisurely time, and, most important, a time when white southerners controlled and owned black lives and labor.[38]

Aunt Jemima's "Famous Southern Recipe"

In 1893, Nancy Green, a fifty-nine-year-old former slave working as a domestic worker in Chicago, was hired to promote Aunt Jemima Pancake Flour at the World's Columbian Exposition in Chicago.[39] Dressed in traditional mammy garb, Green stood in a giant flour barrel—twenty-four feet high and sixteen feet wide—where she greeted guests, sang songs, and told stories of the Old South. Green reportedly served more than a million pancakes and took 50,000 orders for the pancake mix. Her mammy impersonation was inspired by a white minstrelsy figure who dressed in black face and sang Billy Kersand's hit tune of 1875, "Old Aunt Jemima."[40] This caricature of an enslaved black woman was soon registered as a trademark and became the most recognizable, longest-lived mammy stereotype.[41]

Aunt Jemima advertisements of the 1920s featured artist N. C. Wyeth's romanticized illustrations of the plantation South in a popular "social tableaux" style.[42] Much as they listened to a serialized radio drama, loyal consumers followed a developing story line from ad to ad for the pancake mix created by copywriters at the New York advertising firm of J. Walter Thompson. Customers were hooked by the fictional story of a female slave born on a Louisiana plantation, where she was owned by the "kindly" Confederate Colonel Higbee. Aunt Jemima's delicious pancakes were at the heart of the advertisements, where time and again the black cook's superior culinary skills saved both starving Confederate soldiers *and* contemporary housewives struggling to please their busy husbands at breakfast time.

Advertising executives targeted the Aunt Jemima campaigns at white middle-class housewives, especially those without "help"—the dehumanizing colloquial term for black women domestic workers. The ads portrayed white women as the mistresses of their own households and Aunt Jemima as their loyal servant—as M. M. Manring suggests, their "slave in a box."[43] "Spokesservants" like these appeared on hundreds of domestic products, as well as on print advertisements and trade cards.[44] The advertising figure of Aunt Jemima also served as a cultural ambassador of sorts, moving between the North and the South with goodwill and "good taste," heralding a reconciled future between once-embattled regions with a peace offering of pancakes.[45] A popular Aunt Jemima rag doll promotion aimed at American children in the 1920s encouraged housewives to "Get this jolly family for your children!"[46] "Everybody knows good old Aunt Jemima!" stated a Quaker Oats brochure. "But did you ever stop to think about her family? Well, here they are, just the jolliest family of rag dolls you can imagine! Aunt Jemima, Uncle Mose, Wade and Diana."[47] Therein lies the painful irony of this ad copy. White middle-class America had definitely not thought about "Aunt Jemima's family" or the traumatic history this "cheerful" figure and her imaginary kin represented.

Mammy Goes to Hollywood

The redemptive power of a southern black female cook appeared on the Hollywood screen in the 1934 film adaptation of Fannie Hurst's novel *Imitation of Life*.[48] The film featured Claudette Colbert as the white widow Bea Pullman, who takes in a homeless black domestic worker, Delilah Johnson, played by Louise Beaver. In the plot, the two struggling mothers work together to provide for their daughters by creating a successful pancake restaurant inspired by the black woman's cooking skills. Not surprising, the nurturing black figure of Delilah Johnson also provides advice about men to the ambitious white widow, Bea Pullman. The film, like the Aunt Jemima advertising campaigns, implied that young white housewives—inexperienced in both the kitchen and the bedroom—could learn valuable skills from the stereotyped figure of a wise, maternal, sexually savvy mammy. Some scholars have argued that the popular caricature of a heavyset, maternal mammy desexualized the figure to counter accusations of white men's sexual exploitation of African American women throughout slavery, but the sexuality of the stereotyped mammy cannot be denied. Historian Catherine Clinton writes, "Mammies were to be milked, warm bodies to serve white needs—an image with its own sexual subtext."[49]

At the height of the Depression, Hollywood producers David Selznick and William Wyler recognized the box office appeal of motion pictures that offered an escape to a southern "place out of time," filled with romance, feisty southern belles, handsome suitors, loyal servants, and evil carpetbaggers.[50] Their greatest achievement, the 1939 film version of Margaret Mitchell's wildly successful novel, *Gone with the Wind* (1936), locked images of southern hospitality firmly into the American mind—a make-believe world of gracious plantation picnics and spoon-wielding mammies—yet the film, like Mitchell's novel, also depicted the suffering and horrors of the wartime South.

In the film's opening scenes, the white plantation elite of Georgia enjoys traditional southern foods prepared by genial African American cooks, but this "paradise" is soon torn asunder by the outbreak of war. Scarlett O'Hara, the daughter of a once well-to-do white planter, resorts to digging turnips and "straggling butter beans" she finds in the garden patch of an abandoned slave quarters near her beloved Tara. She hungrily eats a dirty radish and then, unable to handle the rough food, falls to the ground and recites the memorable lines, "If I have to steal or kill—as God is my witness, I'm never going to be hungry again."[51] As a southern woman writing during the Depression, Mitchell deeply understood the powerful connection between food and memory, especially in times of want. In Mitchell's text, even Scarlett O'Hara longs for a golden era of plenty at Tara: "Food! Food! Why did the stomach have a longer memory than the mind? Scarlett could banish heartbreak but not hunger."[52] She dreamed of hot breads "dripping in butter," platters of ham and fried chicken, steaming bowls of southern vegetables, and delectable desserts.[53]

Because the South and its history were so unfamiliar to the general public, executives at Metro-Goldwyn-Mayer worried that the plot of *Gone with the Wind* would confuse its audiences. A short trailer, *The Old South* (1940), directed by Fred Zinnemann, explained the rise of "King Cotton" and the South's devastation following the Civil War.[54] Filled with images of a noble, grand South, the trailer re-created lavish scenes of plantation dining, as described by the narrator: "There came to the

South an era of wondrous beauty, of moonlight and magnolias and mint juleps—an era of chivalry and true hospitality, a gallantry of devil-may-care cavaliers and their lovely ladies fair."[55] Moviegoers loved a spectacle, and what images better displayed the debauchery and wealth of elite white southerners than those of doting black servants, grand candelabra, domed silver food warmers, fine china, and starched linens?

That Old Plantation Flavor

Hattie McDaniel's Oscar-winning performance of "Mammy" in *Gone with the Wind*—the first Oscar received by a black American—reinforced Aunt Jemima and her powers, in and outside the kitchen. Advertisements for Aunt Jemima pancake mix emphasized the special flavor of its "famous southern recipe," suggesting that female customers were purchasing not only an easy-to-prepare convenience product but also a closely held culinary secret coaxed from talented African American cooks, like Scarlett's Mammy.[56] An ad from the J. Walter Thompson Company emphasized the "sixth sense for flavor" of the "mammy cook," like the improvisation of the "talent of born [black] musicians."[57] By the 1930s, the majority of Aunt Jemima ads promoted the special taste of "plantation flavor."[58] In the expanding world of advertising-driven consumption, as American studies scholar Kimberly Wallace-Sanders has argued, "the plantation kitchen validated the South as a region with superior appreciation for good food and for the good life."[59]

A 1950s promotional pamphlet from the Savannah Sugar Refining Corporation offered "A Dozen Dixie Recipes" featuring Dixie Crystals Sugar. Iconic images in the pamphlet reinforced the company's Old South brand—a slave log cabin, a Mount Vernon–style plantation house, magnolias, black laborers picking cotton, white belles and beaus, and loyal black servants. Ad copy exclaimed, "There's magic in the name—'Dixie'! Celebrated in song and story, it brings to mind a romantic land of warm sunshine and entrancing moonlight. . . . A splendid part of the rich heritage which the Old South has bequeathed to the new, is the talent for fine cooking. From the many recipes popular in Southern homes, a few of the most representative have been selected for presentation in this booklet."[60] This marketing implied that consumers were buying exclusive food products once reserved for the white plantation elite. Sourced from special stock, the product was now available in limited quantities for the middle-class homemaker with discerning taste. Pamphlet illustrations of blacks waiting on whites promoted a life of "perpetual servitude" for African Americans in the South.[61]

Executives at the Virginia Dare Company, which manufactured "home-made" chocolates and other confections in Baltimore, turned to the early southern past for an evocative story to sell their candies. The company was named in honor of Virginia Dare, the granddaughter of Captain John White and the "First [white] child of English Parentage born on American soil"—a brand name that evoked purity, Anglo-Saxon roots, and wholesome Christian values.[62] Copy from a company brochure revived the 1587 story of Virginia Dare's birth and baptism, which took place soon after the arrival of Sir Walter Raleigh's ships near the Outer Banks. Advertisers assured customers of the quality of the product, with the vaguest hint of exasperation in their copy: "Just try and make this at home as a novice, and see how much it costs you: Virginia Dare candy is just so good and pure as you would have them if you yourself had set about to make some at home, except that with our long years of experience we know how to make them a whole lot better, and besides you couldn't make a single pound for twice the price if you had to buy the same ingredients in such small quantities."[63] In a similar advertising campaign, the Southern Biscuit Company of Richmond packaged its baked goods in decorative tins under the trademark of "FFV"—"Famous Foods of Virginia." Advertising executives hoped customers would purposely associate their "FFV" with another "FFV"—the Victorian-era "First Families of Virginia," a hereditary society composed of the descendants of the first English colonists and Pocahontas. In 1939, the Southern Biscuit Company became the licensed bakers of Girl Scout cookies.[64]

Southern food brands gained strength from the popular and academic identification of the region as the taproot of authentic culture, the mother lode of the nation's purest music, stories, and food traditions—particularly in the "isolated" southern mountains and Carolina's "Lost Colony." Here existed an otherworldly South of culinary delights, such as the "mother vineyard," the scuppernong vine of the Carolina Outer Banks, described by writer Clementine Paddleford as "America's first grape."[65] "No other fruit except maybe peaches," wrote Paddleford, "is as all-southern as solidly southern as the old Confederacy itself."[66] This same ideology of the South as the most "bona fide" region in America drew documentarians like John C. Campbell, Lafcadio Hearn, and Lyle Saxon to document the South's "authentic" folk cultures.

The J. Walter Thompson Company and food manufacturers such as Penick and Ford, who produced molasses syrup in New Orleans, used social tableaux ads to market other southern-themed food and drink products beyond pancake mix. Advertising executives promoted a secret recipe for Maxwell House Coffee—associated with its namesake, a fashionable nineteenth-century hotel in Nashville; Baker's "southern-style" coconut, once only available from "the old coconut man"; nutritious, "rich in iron" Brer Rabbit molasses; and the leisured lifestyle of elite whites associated with Kentucky bourbon and Tennessee whiskey.[67] In Brer Rabbit's "Modern Recipes for Modern Living," the Penick and Ford copy urged homemakers to "let my old plantation molasses help you with mealtime problems."[68] A 1948 Brer Rabbit recipe pamphlet described molasses's origins in the "early Mississippi steamboat days": "As if dripping with the sunshine that warms the rich soil of its plantation home, New Orleans molasses gives spun-gold richness to fine, homemade ginger bread, cakes, and cookies. Treasured by the fine cooks of early crinoline days, this special golden richness is yours today in Brer Rabbit Molasses."[69] Maxwell House coffee reinforced its Old South origins as a sponsor for the popular 1930s radio comedy and musical program *Show Boat*.[70] Set on a Mississippi paddle wheeler, two of the white actors in blackface played African American male servants, "Molasses" and "January."[71]

Noticing the success of the Aunt Jemima trademark, other manufacturers created black characters associated with their products, such as the Cream of Wheat chef "Rastus," the Gold Dust Twins, the Luzianne Coffee Lady, Rinso's housekeeper, and in the 1940s, Uncle Ben's Rice.[72] When this culturally coded material culture entered the homes of white southerners, the images of servile African Americans, the advertising copy, and the catchy jingles in black pidgin dialect reinforced ideas about black inferiority, especially for white children.[73] Grace Hale states: "Childhood was the crucial period when whites learned racial difference. The white home in the American South became a central site for the production and reproduction of racial identity."[74]

Black kitchen "collectibles" were the three-dimensional offspring of American racial advertising and mass-marketing strategies developed at the turn of the twentieth century.[75] The inexpensive kitsch of their time, objects such as mammy-shaped cookies jars appeared in middle-class white homes in the South and across the nation, valued as both decorative and functional ephemera. From the 1920s to the 1950s, American pottery companies (McCoy, Red Wing, Shawnee, and Weller) and Japanese manufacturers transformed plantation-era stereotypes of African Americans into designs for cookie jars, salt and pepper shakers, syrup pitchers, condiment sets, measuring cups, grocery reminder pads, linen dishtowels, and tablecloths. Black figures raised poached eggs and candlesticks aloft, released kitchen string through their mouths, stored sugar cookies in their skirts, and received straight pins in their stomachs. They were molded into human-shaped teapots, syrup pitchers, and dinner bells. Seemingly "innocent," these popular domestic objects, like the racist advertising on thousands of food products, reinforced a culture of segregation and racial subservience in the American home.

Middle-class blacks in the South encountered the offensive stereotypes of African American figures in kitchen objects, advertisements, and product labels and consciously rejected these food brands and ephemera. In a landmark market research study, *The Southern Urban Negro as Consumer* (1932), African American economist Paul Edwards of Fisk University collected data on the buying habits of southern black consumers. A central question of his study asked, "Does the use of racial elements that might be distasteful to the Negro serve to gain his ill will and build up sales resistance?"[76] Edwards examined the reaction of both professional and working-class African Americans in Nashville and Richmond to advertisements for Aunt Jemima's pancake mix and other products that used "racial elements."[77] The majority disapproved of the "use of the Negro mammy and the log cabin plus the reference to Aunt Jemima's master—all of which savored too much of slavery days."[78] Comments ranged from "Would not look at it twice because of picture" to "I hate the picture of Aunt Jemima, the log cabin, and the idea that all colored women are cooks."[79] Edwards included quotes from noted African American educator Nannie Burroughs, who argued, "The Gold Dust Twins, Aunt Jemima, and Amos and Andy have piled up millions for two business concerns and two white men. Aunt Jemima and the Gold Dust Twins cook and wash dishes while Amos and Andy broadcast subtle and mischievous propaganda against Negro business."[80]

The Atlanta-based Coca-Cola company deliberately shunned the African American market from the 1880s invention of the popular soft drink to the 1930s because of segregationist politics and white hysteria fueled by fears of black abuse of the cocaine-laced beverage.[81] Pepsi, Coke's chief competitor, recognized the value of the neglected African American market.[82] Pepsi's liberal chief executive Walter Mack hired African American men to staff its newly formed "negro markets" department.[83] For their ads, the team used professional black models, who represented working-class and middle-class African American *citizens* rather than the Old South stereotype of grinning blacks in service.[84] Pepsi ads appeared in black publications and store displays in southern markets that catered to black customers.[85] Coke officials slowly removed their racial blinders by the 1950s and, as Grace Hale notes, "quietly began to market to African Americans" and to foster the company's tactical support of black organizations, including the NAACP.[86]

The New South's Old South Cookbooks

A genre of regional cookbooks flourished from the late 1920s to the 1950s that were imprinted with the same Old South brand and sentiment for a "bygone era" seen in earlier cookbooks published during Reconstruction and throughout the first decades of the New South. Laced with racial nostalgia, the cookbooks reinforced white authority in a modernizing South. These cookbooks were written largely by aspiring, white, working women—from middle-class housewives to society elites—but also by professional writers. Journalist Henrietta Stanley Dull was widely known for her food columns in the *Atlanta Journal* and her best-selling *Southern Cookbook* (1928). Pulitzer Prize–winning novelist Marjorie Kinnan Rawlings wrote *Cross Creek Cookery* (1942), based on her popular memoir of rural life in Florida. Rawlings's failure to give credit and financial compensation to Idella Parker, the African American cook who created many of the recipes, and tested all of them—was typical of white-authored cookbooks of this era.[87] Over five decades later, Parker published her autobiography, *Idella: Marjorie Rawlings' "Perfect Maid"* (1992), a powerful narrative of her experience as a domestic worker in the Jim Crow South and her complex relationship with Rawlings.

Even Wallace Simpson, the Duchess of Windsor, a native of Maryland, contributed to this canon of New South culinary texts. *Some Favorite Southern Recipes of the Duchess of Windsor* (1942) included an introduction by ever-practical Eleanor Roosevelt, who praised the "simplicity" of the recipes in contrast to the "elaborate and extravagant menus which marked our entertaining as recently as the General Grant period."[88] A "typical southern" dinner menu from the Duchess included regional favorites and a 1940s-style frozen salad: "Gumbo soup, Maryland fried chicken, orange sweet potato, eggplant sautéed, watermelon rind preserve, southern spoon bread, frozen tomato salad, and charlotte russe."[89]

There were also amateur authors of the Old South–style cookbooks, such as Georgia native Patsie McRee. Her publication, *The Kitchen and the Cotton Patch* (1948), combined local color, plantation stories, "Negro dialect," recipes, and racial drawings by illustrator Kathryn Burke in a genre of minstrelsy-inspired cookbooks. Endorsements of McRee by Georgia's poet laureate Ollie Reeves and Louise Hays, the Wesleyan College–educated director of the Georgia Department of History and Archives, reflect the white acceptance of these "dialect" cookbooks. "These hitherto unpublished and closely guarded recipes," wrote Reeves, "make this an invaluable book for those whose poetry is made in the sacred precincts of the kitchen."[90]

Martha McCulloch-Williams's *Dishes and Beverages of the Old South* (1913) is a post-Reconstruction example of this "mammy tribute" cookbook genre. Her privileged childhood on a Tennessee plantation and the family's descent into "'genteel poverty'" after the Civil War provided a cache of rose-colored memories for McCulloch-Williams, who moved to New York, where she embarked on a successful writing career.[91] At age sixty-five, she published *Dishes and Beverages of the Old South*, an unusual text that is both a detailed description of antebellum foodways and folk cultures and a sentimental, racial homage to "Mammy's Kitchen." Her "affectionate" description of "my individual Mammy" was brutal: "An oblate spheroid . . . she stood five feet, one inch high, weighed two hundred and fifty pounds, had a head so flat buckets sat on it as of right," yet it was her cookery that McCulloch-Williams credits with saving the Confederacy.[92] "We might have been utterly crushed but for our proud and pampered stomachs," she wrote, "which in turn gave the bone, brain and brawn for the conquests of peace. So here's to our Mammys—God bless them! God rest them! This imperfect chronicle of the nurture wherewith they fed us is inscribed with love to their memory."[93]

In the interwar period, southern cookbooks reflected national trends and issues, from the growth of domestic science and home economics to improved highway systems and the corresponding rise in tourism and interest in America's diverse regional cultures.[94] A fascination with the colonial revival and America's "pioneer heritage"—again, indicative of a national response to modernity and postwar patriotism—was also seen in the nostalgic tone of these cookbooks, which offered a temporary escape into an idealized southern past.[95] The readers of this genre of southern cookbook were white working mothers and stay-at-home housewives. Many had "help" at home—the labor of an African American domestic worker, who was paid less than a living wage to clean, assist with child care, do yard work, and prepare some or all of the daily meals, from breakfast to evening supper. Commercially published southern cookbooks of this era were used largely as middle-class, aspirational guides for entertaining or as a recipe source for a hired cook or were purchased as a souvenir-collectible of the South by tourists and armchair travelers.[96] Depictions of servile, contented blacks in these cookbooks continued to reinforce the racist dynamics in white middle- and upper-class homes, not only in the South but across the country.[97] Writer Toni Tipton-Martin argues that the image of an enslaved woman in a bandanna obscured African American women's authority, skill, and knowledge.

Georgia-born Henrietta Stanley Dull (1863–1964) was a successful caterer and journalist and the editor of the "Home Economics" page of the *Atlanta Journal*'s Sunday magazine from the 1920s to the 1940s. Dull bridged a pivotal era between the Old South and the New South with her iconic text, *Southern Cooking* (1928).[98] When her husband's health declined in the early 1900s, Dull turned her domestic talents into money-making skills to support her family.[99] She sold homemade goods to church friends and learned to cater. She demonstrated gas-fired ranges for the Atlanta Gas Light Company.[100] In 1916, Dull led a series of cooking classes for 800 African American female domestic workers and cooks in Atlanta, sponsored by the gas company and the white Atlanta Women's Club, who sent representatives to show their support of the venture.[101] Attendees who completed the class received a "certificate of efficiency" signed by Mrs. Dull and members of the Domestic Science Committee of the Atlanta Women's Club. By arbitrarily claiming authority for black women's standards of professionalization, white women disguised racial disempowerment as job training and education.

Over Henrietta Dull's lifetime, southern cookbooks evolved from fund-raising novelties for Confederate women's organizations during the Civil War to the Lost Cause cookbooks of the Reconstruction period to the domestic science–focused texts of Dull's early career in the 1920s and the Junior League cookbooks of the 1950s. Dull dedicated her cookbook to "My friends, the Women of Atlanta, of Georgia, and of the South."[102] Her readers, Dull explained, were housewives who "have no cooks, at all, and are really and truly trying to have nice, well-prepared meals, and want to learn to cook."[103] She did not suffer fools *or* young women who imagined themselves to be southern belles: "This is the day of efficiency, and the woman who admits she can never get through the kitchen is a thing of past. In order to be efficient, she must know how to manage."[104]

From the 1920s through the 1950s, southern cookbook authors branded regional cuisine as a unique commodity, once enjoyed only by native southerners but now available to interested readers across the United States. This message was steeped in coded notions of tradition (slavery/racism), reputation (class), taste (southern recipes), service (African American cooks and servants), artistry ("wizardry" of black women), quality (white plantation elite), and heritage (the Confederacy).

The Dixie culinary brand reinforced in the introduction to *The Southern Cook Book of Fine Old Recipes*, an inexpensive pamphlet cookbook sold by the Culinary Arts Press of Reading, Pennsylvania, in the 1930s, is an example: "All your life you have heard of the traditionally famous dishes of the Southland. No names appear so frequently on hotel menus as Dixie names. No cooking seems more famous or synonymous with quality and deliciousness than Southern cooking. You will find here, published for the first time in book form, we believe, the truly amazing recipe for 'Kentucky Burgoo,' and the celebrated recipe for 'Pot Likker,' which is a famous dish in almost every part of the South, particularly in the homes of the poor white and the negro."[105] The reference to these two dishes implied a sense of adventure and the rare opportunity for readers who, like intrepid anthropologists, could taste celebrated foods seldom available to outsiders. The "vision of the old mammy" was there, too, tied to the Old South trope of magical black cooks who transformed simple ingredients into delicious fare, "head tied with a red bandanna, a jovial, stoutish, welcome personage . . . a wizard in the art of creating savory, appetizing dishes from plain everyday ingredients."[106]

Claire Sondheim, one of the three editors of *The Southern Cook Book of Fine Old Recipes*, was married to Leonard Davidow, founder of the Culinary Arts Press, which produced domestic "how-to-guides," such as *Hot Dishes to Delight Guests* and *Candy Cookery*, plus a series of cookbooks on ethnic, regional, and international food topics from the "Pennsylvania Dutch," to New England, the American West, and "Round the World."[107] The company's slogan, "Attractive Ideas to Make the World a Better Place to Eat in," appeared on a promotional butter dish in 1935.[108] The Culinary Arts Press successfully marketed Americana at a particularly sensitive time for Jewish Americans like Sondheim and Davidow, who were deeply aware of rising anti-Semitism and the forces building toward war with Nazi Germany.

The northern-born Jewish authors of *The Southern Cook Book of Fine Old Recipes* called upon all the stereotypes, fictional figures, imagined landscapes, and language associated with the Old South: "People think of the Southland as the place where the sun shines brighter, the breezes are gentler, the birds sing sweeter and the flowers are fairer. We, who have edited this cook book, which we hope you will find helpful, think of the Southland as the hearthstone of superb cooking."[109] The cover of the 1935 edition of the cookbook is notable for a modern twist on the traditional southern kitchen scene and the black women typically depicted there. In the illustration, an African American cook dressed in stereotypical mammy attire prepares a dish, while a young black girl with pigtails looks on. A stylish, thin, youthful black woman stands nearby, dressed in a fashionable contemporary floral dress and matching head scarf. She appears confident—one hand on her hip, the other on the table—engaged in conversation rather than labor. The image implies that she is the next generation, a modern *New* Black Woman. Not surprising, this image, suggestive of a modernizing South, disappeared in 1940s reprints of the cookbook, replaced by the typical mammy figure, alone with bowl and spoon in hand.[110] Publisher Leonard Davidow must have realized that the old-fashioned, familiar mammy was the stronger brand for his southern cookbooks.

The images of mammy and the Old South used by the Culinary Arts

Press were the same used by Jewish songwriters of New York's Tin Pan Alley in southern-themed music of the early twentieth century. Popular songs such as Jean Schwartz's "Rock-a-Bye Your Baby with a Dixie Melody" (1918) and Irving Caesar's "Is It True What They Say about Dixie?" (1936) were made famous by singer Al Jolson.[111] Whether creating text for southern cookbooks or penning popular song lyrics about Dixie, these Jewish writers "followed a tradition of outsiders," as historian Stephen Whitfield explains, who "created and sustained the image of the South."[112] With their names so firmly tied to an American place—and what place had more regional gravitas than the South?—Jewish producers of popular culture reinforced their American citizenship and loyalties. The strong presence of Jewish Americans in both the music and the literary publishing worlds of the East Coast in the early twentieth century, combined with their recognition of the value of the Dixie brand, helps explain the number of Old South cookbooks by nonsouthern Jewish writers.

The power of the Dixie brand is evident in the persistence of Old South symbols, imagery, and language in southern cookbooks of the 1950s. This era was dominated by fund-raising cookbooks produced by churches, clubs, schools, and Junior League chapters throughout the South.[113] Many of these regional publications were so successful that multiple editions and thousands of copies have been printed. Examples include the Baton Rouge, Louisiana, Junior League's *River Road Recipes* (1959) and the Charleston, South Carolina, Junior League's *Charleston Receipts* (1950)—considered the "Bible of all Junior League cookbooks."[114] These regional classics still hold iconic status, largely among white southerners, and remain "authoritative" reference texts for both experienced cooks and new homemakers. Writers Matt Lee and Ted Lee, residents of both Charleston and New York City, describe *Charleston Receipts* as the "definitive twentieth century cookbook for the region."[115] Mary Vereen Huguenin oversaw the Junior League committee that assembled the cookbook's over 400 recipes, which are clearly suggestive of the city's ethnic and racial diversity, although, as the Lee brothers explain, the text remained "lily white in perspective."[116]

Clementine Paddleford featured *Charleston Receipts* in her column in the *New York Herald Tribune* and in a May 1951 column for *This Week*, a weekly newspaper supplement. "I wanted to borrow from this collection, to pass the good eating on to THIS WEEK readers—and not just the recipes, I wanted to introduce some of the people who serve these traditional foods of the Old South," wrote Paddleford. Huguenin welcomed Paddleford: "Come to Charleston, meet everyone, eat the book if you like. Take your pick of the dishes; I'll arrange for the parties."[117] The column included two photographs that symbolized the racial history of Charleston's food heritage. One was of Paddleford's Charleston host—a modern "Cotton Planter's Daughter—"Mrs. Stuart Dawson," who stood at the base of a gracious staircase in the foyer of her home. The other was of an older female black cook referred to only as "Patsy," at the Otranto Club, a private hunting facility.[118] The black cook, dressed in an old-fashioned gingham apron and head scarf, was posed sitting in front of the fireplace, stirring a pot of "Pine-Bark Stew"—a dish made from fish, potatoes, and bacon and flavored with curry powder. The recipes chosen for the article suggested the sophistication of urbane Charleston, the exoticism of African-inspired dishes, and the tony hunting worlds of Low-country plantations: "Lady Baltimore Cake," "Mrs. Dawson's Shrimp Mold or Paste," "Otranto Pine-Bark Stew," "Benne Seed-Wafers," and "Charleston Okra Soup."[119]

More "modern" regional cookbooks of the 1950s relied less on the symbols of the Old South, such as Marion Brown's *Southern Cookbook* (1951), Elizabeth Hedgecock Sparks's *North Carolina and Old Salem Cookery* (1955), and a contemporary expression of the classic community cookbook, the *Dillard Women's Club Cookbook* (1958). Marion Brown was one of the first southern authors to recognize in print the influence of African Americans and ethnic southerners on regional foodways. She argued, "The art of cooking in the South has never stood still."[120] Elizabeth Sparks—pen name Beth Tartan—was the award-winning food editor, home economist, and features writer for the *Winston-Salem Journal* from 1947 to 1991. She was a graduate of Old Salem College, where she also directed the home economics department, and her Moravian heritage and incisive voice as a working newspaper woman resulted in her iconic *North Carolina and Old Salem Cookery*, as well as a number of cookbooks focused on entertaining and "the good old days."[121]

The Dillard Women's Club Cookbook: A Collection of Fine Recipes, Including Louisiana Cuisine, Foreign Dishes, and Favorite Family Recipes reflects the historic presence of an educated black elite, not only in New Orleans but in cities across the South.[122] Dillard University was formally founded in 1930, but its history is rooted in the city's nineteenth-century black colleges. Recipes for this eclectic volume were gathered from black celebrities and white friends of this cosmopolitan community, including civil rights activist Ralph Bunche; educator Mary McLeod Bethune; writer William Faulkner; Freda DeKnight, food editor for *Ebony Magazine*; opera singers Leontyne Price and Marian Anderson; jazz artist Lena Horne; and First Lady Eleanor Roosevelt.

Old Southern Tearooms, Cafés, and "Fine Dining"

From the early twentieth century through the protests of the civil rights movement, segregated white-owned restaurants cashed in on the popularity and embedded racism of the Old South brand and aesthetic, including iconic regional dishes described in dialect on their menus, female African American cooks and wait staff dressed in mammy costumes and bandannas, and southern plantation–style architectural details and ephemera. The Old South brand crossed class and regional boundaries, successfully selling a storied regional cuisine at white-tablecloth restaurants, down-home "meat 'n' three" cafés, and luncheon tearooms.

Even the management at B. Altman's, the legendary department store in New York City, clearly understood the selling power of the Old South brand. Charleston Gardens, the novelty restaurant at Altman's Fifth Avenue location and later in other store locations in the New York metropolitan region, included a full-scale facade of a plantation home and murals depicting an enclosed southern garden. Matt Lee and Ted Lee believe the restaurant concept was inspired by Charlestonian Blanche Rhett's cookbook, *Two Hundred Years of Charleston Cooking* (1931), edited by New Yorker Lettie Gay.[123] Customers enjoyed club sandwiches and tomatoes stuffed with chicken salad in the courtyard tables set amid the Tara-like columns of a faux southern mansion. Shoppers could buy Altman's "southern-style" foods, Charleston cookbooks, and decorative items to enjoy at home.[124]

When the ten-story Piedmont Hotel opened in Atlanta at the corner of Peachtree and Luckie Streets in 1903—a half-million-dollar investment by local investors—a promotional pamphlet detailed the special features of this first "thoroughly modern" yet distinctly southern edifice.[125] To assure customers that modern standards were not sacrificed for the sake of Old South charm, advertising copy emphasized the up-to-date technology, scientific efficiency, and sanitation of the New South's latest restaurant and hotel. The kitchen and storeroom were separate from the main hotel building, and dining facilities for the hotel's 250 laborers were located in the basement. "All of the white cooks and helpers know their parts as well as actors in a play."[126]

Creighton's operated restaurants in Asheville and Charlotte, North Carolina, and in Chattanooga, Tennessee, and touted their modern, efficient service and cleanliness in the late 1930s: "Even the air you breathe at Creighton's has been washed, dehumidified and cooked for your ultimate comfort, by Frigidaire's powerful machinery."[127] Despite the restaurants' emphasis on modernity, Creighton's embraced the Old South for its out-of-town tourists during the region's annual Rhododendron

HEADACHE SILENCERS

Vegetable Soup	10c
Okra and Tomato Soup	15c
Orange Juice	10c
Tomato Juice	10c
Grapefruit Juice	10c
Fruit Cocktail	15c
Olives or Celery Hearts	20c
Shrimp Cocktail	35c
Half Grapefruit	15c

GONE WITH THE WIND COLD PLATES

25c—AUNT PITTYPAT—25c
Cold Salmon, Sliced Tomatoes, Lettuce, Pickles and Whole Wheat Toast

25c—CARREEN—25c
Boiled Ham, Cole Slaw, Lettuce, Pickles and Saltines

25c—MAMMY—25c
Gooseliver, Sliced Tomatoes, Lettuce, Pickles and Saltines

35c—ASHLEY WILKES—35c
Imported Sardines, Potato Salad, Lettuce, Sliced Tomatoes, Pickles and Saltines

40c—BELLE WATLING—40c
Boiled Ham, Swiss and American Cheese, Potato Salad, Tomatoes, Lettuce, Dill Pickles and Saltines

40c—GERALD—40c
Gooseliver, Sliced Ham, Potato Salad, Tomatoes, Lettuce, Pickles and Saltines

45c—ELLEN—45c
Sliced Ham, Gooseliver, Swiss & American Cheese, Potato Salad, Tomatoes, Lettuce, Pickles and Saltines

45c—MELANIE—45c
Little Vienna Sausages, Potato Salad, Deviled Egg. Tomatoes, Lettuce, Pickles and Buttered Rye Toast

50c—RHETT BUTLER—50c
Lucious Ripe Tomato Stuffed with Fresh Shrimp Salad, Head Lettuce, Thousand Island Dressing, Pickles, Hot Rolls and Butter

50c—SCARLETT—50c
Delicious Chicken Salad, Deviled Egg, Sliced Tomatoes, Lettuce, Mayonnaise, Pickles, Peanut Butter and Jam Sandwiches

BUILDER UPPERS

Potato Salad	10c
Combination Salad	20c
Head Lettuce, Dressing	25c
Sliced Tomato and Lettuce	25c
Pear, Cream Cheese and Nuts	35c
Tomato, Stuffed with Chicken Salad	35c
Chicken Salad	40c
Shrimp Salad	40c

Hot Roast Beef Sandwich, Mashed Potatoes and Brown Gravy	30c
Hot Sliced Chicken Sandwich, Mashed Potatoes and Cream Gravy	35c

Rhododendron Festival—Asheville, N. C.—June 14-18th

❖ CREIGHTON'S ❖

SOUTHERN MAMMY DINNERS

SATURDAY, MAY 29, 1937

WE SERVE A SPECIAL 25c DINNER EVERY NIGHT

No. 1—25c

Browned Corned Beef Hash
Green Steamed Cabbage
Sliced Pickled Cucumbers
Clover Leaf Rolls — Bran Muffins with Raisins
Old Timey Buttermilk Biscuits

Choice One Extra Vegetable or any 10c Dessert Except Ice Cream

Coffee or Tea (Milk 5c Extra)

No. 2—50c

Stuffed Pork Chops—or—Fried Yellow Perch
Escalloped Tomatoes — French Fried Egg Plant
Sliced Pickled Cucumbers
Clover Leaf Rolls — Bran Muffins with Raisins
Old Timey Buttermilk Biscuits
Green Apple Pie

Coffee or Tea (Milk 5c Extra)

No. 3—75c

Choice of Soup or Tomato Juice

Minute Steak Broiled
Stringless Green Beans — Hashed Browned Potatoes
Sliced Pickled Cucumbers
Clover Leaf Rolls — Bran Muffins with Raisins
Old Timey Buttermilk Biscuits
Coconut Custard Pie

Coffee or Tea (Milk 5c Extra)

TONIGHT'S FRESH VEGETABLES

. . . Choice of Two . . .

Tomatoed Northern Beans — Green Garden Peas — Pickled New Beets
Stringless Green Beans — Green Steamed Cabbage
Escalloped Tomatoes — Au Gratin Onions — Fresh Turnip Greens
French Fried Egg Plant — Baked Summer Squash

20c—GEORGIA CAMP MEETING PIE—20c
Fresh Georgia Peaches Candied to Bring out the Southern Sweetness, Blended with a Short Crust that Melts in Your Mouth and Topped with Whipped Cream.

Open Sandwich with Boiled Ham, Crisp Lettuce, Toasted Buttered Rye Bread and Potato Salad	25c

PROHIBITIONIST'S DREAM

Sweet Milk	05c	**Coca Cola**	05c
Buttermilk	05c	**Dr. Pepper**	05c
Chocolate Milk	05c	**Iced Coffee with**	
Hot Coffee	05c	**Whipped Cream**	10c
Tea—Hot or Iced	05c	**Postum**	10c
Orangade	05c	**Beer**	15c

STEAKS—CHOICE U. S. BRANDED STEERS

Hot Rolls and Butter, Coffee or Tea Served with All Steak Orders.

45c—NUMBER ONE—45c
Chopped Sirloin Patty, with Fried Onions

50c—NUMBER TWO—50c
Minute Steak, Shoestring Potatoes, Sliced Tomatoes, Mayonnaise.

85c—NUMBER THREE—85c
Small T-Bone Steak, French Fried Potatoes.

$1.25—NUMBER SIX—$1.25
Thick T-Bone Steak, French Fried Potatoes.

$1.45—NUMBER SEVEN—$1.45
Extra Thick Porterhouse Steak, French Fried Potatoes

WOODMAN SPARE THAT TREE

60c—CHOP A—60c
Broiled or Fried Pork Chops, Hot Rolls and Butter.

65c—CHOP B—65c
Broiled Spring Lamb Chops, Green Sugar Peas, Hot Rolls and Butter.

65c—CHOP C—65c
Native Veal Chops or Veal Cutlets, Breaded or Plain, French Fried Potatoes, Hot Rolls and Butter

SOUTHERN SPECIALS

75c—FRIED CHICKEN—75c
Southern Fried Chicken, Green Sugar Peas, Steamed Rice and Gravy, Today's Salad, Hot Rolls and Butter.

75c—CHICKEN PIE—75c
(Made the Good Old Southern Way)
Individual Casserole, Biscuit Cover. Choice of any Vegetable, Hot Rolls and Butter.

75c—FRIED COUNTRY HAM—75c
Native Cured, an old Southern Custom Handed Down for Generations, with the South's Sweetest Sweet Potatoes, Hot Rolls and Butter.

75c—FRIED SOUTHERN SHRIMP—75c
(As Southern as Swannee)
Sweet Juicy Shrimp, Fried in Butter, Crisp Bacon, Shoestring Potatoes, Tartar Sauce, Hot Rolls and Butter.

THE SWEETEST THINGS

Georgia Peach Cobbler	10c
Cherry Brown Betty	10c
Apricot Whip	10c
Sweet Potato Custard Pie	15c
Green Apple Pie	10c
Fresh Strawberry Tart	15c
Fresh Pineapple Tapioca	10c
Coconut Custard Pie	15c
Pineapple Upside Down Cake	15c
Fresh Strawberry Short Cake	15c

10c—ICE CREAM—10c

Chocolate — **Vanilla** — **Peach**
Pineapple Sherbet

"Creighton's Southern Mammy Dinners," menu, Asheville, North Carolina, May 29, 1937. Pack Memorial Library, North Carolina Collection, Asheville, N.C.

Festival. Although Asheville was far removed from the plantation history of eastern Carolina, the entire state—including the Piedmont and the mountains—attracted northern visitors with descriptions of its "Deep South" food and manners. The Saturday, May 29, 1937, menu at Creighton's was an antebellum extravaganza of "Southern Mammy Dinners," including "Chicken Pie—Made the Good Old Southern Way," "Fried Southern Shrimp—as Southern as Swannee," "Old Timey Buttermilk Biscuits," and "Georgia Camp Meeting Pie—Fresh Georgia Peaches Candied to Bring Out the Southern Sweetness."[128] A selection of "Gone with the Wind Cold Plates" were named in honor of Margaret Mitchell's leading characters, such as the "Mammy" (goose liver and sliced tomatoes), the "Aunt Pittypat" (cold salmon), the "Melanie" (Vienna sausages and potato salad), the "Ashley Wilkes" (sardines), the "Belle Watling" (ham and cheese), the "Rhett Butler" (tomato stuffed with shrimp salad), and the "Scarlett" (chicken salad and a deviled egg).[129]

In Mississippi, entrepreneurs opted for the selling power of the past as they developed tourism campaigns to attract visitors to the state's former plantation district. In the late 1930s, Vicksburg's white society women and civic leaders established the Vicksburg Pilgrimage—an annual fund-raising event in which residents opened the city's antebellum homes to tourists for several weeks each spring. Tours had helped to revive Natchez's sagging economy after the Depression, and Vicksburg hoped for the same boost as its citizens and the rest of the nation faced World War II. In 1941, Mary McKay, the wife of a local Vicksburg attorney, opened the Old Southern Tea Room in downtown Vicksburg. In keeping with the city's celebration of its antebellum and Civil War history, she created an ambience steeped in plantation lore.

Although McKay had no business experience and little cooking ability, she hired excellent African American staff, including Elvira Williams, a skilled cook, and Alberta Jackson, who waited on customers and assisted in the kitchen.[130] Five years later, the Old Southern Tea Room was included in Duncan Hines's *Adventures in Good Eating*: "I doubt if you will find more delicious food in a public eating place between St. Louis and New Orleans. . . . Mammy's fried chicken, Southern corn pudding, Aunt Carrie's jellied apples, old-fashioned lemon filling cake, ice cream with chocolate cherry sauce. That should satisfy either hungry men or women, at least I found it did."[131] Clementine Paddleford also visited: "I speak of home cooking; little of the sort could be found in restaurants, not until Mary McKay opened the Old Southern Tea Room."[132] The Tea Room's bar was as popular as its dining room. Shelby Flowers Ferris recalls McKay's spunk when a Texan requested a "Texas Razoo" from his waitress. "Tell him we don't have a Texas Razoo but we'll fix him a Yazoo Razoo—and you just put everything from the bar in it."[133]

The Old Southern Tea Room's menu featured an illustration of a mammy figure on the front and, in another edition, a cover photograph of McKay's daughter, Eulalie, clad in an antebellum-style ball gown. On the back of the menu, McKay's invented history of the new "old" Tea Room carefully matched the "moonlight and magnolia" narratives repeated by hoop-skirted guides at the town's antebellum venues: "Colored waitresses in bright 'Mammy' costumes, bandannas and hoop earrings, bring you steaming shrimp gumbo with crisp corn sticks, tempting salads, *Southern* stuffed ham for which Vicksburg is famous, and above all else—piping hot biscuits!"[134] Even Mary McKay needed a refashioned past more in keeping with the Tea Room's mythic plantation roots. Charlotte Kahn's introduction for the Tea Room cookbook transformed McKay from the daughter of a hardworking mill town mayor in central Mississippi into a "Southern Lady . . . from a cream puff existence on the old plantation where third-generation-in-the-family cooks produce epicurean dishes by an art handed down from the days of slavery."[135]

The Old South was fully on display when the Carolina Inn opened in Chapel Hill adjacent to UNC in late December 1924. The new inn and its dining facilities were reminiscent of a plantation home, complete with a two-story portico, columns, and a glazed cupola copied from Mount Vernon, the Virginia home of George Washington.[136] Symbolism, rather than an accurate historical reflection of the region's economy, drove the design decisions of the Carolina Inn architects and university administrators from the 1920s to the 1960s. The inn was promoted as a "cross between the real Mount Vernon and the mythical Tara," states historian Kenneth Zogry, and traditional southern foods on the menu were central to this narrative.[137] Restaurant dishware manufactured by Shenango China in New Castle, Pennsylvania, featured the plantation-like facade of the inn in the center of the dinner plate.[138]

By the 1940s, UNC was holding tight to the Old South symbols on campus to counter its growing reputation as a bastion for liberal agitators, including its progressive president, Frank Porter Graham.[139] A 1950 menu for the inn's Hill Room included the text, "The Old South . . . God bless it and keep it. . . . The Land of Cotton, tobacco, plantation mansions, magnolias, moonlight and music is not altogether gone with the wind. . . . The atmosphere of the good old days—the informality, the conviviality, the high spirits—still lives in a few places like the Carolina Inn."[140] Carolina Inn brochures illustrated with "welcoming" images of African American waiters, chefs, and porters in service to white alumni, students, and faculty supported the inn's message of southern hospitality in its segregated facilities. These images remained in use until the early 1970s, long after the university was required to admit African American undergraduates, beginning in 1955, and the civil rights activism of the 1960s.[141]

The economic prosperity that followed World War II brought televisions into thousands of homes, introducing Americans to new timesaving food products and appliances, as well as travelogue programs and commercials that inspired families to explore the country, including the South.[142] On her weekly televised variety show, Tennessee-born star Dinah Shore sang the snappy lyrics, "See the USA in your Chevrolet, America is asking you to call."[143] Americans took Shore's lyrics to heart. Expansion of the nation's transportation infrastructure allowed more car-owning Americans to travel to the South and to taste the region's rich culinary cultures. Southern cookbooks stamped with the familiar symbols of the Old South—sentimental drawings of black servants and plantations, recipes formally attributed to white matrons using their husbands' names, and the conspicuous absence of the African American cooks largely responsible for this cuisine—were popular souvenirs to bring home as a memento from a family vacation or to give as a gift to neighbors and friends.

The chapter that follows reveals that southern cuisine is a key component of regional historic preservation efforts and a growing tourism economy in the New South. These forces appealed to both locals and outsiders by marketing and selling the taste of the Old South in Williamsburg, Virginia, the Lowcountry flavors of Savannah and Charleston, the fashionable Creole cuisine of New Orleans, and the "authentic" "hillbilly" and "Highlands" foods of the mountain South.

14

A Journey Back in Time

FOOD AND TOURISM IN THE NEW SOUTH

A public relations machine operated by automobile clubs, railroad companies, hotels, restaurants, and city- and state-sponsored travel organizations pumped out a sea of tourist guides steeped in the romance and flavors of the southern colonies, the antebellum plantations, the colorful Creole landscapes, and the "isolation" of the mysterious mountain South.[1] A constructed historical narrative of white nobility, black service, and exceptional hospitality enlivened this invented South, as seen in an early twentieth-century tourist brochure from the Seaboard Air Line Railway. Self-advertised as "The Progressive Railway of the South," the rail company's promotional materials included a map of train routes that stretched from Maine to the Florida Keys, alongside information for "Attractive Winter Resorts," "Winter Golf in Dixie," and recommendations for lodging and dining.[2] Visitors enjoying the pleasant air of Dixie in the brochure illustrations were white, well-dressed men and women on horseback and in touring cars set amid a palm tree–studded landscape.[3] In the distance, golfers played on a manicured green, and behind them, a commodious resort hotel beckoned with comfortable lodging and fine dining.

By the 1940s, Seaboard and other rail companies with southern passenger trains had created promotional travelogues for these vacation routes, often viewed as short subject films shown with feature-length movies in theaters across the country. These films tempted viewers with escapes to worlds where they, too, could truly experience—and taste—the "Southland."[4] In a dining car scene filmed on Kansas City Southern Railroad's Southern Belle, the narrator says, "Get your feet under these tables and you'll be reluctant to withdraw them. . . . Here are the best of good things prepared in famous southern style, and the check won't put a dent in your pocketbook either."[5]

No one packaged and sold the Old South better than the region's historic colonial cities, particularly Charleston and Williamsburg, which fashioned themselves as epicenters of southern hospitality, culinary artistry, authenticity, and antiquity.[6] In New Orleans, alluring descriptions of the Creole city and its unique cuisine and history drew tourists, while the mountain South of western North Carolina attracted paying visitors with stories of the region's hardy restorative food and the "pioneer" spirit of the Appalachian people. Popular home and travel magazines drew upon these constructed narratives of the Old South, Creole Country, and the Southern Highlands in product advertisements, marketing, and articles that offered readers an inside view of southern homes and kitchens. *House and Garden* magazine featured a special series that explored the architecture, decorative arts, gardens, and cuisine of the South, dedicating entire issues to Williamsburg, Charleston, and the Southern Highlands in western North Carolina. A blockbuster "Gone with the Wind" edition in November 1939 revealed "Interiors in Full Color" from the film premiere in Atlanta that December.

"A Visit to Old Williamsburg Yields Many Fine Recipes"

House and Garden's November 1937 special issue introduced its middle- and upper-class white readers to the region "South from Williamsburg" and to "routes revealing the Old South and the new that beckon travelers who leave Virginia's most historic peninsula."[7] Founded at the height of New South civic boosterism, Colonial Williamsburg was shaped by both Old South ideologies and the Americanization efforts of the colonial revival, the antimodern design movement.[8] From the late 1920s onward, generations of tourists who visited Colonial Williamsburg enjoyed a southern narrative of abundance, skilled black cooks, loyal servants, and the generous hospitality of gracious planters and their wives. Advertisements throughout *House and Garden*'s Williamsburg issue welcomed automobile tourists to "Old Virginia, Land of Romance. . . . Here you may live in the spirit and grace of the past."[9] Food and entertainment writer June Platt wrote a monthly column in *House and Garden* during the 1930s and also contributed upbeat travel pieces on regional food for the magazine's special southern issues, including an essay for the Williamsburg edition entitled "Good Old Southern Dishes."[10]

As Platt walked about the carefully restored colonial capitol of Virginia, she had difficulty finding a simple kitchen to visit in the historic area of the city.[11] "I was terribly disappointed," Platt wrote, "because somehow there didn't seem to be any kitchens anywhere."[12] Given the national interest in all things patriotic in the interwar years, including the Founding Fathers, museum curators at Williamsburg emphasized the "gracious" homes of the white elite of the colonial city rather than ordinary kitchens dominated by enslaved African American labor. The one kitchen presented in its colonial revival splendor was at the

Governor's Palace, a virtually new building reconstructed by Colonial Williamsburg in 1934. As Platt explained, "We found ourselves in a perfect dream of a kitchen . . . presided over by an honest-to-goodness Mammy."[13] A photograph for Platt's column featured a costumed African American woman seated in front of a large fireplace, operating a coffee grinder on her lap. White costumed female staff were referred to as "hostesses." The caption for the photo read, "Mammy knows many secrets."[14] And certainly she did, but largely about unfair labor practices at Colonial Williamsburg in the 1930s, which kept African Americans in working-class, service jobs throughout their careers with limited opportunities for promotion.[15]

Inside the museum's commercial taverns and inns, one could taste the "plantation flavor" of a conflated colonial and antebellum South at tables set with spit-roasted chickens, baked Virginia hams, puffy loaves of Sally Lunn bread, and cherry-topped trifles. Thanks to Williamsburg's many gift shops, it was possible to bring a bit of this plantation past back home in reproduction tableware, textiles, and furniture, as well as in colonial-style food products, mob caps, and aprons.[16] Popular books such as Helen Bullock's *The Williamsburg Art of Cookery* (1938) and Letha Booth's *The Williamsburg Cookbook* (1971) taught visitors how to entertain, decorate their homes "Williamsburg-style," and recreate both tavern fare and "meals fit for a King—or a Queen."[17]

Colonial Williamsburg's popular orientation film, *Williamsburg: The Story of a Patriot* (1956), reinforced this pleasing world of southern hospitality and fine living in the story of patriot-planters in the years leading up to the Revolution. In scenes filmed at majestic Westover Plantation (1730) overlooking the James River, Hollywood actors played Virginia planters discussing their growing concerns about the British as they enjoyed glasses of Madeira and frosty mint juleps. Scenes set in Williamsburg's restored taverns featured stoneware mugs, ceramic pipes, pewter bowls, glassware, and table linen. Reproductions were conveniently available for visitors to purchase in the museum's gift stores.

Story of a Patriot is still shown at Colonial Williamsburg today in the midcentury modernist Information Center and "motion-picture" theater built in 1957.[18] Winthrop Rockefeller, chairman of the museum's board of trustees at the time, noted that the film and the new facilities—including the 220 "spacious, air-conditioned rooms" of the Motor House and its restaurant, the Cafeteria—would provide "a bridge of understanding over which Americans can walk from the twentieth century into the past."[19] The choice of a modernist design for the first building that Colonial Williamsburg visitors experience on their journey "into the past" reinforced the museum's embrace of the 1950s consensus history of the Cold War era that celebrated freedom, individualism, private property, progress, and capitalism.

The appealing kitchens and tables of Colonial Williamsburg contrasted sharply with the reality of slavery and the antebellum household later documented by historians Eugene Genovese and Elizabeth Fox-Genovese in the 1970s and 1980s.[20] The softer, more palatable story of southern colonial foodways that was told at Colonial Williamsburg for over fifty years originates in the politics of race, region, and consumer culture. A rising white middle class embraced the Old South narrative at Dixie's most popular tourist destinations and in the branded products they used at home.

Charleston "The Home of Southern Hospitality"

In June Platt's March 1939 food column for a special *House and Garden* issue on Charleston, South Carolina, the author enthused over the city's cooking in a manner sure to attract hungry gourmands to the Lowcountry. "This is *my* Charleston," wrote Platt, "and it's a mouth-watering mélange—of far-reaching rice fields, of nets spilling over with fat crabs and shrimps, of green okra and golden yams, of plump, tender chickens and rich cream. It's a dream of cornbread, coconuts, of Hopping John, Pilaus and Daubes, of hams, hotbreads and honey!"[21] Platt provided a few "typical and delicious" Charleston recipes for American foodies of the 1930s, "those who also see the South framed with knife and fork."[22] Her selection included "shrimps in cream," roast chicken, cornbread dressing, "Mulacolong"—a curried chicken dish, yams and oranges, "okra daube"—like a gumbo, "ratifia cream"—flavored with almond liqueur, and "zephryinas"—a baked, puffed cracker.[23]

The popular tourist venue of Historic Charleston was masterminded by white elites and a network of city organizations and businesses following World War I.[24] The reinvented city on display to tourists was awash in the colonial and antebellum past of the Old South—described by historian Stephanie Yuhl as a "sanitized interpretation of Charleston's past and present" that rejected the changing racial politics of the era.[25] In the early twentieth-century paintings and drawings of the Charleston Renaissance—an emerging art colony that flourished at the same time as the city's tourism industry—food and its material culture capture this sentimental, romantic South.[26] Paintings by Alice Ravenel Huger Smith depict the softly hued rice fields of the Lowcountry at harvest time, while Anna Heyward Taylor's bold block prints capture scenes of African American vendors in Charleston's markets and agricultural laborers at work outside the city.[27]

By selectively choosing which elements of the past to remember and commemorate as the city's "official history," white civic leaders such as Susan Pringle Frost, founder and president of Charleston's Society for the Preservation of Old Dwellings, effectively controlled how the city was packaged and sold to tourists. Missing from this constructed past was Charleston's vital commercial and mercantile history, including several generations of Jewish merchants and grocers and the presence of a free black middle class, many of whom were food entrepreneurs.[28] Ultimately, Charleston's pervasive plantation narrative of slavery and service reinforced racist ideas of black inferiority and white supremacy in the segregated South.[29]

The Lowcountry's rich culinary heritage was central to this constructed narrative. Brochure copy, tour guides, and historic house docents told stories of the region's distinctive seafood and rice country dishes, such as pilau (rice cooked in a flavorful broth with meat or seafood) and "hoppin' John" (field peas and rice) and the "mammies" who prepared these delights. In these mythologized accounts, African American cooks oversaw "quaint" kitchens at picturesque Lowcountry plantations and in the back lot courtyards of the city's historic homes on the Charleston Battery beside the Ashley and Cooper Rivers.

The following passage from an Edgefield, South Carolina, publication reflects these invented tales of region, race, and food. "Recipes of Yesteryear" in the *Edgefield Guest Book: A Handbook for Hostesses* (1953) included this description of Colonel Bacon's "legendary" wedding barbecue: "Hundreds of women, hundreds of little children in white; hundreds of vehicles, hundreds of Negroes, hundreds of roast turkeys and baked hams, mounds of salad, mountains of delicious homemade bread, great gulfs and deep seas of ice-lemonade, piles and pyramids of ice cream, East Indian groves of fruit, heavy coffers of splendid bridal presents, and hospitality that vaulted up to the skies."[30] The *Edgefield Guest Book* opens with a photograph of "Aunt Mittie Wigfall," a black servant of the Augustus Thompkins family, standing at a cookstove where she "cooks 'victuals' beyond compare" and also keeps an eye on a young white boy who sits nearby with spoon and bowl in hand. The photograph caption notes, "In the tradition of all small boys, drawn irresistibly by a spoon to lick, 'Joe Boy' Holland Scavens represents the fourth generation which Aunt Mittie has given a prevue of her delicacies before they reach the table. Aunt Mittie cooks 'by ear,' but insists she measures every ingredient, 'Right in de palm of my han.'"[31] Selectively depicting blacks in this manner—at labor, serving and feeding the city's elite, dressed in traditional work clothing, and speaking in pidgin dialect—emphasized a sense of "primitivism" that appealed to white tourists.[32]

Charleston's museums, historic homes, and southern-style restaurants and "olde" tearooms functioned as what historian Fitzhugh Brundage characterizes as the city's "memory theaters."[33] In and around these venues, the "authentic" food-related folkways of historic Charleston and the Lowcountry were transformed into popular tourist attractions in the 1930s. African American produce and shrimp vendors competed in city-sponsored contests where they performed street cries and chants advertising their wares, while Charleston's historical organizations hired local blacks to demonstrate traditional methods of flailing and husking rice.[34] In the 1920s, white businessman Clarence Legerton marketed the distinctive Lowcountry sea grass baskets handcrafted by local African American men and women and associated with rice production and food storage.[35] Promoted as handmade "artifacts of slavery," the baskets were transformed from practical food-related wares to decorative crafts and plantation-era souvenirs for tourists to buy and remember their visit to the Lowcountry.[36] Legerton dominated the sea grass basket market until the 1930s, when local African American basket makers built their own stands alongside the coastal highways and regained control of the pricing and aesthetic design of their work.

Joseph B. Platt, a talented artist, stage and screen set designer, and decorating consultant for *House and Garden*, also contributed to the magazine's Charleston issue, and like his wife, June, he reinforced the Old South brand, but with his designs for home interiors geared to suburban housewives. Platt presented a design for a dining room in a small home, adapting a Charleston slave quarters into a "charming modern house for today."[37] Interested readers could purchase the furniture from Kittinger, the carpet from Mohawk, the Astral china pattern from Royal Worcester, and the King Edward silver from Gorham, "a favorite design in the South."[38] Additional "Charleston-themed" objects were advertised in the back of the magazine, including camellia-decorated china and "a gay luncheon cloth" inspired by the "brilliant bandanas" of "mammy" cooks, both available from B. Altman's in New York City.[39] The rebranding of Charleston's historical narrative was so effective in this era that slave housing and a black cook's head scarf were stripped of any guilt-inducing memories, transformed from artifacts of enslavement into "cheerful" souvenirs of Charleston's plantation past.

The Flavor of "Creole Country"

From the late nineteenth century to the present, hints of New Orleans's infamous hedonism underlay promotions of the city as a romantic, picturesque relic—a "lost" historic place that had survived the ravages of time with its food, scenery, and colorful people preserved for posterity.[40] After Hurricane Katrina, historian Lawrence Powell referred to New Orleans as "an American Pompeii," a moniker that captures the historic sense of threat against this vulnerable place out of time.[41] Early twentieth-century advertising copy emphasized the restorative powers of the city, imagined as a grand yet mysterious lady with a discerning palate: "If you are bored and stale, let New Orleans renovate and divert you. . . . She adores food, and the cuisine of her antique French restaurants will give fillip to the most jaded appetite."[42] As in Williamsburg and Charleston, tourists were encouraged to time travel to the glory days of New Orleans's past and experience its authentic tastes while enjoying the modern conveniences of an evolving New South city. The Crescent City also allowed visitors to daringly experience and *taste* foreign worlds, but safely within the confines of their own country: "A foreign patois is spoken in her highways; her beautiful Spanish courtyards are embowered in tropical vegetation and flowers; heralded in her streets by musical negro criers are unique vegetables, fruits, and sweets. 'Belle des figues!' 'Comfitures coco!' 'Pralines, pistache, pacanes!' [Beautiful figs! Coconut jam! Pralines, pistachios, pecans!]."[43]

New Orleans was at the epicenter of the South's modern tourism industry as it blossomed in the interwar years of the twentieth century, invigorated by a rich culinary narrative that emphasized the city's Creole exoticism, its ties to the Old South, its continental flair, and the natural bounty of the bayous and the Gulf of Mexico.[44] A 1911 advertisement for the Panama Limited evoked both the plantation South and the imagined foreign worlds of New Orleans. The Panama Limited, the Illinois Central Railroad's newest train route, was described as a "streak of luxury," which swept passengers overnight from Chicago—"the doorstep of the Middle West"—to New Orleans—"the Paris of the Mississippi."[45]

An advertisement promoting "A New Train to the South" pictured the speeding Panama Limited supported by plantation-style columns and other iconic southern symbols—"mammy," a petticoat-clad "belle," a steamboat, and a black stevedore posed atop a bale of cotton, strumming a banjo. Savvy advertising copywriters blended Old South romance with the efficiency of modern train travel and the lure of New Orleans's famous cuisine: "This morning in Chicago—tomorrow, lunching, if you will, at some famous New Orleans café, where such marvels of French cookery as Creole Gumbo, Cray-fish Bisque and Coffee Brulo, are at your command. . . . An afternoon of rest, a delicious dinner, a sound night's sleep, and the next morning already in another land, where one side of the street is a glimpse of the old world and the other a striking example of twentieth century progress."[46] New Orleans was also the star city of the Kansas City Southern Railroad's 1940 travelogue film, which culminated in a beauty pageant of "southern belles" staged at the rail terminal.[47] The young white women who competed for the title boarded the train from their home cities and towns en route from Kansas City, Missouri, to New Orleans, clad in hoopskirts and sunbonnets.

Creole heritage was at the heart of New Orleans's tourism narratives, and no aspect of this tradition spoke with more élan than the city's classic cuisine.[48] The term "Creole" refers to the historical interaction of Native Americans, Europeans, enslaved Africans, and their descendants, including free persons of color in New Orleans and the Lower Mississippi Valley.[49] Bolstered by a prospering tourism economy in the late nineteenth century, Creole culture evolved to include ambitious white citizens who invented their own self-styled royalty and pageantry, which culminated in the city's annual Mardi Gras festival.[50] Over time, "Creole" came to refer to the cultural products, including cuisine, born of the voluntary and forced contact among New Orleans's eclectic citizenry.

"Creole cookery," wrote Clementine Paddleford, "is the best-known single type of cooking in the nation. . . . It's a cuisine unique, based on the belief that eating should be a pleasure and not a task to be hurried through, that food and drink are fine things to be talked about, and that recipes are meant to be shared."[51] Creole cuisine began with the "holy trinity" of bell peppers, celery, and onion, enlivened by garlic.[52] Wine and butter formed the base of classical French sauces. Okra, sweet potatoes, beans, and other seasonal vegetables were combined with local fish, shellfish, pork, and poultry. While locals cherished New Orleans's unique culinary culture at home and in their favorite restaurants, food entrepreneurs did not hesitate in packaging and selling this enticing commodity to outsiders.

The term "Creole" connoted New Orleans's unique flavor and authenticity to tourists, but to born-and-bred New Orleanians, "Creole" represented bloodlines and a way of life in which the rituals of daily meals and dining were key to one's position in the city's complex social society. Food in New Orleans, as historian Frederick Starr explains, was not a "mere adornment of life . . . but a core part of life itself."[53] Locals demonstrated their credentials by eating Creole cooking, regardless of their racial or ethnic roots.[54] Historian Rien Fertel describes loyal "eater-citizens," whose culinary literacy reinforced identity and position in New Orleans's society.[55] Visitors to the city quickly learned that to eat local was to act local, a message emphasized in vast numbers of Creole cookbooks sold to tourists, restaurant advertisements, menus, guidebooks, regional literature, newspapers, markets, and casual conversation on the street. The city's Creole cuisine was valuable cultural capital, as important as New Orleans's renowned architecture and landscape.

The spicy Creole flavor and cuisine associated with the urbane sophistication of the polyglot city of New Orleans and the more rustic, informal dishes of the agrarian Cajun countryside were essential aspects of branding and marketing Louisiana to visiting tourists and middle-class consumers throughout the nation. In New Orleans's food service economy, this evocative narrative unfolded in the stories of working-class people—the bartenders, chefs, farmers, grocers, hoteliers, maître d's, restaurateurs, waiters, and street vendors—including costumed African American "Aunties" who sold pralines to tourists. These stories were staged in the city's beloved eating and drinking venues—the bars, bordellos, cafés, corner markets, food carts, grocery stores, historic market halls, and restaurants. The iconic foods of New Orleans's culinary brand ranged from beignets and cala to chicory coffee and pralines, gumbo and pompano en papillote to "snoballs" and Lenten Friday catfish fries at Catholic parish halls throughout the city.

From a term that signaled the taste of New Orleans's cuisine, as well as the city's multinational heritage, "Creole" evolved into a trademark that signified "home-raised or home-made."[56] Louisiana writer Mary Land wrote, "In a New Orleans market you will find 'Creole Cabbage,' 'Creole lilies,' 'Creole shallots,' and other commodities, which label indicates 'superior' or indigenous in Louisiana."[57] Today, "Creole" indicates "locally made," seasonal products found in New Orleans farmers' markets and other venues, such as the city's noted Creole cream cheese and garden-raised Creole tomatoes.

Canonizing Creole Cuisine New Orleans's Cookbooks

New Orleans's many food writers created their own origin myths for the city's distinctive cuisine, beginning with the first Creole cookbooks, published in 1885—the Christian Women's Exchange's *The Creole Cookery Book* and journalist Lafcadio Hearn's *La Cuisine Creole*.[58] These texts were written in anticipation of a growing tourist market and the thousands of visitors who attended the World's Industrial and Cotton Centennial in New Orleans, in 1884 and 1885.[59] By 1900, an encyclopedic guide to New Orleans's cuisine, the *Picayune's Creole Cook Book*, was in print, and it soon became a definitive text for local cooks.[60] That the publisher of this best-selling cookbook was the newspaper of record in the city, the *Daily Picayune*—today's *Times-Picayune*—suggests the weighty significance of Creole food, meal preparation, and dining in the daily life of New Orleanians.[61] These Creole cookbooks addressed the changed circumstances of white households, no longer assured of African American domestic labor. As stated in the introduction of the *Picayune's Creole Cook Book*, "She who had ruled as the mistress of yesterday became her own cook of to-day."[62]

According to the *Picayune's Creole Cook Book*'s particular origin narrative, Creole cookery was the creation of white mistresses of French descent who "carefully instructed and directed" African American cooks in the art of their cuisine, followed by the influence of Spanish rule, and finally the "gradual amalgamation of the two races on Louisiana soil."[63] The author claimed to have gathered culinary secrets from "the lips of the old Creole negro cooks and the grand old housekeepers who still survive, ere they, too, pass away, and Creole cookery . . . will have become a lost art."[64] This rescuing of culinary culture in the nick of time reinforced the characterization of New Orleans as a fragile, mysterious world that could be lost, and with it, the city's great food traditions. Rien Fertel notes that this "duality of being exceptional and facing extinction" endures in New Orleans, where city residents rallied to remember and preserve family recipes and cookbooks destroyed by Hurricane Katrina in 2005.[65]

Not to appear hopelessly adrift in the past, the author changed the style and tone of the introduction to the *Picayune's Creole Cook Book* at this point, suggesting the dawn of a progressive New South and the reform- and domestic science–inspired language of the era. The enlightened "New Woman" of the turn-of-the-twentieth-century South was no longer strictly white. As the author explained, "There is a 'new colored woman' as well as a new white."[66] These women of the growing black middle class in the South were less likely to choose domestic service and cooking as their professions. The *Picayune's Creole Cook Book* stepped into the void of this new racial and social order and the "vexing problem" of finding a good cook.[67] "*The Picayune*," the author explained, "has been animated by the laudable desire to teach the great mass of the public how to live cheaply and well."[68] With this middle-class audience in mind, recipes for the "simple, every-day home dishes of the Creole," such as gumbos, ragouts, and jambalaya, were included, rather than the "elegant novelties or fancifully extravagant recipes" once enjoyed by "the gourmet and epicureans in the palmiest days of old Creole cookery."[69]

New Orleans "Gourmet" Guides

As tourism thrived in New Orleans in the first decades of the twentieth century, a generation of food writers followed in the footsteps of the authors of the city's first cookbooks and continued to promote culinary tales of Creole life and the Old South. Popular cookbooks by

New Orleanians, such as Natalie Scott and Caroline Merrick Jones's *Gourmet's Guide to New Orleans* (1933) and Merlin Samuel "Scoop" Kennedy's *Dining in New Orleans: A Gourmet's Guide* (1945)—a how-to-manual for tourists unfamiliar with the city's cosmopolitan restaurant culture—crossed genres as epicurean guidebooks, recipe collections, and collectible souvenirs. In the foreword to Scott and Jones's *Gourmet's Guide*, journalist and *Picayune* advice columnist Dorothea Dix (pen name for Elizabeth Meriwether Gilmer) argued that New Orleans's food had "reached a degree of perfection" not experienced in the rest of the country.[70] She argued that tourists came to New Orleans to *eat*, as they went to New York for theater, or to Washington, D.C., to "behold the seat of government," or to "Hollywood to gape at the movie stars."[71]

In an earlier cookbook, *200 Years of New Orleans Cooking* (1931), Natalie Scott created a tourist-friendly cookbook for white visitors. Scott, a noted local newspaperwoman and preservationist, invented an African American cook, "Mandy," as the narrator of the text, inspired by "the Mandys of all my friends."[72] The cookbook included line drawings of the French Quarter by Scott's friend William Spratling. A former Tulane University architectural instructor and New Orleans's expatriate, Spratling advanced the revival of Mexico's silversmithing industry in the 1930s and 1940s. Scott, Dix, and Spratling were leading figures of the French Quarter Renaissance in New Orleans in the 1920s, an intellectual colony of writers and artists that sociologist John Shelton Reed refers to as "Dixie Bohemia."[73]

Scoop Kennedy's *Dining in New Orleans* (1945), another insider's guide geared to postwar white tourists, included his descriptions of the city's best-known dining establishments, illustrated by Tilden Landry and Bob Riley, who hand-carved tint blocks for the text.[74] Merlin "Scoop" Kennedy, a former sportswriter for the *Times-Picayune*, gourmet, and public relations specialist, later became a favorite New Orleans television chef on the local network, WDSU-TV. The block prints highlighted the flavor and ambience of each restaurant, while emphasizing the city's character and sensuality. Selected scenes included a couple dancing at the Court of Two Sisters, where the "patio is a fairyland of tropical foliage"; Arnaud's "flaming brandy dipped in mysterious spices"; Café Lafitte, "If it's Bohemia you're looking for . . . "; and Maison Blanche, whose waitresses are "well uniformed, well informed . . . and . . . ," leaving the reader to fill in the implied sexist quip about shapely female staff.[75] If a tourist preferred more conventional dining, a classic American meal of steak and potatoes was available, too. A drawing for Chris Steak House and Crescent City Steaks on North Broad

Street pictured two wide-eyed diners as they gazed upon a grilled steak as big as the serving platter, delivered by a smiling waiter. The caption read, "Sirloins fit for a hungry Bankan king."[76] If a tourist was hungry for down-home dishes, New Orleans's classic Monday night meal of red beans and rice was available at the historic French Quarter hotel, the St. Charles, which opened in 1837.

Kennedy's guide also suggested the cosmopolitan "otherness" of New Orleans, a place where tourists could take on new identities and play at being Old South elites, devil-may-care bohemians, or well-traveled sophisticates. For Antoine's—the oldest restaurant in New Orleans—Landry and Riley depicted a horse-drawn carriage driven by a black man in top hat and livery as it brought fashionable diners to the quaint, gas-lit Rue St. Louis address in the French Quarter. At Delatour's, on Robert E. Lee Boulevard—famous for its southern cuisine—happy diners were encouraged to revel as native bon vivants: "Take your hair down and loft your chicken."[77]

Corinne Dunbar's, a Creole-style restaurant on St. Charles Avenue, was described in Kennedy's guide as "a restaurant unique in many respects."[78] Corinne Dunbar converted the elegant residence into a restaurant after her husband's extended illness during the Depression. In the tradition of southern tearooms operated by resourceful women, Mrs. Dunbar treated her customers as "guests" in her home. Upon ringing the doorbell, an African American butler greeted diners and escorted them to tables set with family silver and linens, allowing tourists-voyeurs to experience a performance of New Orleans's hospitality usually reserved for family and close friends.

Concerning clubby Galatoire's on Bourbon Street—no reservations accepted—Scoop Kennedy commented on the legendary service of its famed waiters, "reminiscent of the continent."[79] Another Landry-Riley illustration captured the comfortable melding of the French Quarter's old-style decorative iron railings and the modern Art Deco sign of the Vieux Carre Restaurant, suggesting the city's embrace of both old and new. Kennedy's caption noted the location of the popular restaurant as the "very hub of the city's hub-bubiest section."[80]

Lena Richard and Mary Land

Women and the Business of Louisiana Cuisine

Lena Richard (1892–1950) and Mary Land (1908–1991) were central figures in the branding of Louisiana cuisine from the 1930s through the 1970s. Land, the daughter of a prominent white family in northern Louisiana, learned to hunt and fish at Rough and Ready Plantation, where she developed a deep love for the state's rich wildlife and natural environs.[81] Educated at the University of Chicago's School of Journalism, Land advanced in a field dominated by men, where she was highly regarded for her syndicated outdoors columns, which appeared in regional papers and magazines.[82] An accomplished figure in sport fishing, Land excelled in the challenging tarpon rodeos of the coastal South (tarpon are large powerful game fish), and she encouraged other women to compete in these largely male worlds.[83] Her strong attachment to nature was also reflected in her poetry, including *Shadows of the Swamp* (1941). In a 1954 interview, Land noted, "My hobbies are fishing, hunting, cooking, and people. My work is writing."[84] Lena Richard was a successful African American caterer, restaurateur, and television chef on New Orleans's WDSU-TV.[85] She learned to cook from the women in her family, and later at cooking schools in New Orleans and the Fannie Farmer Cooking School in Boston.[86] Land's notoriety as an outdoor journalist and Richard's reputation as a talented cook positioned both women to publish commercially viable cookbooks. Today, Land and Richard are still heralded among the culinary elite of New Orleans for their iconic books and their skillful negotiation of sexist and racial barriers as women food writers and culinary professionals in a modernizing South.

LENA RICHARD: AFRICAN AMERICAN WRITER, CHEF, ENTREPRENEUR

Lena Richard's *New Orleans Cook Book* (1940) made her recipes and menus widely available, even to the novice cook and tourist. "To the ordinary homemaker," wrote Richard, "Creole Gumbo, Court Bouillon, Crawfish Bisque, Grillade a la Creole, are no longer dishes prepared in secrecy by French chefs, to be eaten by the rich. These may be prepared by anyone following my simple directions."[87] For her black readers, Richard had another purpose in sharing her recipes. By training black women and men in "the art of food preparation and serving . . . for any occasion, . . . they might be in position to demand higher wages."[88] In 1949, 3,000 African American women entered the auditorium of the Booker T. Washington High School in New Orleans to attend Lena Richard's Cooking and Baking School, sponsored by local Norge appliance distributors—"the first of its kind to be presented . . . for Negroes."[89]

Clementine Paddleford bolstered Richard's fame with columns in the *New York Herald Tribune*. One began like this: "Lena Richard, one of New Orleans's ace kitchen performers, has come to New York with her suitcase bulging with ten pounds of dried shrimp, pure cane syrup, Louisiana shelled pecans and old-fashioned brown sugar. Under her

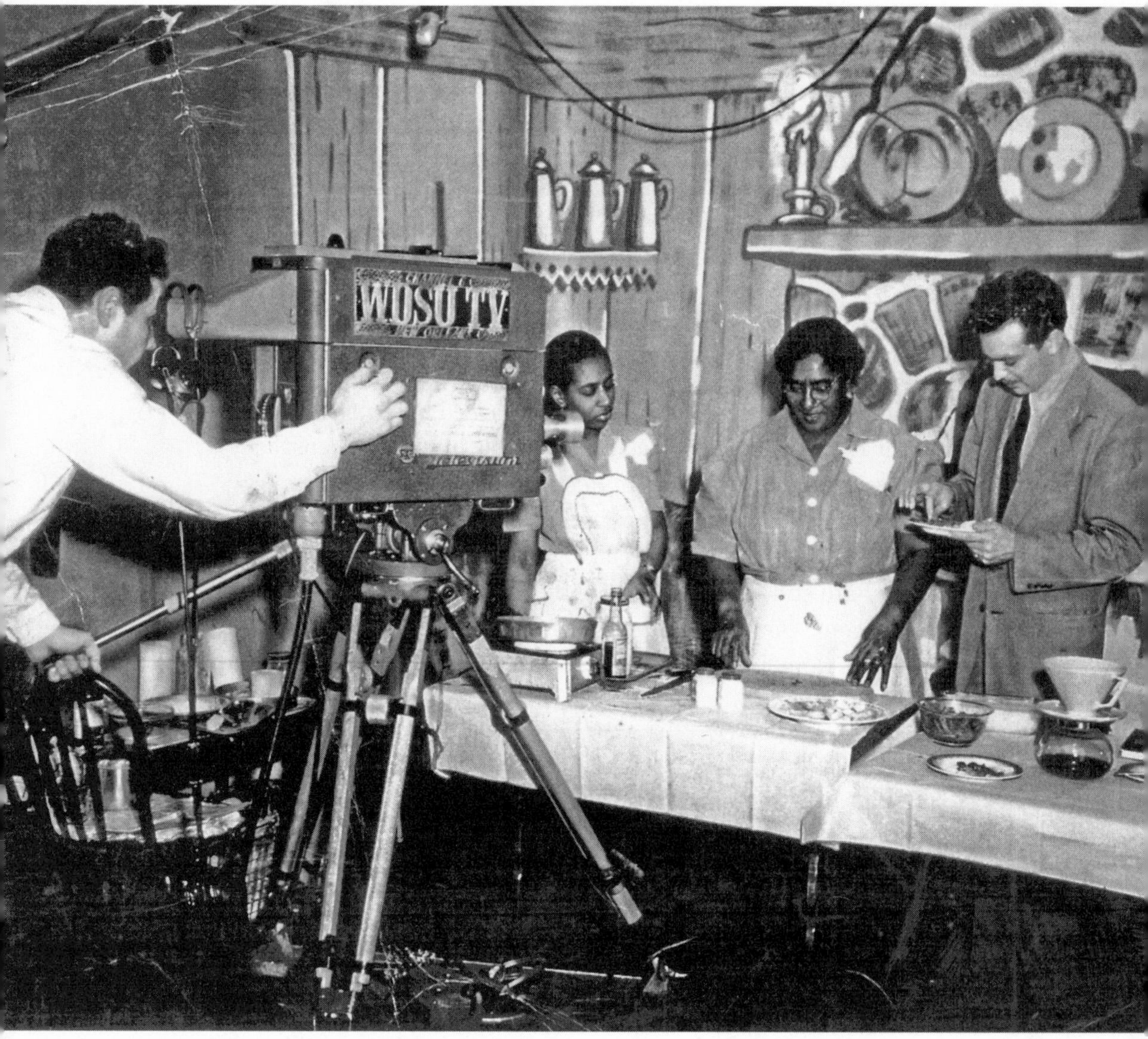

Television chef Lena Richard, WDSU TV, New Orleans, Louisiana, ca. 1949–50. Newcomb College Center for Research on Women, Tulane University Special Collections, New Orleans, La.

arm she carries the pride of her life, 'Lena Richard's Cookbook.'"[90] Unlike most writers of her time, Paddleford credited the central role of African Americans in creating southern cuisine: "Delicacies originated by the Negro cooks of the past generations shall not be lost to posterity, for Lena has collected some 350 of these savory concoctions."[91]

After the publication of Richard's cookbook, Charles and Constance Stearn recruited the author for their colonial-era inn and restaurant, the Bird and Bottle, in Garrison, New York. Constance Stearn wrote an homage to Richard in the inn's guestbook: "To Queen, who in 3 short weeks has done more for us than we can every repay."[92] The popularity of Richard's cooking was evidence of her talent, as well as the power of the Creole brand. The Stearns capitalized on Richard's reputation with a mail-order selection of five specialty foods from the inn. For seven dollars, postage included, a discriminating gourmet could sample Richard's "Shrimp Soup Louisiana" and a box of New Orleans–style cheese straws, described by Clementine Paddleford as the "richest, tangiest, meltingest cheese sticks that ever fluttered away on the tongue."[93] The Bird and Bottle's specialty southern foods were also sold at B. Altman's in New York City. In 1943, Richard was hired by the John D. Rockefeller Foundation in Williamsburg, Virginia, where she brought her southern and Creole recipes to the Travis House tavern in Colonial Williamsburg.[94]

In New Orleans, Richard operated a number of her own restaurants, including the Gumbo House. She appeared twice-weekly on her own cooking show on WDSU-TV from 1949 to 1950, a period in which she was the sole black "personality" on a local station and a captivating presence on television more than a decade before Julia Child.[95] In an era long before prepared specialty foods, New Orleanians could stop by Richard's restaurant on Louisiana Avenue and purchase her turtle soup, okra gumbo, grillades, chicken fricassee, and beef stew by the pint and the quart.[96] Richard also created a line of Creole-style frozen foods prepared from her recipes at a plant in Metairie, Louisiana, and then shipped across the country.[97] Richard is emblematic of many African American independent chefs and caterers in this era who used food as a tool of social and economic empowerment in the South, improving not only the lives of their own families, but those of the larger black community.[98]

MARY LAND: LOUISIANA'S OUTDOORS WOMAN AND FOOD WRITER

Mary Land's *Louisiana Cookery* appeared in 1954, followed by *New Orleans Cuisine* in 1969.[99] James Beard, restaurant reviewer and critic for the *New York Times*, encouraged publication of Land's work.[100] After a visit to her Louisiana home, Beard wrote Land, "I loved your house; I loved the parties; I liked your husband immensely; I adored you."[101] (Land's marital ups and downs—she married and divorced five times—reflect the restraints independent women of the era experienced as they attempted to blend marriage and professional lives.)[102] Land's cookbooks introduced readers to the Creole food of New Orleans as well as the rich culinary heritage of the state's fields, bayous, streams, and coastal waterways. Historian Karen Leatham notes Land's anthropological-like approach to food documentation, gathering ma-

Outdoors columnist Mary Land, bass fishing, Lake Hamilton,
Hot Springs, Arkansas, 1959. Pat Stevens Collection.

terial from local people who learned to cook from family and neighbors.[103] She had no qualms about including street foods, such as *calas tout chaud* (rice cakes), instructions on "outdoor fish cookery," and New Orleans's "potables," the city's famous alcoholic drinks and cocktail culture.[104] In *Louisiana Cookery*, Land recognized by name the African American domestic workers and "faithful retainers" who worked for her family and taught Land the "artifice of Louisiana's *coquemar* [kettle]." Local biologists, chefs, conservationists, cooperative extension agents, fishing experts, and restaurateurs influenced Land's rich descriptions of Louisiana cuisine.[105] She entertained this colorful salon of regional authorities—including a baby alligator—in her French Quarter apartment located in the historic Pontalba Building.[106] Her daughter Pat Stevens said, "Mother didn't set out to be unconventional, she was simply born that way."[107]

The Taste of the Mountain South

The New South consumer culture of products, language, and visual imagery that marketed colonial and Creole flavors was joined by a third culinary narrative in the early twentieth century centered in the Southern Highlands. As highway development programs expanded tourism into the mountain South, popular images of the region's people and their folkways, food, and culture were transformed into a powerful consumer brand. Over time, the edible components of this brand included not only the hearty foodways of "simple mountainfolk" and the lampooned "vittles" of "hillbillies," but a more complicated culinary culture centered in pristine National Park landscapes, modern dairies and working farms, grand estates of wealthy industrialists, restorative health retreats, and hundreds of inns, resorts, and mountain dining venues.

Descriptions of the mountain South and its foodways first appeared in late nineteenth-century local-color writings and magazine articles that emphasized the region's isolation, the "pure" Anglo-Saxon ancestry of its people and their rugged, pioneer nature, and again, the authenticity of a place "frozen in time," a "pre-industrial Eden."[108] This imagined world was reinforced in Allen Eaton's *Handicrafts of the Southern Highlands*, published by the Russell Sage Foundation in 1937. Eaton's intervention in the southern mountain culture focused on "reviving" and preserving regional arts and crafts. He traveled with noted photographer Doris Ullman, whose romantic images of highlanders at work, including scenes of food preparation, suggest a place from an earlier era. In one photograph, Ullman posed the granddaughters of William Creech of Pine Mountain, Kentucky, to grind grain in front of an old cabin. She asked them to don old-fashioned, long linsey-woolsey dresses and to use a quern, the "home-made hand-power grinding mill used by pioneers for preparing corn meal and hominy grits."[109] These were contemporary young women of the mountain South—one later became a physician—but their modern dress and aspirations did not suggest the untouched, "old timey" worlds that Eaton and Ullman hoped to convey.[110] Their families most likely had long ago abandoned grinding their own grain and instead gladly purchased commercial packaged cornmeal at a nearby store, as did their neighbors.

The sentimental, romantic, mysterious, even humorous and derisive depictions of the mountain South and its folkways and foodways were central to the potency of this regional culinary brand in advertising and consumer culture. Historian Patrick Huber explains that the imagery of an honorable, indigenous mountain people "didn't last long," and by the turn of the twentieth century, white southern mountaineers were popularly perceived as "hillbillies."[111] This flattened stereotype of hillbillies was patently derogatory, portraying the typical southern mountaineer and his family as dirty, ignorant, shiftless, lazy, violent, sexually promiscuous, hungry, and drunken.[112] Like the Old South imagery on boxes of pancake mix and in southern tearooms, the hillbilly brand became a racially charged symbol of white culture. For example, the popular soft drink Mountain Dew (slang for moonshine), created in Knoxville, Tennessee, in 1948, appealed more to working-class southerners than to the elite descendants of the colonial and plantation South.[113] Tourist restaurants and souvenir shops were stocked with hillbilly ephemera and food products. A quick walk through a contemporary version of these venues, such as Stuckey's or Cracker Barrel, indicates the tenacity of southern "mountain flavor" in bins of old-fashioned candy and down-home jars of apple butter and chow chow.

The National Park Service
Overseeing "Mountain Flavor"

The U.S. government had a strong presence in shaping the mountain South narrative tourists encountered at the newly created Great Smoky Mountains National Park in the 1930s, including what was considered "authentic" mountain food. Park officials promised to use "every ounce of energy to prevent the hot-dog stand, the soft drink stand, the gaudy filling station, the stand selling celluloid dolls, and the bill boards from marring the natural beauty of our gates."[114] Secretary of the Interior Harold Ickes ruled that park concessions must focus on native mountain crafts.[115] Food and lodging venues adhered to the Park Service's southern mountain–style aesthetic, as seen in blueprint drawings for a "Typical Coffee Shop and Gas Station" on the Blue Ridge Parkway, which featured log exteriors, stone fireplaces, and casement-style windows.[116] The Bluffs Coffee Shop and Gas Station on the Parkway in Doughton Park, North Carolina, at milepost 241, from the 1950s, is very similar in execution to the proposed design for "typical" facilities.[117]

Ignoring the region's evolving agricultural history, rich culinary traditions, and long-existing tourism economy, park administrators manipulated the landscape to tell a story of rural isolation, simple rations, and hardworking pioneer families far removed from commercial development and exchange.[118] In the late 1930s, the National Park Service purchased land at the Peaks of Otter in Virginia for the scenic Blue Ridge Parkway, which would connect the Shenandoah National Park and the Great Smoky Mountains National Park.[119] Historian Anne Mitchell Whisnant states that by 1940 park officials had removed evidence of the active crossroads community that had once existed there, including the popular Hotel Mons and its busy dining room, leaving a retrofitted farmhouse-turned-log-cabin in an isolated field to reinforce the park's narrative of a pristine rural landscape.[120]

In 1949, the National Park Service received ownership of Flat Top Manor, the Blowing Rock, North Carolina, mountain estate of Moses and Bertha Cone, a gift from the Jewish textile magnates. The magnificent twenty-three-room colonial revival mansion and country estate was built in 1900 and overlooked nearly 3,500 acres of mountain land acquired by Moses Cone.[121] Bertha Cone entertained guests in a formal style, complete with silver service, starched linens, and multiple sets of fine china.[122] A butler served each course separately, "à la russe"—in the Russian style.[123] A typical dinner at Flat Top Manor began with a fruit course, followed by soup, an entrée such as lamb, and many vegetables grown on the estate.[124] A trained cook and staff oversaw Flat Top Manor's modern kitchen and pantry, which included the latest equipment and materials lauded by proponents of domestic science.[125]

In the early 1950s, the National Park Service turned the mansion (located beside the Blue Ridge Parkway) into a center featuring regional crafts managed by the Southern Highland Handicraft Guild. A museum of "pioneer life" was established on the grounds of the mansion/craft center. The story of a Jewish-owned mansion, of fortunes built from industry, and of wealthy southerners who vacationed and dined in the mountains did not fit the National Park Service's rural narrative for the Blue Ridge Parkway. Although absent from the park's interpretive materials and signage from the 1950s until recent efforts to present a more accurate history, the story of families like the Cones and their elegant entertaining and working agricultural estates is central to the historical narrative and culinary heritage of the mountain South.[126]

Southern Highlands Cookery

The popularity of the southern mountain brand and aesthetic is illustrated in *House and Garden*'s June 1942 "Southern Highlands Issue."[127] The magazine editors described "a whole pioneer way of life, a separate civilization" hidden "in the steeps of the mountains."[128] The unsullied values of the "isolated" southern mountains were transposed onto a design aesthetic, traditional crafts, new consumer products (furniture, textiles, ceramics), and regional "cookery." Emphasis on "the Anglo-Saxon traditions of Appalachian America" was a racial subtext of the mountain South brand in an era dominated by wartime ethnocentrism and white supremacy.[129]

A feature article, "Highlands Cookery," in the special *House and Garden* issue mixed mountain South and Old South narratives with "Pennsylvania Dutch," "olde" England, and colonial revival aesthetics: "Its cookery has overtones of the Deep South here, of the tidewater area there, of the plantation and the manor house: sweet potato pecan pie, hickory-smoked country ham and grits, banana fritters, spiced grapes, walnut strips, blueberry fool, peas and chinquapins, spiced beef, 'tipsy squire' and strawberry dumplings, even beaten biscuits."[130] Native American foods of the mountain South were largely ignored, except for a brief mention of "Cherokee bread, a pioneer survival made of corn, beans and acorns."[131] A photograph of a Southern Highlands–style dining room featured a stylish housewife in a "black playskirt with multicolor stripes adapted from Highlands 'Balmoral' petticoat," tossing a salad (oak salad bowl and servers), at a graceful walnut table "by Drexel," decorated with "Mansure's woven rope tablemats," earthenware pottery (Southern Highlanders, Inc.), "hurricane candlesticks," handwoven linens, "Heifetz Wood-Art," "Imperial Glass pinched tumblers," and "Fiddle Thread sterling silver flatware."[132] The caption reads, "Heartwarming simplicity is the essence of this supper table."[133] For consumers anxious to purchase this "simplicity," Southern Highlanders, Inc., a cooperative marketing organization for the Southern Highland Handicraft Guild, operated a sales shop in New York City in Rockefeller Center, as well as outlets in North Carolina, Tennessee, and Virginia.[134]

Dining, Southern Mountain–Style

Grand Hotels, Sanitariums, Inns

Popular magazines like *House and Garden* brought the attention of thousands of tourists and consumers to the resorts, inns, and sanitariums of western North Carolina. From larger venues such as the Grove Park Inn in Asheville and the High Hampton Inn in Cashiers to more modest venues such as Tapoco Lodge near the Tennessee border and the Nu-Wray Inn in Burnsville, a mixture of the Southern Highlands and Old South brands attracted tourists to vacation and eat in the mountain South. Motorists were a special market for commercial lodging and dining venues located near the Blue Ridge Parkway, which was under construction for nearly forty years between the 1930s and the 1970s. Since the early 1800s, well-to-do white families from the South Carolina Lowcountry had come to the North Carolina mountains to escape the summer heat, and this tradition continued well into the early twentieth century.[135] In the tourist season, Flat Rock was called the "Charleston of the Mountains."[136] When guests arrived in western Carolina, they encountered a range of mountain-style accommodations, from Swiss chalet lodges to rustic cabins and southern colonial homes transformed into quaint wayside inns. A variety of dining options from down-home tourist cafés to white-tablecloth restaurants reflected the tastes of both modest middle-class travelers and well-heeled summer people.

THE GROVE PARK INN: "THE FINEST RESORT HOTEL IN THE WORLD"

A vast network of southern "mineral resorts" fostered a tourist economy fueled by expanding train travel to the region.[137] Their focus on healing food and waters flourished nearly a hundred years before today's vibrant culinary revival in the mountain South.[138] At the turn of the twentieth century, western North Carolina was known for its sprawling Victorian-era inns and resorts, as well as spa treatments, mineral springs, and health food menus at hotels such as the Grove Park Inn. Edwin Wiley "E. W." Grove, a successful chemist from Tennessee, developed the magnificent mountainside property that became the Grove Park Inn in 1913.[139] His wealth came from the invention of Grove's Tasteless Chill Tonic, a medicinal quinine syrup for treating malaria and other ailments.[140] The large sales of the product—allegedly more bottles were sold than Coca-Cola—encouraged Grove to acquire property in Asheville, whose mountain climate was suitable for a health resort.[141] In an era plagued by "failing" diseases like tuberculosis, which led to weight loss and diminished strength, advertisements for the popular remedy guaranteed weight gain. Packaging and ads for the tonic featured a "laughing baby," actually a pig with the baby face of a child, emblazoned with the words, "GROVE'S TASTELESS CHILL TONIC: MAKES CHILDREN AND ADULTS AS FAT AS PIGS."

"Health food" products for the Grove Park Inn's guests came largely from the Battle Creek Food Company in Battle Creek, Michigan, where John Harvey Kellogg operated his famous late nineteenth-century sani-

Grand opening banquet, Grove Park Inn, Asheville, North Carolina, July 12, 1913. Secretary of State William Jennings Bryan delivered the opening address. Grove Park Inn Historical Photographs, 1913–20, photograph album #3, D. H. Ramsey Library, Special Collections, University of North Carolina–Asheville.

tarium. Fred Seely, Grove's son-in-law, who oversaw construction of the inn, adamantly stated that the Grove Park was not a sanitarium and did not welcome ill patients.[142] "It is a resting place for tired people who are not sick, who want good food well-cooked and digestible, with luxurious . . . surroundings."[143] In May 1925, Seely received a letter from Battle Creek describing a complimentary selection of whole grain, vegetarian products to be sent to the inn, such as "Branola"; "Minute Brew," a cereal drink; malted nuts; gluten biscuits; whole wheat wafers; fruit crackers; bran biscuits; "Protose," "vegetable meat rich as choicest beef"; and "Psylla," "seeds that provide bulk and lubrication."[144]

A local Asheville company, Biltmore Wheat-Hearts, also contacted Seely about carrying their "positively delicious" whole wheat cereal. H. M. Love, general manager of Wheat-Hearts, was anxious to add the Grove Park Inn as a patron of their product. In May 1925, Love assured Seely that eight hotels in Asheville had already agreed to print a special line on their menus: "Asheville is the home of Biltmore Wheat-Hearts."[145] The inn did order Wheat-Hearts, but things did not go quite as well as expected. Mr. Love believed the hotel steward (an employee who supervised food arrangements) was "set against" the product.[146] Fred Seely argued they had done everything possible to promote the cereal. "I don't see how we could possibly send Wheat-Hearts to guests who had not ordered it. The average patron of a Hotel is very quick to tell you that they know what they want."[147]

Fred Seely handled all the food accounts for the Grove Park Inn, ordering supplies from purveyors across the country, including Golden Blue Ribbon celery from the Eagle Celery Company in Kalamazoo, Michigan, Fleetwood Coffee from Chattanooga, Tennessee, the "best quality" beef, duck, lamb, and pork from T. T. Keane, a wholesale provisioner in Washington, D.C., and one hundred pounds of live lobsters from Blackford's at the Fulton Fish Market in New York City.[148] Apples of many varieties—Stayman, Rome Beauty, Starks Delicious, Winesap, Golden Delicious, and Black Ben Davis—came from nearby orchards in Saluda, Waynesville, and Valle Crusis.[149]

For guests with a sweet tooth or a traveler looking for a gift and reminder of their stay at the grand hotel, the news stand at the Grove Park Inn sold fine "bon bons" and chocolates "tied with lavender ribbon" from Huyler's, a New York City candy manufacturer.[150] John S. Huyler, the millionaire founder of the successful candy company, already had a North Carolina connection as a major donor to Montreat, a Christian retreat center in nearby Black Mountain, and as the investor behind the local Hotel Montreat, built in 1900.[151] Fred Seely requested Huyler's recipe for hot chocolate sauce to serve with Grove Park's ice cream: "As you are probably aware, we use your candies exclusively on our newsstand here, and as we want the very best chocolate sauce to be had, it occurred to us to ask you for your formula."[152] In just five days, the chocolate sauce recipe arrived from Huyler's with a note, "Subject: Chocolate Fudge. . . . This recipe is used at all of our stores."[153]

THE QUISISANA NATURE CURE SANITARIUM: "NO MEDICINE, NO OPERATIONS!"

Although Fred Seely was loath to care for sickly guests at the Grove Park Inn, Asheville had a number of sanitariums devoted to the "unwell," and each promoted its particular approach to healing. Diet was central to these regimes. The Quisisana Nature Cure Sanitarium on French Broad Avenue in Asheville advertised the "Latest German Method. No Medicine! No Operations!" and in 1899, published its own cookbook.[154] Lina Kuepper, secretary of the sanitarium, noted in the introduction to the *Quisisana Hygienic Cook Book*, "Since our hygienic cooking has . . . called forth so many favorable comments from our guests, because of its wholesomeness and palatableness, we decided to write a cook book. . . . Only a well nourished body can be healthy and strong, and in order to be well fed we ought to know what to eat and how to prepare it."[155] A sample breakfast menu differed little from a traditional, southern-style breakfast, except for the absence of real coffee: "fresh fruit, grits with sugar, cream, and milk, poached eggs, corn bread and honey, caramel cereal-coffee or Dr. Lahmann's cocoa."[156] Soup recipes included restorative fruit and vegetable broths such as cranberry or carrot, as well as instructions for an unappetizing "brown soup."[157] A sample dinner menu of roast beef served with red cabbage with apples and mashed potatoes suggests that a local cook was overseeing the German-inflected spa cooking. This cook begrudgingly added Dr. Lahmann's "Naehrsalz"—a special mineral salt derived from plants—when directed by the sanitarium staff.[158]

THE NU-WRAY INN—"HOT BISCUITS AWAIT YOU"

Middle-class travelers and tourists in search of a comfortable bed, a hearty meal, and pleasant mountain scenery, rather than a cure or an expensive night in the region's exclusive resorts, sought out the many smaller, affordable inns and dining venues in North Carolina's western mountains. Innkeepers understood the value of a good story to promote their businesses. The Nu-Wray Inn in Burnsville, North Carolina, claimed its southern provenance in the origin tale of founder Garrett Ray, who established a hotel on the village green in 1850.[159] When a descendant of Ray married a Wray, the facility was modernized and the name changed to the "Nu-Wray." By the 1940s, the early nineteenth-century log structure was refashioned into an expansive white-clapboard–covered inn with a brick-columned portico. Inside and out, the décor was southern-style colonial revival—a mishmash of oil lamps, hooked rugs, spinning wheels, iron kettles, and "Colonial Williamsburg blue"–painted trim.

Many hotels and inns in the mountains published souvenir cookbooks for guests. The preface of *Old-Time Recipes from the Nu-Wray Inn* (1940s) reinforced the inn's white southern heritage, especially in the dining room. "The same family for three generations has preserved the true spirit of Southern hospitality. Here it is that home-cured ham, fried chicken and hot biscuits await you."[160] Recipes in the inn's cookbook were a mix of plantation-style dishes, from "Southern Fried Chicken and Cream Gravy" and "Mis Sallie's Candied Yams" to more authentically local mountain foods, such as apple butter, fried cabbage, chow chow pickle relish, smothered lettuce, cured ham, and liver mush. A photograph of "Will, the colored chef" shows him clad in cook's whites carrying the hotel's choice hams from the smokehouse. The caption states, "He has been part of the Nu-Wray establishment over thirty years and is handing the art of southern cooking to his sons."[161] In another photo, white waitresses "Belle and Irene"—dressed in tidy uniforms with starched aprons—pose in the Nu-Wray's dining room, ready to serve guests the evening family-style meal.

Race divided service jobs in the segregated mountain hotels and inns. Black workers who came to the mountains found employment as cooks, chambermaids, handymen, and groundskeepers.[162] Local white women were hired largely as front desk staff, bookkeepers, and waitresses.[163] Four hundred black laborers were brought from Atlanta, Charleston, and Columbia to complete the heavy construction of the all-stone Grove Park Inn in Asheville in the 1910s.[164] After the hotel opened, African Americans were hired for the highly sought after positions of bellmen, porters, and wait staff.[165] Booker T. Sherrill, a black resident of Asheville, followed in the steps of his father, who worked at the Grove Park Inn for over forty years. In 1920, Sherrill was hired as a "bread and butter boy."[166] Despite low salaries and daily inspections of their uniforms and hygiene, black bellmen and wait staff valued the steady work.[167] Sherrill continued in the local hotel business for almost as long as his father.[168] Grove Park waiter Boyce Layton remembered Asheville's Waiter's Club, a local African American social club formed for area tourism workers and their families.[169]

TAPOCO LODGE: "GOOD THINGS TO EAT"

Railroad and highway expansion into the rugged logging regions of western North Carolina and eastern Tennessee brought industry and tourism further into the southern mountains. After hydroelectric dams were built in Graham and Swain Counties in western North Carolina in the late 1920s, the Aluminum Company of America (Alcoa) built the Tapoco Lodge on the Cheoah River in 1930 to use for company functions.[170] "Tapoco" was an acronym for the Tallassee Power Company, just one of several power companies that Alcoa purchased in the area. Financier Andrew W. Mellon, a leading investor in Alcoa, frequently stayed at Tapoco Lodge, allegedly built for him. The inn retains its original aluminum roof.

Less than fifteen miles to the west of Tapoco, the Tennessee Valley Authority (TVA) and Alcoa joined forces to build Fontana Dam on the Little Tennessee River in 1941, the largest dam in the eastern United States.[171] Alcoa needed a massive source of electricity to meet the rising wartime demand for aluminum. Thousands of Smoky Mountain residents lost homes, ancestral land, and access to family cemeteries as communities were flooded to create Fontana Lake and Fontana Dam. The TVA brought in "experimental trailer-houses" with built-in kitchens and furnishings as a housing option for the thousands of workers who lived in the newly created Fontana Village during construction of the dam. A cafeteria in the village provided over 6,000 meals a day for three round-the-clock shifts of workers on the accelerated wartime schedule.[172] Many TVA structures built in the region—temporary housing, grocery stores, restaurants, refreshment concessions in visitor centers servicing the new dams—were designed in the modernist style, reinforcing Atomic Age ideas of progress, organization, and efficiency. Fontana Dam was built in less than three years. By 1937, management at the Tapoco Lodge sidestepped any issues of local conflict surrounding the social upheaval tied to the hydroelectric dams. Promotional materials for Tapoco Lodge celebrated modernity, the romance of the mountains, the "great outdoors," Indian lore, and southern hospitality. The lodge advertised its "Wear-Ever Aluminum Utensils—The Mark of the Modern Kitchen."[173]

While praising its up-to-date equipment and facilities, Tapoco, like the Nu-Wray Inn, also emphasized ties to the Old South. The cookbook *Good Things to Eat at Tapoco Lodge* (1937) featured Eli "Trix" Williams, an African American porter, janitor, and lodge fireman who first came to the area with black construction workers who built the dams and local facilities. "Trix" is pictured in the cookbook ringing a dinner bell. "With his contagious laugh, always ready to meet the guests. He is always on time to ring the dinner bell, and gives it a mellow tone that no one else can."[174] With their friendly photographs and nicknames, African American cooks, wait staff, and porters like Eli Williams were one more attraction included in the advertisements for southern restaurants, hotels, and resorts from the 1920s until the 1970s. Duncan Hines listed the Tapoco Lodge in *Adventures in Good Eating* in the 1940s, describing it as a fisherman's paradise, although "the ladies enthuse over the place as well. . . . A good standard of Southern cuisine is maintained and in general life is very pleasant."[175]

THE HIGH HAMPTON INN: "SOUTHERN HOSPITALITY AT ITS FINEST"

Duncan Hines also praised the southern cuisine of another historic North Carolina mountain retreat, the High Hampton Inn in Cashiers, near the South Carolina border. Although the High Hampton Inn opened to the white public in the 1930s, former South Carolina governor and U.S. senator Wade Hampton III and his descendants owned the original estate and hunting lodge in the mid-nineteenth century. Under the ownership of the McKee family, the High Hampton has remained a beloved family summer haven in the mountain South, well known for "southern hospitality at its finest," including the inn's "famous fried chicken."[176] For more than thirty years, meals were served family-style at long tables in the dining room and guests were expected to dress for dinner in the evening.

When the High Hampton Inn was left out of Hines's annual guide in the 1950s, the hotel manager wrote to inquire. He began by thanking Mr. Hines for his praise of the inn's broiled chicken and then got to the issue at hand. Why had the inn been left out of *Adventures in Good Eating*? "Have we sinned in some manner or was it just an oversight? We have always been proud of our listing among the good places to eat and regret very much that we have been dropped. Perhaps you can tell us the reason."[177] It is possible there was an "oversight," or Mr. Hines happened to dine at the inn on an *off* night, but management of the High Hampton Inn clearly understood the dollar value of inclusion in Hines's annual guide. Today, promotional materials for the inn still reflect the mountain South and Old South narratives of southern hospitality, bountiful meals, family, tradition, and the majesty of nature.

"What's Wrong with Southern Cooking?"

Despite the national reputation of the South's many celebratory food narratives—from colonial and Old South to Lowcountry, Creole Country, and the mountain South—some critics took southern culture and its cuisine to task. Isabelle Post's critical essay "Dyspepsia in Dixie: The Truth about Southern Cooking" (1939) was published in H. L. Mencken's *American Mercury*. Mencken was well known for his diatribe against the South, in which he bemoaned its lack of culture.[178] In a similar voice, Post railed against southern cooking, its "rank rations and still ranker cooking," the absence of fresh vegetables and quality meat, its ill-trained service, and the incessant use of the frying pan.[179] She had no patience for the sentimental fans of southern cuisine, such as the families who returned year after year to High Hampton to enjoy the inn's "crystal clear mountain lake" and local rainbow trout. "Are you one of that vast American contingent whose mouths water at any reference to good ole Southern Cooking?" asked Post. "Do the strains of Dixie conjure up before your eyes visions of white-haired colonels and crinolined belles seated at a festive board groaning beneath mountains of delectable fried chicken, hot biscuits and sweet potato pie?"[180] She then took aim at "mammy," mocking her magical talents yet also commenting on the paltry wages of African American cooks: "Evidently those celebrated secret recipes have been so successfully concealed that not even the South can find them. Mammy's granddaughter, for the princely sum of three dollars a week, rules the kitchen today, and despite her wide, white smile and her general air of well-being, she is the world's worst cook."[181]

Tennessean Ralph McGill, the Pulitzer Prize–winning editor and publisher of the *Atlanta Constitution* and an avowed antisegregationist, enjoyed poking fun at southern cooking, particularly as a foil to the overly sentimental and romantic press that the region's cuisine enjoyed. Rather than maintain an unrelenting attack on the South's social and economic conditions and risk losing his readers, McGill "mixed his pitches" like a skilled baseball player, varying his columns with essays on food and a variety of other topics.[182] McGill's essay "What's Wrong with Southern Cooking?" appeared in the *Saturday Evening Post* in March 1949. Unlike Isabelle Post's heavy-handed attack on southern cuisine and the region's African American cooks, McGill engaged in a more insightful critique.

Condemning forces he believed were destroying southern cooking, McGill praised the region's home cooks and their unpretentious preparation of local foods. "Poor cooking has become standardized across the nation, but in the South it has been glamorized," wrote McGill. "The shadow of a legendary mammy and her skillet stands athwart it. Beneath the tinsel are grease and indigestion."[183] McGill blamed the "luridly lit Dixie Diners, Chicken shacks, Catfish Castles and Bar-B-Q traps" that unsuspecting tourists encountered on southern highways.[184] He believed "thrifty Midwesterners and New Englanders" operated a "goodly number" of these roadside venues.[185] McGill also criticized food writers, whom he described as "fiction writers who have turned to the field of food . . . luring good regional cooking into strange pastures."[186] He even knocked the work of "Brother [Duncan] Hines": "There is no reason to believe culinary surveys are any more infallible than political ones."[187] McGill lauded southern cooks who ignored critics' advice to make their food more cosmopolitan and continued to prepare the region's "indigenous vegetables, such as turnip greens, the lowly cowpea,

Lloyd's Motor Court and Restaurant, Myrtle Beach, South Carolina. 4-W-172, South Caroliniana Library, University of South Carolina, Columbia, S.C., photographs 12452.9.

sweet potatoes, rice and string beans . . . hot breads and desserts."[188] "The best Southern cooking is little known to the average Southerner," concluded McGill. "Yet I strongly suspect that this cooking is the best in the nation."[189]

Like Ralph McGill, journalist Clementine Paddleford, food editor of the *New York Herald Tribune* for thirty years, also celebrated the South's home cooks. Throughout her "gustatory wanderings" documenting America's regional food culture from the 1940s to the 1960s, Paddleford made an annual pilgrimage to the South, where she interviewed homemakers and chefs in Alabama, the Carolinas, Kentucky, Louisiana, Maryland, Mississippi, Tennessee, Virginia, and West Virginia.[190] She noted the "subtle differences" in the cooking traditions across the region and also helped dispel the notion that all southern food was greasy, heavy, and fried: "I have learned about mint juleps and syllabubs, southern hams, grits and gravy, hot breads and innumerable ways to do the yam and the ham. I learned about mustard greens cooked with a streak o' lean. I learned that contrary to general opinion real southern cooking does not have an excess of grease."[191] Despite her attention to detail and narrative, or perhaps because of it, Paddleford was seduced by the Old South.[192] She located southern food's origins in the "lavish tradition of plantation days."[193] The parlance of the plantation legend—descriptions of "landed gentry," "colonial pillars," and "great sideboards"—imbued southern travel and food writing of the era, and even Paddleford, a no-nonsense newspaperwoman, could not resist the most powerful of the region's food narratives.[194]

III

Modern South

The 1940s and the 1950s found southerners adjusting to a rapidly changing cultural landscape shaped by postwar affluence, industrialization, urbanization, agribusiness, and a vigorous consumer economy. John Egerton describes this period as a "hinge of time" in which the closing of a "constricted past" and the opening of an "expansive future" entwined.[1] The opportunity to voluntarily come to terms with its past would disappear in this era, requiring outside forces to intervene and force the South to protect and serve all its citizens.[2] New white-tablecloth restaurants, downtown cafeterias, five-and-dime store lunch counters, and fast-food venues were symbols of this evolving modern South, a contradictory world still mired in racism and class struggle. The insularity that previous generations had known in the South faded as soldiers returned from World War II. Two and a half million African American men registered for the draft when the war began. The African American draftees and volunteers who served their nation on the battlefields of Europe and in the South Pacific expected to be treated as full citizens when they came home.[3] They continued to be denied these rights and privileges in the South, despite the efforts of black newspapers and the "Double V" campaign that called for victory at home—the fight for civil rights—and abroad in the war effort.[4]

Civil rights activist Pauli Murray, a young law student at Howard University during the war, participated in an interracial sit-in at Thompson's Cafeteria near the White House on April 22, 1944.[5] The students held picket signs that read, "WE DIE TOGETHER? WHY CAN'T WE EAT TOGETHER?"[6] The infiltration of radio and television in the South exposed the brutal racial codes of Jim Crow segregation to the critique and view of outsiders. The completion of interstate highway systems, including I-95 from Maine to Florida, coupled with national campaigns to promote southern-branded products and the South as a tourist destination, drew consumers to the region. Modernity slowly cracked open the South's "closed society."

In the chapters that follow, powerful narratives of food give voice to this explosive era, as civil rights activists, antihunger reformers, politicians, counterculture revolutionaries, and feminist advocates fought to build a progressive South. In this vision, all southerners were equally recognized as citizens—blacks, whites, men, and women—and could expect the benefits of citizenship, including three meals a day for themselves and their children. Part 3 ends with a discussion of the late twentieth-century southern food movements born of the blending of nouvelle cuisine and "new American cuisine" in the 1980s and the locavore politics and culinary entrepreneurship of the contemporary South.

15

I'm Gonna Sit at the Welcome Table

SOUTHERN FOOD AND THE CIVIL RIGHTS MOVEMENT

> *I'm gonna sit at the welcome table one of these days. . . .*
> *I'm gonna feast on milk and honey one of these days. . . .*
> *I'm gonna sit at the Woolworth counter one of these days. . . .*
> *Hallelujah! I'm gonna sit at the Woolworth counter (and eat!).*
> *— "I'm Gonna Sit at the Welcome Table," from*
> We Shall Overcome! Songs of the Southern Freedom Movement,
> *compiled by Guy and Candie Carawan*

Stories of food in the civil rights era begin in the Jim Crow South of the 1930s and 1940s, with the daily injustices and horrors that African Americans experienced as a result of institutionalized racism and white supremacy. Consider the lynching of Rubin Stacy, murdered in Fort Lauderdale, Florida, on July 19, 1935, after he asked a white woman, Marion Jones, for food.[1] A homeless black tenant farmer, Mr. Stacy was hungry and desperate. He must have believed a southern sense of charity would prevail when he approached Jones's home. She screamed. Rubin Stacy was arrested and lynched by a mob, and his "corpse was hung in sight" of Jones's home, a clear reminder of the power of white patriarchy and its steely control of female purity.[2] The 1929–30 minutes for the Phillis Wheatley Club, an African American women's service organization in Charleston, South Carolina, reflected the recurring nightmare of lynching in the era and club women's attempts to provide food and other necessities to the families of victims: "We counted it a great privilege to be of service to all the orphans but it was a special privilege to be of service to two girls whose mother was lynched in Aiken, S.C. The women vied with each other to have one of these girls as her particular charge."[3]

With food as our lens in looking at this historic time of change, thousands of discrete "moments" reveal both the racial discrimination and the empowerment that African Americans experienced as the civil rights movement swept across the American South. Hundreds of segregated eating places dotted the southern landscape. Separate, and far from equal, school lunch programs existed for African American children. Black domestic workers and cooks took home "tote" pans of white families' leftover food as "payment." The capricious violence of white supremacist groups such as the Ku Klux Klan escalated as those who defied racial codes preventing blacks and whites from eating together were viciously punished. The era culminated in massive displays of citizen-led protest as justice was demanded by and for African Americans—including the right to eat in public facilities—through bus boycotts, sit-ins, and protest marches across the South.

As civil rights activists attempted to break open the segregated South, both quiet and bloody battles ensued at kitchen tables and lunch counters across the region. Kafi Robinson describes the daily injustices that her great-grandmother, Mrs. Roxie Johnson, experienced as a domestic worker in the home of a well-to-do white family in Oxford, North Carolina, in the 1950s.[4] A small Piedmont town near the Virginia border, Oxford was the location of the racially motivated murder of Henry Marrow, an African American man who was killed by local whites in May 1970.[5] The atmosphere of racial tension and violence that led to Marrow's murder had a deep history that reached back to slavery. This historical arc shaped the work experience of Mrs. Johnson and thousands of other domestic workers in the South. "Rain, sleet or snow, every day at the same time she walked to their house to cook, clean and take care of their kids," said Kafi Robinson.[6] "[Her great-grandmother] was like their mother in many ways. It got to the point where the kids wouldn't eat their real parents' [cooking]—they would wait until 'Mrs. Roxie' came."[7]

Novelist Kathryn Stockett's wildly popular but controversial novel *The Help* (2009) uses the segregated worlds ruled by white club women in 1950s Jackson, Mississippi, as the backdrop for her sentimental story about black domestic workers and the political coming-of-age of Eugenia "Skeeter" Phelan, a recent graduate of the University of Mississippi, who has literary ambitions.[8] The book and the film adaptation use black dialect, exaggerated southern accents, a sea of colorful party dresses, bridge luncheons, and country club functions to expose what black housekeepers endured in white homes. Beyond this flattening of a much-more-complex history, Stockett turns to food to give her black characters voice. The trope of a black servant duping a powerful white figure—of mammy playing the trickster—appears in *The Help*.[9] As historian Harry Watson explains, in this guise, mammy uses "enigma instead of defiance to defend her core."[10] In a climactic moment in *The Help*, housekeeper Minny Jackson taints her "famous chocolate pie" to seek revenge on her cruel employer, Hilly Holbrook, acting out the white fear of racial defilement by black hands. Here again, whites cannot resist the black cook's culinary powers.[11]

As Holbrook slowly enjoys her pie, devouring not one, but *two* pieces, she asks, "What do you put in here, Minny, that makes it taste so good?"[12] Minny Jackson reveals the "special" ingredient: "I tell her to eat my shit."[13] The moment is dramatic—who doesn't like to see an evil Junior Leaguer get her comeuppance—yet it reduces the very real agency and courage that black women exhibited during the civil rights movement to a catfight between mean white girls and their vulnerable black female prey. In the real Mississippi rather than in the Hollywood version, revenge was never as sweet as the moment African Americans secured the right to vote, worked an eight-hour day for fair wages, sat wherever they chose on a bus, and entered a restaurant and were served like anyone else.

In her iconic civil rights–era memoir, *Coming of Age in Mississippi* (1968), author Ann Moody describes a more accurate tableside moment of racial awakening in her childhood as she accompanied her mother, a domestic worker, to the white home where she cooked and cleaned. "One Saturday the white lady let Mama bring us to her house," wrote Moody. "We sat on the back porch until the white family finished eating. Then Mama brought us in the house and sat us at the table and we finished up the food. It was the first time I had seen the inside of a white family's kitchen. That kitchen was so pretty, all white and shiny. "If Mama only had a kitchen like this of her own," I thought, "she would cook better food for us, too."[14] Not once, but a thousand times over, incidents like this occurred in the white kitchens of the segregated South. With few employment options beyond housework and cooking, black women were trapped in unbearable positions that provided only minimal pay to help support their families. Change and resistance lay in youth like Moody, who witnessed these scenes and later channeled anger into activism in the civil rights movement.

Jim Crow and the Southern Table, at Home and on the Road

Eating and drinking were at the heart of the exclusionary Jim Crow laws that dictated "separate but equal" facilities for blacks and whites. In the private domestic worlds of the segregated South, black cooks could prepare and serve food to white employers and their families but not eat with them, a ritual that suggested familiarity and equality.[15] But what to do in public about eating and the "problem" of a rising middle class of black southerners who could suddenly participate in the region's consumer culture as paying *citizen*-shoppers and diners? Whites were increasingly threatened by blacks' changing economic position in society, and also by their demeanor. The old plantation-style deference exhibited by blacks toward whites was fading.

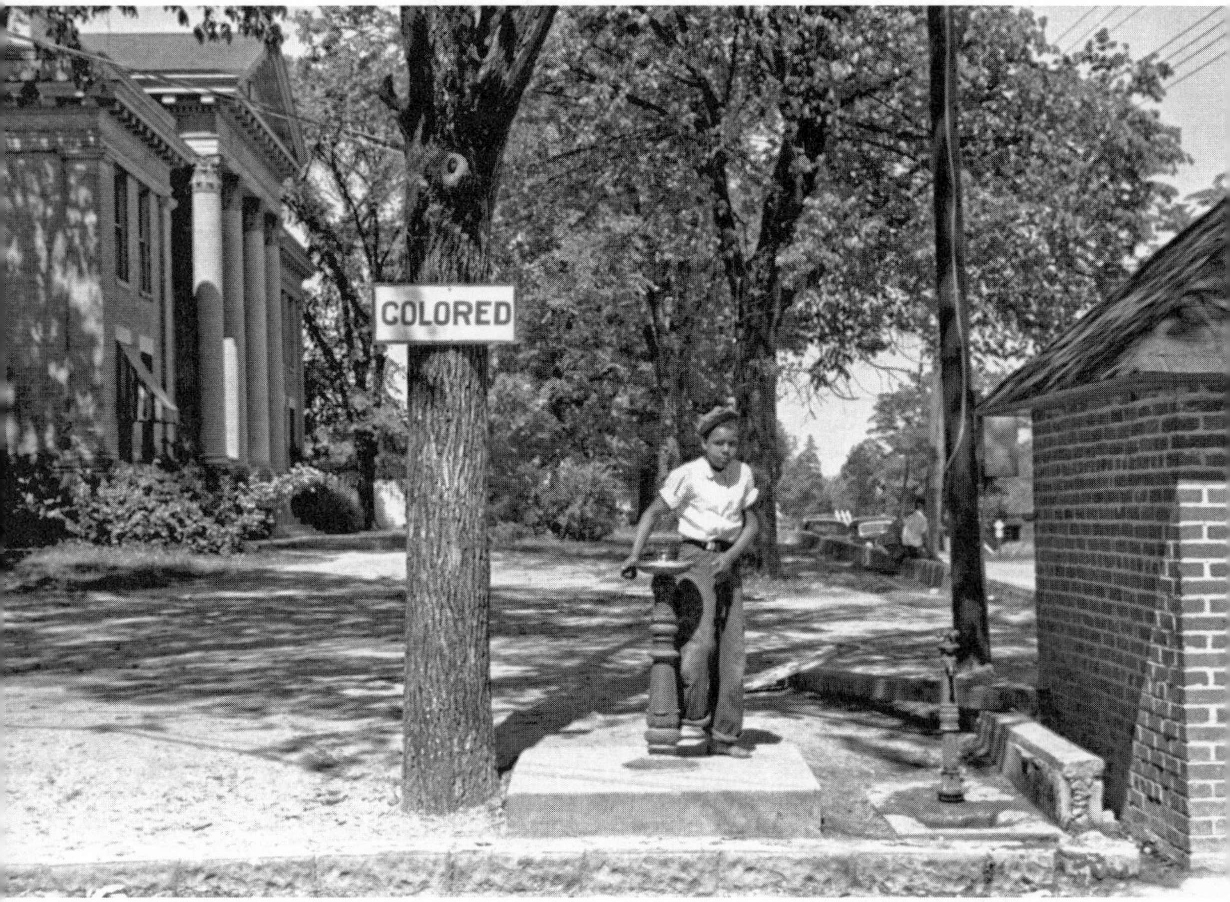

"Drinking fountain on the county courthouse lawn, Halifax, North Carolina." Photograph by John Vachon, April 1938. LC-USF33-T01-001112-M1 (b&w film nitrate neg.), U.S. Farm Security Administration/Office of War Information, Prints and Photographs Division, Library of Congress, Washington, D.C.

Persistent Jim Crow laws offered a solution for whites who would not release the mythology of "our Negroes." If blacks could not be controlled completely, as they were in slavery, Jim Crow at least allowed whites to control their access to the material South and the rights of citizenship. "Eating, a particularly intimate yet increasingly public activity, was especially controlled," says Grace Hale. "African Americans dined at blocked-off, racially marked, and inferior tables, or, as was often the case with department stores that otherwise welcomed their dollars, they did not eat at all."[16] While blacks and whites continued to mix in the shopping districts of southern cities and towns, the restaurants, cafés, dime store lunch counters, and recreational areas remained segregated.[17] City ordinances regulating segregation increasingly conflated health and sanitation codes with white fears about moral propriety and racial purity.[18] In Birmingham, segregation ordinances in the

1950s outlawed whites and blacks from being served in the same room in a restaurant, unless they were separated by a "7-foot or higher" partition.[19] The law also stipulated separate street entrances for whites and blacks into segregated dining facilities.

Traveling for middle-class African Americans was particularly challenging. The late distinguished historian John Hope Franklin remembered a car trip with his wife, Aurelia, on December 7, 1941, when they drove from Charleston, South Carolina, to Raleigh, North Carolina. They did not learn about the Japanese attack on Pearl Harbor until they arrived at home after many hours on the road. Black-owned service stations were difficult to find between Charleston and Raleigh, so the Franklins packed a lunch and "made do," as did other black families who traveled in the segregated South.[20] "You took your life into your hands every time you went out on the road," he said.[21]

The Negro Motorist Green-Book provided an important service to African Americans like the Franklins, who found Duncan Hines's segregated *Adventures in Good Eating* of little use in their travels.[22] Victor Hugo Green, a former postal carrier in Harlem who created a travel agency in the late 1930s to serve African Americans, developed the guide for his clients. He wrote in the book's introduction: "The Jewish press has long published information about places that are restricted."[23] For seventy-five cents, travelers could purchase Green's listing of businesses that served African Americans across the country, including restaurants, hotels, and taverns. For example, until the 1930s, lodging and concessions in Virginia's Shenandoah National Park were for "Whites Only." Pressure from Secretary of Interior Harold Ickes forced the National Park Service to develop facilities for African Americans, such as the "Lewis Mountain Picnic Grounds for Negroes," which opened in 1939.[24] An architectural blueprint for a "Tea Room and Motor Service Station" on the Blue Ridge Parkway in Franklin County, Virginia, designated segregated restroom facilities for "white ladies," "white men," "colored women," and "colored men."[25] The restrooms for blacks were smaller and relegated to the far corner of the building. Victor Green discontinued his guidebook after the passage of the Civil Rights Act in 1964.

The Club from Nowhere Cooking for the Movement

The attention of the nation turned to Montgomery, Alabama, on December 1, 1955, when Rosa Parks, a forty-two-year-old black seamstress and civil rights activist, refused to give up her seat in the back of a crowded city bus to a white man and was arrested. That day marked a historic turning point in the evolving civil rights movement, as Montgomery's black community, from well-known leaders such as Ralph Abernathy and Martin Luther King Jr., to little-known figures such as Georgia Theresa Gilmore, a local cook, organized mass meetings and bake sale fund-raisers to protest the city's segregation laws.

Georgia Gilmore recalled listening to a broadcast of the local black radio station when Rosa Parks was arrested: "They decided to get together because we had gotten tired of having so many things happen and nothing being done about it. . . . They decided that they wouldn't ride the bus until they could get something done about it."[26] Gilmore and other black women organized the highly effective carpools and pick-up stations for workers without transportation during the 381-day boycott.[27] As service workers, cooks, and housekeepers, Montgomery's 40,000 black residents were the primary customers of the bus system. If they did not ride the buses, there was no business.

Georgia Gilmore walked to and from the National Lunch Company every day during the boycott until she was fired after testifying in court in Montgomery.[28] Undeterred, she cooked from her own home and organized the "Club from Nowhere," a name chosen to ensure the anonymity and safety of its members. The working-class black women "from nowhere" raised funds to support the carpools by selling homemade pies and cakes at local beauty parlors, laundromats, and gas stations. Each week, Gilmore reported the club's success to the standing ovations of volunteers gathered at the mass meetings led by the Reverend King.[29] The pie and cake money bought station wagons used in the boycott carpools. Gilmore eventually turned part of her home into a public dining area, thanks to encouragement and start-up funds from King and the Montgomery Improvement Association, which coordinated the boycott. She created a "back door restaurant," where black and white customers—attorneys, activists, barbers, doctors, preachers, and politicians alike—could enjoy her fried chicken, pork chops, stuffed bell peppers, macaroni and cheese, and chitlins.[30] In November 1956, the U.S. Supreme Court declared segregation on public buses to be unconstitutional, and the boycott ended.

Georgia Gilmore continued to feed the civil rights movement. Ten years after the Montgomery bus boycott, she prepared food for participants in the historic Selma to Montgomery March. By the time protesters finally reached the state capitol on Thursday, March 25, 1965, they were 25,000-strong. "You cannot be afraid if you want to accomplish anything," said Gilmore. "You got to have the willing, the spirit and above all, you got to have the get-up."[31] Gilmore died on the twenty-fifth anniversary of the Selma to Montgomery March as she was preparing food for those who gathered to commemorate the historic day.[32] The

Alabama Historical Association erected a historical marker at the site of Georgia Gilmore's home in 1995. The inscription reads: "Her culinary skills continued to aid the cause of justice as she actively worked to encourage civil rights for the remainder of her life."[33]

Lunch Counter Wars The Sit-In Movement

Lunch counters and cafés, the seemingly benign settings of everyday life in the South, became battlegrounds of the civil rights movement. "Food means power, power means food," wrote American studies scholar Warren Belasco. "And power means conflict, even violence."[34] Sit-ins, a form of nonviolent, direct-action protest, staged from the 1940s on, were used in the South to protest the Jim Crow racial practices and laws that did not allow blacks to sit down in public and private eating venues. Blacks were sometimes allowed to eat in a separate section or, in many places, not allowed inside and forced to purchase food at a walk-up window at the side or in the back. The omnipresent "Whites-Only" and "Colored" signs symbolized the racial subjugation of southern blacks. The Golden Gate Quartet, a popular African American singing group from Norfolk, Virginia, imagined a world free of these rules in their 1947 hit "No Restricted Signs in Heaven":

Knock a Knock a Knock a Knock—knock knock,
Folks were knocking at the Pearly Gates . . .
Askin' 'bout the rooms and 'bout the rates.
Old St. Peter was the official greeter,
He was present to let them in;
Some looked down 'cause their skins was brown,
But Pete hollered with a great big grin:
"You're welcome! Welcome! There are
NO RESTRICTED SIGNS IN HEAVEN,
"And there's no selected clientele,
"There are NO RESTRICTED SIGNS IN HEAVEN,
"And, brother, brother, that goes double for Halleluyah!"[35]

During a sit-in, protesters simply sat down inside the eating establishment, politely asked to be served, and remained in place after they were denied service. Most sit-in participants were arrested for trespassing. The sit-in protesters became steadfast soldiers in the fight for the most basic of civil rights—unhindered access to "public accommodation," or to facilities that served the general public. After meeting with student leaders of the sit-in movement at Shaw University in Raleigh, North Carolina, in 1960, activist Ella Baker spoke of their conviction: "Sit-in and other demonstrations are concerned with something much

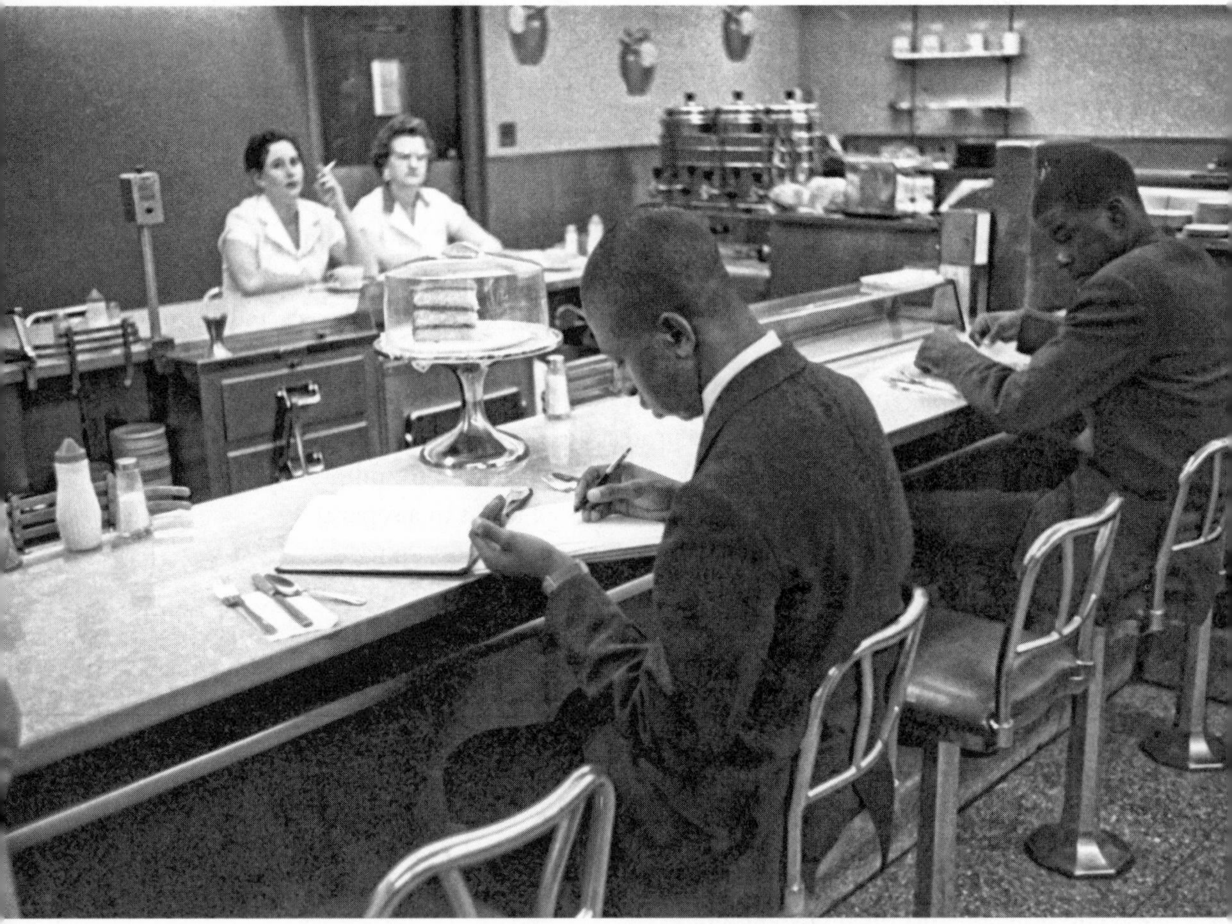

African American students from Saint Augustine College study while participating in a sit-in at a lunch counter reserved for white customers in Raleigh, North Carolina, February 10, 1960. © Bettmann/CORBIS.

bigger than a hamburger or even a giant-sized Coke."[36] They were fighting for "First Class Citizenship," and being spat on, jailed, and threatened with physical violence would not hold them back.[37]

Sit-ins took place at lunch counters throughout the South, especially at five-and-dime stores like Woolworth's and Kress Stores, because they were popular public venues. Boycotts of the stores and nearby merchants after the sit-ins deepened the economic impact of denying service to blacks, who were an important clientele for downtown shopping districts. A particular irony of the segregated lunch counters and restaurants was that the food in the midst of these violent confrontations was a product of the shared culinary heritage of black and white southerners. Rosa Washington, an African American worker, was sweeping the white waiting room of the segregated Birmingham, Alabama, Greyhound Bus Station on Mother's Day, May 10, 1961, when a group of civil rights activists—the first Freedom Riders—arrived and entered the building. In the panic that ensued, she remembered that the first thing the white restaurant manager did was "yank the wiring" of the water fountains out of the wall. "That brought a lump to my throat . . . that meant no cool water for white or black."[38] Next he rushed down to the restaurant, demanding that the workers remove food from the steam tables and leave menus out for the whites. "That brought tears, because black and white hands prepared the food, black and white hands were removing the food, but black and white could not sit in the same room and eat the food."[39]

Virginia Lee Williams was one of the Royal 7, a group of young African Americans who protested the whites-only dining room at the Royal Ice Cream Parlor at 904 North Roxboro Street in Durham, North Carolina, on June 23, 1957.[40] The daughter of a sharecropper in eastern North Carolina, Williams came to Durham in 1956 and found a job in the kitchen of the segregated Duke Hospital. She lived in the Harriet Tubman YWCA, where she and her friends became involved in the growing civil rights movement. Led by the Reverend Douglas Moore of the Asbury Temple Methodist Church, they decided to integrate a restaurant and chose Royal Ice Cream because of its location in one of Durham's black neighborhoods.[41] Mary Elizabeth Clyburn Hooks remembered eating ice cream at the popular store, but never in the main dining room.[42] "They were located in the middle of a colored section [of town]," said Hooks, "but they had signs up on the doors. And they had [a] colored side. But the colored side, when you go over there, you couldn't sit down. You'd just get your stuff. And another thing—it was dirty and dingy."[43] The demonstrators were arrested, which led to lifetimes of activism on picket lines to fight for black civil rights.

Virginia Williams retired in December 2009 after forty years of serving college students in a Chapel Hill cafeteria.[44] Williams was present at Martin Luther King's "I Have a Dream" speech at the March on Washington in 1963, and she gathered with friends in 2008 to watch Barack Obama take the oath of office as the first African American president of the United States.[45] A state highway historic marker commemorating the Royal Ice Cream civil rights protest in June 1957—North Carolina's first sit-in—was dedicated at the site of the restaurant on November 29, 2009.

The segregation of lunch counters was contested in a Woolworth's in downtown Greensboro, North Carolina, on Monday, February 1, 1960, considered to be the "inauguration" date of the modern civil rights revolution and the student movement in America.[46] Four seventeen-year-old African American students at the Agricultural and Technical College of North Carolina (A&T)—Ezell Blair Jr., Franklin McCain, Joseph

McNeil, and David Richmond—staged a sit-in at the whites-only lunch counter. They were prepared for this day, raised by parents, teachers, and preachers in a black community that emphasized education, civil rights activism, and personal excellence.[47]

The four A&T students entered the store about 4:30 P.M., purchased a few school supplies, quietly sat down at the Woolworth's lunch counter, ordered coffee, and were refused service.[48] Showing their receipts from their earlier purchases, Ezell Blair said, "I beg your pardon, but you just served us at [that] counter. Why can't we be served at the [food] counter here?"[49] Throughout the week, hundreds of students from local black colleges and a few white students—all tastefully dressed and carrying study materials with them—joined the protest in a demonstration of solidarity. F. W. Woolworth's national headquarters issued a statement that the company policy was "to abide by local custom."[50] The sit-in spread to the nearby S. H. Kress store. In April, both stores closed their lunch counters. In the following months, over 50,000 people participated in sit-ins at lunch counters in more than fifty cities across the South. On July 21, 1960, the Woolworth's management informed the city that the store would "serve all properly dressed and well-behaved people."[51] Woolworth's employees Charles Bess, Mattie Long, Susie Morrison, and Jamie Robins were the first African Americans to eat at the lunch counter, on Monday, July 25, 1960.[52] The Kress lunch counter was integrated on the same day.[53]

The Congress of Racial Equality (CORE) helped local groups organize nonviolent demonstrations—largely sit-ins and picketing—at southern dime stores and cafés that continued to operate segregated lunch counters, including Grant, Kress, Kresge, McCrory, and Woolworth's. The April 1961 issue of the CORE newsletter, the "CORE-LATOR," included reports of efforts to make "Kresge's 100%."[54] The national variety store had desegregated all but three of its southern stores. CORE encouraged its members to support Kresge stores that had successfully integrated by "patronizing the lunch counters and by commending the local managers."[55] Registered as minority stockholders, CORE staff members also attended annual stockholder meetings of the variety chain stores in the early 1960s, where they spoke out about the corporations' discriminatory racial policies.[56]

The F. W. Woolworth's store in Greensboro, North Carolina, closed permanently in 1993. On the final day of business, the A&T students who had led the 1960 sit-in, Blair, McCain, McNeil, and Richmond, returned and ate a meal at the counter together.[57] The 1960s menu prices were honored.[58] Today, the old "F. W. Woolworth Co." at 132 South Elm Street is the location of the International Civil Rights Center and Museum, which opened on February 1, 2010, the fiftieth anniversary of the sit-in. The museum exhibition includes a section of the original lunch counter, with period plates, silverware, milk shake machines, and cash register, as well as a double-sided Coca-Cola machine used in segregated waiting rooms—one side for whites, and the other for "colored." Some soda machines from the era sold cokes to "whites only" and were modified with a segregated water fountain on the side for blacks.

Ann Moody participated in one of the most violent and highly publicized sit-ins of the 1960s. As Moody and her friends from Tougaloo College sat in protest at the lunch counter of the Woolworth's store on Capitol Street in downtown Jackson, Mississippi, on May 28, 1963, an angry mob of white high school students gathered behind them. Police stood outside and watched as the enraged students pulled the protesters from their seats and beat them severely. Moody described the scene in her memoir: "We were called a little bit of everything. . . . A couple of boys took one end of [a] rope and made it into a hangman's noose. Several attempts were made to put it around our necks. The crowd grew as more students and adults came in for lunch. . . . We bowed our heads [to pray], and all hell broke loose. . . . The mob started smearing us with ketchup, mustard, sugar, pies, and everything on the counter."[59] The very food the protesters had peacefully demanded the right to order and be served was used to humiliate and hurt them. The politicization of food in the American South was never more vivid, as newspapers and television publicized this incident around the world.

"Let Us Break Bread Together on Our Knees"

The Freedom Rides

Led by CORE director James Farmer and civil rights activist James Peck, carefully selected and trained volunteers—seven blacks and six whites and three journalists—participated in the historic Freedom Rides that left Washington, D.C., for "points South" on May 4, 1961.[60] The purpose of the Freedom Rides was to test compliance with the December 1960 Supreme Court *Bruce Boynton v. Virginia* ruling that banned segregated facilities for interstate bus and train passengers. Farmer explained: "Participants will challenge every form of segregation met by the bus passenger: in the buses themselves, in restaurants, and in rest rooms. Whites will sit and eat in 'Colored Sections' and Negroes will sit and eat in 'White Sections.' They will refuse to accept segregation in any form: if need be they will accept threats, violence, and jail sentences."[61]

The worst violence of the 1961 Freedom Rides unfolded outside Anniston, Alabama, when white vigilantes attacked the bus near a road-

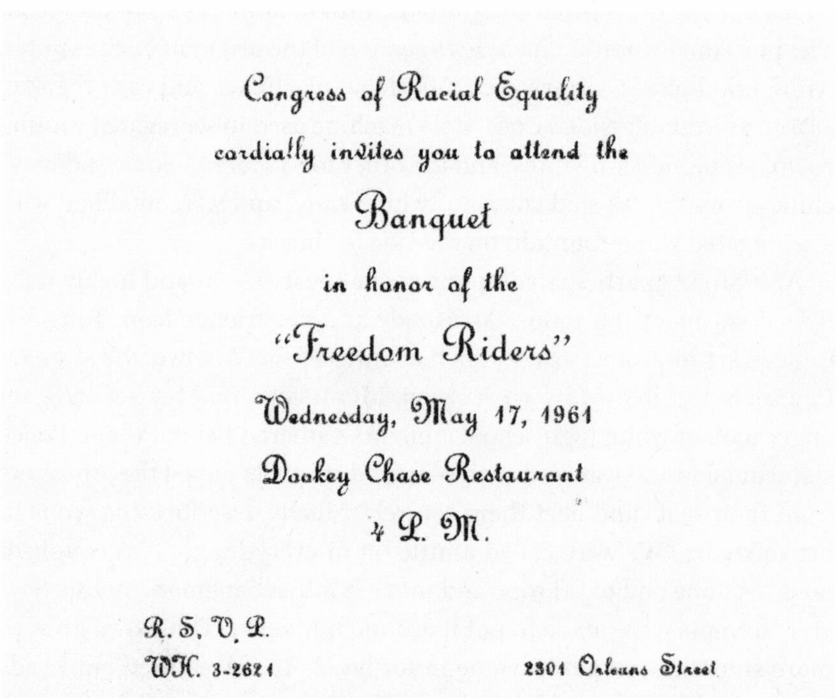

Congress of Racial Equality
cardially invites you to attend the
Banquet
in honor of the
"Freedom Riders"
Wednesday, May 17, 1961
Dookey Chase Restaurant
4 P. M.

R. S. V. P.
WH. 3-2621

2301 Orleans Street

Banquet invitation in honor of Freedom Riders, Dooky Chase Restaurant, 2301 Orleans Street, New Orleans, Louisiana, May 17, 1961, sponsored by the Congress of Racial Equality. Constance B. Harse Papers, Amistad Research Center, New Orleans, La.

side gas station and grocery. A flaming bundle of rags was thrown into the bus through a broken window damaged earlier by violent crowds at the Anniston bus station.[62] The vehicle instantly filled with smoke and fire, trapping the passengers as the mob held the door shut.[63] "They tried to cook the people," wrote Bernard Lafayette, a founder of the Student Nonviolent Coordinating Committee (SNCC).[64] Men in the crowd yelled, "Burn them alive" and "Fry the goddamn niggers."[65] When a gas tank exploded, the mob retreated, and the remaining riders who had not been able to escape through windows staggered from the bus.[66] The second Trailways bus drove into another nightmarish scene in Alabama. At the Trailways terminal in Birmingham, several of the Freedom Riders attempted to enter the whites-only waiting room and sit at the lunch counter.[67] They were severely beaten by a white mob. Birmingham police commissioner Eugene "Bull" Connor carefully orchestrated the logistics of the attack on the riders, with the help of white supporters, from local police to Klansmen to "upstanding" civic leaders.[68]

When no bus driver could be found to drive the battered riders to Montgomery, CORE leaders temporarily ended the Freedom Ride and flew the remaining riders to New Orleans. Chef Leah Chase had planned a banquet in honor of the Freedom Riders for the evening of their arrival, but after the violence in Alabama prevented the buses from continuing on to Louisiana, the special dinner never occurred.[69] Dooky Chase, the beloved Creole restaurant in New Orleans's Treme neighborhood, had long been an important meeting and eating place for civil rights leaders in the city.[70]

Freedom Summer "Love, Housing, Food, Fellowship Must Be Met by Us Whom They Come to Help"

The volatile reaction of whites across the South during Freedom Summer 1961 had less to do with the loss of racial control than the perception that the protesters were "outside agitators."[71] White segregationists built on Cold War fears, connecting the civil rights activists to an imagined communist plot to "subvert the Southern way of life."[72] "Distant enemies"—whether communists, "northern liberals," or members of the National Association for the Advancement of Colored People (NAACP)—were seen as the troublemakers behind the civil rights movement, particularly as the direct-action campaigns, including the Freedom Rides and sit-ins at lunch counters, ramped up in the 1960s.[73]

In stark contrast to the belligerence and fear of conservative white southerners were individuals like Clarie Collins Harvey, a local African American businesswoman and activist in Jackson, Mississippi, who organized Womanpower Unlimited soon after the first Freedom Riders arrived in the state. Harvey drew on the skills and talents of black women and their churches, who provided food, clothing, housing, and fellowship for out-of-state civil rights workers. Womanpower Unlimited partnered with other civil rights organizations to establish "freedom houses" as living quarters for the activists engaged in voter registration drives throughout the state.[74] Supplying nourishing hot meals was an important aspect of this women-led activism, which literally and spiritually fed the movement.

Seeking support for the 1964 "FOOD PROJECT" of Womanpower Unlimited, Clarie Harvey and her female officers wrote donors expressing gratitude for their contributions. She explained that civil rights activists remained in the state to strengthen the Mississippi Freedom Democratic Party—the black delegates who challenged the all-white Mississippi delegation to the Democratic National Convention in Atlantic City, New Jersey, in 1964—but to also tutor students, attend college, establish community centers, and rebuild churches destroyed in Klan-related church bombings.[75] "Their need for love, housing, food, fellowship must be met by us whom they come to help," wrote Harvey. "May we urge you to seek additional funds and bring to us more food supplies so that the project may continue."[76] An article in the fall 1964 Womanpower Unlimited newsletter reported that a local black church was feeding up to forty volunteers a day: "Visitors working here in the Jackson community MUST feel our support of their efforts. Supplying them with well-balanced meals has been proven to be of substantial help to their well-being."[77]

"Wednesdays in Mississippi," a project founded in 1964 by Dorothy Height, president of the National Council of Negro Women, and Jewish philanthropist and activist Polly Spiegel Cowan (whose children were Freedom Summer volunteers), similarly sought support from American women for the civil rights movement in Mississippi.[78] From 1964 to 1967, interracial and interfaith teams of "Wednesdays Women" met in Mississippi, where they formed alliances, raised funds, and distributed supplies, including food, to antipoverty projects throughout the state.

Adhering to the "jail—no bail" policy of CORE and SNCC, more than 300 Freedom Riders from across the country and a number of local supporters spent the summer of 1961 in Mississippi's dreaded Parchman Penitentiary, including Carol Ruth Silver, a twenty-three-year-old Jewish woman from Boston.[79] As Silver weighed her decision to participate in the Freedom Rides, she recalled a talented black professor she had studied with in the North: "I could sit in his office, across a desk littered with term papers and erudite books, trying to catch and hold the ideas and criticisms he was throwing at me ten miles a second. But he could not eat in the same restaurant with me in Mississippi."[80] On June 2, 1961, Silver boarded a bus in New York City for Jackson, Mississippi. Minutes after she and other Freedom Riders walked into the "Colored" waiting room of the Jackson bus station, on June 7, they were arrested and sent to the city jail.[81]

Silver spent forty days in jail in Mississippi, first in the Hinds County Jail and then in Parchman, the state prison. Silver described her initial encounter with southern food prepared by experienced black cooks: "June 7, 1961: It was now dinnertime and I had my first experience with prison food. Surprisingly, it was hot, and the three biscuits were excellent. . . . June 8, 1961: My second prison meal, breakfast—at about 6 A.M.—was three more biscuits, some thin molasses syrup, grits and coffee. Aside from the grits, which I ignored studiously, I was almost embarrassed to pronounce it much to my liking. The coffee was black and sweet and not too strong, the biscuits were light and hot, and the syrup in which they were to be dipped was quite palatable."[82] Civil rights activist Joan Trumpauer noted the same prison food in her diary that summer—a monotonous diet of "grits & gravy," prunes, hot biscuits, hominy, black-eyed peas, beans, cabbage, cornbread and molasses—food not dissimilar to that of Mississippi's working poor.[83]

Bernard Lafayette was also in Parchman Penitentiary during the summer of 1961. Lafayette remembered Reverend King's philosophy: "Martin Luther King had a method about this thing—an incredible philosophy about how you defeat your opponents and people who would be your enemies by making them your friends."[84] Lafayette and his activist friends "experimented" with King's philosophy at Parchman. "We made friends with the folk who brought us the food. . . . We called them 'professor' because we were students. We honored them. . . . Now some people don't believe this, but they brought us ice cream at night. . . . The jailer in Jackson would send a trusty out to get some ice cream."[85] (A "trusty" was a "trusted" convict, who was granted special privileges.) The jailer had a high school–age daughter and was uncertain how to help her get into college. Lafayette and other imprisoned college students shared helpful advice with him. The trusty hid the pints of ice cream for the students in his mop bucket. "We had ice cream every night. Mississippi jail—you got to know how to work it," said Lafayette. "I am telling you now that when we got ready to leave the jail he looked like he was losing his best friends. . . . I remember the very words; he said, 'Y'all come back to see me hear?'"[86]

When Carol Silver and her cohort were released from Parchman on July 15, they experienced the full hospitality of Mississippi's black community at a dinner prepared by the women of the church in Jackson: "We were taken to the house of a Rev. Mays, where some of the church ladies had prepared a dinner of fried chicken, coleslaw, potato salad, etc., the works. And for dessert we had peach ice cream! It was Fourth of July ten times over, even without the chocolate sprinkles."[87]

In the months following Freedom Summer in 1961, members of the Justice Department persuaded officials at the Interstate Commerce Commission to outlaw separate facilities for blacks and whites at bus and train terminals. Long after the ruling was instituted, on November 1, 1961, white civic leaders and businesspeople in southern cities and towns defied the policy by maintaining segregated facilities. In Greenville, Mississippi, "two white air force couples [a U.S. Air Force Base was located outside of town] and two Negro voter registration workers" were arrested when they tried to eat together at a local black-owned restaurant.[88] Municipal court judge Earl Solomon Sr. sentenced them to fifty-five-dollar fines and thirty days in jail and then suspended their jail sentences, "after a stern warning [that] the terms would be reinstated if the couples tried again to seek services at a Negro café."[89]

Earl Solomon's sentence upheld the state law of Mississippi while only slapping the wrists of the offenders and warning them of the dangerous repercussions of their actions. As a southern Jew and a municipal judge appointed by the city council, Solomon walked a difficult line between conforming to white racial attitudes and opposing segregation, yet Greenville was unusually enlightened in its racial attitudes.[90] "Although segregation was the law," explains David Orlansky, a retired U.S. magistrate judge in northern Mississippi, "blacks voted freely in Greenville and the rest of Washington County."[91] White leaders in Greenville hoped to avoid the demonstrations, arrests, and violence occurring in other cities and towns throughout the state.[92] The local presence of Pulitzer Prize–winning liberal journalist Hodding Carter Sr., a strong civil rights advocate and the editor of the progressive *Delta-Democrat Times*, exerted something of a "moderating influence" on the racial politics of Greenville and the county.[93]

In a case that revealed the clash of federal and state laws, Mayor M. C. Billingsley of Winona, Mississippi, agreed to obey the new Interstate Commerce ban and integrate the segregated waiting room in the local Trailways bus station.[94] Plans were in place to enlarge and improve the former "Negro Waiting Room" to serve both races. Although the café remained "whites-only," by integrating the waiting room Billingsley defied his own state's segregation laws and became the first Mississippi official to comply with a federal integration order. "We're going along with what Trailways thinks is the best for us," said the mayor. "I don't like it, but it looks like the best of the two evils."[95]

Chapel Hill "We Do Not Picket . . . Just Because We Want to Eat"

In North Carolina, the news of the February 1, 1960, sit-in at the Greensboro Woolworth's store and the demonstrations that followed reverberated throughout the state. The fight for "equal accommodation" rippled outward from Greensboro to touch eating establishments at the state's flagship campus in Chapel Hill. The first protests in Chapel Hill were instigated not by college students but by black high school students from segregated Lincoln High School, who walked into Colonial Drug at 450 Franklin Street on February 28, 1960, and sat down in a booth reserved for white clientele.[96] John Carswell, owner of the drugstore and lunch counter and a 1943 UNC graduate, refused to serve the students, who were arrested and charged with trespassing.[97] This event inspired an active campaign of picketing, sit-ins, marches, fasts, and arrests involving students from UNC and nearby North Carolina College in Durham (now North Carolina Central University), a few dedicated faculty, the black community in Chapel Hill, and a small number of local white citizens.[98] A leaflet from March 1960 seeking UNC students to participate as picketers explained the motivations of the group: "WHY WE

PICKET—WE DO NOT PICKET . . . just because we want to eat. We can eat at home or walking down the street. . . . WE DO PICKET . . . to enlist the support of all (whatever their color) in getting services in business places that will grant us dignity and respect."[99]

Karen Parker, the first black female graduate of UNC in 1965, was an active participant in the sit-in movement.[100] Parker kept a diary in a UNC spiral notebook describing her feelings as an African American student and her participation in the local civil rights movement. In December 1963, Parker and two friends attempted to integrate Leo's, a restaurant in nearby Carrboro. "On Saturday, the 14th, I decided to go to jail. It was no fun at all. There were 3 of us—James Foushee, a Negro and Rosemary Ezra, a Jew. We went to Leo's, were arrested, and hauled to jail. The police were nice except for the one who dragged me into the car."[101]

The young activists encountered little of the reputed liberalism long associated with UNC as the majority of the campus community failed to support their actions.[102] National leaders of the civil rights movement imagined that Chapel Hill would lead the fight and become the first southern town to desegregate its restaurants.[103] This was not to be the case. In spite of its reputation for progressivism—Jesse Helms called UNC the "University of Negroes and Communists"—Chapel Hill remained a small southern town ruled by white conservatives throughout the civil rights struggle, and university administration followed in lockstep.[104] Local organizer Quinton Baker described Chapel Hill as a "wine sipping, cheese eating, liberal community . . . that talked about desegregation and believing in our cause, but disagreed with how we were doing things."[105]

The *Daily Tar Heel*, UNC's student-run newspaper, documented the unfolding student activism in Chapel Hill. Staff writers and photographers captured the movement for their paper and also served as local "stringers" for national newspapers and news services like UPI.[106] UNC journalism major Jim Wallace, who graduated in 1960, joined the *Daily Tar Heel* staff as a photographer in his freshman year. He was privy to the meetings of leaders of the movement, who often met at Harry's, a New York–style delicatessen on Franklin Street owned by Harry and Sybil Macklin.[107] The business was one of the few integrated restaurants in town that welcomed the young demonstrators.

Wayne King, editor of the *Daily Tar Heel*, who gave Jim Wallace his first civil rights assignment, was persuaded to experience the picket line at the College Café.[108] When a white passerby insulted him and attempted to block his path, King said, "Perhaps I need to point out to you that I am not one of those nonviolent protestors you've been reading about."[109] Jim Wallace and other student photographers such as Jock Lauterer, who went on to teach journalism at UNC, took hundreds of photographs of student protests and sit-ins at Chapel Hill restaurants, cafés, convenience stores, and ice cream shops.

In the early 1960s, the Chapel Hill Board of Aldermen hotly debated but failed to approve a local public accommodations ordinance, due to pressure from conservative, prosegregation business leaders.[110] The ordinance would have prohibited racial discrimination in local businesses, including eating establishments, which were the most egregious offenders. Current Chapel Hill city councilwoman Sally Greene reflected on this time: "While Franklin Street roiled with demonstrations . . . elected leaders did not lead."[111] Over forty years later, on Martin Luther King Jr. Day, former alderman Roland Giduz apologized for the actions of the board: "We focused on trying to persuade individual businesses to drop their racial barriers, when the bigger picture was to eliminate all discrimination. . . . It was a time of great strife that we could have and should have avoided by leading the way."[112]

On January 18, 1963, five days after the defeat of the public accommodations ordinance, North Carolina governor Terry Sanford delivered what was later called the Second Emancipation Speech to the North Carolina Press Association at Chapel Hill's Carolina Inn.[113] (The Inn had "quietly" integrated when Dr. Martin Luther King was honored at a dinner there in May 1960.)[114] In this historic talk, Sanford noted the one-hundredth anniversary of the Emancipation Proclamation and called on the citizens of his state to begin a new era of racial equality in North Carolina. As black waiters stopped in place and listened to Sanford, he urged North Carolinians "to quit unfair discrimination and to give the Negro a full chance to earn a decent living for his family and to contribute to the higher standards for himself and for all men."[115] Sanford aide John Ehle stated that the governor gave the speech in the most public forum he could find, "and in the town he must have known was best able to lead the way."[116]

Sit-ins and protests continued throughout 1963 and 1964 in Chapel Hill, including a march in front of the segregated Long Meadow Dairy Bar on Franklin Street's West End. Jock Lauterer worked there as a "soda jerk": "I was shamefully naïve of the Dairy Bar's segregationist policy—blacks were served at the ice cream counter but couldn't sit down in the dining room."[117] By the following autumn, the Dairy Bar had changed its policy: "I, a freshie at UNC, was out in the streets, protesting, too."[118] Violence escalated during the December 1963 protests in Chapel Hill, as segregated business owners retaliated in anger.

In January 1964, Quinton Baker, Lou Calhoun, and John Dunne

walked into Carlton's Rock Pile, a gas station and store outside of Chapel Hill. When the young men were refused service, they sat down on the floor of the business. Instead of calling the police, storeowner Carlton Mize locked the front and back doors and brought out bottles of bleach and ammonia.[119] Charles Thompson, a student protester from the university, described what happened next: "He poured them [the bottles] over the protestors' heads. When they gasped for air, streams of ammonia and bleach ran into their mouths."[120] Trained in nonresistance, the students "neither moved nor fought Mize."[121] The protest leaders always notified law enforcement of their plans for a sit-in location. After Chapel Hill's police chief William Blake arrived and forcibly broke up the protest, the demonstrators were taken to the hospital, where they were treated for burns from the toxic chemicals.

At an infamous sit-in at the segregated restaurant of the Watts Motel on Highway 15-501 outside Chapel Hill, Jeppie Watts, wife of owner Austin Watts, demanded that the students leave. She began to kick Lou Calhoun, who dropped to the floor, and then squatted over the young man and urinated on him. "This was so disgraceful," wrote Karen Parker in her diary. "No one really wants to believe it."[122] Thompson recalled that the white customers applauded Mrs. Watt.[123]

A series of February 1964 demonstrations in Chapel Hill—marking the fourth anniversary of the Greensboro Woolworth's sit-in—were the largest and most disruptive experienced in the city. The protests followed the unsuccessful passage of the public accommodations ordinance in the city. James Farmer, national director of CORE, promised to shut down Chapel Hill if the ordinance failed to pass. Following the UNC–Wake Forest basketball game on February 8, protesters blocked the exits to the Woolen Gymnasium parking lot and nearby streets, while hundreds of demonstrators marched through the city and blocked traffic by sitting and lying down at busy intersections.[124] As they marched, demonstrators pointed in unison at segregated businesses. Protest signs proclaimed, "CHAPEL HILL: HOME OF CANDY-COATED RACISM," "WE RESERVE THE RIGHT TO REFUSE SERVICE TO JIM CROW," "FOR ALL—SUPPORT A PUBLIC ACCOMMODATION LAW," and "OPEN OUR FUTURE NOW."[125]

Despite violent confrontations between the white public and the demonstrators, Chief "Bill" Blake was committed to keeping police brutality to a minimum in Chapel Hill. He understood the core principles of civil disobedience, having read Gandhi's works on nonviolence.[126] Police detective Lindy Pendergrass worked with Blake and learned to handle protesters as fairly as possible. After viewing photographs of arrests, Chief Blake commanded police officers to carry, not drag, protesters.[127]

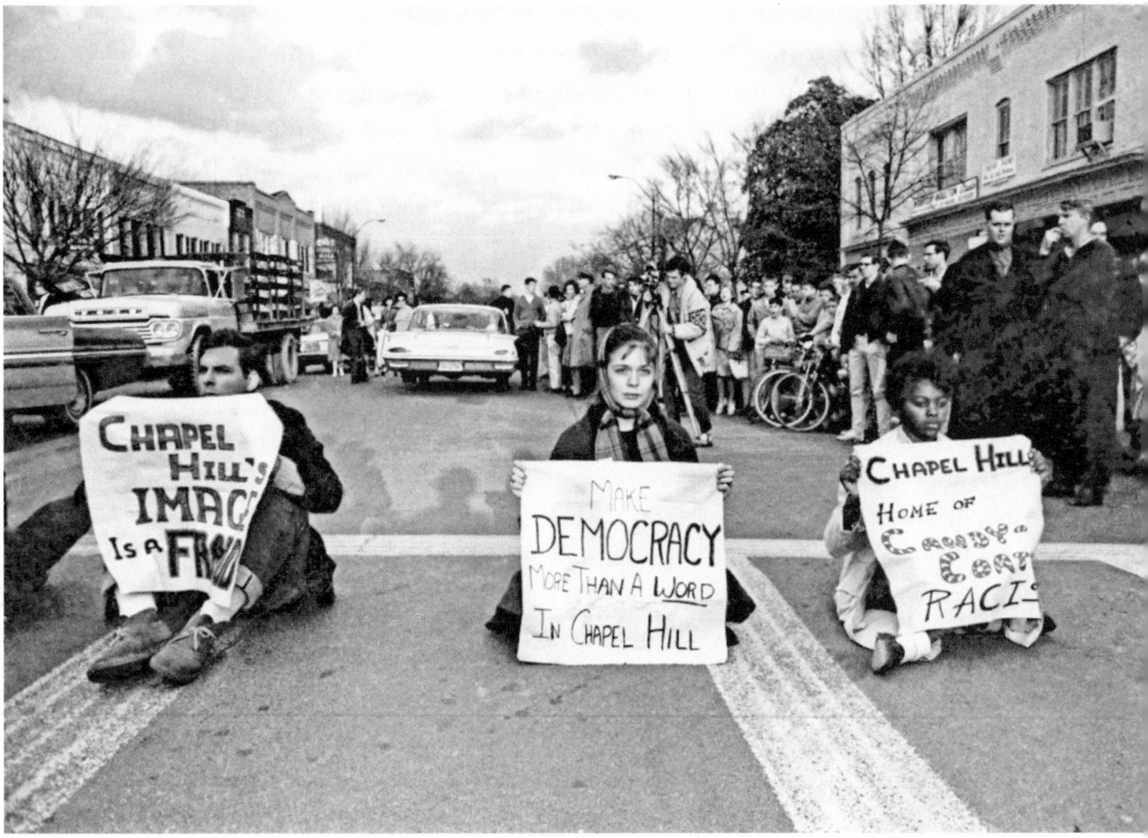

"*Daily Tar Heel* staffers Mickey Blackwell and Wayne King, at far right, observe sit-in that blocked Franklin Street in Chapel Hill, North Carolina, Feb. 8, 1964." Photograph by Jim Wallace, © J&J Wallace Photography LLC.

Pendergrass remembered Blake's orders: "Treat the demonstrators like we wanted to be treated ourselves."[128] A May 1964 letter from Joe Straley to Blake reflected the largely cordial relations the police chief fostered with protesters in Chapel Hill. Writing on behalf of the Committee of Concerned Citizens, Straley explained a change in their picketing schedule at local restaurants: "There will be no picketing for a while at Clarence's and at Brady's. When this is resumed, we will, of course let you know. . . . The Committee of Concerned Citizens . . . want you and your officers to know how much we appreciate the care which has been given to keep the picketing as peaceful as it has mostly been."[129]

In the late 1950s, several years before the desegregation protests gained momentum in Chapel Hill, the Reverend Robert Seymour, the progressive minister of the Olin T. Binkley Baptist Church, realized the power of UNC's beloved sport to initiate social change. Binkley called upon the new UNC assistant basketball coach, Dean Smith, to help integrate the Pines, a popular steak house owned by Frances and Leroy

Merritt.[130] The restaurant was the favorite of Smith's boss, legendary Coach Frank McGuire, and the basketball team ate all of its pregame meals there.[131] Reverend Seymour invited Smith to join him for dinner at the Pines, along with James Forbes, a young African American theology student.[132] "We asked to be served and with Dean Smith at the door, they could not say no," said Seymour. "That was the opening of the door of The Pines restaurant."[133] Years later in an interview with Dean Smith, sportswriter John Feinstein recounted this story and commented on how proud Smith should be of his actions. Dean Smith replied, "You should never be proud of doing what's right. You should just do what's right."[134]

On August 28, 1963, 250,000 people participated in the historic March on Washington in the nation's capitol, organized by a coalition of civil rights, labor, and religious organizations. The massive demonstration of support for social justice solidified support for President Kennedy's proposed civil rights bill. The march began at the Washington Monument and ended at the Lincoln Memorial, where thousands heard impassioned speeches and performances delivered by the nation's leading civil rights activists, religious leaders, and singers. North Carolina's Floyd McKissick read a speech on behalf of James Farmer, who was in prison in Louisiana for protesting police brutality. At the end of the day, Martin Luther King Jr. delivered his moving "I Have a Dream" speech, in which he imagined that, "one day, on the red hills of Georgia, sons of former slaves and sons of former slave owners will sit down together at the *table of brotherhood*."[135] This historic call to action to the nation reverberated in continued protests and demonstrations that spread across the South, even to its most sacred institution, the barbecue café.

16

Culinary Landmarks of "The Struggle"

On January 25, 1964, black community leaders staged a sit-in at Hop's Bar-B-Q in the mill town of Asheboro, North Carolina, to protest the segregationist practices of its white owner, Burrell Hopkins. Four years after the February 1, 1960, Woolworth's sit-in, writes Sarah McNulty Turner, Hopkins's granddaughter, "the civil rights movement finally traveled the thirty miles between the two cities" of Greensboro and Asheboro.[1] A crowd of white onlookers gathered outside Hop's. Members of the local Ku Klux Klan chapter taunted the protesters.[2] By the end of the day, sixty protesters were arrested in the Asheboro sit-ins and taken to the Randolph County jail.[3] Protester Melvin Marley recalled that for those who stayed overnight in jail, supper was Hop's famous ten-cent hotdogs.[4] Fifty years later, surviving protesters who participated in the sit-ins commemorated this local battle in the national struggle for civil rights with the installation of a memorial plaque at the site of the downtown confrontation.[5]

Black and white customers alike enjoyed Hop's "Lexington-style" (western North Carolina) pork barbecue, but only whites could sit and dine inside the café during the 1950s. Hopkins's first restaurant in Asheboro, the Meal-a-Minute Grill, catered to workers at the McLaurin Hosiery Mill, whose shifts allowed little time for full meal breaks.[6] Lunch orders from Meal-a-Minute were delivered on rolling "dope carts," which moved through the workplace at shift and lunch breaks. Hopkins sold the business in 1952 and two years later opened Hop's Bar-B-Q, a "luncheonette" in the center of Asheboro's busy downtown.[7] Blacks were served take-out orders at the back door of the restaurant, in keeping with the same practice at the nearby Woolworth's store and other downtown cafés. "Short-order" restaurants like Hop's grew in popularity in the post–World War II South, a precursor to the fast-food revolution, providing inexpensive, quick, hearty meals to working people.[8]

Six months after the Asheboro sit-ins, the historic Civil Rights Act of 1964 passed, shepherded through Congress by President Lyndon Johnson after the assassination of John F. Kennedy in the fall of 1963. Fol-

Hop's Bar-B-Q, Asheboro, North Carolina. Courtesy of Sarah McNulty Turner.

lowing the violence unleashed by Birmingham police, who used dogs and fire hoses on black civil rights demonstrators in the spring of 1963, President Kennedy had proposed civil rights legislation in a nationally televised address on June 11, 1963. After the House of Representatives voted to approve the bill in February 1964, it was filibustered by Democratic southern senators for another three months, including by North Carolina senator Sam Ervin.[9] The Senate finally passed the legislation on June 19, and the Civil Rights Act was signed into law by President Johnson on July 2, 1964. Title II of the act granted all Americans—regardless of race—the right to use and be served in "public accommodations," from restaurants to lodging to retail stores, theaters, swimming pools, and recreational areas.[10] Discrimination on government property was illegal, as well as in any business that involved interstate commerce. White business owners like Hopkins were encouraged to desegregate voluntarily.[11] By 1965, Hopkins had fully integrated his restaurant.[12] Although the Civil Rights Act was a transformative moment in American history, enforcement of the act was weak. Divisive racial practices remained, evidence of which is still present in resegregated communities in the contemporary American South. On August 6, 1965, the Voting Rights Act passed, a landmark in civil rights legislation, which prohibited discriminatory voting practices based on race and prerequisite qualifications.

Forty-eight years later, on June 25, 2013, the U.S. Supreme Court overturned a critical section of the Voting Rights Act, thus allowing nine states with previous histories of racial discrimination—the majority in the South—to change election laws without federal preapproval. Justice Ruth Bader Ginsberg, a dissenting voice, referred to the Reverend Martin Luther King's words in a rare summary of her decision from the bench: "'The arc of the moral universe is long,' he said, but 'it bends toward justice,' if there is a steadfast commitment to see the task through to completion."[13]

The story of the civil rights movement includes hundreds of southern lunch counters, restaurants, and cafés where black and white demonstrators protested segregation before the Civil Rights Act of 1964 and after its passage bravely tested the compliance of once-segregated businesses with the new law. These places symbolize the long spectrum of "the struggle" and leaders who faced each other from opposite sides of the picket lines and protest marches. Of these, the following stand out as landmarks in the historic landscape of the civil rights movement: Atlanta's Paschal's—an integrated meeting place that welcomed civil rights leaders and activists; Lester Maddox's Pickrick restaurant, also in Atlanta, infamous for the violent racial confrontations that occurred there and were broadcast to a horrified nation; and Ollie's Bar-B-Q in Birmingham, a modest café at the center of a Supreme Court case that contested the constitutionality of the new Civil Rights Act.

Paschal's Restaurant

The Kitchen of the Civil Rights Movement

Paschal's Restaurant, one of the most successful black-owned business empires in America, became a significant site of the civil rights movement as a popular meeting and dining venue for Martin Luther King Jr. and other leaders before and after the desegregation of public accommodations.[14] The Atlanta restaurant was founded by brothers

Robert and James Paschal, the children of African American sharecroppers Henry and Lizzie Paschal, who raised cotton, peanuts, and sweet potatoes in McDuffie County in northeast Georgia.[15] Opened in 1947 as a thirty-seat luncheonette, Paschal's was part of a growing black business district that served working people, middle-class families, professionals, and students.[16] Food businesses like Paschal's were vibrant symbols of black self-reliance and economic independence that persevered despite the racial barriers of the Jim Crow South.[17]

James Paschal managed the business side of the restaurant, while Robert Paschal oversaw the restaurant kitchen, having learned to cook alongside his mother.[18] James Paschal recalled their mother's reputation as a resourceful cook and baker who transformed typical sharecroppers' rations into tasty meals.[19] From tins of canned pink salmon bought in town each Saturday, Mrs. Paschal made salmon croquettes, which she served with buttermilk biscuits, homemade butter, fresh cane syrup, and "smoked, streak of lean bacon."[20] Whites and blacks alike clamored for her pound cakes, cobblers, sweet potato pies, tea cakes, and peanut brittle.[21] "Each time I heard our landowner's wife and other white women around town say, 'Lizzie, I want a cake for Sunday's dinner,' I was filled with rage," wrote James Paschal. "I never heard, 'Mrs. Paschal, will you please bake me a pound cake for Sunday's dinner?' or even 'Miss Lizzie.'"[22]

Described as the "kitchen of the civil rights movement," Paschal's provided a comfortable and safe gathering place for activists to plan critical events, from the 1963 March on Washington to the 1965 Selma to Montgomery Voting Rights March.[23] Former ambassador to the United Nations and mayor of Atlanta Andrew Young described the "sacramental meal" he and other activists shared at Paschal's.[24] "It was the place for the South's best fried chicken, greens, black-eyed peas, cornbread, lettuce and tomato salad, sweet iced tea, and homemade peach cobbler and ice cream," said Young. "This was comfort food, food for the soul and body. This provided the energy and spirit that gave birth to freedom."[25] Ralph Abernathy referred to Paschal's as the "war room for a nonviolent revolution."[26] Defying segregation laws in the 1950s, the restaurant allowed white and black patrons to sit together.[27] "We operated an integrated facility in a segregated community," said James Paschal. "On our license was printed 'for colored people only,' but we violated those city ordinances."[28]

In December 1960, Paschal's opened an adjacent jazz club, La Carrousel, which attracted top performers such as Aretha Franklin, Dizzy Gillespie, Ramsey Lewis, Hugh Masekela, Nina Simone, and Billy Taylor.[29] Orah Belle Sherman was the glamorous hostess of the club for over forty years.[30] Sherman took care of the entertainers, providing after-hours meals and gatherings at her home that went into the early hours of the morning.[31] She knew the "regulars" at the club, as well as the FBI and Secret Service agents sent there to spy on Reverend King.[32]

Civil rights activists met in Paschal's during good times and bad, including leaders and ground troops of the Southern Christian Leadership Conference (SCLC), SNCC, and CORE.[33] After long hours of picketing, or even jail time, protesters were comforted by a bowl of Paschal's vegetable soup, one of Martin Luther King's favorite dishes.[34] "You'd leave the front lines of the movement, in South Georgia or Alabama," said Georgia congressman John Lewis, "and when you made it to Paschal's you were safe."[35] James Paschal recalled that each "soldier" who returned safely to Paschal's "received a hero's welcome, free chicken sandwiches and soft drinks."[36]

The Paschal brothers extended restaurant hours and provided complimentary meals for parents while they waited to ensure the safety of their college-age children who were involved in local protests and sit-ins.[37] These students were enrolled in local schools such as Atlanta University, Clark, Spelman, Morris Brown, and Morehouse College. "We knew, if their minds would dream in peace and with faith," wrote James Paschal, "their bellies needed food to help them keep those dreams alive, sensible, and possible."[38] When necessary, the Paschal brothers posted bond for arrested protesters.[39] Field reports from across the South were shared each morning at Paschal's.[40] "Before CNN and *Jet* covered the Movement," wrote Andrew Young, "you could get the news at Paschal's. We could argue about what it all meant over grits and eggs, sausage and biscuits, pancakes, waffles, and always, fried chicken—breakfast, lunch, dinner, and late night."[41]

In early 1962, the Paschal brothers designated a special meeting room for King in their new and more sophisticated "white-tablecloth" restaurant, across the street at 830 Hunter Street.[42] The 1965 Selma to Montgomery March was largely planned there. "Key decisions were made over fried chicken at the restaurant," said John Lewis, "and that decision to march was one of them. We drove right from Paschal's to Selma."[43] Much of the planning for the Poor People's Campaign in 1968 occurred at Paschal's. This event culminated in a major protest on the Washington Mall, on May 12, 1968, a month after King's assassination in Memphis on April 4, 1968.[44]

On February 4, 1968, King delivered his last sermon at Ebenezer Baptist Church in Atlanta. In the closing stanzas of his sermon, King imagined his own funeral—a powerful foreshadowing of his death just three months later. Coretta Scott King requested that excerpts from the speech be included in her husband's nationally televised funeral on April 9, 1968. In the sermon, "The Drum Major's Instinct," King asked his congregants not to focus on his awards and achievements but to remember him as a man who "tried to love and serve humanity. . . . I want you to say that day that I've tried to be right on the walk with them. *I want you to be able to say that day that I did try to feed the hungry*. . . . Yes, if you want to say that I was a drum major. Say that I was a drum major for justice. Say that I was a drum major for peace. I was a drum major for righteousness."[45] The night of King's death, such large crowds gathered at the restaurant that the Paschal brothers were forced to lock the doors to ensure their customers' safety.[46] Coretta Scott King said of this landmark: "Paschal's is as important a historical site for the American civil rights movement as Boston's Faneuil Hall is to the American Revolution."[47]

Paschal's remained a meeting place for Atlanta's black political elite in the 1980s, including Mayor Andrew Young, who announced his decision to run for Congress there, and the Reverend Jesse Jackson, who ran his presidential campaign from Paschal's adjoining hotel.[48] The original Paschal's closed in 2003 when the property was purchased by Clark Atlanta University. The restaurant continues today in a central Atlanta location and at the Hartsfield-Jackson Airport.[49] Robert and James Paschal died in 1997 and 2008, respectively. "To shouts of 'Amen' and 'Oh, yes' at James Paschal's funeral, veterans of the civil rights movement told how the son of a sharecropper became a millionaire without forgetting his roots or his community."[50] For over sixty years, the Paschal brothers fed those at the heart of "the struggle."

"My Dream Came True. I Was Mr. Maddox. I Was Mr. Pickrick. I Was Mr. Somebody."

Less than five miles across town, another Atlanta restaurant, the Pickrick, stood in stark contrast to Paschal's. The owner, Lester Maddox, grew up in a large working-class white family, besieged by poverty and hunger.[51] With savings from his World War II defense plant job, Maddox and his wife, Virginia, opened a restaurant on property they owned near the Georgia Tech campus.[52] The catchy name, Pickrick, was explained in a slogan printed on the restaurant's ads and menus: "PICK—TO SELECT—TO FASTIDIOUSLY EAT; RICK—TO PILE UP OR TO HEAP, TO AMASS. You PICK it out . . . we'll RICK it up."[53] The restaurant offered a classic southern "meat 'n' three" menu that featured fried chicken and barbecue and daily specials like fried calves' liver and pork chops, served with field peas, green beans, hot biscuits and cornbread, a piece of pie, and iced tea.

Maddox quickly became known for his passionate prosegregation views, touted in his "Pickrick Says" advertisements in the Saturday edition of the *Atlanta Journal*.[54] The popular ads featured Maddox's critique of local politics peppered with prayer, patriotism, and promotion of the Pickrick menu and souvenirs, including Confederate auto tags, American flags, and "Pickrick Drumsticks," available in "Mama, Daddy, and Junior sizes."[55] When a smiling photograph of Maddox was added to the ad banner in 1955, it became "a political column posing as a restaurant ad."[56] The "drumsticks" were a promotional device and warning to demonstrators, who had attempted to organize sit-ins at the segregated restaurant since 1962. Customers could purchase these wooden pickax handles for a dollar or two. Atlanta, "the city too busy to hate," which took pride in its progressive commercial environment, found an exception in figures like Lester Maddox and other whites unwilling to accept a progressive racial landscape.[57] In an effort to demonstrate the solidarity of segregationist whites in business like himself, Maddox formed Georgians Unwilling to Surrender (GUTS) in 1960.[58]

On July 3, 1964, just a day after President Johnson signed the Civil Rights Act into law, three African American theology students from Atlanta's Interdenominational Theological Center pulled into the Pickrick parking lot. The driver was George Willis of Youngstown, Ohio.[59] Joining him were Albert Dunn of Hillsboro, Texas, and Woodrow Lewis of Sumter, South Carolina.[60] Maddox greeted them outside their car with his revolver, where he was backed by a group of white diners, including women, who carried ax handles from the restaurant.[61] An enraged Maddox kicked the side of the vehicle and then struck the top of the car with an ax handle as it pulled out of the parking lot.[62] The gathered reporters and photographers questioned the black men as they drove slowly by the restaurant. "We are still hungry," said Willis. "We'll be back."[63] The image of Maddox brandishing a gun and whites threatening the well-dressed African American men with ax handles appeared in newspapers across the country, including on the front page of the *New York Times*.[64] The men filed charges against Maddox, who continued to stop other African Americans from entering his restaurant. The event solidified his support among conservative whites, who flocked to the restaurant, encouraged by Maddox's weekly request to "Please come by" in his newspaper ads.[65] After the parking lot confrontation, business at the Pickrick was reportedly up by 40 percent.[66]

Maddox believed "forced" integration was nothing less than communism and that it violated the hallowed American right to own and control private property, both at home and in business.[67] Communism gave Maddox a convenient bogeyman to finger as the instigator of the protests.[68] When he looked at the young black demonstrators, he saw sinister forces behind them and convinced himself that he was defending his personal rights, his country, his home, and the ideals of racial purity.[69] He employed many blacks in his business, and like other southern whites, he thought he knew them well and believed many to be his friends. To question that truth was unthinkable. Maddox chose to believe that "his negroes" were satisfied with their situation. Historian Jason Sokol describes the "revolution in consciousness" that rumbled across the South, as white southerners like Maddox encountered activist blacks who "shattered stereotypes."[70]

In a federal case against Maddox and a white hotel owner who also defied the new law, the courts upheld the 1964 Civil Rights Act and issued an injunction prohibiting the business owners from denying service based on race.[71] Maddox's attorneys argued that the Pickrick fell outside the purview of the public accommodations section of the Civil Rights Act, arguing that the restaurant had little to do with interstate customers and commerce.[72] The prosecuting attorney merely pointed to the Pickrick's location on U.S. Highway 41, which ran from Miami to Michigan, and to the number of out-of-state cars in the restaurant's parking lot.[73]

The presiding justice for the case was Elbert Tuttle, who had been appointed by President Eisenhower to the Fifth Circuit Court of Appeals soon after the historic *Brown v. Board of Education* Supreme Court decision in 1954, which ended legal segregation in public schools.[74] Tuttle and his judicial colleagues of the "Fifth Circuit Four"—John Robert Brown, Richard Rives, and John Minor Wisdom—were well known for their historic advocacy of the civil rights of African Americans in the 1950s and 1960s. Historian Justin Nystrom recounts Justice Tuttle's encounter with Dick Rich, president of Rich's Department Store, the most prominent retail business in downtown Atlanta during this era.[75] The justice asked why Rich refused to integrate his lunch counter. Rich stated that he did not "do anything under pressure,'" to which Tuttle replied that he did not "believe any progress is ever made except by pressure."[76]

Rather than comply with the court-ordered desegregation, Maddox closed the Pickrick on August 13, 1964, but continued to sell souvenirs from the location, this time to both whites and a few curious blacks.[77] "The only thing I regret," said Maddox, "is that Bobby Kennedy [attorney general at the time] could not come down here and get some chicken."[78] A month later, Maddox opened another restaurant, the Lester Maddox Cafeteria, in the same location, and again, turned away "integrationists" and welcomed "acceptable" Georgians.[79]

Maddox remained embroiled in legal battles and was found in con-

"View of the staff at the Pickrick Restaurant," Hemphill Avenue, Atlanta, Georgia, ca. 1955. Lester Maddox Photographs, VIS 105.06.08, Kenan Research Center, Atlanta History Center, Atlanta, Ga.

tempt of court for disobeying the injunction.[80] He shut down the Lester Maddox Cafeteria on February 7, 1965, and hung a sign on the door: "Closed. Out of business resulting from an act passed by the U.S. Congress, signed by President Johnson and inspired and supported by deadly and bloody Communism."[81] At a news conference to announce his decision, black employees brought out complimentary fried chicken and biscuits for the gathered newsmen while an emotional Maddox said, "I want to serve my last chicken to members of the news media—regardless of race, color, creed or national origin. You might call it the last supper."[82] He eventually sold the business to former employees.[83] The renamed Gateway Cafeteria served both whites and blacks.[84] The Pickrick launched Maddox into a world of political celebrity, ratcheted up by his racism, bravado, and talent for southern-style showmanship. As Maddox said of the Pickrick, "My dream came true. I was Mr. Maddox. I was Mr. Pickrick. I was Mr. Somebody."[85]

Maddox turned his attention to politics, an ambition he had cultivated since unsuccessfully challenging incumbent William Hartsfield in the Atlanta mayoral race in 1957 and Ivan Allen Jr. in 1961.[86] In a surprising runoff for the gubernatorial election in 1966, Maddox was elected governor; in 1971 he became lieutenant governor under Governor Jimmy Carter. Despite his segregationist past, Maddox was moderately progressive, and he appointed many African Americans to government positions; yet he remained an unreformed racist.[87]

Maddox revived the Pickrick one more time when he reopened the cafeteria-style restaurant in a new location in 1975 following his defeat in the gubernatorial primary. Pulitzer Prize–winning journalist Wayne King, former editor of UNC's *Daily Tar Heel*, reported the story for the *New York Times*. He described the sense of déjà vu at the new Pickrick, "the rich smell of turnip greens, biscuits, hominy and fried chicken haunting the air, the Confederate Stars and Bars unfurled over the tables, Mr. Maddox at the door greeting guests with 'Now don't y'all spend your lunch money anywhere else, heah?'"[88] Customers could still purchase souvenirs, including the "Pickrick Drumstick," although it was a bit pricier at five dollars apiece. Despite preserving its popular menu and selling the same self-promotional ephemera, one thing had changed at the Pickrick. A few African American customers were in the cafeteria line, helping themselves to the same food that whites and blacks had eaten in the South for generations. "If its something you can't do anything about," Maddox said, "you go along with it. The battle is all over."[89]

James Paschal recalled Governor Maddox's visit to Paschal's in the 1960s to settle the question of which of the two restaurants served the best fried chicken.[90] "Of course ours was better," Paschal said, "but I never went to test his out."[91] In 2009, Congressman John Lewis argued that the Pickrick should be saved as part of a civil rights trail, which included the original Paschal's restaurant.[92] Although the building was eventually razed, a historical marker was planned to recognize the Pickrick as an important site in the battle for African American civil rights.

Ollie's Bar-B-Que Goes to the Supreme Court

In Alabama, the leadership of the Birmingham Restaurant Association watched white owners of segregated businesses try to hold off integration, as Maddox had unsuccessfully attempted to do in Georgia. Instead of passively accepting the Civil Rights Act, inciting the wrath of black protesters, or worse, being sued by the federal government to force integration, a restaurant could possibly turn the tables and file a suit against the U.S. Justice Department.[93] The loophole in the Civil Rights Act was the interstate commerce clause. If an eating establishment could prove it was not involved in interstate commerce and catered solely to nearby customers to whom they served locally sourced food, a case could be built to oppose the new law. Ollie's Bar-B-Q in Birmingham fit the bill.[94] The restaurant relied on word of mouth to publicize its barbecue, rather than paid advertising, and it was located some distance from interstate highways, train and bus stations, and the airport.[95]

Founded by the McClung family on the South Side of Birmingham in 1956, the small barbecue café grew into a successful operation that catered to working-class whites and businessmen, although the neighborhood surrounding the café was largely black.[96] Racial privilege and social custom allowed whites to comfortably drive across town to a black neighborhood to enjoy a meal at a favorite diner or a barbecue café. Racial boundaries separated businesses and neighborhoods, but not white and black southerners' taste for the same food. Blacks could not sit down and eat in Ollie's dining room but were allowed to purchase food from a take-out window in the back. On July 3, 1964, four black men decided to test Ollie's compliance with the newly passed Civil Rights Act and sat down at the counter to be served.[97] Unlike the Pickrick, there was no violence, but the black customers were still denied service.[98]

On July 31, 1964, with the encouragement of the Birmingham Restaurant Association, Ollie McClung Sr. filed suit against the Justice Department in *McClung v. Kennedy*.[99] McClung's legal counsel argued that the interstate commerce clause did not apply to Ollie's and that if the restaurant was forced to integrate, Mr. McClung expected to lose $200,000 in business from the departure of white customers.[100] Mr. McClung and his son, Ollie Jr., testified that they were defending their property rights as business owners rather than their racial opinions.[101] A sense of personal "stewardship" for the comfort and well-being of their white customers was central to their defense.[102] The Fifth Circuit U.S. Court of Appeals ruled in favor of Ollie McClung Sr. and his son on September 17, 1964. Like Lester Maddox, the McClungs were hailed as heroes by segregationists in the fight for "white rights."[103] A three-judge federal panel in Birmingham stated that "the public accommodations section was unconstitutional when applied to a restaurant not engaged in interstate commerce."[104] If this ruling held, it would create a "landside" of similar suits by other southern eating establishments arguing that they, too, were not engaged in interstate commerce and thus not subject to the terms of the new Civil Rights Act.[105]

Less than a week later, U.S. Supreme Court justice Hugo Black—a native of Alabama who had been part of the unanimous Court decision in *Brown v. Board of Education* case in 1954—"granted a stay" and temporarily suspended the Birmingham court order regarding Ollie's and the enforcement of the Civil Rights Act.[106] (Hugo Black was married to Josephine Foster, sister of civil rights activist Virginia Foster Durr.)[107] The case questioned the constitutionality of the new law, and it moved forward to the Supreme Court.[108] On October 5, 1964, *McClung v. Katzenbach*—Nicholas Katzenbach became attorney general after Robert Kennedy's resignation—was heard by the nation's highest court.[109] On December 16, 1964, the Supreme Court overturned the federal panel's ruling and declared the act constitutional as applied to Ollie's.[110] With this decision, the Supreme Court upheld Title II of the Civil Rights Act, the public accommodations section, which prohibited "refusal of service or segregation in hotels, motels, restaurants, places of amusement and gasoline stations if the discrimination or segregation is supported by state action."[111] Justice Tom Clark, who also supported the *Brown v. Board of Education* decision, wrote the opinion of the Court for the *McClung v. Katzenbach* case.[112] Two days after the Supreme Court ruling, five African American customers were served at Ollie's Bar-B-Q.[113] One of the customers reported: "Everything was lovely. Lovely. Not a single incident. We sure enjoyed Ollie's good barbecue."[114] Ollie's closed permanently in 2001.[115]

Culinary Compliance across the South

Restaurant owners' compliance with the Civil Rights Act was a slow, contested process that played out in different ways across the South.[116] The varied responses of eating establishments to the public accommodations section of the act—from peaceful acceptance of integration to stubborn adherence to segregation—depended in large part on the behavior of local leaders in both the black and white communities, from law enforcement to influential business owners.[117] J. H. Gibbons, president of Morrison's cafeteria, a popular chain that operated forty-one restaurants across the South, announced that his cafeterias would obey the law.[118] Surprisingly, compliance occurred relatively peacefully in Memphis, Tennessee, and Jackson, Mississippi, where the local restaurant association and the Chamber of Commerce encouraged businesses to honor the new law.[119]

Black and white leaders and activists in the civil rights movement personally tested the compliance of many eating establishments, hotels, and motels throughout the South after the passage of the Civil Rights Act. Charles Evers, field secretary of Mississippi's NAACP chapter, coordinated this effort in his state. Evers stepped into this position after his brother, Medgar Evers, was murdered in 1963 by white supremacist Byron De La Beckwith, who was convicted thirty-one years later in a third trial, in 1994, and sentenced to life in prison. On July 5, 1964, twelve national directors of the NAACP flew into Jackson and traveled together to cities and towns throughout the state to test the enforcement of the newly passed Civil Rights Act. Jackson police officers personally escorted the members of the group from the airport to their hotels and "kept watch" while they registered without incident at the formerly segregated King Edward and the Heidelberg, facilities that were popular with Mississippi legislators.[120] The black men dined peacefully at the Heidelberg coffee shop.

The NAACP leaders also went to McComb, a center of civil rights activism and severe racial violence in southwest Mississippi, including more than a dozen bombings and the burning of African American churches.[121] The group stayed at the Continental Motel and ate lunch in the adjoining restaurant, across the street from the police station. Later that afternoon, the NAACP leaders split into smaller groups and visited the local Woolworth's lunch counter, the bus station café, and a downtown movie theater. Despite the "icy stares from whites" when they entered the formerly segregated businesses, "in all cases, they were received quietly."[122] Later that fall, thirteen white and black civil rights workers were arrested for eating together in the local Freedom House in McComb.[123] They were charged with "operating a food-handling establishment without a health certificate."[124] The charges—designed to intimidate and frighten the activists—were benign compared to the daily violence inflicted on the black community of McComb throughout the voter registration campaigns of the summer and fall of 1964. Oliver Emmerich, editor of the *McComb Enterprise-Journal*, recalled that "almost everybody was hysterically afraid."[125]

Six months after the passage of the Civil Rights Act, on December 24, 1964, a racially mixed group entered the Pinehurst Coffee Shop in Laurel, Mississippi, described in Duncan Hines's *Adventures in Good Eating* as "a good place for this section of the country. Shrimp remoulade, fried chicken and steaks."[126] When the group was asked to leave, the members refused, and they were arrested by local police officers for "breach of the peace."[127] A news report of this incident noted: "The arrests came as Governor Paul B. Johnson declared in Jackson that the U.S. Supreme Court gave a 'green light to anarchy' by upholding the public accommodations section of the 1964 Civil Rights Law."[128] That same month, Charles Evers, representing the NAACP, sued restaurant owner Angelos Primos, a past president of the Jackson Citizens' Council, a prosegregation, white-supremacist organization that opposed the Supreme Court decision in *McClung v. Katzenbach*.[129] Primos owned two popular restaurants in Jackson, which he refused to integrate.[130]

Owners of the thirty-year-old Robert E. Lee Hotel, Jackson's second-largest hotel, named in honor of the "renowned Confederate hero and a true gentleman of the South"—closed their business on Sunday, July 6, 1964, rather than integrate.[131] The business eventually reopened, but as a segregated private club, an option chosen by many white-owned venues as a means to avoid integration. Throughout the state, violent resistance to the Civil Rights Act was seen in bombings of both white and black grocery stores and cafés. In Canton, Mississippi, bombings destroyed a white-owned grocery store that served blacks in their neighborhood.[132] The violence occurred after a successful black boycott of Canton's white downtown merchants who refused to integrate their businesses.

A fall 1964 newsletter from Womanpower Unlimited—the Jackson-based African American women's organization—encouraged its members to support the newly integrated local restaurants after the passage of the Civil Rights Act. "Have you been to SUN and SAND, MORRISON'S, THE GREEN DERBY, and many of the other places? If not, WHY NOT? WU [Womanpower Unlimited] suggests that you and some of your friends go to these places immediately. The only way to keep them open to us is to keep using them."[133] This entreaty from Womanpower Unlimited points to the complicated effects of desegregation, whose economic implications were not always positive for either black or white business districts. As African American customers were increasingly able to eat where they chose, many black businesses, including restaurants, saw a decline in income and the eventual abandonment of shopping districts that exclusively served blacks prior to integration.[134] Adrian Miller notes that soul food restaurants were often "casualties of change" as African Americans moved from all-black neighborhoods.[135]

By April 1964, one hundred formerly segregated restaurants in Memphis had changed their policies and now served blacks.[136] Harlan Fields, president of the Memphis Restaurant Association and owner of popular local restaurants such as the Four Flames and the Pancake Man, represented the position of many white leaders at the time.[137] He vehemently opposed integration and the Civil Rights Act in principle but feared serious loss of revenue from disruptions by civil rights protesters, as well as from the legal system and law enforcement, if he failed to comply.[138] Jason Sokol explains that southern cities generally complied more easily with the new Civil Rights Act than small towns, including supposedly liberal bastions such as Chapel Hill.[139] A July 4, 1964, Associated Press column in the *Atlanta Journal and Constitution* stated, "The calm with which some hold-out segregationists accepted the change almost matched the historic enactment of the sweeping legislation a century after Lincoln emancipated the slaves."[140] Community Relations Services, a government agency established to help communities peacefully comply with the Civil Rights Act, brought conciliators into communities where trouble was expected.[141] In October 1964, a Community Relations Services survey was conducted in nineteen states, examining the compliance rates in fifty-three cities of populations of 50,000 or more.[142] More than two-thirds of the hotels, motels, chain restaurants, theaters, sports facilities, public parks, and libraries had desegregated.[143]

Daniel H. Pollitt, the Graham Kenan Professor of Law Emeritus at UNC, was a passionate advocate for social justice in Chapel Hill during the 1950s and 1960s. Besides helping to desegregate Chapel Hill restaurants, Pollitt and his wife, Jean Ann, joined Martin Luther King and Coretta Scott King in the 1960s for a meal at the Magnolia Room, the segregated restaurant in Rich's Department Store in Atlanta.[144] Civil rights activist and politician Julian Bond noted, "If Rich's went, so would everybody else."[145] As members of the Southern Regional Council, a group dedicated to working against racial injustice, the Pollitts and the Kings were also the first racially mixed group to eat at the fashionable Top of the Mart restaurant in Atlanta in the fall of 1964.[146] Pollitt remembered the elevator man who feared trouble if he took them to the restaurant, so they used a freight elevator. The group was seated near the kitchen. Leslie Dunbar, executive director of the Southern Regional Council, objected: "No, no, no. I have reservations for the outer area where we can observe the city."[147] The distinguished guests were moved to a proper table, and the meal continued without incident. "Nobody said, 'Get out of here' or threw a roll at us or anything," Pollitt noted. "I think people are pretty civilized in expensive restaurants."[148]

Humorist and journalist Harry Golden, who published the *Carolina Israelite* in Charlotte, North Carolina, from 1942 to 1968, frequently spoke out against segregation and the Jim Crow laws of the South and about the challenge of integrating white-only restaurants. In the satirical voice his readers loved, Golden proposed a solution, the "VERTICAL NEGRO PLAN."[149] He observed that southern whites and blacks stood at the same grocery counters, deposited money at the same bank teller's windows, and *walked* through the same dime stores.[150] "It is only when the Negro 'sets,' wrote Golden, "that the fur begins to fly."[151] Golden suggested removing all seats from the South's contested public accommodations, from schools to lunch counters and movie theaters. "Since no one in the South pays the slightest attention to a VERTICAL NEGRO, this will completely solve our problem."[152]

To end the duplication and expense of separate water fountains for whites and blacks, Golden announced his "OUT-OF-ORDER PLAN."[153] He allegedly tried it out in a North Carolina city, where the manager of a department store shut off the water in his "white" water fountain and put up a sign that said, "Out-of-Order."[154] "For the first day or two the whites were hesitant," explained Golden, "but little by little they began to drink out of the water fountain belonging to the 'coloreds'—and by the end of the third week everybody was drinking the 'segregated' water; with not a single solitary complaint to date."[155] Golden believed that whites might accept desegregation if they were "assured that the facilities are still 'separate,' albeit 'Out-of-Order.'"[156]

In Durham, North Carolina, E. J. "Mutt" Evans, who served six terms as the city's mayor from 1951 to 1963, disregarded the Jim Crow laws in his department store, Evans United, which catered to a largely black clientele. When Evans was ordered to stop feeding whites and blacks together at his lunch counter, his attorney realized—like Harry Golden—that seats were the heart of the integration problem. In his classic memoir of growing up in the Jewish South, Eli Evans, son of E. J. Evans, wrote: "My father agreed to remove all the stools at the counter and instructed the carpenters to raise the counter top to elbow-leaning height so that United could proudly retain the only integrated lunch counter in downtown Durham."[157]

The threat of physical violence and destruction of property posed by racial terrorist groups like the Ku Klux Klan made compliance very difficult in some communities, where white-owned businesses that tried to integrate were intimidated by picketing and bomb threats. In St. Augustine, Florida, the Monson Motor Lodge and its restaurant became the epicenter of a violent battle between civil rights supporters and white supremacists after blacks were banned from the facility in June 1964.[158] The business bounced back and forth between segregation, integration, resegregation, and reintegration as the manager, James Brock, attempted to keep his business afloat in the escalating racial violence that followed the passage of the Civil Rights Act that summer.[159] In a matter of weeks, the business experienced the picketing of thousands of civil rights supporters—including seventeen rabbis and Jewish activists who came at the request of Reverend Martin Luther King Jr.—a Klan-sponsored fire bombing of the restaurant, and Brock's dousing of black customers in the motel pool with muriatic acid.[160]

"L. J." (John Leoniadas) Moore was adamant about not integrating his popular barbecue restaurant in New Bern, North Carolina.[161] He wrote Senator Sam Ervin in June 1964, asking his support to maintain a segregated facility, arguing, like Ollie McClung, that integration would destroy his business.[162] An NAACP Legal Defense Fund attorney eventually demanded an injunction in the local district court to end discrimination at Moore's in November 1964.[163] When Moore was forced to integrate in 1967, he bulldozed the restaurant.[164] Seeking a loophole to avoid integration, Moore built a new walk-up-service restaurant on another lot.[165] In 1973, Moore's Barbecue opened in its seventh and last location on Highway 17 South in New Bern with a new dining room. After almost thirty years in business, black and white customers, seated at tables side by side, could finally enjoy Moore's barbecue, a recipe perfected by black and white hands. Today, Tommy Moore, L. J. Moore's son, carries on the barbecue tradition begun by his father. Highway 17 South (Clarendon Boulevard) became Martin Luther King Jr. Boulevard on January 17, 2000.[166]

Everything and Nothing

"The Civil Rights Act, like many other victories of the civil rights movement, changed everything and nothing in southern life," writes Jason Sokol. "The law could not compel African-Americans to *desire* to integrate many places, much less compel whites to embrace them when they did."[167] The process of desegregation went on for years, again determined by the particular racial dynamics of communities throughout the South, often ending in lawsuits and court orders that forced businesses and schools to integrate.[168] Racial violence escalated in 1964, culminating in the discovery of the bodies of three civil rights workers who were murdered by Klan members and buried in an earthen dam outside of Philadelphia, Mississippi.[169] Attention turned from compliance logistics of the Civil Rights Act to a national call for the full recognition and protection of African Americans as citizens of the United States of America.[170] Blacks continued to live in great danger as they carefully negotiated the racially volatile worlds of the American South.

The same year that Lester Maddox was elected governor of Georgia, a brutal racially motivated murder took place, on June 10, 1966, in Natchez, Mississippi, ending the life of Ben Chester White, a sixty-seven-year-old African American caretaker of the Carter family farm. Ernest Avants, Claude Fuller, and James Jones, who called their Klan group the Cottonmouth Moccasin Gang, devised the murder of White to purposely attract the attention of Martin Luther King Jr.[171] They hoped to lure Dr. King to Natchez and then assassinate him. They assumed

King was in Mississippi to support civil rights activist James Meredith in his June March against Fear from Memphis to Oxford.

The Klansmen found Ben Chester White on the farm where he worked and asked him to help them find a lost dog.[172] They promised to pay him two dollars for the chore. Stopping at a nearby country store, they asked if White wanted a cold beer.[173] He said no, but that he would sure like a red pop.[174] White drank his strawberry soda as the group drove to their remote destination—Pretty Creek in the Homochitto National Forest outside Natchez. Avants and his friends murdered White with an automatic rifle and a shotgun. James Jones, one of the Klansmen, testified that White cried out as he was shot, "Oh Lord, what have I done to deserve this?"[175] His body was thrown into Pretty Creek, and the vehicle was burned to destroy evidence of the murder.[176] When White's corpse was found, police had difficulty determining the number of times he was shot; his body was riddled with bullet holes.[177] Adding to the horror of this case was White's trust of the white men and his innocent acceptance of their "hospitality," a "red pop," a popular drink among African Americans, who enjoyed the sweet, affordable refreshment and the vivid color.[178]

In March 2003, the United States retried the 1967 case in which Ernest Avants had been acquitted by the state of Mississippi for the murder of Ben Chester White.[179] The fact that White was murdered on federal land enabled prosecutors to remand the case for trial. Recorded testimony from one of the long-dead Klansmen who witnessed the killing was verified by the statement of a former FBI agent, Allan Kornblum, who heard Avants confess to the murder in 1967.[180] Kornblum returned to Jackson to testify in the 2003 trial.[181]

After three hours of deliberation, the jury of nine whites and three blacks found Avants, the only surviving suspect in the case, guilty of Ben Chester White's murder.[182] "For Mr. White's son, Jessie White [sixty-five years old by this time]," wrote *New York Times* journalist Rick Bragg, "it was like being fed after living his whole life hungry. 'Like a good meal,' said Mr. White. 'It feels good.'"[183] U.S. district judge William Barbour Jr. sentenced Avants to prison as he listened from a wheelchair. "Justice in this country can and sometimes has to wait," said Judge Barbour. "Times have changed since 1966. When Ernest Avants's generation is finally dead, I hope most of the hatred will have died with it."[184] Avants died in prison on June 14, 2004, at age seventy-two.[185]

Ben Chester White's senseless murder was just one in a string of violent killings organized by white terrorist groups that targeted African Americans in the tense years following the passage of civil rights legislation in 1964 and 1965. Increased attention on the South as a result of this tragic violence, televised news reports, and firsthand experience of student activists awakened Americans to another desperate situation in the South—the endemic hunger that had long been the lot of the working poor of the region. A consequence of poverty, the systematic denial of African American civil rights, and government policies that favored industrial agriculture, malnutrition devastated thousands of southern families in the 1960s. The desperate situation of hungry southerners was unfathomable in America, "the greatest country on earth."

17

A Hungry South

Not until President Lyndon Johnson's introduction of the Great Society campaign did policy makers, and the nation, finally recognize the real problem of hunger that existed within the country.[1] Johnson announced his "unconditional war on poverty" on the front porch of the modest hillside home of Tom Fletcher and his wife and their eight children in Inez, Kentucky, on April 24, 1964.[2] Fletcher, an unemployed sawmill operator, had been out of work for two years. His last yearly earnings had been $400. "For the first time in our history," stated Johnson, "an America without hunger is a practical prospect. . . . It must . . . become the urgent business of all men and women of every race and every religion, and every region."[3] The president's visit to eastern Kentucky was part of a "fact-finding" trip examining the poverty-stricken counties of Appalachia. A *Time* magazine cover story documented the presidential motorcade: "People surged into the street. The President's right hand began to bleed, but he kept on shaking. Once he snatched a bullhorn from a cop and bellowed to the delighted crowd, 'The one good thing about America is that our ambitions are not too large! They boil down to food, shelter and clothing!'"[4] In a 1994 interview marking the thirty-year anniversary of President Johnson's visit to Kentucky, a physically weakened Tom Fletcher noted that his family had never fully escaped poverty.[5]

The War on Poverty and Southern Hunger

The Economic Opportunity Act, passed by Congress on August 20, 1964, became the centerpiece legislation of Johnson's campaign against poverty. Sargent Shriver, the founding director of the Peace Corps during the Kennedy administration, drafted the legislation for President Johnson and was appointed director of the Office of Economic Opportunity (OEO). The OEO implemented programs such as VISTA (Volunteers in Service to America), the Job Corps, and Head Start. Increased focus on poverty in America in the 1960s forced Washington leaders to examine oversight of antihunger programs in the South. In April 1964, Mississippi senator James Eastland denied charges that African Ameri-

President Lyndon Johnson speaking to unemployed sawmill operator Tom Fletcher at his home in Inez, Kentucky, where Johnson announced his "unconditional war on poverty," April 24, 1964. © Bettman/CORBIS.

can children had little access to food in the federal school lunch program in his state.[6] The National School Lunch Program, established in 1946, was criticized for reaching only small numbers of children, and particularly for not reaching those in the most need.[7]

The chief problem of the national program to provide free or low-cost lunches to needy children lay in the agenda of its creators, southern senators Richard Russell (Georgia) and Allen Ellender (Louisiana), both members of the powerful Senate Agriculture Committee. Rather than providing for hungry children, historian Susan Levine argues, the National School Lunch Program most benefited white farmers in Russell's and Ellender's districts through federal commodity support.[8] Eligible families received a monthly supply of commodity-driven products, such as flour, cornmeal, dried milk, rice, and, sometimes, butter and cheese.[9] By the 1960s, these programs had laid the economic foundation for industrial agriculture. Agricultural policy "shifted from the small producer, the family farmer, to the large producer, the commercial and corporate farmer."[10] In 1963, Harry McPherson Jr., counsel and speechwriter for President Johnson, argued that "gross inequities" existed because the National School Lunch Program was "administered as a surplus food distribution activity and the methods of administration largely ignore the question of need."[11]

Studies in the Deep South in the early 1960s reported that most black schools had no lunchroom facilities.[12] Wisconsin senator William Proxmire argued that 43 percent of students in the Greenwood, Mississippi, schools were African American, yet they received only one-fifth of subsidized lunches distributed at the school.[13] In 1966, the Child Nutrition Act passed, extending the impact of the National School Lunch Program by enforcing the provision of free lunches. In line with the Civil Rights Act of 1964, the Child Nutrition Act attempted to end racially discriminatory practices that prevented the efficient and fair delivery of food to children in need.[14]

Throughout his presidency, John F. Kennedy pushed for legislation to create a national food stamp program. After Kennedy's assassination, President Johnson continued to lobby for the program in his antipoverty initiatives. On August 31, 1964, Congress authorized a food stamp program—today, known as SNAP (Supplemental Nutrition Assistance Program)—to enable low-income households to receive "a greater share of the Nation's food abundance."[15] People eligible for food stamps, in theory, were given "an opportunity more nearly to obtain a nutritionally adequate diet through the issuance to them of a coupon allotment which shall have a greater monetary value than their normal expenditures for food."[16]

"Fast for Freedom"

Students and Communities Face South

As more Americans became aware of the extent of hunger in the Deep South, volunteer resources were mobilized to send food support to the Mississippi Delta. National student organizations and campus religious associations, as well as the civil rights groups CORE, the NAACP, and SNCC, jointly sponsored "Fast for Freedom" at Brandeis University in 1963.[17] Student activism began in the spring of 1960 following the Greensboro, North Carolina, sit-ins, as Brandeis University students demonstrated solidarity with southern student activists through protests at Boston-area Woolworth's stores.[18] In "Fast for Freedom," students with prepaid meal contracts voluntarily gave up one dinner. The collected funds purchased 80,000 pounds of food—enough to feed 600 families for two weeks.[19] The Teamsters Union contributed shipping costs and scheduled members to drive food to distribution centers in Mississippi and Alabama. President Lyndon Johnson and Reverend Martin Luther King endorsed the successful program.[20] Across the country, volunteer community groups and college students organized similar "Food for Freedom" drives to raise funds and collect food and clothing for African Americans denied relief from federal surplus programs.

During the spring of 1963, food donations and money flowed into Mississippi as a growing crisis in Leflore County unfolded. White administrators halted the distribution of surplus food supplies to needy black families in retaliation against a local voter registration drive.[21] Only minimal quantities of food and welfare aid were available, and only for the "docile poor who 'stayed in line,'" wrote journalist Nick Kotz.[22] Benefits were denied to those who challenged the southern racial code "by demanding full participation in society."[23] After the Chicago Friends of SNCC sent 79,000 pounds of food for distribution in Leflore County, student volunteer James Travis was wounded by a bullet fired into his car outside of Greenwood. SNCC asked Mississippi officials to help protect their workers and supplies.[24] Fred Ross, commissioner of Mississippi's Department of Public Welfare, responded by calling the food aid, including donations by black entertainer Dick Gregory, "publicity stunts, calculated to produce, not avoid, racial violence. The primary beneficiary is Khrushchev and his worldwide propaganda ministry."[25] Private food donations continued to pour into the state from around the country, particularly from regions with significant black populations that had ancestral ties to the South, such as Detroit.[26]

Washington Discovers Hunger in the American South

National exposure of the severe hunger and poverty in the South reached its zenith during the Mississippi tour of Senators Robert Kennedy (New York) and Joseph Clark (Pennsylvania) in April 1967. Marian Wright Edelman, a young civil rights attorney for the NAACP in Mississippi and the first African American woman admitted to the Mississippi bar, testified before the Senate Subcommittee on Employment, Manpower, and Poverty in Washington, D.C. She spoke of the growing hunger in her state at hearings held at the Heidelberg Hotel in Jackson, Mississippi.[27] Edelman urged the senators to not just sit in session, but to meet the hungry poor of Mississippi and see the problem with their own eyes. "They are starving," she said, "and someone has to help them."[28] The senators also heard from local civil rights leaders Unita Blackwell, Charles Evers, Fannie Lou Hamer, and Amzie Moore. Hamer had served as vice chair of the Mississippi Freedom Democratic Party (MFDP), which challenged the all-white delegation chosen to represent the state at the Democratic National Convention in 1964.[29] When the MFDP was offered only two seats at the convention, Hamer famously responded, "We didn't come here for no two seats when all of us is tired."[30]

In the fall of 1967, hearings in Columbia, South Carolina, sponsored by the national Citizens Board of Inquiry into Hunger and Malnutrition in the United States—a group of physicians sponsored by the Field Foundation—revealed egregious conditions and dire stories of impoverished Africans Americans sick and dying from starvation and intestinal parasites.[31] Governor and later senator Ernest "Fritz" Hollins brought the state's devastating conditions to light in his book *The Case against Hunger* (1970).[32] Hollins credits Sister Mary Anthony Monahan of Charleston for making him aware of hunger in his state: "She said, 'No, you don't understand it. I want you to come with me. Come with me.' Well, you can't refuse a Sister. You can be a big shot and busy, but you can't be that big and that busy. I said, 'Yes, ma'am.'"[33]

Journalist Nick Kotz underscored the human consequences of the "Delta area revolution" in the 1960s by comparing white landowner Senator James Eastland and his longtime field worker Atley Taylor.[34] After the government cut Mississippi's cotton allotment by 30 percent in 1966, Eastland received a federal subsidy of $160,000 in 1967 for planting less cotton.[35] The senator reduced his labor force from several hundred farmworkers to ten tractor drivers.[36] The peak work season dropped from 120 days to 50, yet the $1 per hour minimum wage laws still made it cheaper for Eastland to spray chemical weed control than to pay workers to hand-weed his cotton crop.[37] When Taylor lost his job, he was no longer eligible for food stamps, and his family often went hungry with no access to the former food commodity program.[38] In county after county, participation in federal food aid programs dropped by thousands of people.

Kennedy's encounter with a starving child in Mississippi put a face on American hunger. Until that moment, hunger in the American South had been a distant and vague problem for the New York senator. Amzie Moore, who lived and worked in Cleveland, Mississippi, escorted the senators through his town.[39] They entered the run-down home of Annie White, a mother of six children. The family survived on rice and biscuits made from leftover surplus commodities.[40] Kennedy knelt to speak to a toddler sitting on the floor. As much as he tried to connect to the child, she never responded and sat "as if in a trance."[41] The two senators "discovered hunger that day," wrote Nick Kotz, "raw hunger imbedded in the worst poverty the black South had known since the Depression of the 1930s."[42] When Kennedy returned home to Washington that night, his family was eating dinner. Kathleen Kennedy Townsend remembers her father "ashen faced" as he said to them, "In Mississippi a whole family lives in a shack the size of this room. The children are covered with sores and their tummies stick out because they have no food. Do you know

Senator Robert Kennedy shaking the hand of a Catholic nun as he is surrounded by elementary school students during a visit to Greenville, Mississippi, April 11, 1967. © AP/CORBIS.

how lucky you are? Do you know how lucky you are? Do something for your country."[43]

Children and adults exhibited the listlessness associated with malnutrition, as well as hunger-related anemia, growth retardation, protein deficiency, rickets, scurvy, pellagra, and parasitic diseases.[44] Hunger presented itself in schoolchildren's apathy, "fights over food, inattentiveness, acute hunger pangs, withdrawal, and a sense of failure."[45] When children go to school hungry—no breakfast, no money for lunch—"hunger for food overrides hunger for knowledge."[46] One Mississippi mother reported having no food at home but choosing to keep her children at home, rather than sending them to school hungry: "I felt that if I kept them at home with me, at least when they cried and asked for a piece of bread, I would be with them and put my arms around them."[47] Robert Coles, a child psychiatrist and professor at Harvard, worked with poor families in Mississippi and the rural South in the 1960s. In 1969, Coles and southern photojournalist Al Clayton published *Still Hungry in America*, which included their graphic documentation of

Photograph of an empty refrigerator, Mississippi Delta, in Robert Coles and Al Clayton, *Still Hungry in America* (1969). Al Clayton Photographs, 1960s–1980s, #04859, folder 4859/37-38, Southern Historical Collection, Wilson Library, University of North Carolina at Chapel Hill.

southern hunger and poverty shared at the U.S. Senate "Hunger Hearings" in July 1967. Ultimately their work pushed the Senate subcommittee to increase funding for antipoverty programs.[48] Cole's description of the emotional, physical, and cognitive damage children experienced from long-term hunger mirrored Senator Kennedy's encounter with the starving, unresponsive baby in the Delta: "The children . . . ask themselves and others what they have done to be kept from the food they want or what they have done to deserve the pain they seem to feel. . . . Their kind of life can produce a chronic state of mind, a form of withdrawn, sullen behavior."[49]

After returning to Washington, Senators Kennedy and Clark immediately met with Secretary of Agriculture Orville Freeman to request emergency food aid for the people of Mississippi.[50] After Freeman described the complicated procedures that restricted his power, "Robert Kennedy was incredulous. 'I don't know, Orville,' he said. 'I'd just get some food down there.'"[51] Although Freeman promised to send staff to investigate the crisis, the following months and years revealed a maddening display of government inefficiency and racial politics as the United States failed to help thousands of hungry and malnourished citizens.[52] Freeman realized that conservative white leaders of the congressional appropriation and agricultural committees—including Mississippi's Jamie Whitten and James Eastland—would reject social welfare legislation, particularly for African Americans.[53] Later that month, Kennedy spoke to Senator Ellender's subcommittee on agriculture and pushed the members to expand the food stamp program.[54] He again described what he had seen in the Delta: "Here in the United States in 1967 we saw a lot of children with swollen stomachs just as you see them in India or Africa."[55] Senator Everett Jordan of North Carolina replied, "That might be overeating. You cannot tell."[56] Kennedy countered, "No, no it wasn't, because I asked them what they ate. . . . It is a serious problem as to how they are going to get any food."[57] Few Americans were familiar with the bulging stomachs and other symptoms of diseases caused by nutritional deficiencies and thus, like Jordan, were quick to blame the victims for their condition.

The Poor People's Campaign

When Marian Wright Edelman voiced her frustration about federal inaction regarding hunger in Mississippi, Senator Kennedy encouraged her to speak to Reverend Martin Luther King in Atlanta. "He urged me to tell Dr. King to bring the poor people to Washington to make hunger and poverty visible," wrote Edelman.[58] Following King's assassination in 1968, the Poor People's Campaign came to Washington, led by Ralph Abernathy and others, including Edelman, who served as counsel and federal policy liaison for the initiative.[59] Beginning on May 12, 1968, and lasting six weeks, thousands of protesters camped in "Resurrection City" on the National Mall. The Poor People's Campaign's "nonviolent army of the poor" demanded that the government respond to economic inequality, poverty, and hunger in America. Nearly round-the-clock demonstrations at the USDA pressed Orville Freeman and his staff into negotiations with President Johnson and his aides, who were attempting to radically cut government spending.[60] Johnson was loath to approve more money for food, and he told Freeman: "Food comes and food goes. You don't get anything for it. Education and job training get more for the money."[61] Ultimately, the Johnson administration agreed to expand the commodity distribution program, increase appropriations for free and discounted meals for needy children, reform the food stamp program, and create a Senate committee to study hunger.[62]

Hunger, USA—Hunger, the South

The reports of acute malnutrition and hunger as witnessed by Senators Kennedy and Clark led to independent investigations beyond government bureaucracy. The Citizens' Crusade against Poverty, a liberal coalition of educators, physicians, religious leaders, unions, foundations, and social action groups, began an in-depth examination of American hunger and the effectiveness of federal food programs.[63] In the coalition's groundbreaking study, *Hunger, USA*, (1968), co-chairmen Benjamin Mays (president emeritus of Morehouse College) and Leslie Dunbar (executive director of the Field Foundation) presented information from hearings held in the South and throughout the country at which impoverished Americans, medical observers, and public officials spoke. "If you will go look," said Mays and Dunbar, "you will find America a shocking place."[64] Inspired by the powerful images and words of *Hunger, USA*, CBS presented a controversial televised report, "Hunger in America," which aired in 1968.[65] These initiatives galvanized a Senate committee on "Nutrition and Human Needs," chaired by Senator George McGovern of South Dakota in July 1968.[66] McGovern described hunger as "the cutting edge of the problem of poverty."[67] *New York Times* journalist Walter Rugaber explained that "unemployment and welfare problems show up at meal time."[68]

In May 1967, the Citizens' Board of Inquiry into Hunger and Malnutrition traveled to Mississippi to examine its poorest children. The members visited homes where children ate only one meal a day and were severely lacking in necessary vitamins, minerals, and protein: "We saw children who don't get to drink milk, don't get to eat fruit, green vegetables, or meat. They live on starches—grits, bread, Kool Aid. Their parents may be declared ineligible for commodities, ineligible for the food stamp program, even though they have literally nothing."[69] The severity of malnutrition stunned physicians, who identified medical conditions largely seen in underdeveloped countries.[70] Dr. Joseph Brenner of MIT compared conditions in the Mississippi Delta to the worst hunger he had observed in eastern Kenya.[71]

The dire food scenario observed in Mississippi was not confined to that state. Investigators observed hunger in Alabama, Arizona, Florida, Georgia, Kentucky, South Carolina, Texas, Virginia, and West Virginia, and for that matter, in Boston, Washington, D.C., and New York City. One survey examined 1,800 African American households in Alabama (over 10,000 people) and found babies who were given no milk and a daily diet of pork products, fatback, cornbread, beans, and grits—the same substandard meal plan poor whites and blacks had eaten since Reconstruction.[72]

At the 1967 Hunger Hearings in Washington, D.C., Senators James Eastland and John Stennis of Mississippi and Mississippi's Board of Health officer, A. L. Gray, clashed with Senators Kennedy and Clark, as well as committee member Senator Jacob Javits of New York and the Field Foundation medical observers.[73] One of the investigative medical team members, Dr. Raymond Wheeler of Charlotte, North Carolina, described "an unwritten policy on the part of those who control the State to eliminate the Negro Mississippian either by driving him out of the State or starving him to death."[74] Eastland and Stennis denied these charges and accused the southern doctor of libel against the welfare workers of Mississippi.[75] Dr. Wheeler invited the senators and other state officials to "come with me to the delta and I will show you the bright eyes, the shriveled arms and swollen bellies of the children."[76] Journalist Nathan Miller reported, "He had no takers."[77] A shouting match erupted between Javits and Orville Freeman as the senator prodded the secretary to disregard the ineffectual local authorities in Mississippi, declare an emergency, and get food to Mississippi immediately.[78] "We seem to be able to send airplanes to the Congo in a terrible hurry," said Javits. "We first heard of the desperation point of poor Mississippi Negroes 18 months ago . . . and we are still hearing that there is starvation in Mississippi."[79]

"I'd Like to Feel That I'd Done Something to Lessen the Suffering"

On March 25, 1968, British journalist Sir David Frost interviewed Senator Robert Kennedy—the last personal interview of Kennedy before his assassination. Frost asked Kennedy how he would want to be remembered. Kennedy, like King, spoke of making a contribution to his country and helping to improve the lives of others: "We can lessen the number of suffering children, and if you do not do this, then who will do this? I'd like to feel that I'd done something to lessen the suffering."[80] Despite the issues that divided the country, Kennedy believed Americans were surely united on one necessity, "*that starvation in this land of enormous wealth is nothing short of indecent*—and that policy which fails to use the tools at hand to feed the hungry is a policy unworthy of our support."[81] On June 5, 1968, Kennedy was assassinated as he walked through the kitchen of the Ambassador Hotel in Los Angeles after winning the Democratic nomination in the California primary election for the presidency.

"Freedom from Hunger and Poverty"

Pig Banks and Southern Cooperative Farms

In Mississippi, Fannie Lou Hamer continued her activism as a community organizer committed to economic equity for African Americans and, ultimately independence from white-controlled agriculture and industry. The daughter of sharecroppers, Hamer grew up in the rural worlds of the Delta and intimately understood the impoverishment, hunger, and racial disfranchisement in the region. In 1969, with the support of the National Council of Negro Women, Hamer created a "Pig Bank" in Sunflower County in Mississippi.[82] She purchased forty gilts (females) and five boars (males).[83] As soon as the pigs had piglets, babies were given to local families, who built up their own livestock herds and eventually gave pregnant sows to other needy families. Hamer's Pig Bank was not unlike the Heifers for Relief program established in 1944 by Dan West, a midwestern farmer and relief worker. Today, Heifer International, a global nonprofit headquartered in Little Rock, Arkansas, remains committed to ending hunger *permanently*. Families are given livestock and training to free them from the "indignity of depending on others to feed their children."[84]

After the success of the Pig Bank, Hamer founded the Freedom Farm Cooperative in Sunflower County.[85] The goal of the farm was to provide "FREEDOM from hunger and poverty" and to secure long-term economic independence for local African American families through cooperatively owned land, food production, and decent housing.[86] Hamer knew that if people controlled their land, they controlled their destiny: "You can give a man some food and he'll eat it. Then he'll be hungry again. But give a man some ground and he'll never be hungry no more."[87] Singer and civil rights activist Harry Belafonte was a strong supporter of Hamer and participated in fund-raising efforts for the Freedom Farm.[88] Between

1969 and her death in 1976, Hamer increased the original forty acres to several thousand, which was used for food production, cash crops of cotton and soybeans, housing, and entrepreneurial activities. Food crops such as butter beans, snap beans, collard greens, field peas, tomatoes, turnips, mustard greens, and sweet potatoes were used by farm members, given to needy families in Sunflower County, and marketed locally in the Delta.[89] Management and financial setbacks ultimately led to the closure of the Freedom Farm. Writer John T. Edge argues that Hamer's intrepid commitment to black food production in the 1960s and 1970s set precedents for "current dialogues about food sovereignty."[90]

Another agricultural and food cooperative in the Mississippi Delta, the North Bolivar Farm Cooperative, was established on 120 acres of rented land in Bolivar County in the mid-1960s.[91] An initiative of the Delta Health Center in Mound Bayou, the cooperative was one of the first community health centers in the nation, initially sponsored by Tufts University. Dr. Jack Geiger, civil rights activist and director of the Delta Health Center, described the "enormous futility" of tackling health problems, including hunger and malnutrition, without building an economic infrastructure for the local African American community.[92] A soul food cannery was planned to process collards, gumbos, and mustard greens for the "ethnic market."[93]

The founding of the Federation of Southern Cooperatives in February 1967 was an important milestone in securing the economic future of black-owned food production. The organization expanded the rapidly dwindling landholdings of African American farmers throughout the South.[94] The Federation of Southern Cooperatives was rooted in earlier southern cooperative farming initiatives inspired by New Deal programs, which in large part were a "bad deal for black farmers" because of reduced cotton acreage for black and white tenants and sharecroppers.[95] Many of the early members of the interracial Delta and Providence Cooperative Farms founded in the Mississippi Delta in the late 1930s were unemployed and evicted sharecroppers, who had suffered from the impact of the Agricultural Adjustment Act, as well as strikes in eastern Arkansas.[96] At the Delta Cooperative Farm in Hillhouse, Mississippi, working members signed a contract stating they would "share and share alike . . . from the net sale of all crops."[97] Beyond growing cotton, the cooperatives included beef cattle, a dairy farm, and a pasteurizing plant. In Arkansas, segregated cooperative farms—Lake Dick and Dyess Colony for white families and Lake View for black families—were founded by the Resettlement Administration to encourage independent landownership. Renowned singer and songwriter Johnny Cash was just a toddler when his family moved to Dyess in the early 1930s. Farm

Security Administration photographs of the cooperative farms featured model electric kitchens, farmwives preserving food, and healthy schoolchildren receiving cod liver oil and orange juice. The Clarendon County Improvement Association (founded in North Carolina in 1956) and the Grand Marie Vegetable Producers Cooperative, Inc. (founded in Louisiana in 1965), offered education and assistance to black growers discriminated against for their involvement in civil rights activities.[98]

In Lafayette, Louisiana, Father A. J. McKnight helped low-income community members organize the Southern Consumers Cooperative (founded in the 1960s).[99] This successful initiative spun off several businesses, including the Acadian Delight Bakery, whose fruitcakes and pastries were distributed nationally from Lake Charles.[100] In 1969, McKnight and Charles Prejean, the first director of the Federation of Southern Cooperatives, were invited by the Israeli labor movement to visit kibbutz and moshav farming cooperatives.[101] Ford Foundation funding followed, bringing Israeli agricultural specialists to the South to consult with African American farmers.[102]

Like Fannie Lou Hamer, early leaders of the Federation of Southern Cooperatives were trained in the civil rights movement.[103] Charles Prejean recalled conversations between black farmers and VISTA volunteers and SNCC and CORE workers in the 1960s regarding land preservation.[104] Black farmers were committed to education, but getting food on family tables was their first priority.[105] "They wanted to learn how to do that," noted Prejean. "Right away. And we didn't know how to teach it. So we started looking for solutions, looking into things like credit unions and the whole co-op movement."[106] Ezra Cunningham, a black farmer and activist from Monroe County, Alabama, said, "You can't eat freedom. And a ballot is not to be confused with a dollar bill."[107]

In the late 1960s, financial support from the Field Foundation, the Ford Foundation, and the Office of Economic Opportunity funded agricultural co-ops throughout the South that helped farmers work as one entity to market their sweet potatoes, field peas, and cabbage crops. Food-processing companies had to negotiate a fair price for all, rather than playing "one struggling farmer against another."[108] The cooperatives assisted farmers in building livestock operations, constructing catfish ponds, and planting fruit orchards. In 1985, the Federation of Southern Cooperatives merged with the Land Assistance Fund. The successful settlement of class-action lawsuits against the USDA for the systematic discrimination against African American farmers on the basis of race occurred in 2010. The largest civil rights settlement to date, $1.25 billion, was allocated to pay thousands of southern black farmers who failed to receive farm loans and federal assistance from the USDA.[109] Although the USDA settled the case, Pete Daniel argues the agency never admitted its discrimination against black farmers.[110]

The Changing Appearance of Southern Hunger

Today, as the nation reels from daily reports of food insecurity, food deserts, and the new malnutrition—obesity complicated by diabetes, heart disease, and hypertension—critics of America's troubled food system continue to call for the removal of federal food programs from the USDA. Consider the contrasting physical appearance of malnutrition and hunger in the South in the 1960s and today. As the reports of policy makers and physicians confirmed in the 1960s, hungry southerners suffered from scarcity rooted in acute poverty. Many had little or no access to food for several days each month.[111] From the Depression-era photographs of the Farm Security Administration in the 1930s and 1940s to the documentary photography of antihunger reports in the 1960s, low-income white and black southerners' hunger was reflected in adults' gaunt frames and children's swollen bellies. In the *Hunger, USA* report, numerous cases were documented of malnourished pregnant mothers in Louisiana and Alabama who ate laundry starch and clay—a practice called geophagy—to satisfy nutritional deficiencies.[112] Dr. Milton Senn, a professor of pediatrics at Yale, observed, "Children in Mississippi appeared uniformly thin. . . . I would judge that more than 50 percent are less than the third percentile in weight."[113]

Monthly food allocations were scant, and were largely staples—surplus commodities such as cornmeal, grits, flour, powdered milk, peanut butter, rice, and oatmeal. If a low-income family acquired these supplies once a month at a distribution site, it was then necessary to cook and prepare the food at home, which assumed a working kitchen to assemble meals.[114] And, even with access to these supplies, food from government programs in the 1960s provided less than half the calories an adult needed to survive, and poor families could not afford food stamps.[115] In 1967, 29.9 million Americans were impoverished.[116] Food programs reached only 18 percent of this number, or 5.4 million people.[117] The majority of impoverished Americans received no food aid, and the small numbers that did were still grossly underfed. From the early 1900s to the 1960s, impoverished southerners were emaciated due to inadequate calories and nutrients and the infectious diseases and conditions associated with hunger and malnutrition.

In the late 1970s, the appearance of hunger and malnutrition in the South, as in the rest of the nation, began to change radically.[118] Malnourished southerners were increasingly obese rather than fitting the traditional image of "skin-and-bones" impoverishment. The economic problems underlying hunger in the South did not change. Hungry southerners continued to suffer from acute poverty, and many had even less than the impoverished of a generation ago. The work of low-income southerners changed from the strenuous manual labor of field work to less physically demanding factory and assembly-line jobs. Substandard facilities in which to prepare food, a loss of cooking skills, less time due to multiple jobs, little or no physical activity, no fresh foods or gardens, lower prices for unhealthy processed foods, and urban neighborhoods and rural areas with few or no grocery stores made poor southerners more reliant on processed and packaged prepared foods. Thousands of southerners continued to have reduced access to food for several days every month, and when they did obtain food, it was cheap and fattening. Calorie-dense, packaged, and processed convenience foods and sugary drinks—the foods most readily accessible in fast-food venues and urban and rural markets—became the most affordable and quickest means of feeding a hungry family in the 1980s. Even the region's beloved "sweet tea" (heavily sugared ice tea, consumed year-round) was a major component in malnutrition and obesity.

This pattern continues in the contemporary South, where low-income southerners eat a diet high in fat and refined sugars and grains. Global nutrition scholar Barry Popkin refers to the "diseases of civilizations" that are a result of this diet—heart disease, hypertension, diabetes, obesity, and cancer—conditions exacerbated by the stripping of vitamins, minerals, and fibers from processed rice, wheat, and corn.[119] These refined grains and excess fat and sugar comprise the highly processed food products that dominate the southern plate. Malnutrition in the South today is the result of a diet largely composed of substandard, non-nutritive foods combined with minimal physical activity, rather than the problem of grossly inadequate food supplies experienced in the 1930s and 1960s. In 1969, Nick Kotz described the "politics of hunger" as a "dismal story of human greed and callousness, of immorality sanctioned and aided by the government of the United States."[120] Tragically, his statement remains largely true today.

In the late 1960s, civil rights activism and the antipoverty/hunger initiatives were gradually eclipsed by a growing counterculture rooted in the anti–Vietnam War protests and escalating movements focused on black power, women's rights, sexual freedom, the environment, and ecology. These political ideologies found expression at many southern universities, colleges, and liberal enclaves throughout the region, where students, faculty, and community activists awakened their neighbors to a social revolution focused on ecology, military disengagement, gender equality, and black rights. Food was a powerful symbol as well as the fuel that supported a small but vocal counterculture movement in the American South.

18

A Food Counterculture, Southern-Style

The southern counterculture of the late 1960s and early 1970s was shaped by political activism reverberating from strongholds of the student movement in Berkeley, Ann Arbor, and Cambridge. Food was central to new ideologies as activists turned eating into a political act and created what Warren Belasco describes as a "countercuisine."[1] Members of this vibrant youth culture rejected the patriarchy and "near orgiastic consumerism" of their parents' generation, including the commercially processed food they associated with the establishment.[2] The fuel of the counterculture became "natural" foods—a cornucopia of unprocessed grains and beans, homemade yogurt, sprouts, fermented goods, home-baked bread, farm-grown fruits and vegetables, cheeses, and soy products—considered an antidote to a "tasteless and odorless America."[3] Although finding and preparing these foods was challenging in the South, this effort was often the first step in building a committed and dedicated "alternative" community that addressed local issues of social inequity and reform.

Radical Food Reform Southern Cooperative Farms, Communes, and "Intentional Communities"

In progressive pockets of the South, farmers' markets, buying clubs, food cooperatives or "co-ops," vegetarian, health, and natural food restaurants, bakeries, communes, group houses, and alternative bookstores were evidence of the emerging counterculture. In the hills of Tennessee, the Ozarks of northwestern Arkansas, the Blue Ridge Mountains of Virginia, the North Carolina Piedmont, and many other locations throughout the mountain and rural South, a devoted core of "back-to-the-landers" embraced an agrarian-focused philosophy that emphasized self-sufficiency, environmentalism, women's rights, and sustainable, small-scale food production.[4] Kentucky writer and activist Wendell Berry's critique of industrial agriculture and the loss of small-scale farming inspired many southern activists to reject conventional careers and "return to the land" to grow their own food and raise small livestock.[5] One commune in Georgia had houses in both Athens and Atlanta and a working farm in the countryside. Janice Walker, a professor at Georgia Southern University, joined the Athens Family commune in 1970 and recalled visiting the farm: "We'd go out there and work sometimes, because if you wanted to eat, you helped."[6]

These were not the first southerners to participate in cooperative initiatives and homesteading or to engage in radical food reform—consider the home economists, nutritionists, agriculture faculty, and settlement schoolteachers of the early twentieth-century South, as well as the many cooperative farm initiatives of the civil rights era.[7] New Deal–inspired farms and housing cooperatives in the 1930s and 1940s, such as the interracial Delta and Providence Cooperative Farms in Mississippi and Eleanor Roosevelt's pet projects—the planned homestead community of Arthurdale, West Virginia (1934), and that same year, Penderlea Homesteads in Pender County, North Carolina, and Cumberland Homesteads in Crossville, Tennessee—were dedicated to helping impoverished white southerners live more economically yet remain active consumers.[8] Penderlea was the utopian vision of Wilmington businessman Hugh MacRae, who believed planned small farming communities were a solution to the collapse of the American family farm during the Depression. Government agents removed black farmers by purchasing their land below value and then chose the new Penderlea participants—white, Christian, poor families with children—the more boys, the better one's chances of being chosen.[9] Federal dollars for the segregated homestead projects, which settled displaced families on land where they were expected to grow much of their own food, came from the Subsistence Homestead Fund, which was included in President Roosevelt's National Industrial Recovery Act of 1933. Government funding ended by the 1940s due to the prohibitive cost of maintaining the homestead projects, plus the growing conservative critique of these initiatives as socialism.

The influential School of Living in rural Freeland, Maryland, represents a political transition from the New Deal projects created to "supplement, not subvert, capitalism" and the radicalized cooperatives of the 1960s and 1970s.[10] Founded by agrarian activist Ralph Borsodi in 1936, the program promoted self-sufficient cooperative homesteads and "simple living" that reclaimed home food production.[11] Under the leadership of Borsodi's student Mildred Loomis, the school became the Heathcote Center in the 1960s, an intentional community that was an important model for communes of the counterculture generation, including several southern venues.[12]

Another influential southern cooperative farming project was Koinonia Farms, a small interracial "intentional Christian community," located outside Americus, Georgia, in rural Sumter County. Activists Clarence and Florence Jordan and Martin and Mabel England founded

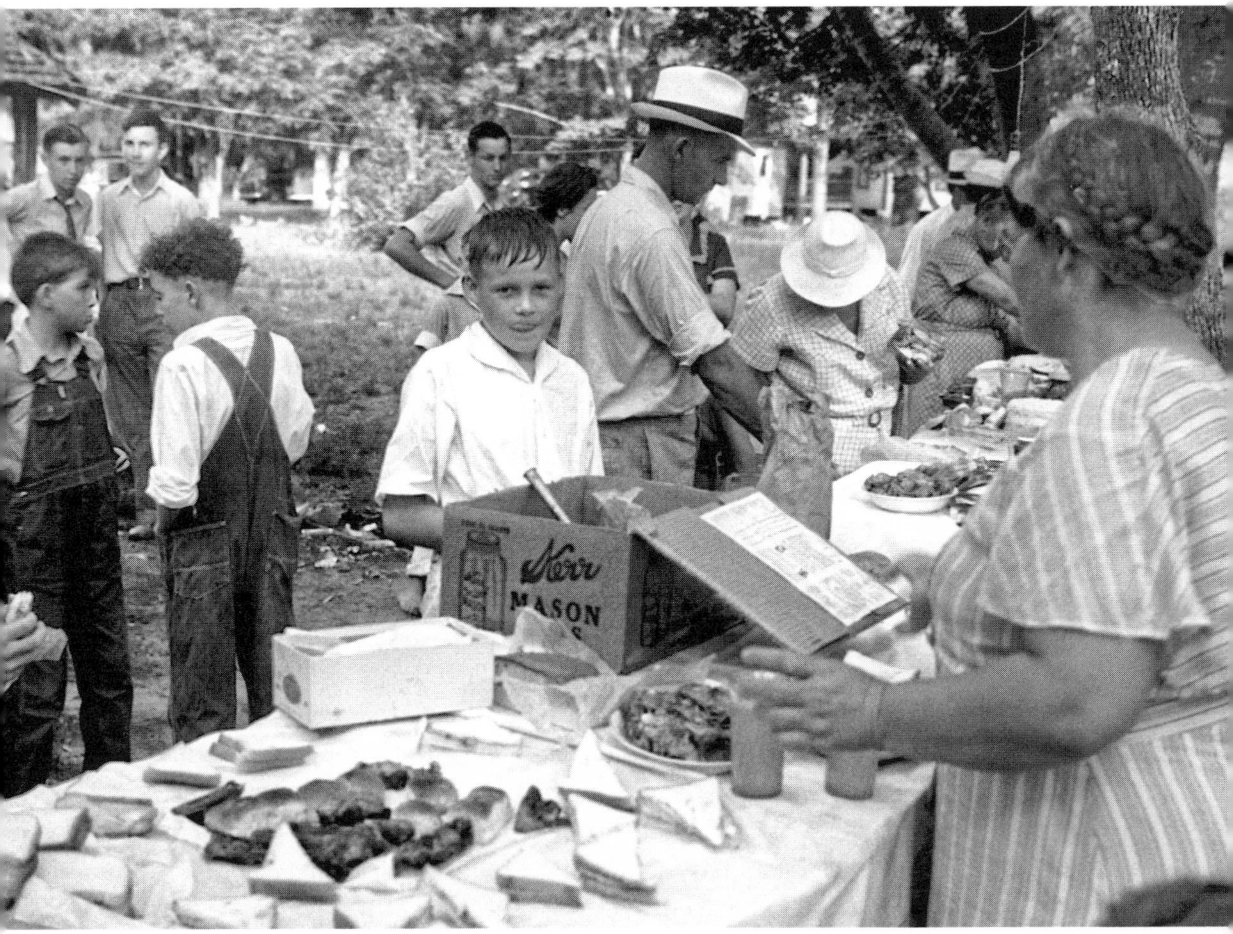

"Sunday School Picnic, Penderlea Homesteads, North Carolina." Photograph by Ben Shahn, 1937. LC-USF33-006316-M5 (b&w film nitrate neg.), U.S. Farm Security Administration/Office of War Information, Prints and Photographs Division, Library of Congress, Washington, D.C.

the farm in 1942.[13] In the heart of the Jim Crow South the two couples created a "demonstration plot for the Kingdom of God" to assist the region's poor white and black sharecroppers and tenant farmers.[14] Conservative whites and local chapters of the Ku Klux Klan opposed Koinonia's support of African Americans, expressed in violence, from firebombs to death threats. As a means of survival in a hostile region, Koinonia created a mail-order business to market its homegrown peanuts and pecans.[15] Today the successful business includes a bakery and on-line store that generate much of the farm's revenue. Koinonia was also the birthplace of the idea for Habitat for Humanity, an affordable housing initiative founded by Millard and Linda Fuller, who visited the farm in 1965.[16]

One of the best-known and longest-lived communes or "intentional communities" from the counterculture era exists in the South. In 1971, teachers and social activists Stephen and Ina May Gaskin and their counterculture followers founded The Farm in Summertown, Tennessee. The Gaskins led two hundred individuals in a caravan of sixty school buses from Haight-Ashbury in San Francisco on a cross-country journey to acquire land and build "the community of their ideals."[17] In middle Tennessee, the collective purchased a 1,000-acre former cattle ranch, where members established homesteads and farmland and began initiatives focused on environmentalism, natural childbirth, alternative technologies, nonviolence, and vegetarianism. Religious studies scholar Timothy Miller describes The Farm as "the one commune that most perfectly epitomized the spirit of the communal 1960s era."[18]

The kitchen was the heart of most communes, and this was certainly the case at The Farm, both in communal housing shared by members and in the single-family homes on the property.[19] Veganism was the dietary practice of members of The Farm, who, in accordance with their nonviolent philosophy regarding animals, did not eat meat, eggs, milk products, or honey or use any products derived from animals.[20] Today, over two hundred residents spanning four generations live at The Farm, which has expanded to 2,000 acres. They work in businesses that support the community, including food-related commerce such as a mail-order "Healthy Eating Catalogue" and companies that manufacture soy products and grow-your-own mushroom kits. The first commercial soy ice cream, "Ice Bean," was developed at The Farm.[21] The wholesome diet and vegetarian cuisine at the heart of The Farm's mission is featured in several macrobiotic and vegan cookbooks published by the community. The Farm's Ecovillage Training Center, built in the 1990s, offers courses in sustainable development to thousands of visitors each year, including intensive organic gardening workshops and vegan cooking retreats.[22]

Twin Oaks is another historic intentional community in the South. Located in Louisa County, in rural central Virginia, this "eco-conscious" sustainable co-housing community was founded in 1967. (Co-housing refers to a collaboratively administered cluster of single-family homes, supported by shared facilities, such as a common building for cooking/dining, garden plots, and recreational areas.) Twin Oaks is not organized around a religion or charismatic leader. Its website explains: "We may get close to worshiping a dinner made from our tofu and organic garden fare, but that's as far as it goes."[23] Like at The Farm, the one hundred or so members who live at Twin Oaks participate in income sharing by working in one of the community businesses. Twin Oaks Community Foods, a worker-owned cooperative, generates much of the income for the organization through its popular tofu line and other soy products distributed throughout the East Coast at major retailers like Whole Foods. Twin Oaks Community Seeds, a certified organic, heirloom seed operation, grows over fifty varieties of plants each year, including traditional southern food crops such as field peas, okra, peanuts, pole beans, sorghum, and watermelon.

Food and Feminism

In New Orleans, regional voices of the counterculture came alive in the *Distaff* (1973), one of the South's first feminist newspapers. The political power of food was clearly visible in the paper, which featured articles about the city's first food co-ops, announcements of women's potluck gatherings, and reports on "alternative lifestyles," including a feminist farm in northwestern Arkansas. Leaders of the local women's movement in New Orleans edited the paper, including journalist Mary Gehman and teacher and social activist Suzanne Pharr.[24] Gehman came to New Orleans via New York City, where she was active in the women's movement, including taking part in protests against the Miss America Pageant in 1968 and 1969.[25] Pharr, from a working-class farming family in rural Georgia, moved to New Orleans in 1969, inspired to work for social change in the local counterculture.[26] A women's center was founded in New Orleans, followed by consciousness-raising groups, housing collectives, food-buying cooperatives, street theater, and the *Distaff* newspaper.[27] Food-related events in the community confirmed that the "personal is political," the rallying cry of the feminist movement. A *Distaff* notice entitled "Don't Ms," invited locals to a potluck supper sponsored by the National Women's Political Caucus: "Bring a covered dish. No admission. Supper begins 7 pm."[28]

In November 1973, Mary Gehman reported on protests against New Orleans's old-line dining clubs and restaurants that prohibited women as members, such as Hotel Monteleone's Men's Grille in the French Quarter and Hotard's in Gretna.[29] Attorney Debra Millenson filed suit against Hotel Monteleone in May 1972 for sexual discrimination, but the Fifth Circuit Court of Appeals ultimately dismissed the case. "Contacts and decisions are made in the business world over drinks and meals," noted Gehman. "As long as women are excluded from such bars and eating accommodation, the idea of equal opportunity for women in business careers is just an idea."[30] After women sociologists attended a convention at the Monteleone and were barred from the restaurant, the National Organization for Women joined the academics in protesting the "men's only" policy.[31] Before the week ended, the Men's Grille had changed its policy. Gehman titled her piece for the *Distaff* "'People's Grille' Open to the Public."[32]

Suzanne Pharr reported on her "back-to-the-land" farming experience in northwestern Arkansas in 1973.[33] Fired from a private school teaching position in New Orleans after coming out as a lesbian, Pharr moved to Huckleberry Farm, one of many communes and collective organizations centered in and around Fayetteville where the women's movement was "raging."[34] Rural projects were particularly compelling after the Kent State student shootings in May 1970. "Antiwar activists were going back to the land, to try to create another kind of society," wrote Pharr, "trying to figure out some other way to live . . . [after] understanding we had a government that would shoot us."[35] Women-only communes and housing collectives also countered sexism in the male-dominated counterculture, where supposedly "enlightened" men expected women to cook, clean, *and* be willing sexual partners.[36]

Pharr and her friends lived in an old log home at Huckleberry Farm, where residents came and went. "We were part of this network where people knew that there were folks like us all over the South," wrote Pharr, "and I guess all over the country."[37] They planted a small garden, built chicken houses, fenced the yard, canned tomatoes, and put up jars of jelly and apple butter.[38] Growing, preparing, and preserving food was an important statement of their independence, including plans to purchase a wood-burning cookstove.[39] "When a problem or task arises, we set ourselves to it without first thinking of how we can get outside help," wrote Pharr. "Consequently, we feel strong in body and mind. . . . A month begins to set one free."[40] Pharr was a back-to-the-lander for four years in Arkansas, eventually directing the local Head Start program. In 1999, Pharr became the first female director of the Highlander Center in Monteagle, Tennessee, a nonprofit dedicated to social and economic justice, co-founded by educator-activist Myles Horton in 1932.

An equally vocal antifeminist cohort in the region existed, which included white female representatives of STOP ERA, Phyllis Schlafly's campaign against the Equal Rights Amendment. Schlafly and her arch-conservative followers believed the ERA would end protective legislation for women and subject them to the military draft.[41] In Georgia, STOP ERA members presented fresh loaves of bread to Georgia legislators in 1974 in a publicity effort to defeat the amendment. Historian Robin Morris describes how each "homemade" loaf was labeled, "From the breadmaker to the breadwinner," although the loaves came from a commercial Atlanta business, Mom's Bakery.[42] The busy committeewomen did not have the time, or the inclination, to bake the bread themselves. Kathryn Dunaway, chair of Georgia STOP ERA, thanked the male owner of the bakery: "Through your generosity we were able to impress upon the legislators that we breadmakers depend on the bread winner and we want our laws to remain as they now protect us."[43] The success of the "Bread Project" in several states was noted by Schlafly: "All the legislators loved it, the publicity was fabulous, our girls had lots of fun and the project put the libbers on the defensive."[44] Journalist Carole Ashkinaze covered the ERA campaign while working at the *Atlanta-Journal Constitution*. She remembered Schlafly and her "confederates" in Georgia, dressed in feminine pink, bringing cookies, cupcakes, and brownies to legislators and accusing ERA "militant radicals" of "trying to destroy the family."[45] In 1982, the State of Georgia opposed the final ratification of the federal ERA.

Elsewhere in Atlanta in the 1970s, "libbers" were gaining strength and numbers in Georgia's growing women's movement and counterculture. The local underground newspaper, the *Great Speckled Bird*, like New Orleans's *Distaff*, was an important weekly venue for news of the New Left, including food-related events. The *Bird*, as it was commonly known, listed area coffeehouses, natural food co-ops like Sevananda in Little Five Points, and health food venues such as the "gourmet ethnic vegetarian cuisine" of the Morningstar Inn, located by the Emory Cinema.[46] A special Food Day issue of the *Bird* (April 17, 1975) examined the exploitative "Politics of Food" in America and advocated food co-ops over "your faceless grocer."[47] The issue published a recipe for granola and commended the soybean-based diet of The Farm's residents in Tennessee. Readers were warned to avoid the "terrible ten," including foods such as "Wonder Bread," bacon—"perhaps the most dangerous food in the supermarket" (carcinogenic "nitrosamines")—table grapes (the United Farm Workers' boycott was under way), and Coca-Cola ("no nutrients").[48] This 1970s critique of America's "mammoth" food corporations, which "shoot up cattle and chicken with chemicals" and "dye fruit bright shiny colors . . . because they sell better," laid the foundation for the contemporary local-food movement in the South and its opposition to industrial agriculture.[49] The *Great Speckled Bird* connected the counterculture worlds of Atlanta to similar communities across the Southeast, where like-minded students and activists found one another at potluck meals, organic markets, vegetarian restaurants, and food co-op meetings.[50]

Rainbow Politics Southern Co-Ops, Buying Clubs, Restaurants, Grocery Stores

In the early 1970s, natural foods–advocate John Deming came to Mississippi, where he hoped to foster a community committed to vegetarianism and to spread interest in the counterculture ideology throughout the South.[51] Deming had deep family roots in the South, having grown up in Louisiana, where he attended Tulane University and became active in Students for a Democratic Society.[52] After dropping out of school in 1969, he helped found communes in Vermont and California before returning to the South. In Jackson, Mississippi, Deming met Renee Rosenfeld, a committed macrobiotic cook and a skilled herbalist.[53] The study of herbs and their medicinal and nutritional properties was a specialty area that many women gravitated to in the counterculture, inspired by not only the herbs but a feminist reclaiming of a "lost" women's art.[54] Deming and Rosenfeld began a small macrobiotic restaurant in Rosenfeld's home and eventually opened a natural foods store, Singing River Granary.[55] Managers from Erewhon, a national leader in the macrobiotic and natural foods industry, visited the store, curious about the success of a counterculture business in Mississippi.[56] Impressed by Deming's vision, they asked him to work for Erewhon, where he became a leading figure in the company until the early 1980s.[57]

The natural foods movement—energized and supported by counterculture activists in the South such as Suzanne Pharr and John Deming—is now more than forty years old. In the early days, like-minded southerners found one another at the same political gatherings, marches, potluck dinners, coffee shops, and independent movie houses, such as Ron Shapiro's 1970s-era Hoka Theater and Moonlight Café in Oxford, Mississippi, near the University of Mississippi. Famous for its alternative films and a menu that ranged from "sprout and bean" fare to hot fudge pie, the Hoka had a laid-back atmosphere that was best expressed in its sign: "No Shoes. No Shirt. Who Cares."[58] In neighborhoods near universities and colleges and in student ghettos in low-rent districts, friends and families created food-buying clubs and co-ops to purchase bulk goods from a wholesaler. In the early 1970s, Ellen Weiss organized a food co-op near Vanderbilt University in Nashville with a group of friends, including my sister, Jamie Cohen. "We had a meeting at our house," said Weiss. "Susan Schewel looked around and said, "It's the same old people."[59] Inspired by their small but loyal crew, they named their co-op SOP (Same Old People).[60]

Many first-time members of southern food co-ops became more deeply entrenched in the counterculture, as well as in the continuing civil rights movement, in part because of food and the radical politics shared over a meal with friends. Mealtime was central to both activism and community building *because* of conversation. "Dinner was prime communal time," writes Timothy Miller, the "glue that held the community together."[61] In Richmond, Virginia, the 1970s Mulberry Family commune encouraged members to use chopsticks at all meals to create a less hurried pace and to promote more discussion.[62]

Local counterculture activists were loyal customers of ethnic restaurants, bars, and grocery stores in southern cities—usually Greek-, Lebanese-, Indian-, or Asian-owned venues. They appreciated the opportunity to purchase difficult-to-find supplies of bulk rice, grains, beans, olive oil, hummus, and fresh-roasted coffee south of the Mason-Dixon Line.[63] They also embraced inexpensive and filling soul food—the "urbanized food of rural southern blacks"—in African American-owned cafés, snack shops, and juke joints.[64] These businesses marked the borders between the white and black neighborhoods of southern cities, and counterculture followers congregated to the liminal worlds between high- and low-rent areas.

Newly arrived back-to-the-landers and start-up farmers in the rural South created a demand in unlikely places for natural foods and specialty products, from black beans and brown rice, to imported wine and beer, to gourmet cheeses. In the mid-1970s in Alamance County, North Carolina, Cornucopia Country Store, owned by Marti and John Doyle and later by Susan Ripley and Verne Dregalla, reflected this transition, as bins of dried beans and nuts, fresh-baked bread, local milk, and produce were offered alongside canned pork and beans, candy bars, and cold sodas.[65] Community members nicknamed Cornucopia the "fatback to tofu" store, as those items sat side by side in the cooler.[66] In the 1980s, the gourmet food portion of the business evolved into Cornucopia Cheese and Specialty Foods, founded by former employee Noland Thuss.

Food-buying clubs and co-ops organized by individuals and families in smaller southern communities often ordered wholesale and bulk supplies from natural foods companies such as Erewhon in Boston and Walnut Acres in Penns Creek, Pennsylvania. In 1976, scholars Ted and Dale Rosengarten moved from Somerville, Massachusetts, to the small town of McClellanville, South Carolina. They chose the community in part, writes Dale Rosengarten, because of people they met there: "Counterculture types who hated the war in Vietnam, loved the marsh and woods, and ate wholesome foods, not exactly what we expected to find in the Deep South in those days."[67] In the following year, the Rosengartens and friends began a food co-op: "I remember 5-gallon vats of honey, bulk grains, nuts, raisins.... On distribution days we would have pot luck dinners."[68] Enthusiasm for the co-op was high but waned as many members "got 'real jobs' and didn't have the time for the collective work and enforced socializing that went along with membership."[69]

James Beard Award–winning food writer and children's author Crescent Dragonwagon moved from New York City to the Ozark Mountains, first to southern Missouri, then to northwest Arkansas, in the early

Ted and Dale Rosengarten and their son Carlin, McClellanville, South Carolina, 1984. Photograph by Greg Day, Dale Rosengarten Collection.

1970s. Born Ellen Zolotow, as a young feminist and participant in the late 1960s counterculture she chose the name "Crescent Dragonwagon" to reflect her independence from patriarchy.[70] Dragonwagon's *The Commune Cookbook* (1972) described her earlier experience in a Brooklyn commune in the late 1960s. In 1970, she began a thirty-six-year adventure in the Ozark Mountains, where she and others established a commune. "But where to?" she wrote at the conclusion of *The Commune Cookbook*. "To the country, to new worlds. . . . It's in the Ozarks and it's a beautiful farm. . . . Open to people who want to build a new way of life, set up an example of how things will maybe be after the revolution . . . growing our own food."[71] Dragonwagon later established Dairy Hollow House, an inn in Eureka Springs, Arkansas, whose "Nouveau 'Zarks" menu drew from heritage Ozark recipes but reflected the food politics of the counterculture.[72]

Although counterculture-related businesses were nowhere as vibrant as in the Northeast or on the West Coast, many moderate-sized southern cities had a food co-op or health food restaurant during the 1960s and 1970s. Some failed to last more than a few months or a year, while others became beloved institutions that continue to thrive today.[73] Eight food co-ops existed in New Orleans by 1974.[74] The *Distaff* reported that VISTA staff members were organizing the co-ops and had plans to open a central food warehouse.[75] For those unfamiliar with this alternative to commercial grocery stores, a *Distaff* writer explained that "a food

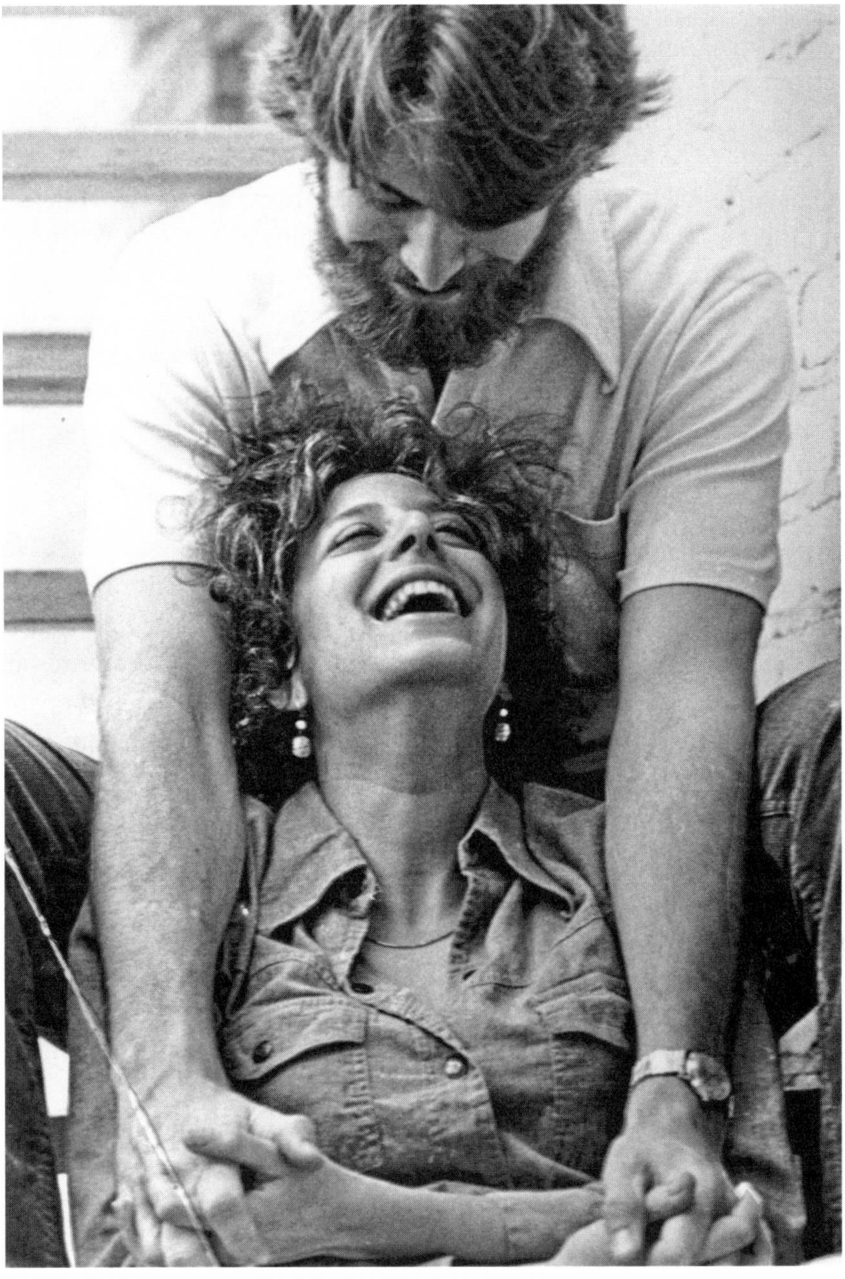

Crescent Dragonwagon and Ned Shank, Little Rock, Arkansas, 1977.
Photograph by Louise Terzia, Crescent Dragonwagon Collection.

co-op is a group of people in a community who get together and buy food wholesale, such as the French Market."[76] Plans were also in place for a New Orleans "Community Co-op Food Store" that would sell bulk "grains, flours (whole and cracked grain, of course), seeds, honey, oils, spices, dried beans, etc."[77] The buying power of a larger venue provided selection and savings that smaller co-ops or food-buying clubs in the city could not offer members. These initiatives suggest the evolution of a southern counterculture natural foods economy, particularly in southern cities and university communities such as New Orleans and Atlanta. For activists unfamiliar with the lingo of doing business, the reporter explained: "In order to stock the store in the beginning . . . it is necessary to have capital (that's money) for the initial order."[78]

The western mountains of North Carolina became a center of counterculture activity in the 1960s and 1970s, and remain so today. As back-to-the-landers and spiritual seekers moved to the region, they created alternatives to commercial food venues, such as Asheville's French Broad Food Co-op (1975), which began as a local buying club for friends and families. The same year, Roger Derrough founded Dinner for the Earth, a natural foods grocery in Asheville. Locals at the time considered the "health food" a bit pricey and nicknamed it "Dinner for the Rich," not unlike today's moniker for Whole Foods, "Whole Salary." In the 1990s, the business evolved into the multi-store, natural grocery chain Earth Fare. Another successful food entrepreneur, Great Eastern Sun, began in Asheville in 1981 and imports and manufactures an extensive line of largely Asian natural and organic foods. The company website attributes Asheville's "focused spiritual power" to the presence of a vortex, or magnetic energy, that is "still potent today."[79]

Nearby Hendersonville, North Carolina, was the headquarters for *Mother Earth News* (1970), the bible of believers committed to simple living and careful stewardship of planet Earth. The magazine became the go-to, how-to source for those seeking what 1950s homesteaders and back-to-the-land pioneers Scott and Helen Nearing described as "the good life." Many articles focused on do-it-yourself food projects, from instructions for growing an organic garden to home canning, baking bread, planting an orchard, and raising honeybees.

Throughout the 1970s and 1980s, owners and membership of southern natural foods co-ops opened restaurants and cafés, and other freestanding vegetarian restaurants located nearby, particularly in progressive pockets near universities.[80] A number of natural foods restaurants were founded in this era in Chapel Hill and Durham, North Carolina.[81] Their names suggest the counterculture politics of the founders—Aurora, Harmony, Somethyme, Wildflower Kitchen, Pyewacket, and Anotherthyme. Chef Bill Smith, who today oversees the kitchen of Chapel Hill's iconic Crook's Corner, worked in the area's budding culinary scene of the 1970s. He remembers the Wildflower Kitchen's savory bowls of brown rice topped with shredded cheddar cheese and owner Elizabeth Anderson's Asian-style umiboshi plum house dressing, miso soup, lentil dishes, and carob ice cream sandwiches made with gingerbread.[82] Oxford, Mississippi, had the Harvest Restaurant, whose tempeh and vegetable dishes I enjoyed with my family in the 1990s. In Athens, Georgia, the El Dorado (later, the Bluebird) was one of the city's first vegetarian restaurants in 1975.[83] The restaurant was located in the back corner of the historic black-owned and -operated vaudeville venue, the Morton Theatre. Celebrity wait staff at the El Dorado included members of Athens's famous rock band, the B-52's.[84] In Charlottesville, Virginia, Integral Yoga Natural Foods has served the university community since 1980, when followers of Sri Swami Satchidananda founded an ashram (spiritual center) and a yoga retreat center, Yogaville, in nearby Buckingham County.

In 1978, John Mackey and Rene Lawson Hardy opened a small natural foods store in Austin, Texas, called SaferWay (a play on the name Safeway), which evolved into the first Whole Foods Market in 1980.[85] In the 1990s, Whole Foods began its ascendancy to becoming the world's largest retailer of natural and organic products as it acquired alternative food businesses, including successful southern venues such as North Carolina's Wellspring Grocery, founded by local food activists and entrepreneurs Lex and Ann Alexander.

A quick look at "family photos" of the southern food counterculture over time reveals an evolution from the natural wood exteriors, homemade signs, bulk bins, and earth tones of the 1970s to upscale, contemporary stores that are indistinguishable from commercial chain stores, *except* for the persistent bulletin boards, book sections, and café-coffee "hang-outs" that speak of a deeply networked and political community.[86] Even one late to the counterculture, like me, who grabbed onto the movement just before it faded in the late 1970s, still judges a community's livability by the presence of a healthy food co-op and farmers' market. When we arrived in Chapel Hill on a fall weekend in 2002, I knew we would be happy as soon as we entered Weaver Street Market in nearby Carrboro. Baskets of hand-knit hats and gloves, bulk containers of granola, local pumpkins, home-baked bread, the smell of good coffee, and a stack of the *Independent Weekly*, a local newspaper, were evidence of the community's progressive politics.

The social revolutions of the 1960s and early 1970s inspired a generation of activists, including a small dynamic community of southerners, who challenged industrial food production and sought an alternative vision of counterculture eating. These culinary worlds ultimately merged with a defining food movement in the 1980s, the "New American Cuisine."

This movement, born of another revolution, the French-born nouvelle cuisine of the early 1960s, spread to America in the 1970s, where it fostered a renaissance of regional American cooking. In the American South, a new group of young, native-born chefs, farmers, and entrepreneurs created the "New Southern Cuisine."

19

New Southern Cuisine

Nouvelle Meets Southern

In 1976, Bill and Moreton Neal opened La Residence just outside Chapel Hill. Located in a historic farmhouse property developed by R. B. and Jenny Fitch, the restaurant combined southern-sourced ingredients and flavors with both classical and new French techniques. A native of south Mississippi, Susan "Moreton" Hobbs Neal had an understanding of fine dining as French cuisine shaped by the powerful influence of nearby New Orleans, a culinary perspective she introduced to native North Carolinian Bill Neal on their first visits to the city. In Durham and Chapel Hill, they trained under old-school "continental" chefs Jacques Condoret and Henry Schliff.[1] As young educated southerners, the Neals traveled to France and Europe in the early 1970s, where they experienced a culinary epiphany much like that of Alice Waters, the legendary founder of Chez Panisse in Berkeley, California.[2] In France, the Neals enjoyed simple meals, prepared from the freshest, highest quality ingredients, sourced from local farmers who knew the café owners and restaurateurs. Vegetables and fruits *looked* different in the markets. Colors were more vivid and flavors more intense than the highly processed produce available in commercial American grocery stores. The tastes of France reminded the Neals of the food of their childhoods in Mississippi and South Carolina in the 1950s—a liminal moment before homegrown and farm-raised food disappeared. "I had to go abroad to appreciate the mystery of food and its rituals in my native southland," wrote Bill Neal in 1985. "At some point I realized my food always had been telling who I was, when, and where; how I felt about my family, and I related to nature. I saw it first in the lives of people whose language, customs, and culture were foreign, but whose values were mine, before I saw the richness in my, my family's, my region's life."[3]

The Neals represented a southern outpost of the growing "good food movement" across the country in their passion for preserving regional cuisine while offering a vibrant reinterpretation of that cuisine. In Chapel Hill, Bill and Moreton Neal created a culinary community inspired by the French concept of *terroir*—"taste of place"—and the en-

Bill and Moreton Neal, La Residence at Fearrington House, Pittsboro, North Carolina, ca. 1976. Moreton Neal Collection.

couragement of friends, such as local scholars and Francophiles Ellie and Jim Ferguson. La Residence, explained Moreton Neal, embodied their regional efforts to "imitate the French way of life, which we were convinced was heaven on earth."[4] The South had its own *terroir*, and although it had been diminished by industrial agriculture and the dominance of commercial food suppliers by the closing decades of the twentieth century, the Neals and a community of like-minded young farmers and eaters were determined to bring it back to life. *New York Times* journalist R. W. "Johnny" Apple described the "real Neal deal" as "traditional regional recipes, heightened and brightened by an innovative twist here and there, and by the use of the best available ingredients, however prosaic."[5] The publication of *Bill Neal's Southern Cooking* (1985) marked a turning point in regional food as Neal and his protégées expanded and redefined southern cuisine, yet honored its history and culture.

La Residence, followed by Bill Neal's second venue, Crook's Corner (1982), created with partner Gene Hamer in Chapel Hill, became the mother ship of new southern cuisine from which a long line of award-winning contemporary southern chefs and restaurants are descended—a legacy built on simplicity, taste, imagination, and heritage.[6] The Neals' influence on southern cuisine continues in Neal's Deli in Carrboro, which opened in 2008 and is owned and operated by son and daughter-in-law Matt and Sheila Neal. The *New York Times*–noted venue enlivens classic delicatessen-style dining with local and seasonal ingredients, such as the deli's lauded house-cured pastrami served on a buttermilk biscuit.[7]

Craig Claiborne

When Craig Claiborne, food editor of the *New York Times*, visited Chapel Hill in 1983, Bill Neal joined him as they sampled the region's best barbecue together.[8] A native of Mississippi, Claiborne had a deep love for southern food. He helped Neal appreciate the traditional ingredients and regional recipes of the South, and to do so with the same passion he had for French provincial cuisine.[9] In 1985, Claiborne returned to North Carolina to write a *New York Times* review of the burgeoning food scene in the Piedmont. While he noted "some of the finest barbecue and down-home cooking" of the state, including Mildred Council's Mama Dip's, Claiborne heralded the newest establishments of the Piedmont as "marvels of sophistication" and important venues in the new American cuisine.[10] He praised Bill Neal's food and artistry at Crook's Corner, forever associating the restaurant and the chef with his "splendid blend of sautéed shrimp served on a bed of cheese grits."[11] At the Fearrington House Restaurant in nearby Pittsboro, Claiborne described Ben Barker's appetizer of pepper pasta with crab, sweet peas, and scallions, followed by a cold cream soup enriched with "sugary Vidalia onions from Georgia."[12] This was food clearly grounded in sense of place but not limited by it.

Claiborne's *New York Times* review "anointed Chapel Hill as the heartbeat of Southern cooking" and simultaneously created a new brand of authenticity and innovative heritage cuisine.[13] This homage from a respected food editor to his home region and its chefs and cooks captured the blending of culinary tradition and an imaginative interpretation of southern cuisine focused on the freshest seasonal and local ingredients. "Here, young chefs display a natural feel for many of the native ingredients," wrote Claiborne, "but they bring to them the same sense of adventure and tastefulness as do their contemporaries elsewhere in the United States."[14] Claiborne's adulation for Neal's shrimp and grits illustrates how a deeply placed, storied dish like "breakfast shrimp," a working-class meal of fresh Lowcountry creek shrimp, cooked in butter, flavored simply with salt and pepper, and served over plain grits, assumed a more cosmopolitan narrative and presentation in the evolving southern food landscape of the 1980s.[15] Rising young chefs like Bill Neal and Ben Barker were touched by this phenomenon, too. They experienced the beginnings of a cult of celebrity as both media and a largely white, affluent clientele lauded restaurants at the heart of "new southern cuisine."

Ben Barker and his wife and partner, pastry chef Karen Barker, became visionaries in the new southern cuisine that Claiborne encountered in North Carolina. After working at La Residence and Fearrington House, the Barkers began their own culinary empire with the opening of Magnolia Grill in Durham in 1986. The beloved institution received national acclaim for its sophisticated local cuisine, including two James Beard awards for its owners. After twenty-six years of dedicated service, the Barkers closed the restaurant in 2012. Like Crook's Corner and La Residence, Magnolia Grill was an important training ground for the next generation of young southern chefs, butchers, cheese makers, pastry chefs, and restaurateurs.[16]

Southern Farmers' Markets Reborn

Farmers' markets were a crucial piece of the reinvigorated southern regional cuisine that the Neals, the Barkers, and their followers envisioned for Chapel Hill and the surrounding communities. Supported by farmers, chefs, city officials, and community members, a successful farmers' market provided the quality seasonal raw ingredients that were

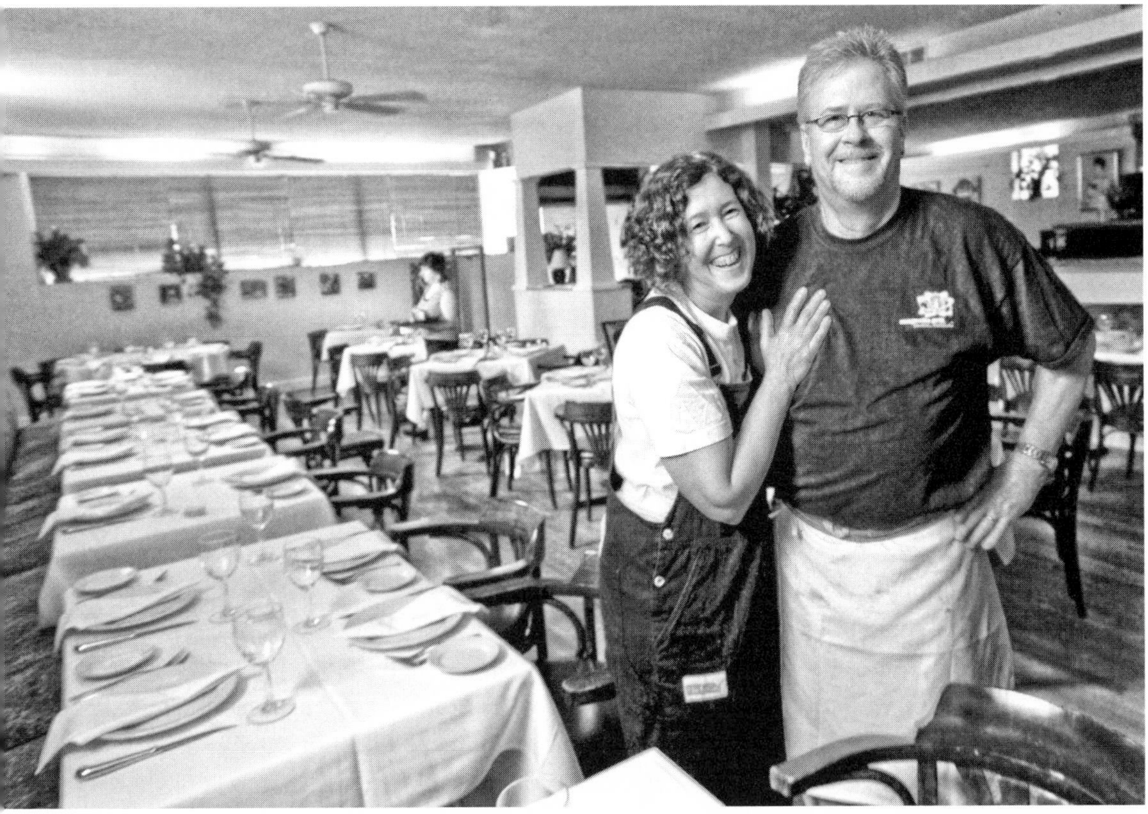

Karen and Ben Barker, Magnolia Grill, Durham, North Carolina, October 2010. Photograph by Kate Medley.

the essential foundation of the new southern cuisine. Farmers' markets sprang to life in the evolving local food movement of the last decades of the twentieth century, revitalizing the old curb markets of the 1930s and 1940s South. The Carrboro Farmers' Market—less than two miles from downtown Chapel Hill—opened in 1979, a joint project of city officials and graduate students at the university's School of Public Health. Ben Barker, one of the early chef supporters of the market, described its leaders as "a redoubtable group of hippies, back-to-the-land movement disciples, traditional farmers, and true visionaries like Ken Dawson of Maple Springs, Alex and Betsy Hitt of Peregrine Farm, and Bill Dow of Ayrshire Farm."[17] Barker recalled a crucial order to their culinary decision making at La Residence in Chapel Hill: "We shopped and then we created menus, handwriting them minutes before the doors opened."[18] Barker describes a "symbiosis" between the farmers and chefs who participated in the market. The restaurants created a new demand for best-quality, locally grown ingredients, and the growers met that demand. This relationship, states Barker, "transformed menus and created an environment that taught us how to cook locally and seasonally."[19]

"Gourmet," Southern-Style

Craig Claiborne recognized another aspect of the changing North Carolina culinary scene in the 1980s, a thriving specialty food market called A Southern Season. Begun by North Carolina native Michael Barefoot as a small coffee-roasting business in the 1970s, the company expanded rapidly, reflecting a significant evolution in the regional and national food scene at the time. It was a "local version of Dean & DeLuca," wrote Claiborne, "vast and splendidly stocked with specialty items: imported and domestic oils, mustards, wines, teas, coffees, vinegars, cheeses, baked-on-the-premises pastries and breads."[20] As interest in the new American and new southern cuisine grew, so too did the appreciation for specialty foods and supplies, particularly in southern cities and university towns. "Gourmet" became a catchall term for ethnic foods and products from around the world, as well as high-end American foodstuffs. The convergence of other factors—the success of Julia Child's popular cooking show, *The French Chef,* and the televised cooking programs that followed, the rise of affordable American travel to Europe, nouvelle cuisine's use of high-quality, less-processed ingredients, and a burgeoning cookbook market—contributed to a turn away from the southern-style, continental cuisine of the post–World War II years.[21] High-end southern chefs and sophisticated home cooks alike sought out the trending ingredients of the era—pesto, pink peppercorns, and imported cheeses—to appear au courant.

South Carolina writer Pat Conroy captured this transformative time in regional culinary history: "Extra virgin olive oil had started to appear in southern supermarkets, bringing sex, at last, to southern kitchens. Arugula, watercress, and daikon radishes were making shy appearances in produce departments in my part of the world. . . . Cuisine was breaking out all over the South, as luxuriant and uncontrollable as kudzu."[22] White suburban housewives and bookish academics alike in the South joined the craze for international flavors, unusual ingredients, and global cooking techniques. These cosmopolitan trends were embraced by the region's popular lifestyle magazine, *Southern Living,* in fondue-style recipes and designs for southern kitchens with "old world" flair.

Kay Goldstein, a graduate of UNC in Chapel Hill, who later founded a successful catering company in Atlanta, recalled the changing food scene of the 1970s and 1980s in Chapel Hill: "Educated professors and their families traveled and returned with a taste for ethnic flavors. Danziger's [Candy] Shop on Franklin [Street] served European pastries. There was a Greek restaurant. Villa Teo was upscale Italian."[23] Goldstein made handmade fresh pasta, which she sold at Danziger Design, Bibi Danziger's new kitchen store, which sold high-end cookware and supplies and also had a modern demonstration kitchen for instruction, including one of the first Viking ranges created by Fred Carl Jr. at his new plant in Greenwood, Mississippi.

Ann Stewart, a Chapel Hill native and granddaughter of a former university chancellor, remembers the "life-changing" cooking classes she took at Danziger Design in the 1970s, organized by Carroll Kyser and Judith Olney (sister-in-law of food writer Richard Olney, known for his work on French country cooking): "Among many things, I learned to: chop things, to make Peking Duck and scallion pan cakes with hoisin sauce (this involved a bicycle pump to inflate the duck before hanging it on a clothesline to dry and thus to crisp the skin); to stuff chicken under the skin; and to make chicken w/ 40 cloves of garlic in a hermetically sealed pot."[24] Many of Chapel Hill's leading cooks and chefs socialized and participated in the classes, which created a strong local following for new southern cuisine. The culinary enlightenment of middle- and upper-class white southerners, including their experimentation with international cuisines, contributed to a growing appreciation for high-quality southern ingredients. "It produced a heightened creativity with food in general and a willingness to break away from the "meat 'n' three" model prevalent in the South," writes Goldstein. "It increased the desire for better quality ingredients. Eventually home cooks and restaurateurs found them [these ingredients] right at home."[25]

John Egerton's *Southern Food: At Home, on the Road, in History*

The path to this new style of southern cooking—which laid the foundation for the local food movement and farm-to-table restaurants of the new millennial South—was not without its bumps. When the groundbreaking *Southern Food: At Home, on the Road, in History* was published in 1987, author John Egerton took issue with the "so-called new American cuisine."[26] Egerton's work celebrated the history and culture of southern restaurants, cafés, diners, and home cooks—culinary worlds embraced by black and white southerners because of their respectful and knowledgeable use of "old and authentic southern recipes" prepared, when possible, with fresh ingredients.[27] These were moderately priced establishments that did not require reservations and dress codes. Egerton feared that the "arty, trendy, chic world of nouvelle cuisine"—and its offshoot of new American cuisine—would hasten "the decline and disappearance of Southern cookery and other distinctive regional foods of high quality and historical importance."[28]

John Egerton valued tried-and-true southern recipes and meals and the anticipation of familiar tastes *worth* repeating.[29] The best southern foods were classics—like the country cuisine that Bill and Moreton Neal had fallen in love with in France—dishes to be repeated again and again, whether at the Sunday dinner table or to mark meaningful life passages. What is good southern food, if not ritual? The new movement's embrace of constant novelty and originality, Egerton believed, would be the death of southern food, an art form that thrived on tradition and time.[30] The number of ambitious celebrity chefs and investor-driven regional restaurants that abandoned southern food to embrace more cosmopolitan nouvelle techniques and flavors gave credence to Egerton's fears. Time and the unparalleled cuisine that began to grace tables between the 1980s and the turn of the century slowly convinced John Egerton that southern food was in the hands of good stewards, largely committed to the region's core culinary grammar.

Spreading the Gospel of New Southern Cuisine, 1980s–1990s

A new southern food movement based on seasonality, the soil, and a growing number of passionate farmers, chefs, and artisanal food producers—the keepers of southern *terroir*—shaped the taste and texture of the region's culinary landscape in the 1980s and 1990s. The young leaders of southern cuisine shared a similar southern upbringing and paths that took them via France and California back home to the South.

After traveling in Europe in the early 1970s, Alabama native Frank Stitt was drawn to San Francisco and Berkeley. He put his philosophy studies aside to work in the cities' French restaurants, and to meet Alice Waters, who was leading the local revolution in regional cuisine.[31] Waters's introduction led Stitt back to Europe and encounters with Chez Panisse's Jeremiah Tower and an indoctrination in seasonal cuisine under the tutelage of Richard Olney in France.[32] Stitt opened Highlands Grill and Bar in Birmingham in 1982, where he served new riffs on old favorites, such as grits soufflé and butter bean crostini.[33] In keeping with the cooking ethic of southern colleagues and mentors, Stitt was passionately committed to seasonal and locally sourced ingredients, enlivened by the flavors of France, Italy, and the Mediterranean. "Highlands Bar and Grill changed the way the people of Alabama thought about food," said Pat Conroy. "The coming of Highlands changed the fate of that part of Birmingham and began its renaissance."[34] After thirty years in business, Highlands remains the culinary heart of Birmingham's vibrant, interracial social scene, a beloved institution known for Frank and Pardis Stitt's commitment to excellence, service, and simplicity of preparation.[35]

In the 1990s, Bill Smith, born in New Bern, North Carolina, carried on Bill Neal's commitment to the best seasonal local cuisine at Crook's Corner in Chapel Hill while reinvigorating the menu with fresh interpretations of classic recipes and inventive new southern dishes. The historic immigration of thousands of Hispanic people to America during this era brought an infusion of talent into professional southern kitchens, like Crook's Corner, where many dishes are inflected with Latin flavors and methods. Bill Smith plans annual trips to Mexico, where he visits with workers' families, eats in their kitchens, and returns inspired to create new dishes for the restaurant's evolving southern table.[36] Down the street from Crook's Corner, at the James Beard award–winning restaurant Lantern, chef Andrea Reusing (born in Washington, D.C., in 1968) and chef de cuisine Miguel Torres (born in Celaya, Guanajuato, Mexico, in 1980) combined North Carolina ingredients with the flavors and methods of Asian cuisine.[37] Torres began to cook with his mother as a young boy and at age eighteen came to Carrboro, where many former residents of Celaya live and work in the bustling restaurant scene.[38]

A New Southern Food Canon

A growing body of southern food literature—from cookbooks to scholarly studies—reflected the national resurgence in regional cuisine beginning in the 1970s. Two early significant voices in this era that first brought national attention to southern cuisine belong to an unlikely pair of southerners, Eugene Walter, a white writer, humorist, and cultural critic, and Edna Lewis, an African American food writer and chef. Both were children of the South. Walter, born in 1921 into a Catholic family in Mobile, Alabama, was steeped in the memories of a lost South and a delectable table serviced by black cooks and tradespeople. Lewis was born in 1916, the granddaughter of free blacks in rural Freetown, Virginia, who purchased land in the area and began to farm after emancipation. Both Walter and Lewis left the South to experience the liberated air of distant places. They joined the bohemian worlds of artists, actors, intellectuals, and writers. These circles fed the mind, but for southerners raised on the memorable food of Mobile Bay and the Virginia countryside, not the body. They remained hungry for the tastes of home.

In New York City, Edna Lewis prepared foods of her childhood for city friends and in 1948 became the chef at the avant-garde Café Nicholson on the East Side of Manhattan, where the "elegant, handsome" woman, as described by Craig Claiborne, was known for her outstanding southern food.[39] Lewis was passionate about the fresh seasonal ingredients of her southern childhood, a love she shared in her cookbook-memoir, *The Taste of Country Cooking* (1976).[40] In a *New York Times* review, Claiborne wrote of Lewis's "self-sustaining" family and community, long

Edna Lewis. Photograph © John T. Hill.

before "sustainability" was an everyday word among food devotees.[41] Lewis's quiet but demanding quest for pure ingredients and authentic flavors caught the attention of the "new regionalists," including Alice Waters.[42] In the early 1980s, Edna Lewis served as guest chef for the Fearrington House Restaurant in Pittsboro, North Carolina. In an interview with oral historian Davia Nelson at that time, she worried about the destructive impact of commercial food production and chemical fertilizers upon flavor, recalling an era in the rural South when composted manure, wood ash, and lime "sweetened" the soil.[43]

Eugene Walter lived in Italy for many years, where the daily culinary pleasures revived memories of his southern food heritage.[44] After nearly twenty years away from the South, Walter came home after he was commissioned to write a book about the South for the popular Time-Life Foods of the World series.[45] The combination of a journalist's skill, an expatriate's point of view, and an ethnographer's eye created one of the most compelling texts on southern foodways to date. The evocative photographs that illustrate Walter's *American Cooking: Southern Style* (1971)—studio shots by Mark Kauffman and those taken across the region by a team of documentary photographers—capture the changing southern food heritage at a moment in time, a surreal mix of the elite Old South and a working-class South less than a decade removed from the passage of the historic civil rights acts.

Food writer Nathalie Dupree published *New Southern Cooking* (1986), whose title further canonized the creative reinterpretation of traditional southern cooking as the "preeminent regional American cuisine."[46] Dupree celebrated the movement's credo of regional foodways prepared with high-quality, fresh, local, and seasonal ingredients. She was also one of the first regional food writers to emphasize the centrality of the African American experience in southern cuisine. Dupree's success led to a public television series, *New Southern Cooking with Nathalie Dupree.* White Lily Flour, the Knoxville, Tennessee, company known for its soft wheat flour—an indispensable ingredient in creating flaky southern biscuits—underwrote the long-running program.[47] The groundbreaking television series presented "new southern cooking" as an art that "emerged from a distinctive regional tradition," fully capable of evolving "in response to the changing South."[48] Dupree surprised viewers who had preconceived ideas of southern food *and* southern women. A stylish, accomplished author and teacher, she was a natural television host and a dynamic spokesperson for the expansive, contemporary South. In the rapidly growing world of food television, Dupree was a modern, educated, working woman, rather than the stereotyped characters viewers associated with popular depictions of the South.[49]

The Southern Food Renaissance A New Millennium

A new generation has embraced the vision of regional food that Edna Lewis and Eugene Walter introduced to America in the 1970s and 1980s, a cuisine shaped by local farms and tradespeople that once ensured a connection between those who grew and crafted food and their communities. The consumers in the new southern food scene—largely middle- and upper-income whites due to access and the price structure of small-scale food production—are buying regionally grown fruits, vegetables, and meat, fresh buttermilk, local wine, beer, and spirits, artisanal cheeses, wood-fired breads, heirloom grains, and traditionally cured bacon and hams.

This passion for local, fresh, unadulterated ingredients suggests a keen alliance between distant generations of discerning southerners. Except where poverty preserved old ways in the rural South, the handmade and homemade food that Edna Lewis describes in *The Taste of Country Cooking* quickly disappeared with late nineteenth- and early twentieth-century "improvements" of cooking stoves, refined flour, cheap manufactured convenience foods, and, most important, the transition of the South's labor force from agriculture to industry. Traditional methods of preserving foods such as drying, salting, brining, and smoking *intensified* flavors, unlike the modern commercial canning and freezing methods, which *diminished* flavors.[50] When a carefully researched facsimile of Mary Randolph's early nineteenth-century cookbook, *The Virginia House-Wife*, was published in 1968, culinary historian Karen Hess bemoaned the loss of the nation's taste for real food such as Randolph would have known in her age. "What can I tell people who have never tasted real cream?" she wrote.[51] Hess encouraged devoted cooks to search for "traditional operations for hams, flour, cornmeal, and so on; they do exist here and there."[52] Today, proponents of the local food movement in the South resonate with Randolph's talent for flavor and her use of regional produce, livestock, seafood, fresh salads, delicately cooked vegetables, homemade preserves and pickles, and fire-roasted meats.

At the time of her death in 2007, Karen Hess had lived long enough to see the burgeoning revival of sustainable farming and entrepreneurial food ventures in the South, including local flour mills, bakeries, cheese-making businesses, chocolatiers, dairies, foragers, hand-crafted bourbon distilleries, and pasture-raised pork operations. Led largely by activists, chefs, environmentalists, farmers' market organizers, seed savers, small-scale farmers and artisan producers, DIY (Do It Yourself) proponents, and "neo-homesteaders," the current southern food movement is rooted in the political activism of the 1960s and 1970s and the new regionalism of the 1980s, yet it is empowered by a contemporary revolution in opposition to America's industrialized food systems.

Sandor Katz, who describes himself as a "fermentation revivalist," exemplifies DIY food activism in the South. Since the 1990s, Katz has lived in rural middle Tennessee and become a national authority on natural fermentation and a vocal advocate for local and seasonal food systems. His popular books, including *The Art of Fermentation* (2012), with a foreword by Michael Pollan, have inspired thousands of consumers, home cooks, and artisanal food entrepreneurs throughout the region and the world.[53] Katz argues that state and federal rules that control food production from industrial processing plants to family cow-milking operations have made "small-scale traditional food production and distribution almost impossible."[54] "Eating well," writes Katz, "has become an act of civil disobedience."[55]

Restoring a Southern "Lost Ark of Taste"

Today, the longing for an authentic agrarian southern past that people can literally taste has been "born again" in the local food movement and activism of southern chefs, farmers, artisan entrepreneurs, food writers, and scholars. "The current renaissance in Southern cooking, somewhere between a movement and a trend," says food writer Jeffrey Steingarten, "is a renewal, a revival, a rebirth, a recapture, retrieval, and return."[56] Contemporary champions of this movement are concerned with flavor, a world of taste they argue once existed in carefully nurtured seeds grown in southern soil by skilled agronomists of the colonial and antebellum eras and which disappeared after the onslaught and homogenization of industrial agriculture.[57] Together they are creating a farm-to-table infrastructure that will restore this lost "ark of taste." Journalist Julia Moskin explains: "They want to reclaim the agrarian roots of Southern cooking, restore its lost traditions and dignity, and if all goes according to plan, completely redefine America's cuisine for a global audience."[58]

The revival of southern foods and methodologies absent for most of the twentieth century represents nothing less than a rebuilding of southern foodways for believers like chef Sean Brock in Charleston, South Carolina. Brock grew up in the coal region of southwestern Virginia, where he helped tend his grandmother's hillside garden.[59] Like Edna Lewis, Bill Neal, Eugene Walter, and thousands of other southerners haunted by the memory of a more flavorful past, those tastes of childhood stayed with him. Brock's mission is to reclaim the old southern food crops and heritage ingredients, a job he cannot do alone. He assembled a dedicated team of scholars, plant geneticists, farmers, and artisan producers to help him, led in large part by University of South Carolina scholar David Shields and Glenn Roberts, the visionary founder of Anson Mills, which grows and mills organic grains in Columbia, South Carolina.[60] Shields chairs the Carolina Gold Rice Foundation, dedicated to education and research on heirloom grains, early ricelands, and historic agriculture.[61] South Carolina is a hotbed of this activity because of its rich agricultural history as well as its strong tourism economy, which creates a healthy financial setting for high-end restaurants, with the presence of receptive consumers who are willing to pay for best-quality food products and culinary expertise.

"Tell about the South"

Selling the Southern Sense of Place

The fervency of contemporary southern culinary narratives and the emphasis on personal connections to the region's rural past, like Sean Brock's Appalachian roots, suggest "the power of a good story" and the value of authentic southern connections to consumers.[62] Rare is the cutting-edge, contemporary southern chef without bona fide rural roots, a regional pedigree, or proof of equivalent time spent "in the field." For many southern chefs and artisan producers, memory—the cache of southern food experiences remembered from childhood—is an essential aspect of their credentials in the local food movement. Linton Hopkins of Restaurant Eugene in Atlanta "grew up with sorghum syrup on the table."[63] In Chapel Hill, April McGreger, proprietor of Farmer's Daughter, creates small-batch, handmade pickles and preserves, using seasonal, local produce. Raised in rural Vardaman, Mississippi, where her family grows sweet potatoes, McGreger remains "in conversation with tradition" as she merges vernacular preservation techniques with a social activist's intense commitment to regional ingredients and real flavor.[64] By switching the ratio of sugar and fruit from the industry standard—more fruit, less sugar—flavors intensify. In the summer, McGreger serves her farmers' market customers icy drinks of fizzy water, brightened with local fruit syrups and flower essences, such as strawberry-hibiscus and muscadine grape-ginger. We take home jars of her Valencia orange marmalade with star anise and rye whiskey.

Chef John Currence of Oxford, Mississippi, recalls his mother's skill in her New Orleans kitchen and his grandparents' abundant vegetable garden in rural North Carolina. Each summer, Currence and his staff honor the iconic preservation techniques of "his people," by canning hundreds of quarts of fruits and vegetables and preparing a stunning variety of homemade sausages, bacon, prosciutto, and ham.[65] John Currence's culinary arc began under Bill Neal's mentorship at Crook's Corner. Atlanta chef and provisioner Anne Stiles Quatrano is tied through many generations to Summerland, the family's ancestral plantation in northern Georgia, which provides much of the produce for her award-winning restaurants.[66] (Quatrano's great-great-grandmother, Eliza Stiles, authored the emancipation-era letter describing her family's challenging journey from south Georgia to Etowah Cliffs, described earlier.) Transforming the land with sustainable farming practices, while nurturing the peach and chestnut trees planted by her forebears, Quatrano reinterprets her culinary heritage for a new era. Donald Link, chef/founder with Susan Spicer of New Orleans's Herbsaint and his own restaurant, Cochon, which honors the Cajun food traditions of southwestern Louisiana, remembers shucking beans and ripping greens as a child with his grandfather.[67]

Another contemporary culinary narrative lies in the coming-home stories of young southerners, who leave the region for education and opportunity but then return, drawn back by family, rural pleasures, new urban initiatives, and the appeal of a more "visceral, purposeful" life.[68] Chef Vivian Howard and her husband, Ben Knight, embody this story in their move from New York City to Kinston, North Carolina, a struggling town in the heart of the state's industrial hog production and former tobacco wealth. Backed by Howard's parents' investment, the young couple opened the Chef & the Farmer (2006), a farm-to-table restaurant in an unlikely location that proved challenging but ultimately was successful. The message—shared with a national audience through a compelling PBS television series, *A Chef's Life*—is how the power of place, personal relationships, hard work, and locally produced and procured seasonal foods tell a southern story, "one ingredient at a time."[69] A moral thread winds through this now-familiar narrative, suggesting that with education, experience, and exposure to artisanship, seasonality, and flavor, hope persists that southerners will reject processed commodity food in favor of their true culinary inheritance. Howard's "ultimate tomato sandwich," prepared with juicy, in-season Cherokee purple tomatoes slathered with smoked corn mayonnaise, served on homemade sweet potato–onion bread, provides potent evidence for locavore activists in the regional debates surrounding food politics.[70] Howard also captures the historical taste of place in her Pepsi-glazed pork belly with country ham–braised peanuts.[71] These ingredients and flavors are a nostalgic, yet contemporary, homage to peanuts added to a bottle of Pepsi, a favorite snack enjoyed by working southerners, who were revived by the sugar and caffeine of this salty-and-sweet inexpensive treat.

John T. Edge commented on the intersection of story and the local food movement in Phoebe Lawless's Scratch, an innovative bakery and sandwich café in Durham, North Carolina: "At this shoe-box storefront . . . each pie pulled from the oven, each brown-bag sandwich handed over the counter, has a backstory. Here the local foods movement is not a mere marketing conceit. . . . The celebration of Carolina farmers and artisans is an operating ideal on which every Scratch dish depends."[72] Similarly, in Arkansas, a new generation of young chefs is revitalizing local cuisine with a strong narrative. Menus are suffused with ingredients produced in the state, such as paddlefish roe from the White River, fresh-milled organic grains from War Eagle Mill in Rogers, and dairy products from Seven Doves Creamery in Mena.[73] Fullsteam Brewery in Durham offers "plow-to-pint" beer, "inspired by the agricultural and culinary traditions of the South." Carver beer is brewed with North Carolina sweet potatoes. Other seasonal beers feature paw paws, persimmons, rhubarb, and scuppernong grapes. Workingman's Lunch, a beer homage to the southern workday snack of an RC Cola and a Moon Pie, is flavored with "biscuity" malt, vanilla, and locally made chocolate. At Lantern in Chapel Hill, chef Andrea Reusing foregrounds the distinctive narrative of local producers, growers, and artisans, who provide the raw ingredients for dishes such as Korean fried chicken, a lemon-grass–grilled local pork chop, and Vietnamese-style caramelized catfish.[74]

Hugh Acheson is a chef and owner of several popular farm-to-table restaurants in Georgia.[75] Born in Canada, he brings an outsider's perspective to southern cuisine and culture, which liberates him from the weight of southern ancestry and regional culinary dogma, yet he captures the essential intersection of place, history, and story in the contemporary food scene of the American South. In a recent interview with *American Food Roots* journalist Michele Kayal, Acheson spoke of "the amazingly storied cuisine" of the agrarian South and argued that "we need to reclaim the food history" and, most important, its debt to enslaved African Americans.[76] By example, Acheson refers to the story behind the creamy "rice grits" he serves with crisped pork belly and kimchi. He describes "middlins"—the broken grains of rice that remained after whole grains were sieved and exported for sale in the nineteenth-century Lowcountry. Gullah people repurposed the "sad crop that brought culinary bounty to the area" by utilizing the rice's starchy quality to best advantage in their daily cooking.[77] What is most exciting to Acheson about southern food today? "Discourse . . . the stories are what has made our food really important."[78] In the early fall of 2013, Acheson joined African American culinary historian Michael Twitty to share the storied foods of slavery in a period meal for the public at Horton Grove, the original slave quarters at Stagville—the remains of the massive nineteenth-century plantation of the Bennehan-Cameron family in Durham, North Carolina. Twitty speaks of the "haunted plate" of southern cuisine, in which lies the rich history, culture, language, and skills of eighteenth- and nineteenth-century African American cooks.[79]

These stories and many more illustrate the symbolic value of sense of place and its expression in the media and consumer worlds of the contemporary southern food movement. The compelling narrative of *real* connection to *authentic* places and people appears in the prefaces and forewords of award-winning, chef-authored cookbooks, the popular food blogs, the long lists of local farms and purveyors on restaurant menus, and the earnest "about us" stories posted on walls, banners, brochures, and websites for small-scale, sustainable farms, artisan food producers, eating establishments, and grocery stores, from local food co-ops to commercial venues like Whole Foods. Strongly aspirational, this longing for a well-crafted, handmade and homemade South, including its foodways, suggests the contours of the region's most recent culinary brand. Its palate is earth tones and natural hues, depicted in spare, highly produced photography of southern food and its environs. "Simplicity," purity of ingredients, labor, and artisanship are central to this brand, not unlike the elite folk revival of southern arts and crafts developed by well-to-do white philanthropists and entrepreneurs in the late nineteenth-century mountain South. At Blackberry Farm, an exquisite luxury hotel in the Smoky Mountains of east Tennessee, the "foothills cuisine" is described as both "rugged and refined," borrowing from "haute cuisine" and "foods indigenous" to the region's mountain heritage.[80] Regional magazines like *Garden and Gun* and the recently redesigned *Southern Living* reflect these romantic worlds of cultivated flavor, rusticity, and sophisticated rural-urban aesthetic. Social and cultural capital lies in the reconnection to a "real," yet carefully distanced, "postracial" South of old-time hog killings, canning, preserving, and distilled whiskey.

The Southern Foodways Alliance

The Southern Foodways Alliance (SFA) has immeasurably shaped this new era in southern food practice, history, culture, and scholarship. This influential organization was founded on July 22, 1999, at the Birmingham, Alabama, corporate headquarters of *Southern Living* magazine.[81] The "fifty founders"—a distinguished group of southern journalists, educators, food writers, editors, scholars, chefs, and restaurateurs—gathered at Frank and Pardis Stitt's Highlands Bar and Grill to mark the historic occasion. The SFA became an institute of the Center for the Study of Southern Culture at the University of Mississippi in Oxford. Georgia native John T. Edge, at the time a recent graduate of the university's master's program in Southern Studies, was appointed director of the SFA. Edge inspired the dynamic and far-reaching initiatives of the SFA, which explore southern foodways as a microcosm of race, class, gender, ethnicity, religion, and region.[82] The SFA has created a stunning body of historical and cultural documentation and research that has single-handedly changed the course of southern and American food scholarship through its award-winning films, oral histories, annual publications, symposia, and courses at the University of Mississippi. In this evolving landscape, the Southern Food and Beverage Museum was founded in 2008 in New Orleans as the region's first permanent exhibition facility dedicated to culinary culture and history.

What Is Southern?

In the early 1990s, Edna Lewis sent an essay entitled "What Is Southern?" to her colleague Eugene Walter. The unpublished, handwritten essay remained in Walter's papers until its recent discovery.[83] In this essay, Lewis led her readers through a cycle of southern seasons and the evocative tastes of New Year's Day "hoppin' John," spring's first wild greens, summer preserves, a slow-cooked Brunswick stew in the fall, and Christmas fruitcake.[84] For Lewis, "southern was" a simple dish, quickly prepared, such as "leftover pieces of boiled ham trimmed and added to a saucepan of heavy cream set on the back of the stove to mull and bring out the ham flavor, then served spooned over hot biscuits, with poached eggs on the side."[85] Yet "southern was" also the slow art of a barbecued pig, "cooked for hours and served with a tomato- or vinegar-based sauce."[86] Lewis argued that something in the South "stimulates creativity in people" and that "the South developed the only cuisine in this country."[87] She noted the region's writers, musicians, and artists and the powerful pull of southern food in their work.[88] Near the end of her essay, Lewis concluded that "southern is" "Dr. Martin Luther King Jr., with a dream."[89]

Even as she wrote this piece, Lewis had become, as Ben Barker states, an "icon" of the regional food movement in the South. With a dedicated group of southern journalists, writers, academics, and chefs, she helped found the Society for the Preservation and Revitalization of Southern Food.[90] Her concern for the future of southern food was reflected in the creation of the society—later replaced by the Southern Foodways Alliance. In the final words of her essay, Lewis wrote: "The world has changed. We are now faced with picking up the pieces and trying to put them into shape, document them so the present-day young generation can see what southern food was like. The foundation on which it rested was pure ingredients, open-pollinated seed—planted and replanted for generations—natural fertilizers. We grew the seeds of what we ate, we worked with love and care."[91] Edna Lewis's poetic description of the foundational elements of southern food reads like a manifesto for both the new southern cuisine of the 1980s and its evolution into the painstakingly sourced cuisine of the contemporary South. Although the quality and flavor of this essential cuisine may be unattainable, even unrecognized by most southerners today, its proponents remain committed to returning this culinary birthright to the people of the region.

Conclusion

Food stands at the center of southern history and culture. From the prehistoric South, where indigenous peoples discovered unparalleled food resources, to the contemporary South, where industrial agriculture and small farms vie for the region's future, food has defined the region for over five centuries. Food narratives spring from the voices of native southerners and from those who came to the region as explorers, travelers, laborers, educators, reformers, tourists, documentarians, and activists. Their history shaped regional food in a process that was negotiated in the crucible of race—the central influence on southern food. The lives of blacks, whites, and Native Americans intertwined with those of newcomers to the South, and nowhere is this more strongly expressed than in foodways. Conversations in this book reveal relationships of power, resourcefulness, and creativity that are key to the region's diverse food cultures.

Southerners honed the art of storytelling for generations, as seen in travel literature from the early South, to tourist campaigns of the twentieth century, to cookbooks by contemporary southern chefs. Their stories promoted and "sold" the South since the first contact between southeastern Indians and Europeans. In the preindustrial South, outsiders discovered the region's food cultures through firsthand encounters, and descriptions of southern cuisine spread through word-of-mouth accounts. Today, media brings southern food to the world, transforming what was once ephemeral—seasonal tastes, a remembered recipe, a cook's voice—into a rapidly developing, contemporary genre of southern culinary practice and performance. Black artists Betye Saar (*The Liberation of Aunt Jemima*, 1972) and Kara Walker (*The Marvelous Sugar Baby*, 2014) have re-empowered "mammy" and her cooking authority in their art as acts of protest and statements of resistance.

The creativity and the crisis of southern foodways are exemplified by two poles in the region today—one of distinctive, innovative foods grounded in tradition, and the other, an inheritance of racial and class trauma, expressed in land loss, poverty, and disease. The vibrant field of southern food studies reflects strong interest in cultural documentation as well as in the historic problems that have plagued the region for centuries.

The evolution of new southern cuisine from the 1980s to the contemporary renaissance in local food economies is the domain chiefly of white, educated, politically progressive southerners, even as the racial and ethnic diversity of this community expands each year. Resurgent interest in traditional southern plants is bringing Native foodways back to the southern table. New organizations like the Southeastern African-American Farmers Organic Network are transforming the racially divided politics of southern agriculture and food production. Despite the growth of these movements, restoring and rebuilding vital, local food systems that sustain and enrich the lives of *all* southerners is an ongoing struggle because of the dominance of industrial agriculture in the region. To visualize a dynamic, just, and healthy future for southern food cultures, we must learn from the region's history, in which progress and resistance to change have done constant battle. Given improbable odds, unimaginable change has already come to the region and will continue.

Notes

Abbreviations

AMRC	Amistad Research Center, Tulane University, New Orleans, La.
BIA	Biltmore Industry Archive, Grovewood Gallery, Inc., Grove Park Inn, Asheville, N.C.
COCSC	College of Charleston Special Collections, Marlene and Nathan Addlestone Library, Charleston, S.C.
DHRL	D. H. Ramsey Special Collections Library, University of North Carolina at Asheville, Asheville, N.C.
GHS	Georgia Historical Society, Savannah, Ga.
HNOC	Historic New Orleans Collection, New Orleans, La.
LOC	Library of Congress, Washington, D.C.
MDAH	Mississippi Department of Archives and History, Jackson, Miss.
MWAC	Margaret Walker Alexander Center, Jackson State University, Jackson, Miss.
NCC	North Carolina Collection, Wilson Library, University of North Carolina at Chapel Hill, Chapel Hill, N.C.
NCCRW	Newcomb College Center for Research on Women, Tulane University, New Orleans, La.
SCHL	Schlesinger Library, Radcliffe Institute for Advanced Study, Harvard University, Cambridge, Mass.
SCHS	South Carolina Historical Society, Charleston, S.C.
SCL	South Caroliniana Library, University Libraries, University of South Carolina, Columbia, S.C.
SFA	Southern Foodways Alliance Oral History Collection, University of Mississippi, Oxford, Miss.
SHC	Southern Historical Collection, Wilson Library, University of North Carolina at Chapel Hill, Chapel Hill, N.C.
SOHP	Southern Oral History Program, Southern Historical Collection, Wilson Library, University of North Carolina at Chapel Hill, Chapel Hill, N.C.
TU	Howard-Tilton Memorial Library, Special Collections, Tulane University, New Orleans, La.
UNC-CH	University of North Carolina at Chapel Hill
WLCL	William L. Clements Library, University of Michigan, Ann Arbor, Mich.
WUL	Washington University Libraries, Film and Media Archive, Henry Hampton Collection, St. Louis, Mo.

Introduction

1. Anne Firor Scott, email to author, May 18, 2009.

2. Prenshaw, "Texts of Southern Food," 12.

3. Sam Bowers Hilliard, *Hog Meat and Hoecake*; Joe Gray Taylor, *Eating, Drinking, and Visiting*; Egerton, *Southern Food*.

4. St. George, *Material Life in America*, 311.

5. Egerton, "Endurance of Southern Food," 18.

6. David Shields, cited in "What We Do and Why We Do It," Anson Mills, Colum-

bia, S.C., http://www.ansonmills.com/what_we_do_pages; Glenn Roberts, email to author, March 4, 2014; David Shields, email to author, March 5, 2014.

7. Wilson and Ferris, *Encyclopedia of Southern Culture*, xv.

Chapter 1

1. Steponaitis, *Natchez District*, 2.

2. Theda Perdue, *Cherokee Women*, 13–17.

3. Ibid., 17.

4. Steponaitis, *Natchez District*, 1.

5. Diamond, "The Worst Mistake," 64–66; Claudine Payne, "Mississippian Period," in *Encyclopedia of Arkansas History and Culture*, http://www.encyclopedia ofarkansas.net/encyclopedia/entry-detail.aspx?entryID=544. See discussion of fostering sustainable perennial polycultures, rather than fertilizer-dependent monoculture agriculture, in Bittman, "Now This Is Natural Food." Anthropologist Benjamin Auberback cautions against "universalizing" patterns of morphological change during the development of agriculture in the Eastern region between the Archaic and Mississippian periods. He argues that agriculture did "not inherently lead to declining health," as measured solely by stature and body mass. See Auberback, "Reaching Great Heights," 228.

6. Diamond, "The Worst Mistake."

7. Horwitz, *A Voyage Long and Strange*; Tony Horwitz, *The NewsHour*, August 19, 2008.

8. Percy, *A True Relation*.

9. Ibid.

10. Wade, "Girl's Bones." The 2012 archaeological discovery at Jamestown was overseen by William Kelso, archaeologist of Preservation Virginia, and analyzed by Douglas Owsley, a physical anthropologist at the National Museum of Natural History in Washington, D.C.

11. Catesby, *Natural History of Carolina*, 87, 98–99. The *Oxford English Dictionary* defines "bonavist" as a "species of tropical pulse; a species of kidney beans."

12. Merrens, *Colonial South Carolina Scene*, 101.

13. Ibid., 102.

14. Hyrne Family Letters, 1701–10, in ibid., 20–22.

15. Ibid.

16. Davis and Morgan, "Collards in North Carolina," 69; Lonnee Hamilton, "Green Goddess," 29.

17. Edward H. Davis, "The Culture of Collards"; Davis and Morgan, "Collards in North Carolina," 67–82; Farnham, Davis, Morgan, and Smith, "Neglected Landraces," 797–801.

18. Sam Bowers Hilliard, *Hog Meat and Hoecake*, 44.

19. "Profitable Advice for Rich and Poor," in Merrens, *Colonial South Carolina Scene*, 38–55.

20. Ibid., 47.

21. Ibid., 46.

22. Loewald, Starika, and Taylor, "John Martin Bolzius," 234.

23. Ibid.

24. Ibid.

25. Ibid., 235.

26. Ibid., 239.

27. Ibid., 232.

28. Ibid., 240.

29. Ibid.

30. Schaw, *Journal of a Lady of Quality.*

31. Ibid., 78.

32. Ibid., 95–100.

33. Ibid., 95–96; see also Yentsch, *A Chesapeake Family*, 151.

34. Yentsch, *A Chesapeake Family*, 151. For further discussion of British foodways of this era, see Fischer, *Albion's Seed.*

35. Schaw, *Journal of a Lady of Quality*, 96.

36. Ibid.

37. Ibid., 97.

38. Ibid., 97–98.

39. Ibid., 95.

40. Ibid., 96. See also Ferguson, *Uncommon Ground*, 94; and Yentsch, *A Chesapeake Family*, 208. For discussion of pepper in African American foodways, see Adrian Miller, *Soul Food*, 208–21.

41. Ferguson, *Uncommon Ground*, 94; Jessica B. Harris, *High on the Hog*, 11; Opie, *Hog and Hominy*, 1–15; Adrian Miller, *Soul Food*, 11–28.

42. Robert White, "Travel Writing," 160–61. White refers to Thomas Clark's edited volumes, *Travels in the Old South: A Bibliography* (1956–59) and *Travels in the South: A Bibliography* (1962), and states that "never again would there be so many [travelers to the South]," as Clark wrote, in "so short a time."

43. Alexis de Tocqueville, *Democracy in America* (1835); Harriet Martineau, *Society in America* (1837); Fredrika Bremer, *The Homes of the New World: Impressions of America* (1853); and Frederick Law Olmsted, *A Journey in the Seaboard Slave States* (1856), *A Journey in the Back Country in the Winter of 1853–4* (1860), and *The Cotton Kingdom* (1861).

44. Robert White, "Travel Writing."

45. Blassingame, *The Slave Community*, 379. In Blassingame's "Critical Essay on Sources," he writes, "Travel accounts were among the most important sources used in this study. Xenophobia, class and race bias, age, sex, intelligence, routes, mode of travel, and numerous other things have to be considered in reading the travel accounts. By and large, the travelers' observations are much more trustworthy in regard to the attitudes of whites than their opinions of slaves."

46. Davis Thacher Diary, SCL. Born in Yarmouth, Mass., on August 4, 1793, Thacher was twenty-three years old when he began his journey to the American South. He returned to New England by 1819 to marry Mary Sellars Nye, with whom he had six children. Thacher, a deacon, died in Fairhaven, Mass., on April 11, 1873, at the age of eighty. Toten, *Thacher-Thatcher*, 389, 547.

47. Davis Thacher Diary, SCL.

48. Ibid.

49. Ibid.

50. Ibid.

51. Ibid.

52. Ibid.

53. Herman, "Drum Head Stew," 37.

54. John Boynton to Isaac Boynton, Lower Marlborough, Md., October 3, 1836, Boynton Papers, WLCL. John Boynton was born in 1810 in Pepperell, Mass. He attended Amherst and Andover academies in preparation for his studies at Middlebury College in Vermont. Discouraged by poor wages teaching in New England, he

followed the advice of friends who encouraged him to seek a position as a teacher in the South. He taught "50 miles back in the country from Vicksburgh," in Mississippi Springs, Miss., from 1836 to 1837. Boynton returned to Pepperell and died there shortly afterward in 1839. See Fischer's discussion of early "New England's 'canonical dish'" of baked beans, in *Albion's Seed*, 136–37, 350.

55. John Boynton to Isaac Boynton, November 6, 1836, Boynton Papers, WLCL.

56. Ibid.

57. John Boynton to Isaac Boynton, Mississippi Springs, Miss., January 25, 1837, ibid.

58. Ibid.

59. Ibid.

60. Ibid.

61. Prucha, "Protest by Petition," 43; Katharine Morton, "Guide to the Evarts Family Papers," Evarts Family Papers, MS 200, Yale University Library, New Haven, Conn.

62. Jeremiah Evarts Diary, MS 240, March 30, 1822, and April 5, 1822, GHS.

63. Ibid.

64. Drum is a large, active, bottom-feeding fish. Southern varieties include the Spotted Sea Trout, the Black Drum (grows up to eighty pounds), Spot, Red Drum (grows up to forty pounds), King Fish, Whiting, and Croaker. I am indebted to professors Bernie Herman (UNC-CH) and David Shields (University of South Carolina at Columbia) for descriptive information regarding drum fish. Herman states that Chesapeake Bay inhabitants prefer Red Drum. According to Shields, the drum fish family is "notable for its short spiny dorsal fin and very long rayed fin along the ridge of the back toward the tail. Most of the species feed off the bottom so they've got barbels (whiskers) and very strong teeth for crunching shellfish and crabs." Shield describes Spot as a "good pan fish." Bernie Herman, email to author, August 18, 2012; David Shields, email to author, August 18, 2012.

65. Jeremiah Evarts Diary, GHS.

66. Ibid.

67. Ibid.

68. Ibid.

69. Ibid.

70. Ibid.

71. Edmund Sears Morgan, *Virginians at Home*, 75.

72. Upton, "White and Black Landscapes in Eighteenth-Century Virginia," 364.

73. Ibid., 363.

74. Ibid., 364.

75. *The Rambler, or, A tour*, WLCL.

76. Ibid.

77. Rogene A. Scott, Grayson, Ky., to her mother, March 11, 1858, Scott Family Papers, SHC.

78. Fischer, *Albion's Seed*, 352.

79. Martin, "Frontier Boys and Country Cousins," 78. Martin notes this citation in the Latrobe journal: Edward C. Carter, ed., *The Virginia Journals of Benjamin Latrobe, 1795–1798* (New Haven: Yale University Press, 1977), 1:79.

80. Smedes, *Memorials of a Southern Planter*, 35.

81. Ibid.

82. Kierner, *Beyond the Household*, 37.

83. Bremer, *America of the Fifties*, 128–29.

84. Ibid.

85. Ibid., 101–2.

86. McInnis, *Politics of Taste*, 28.

87. "Diary of Timothy Ford, 1785–1786," 142–43.

88. Ibid.

89. Diary of Mary Reed Eastman, "Wedding Journey," November 5, 1832–July 4, 1833, SCHS; Mary Reed Eastman Papers, 1834–1987, A/E13r, folder 1, SCHL. Mary Reed Eastman was born in 1806 in Marblehead, Mass., and lived in New York City after her marriage to a Yale-educated minister, Ornan Eastman, in 1832.

90. Diary of Mary Reed Eastman, "Wedding Journey," November 5, 1832–July 4, 1833, SCHS, 6.

91. Ibid.

92. McInnis, *Politics of Taste*, 163.

93. Ibid., 164. The Denmark Vesey slave insurrection was one of the largest American uprisings organized by African Americans, planned for July 22, 1822, in Charleston, S.C. Denmark Vesey, a free man and local Methodist leader, and other African American leaders organized the insurrection after white Charlestonians suppressed the city's African church, which had over 3,000 members. More than one hundred men were investigated for participating in the conspiracy. Denmark Vesey and more than thirty other men were condemned to death and hanged for their involvement in the plot.

94. Diary of Mary Reed Eastman, December 7, 1832, SCHS.

95. McInnis, *Politics of Taste*, 164.

96. For a compelling fictional account of this era in Charleston and the lingering anger and resistance expressed in historical memory over generations, see Durban, *So Far Back*, 74.

97. McInnis, *Politics of Taste*, 172–79, 252–64. See McInnis for detailed descriptions of Charleston's antebellum kitchen and pantry plans, division of enslaved African Americans from public areas of the slaveholding family, and the "buffer zones" of backlot yards, working gardens, toolsheds, storerooms, and livestock pens.

Chapter 2

1. Fox-Genovese, *Within the Plantation Household*, 32, 42.

2. Ibid., 110.

3. Anne Firor Scott led this reinterpretation of slaveholding women's history in *The Southern Lady* (1970), followed by a cohort of women scholars of the plantation South, such as Catherine Clinton, *Plantation Mistress* (1982), Suzanne Lebsock, *Free Women of Petersburg* (1984), Elizabeth Fox-Genovese, *Within the Plantation Household* (1988), and Drew Gilpin Faust, *Mothers of Invention* (1996).

4. See Hall, "Partial Truths," for a discussion of antebellum southern women's historiography and how staple-crop agriculture supported by slavery created a regional history of race, gender, labor, and home life distinctive from that of New England women. Fox-Genovese wrote, "The history of southern women does not constitute another regional variation on the main story; it constitutes another story" (Fox-Genovese, *Within the Plantation Household*, 42).

5. Eliza Lucas Pinckney, *Letterbook of Eliza Lucas Pinckney*, 34–35; Hooker, *Colonial Plantation Cookbook*, 2–3.

6. Schulz, "Eliza Lucas Pinckney and Harriott Pinckney Horry," 105.

7. Ibid., 101.

8. Egerton, *Southern Food*, 17–18.

9. Hooker, *Colonial Plantation Cookbook*, 18–33.

10. Pinckney and Easterby, "Charles Cotesworth Pinckney's Plantation Diary," 136–38; Journal of Charles Cotesworth Pinckney, COCSC. As a member of South Carolina's slaveholding plantation elite, Pinckney was also a noted Federalist politician, a veteran of the Revolutionary War, and a delegate to the Constitutional Convention. Pinckney and his family members divided their time between Charleston and their Sea Island plantation, which they reached by steamboat.

11. Pinckney and Easterby, "Charles Cotesworth Pinckney's Plantation Diary," 145. On April 10, 1818, Pinckney noted that his overseer Mr. Cannon "had planted" 146 acres of cotton, 80 acres of corn, 10 acres of sweet potatoes, 25 acres of oats, and "near" 2 acres of Irish potatoes on "The Crescent," one of several tracts of property making up the larger plantation's total 1,500 acres.

12. Ibid., 136–38. Pinckney's worlds were not unlike those of cotton planter Thomas Chaplin, the St. Helena, S.C., planter whose plantation journal was brought to life by Ted Rosengarten in *Tombee*, 130. Drum fish were caught in the spring, sheepshead in the summer, and bass in the fall.

13. Ibid. 138. For further discussion of fish in African American foodways, see Adrian Miller, *Soul Food*, 70–75.

14. Journal of Charles Cotesworth Pinckney, COCSC.

15. Yentsch, "Excavating the South's African American Food History," 66.

16. McInnis, *Politics of Taste*, 251–52; Mary Motte Alston Pringle Household Inventory Book, SCHS.

17. McInnis, *Politics of Taste*, 251–52.

18. Mary Motte Alston Pringle Receipt Book, October 2, 1826, SCHS.

19. McInnis, *Politics of Taste*, 251; Mary Motte Alston Pringle Household Inventory Book, SCHS.

20. Mary Motte Alston Pringle Household Inventory Book, SCHS.

21. McInnis, *Politics of Taste*, 252.

22. The original diaries of both "Meta" and John Grimball are located in the Southern Historical Collection. See Margaret Ann Meta Morris Grimball Diary, South Carolina, December 1860–February 1866, SHC. Mr. Grimball's seventeen volumes of his diary cover the years 1832 to 1883. See John Berkley Grimball Diaries, SHC.

23. McInnis, "Raphaelle Peale's Still Life," 315–17; McInnis, *Politics of Taste*, 285–88.

24. McInnis, *Politics of Taste*, 286; John Berkley Grimball Diaries, October 16, 1832.

25. McIinnis, *Politics of Taste*, 285–86.

26. John Berkley Grimball Diaries, November 1, 1832.

27. Kemble, *Journal of a Residence*, January 1839, 99.

28. Ibid., 100.

29. Olmsted, "A Journey in the Seaboard Slave States," 89–90.

30. Ibid. Olmsted wrote, "I think the slaves generally (no one denies that there are exceptions) have plenty to eat; probably are fed better than the proletarian class of any other part of the world."

31. Yentsch, "Excavating the South's African American Food History," 67.

32. For further discussion of slave rations, see Sam Bowers Hilliard, *Hog Meat and Hoecake*, 56; Sam Bowers Hilliard, "Hog Meat and Cornpone," 321; Jessica B. Harris, *High on the Hog*, 94–102; Philip Morgan, *Slave Counterpoint*, 134–45; Opie, *Hog and Hominy*, 17–54; and Adrian Miller, *Soul Food*, 20–26, 166–72.

33. Sam Bowers Hilliard, *Hog Meat and Hoecake*, 56; Sam Bowers Hilliard, "Hog Meat and Cornpone," 321; Jessica B. Harris, *High on the Hog*, 94–102; Philip Morgan, *Slave Counterpoint*, 134–45; Opie, *Hog and Hominy*, 17–54; Adrian Miller, *Soul Food*, 20–26, 166–72.

34. Sam Bowers Hilliard, "Hog Meat and Cornpone," 321–25.

35. Kemble, *Journal of a Residence*, February 1839, 167.

36. Ibid.

37. Ibid., March 24–28, 1839, 285.

38. Fanny Kemble Butler to John Fraser, Hamilton Plantation, Couper-Fraser Papers, 1839, GHS. Fanny Kemble Butler refers to the gift of drum fish from the Frasers in her journal entry of April 5–7, 1839. See Kemble, *Journal of a Residence*, 307–8. John Fraser, a native of Scotland, married Anne Sarah Couper in 1816 on St. Simon's Island. There, he managed his brother-in-law John Hamilton Couper's Hamilton Plantation. John Fraser died in 1839, leaving his family in difficult financial straits. He and his wife had five daughters and one son, John Couper Fraser, who was killed at Gettysburg on July 3, 1863. For discussion of the Couper family's agricultural experimentation on St. Simon's Island, including olive tree cultivation, see Shields, "Prospecting for Oil," 60–66.

39. Kemble, *Journal of a Residence*, April 5–7, 1839, 308.

40. Ibid., April 17, 1839, 60, 343.

41. Ibid. Kemble described the other household slaves at Butler's Sea Island plantation: "a dairy woman, who churns for us; a laundrywoman; her daughter, our housemen, the aforesaid Mary; and two young lads of from fifteen to twenty, who wait upon us in the capacity of footmen." Kemble rejected the young boys' service at mealtimes because they were unwashed and improperly clothed.

42. Ibid.

43. Fraser, *Gender, Race, and Family*, 65.

44. Evans, *Judah P. Benjamin*, 8–9.

45. Judah P. Benjamin letter to Dr. Barton, HNOC. From the Oxford English Dictionary, a biggin is "a type of coffee pot containing a strainer, through which coffee infuses without mixing with the water."

46. Judah P. Benjamin letter to Dr. Barton, HNOC.

47. Ibid.

48. "Complimentary Dinner Given to the Hon. J. P. Benjamin," Boston Club, St. Charles Hotel, November 21, 1833, HNOC. The Boston Club was a private social club founded in 1841 by white, elite "gentlemen" of New Orleans. The club initially admitted Jewish men and their sons, but by the late nineteenth century Jews were not allowed. Both the Boston Club and the Pickwick Club were associated with the early history of New Orleans's Mardi Gras organizations. See Fishman and Zweigenhaft, "Jews and the New Orleans Economic and Social Elites," 292; and Korn, *Early Jews of New Orleans*, 228.

49. Mary Elizabeth Pearson Boyce Diary, SCL. Boyce, born in 1820, was married to attorney William Waters Boyce, who served as state legislator and U.S. congressman for South Carolina. The couple and their children lived with Mary Elizabeth's parents, Dr. George Butler and Elizabeth Alston Pearson, in their Fairfield County, S.C., Greek Revival–style home, Fonti Flora ("fountains and flowers").

50. Ibid., October 17, 1855.

51. Mary "Minnie" Pearson Boyce married Robert Marion DuBose on April 13, 1864, and died three years later on March 2, 1867; burial place, Saint John's Epis-

copal Cemetery, Winnsboro, Fairfield County, S.C., findagrave.com, http://www.findagrave.com/cgiin/fg.cgi?page=gr&GSln=DUB&GSpartial=1&GSbyrel=all&GSst=43&GScntry=4&GSsr=881&GRid=53569041&.

Chapter 3

1. "Catherine W. B.," Murfreesborough, Tenn., to Mrs. Clarissa S. Greene, Salisbury, N.H., July 26, 1841, American Travel Collection, WLCL. "Catherine" boarded with "Esquire Rucker" and his wife in Murfreesboro, Tenn., where she was employed in a small school.

2. Wilma King, *A Northern Woman*, xiii. The Mississippi Department of Archives and History in Jackson has over 200 of Fox's letters and a transcription of her diary in its collections. See Fox (Tryphena Holder) Papers, MDAH.

3. Wilma King, *A Northern Woman*, 7.

4. Hastings's letter reassuring her parents about her ability to help them financially was written in January 1853. See "Biography," in Finding Aid, Ruth Newcomb Hastings Papers, WLCL.

5. Rogene Scott to her mother, Hanah Scott Warren, January 13, 1858, Scott Family Papers, SHC.

6. Anne Firor Scott, "The Ever Widening Circle," 3–8.

7. Ibid.

8. Emily P. Burke, *Reminiscences of Georgia*, iii–iv.

9. Plaag, "There Is an Abundance," 27.

10. Ruth B. Hastings, Oaky Hollow, S.C., to Mary Anne Hastings, July 27, 1852, Ruth Newcomb Hastings Papers, WLCL. Oaky Hollow was the summer home of the Williams family.

11. Plaag, "There Is an Abundance," 42.

12. Ruth B. Hastings, Oaky Hollow, S.C., to Mary Anne Hastings, July 13, 1852, Ruth Newcomb Hastings Papers, WLCL.

13. Ibid.

14. Rogene A. Scott, Nashville, Tenn., to her mother, March 29, 1861, Scott Family Papers, SHC.

15. Tryphena Blanche Holder Fox to Anna Rose Cleveland Holder, August 28, 1859, Fox (Tryphena Holder) Papers, MDAH; Wilma King, Columbia, Mo., email to author, May 18, 2011.

16. Gill, "A Year of Residence," 296; Faust, *Mothers of Invention*, 54. Faust writes that nineteenth-century southerners often called slavery "the domestic institution." Slavery was imbedded "in the social relations of the master's household." For a discussion of Governor David Rogerson Williams's cotton seed oil mill operation at the family's Society Hill plantation, see Shields, "Prospecting for Oil," 70–71.

17. Ruth Newcomb Hastings to Mary Anne Hastings, Oaky Hollow, S.C., July 13, 1852, Ruth Newcomb Hastings Papers, WLCL.

18. Ruth Hastings to Hastings Family, Society Hill, S.C., May 9, 1852, ibid.

19. Gill, "A Year of Residence," 296.

20. Ruth Hastings to Mary Anne Hastings and Ruth Washburn Hastings, Oaky Hollow, S.C., August 12, 1852, Ruth Newcomb Hastings Papers, WLCL.

21. Hastings, Society Hill, S.C., October 9, 1852, ibid.

22. Emma Holcombe to Rogene Scott, Grayson, Ky., December 13, 1858, Scott Family Papers, SHC.

23. Rogene A. Scott to her brother, Don, February 27, 1859, Cheneyville, Parish Rapides, La., ibid.

24. Tryphena Blanche Holder Fox to Anna Rose Cleveland Holder, September 8, 1856, in Wilma King, *A Northern Woman*, 37–41.

25. Ruth Hastings to Mary Anne Hastings and Ruth Washburn Hastings, Society Hill, S.C., May 24–25, 1852, Ruth Newcomb Hastings Papers, WLCL.

26. Ruth Hastings to Hastings Family, Society Hill, S.C., May 9, 1852, ibid.

27. Ibid.

28. Ingraham, *Sunny South*, 52–53.

29. Ibid.

30. Ibid.

31. Tryphena Blanche Holder Fox to Anna Rose Cleveland Holder, October 24, 1858, in Wilma King, *A Northern Woman*, 84.

32. Introduction, Wilma King, *A Northern Woman*, 1, 8.

33. Tryphena Blanche Holder Fox to Anna Rose Cleveland Holder, July 7, 1856, in Wilma King, *A Northern Woman*, 31; Fox-Genovese, *Within the Plantation Household*, 110; Yentsch, "Excavating the South's African American Food History," 66–68.

34. Wilma King, *A Northern Woman*, 4–5.

35. Tryphena Blanche Holder Fox to Anna Rose Cleveland Holder, July 14, 1856, in Wilma King, *A Northern Woman*, 33–37.

36. Fox-Genovese, *Within the Plantation Household*, 110, 116.

37. Tryphena Blanche Holder Fox to Anna Rose Cleveland Holder, September 8, 1856, in Wilma King, *A Northern Woman*, 37–41.

38. Sharpless, *Cooking in Other Women's Kitchens*, 44.

39. Ibid., 42–43; Sandra L. Oliver, Isleboro, Maine, email to author, May 15, 2011; see Oliver, "Food History News," http://foodhistorynews.com/index.html.

40. Sharpless, *Cooking in Other Women's Kitchens*, 42–43.

41. Tryphena Blanche Holder Fox to Anna Rose Cleveland Holder, September 8, 1856, in Wilma King, *A Northern Woman*, 37–41.

42. Ibid., November 18, 1856, 41–45.

43. Sharpless, *Cooking in Other Women's Kitchens*, 41.

44. Fox-Genovese, *Within the Plantation Household*, 110.

45. Wilma King, *A Northern Woman*, 5.

46. Tryphena Blanche Holder Fox to Anna Rose Cleveland Holder, December 27, 1857, in ibid., 67.

47. Ibid., December 16, 1860, 105–7.

48. Ibid.

49. Fox-Genovese, *Within the Plantation Household*, 144.

50. Tryphena Blanche Holder Fox to Anna Rose Cleveland Holder, March 29, 1861, in Wilma King, *A Northern Woman*, 113–18.

51. Ibid.

52. Ibid.

53. Faust, *Mothers of Invention*, 61.

54. Jessica B. Harris, *High on the Hog*, 102–5.

55. Vlach, *Back of the Big House*, 43; Fox-Genovese, *Within the Plantation Household*, 98.

56. Tryphena Blanche Holder Fox to Anna Rose Cleveland Holder, July 7, 1856, in Wilma King, *A Northern Woman*, 31.

57. Ibid., February 19, 1866, 76.

58. Vlach, *Back of the Big House*, 44.

59. Lumpkin, *The Making of a Southerner*, 8–9.

60. Ibid.

61. Ibid.

62. Vlach, *Back of the Big House*, 84–86.

63. Tryphena Blanche Holder Fox to her mother, July 7, 1856, in Wilma King, *A Northern Woman*, 31.

64. Rogene A. Scott, Cheneyville, La., to her mother, February 25, 1860, Scott Family Papers, SHC.

65. Ruth Hastings to Mary Anne Hastings, Society Hill, S.C., May 26, 1852, Ruth Newcomb Hastings Papers, WLCL.

66. For further discussion of meal patterns of the white, slaveholding elite in the antebellum South, see Hilliard, "All Kinds of Good Rations," in *Hog Meat and Hoecake*, 37–69.

67. Engelhardt, *A Mess of Greens*, 76.

68. Ruth Hastings to Hastings Family, June 7, 1852, Ruth Newcomb Hastings Papers, WLCL.

69. Ruth Hastings to Ruth Washburn Hastings, June 25, 1852, ibid.

70. Ruth Hastings to Mary Anne Hastings, June 3, 1852, ibid.

71. Ruth Hastings Finding Aid, ibid.

72. Ruth Hastings to Mary Anne Hastings, May 26, 1852, ibid.

73. Ruth Hastings to Hastings Family, June 7, 1852, ibid.

74. Ruth Hastings to Mary Anne Hastings, May 26, 1852, ibid.

75. Ruth Hastings to Mary Anne Hastings, Oaky Hollow, S.C., August 28, 1852, ibid.

76. Ruth Hastings to Hastings Family, June 7, 1852, ibid.

77. Ruth Hastings to Mary Anne Hastings, Oaky Hollow, S.C., August 28, 1852, ibid.

78. Ibid.

79. Carney, *Black Rice*, 114; Carney cites Hess, *Carolina Rice Kitchen*, 2–26.

80. Carney, *Black Rice*, 114–15.

81. Ibid.

82. Rogene A. Scott, Grayson, Ky., to her mother, father, and brother, February 15, 1858, Scott Family Papers, SHC.

83. Ibid.

84. For more information on Cajun foodways, see Gutierrez, *Cajun Foodways*.

85. Rogene A. Scott, Cheneyville, La., to her mother, May 23, 1859, Scott Family Papers, SHC.

86. Rogene A. Scott to her mother, March 14, 1859, Cheneyville, Parish Rapides, La., ibid.

87. Wilma King, *A Northern Woman*, 16.

Chapter 4

1. Margaret Ann Meta Morris Grimball Diary, December 15, 1860, SHC.

2. Ibid., January 10, 1861.

3. Ibid., January 12, 1861.

4. Litwak, *Been in the Storm So Long*, 5. Litwak cites Slave Narrative of Hannah Crasson, interview by T. Pat Matthews, WPA Slave Narrative Project, North Carolina Narratives, Volume 11, Part 1, LOC, 192.

5. Ibid.

6. Andrew F. Smith, *Starving the South*, 12–13.

7. Ibid., 13.

8. Christopher Morris, *Becoming Southern*, 157–58.

9. Andrew F. Smith, *Starving the South*, 6.

10. Kate Stone Journal, May 27, 1861, in John Q. Anderson, *Brokenburn*, 18, 70; Farmer-Kaiser, "Sarah Katherine (Kate) Stone," 80.

11. Kate Stone Journal, May 22, 1862, in John Q. Anderson, *Brokenburn*, 109.

12. Ibid.; Farmer-Kaiser, "Sarah Katherine (Kate) Stone," 76, 79.

13. John Q. Anderson, Introduction, *Brokenburn*, xviii.

14. Hague, *A Blockaded Family*, 17–19.

15. Ibid.; Andrew F. Smith, *Peanuts*, 20–22.

16. James McPherson, *Battle Cry of Freedom*, 620–23.

17. Ibid.

18. William H. Oliver, "Wheat and Flour Wanted," August 15, 1863, Thomas Ruffin Papers, SHC.

19. Ibid.

20. Stern, *Mary Chesnut's Civil War Epic*, 226. For a detailed analysis of the Witherspoon murder, see ibid., "Revolt: Family Troubles in the House Divided," and "Revolt: More Family Troubles in the House Divided," 207–51.

21. Woodward, *Mary Chesnut's Civil War*, October 7, 1861, 209.

22. For a full discussion of the relationships among food, southern history, and racial purity, see Angela Jill Cooley, "To Live and Dine in Dixie." Regarding "racial pollution" and southern consumption, see Hale, *Making Whiteness*, 128. Cooley also refers to theoretical work on this topic in Probyn's *Carnal Appetites*. See also Tompkins, *Racial Indigestion*; and Sharon Holland, *Erotic Life of Racism*.

23. Woodward, *Mary Chestnut's Civil War*, October 7, 1861, 211.

24. Stern, *Mary Chesnut's Civil War Epic*, 236–37.

25. Woodward, *Mary Chesnut's Civil War*, October 18, 1861, 217.

26. Ibid., 218.

27. Ibid.

28. Kate Stone Journal, March 2, 1863, in John Q. Anderson, *Brokenburn*, 170–71; Farmer-Kaiser, "Sarah Katherine (Kate) Stone," 82–83.

29. Kate Stone Journal, March 15, 1863, in John Q. Anderson, *Brokenburn*, 180.

30. Kate Stone Journal, April 15, 1863, in John Q. Anderson, *Brokenburn*, 192.

31. Kate Stone Journal, May 22, 1863, in John Q. Anderson, *Brokenburn*, 209–10; Farmer-Kaiser, "Sarah Katherine (Kate) Stone," 84.

32. Kate Stone Journal, May 22, 1863, in John Q. Anderson, *Brokenburn*, 209–10; Farmer-Kaiser, "Sarah Katherine (Kate) Stone," 84.

33. Kate Stone Journal, May 22, 1863, in John Q. Anderson, *Brokenburn*, 210.

34. Ibid.

35. Ibid.

36. Ibid., April 24, 1863, 193.

37. Litwak, *Been in the Storm So Long*, 5. Litwak cites Slave Narrative of Pauline Grice, WPA Slave Narrative Project, Texas Narratives, Volume 16, Part 2, LOC, 100.

38. Litwak, *Been in the Storm So Long*, 5.

39. Ibid., 31; Van Moore, Houston, Tex., in *Slave Narratives*, Texas Narratives, 1941.

40. Groom, *Vicksburg 1863*, 107.

41. Ibid.

42. Ashkenazi, *Civil War Diary*, May 11, 1862, 360. The Department of the Gulf was created when Union admiral David G. Farragut captured New Orleans in 1862.

43. Ibid.

44. James McPherson, *Battle Cry of Freedom*, 623–24.

45. Ashkenazi, *Civil War Diary*, May 26, 1862, 383.

46. Ibid.

47. Joe Gray Taylor, *Eating, Drinking, and Visiting*, 95. For an excellent discussion of the Union army's attack on southern salt works during the Civil War, see "The War between the Salts," in Kurlansky, *Salt*, 257–75.

48. Kurlansky, *Salt*, 258.

49. Charley Roberts, Perrine, Fla., June 30, 1938, WPA Slave Narrative Project, Florida Narratives, Jacksonville, Fla., LOC.

50. Mary A. DeCredico, "Confederate Impressment during the Civil War," in *Encyclopedia Virginia*, http://www.encyclopediavirginia.org/confederate_impressment_during_the_civil_war.

51. Mary A. DeCredico, "Richmond Bread Riot," in *Encyclopedia Virginia*, http://www.encyclopediavirginia.org/bread_riot_richmond.

52. Andrew F. Smith, *Starving the South*, 53.

53. James McPherson, *Battle Cry of Freedom*, 618.

54. Pryor, *Reminiscences of Peace and War*, 237–39.

55. Ibid.

56. Ambrose, "Bread Riots in Richmond," 203–4. The original Tutwiler letter is in the Netta L. Tutwiler Letters, SHC.

57. Andrew F. Smith, *Starving the South*, 68; James McPherson, *Battle Cry of Freedom*, 618–19.

58. Faust, *Mothers of Invention*, 242–46.

59. Sarah Hillhouse Alexander Lawton Diary, Sarah Alexander Cunningham Papers, folder 4, MS 194, no. 67, GHS.

60. Ibid.

61. Woodward, *Mary Chesnut's Civil War*, December 4, 1863, 498.

62. Ibid., December 2, 1863, 497.

63. Ibid., January 22, 1864, 548.

64. Ibid., March 25, 1861, 33–34.

65. Ibid.

66. Ibid., March 5, 1865, 744.

67. Ibid., February 26, 1865, 733; see also Muhlenfeld, "Mary Boykin Chesnut."

68. Woodward, *Mary Chesnut's Civil War*, March 6, 1865, 748.

69. Ibid.

70. Ibid.

71. Ibid., Samantha Matilda Middleton to Mary Chesnut, April 5, 1865, 778–79.

72. Ibid., August 1, 1861, 124.

73. For a good discussion of Union army rations, see "Rations," in David G. Martin, *Vicksburg Campaign*, 151–53.

74. Curry, *Volunteers' Camp and Field Book*, WLCL.

75. Ibid.; handwritten on front page, "E. S. Hammond, Lynchburg, VA., June 30, 1862."

76. Isaac J. Levy letter to Leonora E. Levy, Adams Run, S.C., April 24, 1864, Amy Hart Stewart Papers, SC-12013, American Jewish Archives, Cincinnati, Ohio.

77. Robert C. Caldwell to Mag Caldwell, June 3, 1864, http://digital.lib.ecu.edu/513. Caldwell served in Company C, 10th Battalion, North Carolina Heavy Artillery.

78. James McPherson, *Battle Cry of Freedom*, 487–88.

79. Ibid., 797.

80. Ibid. McPherson gives the distinction of the worst southern prison to Salisbury, N.C., where 34 percent of the 10,321 imprisoned men died.

81. Sergeant John Bodamer, 24th N.Y. Cavalry in the Virginia Campaigns, transcript of diary, October 26, 1864, John Bodamer Collection, WLCL.

82. Ibid., October 12, October 31, November 1, 1864.

83. Madison Finch to Thirza Finch, Maple Valley, Va., October 25, 1861, Thirza Finch Diary and Copybook, 1858–70, WLCL.

84. Edwin Finch, White House Landing, New Kent Co., Va., to Thirza Finch, March 23, 1865, Thirza Finch Diary and Copybook, 1858–70, WLCL.

85. Ibid., Thirza Finch Diary, May 27, 1862.

86. Ibid., May 30, 1862.

87. Ibid., July 1865.

88. For discussion of the enlistment and treatment of black Union soldiers, see "Black Liberators," in Litwack, *Been in the Storm So Long*, 64–103.

89. Ibid., 81–85.

90. Ibid.

91. Unsigned letter, "New Orleans Camp Parpit Louisiana, [August] 1864, My Dear Friend and x Pre," in Berlin, Fields, Miller, Reidy, and Rowland, *Free at Last*, 477–79.

92. Ibid.

93. Ibid.

94. "Affidavit of Joseph Miller, November 26, 1864," in Berlin, Fields, Miller, Reidy, and Rowland, *Free at Last*, 493–95.

95. Ibid.

96. Andrew F. Smith, *Starving the South*, 45.

97. James A. Graham to his father, William Alexander Graham, October 21, 1863, James Augustus Graham Papers, 283, SHC. I am indebted to Helen Thomas for sharing this diary entry with me, which she discusses on the Wilson Special Collections Library blog, at UNC-CH, "The Civil War Day by Day," http://blogs.lib.unc.edu/civilwar/index.php/2013/10/21/21-october-1863-a-box-of-eatables-and-some-lard/.

98. Andrew F. Smith, *Starving the South*, 79–83. For further discussion of American canning history, see Andrew F. Smith, *Eating History*, 68–73.

99. Andrew F. Smith, *Eating History*, 68–73.

100. Ibid.

101. Andrew F. Smith, *Starving the South*, 187.

102. Groom, *Vicksburg, 1863*, 363.

103. Balfour, *Mrs. Balfour's Civil War Diary*, 25. Emma Balfour was married to Dr. W. T. Balfour and lived next door to the Vicksburg headquarters of Lt. Gen. John C. Pemberton.

104. Groom, *Vicksburg, 1863*, 390.

105. Loughborough, *My Cave Life in Vicksburg*, 60–61.

106. Ibid., 106.

107. Ibid.

108. Groom, *Vicksburg, 1863*, 394.

109. Ibid.

110. Ibid.

111. James McPherson, *Battle Cry of Freedom*, 635.

112. Groom, *Vicksburg, 1863*, 393; Andrew F. Smith, *Starving the South*, 103–5. The *Chicago Tribune* piece appeared on July 25, 1863.

113. Groom, *Vicksburg, 1863*, 393; Andrew F. Smith, *Starving the South*, 103–5.

114. Groom, *Vicksburg, 1863*, 393; Andrew F. Smith, *Starving the South*, 103–5.

115. Groom, *Vicksburg, 1863*, 393; Andrew F. Smith, *Starving the South*, 103–5.

116. Groom, *Vicksburg, 1863*, 401–2.

117. In memory of the Confederate surrender, the July Fourth holiday was not officially celebrated by white citizens of Vicksburg for nearly eighty years.

118. James McPherson, *Battle Cry of Freedom*, 637.

119. David G. Martin, *Vicksburg Campaign*, 136.

120. Ibid.

121. James McPherson, *Battle Cry of Freedom*, 636–37.

122. "From a Private's Diary."

123. Tryphena Blanche Holder Fox to Anna Rose Cleveland Holder, July 3, 1863, Woodburne Plantation, in Wilma King, *A Northern Woman*, 134–35.

124. Ibid.; Christopher Morris, *Becoming Southern*, 184. Morris notes that Union officials counted 136 abandoned plantations around Vicksburg.

125. Faust, *Mothers of Invention*, 197.

126. Samuel A. Agnew Diary, October 6, 1863, folder 9, vol. 7B, 923, SHC. I am indebted to Helen Thomas for sharing this diary entry with me, which she discusses on the Wilson Special Collections Library blog, UNC-CH, "The Civil War Day by Day," http://blogs.lib.unc.edu/civilwar/index.php/2013/10/21/6-october-1863-becky-eliza-were-faithful-and-the-yankees-called-becky-secesh-because-she-told-them-she-was-not-willing-to-leave-her-master/.

127. Samuel A. Agnew Diary, October 6, 1863, folder 9, vol. 7B, 923, SHC.

128. Streater, "She-Rebels," 88–89.

129. Whites and Long, *Occupied Women*, 4–9.

130. Ibid.

131. Faust, *Mothers of Invention*, 234–35.

132. Ibid., 242–47.

133. Andrew F. Smith, *Starving the South*, 200–202.

134. James McPherson, *Battle Cry of Freedom*, 847–48.

135. Ibid., 848.

136. Smith Kitchin, "The Notes and Sketches of a Confederate Soldier of the War of the Rebellion from November 1862–July 1865," SCL. Company A, 17th Infantry Regiment, was organized at Rich Hill, S.C., in 1862, and commanded by John R. Culp.

137. Eliza Clifford Gordon Stiles to William Gordon, July 1, 1865, Terrell Co., Ga., Gordon Family Papers, MS 318, box 1, no. 318, GHS. Eliza C. Stiles was the aunt of Juliette Gordon Low, founder of the Girl Scouts.

138. Ibid.

139. Ibid.

Chapter 5

1. "Testimony of Nancy Johnson before the Southern Claims Commission, Savannah, Georgia, March 22, 1873," in Berlin, Fields, Miller, Reidy, and Rowland, *Free at Last*, 124–29.

2. Ibid., 129.

3. Ibid., 126.

4. Ibid., 129.

5. For discussion of "the liberators" seizing property of both slaves and their owners as Union forces arrived on southern plantations and farms, see Litwack, *Been in the Storm So Long*, 122–25.

6. Sharpless includes an important summary of the first-person narratives, autobiographies, and published letters of African American cooks and domestic workers that followed this era. See Sharpless, "Neither Friends nor Peers," 331–32.

7. See Titus, "Groaning Tables," 13–21; and Warner, "Harriet Jacobs's Modest Proposals," 22–28.

8. Titus, "Groaning Tables," 18.

9. Douglass, *Narrative of the Life of Frederick Douglass*, 299. Douglass included the same story of feeding slave children in his second autobiography, *My Bondage and My Freedom*, 133, http://docsouth.unc.edu/neh/douglass55/douglass55.html.

10. Douglass, *Life and Times of Frederick Douglass*, 181; Genovese, *Roll, Jordan, Roll*, 58.

11. Douglass, *My Bondage and My Freedom*, 107.

12. Harriet A. Jacobs, *Incidents in the Life of a Slave Girl*, 12.

13. Titus, "Groaning Tables," 18.

14. Gwin, *Black and White Women of the Old South*, 64.

15. Yellin, *Harriet Jacobs*, 30.

16. Harriet A. Jacobs, *Incidents in the Life of a Slave Girl*, 12.

17. Ibid.

18. Ibid.

19. Ibid.

20. Ibid., 46.

21. Warner, "Harriet Jacobs's Modest Proposals," 25–26.

22. Washington, *Up from Slavery*, 10.

23. Carody, "Sterling Brown," 820.

24. Ibid., 822.

25. Ibid., 822–25.

26. "Notes . . . on Editing Dialect Usage in Accounts of Interviews with Ex-slaves," Stetson Kennedy Papers, 4193, folder 14, SHC.

27. Ibid.

28. William Ferris, "John Blassingame, 1940–2000," in William R. Ferris, *The Storied South*, 132.

29. Berlin, Favreau, and Miller, *Remembering Slavery*, xix.

30. Ibid.

31. Woodward, Review of *The American Slave*, 474–75.

32. George Fleming, WPA Slave Narrative, Spartanburg, S.C., October 28, 1937, in Mellon, *Bullwhip Days*, 257–62; Berlin, Favreau, and Miller, *Remembering Slavery*, 77–81.

33. Woodward, Review of *The American Slave*, 474–75.

34. Alex McCinney, WPA Slave Narrative, in *Bullwhip Days*, 43.

35. Litwak, *Been in the Storm So Long*, 228. Litwak cites Slave Narrative of Stephen McCray, Oklahoma City, Okla., August 19, 1937, WPA Slave Narrative Project, Oklahoma Narratives, Volume 13, LOC, 209.

36. George Fleming, WPA Slave Narrative, Spartanburg, S.C., October 28, 1937, in Mellon, *Bullwhip Days*, 259; Berlin, Favreau, and Miller, *Remembering Slavery*, 80–81.

37. Anna Wright, interview by Mary Hicks, Wendell, N.C., August 17, 1937, WPA Slave Narrative Project, North Carolina Narratives, Volume 11, Part 2, LOC.

38. Ibid., 424.

39. Ibid, 423.

40. Ibid.

41. Ibid, 424.

42. Ibid, 423.

43. Ibid, 423–24.

44. Louisa Adams, interview by T. Pat Matthews, June 7, 1937, WPA Slave Narrative Project, North Carolina Narratives, Volume 11, Part 1, LOC, 2.

45. Julia (Aunt Sally) Brown, interview by Geneva Tonsill, Atlanta, Ga., July 25, 1930, WPA Slave Narrative Project, Georgia Narratives, Volume 4, Part 1, LOC, 5–6.

46. Henrietta King, West Point, Va., in Perdue, Barden, and Phillips, *Weevils in the Wheat*, 190–92.

47. Ibid.

48. Ibid.

49. Simpson, WPA Texas Slave Narrative, in Rawick, *American Slave.*

50. Litwak, *Been in the Storm So Long*, 11–12.

51. Ibid., 203.

52. Larry Levine, "Meaning of Slave Tales," 83, 102.

53. Foner, *Reconstruction*, 69.

54. Ibid., 81–82.

55. Julia Rollins Holt to her daughter, Emily "Bertie" Burt Holt, Jackson, Miss., June 29, 1868, Holt-Messer Family Papers, SCHL.

56. Ibid.

57. Ibid., August 7, 1868.

58. Ibid., July 5, 1868.

59. Ibid.

60. Ibid., July 10, 1868.

61. Foner, *Reconstruction*, 78.

62. Ibid.

63. Ibid., 257.

64. Litwak, *Been in the Storm So Long*, May 20, 1865, 347. Litwak cites Eppes, *Through Some Eventful Years*, 282–83.

65. Litwak, *Been in the Storm So Long*, 346. Litwak cites a story from Charles Stearns, *The Black Man of the South, and the Rebels* (New York, 1872), 43–46.

66. Burr, *Secret Eye*, May 29, 1865, 273.

67. Ibid.

68. Litwak, *Been in the Storm So Long*, 300.

69. Ibid., 293.

Chapter 6

1. Harland, *Common Sense in the Household*, 14.

2. Censer, *Reconstruction of White Southern Womanhood*, 69.

3. Tryphena Blanche Holder Fox to Anna Rose Cleveland Holder, September 10, 1865, in Wilma King, *A Northern Woman*, 157–58.

4. Burr, *Secret Eye*, May 4, 1871, 370.

5. Ibid.

6. Wilcox, *Dixie Cook-Book*, 499.

7. See "Cookbooks," in Engelhardt, *A Mess of Greens*, 175–82.

8. Hess, "Historical Notes and Commentaries," xiii.

9. Ibid., xxiv; Jessica B. Harris, *High on the Hog*, 105.

10. Hess, "Historical Notes and Commentaries," xxi.

11. Mary Randolph (1762–1828) was the eldest daughter of Anne Cary Randolph and Thomas Mann Randolph of Tuckahoe Plantation in Goochland County, Va.

The family was related to the Custis and Washington families in Virginia by blood and marriage. Mary Randolph's brother Thomas Mann Randolph (wife, Martha Jefferson) was Thomas Jefferson's son-in-law. For further discussion of Mary Randolph and her sister Virginia Randolph Cary, see Kierner, *Beyond the Household*, 203–7.

12. Ibid.; preface to Randolph, *Virginia House-Wife*, facsimile, x.

13. Preface to Randolph, *Virginia House-Wife*, facsimile, x.

14. Ibid.

15. See Damon Fowler's extensive bibliography of nineteenth-century cookbooks by southerners and nonsoutherners who influenced regional cuisine, in Hill, *Mrs. Hill's Southern Practical Cookery and Receipt Book*, 450–59.

16. Rutledge, *The Carolina Housewife*, v. For discussion of African ingredients in *The Carolina Housewife*, see Jessica B. Harris, *High on the Hog*, 106.

17. Jessica B. Harris, *High on the Hog*, 105.

18. Bryan, *Kentucky Housewife*, 153.

19. Ibid., vii–viii.

20. Russell, *A Domestic Cook Book*; Fisher, *What Mrs. Fisher Knows*. For further discussion of Fisher and Russell, see Jessica B. Harris, *High on the Hog*, 164–66. For discussion of African American women cooks and the racial politics of their "invisibility" in print, see Tipton-Martin, "Bluegrass and Black Magic," v–xxxiii.

21. See Williams-Forson, *Building Houses Out of Chicken Legs*, 31–37, for discussion of the racial economies of food negotiated by African American women in the South throughout Reconstruction and into the twentieth century.

22. Ibid., 4.

23. Russell, *A Domestic Cook Book*, 5.

24. Harland, *Common Sense in the Household*, 463.

25. Tryphena Blanche Holder Fox to Anna Rose Cleveland Holder, December 28, 1872, in Wilma King, *A Northern Woman*, 252–53.

26. Harland's *Common Sense in the Household* sold over a million copies and had at least ten printings from 1871 to 1892. Harland published twenty-five books on homemaking and domestic advice and wrote related columns for many women's magazines. See "Feeding America," in Michigan State University Libraries, http://digital.lib.msu.edu/projects/cookbooks/html/books/book_30.cfm; and M. L. Crawford, "Marion Harland" (1830–1922), in *Encyclopedia Virginia*, http://www.encyclopediavirginia.org/harland_marion_1830-1922.

27. Harland, *Common Sense in the Household*, dedication.

28. Ibid., 14.

29. Wilcox, *Dixie Cook-Book*, 499.

30. Ibid., dedication. Italics added for emphasis.

31. Hill, *Southern Practical Cookery*, 12.

32. Fowler, "Historical Commentary," xiv, xxii–xxiv.

33. Warren, Introduction to Hill, *Southern Practical Cookery*, 5–6; Fowler, "Historical Commentary, 447. Damon Fowler states that Warren (1820–93) was a prominent Baptist minister in Macon, Ga., acquainted with Annabella Hill through family connections. For further discussion of Hill's work and its discussion of the "crisis" of the age, see Grubb, "House and Home in the Victorian South," 163, 170–71.

34. Warren, Introduction to Hill, *Southern Practical Cookery*, 6.

35. Ibid.

36. Ibid., 10–11.

37. Joe Gray Taylor, *Eating, Drinking, and Visiting*, 104; Fowler, "Notes on

the Original Introduction and Its Author," in Hill, *Mrs. Hill's Southern Practical Cookery and Receipt Book*, 447–48.

38. Tyree, *Housekeeping in Old Virginia*, vii–viii. The first edition of *Housekeeping in Old Virginia* by Marion Cabell Tyree (1826–1912) was published in New York in 1877. Succeeding editions were published in southern cities such as Richmond and Louisville.

39. Ibid., viii.

40. Ibid., inside back cover.

41. Ibid., 19.

42. Ibid., 374.

Part II

1. Ayers, *Promise of the New South*, 21. This phrase comes from Henry Grady's 1886 speech to the New England Society in New York City, designed as an overly positive "State of the South" report.

2. Archie Green, "Railroad Songs and Ballads," from the Archive of Folk Song, Library of Congress, Recording Laboratory AFS L61, Washington, D.C., 1968, 14–15.

Chapter 7

1. Margaret Mitchell, *Gone with the Wind*.

2. Daniel, *Dispossession*, 9–14.

3. Egerton, *Speak Now against the Day*, 18.

4. Ayers, *Southern Crossing*, 18.

5. Egerton, *Speak Now against the Day*, 20.

6. Ibid., 22.

7. Ayers, *Southern Crossing*, 10–11.

8. Ibid., 26–27; Sharpless and Walker, *Work, Family, and Faith*, 8.

9. Ibid.

10. Johnson, Embree, and Alexander, *Collapse of Cotton Tenancy*, 16–17.

11. Ibid.

12. Ibid.; see also ibid., "What Is a Tenant," 6–11.

13. Ibid.; for period discussion on "Furnishing," see ibid., 17–20.

14. Ibid.

15. Ayers, *Southern Crossing*, 26–27.

16. Egerton, *Speak Now against the Day*, 21.

17. Ibid., 18–23. See "The State of the South," in ibid., for discussion of the social and economic status of southern sharecroppers and tenant farmers in the 1930s.

18. Ibid., 21.

19. Powdermaker, *After Freedom*, 79.

20. Vance, *Human Geography of the South*, 33.

21. Ibid.

22. Johnson, Embree, and Alexander, *Collapse of Cotton Tenancy*, 17.

23. Ibid.

24. Ibid.

25. Federal Writers' Project, *The WPA Guide to 1930s Arkansas*, 131.

26. Ibid., 232.

27. Ayers, *Southern Crossing*, 11.

28. Ibid., 26–28.

29. Melissa Walker, *All We Knew Was to Farm*, 29.

30. Hall et al., *Like a Family*, 9–10.

31. Egerton, *Speak Now against the Day*, 22–24, 70–73.

32. Hall et al., *Like a Family*, 33.

33. Ayers, *Southern Crossing*, 26.

34. Opie, *Hog and Hominy*, 56; Jessica B. Harris, *High on the Hog*, 172.

35. Cobb, *The Most Southern Place on Earth*, 115–17.

36. Opie, *Hog and Hominy*, 57. See also "Traveling the Chicken Bone Express," in Williams-Forson, *Building Houses Out of Chicken Legs*, 114–34.

37. Williams-Forson, *Building Houses Out of Chicken Legs*, 116.

38. Ibid.

39. Wilkerson, *Warmth of Other Suns*, 531.

40. Jessica B. Harris, *High on the Hog*, 174–78; Opie, *Hog and Hominy*, 55–82; Adrian Miller, *Soul Food*, 35–41.

41. Ellison, *Invisible Man*, 262–63.

42. Egerton, *Speak Now against the Day*, 82–85; see also Daniel, *Dispossession*, 9. Daniel examines the systematic, institutional and government discrimination (from the New Deal through the civil rights movement) against southern minority, women, and black farmers that prevented them from sharing equally in federal agricultural programs. See Kuhn's discussion of "high-modernist" efforts of rural New Dealers to transform the southern family farm, in "It Was a Long Way from Perfect," 68–69.

43. Daniel, *Lost Revolutions*, 39; Daniel, *Dispossession*, xi.

44. Council, *Mama Dip's Kitchen*, 19.

45. Ibid.

46. Daniel, *Lost Revolutions*, 39–40; Daniel, *Dispossession*, 9–13; Daniel, "USDA Approved," 103–4.

47. Kirby, *Rural Worlds Lost*, 60.

48. Ibid., 61; Egerton, *Speak Now against the Day*, 154–58. See "Historical Information," Southern Tenant Farmers' Union Records, SHC.

49. William H. Cobb, "Southern Tenant Farmers' Union," in *Encyclopedia of Arkansas History and Culture*, http://encyclopediaofarkansas.net/encyclopedia/entry-detail.aspx?entryID=35.

50. Kuhn, "It Was a Long Way from Perfect," 71.

51. Ibid.

52. Kirby, *Rural Worlds Lost*, 68.

53. Ibid., 338–39.

54. Ibid.

55. Ibid.

56. Daniel, *Lost Revolutions*, 42.

57. Daniel, *Dispossession*, 9.

58. Kirby, *Rural Worlds Lost*, 72.

59. For further discussion of southern agricultural reform and legislation, see Roy V. Scott, *Eugene Beverly Ferris*.

60. Daniel, *Dispossession*, xii.

61. Ibid.

62. Grantham, *Southern Progressivism*, xvii.

63. Ibid., xvi, xvii.

Chapter 8

1. McCleary, "Seizing the Opportunity," 100.

2. Hoffschwelle, *Rebuilding the Rural Southern Community*, 14; Danbom, "Rural Education Reform," 462–74.

3. For more information on Rockeller-funded initiatives to battle hookworm in the American South, see Ettling, *The Germ of Laziness*.

4. Conkin, "The School of Country Life."

5. Ibid.

6. "Canning Tomatoes," in Engelhardt, *A Mess of Greens*, 83–117; Kuhn, "It Was a Long Way from Perfect," 79–83.

7. Hoffschwelle, *Rebuilding the Rural Southern Community*, 97–98.

8. Conkin, "The School of Country Life."

9. Andrew F. Smith, *Eating History*, 117; Elias, *Stir It Up*, 7.

10. Elias, *Stir It Up*, 11; Angela Jill Cooley, "To Live and Dine in Dixie," 34. Cooley explains that Richards preferred the term "Euthenics"—"race improvement through environment"—rather than "domestic science."

11. Engelhardt, *A Mess of Greens*, 54–55.

12. Elias, *Stir It Up*, 8.

13. Ibid., 16.

14. For further discussion of white and black women's involvement in Progressive-Era reform movements in the South, see "Feminism and Reform," in Grantham, *Southern Progressivism*, 200–209.

15. Rieff, "Revitalizing Southern Homes," 204.

16. Anne Firor Scott, *Making the Invisible Woman Visible*, 219.

17. Angela Jill Cooley, "To Live and Dine in Dixie," 43.

18. Ibid.

19. McCandless, *Past in the Present*, 74.

20. Hoffschwelle, *Rebuilding the Rural Southern Community*, 29.

21. Ibid.

22. McCandless, *Past in the Present*, 58.

23. Ibid., 73.

24. Boyer, *Notes and Recipes*, 4.

25. Ibid., 3.

26. Ibid., 4; Georgen Coyle and Susan Tucker, "Newcomb," http://tulane.edu/nccrow/newcomb-archives/history-of-newcomb-college.cfm.

27. Boyer, *Notes and Recipes*, 31.

28. Ibid., 97, 101, 103.

29. Ibid.

30. Product Sample Letters, New Orleans Railway and Light Company to Miss Harriet Boyer, Newcomb College, New Orleans, La., May 6, 1914, Harriet Boyer Papers, NCCRW.

31. J. B. Osborn, H. M. Anthony Company, New York, N.Y., to Miss Harriet Boyer, Newcomb College, New Orleans, La., December 3, 1913, Harriet Boyer Papers, NCCRW.

32. USDA, Bureau of Plant Industry, Foreign Seed and Plant Introduction, Washington, D.C., to "Gentlemen," September 17, 1917, Harriet Boyer Papers, NCCRW.

33. See Dr. Lance Hill, Southern Institute for Education and Research, Tulane University, New Orleans, La., at http://www.mirlitons.org/.

34. "News from the Field."

35. Georgen Coyle and Susan Tucker, "Newcomb," http://tulane.edu/nccrow

/newcomb-archives/history-of-newcomb-college.cfm. See also McCandless, *Past in the Present*, 58. McCandless describes the closure of the home economics program at Converse College in 1927 and the decision to not include such a program at Agnes Scott College in Decatur, Ga., because such studies were considered "peripheral to the 'real' work" of the academy.

36. Elias, *Stir It Up*, 16.

37. Lu Ann Jones, *Mama Learned Us to Work*, 141.

38. Engs, *Educating the Disfranchised and Disinherited*, xiii, 78–79. Engs refers to the "men and women [James] McPherson aptly describes as 'the children of the abolitionists'" in his work *Abolitionist Legacy*.

39. Bacon, "Work and Methods of the Hampton Folklore Society," 17–21.

40. Louise Lane Gilman to Emily Gilman, Hampton, Va., February 17, 1869, Louise Lane Gilman Papers, March 28, 1866–May 7, 1869, WLCL.

41. Cimbala and Miller, *Freedmen's Bureau and Reconstruction*, 135–36.

42. Engs, *Educating the Disfranchised and Disinherited*, 79.

43. Ibid., 80.

44. Armstrong and Ludlow, *Hampton and Its Students*, 41–42.

45. Tillery, *A Taste of Freedom*, 138.

46. Louise Lane Gilman to Emily Gilman and Molly Gilman, Hampton, Va., March 7, 1869, Louise Lane Gilman Papers, March 28, 1866–May 7, 1869, WLCL.

47. Louise Lane Gilman to Emily Gilman, Hampton, Va., February 17, 1869, ibid.

48. Church, "Solving the Problem," 404–5.

49. Tillery, *A Taste of Freedom*, 158.

50. Lindsey, *Indians at Hampton Institute*, 137.

51. Ibid., 139.

52. Ibid., 138.

53. Ibid.

54. Engs, *Educating the Disfranchised and Disinherited*, 122.

55. Ibid.

56. Ibid. See also Lindsey, *Indians at Hampton Institute*, 223.

57. Lindsey, *Indians at Hampton Institute*, 136.

58. Engs, *Educating the Disfranchised and Disinherited*, 122.

59. Ibid.

60. Lindsey, *Indians at Hampton Institute*, 137.

61. Ibid.

62. Neverdon-Morton, *Afro-American Women of the South*, 26; Jones-Wilson, "Home Economics and African-American Education," 214–15.

63. Church, "Solving the Problem," 405.

64. Neverdon-Morton, *Afro-American Women of the South*, 23.

65. Lyford, *A Book of Recipes for the Cooking School*.

66. Ibid.

67. Laura Shapiro, *Perfection Salad*, 86–87. See Shapiro for a discussion of the popularity of white sauce at the turn of the twentieth century and the "fondness for whitening" food in the same era.

68. Church, "Solving the Problem," 402–3.

69. Ibid.

70. Ibid., 402.

71. Ibid., 403.

72. Ibid., 408.

73. Neverdon-Morton, *Afro-American Women of the South*, 36.

74. Dotson, "The Story of a Teacher of Cooking," 204.
75. Ibid., 208.
76. Emma S. Jacobs, "Pioneering in Home Economics," 85.
77. Ibid.
78. Ibid., 86.
79. Ibid., 88–89.
80. Neverdon-Morton, *Afro-American Women of the South*, 1.
81. Barnett, "Nannie Burroughs and the Education of Black Women," 97–108; Sharpless, *Cooking in Other Women's Kitchens*, 27.
82. Alexander, *Images of America*, 58.
83. Ibid.
84. "Colored Cooks Are Given Lessons in Culinary Art."
85. Rieff, "Revitalizing Southern Homes," 137; Jessica B. Harris, *High on the Hog*, 184–85.
86. Theda Perdue, *Race and the Atlanta Cotton States Exposition of 1895*, 148–51.
87. Washington, "The Atlanta Exposition Address," 220, http://docsouth.unc.edu/fpn/washington/washing.html#washing217.
88. Washington, *Up from Slavery*, 127.
89. Ibid.
90. Bacon, *The Negro and the Atlanta Cotton Exposition*, 18.
91. Jones, "Improving Rural Life for Blacks, 107.
92. Ibid., 106–9. The Tuskegee demonstration farm included 2,300 acres by 1915.
93. Ibid.
94. Neverdon-Morton, *Afro-American Women of the South*, 124–25.
95. Jones, "Improving Rural Life for Blacks," 111.
96. Ibid.
97. Ibid., 112.
98. For more information on the Black Farmers Class Action Lawsuit, see the Federation of Southern Cooperatives/Land Assistance Fund, which has fought for the successful resolution of the lawsuit since the 1990s, http://www.federationsoutherncoop.com/. See also Southall, "Senate Approves Payment of Black Farmers' Claims."

Chapter 9

1. Atwater and Woods, "Dietary Studies with Reference to the Food of the Negro"; Frissell and Bevier, "Dietary Studies of Negroes in Eastern Virginia."
2. Anthropologist Robert Dirks and agricultural librarian Nancy Duran describe the "ethnographic dimension" that human nutritional studies assumed in the late nineteenth-century dietaries overseen by Atwater's Office of Experiment Stations. Dirks and Duran, "Experiment Station Dietary Studies," 1253.
3. Ibid. Dirks and Duran explain that Wilbur Atwater "originated American field investigations and set the standards for the period."
4. See "Wilbur O. Atwater's Calorimeter," in Andrew F. Smith, *Eating History*, 114–20.
5. Dirks and Duran, "African American Dietary Patterns," 1881.
6. Dirks and Duran, "Experiment Station Dietary Studies," 1253.
7. Ibid.
8. "Letter of Transmittal from A. C. True, Director of the Office of Experiment Stations, to Hon. J. Sterling Morton, Secretary of Agriculture," Washington, D.C., January 1897, in Atwater and Woods, "Dietary Studies with Reference to the Food

of the Negro," 3–4. John Wesslay Hoffman taught at Tuskegee from 1894 to 1896. He went on to teach in black schools in Orangeburg, S.C., and Prairie View, Tex. See Harlan, *Booker T. Washington Papers*, 414.

9. "Letter of Transmittal from A.C. True, Director of the Office of Experiment Stations, to Hon. J. Sterling Morton, Secretary of Agriculture," Washington, D.C., January 15, 1897, in Atwater and Woods, "Dietary Studies with Reference to the Food of the Negro," 3–4. The Agricultural and Mechanical College of Alabama (Alabama A&M) was created in 1875 under the Morrill Act to extend agricultural education to African Americans. The Alabama legislature sanctioned it as the African American land-grant institution in 1891. See Robert J. Vejnar II, "Land Grant Colleges in Alabama," in *Encyclopedia of Alabama*, http://encyclopediaofalabama.org/face/Article.jsp?id=h-1558.

10. Dirks and Duran, "African American Dietary Patterns," 1882.

11. Ibid.

12. Ibid.

13. Dirks and Duran, "Experiment Station Dietary Studies," 1254.

14. Atwater and Woods, "Dietary Studies with Reference to the Food of the Negro," 28–29.

15. Ibid.

16. Ibid.

17. Washington, *Up from Slavery*, 112–13.

18. Ibid.

19. Ibid.

20. Ibid., 113–14.

21. Ibid., 9.

22. Atwater and Woods, "Dietary Studies with Reference to the Food of the Negro," 19.

23. Ibid.

24. Joe Gray Taylor, *Eating, Drinking, and Visiting*, 139–40.

25. Atwater and Woods, "Dietary Studies with Reference to the Food of the Negro," 19.

26. Dirks, "What Early Dietary Studies of African Americans Tell Us," 10.

27. Kraut, *Goldberger's War*, 222–23.

28. Atwater and Woods, "Dietary Studies with Reference to the Food of the Negro," 19.

29. Ibid.

30. Ibid.

31. Glassie, *Pattern in the Material Folk Culture of the Eastern United States*, 102, 107.

32. Ibid., 115.

33. For further discussion of the "three m" diet of African Americans, see Adrian Miller, *Soul Food*, 19–23.

34. Clark, *Pills, Petticoats, and Plows*, 131–32.

35. Ibid.

36. Sharpless, *Cooking in Other Women's Kitchens*, 41–42.

37. Ibid., 134.

38. Taylor and Edge, "Southern Food," 4; Charles Reagan Wilson, "Cornbread," 152–54; Adrian Miller, *Soul Food*, 186–204.

39. Taylor and Edge, "Southern Food," 4; Egerton, "Grits," 175–77.

40. Taylor and Edge, "Southern Food," 6; Engelhardt, *A Mess of Greens*, 127.

41. Clark, *Pills, Petticoats, and Plows*, 127–28.

42. Atwater and Woods, "Dietary Studies with Reference to the Food of the Negro," 19.

43. Ibid.

44. Ibid.

45. Ibid., 20.

46. Booker T. Washington discussed the meaning of the term "Black Belt" in his autobiography, *Up from Slavery* (1901). He explained that the term referred to "a part of the country, which was distinguished by the color of the soil. The part of this country possessing this thick, dark, and naturally rich soil was, of course, the part of the South where the slaves were most profitable, and consequently they were taken there in the largest numbers. Later, and especially since the war, the term seems to be used wholly in a political sense—that is, to designate the counties where the black people outnumber the white." Ibid., 108.

47. Opie, "Molasses-Colored Glasses," 85.

48. Ibid., 82.

49. Sohn, "Sorghum," 263–64.

50. Clark, *Pills, Petticoats, and Plows*, 127–28. "Ribbon" refers to the distinctive striped pattern of the specific variety of sugarcane.

51. Atwater and Woods, "Dietary Studies with Reference to the Food of the Negro," 19.

52. Frissell and Bevier, "Dietary Studies of Negroes in Eastern Virginia."

53. Frissell, "Dietary Studies among the Negroes in 1897," in ibid., 8.

54. Ibid.

55. Ibid., 10.

56. Ibid., 11, 13.

57. Ibid., 7.

58. Ibid., 7, 8.

59. Ibid., 8.

60. Dirks and Duran, "African American Dietary Patterns," 1884.

61. Ibid., 8, 29.

62. Ibid.

63. Ibid., 17.

64. Ibid.

65. Ibid., 18.

66. Ibid., 18, 41.

67. Ohles, "Isabel Bevier," 127; Bartow, *Isabel Bevier*. For further discussion of Bevier, see Elias, *Stir It Up*.

68. Bartow, *Isabel Bevier*, 27; Bevier, "How I Came to Take Up Home Economics Work," 140.

69. Bevier, "How I Came to Take Up Home Economics Work," 140.

70. Ibid.

71. Bevier, "Dietary Studies among the Negroes in 1898," in Frissell and Bevier, "Dietary Studies of Negroes in Eastern Virginia," 26.

72. Ibid., 40.

73. Ibid., 44.

74. Frissell and Bevier, "Discussion of Results," in ibid., 41.

75. Goldberger and Sydenstricker, "Pellagra in the Mississippi Flood Area," 2712.

76. Kraut, *Goldberger's War*, 5. For further discussion of pellagra in the New

South, see "Mill Work, Pellagra, and Gendered Consumption," in Engelhardt, *A Mess of Greens*, 124–28.

77. Kraut, *Goldberger's War*, 17.

78. Ibid., 99.

79. Ibid., 7.

80. Ibid., 128. See also James A. Jones, *Bad Blood*.

81. Kraut, *Goldberger's War*, 124.

82. Ibid., 128.

83. Ibid., 134.

84. Ibid., 135. See also Minor, "They Ate Their Way to Freedom."

85. Kraut, *Goldberger's War*, 105, 112, 123, 124, 153, 218–19.

86. Ibid., 13.

87. Neverdon-Morton, *Afro-American Women of the South*, 125.

88. Kraut, *Goldberger's War*, 219.

89. Ibid.

90. Ibid.

91. Ibid.

92. Goldberger and Sydenstricker, "Pellagra in the Mississippi Flood Area," 1927.

93. Ibid., 2710.

94. Kraut, *Goldberger's War*, 8.

95. Goldberger and Sydenstricker, "Pellagra in the Mississippi Flood Area," 2712.

96. Ibid., 2724–25.

97. Ibid., 2722.

98. Kraut, *Goldberger's War*, 234.

99. Ibid., 259.

100. Popkin, *The World Is Fat*, 27.

101. Green, "Mother Corn and Dixie Pig," 117.

102. Ibid.

103. Ibid.

104. Kraut, *Goldberger's War*, 259–61. In 1924, research determined that irradiation—exposing food to ultraviolet radiation—produced vitamin D. Food irradiation programs began in the United States in the 1950s.

Chapter 10

1. David E. Whisnant, *All That Is Native and Fine*, 7–8. See Whisnant for an in-depth discussion of the mission and the "cultural intervention" practices of the many schools, academies, and institutes—particularly those with a "cultural preservation and revival focus"—established in the mountain South after 1900.

2. Stoddart, *Quare Women's Journals*, 60.

3. Ibid.

4. Ibid., 49; Engelhardt, *A Mess of Greens*, 55.

5. Camp Cedar Grove, 1899, in Stoddart, *Quare Women's Journals*, 63.

6. Pettit and Stone's descriptions of how the people of the mountain South ate are similar to John C. Campbell's ethnographic writing, including extensive sections on diet published in his *Southern Highlander and His Homeland* in 1921. Dramatic food descriptions that disparaged and exoticized mountain southerners are also seen in the work of local color writers such as Arthur W. Spalding (*The Hill O'*

Ca'Liny, 1921) and Margaret W. Morley (*The Carolina Mountains*, 1913). See Kephart, *Our Southern Highlanders*, 323.

7. Stoddart, *Challenge and Change in Appalachia*, 49.

8. Stoddart, *Quare Women's Journals*, 63.

9. Ibid.

10. Engelhardt, *A Mess of Greens*, 60, 67–68.

11. Stoddart, *Quare Women's Journals*, 71.

12. Ibid., 20.

13. Ibid., 19–20.

14. Ibid., 106.

15. Ibid.

16. Ibid., 84.

17. Ibid.

18. Stoddart, *Challenge and Change in Appalachia*, 117.

19. Ibid., 122.

20. Ibid., 123.

21. Rev. A. J. Beard of the American Missionary Association to Reverend Wheeler, Pleasant Hill Academy, Tenn., July 18, 1900, John Charles Campbell and Olive D. Campbell Papers, SHC.

22. Ibid.

23. Dorothy Hancock Stiles Journal, March 8, 1916, Hindman Settlement School, Hindman, Ky., Dorothy Hancock Stiles Papers, SCHL.

24. Stoddart, *Challenge and Change in Appalachia*, 122.

25. Ibid.

26. Ibid., 123.

27. Ibid.

28. Ibid., 122–23.

29. Ibid., 123; Engelhardt, *A Mess of Greens*, 56–59.

30. Engelhardt, *A Mess of Greens*, 68–70.

31. Becker, *Selling Tradition*, 42–43.

32. David E. Whisnant, *All That Is Native and Fine*, 58–59; C. Brenden Martin, "To Keep the Spirit of Mountain Culture Alive," 254.

33. Dorothy Hancock Stiles Journal, February 15, 1915, Hindman Settlement School, Hindman, Ky., Dorothy Hancock Stiles Papers, SCHL.

34. Ibid., February 17, 1915.

35. Kraut, *Goldberger's War*, 44. Joseph Goldberger devoted much of his work in the early 1900s to battling the typhoid epidemic in the United States. Kraut writes that "typhoid was seventh of the ten leading causes of death in the United States" at the turn of the twentieth century.

36. Dorothy Hancock Stiles Journal, February 21, 1915, Hindman Settlement School, Hindman, Ky., Dorothy Hancock Stiles Papers, SCHL.

37. Ibid.

38. Ibid., March 12, 1915.

39. Engelhardt states that the women reformers' experiences in Appalachia gave them "freedom and mobility" and an "escape from domestic duties awaiting them at home." See "Biscuits and Cornbread: Race, Class, and Gender Politics of Women Baking Bread," in Engelhardt, *A Mess of Greens*, 70.

40. "Will Marry in London."

41. Dorothy Hancock Stiles Journal, March 7, 1916, Hindman Settlement School, Hindman, Ky., Dorothy Hancock Stiles Papers, SCHL.

42. Grace H. Buckingham, Cullman Academy, Joppa, Ala., January 1896, John Charles Campbell and Olive D. Campbell Papers, SHC.

43. Ibid.

44. John C. Campbell to John Glenn, Russell Sage Foundation, March 9, 1910, John Charles Campbell and Olive D. Campbell Papers, SHC.

45. Ibid.

46. Holland Thompson, *From the Cotton Field to the Cotton Mill*, 144. For further discussion of Thompson's mill town study, see Engelhardt, *A Mess of Greens*, 123–25.

47. Becker, *Selling Tradition*, 48–49.

48. John C. Campbell, *Southern Highlander*, 202.

49. Kraut, *Goldberger's War*, 99.

50. John C. Campbell, *Southern Highlander*, 203.

51. Butchart, "Laura Towne and Ellen Murray," 26.

52. Robbins, "Rossa B. Cooley and Penn School," 44.

53. Rossa Belle Cooley, *School Acres*, 37.

54. Ibid., 69.

55. Ibid.

56. Ibid., 76.

57. Ibid., 80.

58. Ibid.

59. P. W. Dawkins's Annual Report, June 18, 1903, Penn School Papers, SHC.

60. Ibid.

61. Ibid.

62. Ibid.

63. J. E. Davis, "Hampton at Penn School," 82.

64. Kellogg, Introduction to *School Acres*, 25.

65. J. E. Davis, "Hampton at Penn School," 82.

66. Ibid.

67. "Mrs. Linnie M. Blanton Obituary."

68. J. E. Davis, "Hampton at Penn School," 85. Blanton served in World War I in France and toured several army camps teaching versions of spirituals to the troops.

69. Dale Rosengarten, "Missions and Markets: Sea Island Basketry and the Sweetgrass Revolution," in Rosengarten, Rosengarten, and Schildkrout, *Grass Roots*, 129.

70. Rossa Belle Cooley, *School Acres*, 161.

71. Della Harvey, Colored Supervisor of Rural Schools, Beaufort County, S.C., Penn School Papers, folder 18, SHC.

72. Rossa Belle Cooley, *School Acres*, 103.

73. Mooney, "The Comfortable Tasty Framed Cottage," 64–65. For further discussion of W. E. B. Du Bois, see Jessica B. Harris, *High on the Hog*, 184–85.

74. Mooney, "The Comfortable Tasty Framed Cottage," 64–65. The cartoon was published in the *Crisis*, September 1913, 247.

75. Kennard, "Personal Notes."

76. For references to the "Better Homes" program and practice houses at Hampton, Tuskegee, and other African American institutions in the South, as well as at institutions in the white mountain South such as Berea College, see Ford and Halbert, *School Cottages*.

77. Hutchison, "Better Homes and Gullah," 106. See also Mooney, "The Comfortable Tasty Framed Cottage," 48–67. The Better Homes Campaign was begun at the

women's magazine, *The Delineator*. It became a national program after receiving support from Herbert Hoover and the Department of Commerce and financing from the Rockefeller Foundation.

78. Hutchison, "Better Homes and Gullah," 111.

79. Ibid., 111–12; Ford and Halbert, *School Cottages*, 17.

80. Ford and Halbert, *School Cottages*, 10.

81. Robbins, "Rossa B. Cooley and Penn School," 46.

82. Ibid., 48; Rossa Belle Cooley, *School Acres*, 107–9.

83. Jacoway, *Yankee Missionaries in the South*, 78–79.

84. Ibid.

85. J. E. Blanton to Francis Cope, March 17, 1921, Penn School Papers, SHC.

86. Ibid.

87. Letter to Penn School Finance Committee from members of the Cooperative Society, May 28, 1923, Penn School Papers, SHC.

Chapter 11

1. Grantham, *Southern Progressivism*, 340.

2. Ibid.

3. Ibid., 342; Carmen Harris, "Grace under Pressure," 204; Engelhardt, *A Mess of Greens*, 107.

4. Elias, *Stir It Up*, 28.

5. Ibid., 12. Elias's phrase "nostalgic modernism" refers to a Progressive-Era ideology that "sought to correct the weaknesses in traditional life so that its strengths . . . could be made all the stronger."

6. "Women's Institutes in North Carolina," 163.

7. Ibid.

8. Ibid., 161.

9. Grantham, *Southern Progressivism*, 334.

10. Harrison, "Southern Railway Company," 21. The Louisville and Nashville Railroad partnered with state agricultural departments in Kentucky, Tennessee, Florida, and Georgia to run trains with special farm exhibition cars; see "Louisville and Nashville Railroad," 15.

11. Butler, "Women's Institutes," 4–5.

12. Lu Ann Jones, *Mama Learned Us to Work*, 109; Engelhardt, *A Mess of Greens*, 85; McKimmon, *When We're Green We Grow*, 1, 4–5.

13. Butler, "Women's Institutes."

14. Ibid., 15.

15. Ibid.

16. Grantham, *Southern Progressivism*, 340–42.

17. Ibid.

18. Lu Ann Jones, *Mama Learned Us to Work*, 15; Rieff, "Revitalizing Southern Homes," 144.

19. Ibid.

20. Rieff, "Revitalizing Southern Homes," 136, 147.

21. Lu Ann Jones, *Mama Learned Us to Work*, 20.

22. Ibid., 18.

23. Ibid., 14, 52.

24. See "Curb Markets," in Engelhardt, *A Mess of Greens*, 183–90.

25. McCleary, "Seizing the Opportunity," 52, 100.

26. Ibid., 122; Lu Ann Jones, *Mama Learned Us to Work*, 52.

27. McKimmon, *When We're Green We Grow*, 164; Engelhardt, *A Mess of Greens*, 184–90.

28. Ibid., 86.

29. McKimmon, *When We're Green We Grow*, 11. Jane Simpson McKimmon was born in Raleigh, N.C., in 1867. She died in 1957. For more information on McKimmon and the history of home demonstration and 4-H youth development in North Carolina, see North Carolina State University's on-line exhibit and digital resources, "Green 'n' Growing," http://www.lib.ncsu.edu/specialcollections/greenngrowing/index.html. See also "Canning Tomatoes," in Engelhardt, *A Mess of Greens*, 83–117.

30. McKimmon, *When We're Green We Grow*, 165.

31. Lu Ann Jones, *Mama Learned Us to Work*, 78–79.

32. Ibid., 74.

33. Kuhn, "It Was a Long Way from Perfect," 73. See also Raper, "Good Gardens and 'Precious' Cookers," 233–42.

34. Kuhn, "It Was a Long Way from Perfect."

35. Ibid.

36. Ibid., 78; Raper, "Good Gardens and 'Precious' Cookers," 234–35.

37. Kuhn, "It Was a Long Way from Perfect," 74.

38. Ibid., 80.

39. Raper, "Good Gardens and 'Precious' Cookers," 237.

40. Ibid.

41. Ibid.

42. Kuhn, "It Was a Long Way from Perfect," 81.

43. Ibid., 83.

44. Ibid., 81–82.

45. Ibid., 82; Raper, "Good Gardens and 'Precious' Cookers," 238.

46. Grantham, *Southern Progressivism*, 333; Elias, *Stir the Pot*, 69.

47. Roy V. Scott, *Eugene Beverly Ferris*, 24; Stark and Kilgore, "Dorothy Dickins"; Ratliff, "Dorothy Dickins," 14–15.

48. Ratliff, "Dorothy Dickins," 15.

49. Ownby, "Gladys Presley, Dorothy Dickins, and the Limits of Female Agrarianism," 219.

50. Ibid., 229.

51. Dickins, "A Study of Food Habits"; Dickins, "A Nutrition Investigation of Negro Tenants."

52. Dickins, "A Study of Food Habits," 3.

53. Dickins, "A Nutrition Investigation of Negro Tenants," 36.

54. Ibid., 37.

55. Dickins, "A Study of Food Habits," 32.

56. Ibid.

57. Dickins, "A Nutrition Investigation of Negro Tenants," 17; Dickins, "A Study of Food Habits," 50.

58. Dickins, "A Study of Food Habits," 50.

59. Dickins, "A Nutrition Investigation of Negro Tenants," 47.

60. Ibid.

61. Angela Jill Cooley, "To Live and Dine in Dixie," 156–57.

62. Ibid.

63. Ibid.

64. Ibid.

65. "Work Progressing Well," news report of Selma Parrish's home demonstra-

tion activity in Kershaw County, S.C., in DeSaussure, Gamewell, Lange, and Parrish Family Papers, SCL.

66. "That Kitchen," news report of Selma Parrish's home demonstration activity in Kershaw County, S.C., in ibid.

67. Ibid.

68. Ibid.

69. For an in-depth discussion of the work of African American female extension agents in county and state home demonstration programs, see "Women in the Middle," in Lu Ann Jones, *Mama Learned Us to Work*, 138–69. For more information on the African American extension workers who oversaw tomato clubs, canning clubs, and home demonstration clubs for black women and girls in North Carolina, see Engelhardt, *A Mess of Greens*, 104–13; and Carmen Harris, "Grace under Pressure," 203–28.

70. Lu Ann Jones, *Mama Learned Us to Work*, 139–40.

71. Ibid., 140.

72. McKimmon, *When We're Green We Grow*, 142.

73. Lu Ann Jones, *Mama Learned Us to Work*, 147. See McKimmon's chapter on African American participation in North Carolina's home demonstration programs, "Negroes Eager Participants," in McKimmon, *When We're Green We Grow*, 137–49.

74. Lu Ann Jones, *Mama Learned Us to Work*, 145; Engelhardt, *A Mess of Greens*, 109.

75. McKimmon, *When We're Green We Grow*, 145.

76. Ibid., 146.

77. Lu Ann Jones, *Mama Learned Us to Work*, 143–44, 147; Engelhardt, *A Mess of Greens*, 107–8.

78. Lu Ann Jones, *Mama Learned Us to Work*, 143–44, 147.

79. Ratliff, "Dorothy Dickins," 15.

80. Hoffschwelle, *Rebuilding the Rural Southern Community*, 101–2.

81. Ibid.

82. Rich Hill Colored School, 1946, Lancaster, S.C., 12363.14, and Blacksburg Grammar Lunchroom, March 3, 1946, Blacksburg, S.C., 12363.7, South Carolina: School Lunch Program, Photographs, SCL.

83. Hoffschwelle, *Rebuilding the Rural Southern Community*, 102.

84. Employment Relief Committee reports, Lucille Cook Watson, Tensas Parish, La., 1933, Cross Keys Plantation Papers, TU.

85. Ashland Plantation, Tensas Parish, La., July 5, 1933, ibid.

86. Ibid.

87. Description of Lucille Cook Watson's visit to Crossgrove home, Tensas Parish, La., October 1933, ibid.

88. Ibid.

89. Mrs. Crossgrove to Unemployment Bureau, Tensas Parish, La., October 31, 1933, ibid.

90. Diana Bell-Kite, "Live-at-Home Program," in *NCpedia*, http://ncpedia.org/live-at-home.

91. Diana Bell-Kite, "Governor O. Max Gardner and the Great Depression," http://www.governoromaxgardner.com/images/TheLiveatHomeProgram.pdf.

92. Diana Bell-Kite, "Live-at-Home Program," in *NCpedia*, http://ncpedia.org/live-at-home.

93. Carmen Harris, "Grace under Pressure," 217–18.

94. Kirk et al., *Emergency Relief in North Carolina*, 289–93.

95. Diana Bell-Kite, "Live-at-Home Program," in *NCpedia*, http://ncpedia.org/live-at-home.

96. McKimmon, *When We're Green We Grow*, 193–94.

97. Ibid., 194.

98. Ibid.

99. Diana Bell-Kite, "Governor O. Max Gardner and the Great Depression," http://www.governoromaxgardner.com/images/TheLiveatHomeProgram.pdf.

100. Ibid.

101. Ibid.

102. Ibid.

103. Ibid. Yaupon is a small evergreen holly, common in the coastal plains of the southeastern United States, and has historical connections to coastal southeastern Native American tribes. The tea has caffeine levels similar to those of Asian tea and American coffee. John Lawson described the tea in *A New Voyage to Carolina* (1709), http://www.duke.edu/~cwcook/trees/ilvo.html.

104. County Federation of Home Demonstration Clubs, *Good Victuals*, 2.

105. Ibid.

106. Diana Bell-Kite, "Live-at-Home Program."

107. Ibid.

108. "Live-at-Home," *Time Magazine*, 19–20. A copy of Holley's winning "Live-at-Home" essay is in the Oliver Max Gardner Papers, Subseries 2.1, Speeches, 1905–47 and undated, SHC.

109. Diana Bell-Kite, "Live-at-Home Program." Governor Max Gardner presented the "Live-at-Home" student essay awards to Holley and Sossamon at a June 23, 1930, ceremony in Raleigh, N.C.

110. "Live-at-Home," *Time Magazine*, 19–20.

Chapter 12

1. Tindall, *Emergence of the New South*, 599. President Franklin Delano Roosevelt's July 1938 statement was made in response to the *Report on Economic Conditions of the South*, produced by the National Emergency Council. Tindall states that the report was "essentially a synopsis of existing analyses by Vance, Odum, and others."

2. Odum, *Southern Regions of the United States*, 541.

3. Ibid.

4. Odum, "New Sources of Vitality for the People," 417–23.

5. "So-Called Scientist Talks," clipping from unknown Mississippi newspaper, ca. 1930s, Joffre Coe memorabilia, http://digital.ncdcr.gov/cdm/singleitem/collection/p16062coll15/id/224/rec/8.

6. Ibid.

7. Tindall, "Significance of Howard W. Odum," 296, 298.

8. Tindall, *Emergence of the New South*, 576–78; Egerton, *Speak Now against the Day*, 61–63.

9. Tindall, *Emergence of the New South*, 576–77; Egerton, *Speak Now against the Day*, 64–69; Hale, *Making Whiteness*, 138–39.

10. Lytle, "The Hind Tit," 227. Lytle (1902–95), a native of Tennessee and a prolific writer and professor of literature at the University of the South, was one of the most important of the Vanderbilt Agrarians. I am grateful to Zackary Vernon for his reflection on this topic, explored further in his essay "The Problematic History and Recent Cultural Reappropriation of Southern Agrarianism."

11. Reed and Singal, Introduction to *Regionalism and the South*, xi.

12. Vance, "Cotton Culture," 21; Vance, *Human Factors in Cotton Culture.*

13. Vance, "Cotton Culture," 22. For further period discussion of the "notorious three M's," see Johnson, Embree, and Alexander, *Collapse of Cotton Tenancy*, 16–17.

14. Vance, *Human Geography of the South*, 411.

15. Ibid.

16. Ibid.

17. Ibid., 415.

18. Ibid., 511.

19. Ibid., 412, 423. Vance sent more than 800 surveys to southern home demonstration agents, in which he asked for sample menus from farm families in their counties for two seasons, representing three socioeconomic levels; 150 agents responded to the survey. Although Vance noted that the menus were filed at UNC-CH's Institute for Research in Social Science, a recent archival search could not locate these materials.

20. Egerton, *Speak Now against the Day*, 133.

21. Couch, *Culture in the South.* William Terry Couch (1901–88), born in Pamplin, Va., entered UNC-CH in 1920 and graduated with a BA in history in 1926. Couch directed the University of North Carolina Press from 1932 to 1945.

22. Couch, "The Negro in the South," in *Culture in the South*, 446.

23. Herring, "The Industrial Worker," 354.

24. Hatcher, "Appalachian America," 384, 385, 387. Hatcher was chair of the Department of Sociology at Berea College in the 1930s.

25. Ibid., 385–87.

26. Ibid., 384.

27. Ibid., 387.

28. Ibid.

29. Fleischauer et al., Introduction to *Documenting America*, 1–2, 4. Stryker's mentor in economics at Columbia University, Rexford Guy Tugwell, became the assistant secretary of agriculture under Franklin Delano Roosevelt and brought Stryker to Washington, D.C., to the Resettlement Administration (RA) in 1935. The photographic section became part of the Farm Security Administration (FSA) in 1937. The RA, and later the FSA, were New Deal agencies, established by Roosevelt beginning in 1933, to address rural poverty through loans to struggling farmers, commodity adjustments, and resettlement programs. Stryker was very familiar with the work of Odum and his colleagues in sociology at UNC-CH. See Egerton, *Speak Now against the Day*, 95–98.

30. Spirn, *Daring to Look*, 32.

31. Ibid., 91.

32. Astrid Boger, *People's Lives, Public Images*, 145.

33. Gordon, "Dorothea Lange," 718.

34. "Stryker to Delano," September 12, 1940, in Carlebach, "Documentary and Propaganda," 23.

35. "From R. E. Stryker to All Photographers," in Stryker and Wood, *In This Proud Land*, 187–88. Sociologist Robert Lynd, co-author of *Middletown* (1929), provided Stryker with subject lists for the photographers. See also Astrid Boger, *People's Lives, Public Images*, 149.

36. "R. E. Stryker to Russell Lee, Arthur Rothstein, in particular," FSA, February 19, 1942, in Stryker and Wood, *In This Proud Land*, 187–88.

37. Ibid.

38. Spirn, *Daring to Look*, 92.
39. Hagood, *Mothers of the South*.
40. Spirn, *Daring to Look*, 91–92; Hagood, *Mothers of the South*, insert after 132.
41. Spirn, *Daring to Look*, 92.
42. Ibid.
43. Harriet L. Herring, "Notes and Suggestions for Photographic Study of the 13 County Subregional Area," in Howard Odum Papers, folder 3638, SHC.
44. Hagood, *Mothers of the South*, 102–4.
45. Ibid., 102.
46. Ibid.
47. Ibid.
48. Gordon, "Dorothea Lange," 699.
49. Astrid Boger, *People's Lives, Public Images*, 156.
50. Spirn, *Daring to Look*, 94. For discussion of Lange's "trademark" photographic captions, see Curtis, *Mind's Eye, Mind's Truth*, 15.
51. Dorothea Lange, "Route 501, Person County, North Carolina," LOC, http://www.loc.gov/pictures/item/2006682428/.
52. Hagood, *Mothers of the South*, insert after 132.
53. Daniel, "Reasons to Talk about Tobacco," 7.
54. Ibid., 10.
55. Ibid.
56. Leonard Rapport was born in Durham, N.C., and graduated from UNC-CH in 1935. Rapport worked for the University of North Carolina Press and for the WPA's Southern Writers' Project in North Carolina, 1938–41. Rapport spent much of his career at the National Archives in Washington, D.C.
57. Daniels, "Reasons to Talk about Tobacco," 9.
58. Ibid.
59. Spirn, *Daring to Look*, 91; Hagood, *Mothers of the South*, insert after 132.
60. Hurley, *Marion Post Wolcott*, 58.
61. Brochure for "A University Conference: Population Research, Regional Research, the Measure of Regional Development, April 30–May 4, 1940, Institute for Research in Social Science, Chapel Hill," Howard Odum Papers, folder 3644, SHC.
62. Hagood, *Mothers of the South*, insert after 132; Hurley, *Marion Post Wolcott*, 62; Brochure for "A University Conference," Howard Odum Papers, SHC.
63. Margaret Jarman Hagood correspondence with Roy E. Stryker, March 27, 1940, Howard Odum Papers, folder 3644, SHC.
64. Panel for the IRSS, UNC-CH, prepared by the FSA for an exhibition at the university in 1940, LOC, http://www.loc.gov/pictures/item/fsa1998020566/PP/.
65. Spirn, *Daring to Look*, 92.
66. Jack and Irene Delano, interview by Richard K. Doud, Rio Piedras, Puerto Rico, June 12, 1965, Archives of American Art, Smithsonian Institution, http://www.aaa.si.edu/collections/interviews/oral-history-interview-jack-and-irene-delano-13026.
67. Egerton, *Speak Now against the Day*, 98.
68. Ibid., 98–100.
69. Hirsch, *Portrait of America*, 163.
70. Ibid., 162.
71. Ibid.
72. Ibid., 167.
73. Ibid.

74. Couch, "Instructors to Writers," in *These Are Our Lives*, 419.

75. "Outline for Life Histories," in ibid., 420–21.

76. Dora Hayes and Anne Fuller, interview by Gertha Couric, Richlands, Ala., "A Day on the Farm," Federal Writers' Project Papers, SHC.

77. Ibid., 88–90.

78. Ibid., 90.

79. Gertha Couric, interview by Woodrow Hand, Eufala, Ala., "Hotel Hostess–WPA Worker," Federal Writers' Project Papers, folder 16, SHC.

80. Robert and Gladys Walker, interview by Sadie B. Hornsby (writer) and Sarah H. Hall (reviser), "The Barbecue Stand," April 10, 19, 1939, Athens, Ga., Federal Writers' Project Papers, folder 193, SHC.

81. Alma Kingland, interview by Mary A. Hicks (writer), January 9, 1939, Raleigh, N.C., Federal Writers' Project Papers, folder 530, SHC.

82. Egerton, *Speak Now against the Day*, 148.

83. Hirsch, *Portrait of America*, 54–55; Powell, "Lyle Saxon."

84. Hirsch, *Portrait of America*, 188.

85. Powell, "Lyle Saxon."

86. Kurlansky, *Food of a Younger Land*, 17.

87. Saxon and Dreyer, *WPA Guide to New Orleans*, 165–73. For further discussion of Saxon as a member of the "French Quarter Renaissance," see Reed, *Dixie Bohemia*, 208–12.

88. Ibid., lxix–lxxviii.

89. Ibid., lxxviii; Stanonis, *Creating the Big Easy*, 8. For more food-related history of Storyville, see Randy Fertel, *Gorilla Man*, 39–40.

90. Powell, "Lyle Saxon."

91. Botkin, *Treasury of Southern Folklore*. Botkin's work also included evocative descriptions of southern food from an excerpt of Ben Robertson's memoir set in South Carolina, *Red Hills and Cotton Country*. Howard Odum praised Robertson's "realistic" and "vivid" descriptions of regional life, which he argued would help "social anthropologists to understand the culture of the South." See Lacy K. Ford Jr., Introduction to Robertson, *Red Hills and Cotton*, xxxi–xxxii.

92. "Eating and Drinking," in Federal Writers' Project, *North Carolina: The WPA Guide*, 105–6.

93. Ibid., 105.

94. Kurlansky, *Food of a Younger Land*, 14.

95. Ibid., 15.

96. Ibid., 99–197.

97. Egerton, *Speak Now against the Day*, 98–100.

98. Welty, "Mississippi Food," 102–9.

99. Ibid., 102.

100. Hurston, "Diddy-Wah-Diddy," 123–25.

101. Ibid.

102. Kurlansky, *Food of a Younger Land*, 17.

103. Ibid., 19.

104. Ibid.

105. Ibid.

106. Ibid., 15; Willard, *America Eats*.

107. Tindall, *Emergence of the New South*, 589; Caldwell and Bourke-White, *You Have Seen Their Faces*; Lange and Taylor, *An American Exodus*; Egerton, *Speak Now against the Day*, 144–50.

108. Agee and Evans, *Let Us Now Praise Famous Men*; Egerton, *Speak Now against the Day*, 144.

109. Agee and Evans, *Let Us Now Praise Famous Men*, 13.

110. Ibid., 154.

111. William R. Ferris, *Images of the South*, 34.

112. For in-depth discussion of Evans's photography of the kitchen in Floyd Burroughs's Hale County home, see Curtis, *Mind's Eye, Mind's Truth*, 40–44.

113. Agee and Evans, *Cotton Tenants*, 85.

114. Ibid., 85.

115. Ibid., 85–102.

116. Ibid., 94.

117. Ibid., 100.

118. I am grateful to my colleagues and friends Joy Kasson and Bobbie Malone for sharing their interest in and research on Lois Lenski with me.

119. Lenski, *Cotton in My Sack*.

120. Lenski, *Journey into Childhood*, 183.

121. Malone, "Lois as Storycatcher."

122. Ibid.

123. Dollard, *Caste and Class*; Powdermaker, *After Freedom*; Davis, Gardner, and Gardner, *Deep South*.

124. Doyle, *Etiquette of Race Relations in the South*.

125. Dollard, *Caste and Class*, 351.

126. Ibid.

127. Ibid. Davis, Gardner, and Gardner also discussed the "taboo" in Natchez against sexual relations between a black man and a white woman and the formal law that prohibited intermarriage between whites and blacks in the state. See Davis, Gardner, and Gardner, *Deep South*, 25.

128. Edward Ayers, quote in reference to Mildred and Richard Loving, a white man and a black woman from Virginia, who defied the state law banning interracial marriage and married in Washington, D.C., in 1958. The couple was arrested in Virginia and convicted on felony charges. See "The Loving Story," a film by Nancy Buirski, director, 2011; "Fourth Row Center," http://www.jason-bailey.com/2011/04/tribecafest-review-loving-story.html; and Ayers, *Promise of the New South*, 140: "The history of segregation shows a clear connection to gender: the more closely linked to sexuality, the more likely was a place to be segregated."

129. Powdermaker, *After Freedom*, 47.

130. Ibid., 33.

131. Davis, Gardner, and Gardner, *Deep South*, 256.

132. Dollard, *Caste and Class*, 353.

133. William R. Ferris, "John Dollard," 8.

134. Powdermaker, *After Freedom*, 119.

135. Ibid., 119–20.

136. Barbara C. Johnson, "Hortense Powdermaker, 1896–1970," in *Comprehensive Encyclopedia*, http://jwa.org/encyclopedia/article/powdermaker-hortense.

137. Ibid.

Chapter 13

1. Frederick Douglass quoted in Blight, "For Something beyond the Battlefield," 1169.

2. For discussion of the United Daughters of the Confederacy and southern

white women's leadership in shaping the historical memory of the Lost Cause, see Karen L. Cox, *Dixie's Daughters*.

3. "Georgia Products Dinner Menu," Georgia Society of the City of New York, Hotel Biltmore, November 15, 1917, Matthews Family Papers, MC 248, folder 4, SCHL.

4. Hale, *Making Whiteness*, 125; Karen L. Cox, *Dreaming of Dixie*, 37.

5. Ownby, *American Dreams in Mississippi*, 82.

6. Ibid. Ownby is referring to Ayers's discussion in *Promise of the New South* of the 1890s as a "turning point in the development of a marketplace for goods in the South."

7. Hale, *Making Whiteness*, 8.

8. Ibid., 7–8.

9. Ibid., 7.

10. Ibid., 185. Hale uses the phrase "geography of consumption" to describe the black and white worlds of southern downtowns in the 1930s, where "overlapping and yet segregated gatherings of family and friends occupied a shared geography of consumption that belied any absolute racial difference."

11. Ibid., 284.

12. Shawn Michelle Smith, "Spectacles of Whiteness," 120–21; Egerton, *Speak Now against the Day*, 360–61; Hale, "Deadly Amusements," in *Making Whiteness*, 199–239.

13. Shawn Michelle Smith, "Spectacles of Whiteness," 122.

14. Ayers, *Southern Crossing*, 99.

15. For discussion of the representation of black figures on nineteenth-century trade cards, see Hale, *Making Whiteness*, 161–64.

16. Selected trade cards, Print Case Advertisements, HNOC.

17. Karen L. Cox, *Dreaming of Dixie*, 3.

18. For further discussion of the Lost Cause ideology, see Blight, *Race and Reunion*, 273.

19. Woodward, *Origins of the New South*, 155.

20. Ayers, *Promise of the New South*, viii.

21. Lears, *Fables of Abundance*, 383.

22. Ibid.

23. Ibid., 382–83.

24. Karen L. Cox, *Dreaming of Dixie*, 5.

25. Ibid., 3.

26. Lears, *Fables of Abundance*, 383.

27. Hale, *Making Whiteness*, 169. See also Tolbert, "Doggeries, Jungles, and Piggly Wigglies," for a discussion of Clarence Saunders, founder of the Piggly Wiggly franchise (1916), one of the first self-service grocery stores in the nation. Tolbert examines the changing social geography of food shopping in the evolving commercial landscape of the New South.

28. Hale, *Making Whiteness*, 173.

29. Tolbert, "Aristocracy of the Market Basket," 181. Saunders opened the first "Piggly Wiggly Self-Serving System" grocery store on September 6, 1916, in downtown Memphis near the busy wholesale cotton markets. By 1918, Piggly Wiggly stores were located in forty American cities, including fifteen in Memphis.

30. Ibid.

31. Ibid., 191.

32. Advertisement, Piggly Wiggly Stores, "Choose for Yourself, Help Yourself," *Ladies' Home Journal*, June 1929, courtesy Lisa Tolbert.

33. Engelhardt, *A Mess of Greens*, 9.

34. Ibid., 78.

35. Ibid., 9. For further discussion of mill workers' diets and foods purchased at stores and prepared at home, see Herman Newton Truitt, interview by Allen Tullos, December 5, 1978, SOHP; Wallace, "Pimento Cheese," 13–16; Wallace, "Eugenia Duke Made Her Name"; and Hale, "When Jim Crow Drank Coke."

36. Karen L. Cox, *Dreaming of Dixie*, 36; Hale, *Making Whiteness*, 138.

37. Karen L. Cox, "Branding Dixie," 55.

38. Karen L. Cox, *Dreaming of Dixie*, 36–37; Hale, *Making Whiteness*, 145–74.

39. Hale, *Making Whiteness*, 150–52; Manring, *Slave in a Box*, 75.

40. Manring, *Slave in a Box*, 64–65.

41. Ibid.

42. Karen L. Cox, *Dreaming of Dixie*, 43–44; Manring, *Slave in a Box*, 112–15.

43. Manring, *Slave in a Box*, 12.

44. Hale, *Making Whiteness*, 164.

45. For further discussion of Aunt Jemima and her products as "reconciliation gifts from the South to the North," see Wallace-Sanders, *Mammy*, 66; Manring, *Slave in a Box*, 115; Jo-Ann Morgan, "Mammy the Huckster," 88; and Hale, *Making Whiteness*, 164–67.

46. "America's Most Famous Recipe," brochure, Aunt Jemima Mills Branch, Quaker Oats Company, Chicago, 1927, Longone Culinary Collection, WLCL.

47. Ibid. For further discussion of the Aunt Jemima rag doll promotion, see Manring, *Slave in a Box*, 676–77.

48. The 1934 film *Imitation of Life* was directed by John M. Stahl. A second film adaptation of the novel was released in 1959, directed by Douglas Sirk. In this version, which appeared at the beginning of the civil rights movement, the white mother—an ambitious actress—rather than the black domestic worker, is responsible for the family's financial success. The pancake theme is absent in the 1959 film.

49. Clinton, *Plantation Mistress*, 202.

50. Edward D. C. Campbell Jr., "Plantation Film," 922–24. See also Clinton, *Tara Revisted*, 21, 205.

51. Margaret Mitchell, *Gone with the Wind*, 408.

52. Ibid., 409.

53. Ibid.

54. Zinnemann, *The Old South*.

55. Ibid.

56. Karen L. Cox, *Dreaming of Dixie*, 42.

57. Manring, *Slave in a Box*, 134–35.

58. Ibid., 145.

59. Wallace-Sanders, *Mammy*, 70.

60. "A Dozen Dixie Recipes," Savannah Sugar Refining Corporation, Savannah, Ga., 1950, Longone Culinary Collection, WLCL.

61. Manring, *Slave in a Box*, 105, 150.

62. "The Story of Virginia Dare," 309 N. Howard St., Baltimore, Md., 1900, Longone Culinary Collection, WLCL.

63. Ibid.

64. Southern Biscuit Company, begun in 1899 in Richmond, Va., is now Inter-

bake Foods, still headquartered in Richmond, Va.; see http://richmondthenandnow.com/Richmond-Then-and-Now-4.html.

65. Paddleford, "The Carolinas," in *How America Eats*, 142.

66. Ibid.

67. Manring, *Slave in a Box*, 95–99; Karen L. Cox, *Dreaming of Dixie*, 43–44.

68. "Brer Rabbit Modern Recipes for Modern Living," no date, Longone Culinary Collection, WLCL.

69. "Brer Rabbit's New Molasses Recipes for Delicious Desserts, Candies, Beverages and Other Tasty Foods," 1948, Longone Culinary Collection, WLCL.

70. Karen L. Cox, *Dreaming of Dixie*, 47.

71. Manring, *Slave in a Box*, 108.

72. Hale, *Making Whiteness*, 160–64; Manring, *Slave in a Box*, 91, 112, 115, 116, 140.

73. Hale, *Making Whiteness*, 94–96.

74. Ibid., 94.

75. See Patricia A. Turner, *Ceramic Uncles and Celluloid Mammies*.

76. Paul K. Edwards, *The Southern Urban Negro*, 48–49. Like Dr. Wilbur Atwater's earlier dietaries conducted in black communities in the South in the late nineteenth and early twentieth centuries, Edwards also discussed the regionally distinctive food patterns of urban blacks in the South. In the 1930s, Edwards noted that black families continued to eat "heavy, energy-producing, muscle-building foods," because of the hard physical labor required of most workers. That diet included large amounts of "salt side pork" for flavoring turnip and mustard greens and other vegetables, shortening to fry foods and prepare hot breads, and bulk flour, sweet potatoes, yams, hominy, and grits.

77. Ibid., 229.

78. Ibid., 234.

79. Ibid., 243, 245.

80. Ibid., 235. Nannie Helen Burroughs's quote is from an article in the *Philadelphia Tribune*, December 1930. Burroughs founded the National Training School for Women and Girls in Washington, D.C., in 1909.

81. Hale, "When Jim Crow Drank Coke."

82. Ibid.

83. Ibid.

84. Capparel, *The Real Pepsi Challenge*, 62–63.

85. Hale, "When Jim Crow Drank Coke."

86. Ibid.

87. Sharpless, "Neither Friends nor Peers," 339.

88. Windsor, *Some Favorite Southern Recipes*, vii.

89. Ibid.

90. McRee, Foreword to *Kitchen and the Cotton Patch*.

91. "Martha McCulloch-Williams—Dishes and Beverages of the Old South," Feeding America: The Historic American Cookbook Collection, Michigan State University Libraries, http://digital.lib.msu.edu/projects/cookbooks/html/books/book_66.cfm.

92. McCulloch-Williams, *Dishes and Beverages of the Old South*, 15.

93. Ibid., 10.

94. Mendelson, "Cookbooks," 300.

95. Ibid.

96. Examples of this genre of early twentieth-century southern cookbooks include Henrietta Dull, *Southern Cooking* (1928), Mary Denson Pretlow, *Old Southern Re-*

ceipts (1930), Blanche Rhett and Lettie Gay, *Two Hundred Years of Charleston Cooking* (1930), Frederick Stieff, *Eat, Drink, and Be Merry in Maryland* (1932), Harriet Ross Colquitt, *The Savannah Cook Book* (1933), Lillie Lustig, Claire Sondheim, and Sarah Rensel, *The Southern Cook Book of Fine Old Recipes* (1935), Blanche Elbert Moncure, *Emma Jane's Souvenir Cook Book* (1937), Helen Bullock, *Williamsburg Art of Cookery* (1938), and Marion Flexner, *Out of Kentucky Kitchens* (1949).

97. Angela Jill Cooley, "Making the McSouth," in "To Live and Dine in Dixie," 202–8; Tipton-Martin, "Bluegrass and Black Magic," v–xxxiii.

98. Tartan, "Cookbooks," 69.

99. Fowler, Foreword to *Southern Cooking*, ix.

100. Sharpless, *Cooking in Other Women's Kitchens*, 30.

101. Ibid. Attendees who completed all the classes received a "certificate of efficiency" signed by Mrs. Dull and members of the Domestic Science Committee of the Atlanta Women's Club. See "Colored Cooks Are Given Lessons in Culinary Art."

102. Dull, *Southern Cooking*, dedication.

103. Ibid., 6.

104. Ibid., 5.

105. Lustig, Sondheim, and Rensel, *Southern Cook Book*, introduction. For further discussion of southern white women's praise of black cooks' "intuitive and artistic" skills in the kitchen, see Angela Jill Cooley, "Making the McSouth," in "To Live and Dine in Dixie," 196–201.

106. Lustig, Sondheim, and Rensel, *Southern Cook Book*, introduction.

107. Daniels, "A Cookbook Lover's Guide," http://www.friktech.com/cai/cai2.htm.

108. Ibid.

109. Lustig, Sondheim, and Rensel, *Southern Cookbook of Fine Old Recipes*, introduction.

110. Daniels, "A Cookbook Lover's Guide," http://www.friktech.com/cai/cai2.htm.

111. Whitfield, "Is It True What They Sing about Dixie," 11, 19.

112. Ibid., 10.

113. Tartan, "Cookbooks," 42–43.

114. Ibid. By the seventieth printing of *River Roads Recipes* in 2007, 1.3 million copies of the cookbook had been sold. *Charleston Receipts*, described as "the Bible of all Junior League cookbooks," remains in print, still published by the Junior League of Charleston. Between 1950 and 1958 alone, the cookbook went through ten printings.

115. Lee and Lee, *The Lee Bros. Charleston Kitchen*, 52.

116. Ibid.

117. Paddleford, "Secret Dishes from Old Charleston."

118. Ibid.

119. Ibid.

120. Marion L. Brown, *Southern Cook Book*, vi.

121. Sparks, *North Carolina and Old Salem Cookery.* The 1955 and 1960 editions were self-published by Sparks in Kernersville, N.C. The seventh edition was published in 1974. In 1992, the year of the author's death, the University of North Carolina Press published an expanded and revised edition of this classic North Carolina cookbook. Other Sparks titles include *The Successful Hostess* (1949), *Beth Tartan's Cook Book* (1952), *Menu Maker and Party Planner* (1957), *The Good Old Days Cook Book* (1971), and *The Korner's Folly Cook Book* (1976).

122. *The Dillard Women's Club Cookbook*, compiled by the Dillard Women's Club, New Orleans, La., 1958, Dent Family Papers, box 9, folder 7, AMRC.

123. Lee and Lee, *The Lee Bros. Charleston Kitchen*, 13.

124. Clementine Paddleford, "Inn for Gourmets Is Accepting Mail Orders for Menu Favorites," *New York Herald-Tribune*, undated clipping, Lena Richard Collection, folder 5, NCCRW.

125. Thomas H. Martin, *Atlanta and Its Builders*, 474.

126. Piedmont Hotel Brochure, Atlanta, Ga., 1903, Longone Culinary Collection, WLCL.

127. Creighton's Restaurant Menu, 34 Haywood Street, Asheville, N.C., May 29, 1937, Creighton's Menus, Special Collections, Pack Memorial Library, Asheville, N.C.

128. Ibid.

129. Ibid.

130. Shelby Flowers Ferris, interview by author, Vicksburg, Miss., December 23, 2011. Ferris, a native of Vicksburg, and McKay's daughter Eulalie were close friends and attended Newcomb College together from 1936 to 1941. Ferris describes Mary McKay as a devoted mother and hard worker in the tough post-Depression years in Vicksburg. She wanted the best opportunities—educationally and culturally—for her daughter during her college years in New Orleans. Opening the Old Southern Tea Room allowed McKay to contribute to the family income and support the dreams she had for her children.

131. Hines, *Adventures in Good Eating*, 170.

132. Charlotte Kahn, "Recipe for Nationally Famous Recipe," back cover, in Kahn, *Old Southern Tea Room*.

133. Shelby Flowers Ferris, interview by author, Vicksburg, Miss., December 23, 2011.

134. Old Southern Tea Room Menu, 1201 Monroe Street, Vicksburg, Miss., Janette Faulkner Ethnic Notions Collection, AMRC.

135. Kahn, *Old Southern Tea Room*, 1–2.

136. Zogry, *The University's Living Room*, 17–19.

137. Ibid., 74.

138. Ibid., 66–69.

139. Egerton, *Speak Now against the Day*, 130–32.

140. Zogry, *The University's Living Room*, 74.

141. Ibid., 87–88.

142. Longone, "Cookbooks," 301.

143. "See the USA in Your Chevrolet" became the theme song for NBC's *The Dinah Shore Chevy Show*, sponsored by Chevrolet from 1957 to 1962. Lyrics and music were written by Leo Corday and Leon Carr for the Chevrolet Division of General Motors Corporation in about 1949.

Chapter 14

1. Karen L. Cox, *Dreaming of Dixie*, 138, 148.

2. "Attractive Winter Resorts," Seaboard Air Line Railway brochure," SoCar 917.5 At6, SCL.

3. Ibid.

4. Karen L. Cox, *Dreaming of Dixie*, 151. The Kansas City Southern Railroad's Southern Belle passenger train traveled between Kansas City, Missouri, and New Orleans. To view sample railroad company southern travelogues, see Dudley and Boxer, Seaboard Air Line Railroad, "New Horizons," 1948, http://www.youtube.com/watch?v=C8M2yU-gdNE; and Kansas City Southern Railroad promotional

film, "Southern Belle," 1940, The Calvin Company, Kansas City, Mo., http://www.youtube.com/watch?v=Ja6zzCL4To4.

5. Kansas City Southern Railroad promotional film, "Southern Belle," 1940, The Calvin Company, Kansas City, Mo., http://www.youtube.com/watch?v=Ja6zzCL4To4.

6. Brundage, *Southern Past*, 22.

7. "South from Williamsburg," 127.

8. Handler and Gable, *New History in an Old Museum*, 31–36.

9. "Welcome to Old Virginia."

10. Platt, "Good Old Southern Dishes."

11. Ibid., 82–83.

12. Ibid.

13. Ibid.

14. Ibid.

15. Handler and Gable, *New History in an Old Museum*, 138–39.

16. Ibid., 35.

17. Bullock, *Williamsburg Art of Cookery*; Booth, *Williamsburg Cookbook.*

18. Willis, "Williamsburg," 235–36.

19. Crowther, "Williamsburg: The Story of a Patriot."

20. Genovese, *Roll, Jordan, Roll*; Fox-Genovese, *Within the Plantation Household.*

21. Platt, "Recipes of the Lowcountry," 48.

22. Ibid.

23. Ibid.

24. Yuhl, *A Golden Haze of Memory*, 6; see "Where Mellow Past and Present Meet," for an in-depth history and chronology of the tourism industry in Charleston, beginning with the 1923 election of Mayor Thomas Stoney. In 1924, Stoney declared that Charleston was "America's Most Historic City" (162). For a broader discussion of the development of a southern tourism infrastructure from the late nineteenth century through the first half of the twentieth century, see Brundage, "Exhibiting Southernness in a New Century," in *The Southern Past.*

25. Yuhl, *A Golden Haze of Memory*, 6, 10.

26. Brundage, *Southern Past*, 206–7.

27. Ibid.; Yuhl, *A Golden Haze of Memory*, 60–73.

28. Yuhl, *A Golden Haze of Memory*, 6.

29. Ibid., 13–14.

30. Mims, *Edgefield Guest Book*, SCL.

31. Ibid., "Photo by Eddings," 1, SCL.

32. Yuhl, *A Golden Haze of Memory*, 14.

33. Brundage, *Southern Past*, 184; Yuhl, *A Golden Haze of Memory*, 167–68.

34. Brundage, *Southern Past*, 184.

35. Ibid., 211–12. See also Jessica B. Harris, "Three Hundred Years of Rice and Recipes in Lowcountry Kitchens," 136; and Dale Rosengarten, "Missions and Markets," 134–40.

36. Brundage, *Southern Past*, 211–12; Dale Rosengarten, "Missions and Markets," 134–40.

37. *House and Garden*, Charleston Houses and Gardens Issue, 38–39.

38. "Southern Accents," *House and Garden*, Charleston Houses and Gardens Issue, 82–83.

39. Ibid.

40. Stanonis, *Creating the Big Easy*, 23, 26.

41. Rien Fertel, "Everybody Seemed Willing to Help," 12; Waddington, "Parades, Bars, Bantering Locals."

42. "Into the Land of the Creole," Illinois Central Railroad advertisement for the Panama Limited, Chicago, 1911, Howard-Tilton Memorial Library, Special Collections, TU.

43. Ibid. These same street cries were later noted and described by Edward Dreyer, Lyle Saxon, and Robert Tallant in *Gumbo Ya-Ya: A Collection of Louisiana Folk Tales*, published in 1945 in conjunction with the Louisiana Writers' Project and the Works Project Administration. See "Street Criers," in ibid., 27–49.

44. Stanonis, *Creating the Big Easy*, 2.

45. "A New Train to the South," Illinois Central advertisement for the Panama Limited, Chicago, 1911, Howard-Tilton Memorial Library, Special Collections, TU.

46. Ibid.

47. Kansas City Southern Railroad promotional film, "Southern Belle," 1940, The Calvin Company, Kansas City, Mo., http://www.youtube.com/watch?v=Ja6zzCL4T04.

48. For discussion of the impact of a hybrid Creole culture upon New Orleans foodways, see Powell, *The Accidental City*, 97–99.

49. Tucker, *New Orleans Cuisine*, 5–7. Tucker writes that the word "Creole" derives from the Latin "creare" (to create) and from the Portuguese "crioulo"—a slave of African descent born in the New World. "The most basic meaning of 'Creole,'" writes Tucker, is "new to the southern French and Spanish colonies" or "born here."

50. Stanonis, *Creating the Big Easy*, 15–16.

51. Paddleford, "The Creole Country," in *How America Eats*, 227.

52. Tucker, *New Orleans Cuisine*, 7.

53. Starr, Foreword to ibid., xi.

54. Rien Fertel, "Creole Cookbooks," 12.

55. Ibid., 5–6. Fertel argues that the new print Creole culinary culture in New Orleans at the turn of the twentieth century created a community of "eater-citizens." He defines "eater-citizens" as "members of a society for which the consumption of a specific food or cuisine has certain 'civilizing' or assimilating possibilities."

56. Tucker, *New Orleans Cuisine*, 13–14.

57. Land, *New Orleans Cuisine*, 9.

58. Hearn, *La Cuisine Creole*; Christian Women's Exchange, *Creole Cookery Book*. Lolis Eric Elie examines the foundational contributions of African Americans to Creole cuisine, as well as the skewed history of New Orleans's foodways, in "Origin Myth of New Orleans Cuisine," 214–25.

59. Rien Fertel, "Creole Cookbooks," 5. Fertel explains that the phrases "Creole cuisine," "Creole food," and "Creole cooking" were not seen in print until the 1885 publication of Hearn's *La Cuisine Creole* and the Christian Women's Exchange, *Creole Cookery Book*, 14. See Rien Fertel, "Everybody Seemed Willing to Help," 16–17.

60. *Picayune's Creole Cook Book*.

61. Judy Walker, "Local Historian Digs Up." Rien Fertel states that the cookbook exists because of the *New Orleans Daily Picayune* publisher, Eliza Jane Nicholson, the first female head of a major metropolitan newspaper, in 1876. Fertel explains, "She feminized the paper and marketed it more toward women readers," adding society news and a domestic column entitled "Household Hints." Fertel believes that the author of the cookbook was *Picayune* reporter and writer Marie Louise Points, a white French Creole, who described Creole cuisine using the same post-Reconstruction tropes of race and memory seen in other turn-of-the-century New

South cookbooks that mourned the "lost" culinary worlds of the Old South. See Rien Fertel, "Everybody Seemed Willing to Help," 13.

62. Introduction to the first edition of *Picayune's Creole Cook Book*, 6.

63. Ibid.

64. Title page of first edition of *Picayune's Creole Cook Book*.

65. Rien Fertel, "Everybody Seemed Willing to Help," 12. Fertel cites the post-storm cookbook Bienvenu and Walker, *Cooking Up a Storm*.

66. Introduction to the first edition of *Picayune's Creole Cook Book*, 6.

67. Ibid.

68. Ibid.

69. Ibid., 7.

70. Dix, Foreword to *Gourmet's Guide to New Orleans*, vii.

71. Ibid.; see also Vella, "Dorothy Dix," 195–214.

72. Natalie V. Scott, Foreword to *200 Years of New Orleans Cooking*. The book was originally titled *Mirations and Miracles of Mandy: Some Favorite Louisiana Recipes* (1929) and was locally printed in New Orleans. A New York publisher reissued the cookbook with its new title, *200 Years of New Orleans Cooking*, with illustrations by William Spratling, in 1931. See Natalie V. Scott Exhibit, Louisiana Research Collection, Special Collections, TU, http://larc.tulane.edu/collections/dig_init/exhibits/nvs/p3.

73. For further discussion of Scott and Spratling and the early twentieth-century intellectual colony at the heart of the "French Quarter Renaissance," see Reed, *Dixie Bohemia*, 125–29.

74. Samuel Merlin "Scoop" Kennedy, *Dining in New Orleans*.

75. Ibid., 30, 49, 68, 74.

76. Ibid., 42.

77. Ibid., 54.

78. Ibid., 56.

79. Ibid., 59.

80. Ibid., 105.

81. Leathem, "Mary Land," 270.

82. Ibid., 270; Karen Trahan Leathem, "Two Women and Their Cookbooks," an exhibit organized by the NCCRW, guide, 8.

83. Leathem, "Mary Land," 274–75.

84. Ibid., 273–74.

85. See Ashley Young, "Case of Lena Richard"; and Jessica B. Harris, *High on the Hog*, 193–95.

86. Karen Trahan Leathem, "Two Women and Their Cookbooks," an exhibit organized by the NCCRW, guide, 2. Richard's mother, Frances Laurence Paul, worked as a cook and housekeeper for Alice and Nugent Vairin in the Mid-City neighborhood of New Orleans on Esplanade Avenue. After school, Lena Paul assisted her mother with her work at the Vairin home. Lena Richard dedicated the *New Orleans Cookbook* to Vairin and described her as "the lady who raised me." Vairin financed Lena Paul's cooking school education in both New Orleans and Boston.

87. Richard, *New Orleans Cook Book*, preface.

88. Ibid.

89. "3,000 Interested Housewives Attend 2 Day Norge Cooking School Sessions at Booker T.," clipping from unidentified New Orleans newspaper, 1949, Lena Richard Collection, folder 5, NCCRW.

90. Paddleford, "Cooks from New Orleans."

91. Ibid.

92. Lena Richard guestbook/diary, ca. 1940s, Bird and Bottle Inn, Garrison, N.Y., Lena Richard Collection, NCCRW.

93. Paddleford, "Food Flashes."

94. Karen Trahan Leathem, "Two Women and Their Cookbooks," an exhibit organized by the NCCRW, guide, 5.

95. Ashley Young, "Case of Lena Richard," 4.

96. Karen Trahan Leathem, "Two Women and Their Cookbooks," an exhibit organized by the NCCRW, guide, 6.

97. Ibid. Richard's mail-order food was distributed by Bordelon Fine Food Company.

98. Angela Jill Cooley, "To Live and Dine in Dixie," 191. See discussion of African American chef-caterers in Marcie Cohen Ferris, *Matzoh Ball Gumbo*: Mary Jordan and her son, Windsor Jordan, Atlanta, Ga., 172–74; Lamar White, Congregation Ahavath Achim, Atlanta, Ga., 175–76; and Shirley Bateman-Barra and her grandmother, Lucy Ater, New Orleans, La., 122–27.

99. Land, *Louisiana Cookery*; Land, *New Orleans Cuisine*.

100. James Andrews Beard, New York, N.Y., to Mary Land, New Orleans, La., October 6, 1969, Mary Land Collection, NCCRW.

101. Leathem, "Mary Land," 278.

102. Ibid., 277.

103. Ibid., 280.

104. Land, *New Orleans Cuisine*, 33, 251, 258.

105. Land's acknowledgments in both of her cookbooks reflect her eclectic world of professional contacts and friends, from Walter McIlhenny, president of McIlhenny Company, manufacturers of Tabasco, to George Lowe, "master mixologist for the Motel DeVille Cocktail Lounge of New Orleans," to business colleagues from the Rice Council, the National Banana Association, and the nationally renowned advertising firm J. Walter Thompson Company. See Land, *New Orleans Cuisine*, 11–13; and Land, *Louisiana Cookery*, xi–xiv.

106. Karen Trahan Leathem, "Two Women and Their Cookbooks," an exhibit organized by the NCCRW, guide, 12.

107. Leathem, "Mary Land," 278.

108. Huber, "Riddle of the Horny Hillbilly," 71–73; C. Brenden Martin, "To Keep the Spirit of Mountain Culture Alive," 251–52.

109. Becker, *Selling Tradition*, 79–81; Eaton, *Handicrafts of the Southern Highlands*, 52.

110. Becker, *Selling Tradition*, 79–81.

111. Huber, "Riddle of the Horny Hillbilly," 73; C. Brenden Martin, "To Keep the Spirit of Mountain Culture Alive," 258–62.

112. Huber, "Riddle of the Horny Hillbilly," 73.

113. Ibid., 78; Egerton, Hanchett, and Abbott, "Beverages," 30.

114. Becker, *Selling Tradition*, 220; "Concession Bids for Park Route," in "Driving through Time: The Digital Blue Ridge Parkway," NCC, http://docsouth.unc.edu/blueridgeparkway/content/9025/.

115. Becker, *Selling Tradition*, 220.

116. "Typical Coffee Shop and Gas Station," in "Driving through Time," NCC, http://docsouth.unc.edu/blueridgeparkway/content/9134/.

117. "Bluffs Coffee Shop & Gas Station," photograph, 1950s, Doughton Park,

N.C., in "Driving through Time," NCC, http://docsouth.unc.edu/blueridgeparkway/content/7695/.

118. Anne Mitchell Whisnant, *Super-Scenic Motorway*, 215, 240; C. Brenden Martin, "To Keep the Spirit of Mountain Culture Alive," 256–57.

119. Anne Mitchell Whisnant, *Super-Scenic Motorway*, 231–33.

120. Ibid., 245.

121. "Public History Project Chronicles Life at Moses Cone Estate." For further discussion of the Cone family and their motivation to build a country estate, see Noblitt, *A Mansion in the Mountains*, 28–29. Noblitt situates the Cones among other wealthy industrialists who built country homes, such as J. Ogden Armour and their Mellody Farm near Chicago and the Vanderbilts and their Biltmore Estate in Asheville, who were inspired by the restorative qualities of residing in a natural setting. Returning to nature was promoted for good health, as well as for "emotional, spiritual, and moral uplift." The grand homes were also conspicuous symbols of the fortunes that industrialists had amassed after the Civil War.

122. Noblitt, *A Mansion in the Mountains*, 66.

123. Ibid.

124. Ibid.

125. Ibid., 69–70.

126. The National Park Service commissioned a research report to more accurately interpret the Jewish origins of Flat Top Manor in 2011. The report and historic furnishings plan was overseen by Appalachian State University's Dr. Neva Specht, associate dean of the College of Arts and Sciences, and graduate research assistants Carrie Streeter and Joseph Otto.

127. For further discussion of the 1942 Southern Highlands Issue of *House and Garden*, see Becker, *Selling Tradition*, 225–30.

128. "Our Southern Highlands," cover, 19; see also Becker, *Selling Tradition*, 225–26.

129. Becker, *Selling Tradition*, 225–26.

130. "Highlands Cookery from Mountain Cove and Knob," 44.

131. Ibid.

132. Ibid., 49.

133. Ibid., 48.

134. Becker, *Selling Tradition*, 90, 156–57. The product endorsements for *House and Garden*'s Southern Highlands dining room also credited Mary Rodney, the manager of Southern Highlanders, Inc.'s New York sales shop.

135. Starnes, *Creating the Land of the Sky*, 13.

136. Ibid., 14.

137. For discussion of "mineral springs tourism" in Appalachia, see Chris Baker, "Golden Age of Health Spring Tourism," 44–46.

138. Ibid., 44, 46.

139. Wykle, "Fred Seely's Women." Grove, a successful real estate developer and entrepreneur, owned extensive property and several businesses throughout the South. He created the fashionable Sunset Mountain residential neighborhood surrounding the Grove Park Inn in Asheville, and he also built two of the city's most recognized downtown commercial buildings, the second Battery Park Hotel (1924) and the Grove Arcade (1929). See Chase, *Asheville*, 46.

140. David W. Webb, "Grove's Tasteless Chill Tonic," http://www.grovearcade.com/groves-tasteless-chill-tonic/.

141. Ibid.

142. Chase, *Asheville*, 55.

143. Ibid.

144. Battle Creek Food Company, Battle Creek, Mich., to Fred Seely, Grove Park Inn, Asheville, N.C., May 8, 1925, BIA, DHRL.

145. H. M. Love, Biltmore Wheat-Hearts, Asheville, N.C., to Fred Seely, Grove Park Inn, Asheville, N.C., May 14, 1925, ibid.

146. H. M. Love, Biltmore Wheat-Hearts, Asheville, N.C., to Fred Seely, Grove Park Inn, Asheville, N.C., August 17, 1925, ibid.

147. Fred Seely, Grove Park Inn, to H. M. Love, Biltmore Wheat-Hearts, Asheville, N.C., August 24, 1925, ibid.

148. Letters of inquiry, orders, and invoices to the Grove Park Inn, Asheville, N.C., from the Eagle Celery Company, Kalamazoo, Mich., July 7, 1922, Fleetwood Coffee, Chattanooga, Tenn., August 28, 1940, T. T. Keane, Wash., D.C., 1920s, and Blackford's at Fulton Fish Market, March 16, 1918, all ibid.

149. Invoices to Grove Park Inn, Asheville, N.C., from R. N. Barber and Co., Waynesville, N.C., November 18, 1938, C. E. Saunders, Saluda, N.C., September 19, 1935, and Valle Crusis Farm School, Valle Crusis, N.C., all ibid.

150. Correspondence between Grove Park Inn, Asheville, N.C., and Huyler's, New York, N.Y., March 14, March 19, 1917, ibid.

151. "The Man Who Saved Montreat," http://www.phcmontreat.org/montreat history-Huyler.htm.

152. Correspondence between Grove Park Inn, Asheville, N.C., and Huyler's, New York, N.Y., March 14, March 19, 1917, BIA, DHRL.

153. Ibid.

154. *Food, Home, and Garden: The Vegetarian Magazine.*

155. Kuepper, *Quisisana Hygienic Cook Book*, iii.

156. Ibid., ix.

157. Ibid.

158. Ibid., x.

159. Wray, *Old-Time Recipes from the Nu-Wray*, 3–4.

160. Ibid., 4.

161. Ibid., end page.

162. Starnes, *Creating the Land of the Sky*, 176–78.

163. Ibid.

164. Ibid., 51.

165. Ibid., 179.

166. Ibid.

167. Ibid.

168. Ibid.

169. Ibid., 180.

170. J. S. Barrett, "History of Tapoco," http://www.grahamcounty.net/gchistory /index.htm.

171. Jabbour and Jabbour, *Decoration Day in the Mountains*, 94; Egerton, *Speak Now against the Day*, 93–94.

172. "Fontana Dam," http://digitalheritage.org/2010/08/fontana-dam/.

173. Daisy B. Walker, *Good Things to Eat at Tapoco Lodge*, back cover.

174. Ibid.; see also Barrett, "The History of Tapoco."

175. Ibid., inside copy.

176. "History—An Historic NC Inn," http://highhamptoninn.com/history.aspx.

177. F. J. Schermerhorn, Cashiers, N.C., to Duncan Hines, Bowling Green, Ky., July 16, 1956, High Hampton Inn Papers, Cashiers, N.C.

178. Literary scholar Fred Hobson writes: "Mencken shocked southerners when he published a severe indictment of southern culture, 'The Sahara of the Bozart,' which first appeared in 1917 in the *New York Evening Mail* and was reprinted in his book *Prejudices, Second Series* (1920). In his essay, he charged that the South was 'almost as sterile, artistically, intellectually, culturally, as the Sahara Desert.'" Other essays by Mencken, also critical of the South, followed. See Hobson, *Serpent in Eden*; and Egerton, *Speak Now against the Day*, 58–61, for further discussion of H. L. Mencken's critique of the early twentieth-century South.

179. Post, "Dyspepsia in Dixie," 30–34.

180. Ibid., 30.

181. Ibid., 32–33.

182. Leonard Ray Teel, "Ralph McGill," in *New Georgia Encyclopedia*, http://www.georgiaencyclopedia.org/nge/ArticlePrintable.jsp?id=h-2769; Egerton, *Speak Now against the Day*, 256–57.

183. McGill, "What's Wrong with Southern Cooking," 38.

184. Ibid.

185. Ibid.

186. Ibid.

187. Ibid., 39.

188. Ibid.

189. Ibid., 105.

190. Paddleford, "I Eat, Drink and Go Merrily Maryland," in *How America Eats*, 121. For further study of Paddleford, see Alexander and Harris, *Hometown Appetites*; and Alexander's revised edition of Paddleford's *How America Eats*.

191. Paddleford, "I Eat, Drink and Go Merrily Maryland," in *How America Eats*.

192. Ibid.

193. Ibid.

194. Ibid., 121–22.

Part III

1. Egerton, *Speak Now against the Day*, 5.

2. Ibid., 10.

3. Jessica B. Harris, *High on the Hog*, 202.

4. Chafe, *Unfinished Journey*, 21–22.

5. Egerton, *Speak Now against the Day*, 232–33. Murray, born in Baltimore and raised in Durham, applied to UNC-CH for graduate studies in social sciences. University president Frank Porter Graham personally reviewed Murray's application after she was rejected for admission. Graham ultimately decided not to admit Murray in 1939.

6. Olson, *Freedom's Daughters*, 20.

Chapter 15

1. Shawn Michelle Smith, "Spectacles of Whiteness," 130–31.

2. Ibid.

3. Phillis Wheatley Club Minutes, 1929–30, Fourteenth Administration, Phillis Wheatley Literary and Social Club Papers, 1916–2011, AMN 103, Avery Research Center, College of Charleston.

4. Lauterer, "Mrs. Roxie, Oxford, 1960s." For further discussion of the narratives

of black domestic workers in the segregated South, see Tucker, *Telling Memories among Southern Women*, and Sharpless, *Cooking in Other Women's Kitchens*.

5. See Tyson's memoir and history of the murder of Henry Marrow in his hometown of Oxford, N.C., *Blood Done Sign My Name*.

6. Lauterer, "Mrs. Roxie, Oxford, 1960s."

7. Ibid.

8. Stockett, *The Help*; Taylor, "The Help."

9. Watson, "Front Porch," 3, 6. Watson's essay introduces the spring 2014 special issue of *Southern Cultures*, which examines the book and film *The Help*. Organized by literary scholar Suzanne Jones, the essays began as conference papers delivered at Vanderbilt University in March 2011.

10. Ibid., 6.

11. I am indebted to my former student Rose Lambert-Sluder for her insight on *The Help* in her essay "Civil Rights and Southern Food," May 1, 2012.

12. Stockett, *The Help*, 339.

13. Ibid.

14. Moody, *Coming of Age in Mississippi*, 34.

15. Jessica B. Harris, *High on the Hog*, 206.

16. Hale, *Making Whiteness*, 284–85.

17. Ibid., 186.

18. Angela Jill Cooley, "To Live and Dine in Dixie," 102.

19. Whitehouse, "Memorial to an Uncivil Era."

20. Williams-Forson, *Building Houses Out of Chicken Legs*, 116–18.

21. Staples, "A Conversation with John Hope Franklin."

22. Seiler, *Republic of Drivers*, 115–16.

23. Magee, "The Open Road Wasn't Quite Open to All."

24. Reed Engle, "Segregation/Desegregation," http://www.nps.gov/shen/history culture/segregation.htm; Egerton, *Speak Now against the Day*, 93. Egerton describes Ickes as the "leading standard-bearer for social change in the early Roosevelt years, breaking the segregationist ice in the Interior Department and the Public Works Administration."

25. Layout Plan Concession, "Tea Room and Motor Service Station," at Smart View Park, Franklin County, Va., in "Driving through Time," NCC, http://docsouth.unc.edu/blueridgeparkway/content/15626/. The design was created by Robert G. Hall and Gilbert Thurlow.

26. Georgia Gilmore, interview by Blackside, Inc., February 17, 1986, for *Eyes on the Prize: America's Civil Rights Years* (1954–65), WUL, 1, 2.

27. Branch, *Parting the Waters*, 128–36; Chafe, *Unfinished Journey*, 162–63.

28. Nelson and Silva, "The Kitchen of a Civil Rights Hero." The City of Montgomery claimed that the bus boycott was an unlawful conspiracy.

29. Garrow, *Montgomery Bus Boycott*, 22.

30. Nelson and Silva, "The Kitchen of a Civil Rights Hero."

31. Ibid.

32. Ibid.

33. "Georgia Gilmore, February 5, 1920–March 3, 1990," 453 Dericote Street, Montgomery, Alabama Historical Marker, http://www.hmdb.org/marker.asp?marker=28197.

34. Belasco, "Food Matters," 4.

35. Golden Gate Quartet, "No Restricted Signs (Up in Heaven)," released June 6,

1946, Columbia Records, matrix no. CO36388-1, label number 37832, recorded in New York, N.Y.

36. Ella J. Baker, "Bigger Than a Hamburger."

37. Ibid.

38. Rosa Washington, interview, April 14, 1995, Birmingham Civil Rights Institute, http://www.bcri.org/resource_gallery/interview_segments/washington.mov.htm.

39. Ibid.

40. Biesecker, "1957 Sit-In."

41. Milliken, "Civil Rights History Marked."

42. Ibid.

43. Ibid.

44. Biesecker, "1957 Sit-In."

45. Ibid.

46. Chafe, *Civilities and Civil Rights*, viii; Jessica B. Harris, *High on the Hog*, 203–5.

47. Chafe, *Unfinished Journey*, 165–66.

48. "The Greensboro Chronology," http://www.sitinmovement.org/history/greensboro-chronology.asp.

49. Chafe, *Civilities and Civil Rights*, 83.

50. "The Greensboro Chronology," http://www.sitinmovement.org/history/greensboro-chronology.asp.

51. Ibid.

52. Ibid.

53. Ibid.

54. "Help Make Kresge's 100%," James Peck, ed., "CORE-LATOR," April 1961, no. 88, CORE Papers, AMRC.

55. Ibid.

56. "McCrory's Stockholders Hear Protest," ibid.

57. Townsend Davis, *Weary Feet, Rested Souls*, 312.

58. Ibid.

59. Moody, *Coming of Age in Mississippi*, 265.

60. Arsenault, *Freedom Riders*, 71–73.

61. "CORE to Test Bus Bias in 'Freedom Ride,' 1961," CORE, 38 Park Row, New York, N.Y., March 31, 1961, copy of press release in Carol Ruth Silver, "The Diary of a Freedom Rider," 1961, Tougaloo Collection, MDAH.

62. Arsenault, *Freedom Riders*, 97.

63. Ibid.

64. Lafayette, "Movement Food," 246.

65. Arsenault, *Freedom Riders*, 97.

66. Ibid.

67. Ibid., 106–7.

68. Ibid.

69. Ibid., 134; Congress of Racial Equality, invitation to banquet "in honor of the Freedom Riders," May 17, 1961, Dookey Chase Restaurant, 2301 Orleans Street, New Orleans, La., in Constance B. Harse Papers, AMRC.

70. Jessica B. Harris, *High on the Hog*, 234–35.

71. Arsenault, *Freedom Riders*, 233.

72. Ibid.

73. Sokol, *There Goes My Everything*, 42, 57; Egerton, *Speak Now against the Day*, 10.

74. Moye, "Discovering What's Already There," 257.

75. "Food Project," Womanpower Unlimited, 1072 Lynch Street, Jackson, Miss., fall 1964, Womanpower Unlimited Collection, MWAC.

76. Ibid.

77. Womanpower Unlimited Newsletter, September/October 1964, ibid.

78. "Wednesdays in Mississippi: Civil Rights as Women's Work," Virginia Center for Digital History, http://www.history.uh.edu/cph/WIMS/; Judith Rosenbaum, "Wednesdays in Mississippi," Jewish Women's Archive, http://jwa.org/teach/livingthelegacy/civilrights/community-organizing-ii-wednesdays-in-mississippi; Holly Cowan Shulman, "Polly Spiegel Cowan," Jewish Women's Archive, http://jwa.org/weremember/cowan.

79. Arsenault, *Freedom Riders*, 201, 247.

80. Carol Ruth Silver, "The Diary of a Freedom Rider," May 23, 1961, Tougaloo Collection, MDAH.

81. Whiting, "Carol Ruth Silver."

82. Carol Ruth Silver, "The Diary of a Freedom Rider," June 7–8, 1961, Tougaloo Collection, MDAH.

83. Mulholland, "Diary of a Freedom Rider," June 9–12, 1961, Hinds County Jail, Jackson, Miss., in Holsaert et al., *Hands on the Freedom Plow*, 75.

84. Lafayette, "Movement Food," 247–48.

85. Ibid., 249.

86. Ibid.

87. Carol Ruth Silver, "The Diary of a Freedom Rider," December 18, 1962, Tougaloo Collection, MDAH.

88. "Six Sentenced in Greenville Restaurant Case," Greenville, Miss., November 6, 1962, in Joan Harris Trumpauer Civil Rights Scrapbooks III, folder 1, MDAH.

89. Ibid.

90. See Webb's powerful analysis of the complex and contradictory position of southern Jews in the civil rights–era South, *Fight against Fear*, xv.

91. Retired U.S. magistrate judge J. David Orlansky, Northern District of Mississippi, email to author, July 9, 2012.

92. Ibid.

93. Ibid.; Egerton, *Speak Now against the Day*, 256–57.

94. "State City to Mix Bus Station Room, but Café to Remain White," October 31, 1961, Joan Harris Trumpauer Civil Rights Scrapbooks III, MDAH.

95. Ibid.

96. Paul Dickson, "The Day Jim Wallace Un-boxed His Negatives," in Dickson, *Courage in the Moment*, 16.

97. Ibid.

98. Karen L. Parker, "I Raised My Hand," 182.

99. Leaflet, "Wanted: Picketers," March 1960, Records of the Office of Chancellor William B. Aycock, Series 40020, Wilson Library, UNC-CH.

100. Karen L. Parker, "I Raised My Hand," 179.

101. Karen L. Parker diary, December 18, 1964, Karen L. Parker Diary, Letter, and Clippings, 5275, SHC. After graduating from UNC-CH in 1964, Karen Parker worked for the *Grand Rapids Press* in Michigan, the *Los Angeles Times*, and other newspapers before returning to work at the *Winston-Salem Journal*.

102. Pat Cusick interview, June 19, 1989, SOHP.

103. Ibid.

104. Sokol, *There Goes My Everything*, 39. Helms, future Republican senator from North Carolina, managed the successful campaign of Willis Smith to defeat former UNC-CH president Frank Porter Graham—a progressive committed to civil rights—in his run for reelection to the U.S. Senate in 1950.

105. Quinton E. Baker interview, February 23, 2002, SOHP.

106. Dickson, *Courage in the Moment*, 10.

107. Ibid., xvii–xviii, 18.

108. Ehle, *Free Men*, 14.

109. Wayne King, Afterword to ibid.

110. Ehle, *Free Men*, 156–64.

111. Sally Greene, "A Local Apology," *GreeneSpace Blog*, February 12, 2008, http://greenespace.blogspot.com/2008/02/local-apology.html.

112. Giduz, "We Should Have Led the Way." Local newspaperman and civic leader Roland Giduz (bachelor's degree in journalism from UNC-CH and master's degree from Columbia University School of Journalism) was also an important photo-documentarian of the movement.

113. Korstad and Leloudis, *To Right These Wrongs*, 53–54; "To Right These Wrongs," Terry Sanford Papers, SHC, www.torightthesewrongs.com.

114. Zogry, *The University's Living Room*, 86.

115. Sanford, "Emancipation," video, January 18, 1963, Terry Sanford Papers, SHC.

116. Ehle, *Free Men*, 62. John Ehle graduated from UNC-CH in 1949 and served on North Carolina governor Terry Sanford's staff from 1962 to 1964.

117. Lauterer, "Picketing the Dairy Bar, 1963."

118. Ibid.

119. Ehle, *Free Men*, 142–44; Charles L. Thompson, "Standing Up by Sitting Down," 171.

120. Charles L. Thompson, "Standing Up by Sitting Down," 171.

121. Ibid.

122. Karen L. Parker diary, January 10, 1964, Karen L. Parker Diary, Letter, and Clippings, SHC.

123. Charles L. Thompson, "Standing Up by Sitting Down," 177.

124. Barksdale, "Civil Rights Organization," 40–41.

125. Dickson, *Courage in the Moment*.

126. Ibid., 20–21; Pat Cusick interview, June 19, 1989, SOHP. Blake was intrigued by the nonviolent tactics of the first CORE-sponsored Freedom Riders, who participated in the "Journey of Reconciliation" that stopped in Chapel Hill on its route through the Upper South in April 1947.

127. Dickson, *Courage in the Moment*, 20–21; Pat Cusick being loaded into a police squad car, photograph, "Part 1: Integration Sit-Ins," "I Raised My Hand to Volunteer: Students Protest in 1960s Chapel Hill," SHC, http://www.lib.unc.edu/mss/exhibits/protests/catalog19.html.

128. Dickson, *Courage in the Moment*, 20.

129. Joe Straley to Police Chief William Blake, May 18, 1964, Joseph W. Straley Papers, SHC.

130. Chansky, *Light Blue Reign*, 152–53.

131. Ibid.; Wolff, "Fanfare for an Uncommon Man."

132. Chansky, *Light Blue Reign*, 152–53.

133. Kelley, "Dean Smith Challenged Chapel Hill's Old Prejudices."

134. Feinstein, "Memories of Dean Smith Linger." Feinstein included this story in his profile of great figures in American sports, *One on One: Behind the Scenes with the Greats in the Game* (New York: Little, Brown, 2011).

135. Martin Luther King Jr., "I Have a Dream," Speech at March on Washington for Jobs and Freedom, Washington, D.C., August 28, 1963.

Chapter 16

1. Sarah E. McNulty Turner, "Hop's Bar-B-Q," 44.
2. Ibid., 46–47.
3. Ibid.
4. Ibid., 50.
5. "Asheboro Sit-In Participants Recall History."
6. Sarah E. McNulty Turner, "Hop's Bar-B-Q," 14.
7. Ibid., 15.
8. Egerton, *Southern Food*, 152.
9. Sokol, *There Goes My Everything*, 183.
10. Jessica B. Harris, *High on the Hog*, 205–6.
11. Sarah E. McNulty Turner, "Hop's Bar-B-Q," 57; Sokol, *There Goes My Everything*, 192.
12. Sarah E. McNulty Turner, "Hop's Bar-B-Q," 57.
13. Liptak, "Justices Void Oversight of States, Issue at Heart of Voting Rights Act."
14. Carman, "Paschal's."
15. Paschal, *Paschal*, 17–19.
16. Ibid., 102–3.
17. Angela Jill Cooley, "To Live and Dine in Dixie," 151. For further discussion of culinary landmarks of the civil rights movement, see "We Shall Not Be Moved," in Jessica B. Harris, *High on the Hog*, 200–206.
18. Paschal, *Paschal*, 3.
19. Ibid., 46–47.
20. Ibid., 47.
21. Ibid., 46–47.
22. Ibid., 24.
23. Gettleman, "A Cherished Civil Rights Site."
24. Andrew Young, Foreword to *Paschal*, xvii–xviii; Jessica B. Harris, *High on the Hog*, 200–201.
25. Carman, "Paschal's."
26. Paschal, *Paschal*, 11.
27. Robbie Brown, "Remembering a Soul Food Legend."
28. "Paschal's Restaurant Founder Dies at 88."
29. Ibid.; Andrew Young, Foreword to Paschal, *Paschal*, xvii–xviii, 120.
30. "Orah Belle Sherman, Hostess at Paschal's."
31. Ibid.; Paschal, *Paschal*, 121.
32. "Orah Belle Sherman, Hostess at Paschal's"; Paschal, *Paschal*, 121.
33. Paschal, *Paschal*, 127.
34. "Paschal's Restaurant Founder Dies at 88."
35. Ibid.
36. Paschal, *Paschal*, 127.
37. Towns, "A Piece of History."
38. Paschal, *Paschal*, 124–26.
39. "Paschal's Timeline—History," http://www.paschalsatlanta.com/.

40. Andrew Young, Foreword to Paschal, *Paschal*, xvii–xviii.
41. Ibid.
42. Carman, "Paschal's."
43. Paschal, *Paschal*, 136.
44. Carman, "Paschal's"; "Paschal's Restaurant Founder Dies at 88."
45. Martin Luther King Jr., "Drum Major Instinct," http://mlk-kpp01.stanford.edu/index.php/encyclopedia/encyclopedia/enc_drum_major_instinct_1968/.
46. Paschal, *Paschal*, 136.
47. Gettleman, "A Cherished Civil Rights Site."
48. Robbie Brown, "Remembering a Soul Food Legend"; "Paschal's Restaurant Founder Dies at 88."
49. Paschal, *Paschal*, xx. In the late 1970s, Paschal's partnered with Dobb's Inc. to become the principal concessionaire at the Atlanta airport.
50. Ibid.
51. Severo, "Lester Maddox."
52. Sokol, *There Goes My Everything*, 184; Severo, "Lester Maddox"; Short, *Everything Is Pickrick*, 28–29.
53. Nystrom, "Segregation's Last Stand," 37, 40.
54. Ibid.
55. Ibid., 40.
56. Short, *Everything Is Pickrick*, 35.
57. Ibid.
58. Ibid., 38.
59. "Maddox Holds Gun, Bars 3 Negroes."
60. Ibid.
61. "Atlanta Restaurant Defies High Court."
62. Milliones, "Negroes in South Test Rights Act."
63. "Maddox Holds Gun, Bars 3 Negroes."
64. Milliones, "Negroes in South Test Rights Act."
65. Nystrom, "Segregation's Last Stand," 44.
66. Sokol, *There Goes My Everything*, 185.
67. Nystrom, "Segregation's Last Stand," 38.
68. Sokol, *There Goes My Everything*, 57, 59.
69. Ibid., 84–85.
70. Ibid., 62.
71. Nystrom, "Segregation's Last Stand," 44; "WSB-TV News Film Clip of Segregationist Lester Maddox," Pickrick Restaurant, Civil Rights Digital Library, University of Georgia, http://crdl.usg.edu/cgi/crdl?query=id:ugabma_wsbn_46919.
72. Nystrom, "Segregation's Last Stand," 45.
73. Ibid.
74. Ibid., 44–45.
75. Ibid., 45.
76. Ibid.
77. Ibid., 47.
78. "Atlantan Shuts His Restaurant to Bar Patronage by Negroes," 25.
79. "WSB-TV News Film Clip of Segregationist Lester Maddox," Pickrick Restaurant, Civil Rights Digital Library, University of Georgia, http://crdl.usg.edu/cgi/crdl?query=id:ugabma_wsbn_46919.
80. "WSB-TV News Film Clip of a News Report," Civil Rights Digital Library, University of Georgia.

81. "Lester Maddox Shuts Cafeteria."
82. Ibid.
83. Sokol, *There Goes My Everything*, 187.
84. Ibid.
85. Ibid., 231; quote from Frady, *Southerners: A Journalist's Odyssey*, 71.
86. Nystrom, "Segregation's Last Stand."
87. Ibid.
88. Wayne King, "Restaurateur Maddox and Passing Scene."
89. Ibid.
90. "Paschal's Restaurant Founder Dies at 88."
91. Ibid.
92. Auchmutey, "Lewis Wants Maddox Restaurant Preserved."
93. Sokol, *There Goes My Everything*, 189.
94. Ibid.
95. Ibid.
96. Ibid., 187–88.
97. Ibid., 188.
98. Ibid.
99. Ibid., 189.
100. Ibid.
101. Ibid., 190.
102. Angela Jill Cooley, "To Live and Dine in Dixie," 250.
103. Sokol, *There Goes My Everything*, 190.
104. "U.S. Court Limits Rights Act Clause."
105. Ibid.
106. Anthony Lewis, "Justice Suspends Rights-Law Curb," 41.
107. Steve Suitts, "Hugo L. Black," in *Encyclopedia of Alabama*, http://www.encyclopediaofalabama.org/face/Article.jsp?id=h-1848.
108. Ibid.
109. Ibid.
110. "Birmingham Café Bows to Decision."
111. Anthony Lewis, "Bench Unanimous," 1.
112. Ibid.
113. Herbers, "Civil Rights."
114. Sokol, *There Goes My Everything*, 191.
115. Edge, "Civil Roots," 52.
116. Sokol, *There Goes My Everything*, 195.
117. "Southerners Gloomily Agree Segregation Is Lost Cause."
118. "Many Doors Open Quietly to Negroes."
119. Sokol, *There Goes My Everything*, 195, 197.
120. Chapman, "Mississippi Racial Bars Fall as Negroes Register at Hotels."
121. James L. Jones, "McComb Serves 20 Negro Diners; Barrier Broken without Incident," Joan Harris Trumpauer Civil Rights Scrapbooks III, folder 1, 1961–64, MDAH.
122. Ibid.
123. "Police Jail 13 Rights Aides."
124. Ibid.
125. Crespino, *In Search of Another Country*, 120; Emmerich quote in *McComb Enterprise-Journal*, October 20, 1964.
126. Hines, *Adventures in Good Eating*, 169.

127. Joan Harris Trumpauer Civil Rights Scrapbooks III, folder 1, December 16, 1964, MDAH.

128. Ibid.

129. Ibid., December 18, 1964, Jackson, Miss.

130. Ibid.

131. Ibid., July 7, 1964, Jackson, Miss.

132. Ibid., "Blast Rips Mississippi Food Store," 1961–64.

133. Womanpower Unlimited Newsletter, September/October 1964, Womanpower Unlimited Collection, MWAC.

134. Edge, "Civil Roots," 52; see also Anna Hamilton, "Documenting Jackson's Farish Street District," 6.

135. Adrian Miller, *Soul Food*, 3.

136. Sokol, *There Goes My Everything*, 195.

137. Ibid.

138. Ibid.

139. Ibid., 204; Shipp, "U.S. Responding Well to Rights Law," 1, 10.

140. Sokol, *There Goes My Everything*, 196; "Many Doors Open Quietly to Negroes."

141. Herbers, "Civil Rights."

142. Ibid.

143. Ibid.

144. John Charles Boger, "Daniel H. Pollitt," 12–13.

145. Matthew Bailey, "Rich's Department Store," in *New Georgia Encyclopedia*, http://www.georgiaencyclopedia.org/nge/Article.jsp?id=h-1888.

146. Easterbrook, "Historic Dinner with King." I am indebted to Professor Daniel H. Pollitt's Chapel Hill family—his son and daughter-in-law, Daniel R. Pollitt and Linda Weisel, and their son, Daniel L. Pollitt—for sharing this article and memories of their father and grandfather with me.

147. Easterbrook, "Historic Dinner with King."

148. Ibid.

149. Golden, *Only in America*, 106.

150. Ibid.

151. Ibid.

152. Ibid.

153. Ibid., 107.

154. Ibid.

155. Ibid., 108.

156. Ibid.

157. Evans, *The Provincials*, 27.

158. Sokol, *There Goes My Everything*, 201.

159. Ibid., 203.

160. Ibid., 198–203; "5 Whites Accused in St. Augustine"; Shapiro, "St. Augustine," 7; Herbers, "Martin Luther King."

161. Sokol, *There Goes My Everything*, 193–94.

162. Ibid.

163. "Rights Act Tested in N. Carolina."

164. Ibid.

165. Ibid.; Edge, "Civil Roots," 54.

166. I am grateful for the date of the naming of Martin Luther King Jr. Boulevard in New Bern that was provided by Victor T. Jones, Special Collections Librarian,

New Bern–Craven County Public Library, New Bern, N.C. See Victor T. Jones, email to author, June 21, 2012.

167. Sokol, *There Goes My Everything*, 213–14.

168. Ibid., 212.

169. Ibid., 210.

170. Ibid.

171. Bragg, "Former Klansman Is Found Guilty"; Jerry Mitchell, "The Last Days of Ben Chester White," http://blogs.clarionledger.com/jmitchell/2010/04/05/the-last-days-of-ben-chester-white-chapter-one/chapter 3.

172. Jerry Mitchell, "The Last Days of Ben Chester White," http://blogs.clarionledger.com/jmitchell/2010/04/05/the-last-days-of-ben-chester-white-chapter-one/chapter 3.

173. Ibid.

174. Ibid.

175. Ibid.; Bragg, "Former Klansman Is Found Guilty."

176. "Ben Chester White," *Mississippi Civil Rights Project*, http://mscivilrightsproject.org/index.php?option=com_content&view=article&id=420:ben-chester-white&catid=8:person&Itemid=2.

177. Jerry Mitchell, "The Last Days of Ben Chester White," chap. 4.

178. Adrian Miller, *Soul Food*, 223–24.

179. "Ben Chester White," Civil Rights and Restorative Justice, http://nuweb9.neu.edu/civilrights/?page_id=768.

180. Ibid.

181. Ibid.

182. Bragg, "Former Klansman Is Found Guilty"; Jerry Mitchell, "Answers to Legal Questions on Cold Cases," *Journey to Justice Blog*, February 21, 2010. Mitchell writes: "U.S. District Judge William Barbour Jr. sentenced Avants to life in prison, where he died."

183. Bragg, "Former Klansman Is Found Guilty."

184. Ibid.; "Ben Chester White," *Mississippi Civil Rights Project*.

185. "Ernest Avants, 72."

Chapter 17

1. *Hunger, USA*, 108.

2. Marcum, "Speak Your Piece."

3. "The Poverty Tours," April–May 1964, LBJ Library Moving Picture Collection, http://www.youtube.com/watch?v=oVyZ_vKuY-M.

4. "The American Dream," 23.

5. Breed, "'Poster Father' Weary of Sour Fate."

6. "Eastland Denies Charge Negro Shorted on Food," Greenwood, Miss., April 19, 1964, Joan Harris Trumpauer Civil Rights Scrapbooks, MDAH.

7. Susan Levine, *School Lunch Politics*, 105.

8. Ibid., 40, 76.

9. Kotz, *Let Them Eat Promises*, 50.

10. *Hunger, USA*, 78.

11. Susan Levine, *School Lunch Politics*, 110.

12. Ibid.

13. "Eastland Denies Charge Negro Shorted on Food," Greenwood, Miss., April 19, 1964, Joan Harris Trumpauer Civil Rights Scrapbooks, MDAH.

14. Susan Levine, *School Lunch Politics*, 116–17.

15. Food Stamp Act of 1964, Public Law 88-525, approved by the 88th Congress of the United States, enacted August 31, 1964.

16. Ibid.

17. "Students Aid Hungry South"; Miyuki, "Seeking Justice," 107–10.

18. Ibid.

19. Ibid., 109.

20. Ibid.

21. Kotz, *Let Them Eat Promises*, 25–26.

22. Ibid.

23. Ibid. See also Daniel, "USDA Approved," 105; and Daniel, *Dispossession*, 17–25. Daniel writes about black farmers in the South who were denied credit and access to government programs in the 1960s as punishment for their participation in the civil rights movement.

24. Larry Still, "Step Up Drive to Aid Hungry Miss. Negroes," February 21, 1963, Joan Harris Trumpauer Civil Rights Scrapbooks, 1961–64, MDAH.

25. Ibid.

26. Ibid.

27. Kotz, *Let Them Eat Promises*, 2–3.

28. Edelman, "Still Hungry in America." In 1973, Edelman founded the Children's Defense Fund, a leading nonprofit child advocacy organization; Norris, "'Still Hungry in America.'"

29. Palermo, *Robert F. Kennedy*, 117.

30. Lee, *For Freedom's Sake*, 99.

31. Bass, "Hunger? Let Them Eat Magnolias," 276.

32. Hollings, *Case against Hunger*.

33. Hartsook, "Well, You Can't Refuse a Sister."

34. Kotz, *Let Them Eat Promises*, 3–4.

35. Ibid.; Rugaber, "In the Delta."

36. Ibid.

37. Ibid.

38. Kotz, *Let Them Eat Promises*, 3–4.

39. Schmitt, *President of the Other America*, 178.

40. Kotz, *Let Them Eat Promises*, 1–2; Irwin, "Senators Visit Poor in Rural Mississippi," 11; Bigarts, "Hunger in America."

41. Kotz, *Let Them Eat Promises*, 1–2; Irwin, "Senators Visit Poor in Rural Mississippi," 11; Bigarts, "Hunger in America."

42. Kotz, *Let Them Eat Promises*, 2; Norris, "'Still Hungry in America.'"

43. Evan Thompson, *Robert Kennedy*, 339.

44. *Hunger, USA*, 18, 22, 31.

45. Ibid.

46. Ibid., 31.

47. Ibid.

48. Coles and Clayton, *Still Hungry in America*; "Abstracts" in Al Clayton Photographs, 4859, SHC; Robert Coles Papers, SHC. See also Norris, "'Still Hungry in America.'"

49. *Hunger, USA*, 31.

50. Kotz, *Let Them Eat Promises*, 7.

51. Ibid., 48; Loftus, "Johnson Is Asked to Rush Food Aid," 51.

52. Irwin, "U.S. Will Probe Food Program in Mississippi."

53. Kotz, *Let Them Eat Promises*, 47; Vincent J. Burke, "Freeman, Javits Clash over Food for Poor," 5.

54. Schmitt, *President of the Other America*, 180. Schmitt cites U.S. Senate, Subcommittee of the Committee on Agriculture and Forestry, *Hearings on Food Stamp Appropriations Authorization*, 10.

55. Ibid.

56. Ibid.

57. Ibid.

58. Edelman, "Still Hungry in America," 2.

59. Kotz, *Let Them Eat Promises*, 154–55; Edelman, "Still Hungry in America," 2.

60. Kotz, *Let Them Eat Promises*, 167.

61. Ibid., 188; Fritchey, "The Ingredients of Hunger."

62. Kotz, *Let Them Eat Promises*, 190–91.

63. Susan Levine, *School Lunch Politics*, 129; Kotz, *Let Them Eat Promises*, 13.

64. Mays and Dunbar, Foreword to *Hunger, USA*, 4.

65. Susan Levine, *School Lunch Politics*, 129.

66. Nestle, *Food Politics*, 38; McGovern, Foreword to Kotz, *Let Them Eat Promises*, iii.

67. McGovern, Foreword to Kotz, *Let Them Eat Promises*, vii.

68. Rugaber, "In the Delta."

69. *Hunger, USA*, 13.

70. Ibid., 21; Kotz, *Let Them Eat Promises*, 31–32.

71. Nathan Miller, "Poverty Hearing Results in Clash."

72. *Hunger, USA*, 18.

73. Schmitt, *President of the Other America*, 181–82.

74. Nathan Miller, "Poverty Hearing Results in Clash."

75. Ibid.; Edstrom, "Visit Starving, Miss. Senators Told."

76. Nathan Miller, "Poverty Hearing Results in Clash"; Edstrom, "Visit Starving, Miss. Senators Told."

77. Nathan Miller, "Poverty Hearing Results in Clash."

78. Vincent J. Burke, "Freeman, Javits Clash over Food for Poor."

79. Ibid.

80. David Frost, interview with Senator Robert Kennedy, March 25, 1968, Armed Forces Radio, http://www.radio4all.net/files/kperron@gmail.com/3101-1-DAVID_FROST_BOBBY_KENNEDY.mp3.

81. Robert F. Kennedy, Introductory Comment to *Hunger, USA*, 7.

82. Asch, *The Senator and the Sharecropper*, 257; Lee, *For Freedom's Sake*, 147–48; Kay Mills, "Fannie Lou Hamer," in *Mississippi History Now*, http://mshistorynow.mdah.state.ms.us/articles/51/fannie-lou-hamer-civil-rights-activist.

83. "Brief Historical Background of Freedom Farm Corporation," ca. 1977, Sunflower County Freedom Farm Co-op Papers, AMRC.

84. "Our History," Heifer International, http://www.heifer.org.

85. Asch, *The Senator and the Sharecropper*, 257–62; Lee, *For Freedom's Sake*, 147–62. See also Nembhard, *Collective Courage*, for the history of black cooperatives in the United States, including Hamer's Freedom Farm.

86. "Brief Historical Background of Freedom Farm Corporation," ca. 1977, Sunflower County Freedom Farm Co-op Papers, AMRC.

87. Asch, *The Senator and the Sharecropper*, 256; Peterson, "Sunflowers Don't Grow in Sunflower County."

88. Mills, *This Little Light of Mine*, 258.

89. "Brief Historical Background of Freedom Farm Corporation," ca. 1977, Sunflower County Freedom Farm Co-op Papers, AMRC; Lee, *For Freedom's Sake*, 148.

90. Edge, "Civil Roots," 53.

91. Lee, *For Freedom's Sake*, 162.

92. Bigarts, "Hunger in America"; see also "Abstract," Delta Health Center Records, Mound Bayou, Miss., SHC.

93. Bigarts, "Hunger in America."

94. "History," Federation of Southern Cooperatives Land Assistance Fund, http://www.federationsoutherncoop.com/history.htm; Bethell, "Sumter County Blues."

95. "Black Farmers in America, 1865–2000," 8. See forthcoming oral history collection of African American farmers in the South, Petty and Schultz, "Breaking New Ground," http://www.lewis.edu/BreakingNewGround.

96. Egerton, *Speak Now against the Day*, 126–27; "Historical Information," Delta and Providence Cooperative Farms Papers, SHC; Fred C. Smith, "Cooperative Farming in Mississippi," in *Mississippi History Now*, http://mshistorynow.mdah.state.ms.us/articles/219/cooperative-farming-in-mississippi. See also Fred C. Smith, *Trouble in Goshen*, for a history of New Deal cooperative farms: in Mississippi, the Tupelo Homesteads and the Delta Cooperative Farm, and in Arkansas, the Dyess Colony.

97. Fred C. Smith, "Cooperative Farming in Mississippi"; "Delta Cooperative Farm Records, 1936–1966," Mississippi Valley Collection 13, box 1, folder 7, University of Memphis Libraries, Memphis, Tenn.

98. "Black Farmers in America, 1865–2000," 10–11.

99. Moore, *Whistling in the Wind*, 26–28.

100. Ibid.

101. Bigarts, "Hunger in America"; Moore, *Whistling in the Wind*, 67–68; "Kibbutz Movement," Jewish Visual Library, http://www.jewishvirtuallibrary.org/jsource/judaica/ejud_0002_0012_0_11103.html. A kibbutz is a voluntary collective community, usually organized around agriculture and the concept of no private wealth. The kibbutz takes care of all needs of the member families. The kibbutz movement began in Israel in 1969, inspired by the Zionist labor movement and the centrality of social justice in the resettlement of the Jewish homeland. A moshav is based on individual agricultural holdings worked by a single family for income, with limited areas of social, economic, and communal cooperative engagement.

102. Moore, *Whistling in the Wind*, 70–71.

103. "History," Federation of Southern Cooperatives Land Assistance Fund, http://www.federationsoutherncoop.com/history.htm.

104. Bethell, "Sumter County Blues," 4.

105. Ibid.

106. Ibid., 5.

107. Ibid.

108. Ibid.

109. For information on the class-action lawsuit, see the Federation of Southern Cooperatives Land Assistance Fund, which has fought for the successful resolution of the lawsuit since the 1990s, http://www.federationsoutherncoop.com/. See also Southall, "Senate Approves Payment of Black Farmers' Claims."

110. Daniel, "USDA Approved," 106.

111. *Hunger, USA*, 16.

112. Ibid., 20.

113. Ibid., 21.

114. Cutler, Glaeser, and Shapiro, "Why Have Americans Become More Obese?," 93.

115. *Hunger, USA*, 50.

116. Ibid.

117. Ibid.

118. Valentine, "Q & A: The Causes behind Hunger"; Berkes, "A Rural Struggle to Keep the Family Fed."

119. Popkin, *The World Is Fat*, 29.

120. Kotz, *Let Them Eat Promises*, 246. In February 2014, federal health authorities reported lowered obesity rates for a tiny percentage of Americans (two- to five-year-olds) in a study to be published in the *Journal of the American Medical Association*. The cause of the decline is attributed to increased funding for whole fruits and vegetables in programs for low-income women and children instead of funding for sugary fruit drinks, eggs, and cheese. See Tavernise, "Obesity Rate for Young Children Plummets."

Chapter 18

1. Belasco, *Appetite for Change*, 4.

2. Braunstein and Doyle, "Historicizing the American Counterculture," in *Imagine Nation*, 8.

3. Belasco, *Appetite for Change*, 40.

4. For the history of the back-to-the-land movement, see Donna Brown, *Back to the Land*, 210–11.

5. Berry, *Unsettling of America*.

6. Agnew, *Back from the Land*, 73–74.

7. See discussion of "1960s themes long before the 1960s," in Timothy Miller, *The 60s Communes*, 7.

8. Belasco, *Appetite for Change*, 87. For information on New Deal–era cooperatives and subsistence homesteads, see "Subsistence Homesteads: The New Deal Goes Back to the Land," in Donna Brown, *Back to the Land*, 141–71; Maloney, *Back to the Land*, 4, 56; "Historical Information," Delta and Providence Cooperative Farms Papers, SHC; Nembhard, *Collective Courage*; and Fred C. Smith, *Trouble in Goshen*.

9. Ann Southerland Cottle, "Penderlea: Yesterday and Today," in *NCPedia*, http://ncpedia.org/geography/penderlea.

10. Belasco, *Appetite for Change*, 87.

11. Timothy Miller, *The 60s Communes*, 9–10; see also "School of Living History," http://www.schoolofliving.org/history.htm#briefhistory.

12. Timothy Miller, *The 60s Communes*, 9–10.

13. "An Introductory History," Koinonia Farms, http://www.koinoniapartners.org/History/brief.html.

14. Ibid.

15. Ibid.

16. "The History of Habitat," http://www.habitat.org/how/historytext.aspx.

17. "History of The Farm," http://thefarmcommunity.com/history_the_beginning.html.

18. Timothy Miller, *The 60s Communes*, 118.

19. Belasco, *Appetite for Change*, 78.

20. Timothy Miller, *The 60s Communes*, 120.

21. Ibid.

22. Ibid., 123–24; "The Farm Ecovillage Training Center," http://www.thefarm.org/etc.

23. "So, What Is Twin Oaks?," http://twinoakstofu.com/twin_oaks_community.

24. *Distaff*, 1973–82, Mary Elizabeth Gehman Collection, NAC 232-244, OV-002-003, NCCRW.

25. Ibid., "Biographical Note—*Distaff*."

26. Suzanne Pharr, interview by Kelly Anderson, June 28–29, 2005, Knoxville, Tenn., preface, Sophia Smith Collection, Smith College, Northampton, Mass., http://www.smith.edu/libraries/libs/ssc/vof/transcripts/Pharr.pdf.

27. Ibid., 38.

28. "Don't Ms," *Distaff*, March 1974, Mary Elizabeth Gehman Collection, NCCRW.

29. Gehman, "'People's Grille' Open to the Public," Mary Elizabeth Gehman Collection, NCCRW.

30. Ibid.

31. Ibid.

32. Ibid.

33. Pharr, "From Distaff to Huckleberry Farm," Mary Elizabeth Gehman Collection, NCCRW.

34. Suzanne Pharr, interview by Kelly Anderson, June 28–29, 2005, Knoxville, Tenn., 42, Sophia Smith Collection, Smith College, Northampton, Mass., http://www.smith.edu/libraries/libs/ssc/vof/transcripts/Pharr.pdf.

35. Ibid.

36. Belasco, *Appetite for Change*, 81–82.

37. Suzanne Pharr, interview by Kelly Anderson, June 28–29, 2005, Knoxville, Tenn., 43, Sophia Smith Collection, Smith College, Northampton, Mass., http://www.smith.edu/libraries/libs/ssc/vof/transcripts/Pharr.pdf.

38. Pharr, "From Distaff to Huckleberry Farm," Mary Elizabeth Gehman Collection, NCCRW.

39. Ibid.

40. Ibid.

41. Angela Jill Cooley, "Kitchen to Classroom: Let Them Eat Bread!," on *Southern Foodways Alliance Blog*, September 27, 2012, http://southernfoodways.blogspot.com/2012/09/kitchen-to-classroom-let-them-eat-bread.html; Robin Morris, "Organizing Breadmakers."

42. Cooley, "Kitchen to Classroom"; Robin Morris, "Organizing Breadmakers," 161–62.

43. Robin Morris, "Organizing Breadmakers," 161.

44. Ibid., 162.

45. Carol Ashkinaze, interview, W008, Georgia Women's Movement Oral History Project, Special Collections and Archives, University Library, Georgia State University, Atlanta.

46. The *Great Speckled Bird* was published weekly in Atlanta from 1968 to 1976, "one of the longest-running and highest quality underground newspapers of the era." See Digital Collections, Georgia State University, Atlanta, http://digitalcollections.library.gsu.edu/cdm/landingpage/collection/GSB; and Christopher Allen Huff, "The Great Speckled Bird," in *New Georgia Encyclopedia*, http://www.georgiaencyclopedia.org/nge/Article.jsp?id=h-3455&hl=y.

47. Silver and Grossman, "Comment: Food Day"; Wiley, "Politics of Food," 8–9.

48. Wiley, "Politics of Food," 8–9.

49. Ibid.

50. Christopher Allen Huff, "The Great Speckled Bird," in *New Georgia Encyclope-*

dia; Christopher Allen Huff, "Student Movement of the 1960s," in *New Georgia Encyclopedia*, http://www.georgiaencyclopedia.org/nge/Article.jsp?id=h-3400&hl=y.

51. Shurtleff and Aoyagi, *History of Erewhon*, 222–23.

52. Ibid.

53. Ibid.

54. Belasco, *Appetite for Change*, 82.

55. Shurtleff and Aoyagi, *History of Erewhon*.

56. Ibid.

57. Ibid.

58. Ron Shapiro, interview by Amy Evans, July 27, 2004, SFA, southernfoodways.org/documentary/oh/oxford/OX05_moonlite.html.

59. Ellen Weiss, email to author, July 18, 2012.

60. Ibid.

61. Timothy Miller, *The 60s Communes*, 199.

62. Ibid.

63. Belasco, *Appetite for Change*, 62.

64. Soul food definition from Taylor and Edge, "Southern Food," 12. For further discussion of the origins of the term "soul food," see Jessica B. Harris, *High on the Hog*, 206–8; Opie, "The Chitlin Circuit," in Opie, *Hog and Hominy*, 121–38; and Adrian Miller, *Soul Food*, 1–10, 265.

65. "History of the Building," Upper Chatham Lower Alamance Community Center, http://uclacc.net/blog/history-of-the-building.

66. Susan Ripley, email to author, November 14, 2013.

67. Dale Rosengarten, email to author, July 20, 2012.

68. Ibid.

69. Ibid.

70. Ethel C. Simpson, "Crescent Dragonwagon and Ellen Zolotow," in *Encyclopedia of Arkansas History and Culture*, http://encyclopediaofarkansas.net/encyclopedia/entry-detail.aspx?entryID=2969.

71. Dragonwagon, *Commune Cookbook*, 186–87.

72. Dragonwagon and Brown, *Dairy Hollow Cookbook*, 11.

73. A brief sampling of southern stalwarts of "countercuisine" include Deep Roots (1976), which began as a small vegetarian buying club in a Guildford College dormitory in the 1960s in Greensboro, N.C.; Ozark Natural Foods (1971) in Fayetteville, Ark.; Good Foods Co-op (1972) in Lexington, Ky.; Sunshine Grocery (1972) in Nashville, Tenn.; Rosewood Market, which evolved from Basil Pot Restaurant (1973) in Columbia, S.C.; Sevananda Natural Food Market (1974), originally the Egg and Lotus, located near Emory University in Atlanta, Ga.; Phoenix Natural Food Market (1970s) in Athens, Ga.; Rainbow Natural Foods (1976) in Decatur, Ga.; and Rainbow Blossom Natural Food Market (1977) in Louisville, Ky.

74. "Food Co-ops Planned," *Distaff* 2, no. 6 (Oct. 1974), Mary Elizabeth Gehman Collection, NCCRW.

75. Ibid.

76. Ibid.

77. "Co-op Food Store," *Distaff* 2, no. 7 (Nov. 1974), Mary Elizabeth Gehman Collection, NCCRW.

78. Ibid.

79. "The Great Eastern Sun Story," www.great-eastern-sun.com/shop/our-story.

80. Important additions to the natural food scene in the South included Three Rivers Market in Knoxville, Tenn.; Harvest Moon Food Store in Floyd, Va.; Rain-

bow Natural Grocery Cooperative in Jackson, Miss.; Wellspring Grocery in Durham, N.C.; Tidal Creek Co-op in Wilmington, N.C.; and Weaver Street Market in Carrboro, N.C.

81. Whitney E. Brown, "From Cotton Mill to Co-op." Brown provides further information on the historical chronology of natural food grocers in the Chapel Hill, N.C., area.

82. Bill Smith, email to author, July 21, 2012.

83. Judy Long, email to author, July 17, 2012; "Athens, Music History Walking Tour," Athens Welcome Center, Athens, Ga., brochure, www.athenswelcomecenter.com/images/Athens_Music_History_Walking_Tour.pdf.

84. Judy Long, email to author, July 17, 2012; "Athens, Music History Walking Tour," Athens Welcome Center, Athens, Ga., brochure, www.athenswelcomecenter.com/images/Athens_Music_History_Walking_Tour.pdf.

85. "Company History," Whole Foods Market, www.wholefoodsmarket.com/company/history.php.

86. I am indebted to Josh Davis for sharing his work with my students and me on counterculture retail food venues in the American South. Joshua Clark Davis, *Head Shops and Whole Foods*.

Chapter 19

1. Moreton Neal, Foreword to *Chefs of the Triangle*, ix–x; Moreton Neal, "The Birth of La Residence," 44.

2. Alice Waters and chef Jeremiah Tower built a network of local farmers, fisherman, and artisans that shaped Chez Panisse into the heart of the nascent organic food movement in California. See "Radical Notions," in Kamp, *United States of Arugula*, 124–65.

3. Bill Neal, *Bill Neal's Southern Cooking*, 2–3.

4. Moreton Neal, Chapel Hill, N.C., email to author, July 21, 2012.

5. Apple, "Bliss from the South."

6. Ibid.; see also Glenn, "Culinary Genealogy of the Triangle."

7. Moskin, "Can the Jewish Deli Be Reformed?"

8. Bryan Miller, "Craig Claiborne."

9. Moreton Neal, *Remembering Bill Neal*, xiv.

10. Claiborne, "Sophistication Spices Southern Food"; Council, "Mama Dip," interview.

11. Claiborne, "Sophistication Spices Southern Food."

12. Ibid.

13. Barker, "Chapel Hill Eats and a Chef Remembers," 172. See also Ben and Karen Barker, interview by Barbara Ensrud, March 14, 2005, SFA.

14. Claiborne, "Sophistication Spices Southern Food."

15. Lee and Lee, *The Lee Bros. Charleston Kitchen*, 169. Before Craig Claiborne included Neal's shrimp and grits recipe in the *New York Times* in 1985, the recipe was well known in the Lowcountry and published in iconic works such as *200 Years of Charleston Cooking* (1934) and *Charleston Receipts* (1950). I am grateful to Elijah Heyward III, doctoral student in American Studies at UNC-CH and a native of the South Carolina Lowcountry, for his discussion of the evolving narratives of iconic regional dishes like shrimp and grits—prepared by his mother, Vernell Heyward, and grandmother, Annie Ruth Smalls—and the origins of these culturally resonant food traditions.

16. The Barkers note over thirty-five chefs and cooks who began at Magnolia

Grill and went on to open their own restaurants and kitchens. See Weigl, "From Two Chefs, Many."

17. Barker, "Chapel Hill Eats and a Chef Remembers," 171.

18. Ibid., 172.

19. Ibid.

20. Claiborne, "Sophistication Spices Southern Food."

21. David Kamp, "California Nouvelle," in Kamp, *United States of Arugula*, 231–66; Francke, Sullivan, and Goldschlanger, "Food: The New Wave," 50; Jessica B. Harris, *High on the Hog*, 228.

22. Conroy, Foreword to *Frank Stitt's Southern Table*, vii–viii.

23. Kay Goldstein, Chapel Hill, N.C., email to author, July 20, 2012.

24. Ann Stewart, Chapel Hill, N.C., email to author, July 25, 2012.

25. Kay Goldstein, Chapel Hill, N.C., email to author, July 20, 2012.

26. Edge, "Southern Foodways," in *New Encyclopedia of Southern Culture: Foodways*, 12–13; Egerton, *Southern Food*, 344.

27. Egerton, *Southern Food*, 52–53.

28. Ibid., 343–44.

29. Ibid., 344.

30. Ibid., 344–45.

31. Stitt, Introduction to *Frank Stitt's Southern Table*, xiv–xv; David Kamp, "California Nouvelle," in Kamp, *United States of Arugula*, 231–66.

32. Stitt, Introduction to *Frank Stitt's Southern Table*, xvi.

33. Edge, "Southern Foodways," in *New Encyclopedia of Southern Culture: Foodways*, 13.

34. Conroy, Foreword to *Frank Stitt's Southern Table*, viii–ix. The James Beard Foundation named Stitt "Best Chef in the Southeast" in 2001.

35. Sifton, "Is There Life after 30?," 73–74.

36. Bill Smith, "The Cooks Who Giggle," 2–4.

37. Andrea Reusing and Miguel Torres, interview by Sara Camp Arnold, September 7, 2011, Lantern Restaurant, Chapel Hill, N.C., SFA.

38. Ibid.

39. Claiborne, "Country Cooking by an Urban Chef." For further discussion of Edna Lewis, see Jessica B. Harris, *High on the Hog*, 231–32; Severson, "Blood and Water," 130–33; and Edge, "Debts of Pleasure."

40. Judith Jones, the acclaimed cookbook editor of Julia Child at Alfred A. Knopf, fostered the publication of Edna Lewis's *A Taste of Southern Cooking* (1976).

41. Claiborne, "Country Cooking by an Urban Chef."

42. Asimov and Severson, "Edna Lewis." See also Alice Waters's Foreword to the thirtieth-anniversary edition of Edna Lewis, *Taste of Country Cooking*.

43. Edna Lewis, interview by Davia Nelson, Chapel Hill, N.C., 1983, http://www.kitchensisters.org/ednalewis.htm.

44. Walter, "The Southland I Remember," 19.

45. Edge, "Eugene Ferdinand Walter," in *New Encyclopedia of Southern Culture: Foodways*, 279–81. See also Walter, *The Happy Table of Eugene Walter*.

46. Dupree, *New Southern Cooking*, xiii.

47. Diane Trap, "Nathalie Dupree," in *New Georgia Encyclopedia*, http://www.georgiaencyclopedia.org/nge/Article.jsp?id=h-3203.

48. Dupree, *New Southern Cooking*, xiii–xv.

49. Nathalie Dupree has received three James Beard awards, including the 2013

Beard Award for American Cooking for *Mastering the Art of Southern Cooking*, co-authored with Cynthia Graubart.

50. Hess, "Historical Notes and Commentaries," xxxiv.

51. Ibid., xliv–xlv.

52. Ibid.

53. See Katz, *Wild Fermentation*; Katz, *The Revolution Will Not Be Microwaved*; Katz, *The Art of Fermentation*; and www.wildfermentation.com/who-is-sandorkraut/.

54. Katz, *The Revolution Will Not Be Microwaved*, xiv.

55. Ibid.

56. Steingarten, "Fresh Prince."

57. Bilger, "True Grits."

58. Moskin, "Southern Farmers Vanquish the Cliches." See also Bilger, "True Grits," 40–53.

59. Bilger, "True Grits," 45; Black, "Home Grown," 126–29.

60. Bilger, "True Grits," 42, 44; "Glenn Roberts," http://www.ansonmills.com/biographies.

61. For further discussion on antebellum agriculture, cuisine, and restoring the Lowcountry's unique food heritage, see Shields, "Charleston Gold"; and Shields, *Southern Provisions*.

62. Regarding the "power of a good story," I am grateful to my colleague Bernie Herman, who raised the question, "What is a story worth?," and to my student Sara Camp Arnold, who developed this concept in her insightful master's thesis in folklore at UNC-CH. The thesis examined the value of narrative and the virtual construction of *terroir* through a vital narrative exchange among farmers, chefs, and customers at the Carrboro Farmers' Market in Carrboro, N.C. See Arnold, "What Is a Story Worth?"

63. Severson, "Sorghum Speaks with a Sweet Drawl."

64. Whitney E. Brown, "Eat It to Save It," 95.

65. Currence, *Pickles, Pigs, and Whiskey*, xii.

66. Quatrano, *Summerland*.

67. "Q & A with Chef Donald Link," Viking Corporation, www.vikingrange.com/consumer/lifestyle/article.jsp?id=prod8360197; Link and Disbrowe, *Real Cajun*, 9.

68. McMinn, *Chickens in the Road*, 127. McMinn writes of returning to her home state of West Virginia: "When I came to the country, I'd been looking for some kind of connection with life that was visceral, purposeful, even sometimes dirty, but most especially difficult."

69. *A Chef's Life*, "About the Show," www.achefslifeseries.com/about. The series is directed and produced by Cynthia Hill, with Rex Miller, director of photography and co-producer, and is associated with SC-ETV.

70. *A Chef's Life*, "You Say Heirloom I Say Old Timey," www.achefslifeseries.com/episodes/5, SC-ETV.

71. *A Chef's Life*, "Peanut Pastime," www.achefslifeseries.com/episodes/9, SC-ETV.

72. Edge, "Sweet Spot" and "Due South," 93–94.

73. Eifling, "What Do Arkansans Eat?," 56–57.

74. Andrea Reusing is the 2011 winner of the James Beard award for Best Chef: Southeast. Reusing's *Cooking in the Moment* captures her philosophy of preparing and eating simple meals prepared from local, seasonal ingredients.

75. Acheson, *A New Turn in the South.*

76. Kayal, "Hugh Acheson Talks Kimchi Collards and Southern Stories."

77. Ibid.

78. Ibid.

79. See Michael Twitty's website and blog, http://afroculinaria.com; Kenan, "Michael Twitty."

80. "Wine and Food," www.blackberryfarm.com.

81. John Egerton, "Founders' Letter," Southern Foodways Alliance, www.southernfoodways.com/about/history.html.

82. Ibid.

83. Reichl, "Pride of the South"; Walter, *The Happy Table of Eugene Walter*, xii; Edna Lewis, "What Is Southern?," 24–30. This essay draws heavily from Lewis's earlier book, *The Taste of Country Cooking*, 28, 30.

84. Edna Lewis, "What Is Southern?," 26–30.

85. Ibid., 28.

86. Ibid.

87. Ibid., 27.

88. Ibid., 30.

89. Ibid.

90. Ben and Karen Barker, interview by Barbara Ensrud, March 14, 2005, Magnolia Grill, Durham, N.C., http://southernfoodways.org/documentary/oh/sfa_founders/ben_barker.shtml.

91. Edna Lewis, "What Is Southern?," 30.

Bibliography

Archival Collections

Ann Arbor, Mich.
  William L. Clements Library, University of Michigan
    American Travel Collection
    R. W. Benson Journal, 1905–6
    John Bodamer Journal, 1864–65
    Boynton Family Papers, 1827–63
    Thirza Finch Civil War Diary, 1858–70
    Louise Gilman Papers, 1866–69
    Ruth Newcomb Hastings Papers, 1852–53
    Edgar H. Klemroth Civil War Sketchbooks, 1864
    Longone Culinary Collection: Culinary ephemera, advertisements, food pamphlets, brochures
    Harry A. Simmons Journal and Sketchbook, 1861–62
    Samuel C. Taylor Journal, 1863, 1890
Asheville, N.C.
  D. H. Ramsey Special Collections Library, University of North Carolina at Asheville
    Biltmore Industries Archive, Grovewood Gallery, Inc., Grove Park Inn
      Grove Park Inn Letters, 1912–13
      Grove Park Inn Photographic Collection, 1913–30
    W. B. McEwen and Caroline Nichols McEwen Wedding Scrapbook (Menus)
  Pack Memorial Library
    Biltmore Dairy Farms Brochure
    Creighton's Menus
    Grove Park Inn Brochures and Menus
Atlanta, Ga.
  Georgia State University Digital Collections
    Great Speckled Bird
  Georgia Women's Movement Oral History Project, Special Collections and Archives, University Library, Georgia State University
Cambridge, Mass.
  Schlesinger Library, Radcliffe Institute for Advanced Study, Harvard University
    Mabel Hall Colgate Papers, 1827–1979
    Mary Reed Eastman Papers, 1834–1987
    Holt-Messer Family Papers, 1809–1962
    Matthews Family Papers
    Dorothy Hancock Stiles Papers, Hindman Settlement School, 1915–16
Cashiers, N.C.
  High Hampton Inn Papers
Chapel Hill, N.C.
  North Carolina Collection, Wilson Library, University of North Carolina at Chapel Hill
    Driving through Time: The Digital Blue Ridge Parkway

Southern Historical Collection, Wilson Library,
University of North Carolina at Chapel Hill
Samuel A. Agnew Diary, 1851–1902, 00923
John Charles Campbell and Olive D. Campbell Papers, 1836–2005, 03800
Al Clayton Photographs, 1960s–1980s, 04859
Robert Coles Papers, 1954–99, 04333
William T. Couch Papers, 1926–88, 03825
Delta and Providence Cooperative Farms Papers, 1925–63, 03474
Delta Health Center Records, 1956–92, 04613
Federal Writers' Project Papers, 1936–40, 03709
Oliver Max Gardner Papers, 1892–1966, 03613
Joseph Goldberger Papers, 1891–1949, 01641
Gordon Family Papers, 1810–1968, 02235
James Augustus Graham Papers, 1861–1901, 00283
John Berkley Grimball Diaries, 1832–83, 00970
Margaret Ann Meta Morris Grimball Diary, 1860–66, 975-z
Harriet L. Herring Papers, 1925–68, 04017
James A. Hutchins Scrapbook and Other Papers, 1927–87, 05439-z
Stetson Kennedy Papers, 1936–78, 04193
Mackay and Stiles Family Papers, 1743–1975, 00470
Howard Washington Odum Papers, 1908–82, 03167
John Milliken Parker Papers, 1902–38, 01184
Karen L. Parker Diary, Letter, and Clippings, 1963–66, 05275-z
Penn School Papers, 1862–2004, 03615
Daniel H. Pollitt Papers, 1935–2009, 05498
Arthur Franklin Raper Papers, 1913–79, 03966
Thomas Ruffin Papers, 1753–1898, 00641
Terry Sanford Papers, 1946–93, 03531
Scott Family Papers, 1839–67, 04638
Southern Oral History Program
Quinton E. Baker, K-0838
Pat Cusick, L-0043
Harriet Herring, G-0027
Daniel H. Pollitt, L-0064-7
Herman Newton Truitt, H-0054
Southern Tenant Farmers' Union Records, 1934–91, 03472
Joseph W. Straley Papers, 1936–2002, 05252
Netta L. Tutwiler Letters, 1861–75, 00452-z
Rupert Bayless Vance Papers, 1926–75, 04014
Charleston, S.C.
Avery Research Center, College of Charleston
Phillis Wheatley Literary and Social Club Papers, 1916–2011, AMN 103
South Carolina Historical Society
Charleston tourism ephemera, advertisements, menus, brochures, pamphlets
Mary Motte Alston Pringle Household Inventory Book, 1834–65
Special Collections, Marlene and Nathan Addlestone Library,
College of Charleston
Journal of Charles Cotesworth Pinckney, 1818–19, Mss 0034-054
Cincinnati, Ohio
American Jewish Archives

Columbia, S.C.
South Caroliniana Library, University Libraries, University of South Carolina
America Eats Papers, WPA Reports for South Carolina
Mary Elizabeth Pearson Boyce Diary, 1854–55
Dean Hall Plantation, Berkeley County Photograph Collection, Digital Collections
DeSaussure, Gamewell, Lange, and Parrish Family Papers, 1757–1925
Hayes Mizell Collection—Basil Pot Calendars, Columbia, S.C.
Smith Kitchin, "Notes and Sketches of a Confederate Soldier of the War of the Rebellion from Nov. 1862–July 1865"
Mary F. Norris Diary, June 18, 1865–March 21, 1866
South Carolina: School Lunch Program, Photographs
Davis Thacher Diary, 1816–18
Tourism ephemera, postcards, photographs
Jackson, Miss.
Margaret Walker Alexander Center, Jackson State University
WomanPower Unlimited Collection, 1946–76
Mississippi Department of Archives and History
Fox (Tryphena Holder) Papers, Z 1708.000 SM, 1826; 1852–85
Tougaloo Collection: Carol Ruth Silver, "The Diary of a Freedom Rider," 1961
Joan Harris Trumpauer Civil Rights Scrapbooks, z22 74.000s
New Orleans, La.
Amistad Research Center, Tulane University
CORE Papers
Dent Family Papers (Dillard University), 1890–2001
Janette Faulkner Ethnic Notions Collection
Fannie Lou Hamer Papers (Freedom Farms Corporation, Inc.), 1962–68
Constance B. Harse Papers, 1959–65
Sunflower County Freedom Farm Co-op Papers
Historic New Orleans Collection
Association of the Army of Tennessee, Louisiana Division, 44th Annual Reunion, Hotel DeSoto, April 6, 1921, New Orleans, TX 739.A7
Judah P. Benjamin letter to Dr. Barton, New Orleans, April 28, 1833
"Complimentary Dinner Given to the Hon. J. P. Benjamin," Boston Club, St. Charles Hotel, November 21, 1833, TX 739.B6
Galatoire's Menu, January 29, 1910, TX 737.G3 1910
Print Case Advertisements (Trade Cards)
Print Cases: Markets, Vendors, Public Markets, Chain Groceries, Neighborhood Stores, Mardi Gras, "Negroes," Restaurants and Hotels, African American, Rural La.
Howard-Tilton Memorial Library, Special Collections, Tulane University
Cross Keys Plantation Papers (Lucille Cook Watson)
Vertical Files: New Orleans tourism ephemera, advertisements, menus, brochures, pamphlets
Louisiana Historical Center, Louisiana State Museum
Cookbook Collection
Newcomb College Center for Research on Women, Tulane University
Harriet Boyer Papers, 1910–18
Mary Elizabeth Gehman Collection (*Distaff* newspaper)

Mary Land Collection
Lena Richard Collection
Oxford, Miss.
Southern Foodways Alliance Oral History Collection, University of Mississippi
Ben and Karen Barker, Durham, N.C.
Mildred Council, Chapel Hill, N.C.
Ken Dawson, Cedar Grove, N.C.
Bill Dow, Pittsboro, N.C.
Alex and Betsy Hitt, Graham, N.C.
April McGreger, Hillsborough, N.C.
Matt and Sheila Neal, Carrboro, N.C.
Andrea Reusing and Miguel Torres, Chapel Hill, N.C.
Ron Shapiro, Oxford, Miss.
Bill Smith, Chapel Hill, N.C.
St. Louis, Mo.
Henry Hampton Collection, Film and Media Archive, Washington University Libraries
Savannah, Ga.
Georgia Historical Society
Couper-Fraser Papers, 1810–94
Sarah Alexander Cunningham Papers, 1803–1939
Gordon Family Papers, 1802–1946
Jeremiah Evarts Diary, 1822
Washington, D.C.
Library of Congress
Farm Security Administration/Office of War Information Collection, Prints and Photographs Division
WPA Slave Narrative Project, Federal Writers' Project, Works Projects Administration, Manuscript Division

Secondary Sources

Acheson, Hugh. *A New Turn in the South: Southern Flavors Reinvented for Your Kitchen*. New York: Clarkson Potter, 2011.

Adams, Louisa. Interviewed by T. Pat Matthews, June 7, 1937, WPA Slave Narrative Project, North Carolina Narratives, vol. 11, pt. 1, LOC, 2.

Agee, James, and Walker Evans. *Cotton Tenants: Three Families*. Edited by John Summers. Brooklyn, N.Y.: Melville House, 2013.

———. *Let Us Now Praise Famous Men*. Boston: Houghton Mifflin, 1939.

Agnew, Eleanor. *Back from the Land: How Young Americans Went to Nature in the 1970s, and Why They Came Back*. Chicago: Ivan R. Dee, 2004.

Alexander, Bill. *Images of America: Around Biltmore Village*. Charleston, S.C.: Arcadia, 2008.

Alexander, Kelly. *Peaches: A Savor the South Cookbook*. Chapel Hill: University of North Carolina Press, 2013.

———. *Southern Living No Taste Like Home: A Celebration of Regional Southern Cooking and Hometown Flavor*. New York: Oxmoor House, 2013.

Alexander, Kelly, and Cynthia Harris. *Hometown Appetites: The Story of Clementine Paddleford, the Forgotten Food Writer Who Chronicled How America Ate*. New York: Gotham Books, 2008.

Algren, Nelson. *America Eats*. Iowa City: University of Iowa Press, 1992.

Ambrose, Stephen E. "The Bread Riots in Richmond." *Virginia Magazine of History and Biography* 71, no. 2 (1963): 203–4.
"The American Dream." *Time*, May 1, 1964, 23.
Anderson, Brett, ed., with Sara Camp Arnold. *Cornbread Nation 6: The Best of Southern Food Writing*. Athens: University of Georgia Press, 2012.
Anderson, Jean. *A Love Affair with Southern Cooking: Recipes and Recollections*. New York: William Morrow, 2007.
Anderson, John Q., ed. *Brokenburn: The Journal of Kate Stone, 1861–1868*. 1955; reprint, Baton Rouge: Louisiana State University Press, 1972.
Andrews, Evangeline Walker, and Charles McLean Andrews, eds. *Journal of a Lady of Quality by Janet Schaw, 1774 to 1776*. Lincoln: University of Nebraska Press, 2005.
Andrews, William L., and Henry Louis Gates Jr., eds. *Slave Narratives*. New York: Library of America, 2000.
Apple, R. W., Jr. "Bliss from the South: A Chef's Grand Legacy." *New York Times*, July 23, 2003, F5.
Arellano, Gustavo. *Taco USA: How Mexican Food Conquered America*. New York: Scribner, 2012.
Armstrong, Mary Frances. *Hampton Institute, 1868–1885, Its Work for Two Races*. Hampton, Va.: Normal School Press Print, 1885.
Armstrong, Mrs. Mary Frances, and Helen W. Ludlow. *Hampton and Its Students, with Fifty Cabin and Plantation Songs, Arranged by Thomas P. Fenner*. New York: G. P. Putnam's, 1874. http://docsouth.unc.edu/church/armstrong/armstrong.html.
Arnold, Sara Camp. "What Is a Story Worth? The Value of Narrative at the Carrboro Farmers' Market." Master's thesis, University of North Carolina at Chapel Hill, 2012.
Arsenault, Raymond. *Freedom Riders: 1961 and the Struggle for Racial Justice*. 2006; reprint, New York: Oxford University Press, 2011.
Asch, Chris Myers. *The Senator and the Sharecropper: The Freedom Struggles of James O. Eastland and Fannie Lou Hamer*. Chapel Hill: University of North Carolina Press, 2008.
"Asheboro Sit-In Participants Recall History." *Asheboro Courier-Tribune*, August 24, 2013. http://courier-tribune.com/sections/news/local/asheboro-sit-participants-recall-history.html.
Ashkenazi, Elliot, ed. *The Civil War Diary of Clara Solomon: Growing Up in New Orleans, 1861–1862*. Baton Rouge: Louisiana State University Press, 1995.
Asimov, Eric, and Kim Severson. "Edna Lewis, 89, Dies; Wrote Cookbooks That Refined Southern Cuisine." *New York Times*, February 14, 2006. http://www.nytimes.com/2006/02/14/national/14lewis.html?pagewanted=all&_r=0.
"Atlantan Shuts His Restaurant to Bar Patronage by Negroes." *New York Times*, August 14, 1964, 25.
"Atlanta Restaurant Defies High Court, Again Bars Negroes." *New York Times*, August 12, 1964, 1.
Atwater, W. O., and Charles D. Woods. "Dietary Studies with Reference to the Food of the Negro in Alabama in 1895 and 1896." Bulletin no. 38, U.S. Department of Agriculture, Office of Experiment Stations. Washington, D.C.: Government Printing Office, 1897.
Auberback, Benjamin M. "Reaching Great Heights: Changes in Indigenous Stature, Body Size, and Body Shape with Agricultural Intensification in North

America." In *Human Bioarchaeology of the Transition to Agriculture*, edited by Ron Pinhasi and Jay Stock, 203–33. Hoboken: Wiley-Blackwell, 2011.

Auchmutey, Jim. "Lewis Wants Maddox Restaurant Preserved." *Atlanta Journal-Constitution*, February 5, 2009, 1A.

Avirett, James Battle. *The Old Plantation: How We Lived in Great House and Cabin before the War.* New York: F. Tennyson Neely, 1901.

Ayers, Edward L. *The Promise of the New South: Life after Reconstruction.* New York: Oxford University Press, 1992.

———. *Southern Crossing: A History of the American South, 1870–1960.* New York: Oxford University Press, 1995.

Ayers, Edward, Patricia Limerick, Steven Nissenbaum, and Peter Onuf, eds. *All Over the Map Rethinking American Regions.* Baltimore: Johns Hopkins University Press, 1996.

Bacon, Alice M. *The Negro and the Atlanta Cotton Exposition.* Baltimore: Trustees of the John F. Slater Fund, Occasional Papers no. 7, 1896.

———. "Work and Methods of the Hampton Folklore Society." *Journal of American Folklore* 11 (January–March 1898): 17–21.

Baker, Chris. "The Golden Age of Health Spring Tourism in the Rural East Tennessee Valley." *Now & Then: The Appalachian Magazine* 29, no. 1 (2014): 44–46.

Baker, Ella J. "Bigger Than a Hamburger." *Southern Patriot* 18 (1960). Excerpted in *Let Nobody Turn Us Around: Voices of Resistance, Reform, and Renewal*, edited by Manning Marable and Leith Mullings, 375. Oxford: Rowan and Littlefield, 1999.

Balfour, Emma Harrison. *Mrs. Balfour's Civil War Diary: A Personal Account of the Siege of Vicksburg.* Edited by Gordon A. Cotton. Vicksburg, Miss.: Old Court House Museum, 2008.

Barker, Ben. "Chapel Hill Eats and a Chef Remembers." In *Cornbread Nation 5: The Best of Southern Food Writing*, edited by Fred Sauceman, 169–73. Athens: University of Georgia Press, 2010.

Barker, Ben, and Karen Barker. Interview by Barbara Ensrud, March 14, 2005, Magnolia Grill, Durham, N.C. http://southernfoodways.org/documentary/oh/sfa_founders/ben_barker.shtml.

Barker, Deborah E., and Kathryn McKee, eds. *American Cinema and the Southern Imaginary.* Athens: University of Georgia Press, 2011.

Barksdale, Marcellus. "Civil Rights Organization and the Indigenous Movement in Chapel Hill." *Phylon* 47, no. 1 (1986): 29–42.

Barnett, Evelyn Brooks. "Nannie Burroughs and the Education of Black Women." In *The Afro-American Woman: Struggles and Images*, edited by Sharon Harley and Rosalyn Terborg-Penn, 97–108. Baltimore: Black Classics Press, 1979.

Bartow, Beverly. *Isabel Bevier at the University of Illinois and the Home Economics Movement.* Urbana: University of Illinois, 1977.

Bass, Jack. "Hunger? Let Them Eat Magnolias." In *You Can't Eat Magnolias*, edited by H. Brandt Ayers and Thomas H. Naylor, 273–83. New York: McGraw-Hill, 1972.

Becker, Jane S. *Selling Tradition: Appalachia and the Construction of an American Folk, 1930–1940.* Chapel Hill: University of North Carolina Press, 1998.

Belasco, Warren J. *Appetite for Change: How the Counterculture Took on the Food Industry.* Ithaca: Cornell University Press, 1989.

———. *Food: The Key Concepts.* New York: Berg, 2008.

———. "Food Matters: Perspectives on an Emerging Field." In *Food Nations: Selling Taste in Consumer Societies*, edited by Warren Belasco and Philip Scranton, 2–23. New York: Routledge, 2002.

Belasco, Warren, and Roger Horowitz, eds. *Food Chains: From Farmyard to Shopping Cart*. Philadelphia: University of Pennsylvania Press, 2009.

Berkes, Howard. "A Rural Struggle to Keep the Family Fed," "Hunger in America" Series, NPR, November 21, 2005. http://www.npr.org/templates/story/story.php?storyId=5018670.

Berlin, Ira. "From Creole to African: Atlantic Creoles and the Origins of African American Society in Mainland North America." *William and Mary Quarterly*, 3d ser., 53, no. 2 (April 1996): 251–88.

———. *Many Thousands Gone: The First Two Centuries of Slavery in North America*. Cambridge, Mass.: Belknap Press, 2000.

Berlin, Ira, Marc Favreau, and Steven F. Miller, eds. *Remembering Slavery: African Americans Talk about Their Personal Experiences of Slavery*. New York: New Press, 1998.

Berlin, Ira, Barbara Fields, Steven F. Miller, Joseph P. Reidy, and Leslie S. Rowland. *Free At Last: A Documentary History of Slavery, Freedom, and the Civil War*. New York: New Press, 1992.

Berlin, Ira, and Philip D. Morgan, eds. *Cultivation and Culture: Labor and the Shaping of Slave Life in the Americas*. Charlottesville: University Press of Virginia, 1993.

Bernhard, Virginia, Betty Brandon, Elizabeth Fox-Genovese, and Theda Perdue, eds. *Southern Women: Histories and Identities*. Columbia: University of Missouri Press, 1992.

Berry, Wendell. *Bringing It to the Table: On Farming and Food*. Introduction by Michael Pollan. Berkeley: Counterpoint, 2009.

———. *The Unsettling of America: Culture and Agriculture*. San Francisco: Sierra Club Books, 1977.

Bethell, Thomas N. "Sumter County Blues: The Ordeal of the Federation of Southern Cooperatives." Washington, D.C.: National Committee in Support of Community Based Organizations, 1982.

Bevier, Isabel. "How I Came to Take Up Home Economics Work." *Home Economist*, May 1928, 140.

Bienvenu, Marcelle, Carl A. Brasseaux, and Ryan A. Brasseaux. *Stir the Pot: The History of Cajun Cuisine*. New York: Hippocrene Books, 2005.

Bienvenu, Marcelle, and Judy Walker, eds. *Cooking Up a Storm: Recipes Lost and Found from the Times-Picayune of New Orleans*. San Francisco: Chronicle, 2008.

Biesecker, Michael. "1957 Sit-In Began a Life of Activism." *Raleigh News and Observer*, February 21, 2010. http://www.newsobserver.com/2010/02/21/350063.html.

Bigarts, Homer. "Hunger in America: Mississippi Delta: Hunger in America: Negroes in Mississippi Delta Poorly Fed." *New York Times*, February 18, 1969, 1.

Bilger, Burkhard. "True Grits: In Charleston, a Quest to Revive Authentic Southern Cooking." *New Yorker*, October 31, 2011, 40–53.

"Birmingham Café Bows to Decision: Ollie McClung Now Says He Will Serve Negroes." *New York Times*, December 17, 1964, 46.

Bittman, Mark. "Now This Is Natural Food." *New York Times*, October, 22, 2013, A29.

Black, Jane. "Home Grown." In *Cornbread Nation 6: The Best of Southern Food Writing*, edited by Brett Anderson, 126–29. Athens: University of Georgia Press, 2012.

"Black Farmers in America, 1865–2000: The Pursuit of Independent Farming and the Role of Cooperatives." Washington, D.C.: USDA Rural Business Cooperative Service, RBS Research Report 194 (2003). http://www.rurdev.usda.gov/rbs/pub/rr194.pdf.

Blassingame, John W. *The Slave Community: Plantation Life in the Antebellum South*. New York: Oxford University Press, 1979.

Blight, David W. "'For Something beyond the Battlefield': Frederick Douglass and the Struggle for the Memory of the Civil War." *Journal of American History* 75, no. 4 (1989): 1156–78.

———. *Race and Reunion: The Civil War in American Memory*. Cambridge, Mass.: Belknap Press of Harvard University Press, 2001.

Boger, Astrid. *People's Lives, Public Images: The New Deal Documentary Aesthetic*. Tübingen, Germany: Gunter Narr Verlag, 2001.

Boger, John Charles. "Daniel H. Pollitt: In Memoriam." *North Carolina Law Review* 89 (2010): 9–16.

Bogle, Donald. *Toms, Coons, Mulattoes, Mammies, and Bucks: An Interpretive History of Blacks in American Films*. New York: Continuum, 2001.

Bold, Christine. *The WPA Guides: Mapping America*. Jackson: University Press of Mississippi, 1999.

Booth, Letha. *The Williamsburg Cookbook*. Williamsburg, Va.: Colonial Williamsburg Foundation, 1971.

Botkin, B. A., ed. *A Treasury of Southern Folklore: Stories, Ballads, Traditions, and Folkways of the People of the South*. New York: Crown, 1949.

Bower, Anne L., ed. *African American Foodways: Explorations of History and Culture*. Urbana: University of Illinois Press, 2007.

———, ed. *Reel Food: Essays on Food and Film*. New York: Routledge, 2004.

Boyer, Harriet Amelia. *Notes and Recipes: Freshman Domestic Science, H. Sophie Newcomb Memorial College*. New Orleans: Tulane University Press, 1915.

Bragg, Rick. "Former Klansman Is Found Guilty of 1966 Killing." *New York Times*, March 1, 2003. http://www.nytimes.com/2003/03/01/us/former-klansman-is-found-guilty-of-1966-killing.html?pagewanted=all&src=pm.

Branch, Taylor. *Parting the Waters: America in the King Years, 1954–63*. New York: Simon and Schuster Paperbacks, 1988.

———. *Pillar of Fire: America in the King Years, 1963–65*. New York: Simon and Schuster Paperbacks, 1998.

Braunstein, Peter, and Michael William Doyle, eds. *Imagine Nation: The American Counterculture of the 1960s and '70s*. New York: Routledge, 2002.

Breed, Allen G. "'Poster Father' Weary of Sour Fate." *Los Angeles Times*, June 26, 1994. http://articles.latimes.com/1994-06-26/news/mn-8651_1_tom-fletcher.

Bremer, Fredrika. *America of the Fifties: Letters of Fredrika Bremer*. Edited by Adolph Benson and Carrie Catt. Carlisle, Mass.: Applewood Books, 1924.

Brown, Donna. *Back to the Land: The Enduring Dream of Self-Sufficiency in Modern America*. Madison: University of Wisconsin Press, 2011.

Brown, Julia (Aunt Sally). Interviewed by Geneva Tonsill, Atlanta, Ga., July 25, 1930, WPA Slave Narrative Project, Georgia Narratives, vol. 4, pt. 1, LOC, 5–6.

Brown, Marion L. *Southern Cook Book*. Chapel Hill: University of North Carolina Press, 1968.

Brown, Robbie. "Remembering a Soul Food Legend Who Nurtured Civil Rights Leaders." *New York Times*, December 6, 2008, A9.
Brown, Whitney E. "'Eat It to Save It': April McGreger in Conversation with Tradition." *Southern Cultures* 15, no. 4 (2009): 93–102.
———. "From Cotton Mill to Co-op: The Rise of a Local Food Culture in Carrboro, North Carolina." Master's thesis, University of North Carolina at Chapel Hill, 2010.
Brown Lung Association, Ala., Ga., N.C., S.C., Va. *Spindles and Spatulas Cookery.* 1982.
Brundage, W. Fitzhugh. *The Southern Past: A Clash of Race and Memory.* Cambridge, Mass.: Belknap Press of Harvard University Press, 2005.
———, ed. *Where These Memories Grow: History, Memory, and Southern Identity.* Chapel Hill: University of North Carolina Press, 2000.
Bryan, Mrs. Lettice. *The Kentucky Housewife.* 1839; reprint, Bedford, Mass.: Applewood Books, 2001.
Bullock, Helen. *The Williamsburg Art of Cookery.* Williamsburg, Va.: Dietz Press, 1938.
Burke, Emily P. *Reminiscences of Georgia.* Oberlin, Ohio: James M. Fitch, 1850.
Burke, Vincent J. "Freeman, Javits Clash over Food for Poor: Dispute Enlivens Hearing by Senate Unit on Plight." *Los Angeles Times*, July 13, 1967, 5.
Burr, Virginia Ingraham, ed. *The Secret Eye: The Journal of Ella Gertrude Clanton Thomas, 1848–1889.* Chapel Hill: University of North Carolina Press, 1990.
Butchart, Ronald E. "Laura Towne and Ellen Murray: Northern Expatriates and the Foundations of Black Education in South Carolina, 1862–1908." In *South Carolina Women: Their Lives and Times*, edited by Marjorie Julian Spruill, Valinda W. Littlefield, and Joan Marie Johnson, 2:12–30. Athens: University of Georgia Press, 2010.
Butler, Tait. "Women's Institutes," in "Report of Farmers' Institute Work, 1906." *Bulletin of the North Carolina Department of Agriculture* 27, no. 10 (1906): 4–5.
Bynum, Victoria. *Unruly Women: The Politics of Social and Sexual Control in the Old South.* Chapel Hill: University of North Carolina Press, 1992.
Byrd, Lily. *High Hampton Hospitality.* 1970; reprint, Chapel Hill: Creative Printers, 1984.
Byrd, William, II. *The Westover Manuscripts Containing the History of the Dividing Line betwixt Virginia and North Carolina, 1728–1736.* Petersburg, Va.: Edmund and Julian C. Ruffin, 1841.
Caldwell, Erskine, and Margaret Bourke-White. *You Have Seen Their Faces.* 1937; reprint, Athens: University of Georgia Press, 1995.
Campbell, Edward D. C., Jr. "Plantation Film." In *Encyclopedia of Southern Culture*, edited by Charles Reagan Wilson and William R. Ferris, 922–24. Chapel Hill: University of North Carolina Press, 1989.
Campbell, John C. *The Southern Highlander and His Homeland.* New York: Russell Sage Foundation, 1921.
Capparel, Stephanie. *The Real Pepsi Challenge: The Inspirational Story of Breaking the Color Barrier in American Business.* New York: Free Press, 2007.
Carlebach, Michael. "Documentary and Propaganda: The Photographs of the Farm Security Administration." *Journal of Decorative and Propaganda Arts* 8 (1998): 6–25.
Carman, Tim. "Paschal's, Once a Civil Rights Landmark, Is in Tatters." *Washington Post*, August 21, 2011. http://www.washingtonpost.com/lifestyle/style/paschals

-once-a-civil-rights-landmark-is-in-tatters/2011/07/25/gIQAY5xFUJ_story .html.

Carney, Judith A. *Black Rice: The African Origins of Rice Cultivation in the Americas.* Cambridge, Mass.: Harvard University Press, 2001.

Carney, Judith A., and Richard Nicholas Rosomoff. *In the Shadow of Slavery: Africa's Botanical Legacy in the Atlantic World.* Berkeley: University of California Press, 2009.

Carody, Todd. "Sterling Brown and the Dialect of New Deal Optimism." *Callaloo* 33, no. 3 (2010): 820–40.

Carson, Barbara G. *Ambitious Appetites: Dining, Behavior, and Patterns of Consumption in Federal Washington.* Washington, D.C.: American Institute of Architects Press, 1990.

Carson, James Taylor. "'The Obituary of Nations': Ethnic Cleansing, Memory, and the Origins of the Old South." *Southern Cultures* 14, no. 4 (Winter 2008): 6–31.

Carson, Jane. *Colonial Virginia Cookery.* Williamsburg, Va.: Colonial Williamsburg, 1968.

Carson, Rachel. *Silent Spring.* New York: Houghton Mifflin, 1962.

Castle, Sheri. *The New Southern Garden Cookbook.* Chapel Hill: University of North Carolina Press, 2011.

———. *The Southern Living Community Cookbook: Celebrating Food and Fellowship in the American South.* Birmingham, Ala.: Oxmoor House, 2014.

Catesby, Mark. *The Natural History of Carolina, Florida, and the Bahama Islands,* vol. 2. Reprinted in *The Colonial South Carolina Scene: Contemporary Views, 1697–1774,* edited by H. Roy Merrens. Columbia: University of South Carolina Press, 1977.

Censer, Jane Turner. *The Reconstruction of White Southern Womanhood, 1865–1895.* Baton Rouge: Louisiana State University Press, 2003.

Chafe, William H. *Civilities and Civil Rights: Greensboro, North Carolina, and the Black Struggle for Freedom.* New York: Oxford University Press, 1980.

———. *The Unfinished Journey: America since World War II.* New York: Oxford University Press, 1999.

Chafe, William H., Raymond Gavins, and Robert Korstad, eds. *Remembering Jim Crow: African Americans Tell about Life in the Segregated South.* New York: New Press, 2001.

Chansky, Art. *Light Blue Reign: How a City Slicker, a Quiet Kansan, and a Mountain Man Built College Basketball's Longest-Lasting Dynasty.* New York: St. Martin's, 2009.

Chapman, William. "Mississippi Racial Bars Fall as Negroes Register at Hotels." *Washington Post,* July 6, 1964, A7.

Chase, Nan K. *Asheville: A History.* Jefferson, N.C.: McFarland, 2007.

Christian Women's Exchange, ed. *The Creole Cookery Book.* 1885; reprint, Gretna, La.: Pelican, 2005.

Church, Virginia. "Solving the Problem." *Southern Workman* 40, no. 7 (1911): 402–8.

Cimbala, Paul A., and Randall M. Miller, eds. *The Freedmen's Bureau and Reconstruction: Reconsiderations.* New York: Fordham University Press, 1999.

Claiborne, Craig. "Country Cooking by an Urban Chef: How Fate Made a Country Cook a Chef and Brought Forth a Book of Recipes." *New York Times,* August 1, 1979, C1.

———. *Craig Claiborne's A Feast Made for Laughter.* Garden City, N.Y.: Doubleday, 1982.

———. *Craig Claiborne's Southern Cooking*. New York: Wings Books, 1987.
———. "Sophistication Spices Southern Food." *New York Times*, June 26, 1985, C1.
Clark, Thomas D. *Pills, Petticoats, and Plows: The Southern Country Store*. 1964; reprint, University of Oklahoma Press, 1991.
Clinton, Catherine. *The Plantation Mistress*. New York: Pantheon Books, 1982.
———. *Tara Revisited: Women, War, and the Plantation Legend*. New York: Abbeville Press, 1995.
———, ed. *Fanny Kemble's Journals*. Cambridge, Mass.: Harvard University Press, 2000.
Clinton, Catherine, and Nina Silber, eds. *Divided Houses: Gender and the Civil War*. New York: Oxford University Press, 1992.
Cobb, James C. *The Most Southern Place on Earth: The Mississippi Delta and the Roots of Regional Identity*. New York: Oxford University Press, 1992.
Coles, Robert, and Al Clayton. *Still Hungry in America*. New York: World, 1969.
"Colored Cooks Are Given Lessons in Culinary Art." *Atlanta Journal-Constitution*, February 29, 1916, 7.
Colquitt, Harriet Ross. *The Savannah Cook Book: A Collection of Old Fashioned Receipts from Colonial Kitchens*. Charleston, S.C.: Colonial, 1933.
"Concession Bids for Park Route." *News and Observer*, August 7, 1940. Digital Blue Ridge Parkway, NCC. http://docsouth.unc.edu/blueridgeparkway/content/9025/.
Conkin, Paul K. "The School of Country Life." *Vanderbilt Magazine*, Spring 2010. http://www.vanderbilt.edu/magazines/vanderbilt-magazine/2010/04/the-school-of-country-life/.
Conroy, Pat. Foreword to *Frank Stitt's Southern Table: Recipes and Gracious Traditions from Highlands Bar and Grill*, by Frank Stitt, vii. New York: Artisan, 2004.
Cook, Harvey Toliver. *The Life and Legacy of David Rogerson Williams*. New York: N.p., 1916.
Cooley, Angela Jill. "To Live and Dine in Dixie: Foodways and Culture in the Twentieth-Century South." Ph.D. diss., University of Alabama, 2011.
Cooley, Rossa Belle. *School Acres: An Adventure in Rural Education*. New Haven: Yale University Press, 1930.
Cooper, Lenna Frances. *The New Cookery: A Book of Recipes, Most of Which Are in Use at the Battle Creek Sanitarium*. Battle Creek, Mich.: Good Health, 1913.
Couch, W. T., ed. *Culture in the South*. Chapel Hill: University of North Carolina Press, 1935.
———, ed. *These Are Our Lives: As Told by the People and Written by Members of the Federal Writers' Project of the Works Progress Administration in North Carolina, Tennessee, and Georgia*. New York: W. W. Norton, 1939.
Council, Mildred "Mama Dip." Interview with Amy Evans, June 2, 2007, Mama Dip's Traditional Country Cooking, Chapel Hill, N.C. http://southernfoodways.org/documentary/oh/chapelhill_eats/mildred_council.shtml.
———. *Mama Dip's Family Cookbook*. Chapel Hill: University of North Carolina Press, 2005.
———. *Mama Dip's Kitchen*. Chapel Hill: University of North Carolina Press, 1999.
Counihan, Carole M. *The Anthropology of Food and Body: Gender, Meaning, and Power*. New York: Routledge Press, 1999.
County Federation of Home Demonstration Clubs, ed. *Good Victuals from the Mountains*. Asheville, N.C.: Inland Press, 1951.

Covey, Herbert C., and Dwight Eisnach. *What the Slaves Ate: Recollections of African American Foods and Foodways from the Slave Narratives*. Santa Barbara, Calif.: Greenwood Press, 2009.

Cox, Craig. *Storefront Revolution: Food Co-ops and the Counterculture*. New Brunswick, N.J.: Rutgers University Press, 1994.

Cox, Karen L. "Branding Dixie: The Selling of the American South, 1890–1930." In *Dixie Emporium: Tourism, Foodways, and Consumer Culture in the American South*, edited by Anthony J. Stanonis, 50–68. Athens: University of Georgia Press, 2008.

———. *Dixie's Daughters: The United Daughters of the Confederacy and the Preservation of Confederate Culture*. Gainesville: University Press of Florida, 2003.

———. *Dreaming of Dixie: How the South Was Created in American Popular Culture*. Chapel Hill: University of North Carolina Press, 2011.

———, ed. *Destination Dixie: Tourism and Southern History*. Gainesville: University Press of Florida, 2012.

Crasson, Hannah. Interviewed by T. Pat Matthews, WPA Slave Narrative Project, North Carolina Narratives, vol. 11, pt. 1, LOC, 192.

Crespino, Joe. *In Search of Another Country: Mississippi and the Conservative Counterrevolution*. Princeton, N.J.: Princeton University Press, 2007.

Cripps, Thomas. *Slow Fade to Black: The Negro in American Film, 1900–1942*. New York: Oxford University Press, 1977.

Crowther, Bosley. "'Williamsburg: The Story of a Patriot' (1956), Screen: Williamsburg Information Center at Colonial Site Opens and Special Film Has Premiere There." *New York Times*, April 1, 1957. http://movies.nytimes.com/movie/review?res=9D01EED81E3EE63ABC4953DFB266838C649EDE.

Crump, Nancy Carter. "Foodways of the Albemarle Region: Indulgent Nature Makes Up for Every Want." *Journal of Early Southern Decorative Arts* 19, no. 1 (May 1993): 1–36.

———. *Hearthside Cooking: Early American Southern Cuisine*. Chapel Hill: University of North Carolina Press, 2008.

Cuadra, Cruz Miguel Ortiz. *Eating Puerto Rico: A History of Food, Culture, and Identity*. Translated by Russ Davidson. Chapel Hill: University of North Carolina Press, 2013.

Currence, John. *Pickles, Pigs, and Whiskey: Recipes from My Three Favorite Food Groups*. Kansas City, Mo.: Andrews McMeel, 2013.

Curry, John P. *Volunteers' Camp and Field Book*. 1862; facsimile compiled and edited by William B. Sargeant and John W. Brinsfield, Macon, Ga.: Mercer University Press, 2009.

Curtis, James. *Mind's Eye, Mind's Truth: FSA Photography Reconsidered*. Philadelphia: Temple University Press, 1989.

Cutler, David M., Edward L. Glaeser, and Jesse M. Shapiro. "Why Have Americans Become More Obese?" *Journal of Economic Perspectives* 17, no. 3 (2003): 93–118.

Danbom, David B. "Rural Education Reform and the Country Life Movement, 1900–1920." *Agricultural History Society* 53, no. 2 (1979): 462–74.

Daniel, Pete. *Dispossession: Discrimination against African American Farmers in the Age of Civil Rights*. Chapel Hill: University of North Carolina Press, 2013.

———. *Lost Revolutions: The South in the 1950s*. Chapel Hill: University of North Carolina Press, 2000.

———. “Reasons to Talk about Tobacco.” Presidential Address at the Organization of American Historians, Seattle, Wash., March 28, 2009. http://www.journalofamericanhistory.org/issues/963/presidential_address/.

———. *Standing at the Crossroads: Southern Life in the Twentieth Century.* 1986; reprint, Baltimore: Johns Hopkins University Press, 1996.

———. “USDA Approved: The Mark of Discrimination in Twentieth-Century Farm Policy.” In *Cornbread Nation 5: The Best of Southern Food Writing*, edited by Fred Sauceman, 101–6. Athens: University of Georgia Press, 2010.

Davis, Adele. *Let's Cook It Right.* New York: Harcourt and Brace, 1947.

Davis, Allison, Burleigh B. Gardner, and Mary R. Gardner. *Deep South: A Social Anthropological Study of Caste and Class.* Chicago: University of Chicago Press, 1941.

Davis, Edward H. “The Culture of Collards.” Paper presented at the symposium of the Southern Foodways Alliance, Oxford, Miss., October 27–29, 2012.

Davis, Edward H., and John T. Morgan. “Collards in North Carolina.” *Southeastern Geographer* 45, no. 1 (2005): 69.

Davis, J. E. “Hampton at Penn School.” *Southern Workman* 46, no. 2 (1917): 81–89.

Davis, Joshua Clark. *Head Shops and Whole Foods: How Activist Entrepreneurs Remade Retail and Public Life in the 1960s and Beyond.* New York: Columbia University Press, forthcoming 2016.

Davis, Townsend. *Weary Feet, Rested Souls: A Guided History of the Civil Rights Movement.* New York: W. W. Norton, 1998.

Davis, William C. *A Taste for War: The Culinary History of the Blue and the Gray.* Mechanicsburg, Pa.: Stackpole Books, 2003.

Deutsch, Tracey. *Building a Housewife's Paradise: Gender, Politics, and American Grocery Stores in the Twentieth Century.* Chapel Hill: University of North Carolina Press, 2010.

Diamond, Jared. “The Worst Mistake in the History of the Human Race.” *Discover Magazine*, May 1987. http://discovermagazine.com/1987/may/02-the-worst-mistake-in-the-history-of-the-human-race#.UxtsGv2AfRo.

“Diary of Timothy Ford, 1785–1786, with notes by Joseph W. Barnwell.” *South Carolina Historical and Genealogical Magazine* 13, no. 3 (July 1912): 142–43.

Dickins, Dorothy. “A Nutrition Investigation of Negro Tenants in the Yazoo Mississippi Delta.” Bulletin no. 254. Mississippi Agricultural Experiment Station, August 1928.

———. “A Study of Food Habits of People in Two Contrasting Areas of Mississippi.” Bulletin no. 254. Mississippi Agricultural Experiment Station, November 1927.

Dickson, Paul. *Courage in the Moment: The Civil Rights Struggle, 1961–1964.* Mineola, N.Y.: Dover, 2012.

Dirks, Robert T. “What Early Dietary Studies of African Americans Tell Us about Soul Foods.” *Repast* 26, no. 2 (2010): 8–18.

Dirks, Robert T., and Nancy Duran. “African American Dietary Patterns at the Beginning of the Twentieth Century.” *Journal of Nutrition* 131, no. 7 (2001): 1881–89.

———. “Experiment Station Dietary Studies prior to World War II: A Bibliography for the Study of Changing American Food Habits and Diet over Time.” *Journal of Nutrition* 128, no. 8 (1998): 1253–56.

Dix, Dorothy. Foreword to *Gourmet's Guide to New Orleans*, by Natalie Vivian Scott and Caroline Merrick Jones, 1. New Orleans: Peerless Printing, 1933.

Dollard, John. *Caste and Class in a Southern Town*. New York: Routledge, 1937.
Dotson, Mary L. "The Story of a Teacher of Cooking." In *Tuskegee and Its People: Their Ideals and Achievements*, edited by Booker T. Washington, 200–210. New York: D. Appleton, 1905.
Douglass, Frederick. *Life and Times of Frederick Douglass*. Boston: De Wolfe and Fiske, 1892.
———. *My Bondage and My Freedom*. New York: Miller, Orton, and Mulligan, 1855.
———. *Narrative of the Life of Frederick Douglass, An American Slave: Written by Himself.* In *Slave Narratives*, edited by William L. Andrews and Henry Louis Gates Jr. New York: Library of America, 2000.
Doyle, Bertram Wilbur. *The Etiquette of Race Relations in the South: A Study in Social Control*. Chicago: University of Chicago Press, 1937.
Dragonwagon, Crescent. *The Commune Cookbook*. New York: Simon and Schuster, 1972.
Dragonwagon, Crescent, with Jan Brown. *The Dairy Hollow Cookbook*. Eureka Springs, Ark.: Cato and Martin, 1992.
Dreyer, Edward, Lyle Saxon, and Robert Tallant. *Gumbo Ya-Ya: A Collection of Louisiana Folktales*. Boston: Houghton Mifflin, 1945.
Dull, Mrs. S. R. *Southern Cooking*. 1928; reprint, Athens: University of Georgia Press, 2006.
Dupree, Nathalie. *Nathalie Dupree's Southern Memories*. 1993; reprint, Athens: University of Georgia Press, 2004.
———. *New Southern Cooking*. 1986; reprint, Athens: University of Georgia Press, 2004.
Dupree, Nathalie, and Cynthia Graubart. *Mastering the Art of Southern Cooking*. Layton, Utah: Gibbs Smith, 2012.
Durban, Pam. *So Far Back*. New York: Picador USA, 2000.
Easterbrook, Michael. "Historic Dinner with King." *Raleigh News and Observer*, February 26, 2004, B1.
Eaton, Allen H. *Handicrafts of the Southern Highlands*. New York: Russell Sage Foundation, 1937.
Edelman, Marian Wright. "Still Hungry in America." *Huffington Post*, February 10, 2012. http://www.huffingtonpost.com/marian-wright-edelman/hunger-in-america_b_1269450.html.
Edge, John T. "Civil Roots." *Oxford American* (Summer 2013): 52–54.
———. "Clarence Saunders, 1881–1953, Creator of Piggly Wiggly Supermarkets." In *The New Encyclopedia of Southern Culture: Foodways*, edited by John T. Edge, 261–62. Chapel Hill: University of North Carolina Press, 2007.
———. "Debts of Pleasure." *Oxford American* (September 16, 2013). http://www.oxfordamerican.org/articles/2013/sep/16/local-fare-debts-pleasure/.
———. *A Gracious Plenty: Recipes and Recollections from the American South*. New York: Berkley Publishing Group, 1999.
———. "Sweet Spot: Scratch Satisfies the Itch for Baked Goods Done Right." *Garden and Gun*, February–March 2011, 93–94.
———, ed. *The New Encyclopedia of Southern Culture: Foodways*. Chapel Hill: University of North Carolina Press, 2007.
Edge, John T., Elizabeth Engelhardt, and Ted Ownby, eds. *The Larder: Food Studies Methods from the American South*. Athens: University of Georgia Press, 2013.

Edstrom, Eve. "Visit Starving, Miss. Senators Told: Doctor Disputes Their Charge He Libeled State." *Washington Post*, July 12, 1967, A4.
Edwards, Laura F. *Scarlett Doesn't Live Here Anymore: Southern Women in the Civil War Era*. Urbana: University of Illinois Press, 2000.
Edwards, Paul K. *The Southern Urban Negro as a Consumer*. 1932; reprint, New York: Negro Universities Press, 1969.
Egerton, John. "The Endurance of Southern Food." *Oxford American* 49 (Spring 2005): 18.
———. "Grits." In *The New Encyclopedia of Southern Culture: Foodways*, edited by John T. Edge, 175–77. Chapel Hill: University of North Carolina Press, 2007.
———. *Side Orders: Small Helpings of Southern Cookery and Culture*. Atlanta: Peachtree, 1990.
———. *Southern Food: At Home, on the Road, in History*. New York: Alfred A. Knopf, 1987.
———. *Speak Now against the Day: The Generation before the Civil Rights Movement in the South*. Chapel Hill: University of North Carolina Press, 1994.
———, ed. *Cornbread Nation 1: The Best of Southern Food Writing*. Chapel Hill: University of North Carolina Press, 2002.
Egerton, John, Tom Hanchett, and Frances Abbott. "Beverages." In *The New Encyclopedia of Southern Culture: Foodways*, edited by John T. Edge, 27–32. Chapel Hill: University of North Carolina Press, 2007.
Ehle, John. *The Free Men*. 1965; reprint, Lewisville, N.C.: Press 53, 2007.
Eifling, Sam. "What Do Arkansans Eat? In Search of a State's Cuisine." Food Issue, guest edited by John T. Edge. *Oxford American* 68 (2010): 56–57.
Elias, Megan J. *Stir It Up: Home Economics in American Culture*. Philadelphia: University of Pennsylvania Press, 2008.
Elie, Lolis Eric. "The Origin Myth of New Orleans Cuisine." In *Cornbread Nation 6: The Best of Southern Food Writing*, edited by Brett Anderson, 214–25. Athens: University of Georgia Press, 2012.
———, ed. *Cornbread Nation 2: The United States of Barbecue*. Chapel Hill: University of North Carolina Press, 2004.
Ellis, Belinda. *Biscuits: A Savor the South Cookbook*. Chapel Hill: University of North Carolina Press, 2013.
Ellison, Ralph. *Invisible Man*. New York: Random House, 1947.
Engelhardt, Elizabeth S. D. *A Mess of Greens: Southern Gender and Southern Food*. Athens: University of Georgia Press, 2011.
Engs, Robert Francis. *Educating the Disfranchised and Disinherited: Samuel Chapman Armstrong and Hampton Institute, 1839–1893*. Knoxville: University of Tennessee Press, 1999.
Eppes, Susan Bradford. *Through Some Eventful Years*. Macon, Ga.: Press of the J. W. Burke Company, 1926.
"Ernest Avants, 72, Plotter against Dr. King." *New York Times*, June 17, 2004. http://www.nytimes.com/2004/06/17/us/ernest-avants-72-plotter-against-dr-king.html.
Estes, Rufus. *Good Things to Eat as Suggested by Rufus*. Edited by D. J. Frienz. 1911; reprint, Jenks, Okla.: Howling at the Moon Press, 1999.
Ettling, John. *The Germ of Laziness: Rockefeller Philanthropy and Public Health in the New South*. Cambridge, Mass.: Harvard University Press, 1981.
Evans, Eli N. *Judah P. Benjamin: The Jewish Confederate*. New York: Free Press, 1988.

———. *The Provincials: A Personal History of Jews in the South.* 1973; reprint, Chapel Hill: University of North Carolina Press, 2005.

Farmer-Kaiser, Mary. "Sarah Katherine (Kate) Stone: 'The Agony and Strife' of Civil War Louisiana." In *Louisiana Women: Their Lives and Times*, edited by Janet Allured and Judith F. Gentry, 73–93. Athens: University of Georgia Press, 2009.

Farnham, M. W., E. H. Davis, J. T. Morgan, and J. P. Smith. "Neglected Landraces of Collard (*Brassica oleracea* L. var. *viridis*) from the Carolinas (USA)." *Genetic Resources and Crop Evolution* 55 (2008): 797–801.

Farr, Sidney Saylor. *Table Talk: Appalachian Meals and Memories.* Pittsburgh: University of Pittsburgh Press, 1995.

Faust, Drew Gilpin. *Mothers of Invention: Women of the Slaveholding South in the American Civil War.* New York: Vintage Press, 1996.

Federal Writers' Project. *North Carolina: The WPA Guide to the Old North State.* 1939; reprint, Columbia: University of South Carolina, 1988.

———. *The WPA Guide to 1930s Arkansas.* 1941; reprint, with a new introduction by Elliott West, Lawrence: University Press of Kansas, 1987.

Feeding America: The Historic American Cookbook Project, Michigan State University Libraries. http://digital.lib.msu.edu/projects/cookbooks/.

Feinstein, John. "Memories of Dean Smith Linger, Even as His Memory Sadly Fails Him." *Washington Post*, "Colleges," March 1, 2014.

Ferguson, Leland. *Uncommon Ground: Archaeology and Early African America, 1650–1800.* Washington, D.C.: Smithsonian Institution Press, 1992.

Ferris, Marcie Cohen. "Culinary Codes of the Plantation South." In *Writing in the Kitchen*, edited by Tara Powell and David A. Davis. Jackson: University Press of Mississippi, forthcoming 2014.

———. *Matzoh Ball Gumbo: Culinary Tales of the Jewish South.* Chapel Hill: University of North Carolina Press, 2005.

———. "The 'Stuff' of Southern Food: Food and Material Culture in the American South." In *The Larder: Food Studies Methods from the American South*, edited by John T. Edge, Elizabeth Engelhardt, and Ted Ownby, 276–311. Athens: University of Georgia Press, 2013.

———, ed. Special issue, "Edible South." *Southern Cultures* 15, no. 4 (2009).

———, ed. Special issue, "Food." *Southern Cultures* 18, no. 2 (2012).

Ferris, William R. *Images of the South: Visits with Eudora Welty and Walker Evans.* Memphis: Center for Southern Folklore, 1978.

———. "John Dollard: Caste and Class Revisited." *Southern Cultures* 10, no. 2 (Summer 2004): 7–18.

———. *The Storied South: Voices of Writers and Artists.* Chapel Hill: University of North Carolina Press, 2013.

Fertel, Randy. *The Gorilla Man and the Empress of Steak: A New Orleans Family Memoir.* Jackson: University Press of Mississippi, 2011.

Fertel, Rien. "Creole Cookbooks and the Formation of Creole Identity in New Orleans, 1885–1900." Master's thesis, New School of Social Research, 2008.

———. "Everybody Seemed Willing to Help: The Picayune Creole Cook Book as Battleground, 1900–2008." In *Cornbread Nation 6: The Best of Southern Food Writing*, edited by Brett Anderson, 10–31. Athens: University of Georgia Press, 2012.

Fieselman, Laura Collier. "The Contemporary Homestead: A Regional Moment in an American Movement." Master's thesis, University of North Carolina at Chapel Hill, 2014.

Fischer, David Hackett. *Albion's Seed: Four British Folkways in America.* New York: Oxford University Press, 1989.
Fisher, Abby. *What Mrs. Fisher Knows about Old Southern Cooking, Soups, Pickles, Preserves, Etc.* 1881; reprint, in facsimile, with historical notes by Karen Hess, Bedford, Mass.: Applewood, Books, 1995.
Fishman, Walda Katz, and Richard L. Zweigenhaft. "Jews and the New Orleans Economic and Social Elites." *Jewish Social Studies* 44, no. 3/4 (1982): 291–98.
Fitzgerald, Gerard, and Gabriella Petrick. "In Good Taste: Rethinking American History with Our Palates." *Journal of American History* (2008): 392–404.
"5 Whites Accused in St. Augustine: Klan Lawyer Is Sought in Cross-Burning Incident." *New York Times*, July 25, 1964, 9.
Fleischauer, Carl, Beverly W. Brannan, Lawrence W. Levine, and Alan Trachtenberg, eds. *Documenting America, 1935–1943.* Berkeley: University of California Press, 1988.
Foner, Eric. *Reconstruction: America's Unfinished Revolution, 1863–1877.* New York: Harper and Row, 1988.
"Food Co-ops Planned." *Distaff* 2 (1974): 3.
Food, Home, and Garden: The Vegetarian Magazine 4, no. 36 (1900). Chicago: Chicago Vegetarian Society, 1900.
Foose, Martha. *Screen Doors and Sweet Tea: Recipes and Tales from a Southern Cook.* New York: Clarkson Potter, 2008.
———. *A Southerly Course: Recipes and Stories from Close to Home.* New York: Clarkson Potter, 2011.
Ford, James, and Blanche Halbert. *School Cottages for Training in Home-Making.* Washington, D.C.: Better Homes in America, 1926.
Fowler, Chris. "My Integrity Means More to Me Than a Dollar Bill: Habitus and Good Farming in an Eastern North Carolina Community." Master's thesis, University of North Carolina at Chapel Hill, 2011.
Fowler, Damon Lee, ed. *Dining at Monticello.* Charlottesville: Thomas Jefferson Foundation, 2005.
———. *Essentials of Southern Cooking.* Guildford, Conn.: Lyons Press, 2013.
———. Foreword to *Southern Cooking*, by Henrietta Stanley Dull. 1928; reprint, Athens: University of Georgia Press, 2006.
———. "Historical Commentary." In *Mrs. Hill's Southern Practical Cookery and Receipt Book*, by Annabella P. Hill. Facsimile of *Mrs. Hill's New Cook Book* (1872). Columbia: University of South Carolina Press, 1995.
Fox-Genovese, Elizabeth. *Within the Plantation Household: Black and White Women of the Old South.* Chapel Hill: University of North Carolina Press, 1988.
Frady, Marshall. "How Lester Maddox at Last Became 'Mr. Somebody.'" In *Southerners: A Journalist's Odyssey*, by Marshall Frady, 44–74. New York: New American Library, 1980.
Francke, Linda Bird, with Scott Sullivan and Seth Goldschlanger. "Food: The New Wave." *Newsweek*, August 11, 1975, 50.
Franklin, Sarah B. "Interview: Tradition, Treme, and the New Orleans Renaissance: Lolis Eric Elie." *Southern Cultures* 18, no. 2 (2012): 32–44.
———. "Judith and Edna: How Two Women Made Culinary History." *Gravy*, no. 50 (December 2013): 24–28.
Fraser, Rebecca J. *Gender, Race, and Family in Nineteenth Century America: From Northern Women to Plantation Mistress.* New York: Palgrave Macmillan, 2013.

Frissell, H. B., and Isabel Bevier. "Dietary Studies of Negroes in Eastern Virginia in 1897 and 1898." Washington, D.C.: Government Printing Office, 1899.

"From a Private's Diary: Jackson, Miss., Captured by Sherman the Second Time." *New York Times*, December 4, 1892. http://query.nytimes.com/mem/archive-free/pdf?res=F50D10FE3C5515738DDDAD0894DA415B8285F0D3.

Gantt, Patricia M. "Taking the Cake: Power Politics in Southern Life and Fiction." In *Cooking Lessons: The Politics of Gender and Food*, edited by Sherrie A. Inness, 63–85. Lanham, Md.: Rowman and Littlefield, 2001.

Garrow, David J. *The Montgomery Bus Boycott and the Women Who Started It: The Memoir of Jo Ann Gibson Robinson*. Knoxville: University of Tennessee Press, 1987.

Gehman, Mary. "'People's Grille' Open to the Public." *Distaff* 1, no. 10 (1973): 5.

Genovese, Eugene D. *Roll, Jordan, Roll: The World the Slaves Made*. New York: Vintage Books, 1972.

Gettleman, Jeffrey. "A Cherished Civil Rights Site Faces Its Doom." *New York Times*, July 26, 2003. http://www.nytimes.com/2003/07/26/us/a-cherished-civil-rights-site-faces-its-doom.html.

Gibbons, Euell. *Stalking the Wild Asparagus*. New York: David and McKay Co., 1970.

Giduz, Roland. "We Should Have Led the Way." *Old Codger Blodger*, January 17, 2008. http://rolandgiduz.wordpress.com.

Gill, Christopher J. "A Year of Residence in the Household of a South Carolina Planter: Teacher, Daughters, Mistress, and Slaves." *South Carolina Historical Magazine* 97, no. 4 (1996): 293–309.

Giltner, Scott E. *Hunting and Fishing in the New South: Black Labor and White Leisure after the Civil War*. Baltimore, Md.: Johns Hopkins University Press, 2008.

Glassie, Henry. *Pattern in the Material Folk Culture of the Eastern United States*. Philadelphia: University of Pennsylvania Press, 1968.

Glenn, C. C. "Culinary Genealogy of the Triangle." *Raleigh Metro Magazine*, April 2013. http://www.metronc.com/article/?id=2528.

Glymph, Thavolia. *Out of the House of Bondage: The Transformation of the Plantation Household*. Cambridge, Mass.: Cambridge University Press, 2008.

Goings, Kenneth W. *Mammy and Uncle Mose: Black Collectibles and American Stereotyping*. Bloomington: Indiana University Press, 1994.

Goldberger, Joseph, and Edgar Sydenstricker. "Pellagra in the Mississippi Flood Area: Report of an Inquiry Relating to the Prevalence of Pellagra in the Area Affected by the Overflow of the Mississippi and Its Tributaries in Tennessee, Arkansas, Mississippi, and Louisiana in the Spring of 1927." *Public Health Reports* (1896–1970) 42, no. 44 (1927): 2706–25.

Golden, Harry. *Only in America*. New York: PermaBook, 1958/59.

Goldstein, Kay, and Liza Nelson. *A Book of Feasts: Recipes and Stories from American Celebrations*. Atlanta, Ga.: Longstreet Press, 1993.

Gordon, Linda. "Dorothea Lange: The Photographer as Agricultural Sociologist." *Journal of American History* 93, no. 3 (2006): 698–727.

Granger, Mary. *Drums and Shadows*. Georgia Writers' Project, 1940.

Grantham, Dewey W. *Southern Progressivism: The Reconciliation of Progress and Tradition*. Knoxville: University of Tennessee Press, 1983.

Green, Rayna. "Mother Corn and Dixie Pig: Native Food in the Native South." *Southern Cultures* 14, no. 4 (2008): 114–26.

Groom, Winston. *Vicksburg 1863*. New York: Vintage Books, 2009.
Grubb, Alan. "House and Home in the Victorian South: The Cookbook as Guide." In *In Joy and in Sorrow: Women, Family, and Marriage in the Victorian South, 1830–1900*, edited by Carol Blesser, 154–75. New York: Oxford University Press, 1991.
Gutierrez, C. Page. *Cajun Foodways*. Jackson: University Press of Mississippi, 1992.
Gutierrez, Sandra A. *The New Southern-Latino Table*. Chapel Hill: University of North Carolina Press, 2011.
Gwin, Minrose. *Black and White Women of the Old South: The Peculiar Sisterhood in American Literature*. Knoxville: University of Tennessee Press, 1985.
Hagood, Margaret Jarman. *Mothers of the South: Portraiture of the White Tenant Farm Woman*. New York: W. W. Norton, 1939.
Hague, Parthenia Antoinette. *A Blockaded Family: Life in Southern Alabama during the Civil War*. Boston: Houghton Mifflin, 1888.
Hale, Grace Elizabeth. "'For Colored' and 'For White': Segregating Consumption in the South." In *Jumpin' Jim Crow: Southern Politics from Civil War to Civil Rights*, edited by Jane Dailey, Glenda Elizabeth Gilmore, and Bryant Simon, 162–82. Princeton, N.J.: Princeton University Press, 2000.
———. *Making Whiteness: The Culture of Segregation in the South, 1890–1940*. New York: Pantheon, 1998.
———. "When Jim Crow Drank Coke." *New York Times*, January 28, 2013, A23.
Haley, Andrew P. *Turning the Tables: Restaurants and the Rise of the American Middle Class, 1880–1920*. Chapel Hill: University of North Carolina Press, 2013.
Hall, Jacquelyn Dowd. "Partial Truths: Writing Southern Women's History." In *Southern Women: Histories and Identities*, edited by Virginia Bernhard, Betty Brandon, and Elizabeth Fox-Genovese, 11–29. Columbia: University of Missouri Press, 1992.
Hall, Jacquelyn Dowd, James Leloudis, Robert Korstad, Mary Murphy, Lu Ann Jones, and Christopher B. Daly. *Like a Family: The Making of a Southern Cotton World*. Chapel Hill: University of North Carolina Press, 1987.
Hamilton, Anna. "Documenting Jackson's Farish Street District." *Southern Register* (Spring 2013): 6.
Hamilton, Lonnee. "Green Goddess: Why We Love Collard Greens." In *Cornbread Nation 6: The Best of Southern Food Writing*, edited by Brett Anderson. Athens: University of Georgia Press, 2012.
Hanchett, Thomas. "Salad Bowl Suburbs: A History of Charlotte's East Side and South Boulevard Immigrant Corridors." In *Charlotte, N.C.: The Global Evolution of a New South City*, edited by William Graves and Heather Smith, 246–62. Athens: University of Georgia Press, 2010.
Handler, Richard, and Eric Gable. *The New History in an Old Museum: Creating the Past at Colonial Williamsburg*. Durham, N.C.: Duke University Press, 1997.
Hariot, Thomas, John White, and Richard Hakluyt. *A Briefe and True Report of the New Found Land of Virginia* (1590). New York: J. Sabin, 1871.
Harlan, Louis R., ed. *The Booker T. Washington Papers, 1889–1895*. Vol. 3. Urbana: University of Illinois Press, 1974.
Harland, Marion. *Common Sense in the Household: A Manual of Practical Housewifery*. New York: Charles Scribner, 1871.
Harris, Carmen. "Grace under Pressure: The Black Home Extension Service in South Carolina, 1919–1966." In *Rethinking Home Economics: Women and the*

History of a Profession, edited by Sarah Stage and Virginia B. Vincenti, 203–28. Ithaca: Cornell University Press, 1997.

Harris, Jessica B. *Beyond Gumbo: Creole Fusion Food from the Atlantic Rim*. New York: Simon and Schuster, 2003.

———. *High on the Hog: A Culinary Journey from Africa to America*. New York: Bloomsbury, 2011.

———. *Iron Pots and Wooden Spoons: Africa's Gifts to New World Cooking*. New York: Simon and Schuster, 1999.

———. "Three Hundred Years of Rice and Recipes in Lowcountry Kitchens." In *Grass Roots: Origins of an African Art*, edited by Dale Rosengarten, Theodore Rosengarten, and Enid Schildkrout, 122–26. New York: Museum for African Art, 2008.

———. *The Welcome Table: African-American Heritage Cooking*. New York: Simon and Schuster, 1995.

Harrison, Bertha N., and Lina R. Godfrey. "Home Economics and African-American Education." In *Encyclopedia of African-American Education*, edited by Faustine C. Jones-Wilson, Charles A. Asbury, Margo Okazawa-Rey, D. Kamili Anderson, Sylvia M. Jacobs, and Michael Fultz, 213–15. Westport, Conn.: Greenwood Press, 1996.

Harrison, Fairfax. "Southern Railway Company." *Railway Journal* 21 (1915): 21.

Harris-Perry, Melissa V. *Sister Citizen: Shame, Stereotypes, and Black Women in America*. New Haven: Yale University Press, 2011.

Hartsook, Herb. "'Well, You Can't Refuse a Sister': Sister Mary Anthony Monahan, Fritz Hollings, and Hunger in South Carolina," January 13, 2012, "A Capitol Blog," University Library, University of South Carolina, Columbia, South Carolina. http://library.sc.edu/blogs/scpc/2012/01/13/well-you-cant-refuse-a-sister-sister-mary-anthony-monahan-fritz-hollings-and-hunger-in-south-carolina/.

Harvey, Shannon. "Vimala Cooks, Everybody Eats." *Southern Cultures* 18, no. 2 (2012): 98–103.

Harwell, Richard, ed. *Hardtack and Coffee: The Unwritten Story of Army Life, by John D. Billings*. Chicago: R. R. Donnelley, 1960.

Hatcher, J. Welsey. "Appalachian America." In *Culture in the South*, edited by W. T. Couch, 374–402. Chapel Hill: University of North Carolina Press, 1934.

Hatchett, Louis. *Duncan Hines: The Man behind the Cake Mix*. Macon, Ga.: Mercer University Press, 2001.

Head, Thomas. Foreword to *The Happy Table of Eugene Walter*, by Eugene Walter. Chapel Hill: University of North Carolina Press, 2011.

Hearn, Lafcadio. *La Cuisine Creole: A Collection of Culinary Recipes from Leading Chefs and Noted Creole Housewives, Who Have Made New Orleans Famous for Its Cuisine*. New Orleans: F. F. Hansell & Bro., 1885. Reprinted in *Lafcadio Hearn's Creole Cook Book: With the Addition of a Collection of Drawings and Writings by Lafcadio Hearn during His Sojourn in New Orleans from 1877 to 1887: A Literary and Culinary Adventure*, by Lafcadio Hearn. Gretna, La.: Pelican, 1990.

The Help. Directed by Tate Taylor. Burbank, Calif.: Walt Disney Studios, 2011. DVD.

Hendricks, W. C., ed. *North Carolina: A Guide to the Old North State*. 1939; reprint, Columbia: University of South Carolina Press, 1988.

Herbers, John. "Civil Rights: South Slowly Yields." *New York Times*, December 20, 1964, E3.

———. "Martin Luther King and 17 Others Jailed Trying to Integrate St. Augustine Restaurant." *New York Times*, June 12, 1964, 17.
Herman, Bernard L. "Drum Head Stew: The Power and Poetry of Terroir." *Southern Cultures* 15, no. 4 (2009): 36–49.
———. "Theodore Peed's Turtle Party." *Southern Cultures* 18, no. 2 (2012): 59–73.
———. *Town House: Architecture and Material Life in the Early American City, 1780–1830*. Chapel Hill: University of North Carolina Press, 2005.
Herring, Harriet L. "The Industrial Worker." In *Culture in the South*, edited by W. T. Couch, 344–60. Chapel Hill: University of North Carolina Press, 1934.
Hess, Karen. *The Carolina Rice Kitchen: The African Connection*. Columbia: University of South Carolina Press, 1992.
———. "Historical Notes and Commentaries on Mary Randolph's *The Virginia House-Wife*." In *The Virginia House-Wife*, by Mary Randolph, xiii. 1824; reprint, Columbia: University of South Carolina Press, 1984.
Hibben, Sheila. *American Regional Cooking*. New York: Gramercy, 1932.
"Highlands Cookery from Mountain Cove and Knob." *House and Garden*, June 1942, 48.
Hill, Mrs. Annabella P. *Mrs. Hill's Southern Practical Cookery and Receipt Book*. Facsimile of *Mrs. Hill's New Cook Book*, 1872, with Damon L. Fowler. Columbia: University of South Carolina Press, 1995.
Hilliard, Emily. "Vimala Cooks, Everybody Eats: Domesticity, Community, and Empowerment." Master's thesis, University of North Carolina at Chapel Hill, 2011.
Hilliard, Sam Bowers. "Hog Meat and Cornpone: Foodways in the Antebellum South." In *Material Life in America, 1600–1800*, edited by Robert Blair St. George, 311–32. Boston: Northeastern University Press, 1988.
———. *Hog Meat and Hoecake: Food Supply in the Old South, 1840–1860*. Foreword by James C. Cobb. 1972; reprint, Athens: University of Georgia Press, 2014.
Hines, Duncan. *Adventures in Good Eating: Good Eating Places along the Highways of America*. Bowling Green, Ky.: Adventures in Good Eating, 1946.
Hirsch, Jerrold. *Portrait of America: A Cultural History of the Federal Writers' Project*. Chapel Hill: University of North Carolina Press, 2003.
Hobson, Fred. *Serpent in Eden: H. L. Mencken and the South*. Baton Rouge: Louisiana State University Press, 1978.
Hoffschwelle, Mary S. *Rebuilding the Rural Southern Community: Reformers, Schools, and Homes in Tennessee, 1900–1930*. Knoxville: University of Tennessee Press, 1998.
Holland, Rupert Sargent, ed. *Letters and Diary of Laura M. Towne: Written from the Sea Islands of South Carolina, 1862–1884*. Cambridge, Mass.: Riverside Press, 1912.
Holland, Sharon. *The Erotic Life of Racism*. Durham, N.C.: Duke University Press, 2012.
Hollings, Ernest F. *The Case against Hunger: A Demand for a National Policy*. New York: Cowles Book Company, 1970.
Holsaert, Faith S., Martha Prescod, Norman Noonan, Judy Richardson, Betty Garman Robinson, Jean Smith Young, and Dorothy M. Zellner, eds. *Hands on the Freedom Plow: Personal Accounts by Women in SNCC*. Urbana: University of Illinois Press, 2010.
Hooker, Richard J., ed. *A Colonial Plantation Cookbook: The Receipt Book of*

Harriott Pinckney Horry, 1770. Columbia: University of South Carolina Press, 1984.

Hoopes, Gulielma M. *Memoir and Letters of Gulielma M. Hoopes*. Philadelphia: Henry B. Ashmead, 1862.

Horwitz, Tony. *A Voyage Long and Strange: Rediscovering the New World*. New York: Henry Holt, 2008.

Houck, Davis W., and David E. Dixon, eds. *Women and the Civil Rights Movement, 1954–1965*. Jackson: University Press of Mississippi, 2009.

Huber, Patrick. "The Riddle of the Horny Hillbilly." In *Dixie Emporium: Tourism, Foodways, and Consumer Culture in the American South*, edited by Anthony J. Stanonis, 69–86. Athens: University of Georgia Press, 2008.

Hudson, Larry E., ed. *Working toward Freedom: Slave Society and Domestic Economy in the American South*. Rochester: University of Rochester Press, 1994.

Huguenin, Mary Vereen, and Anne Montague Stoney, eds. *Charleston Receipts Collected by the Junior League of Charleston*. Charleston, S.C.: Walker Evans and Cogeswell, 1950.

Humphreys, Margaret. *Malaria: Poverty, Race, and Public Health in the United States*. Baltimore: Johns Hopkins University Press, 2001.

Hunger, USA: A Report by the Citizens' Board of Inquiry into Hunger and Malnutrition in the United States. Boston: Beacon Press, 1968.

Hunter, Tera W. *To 'Joy My Freedom: Southern Black Women's Lives and Labors after the Civil War*. Cambridge, Mass.: Harvard University Press, 1997.

Hurley, F. Jack. *Marion Post Wolcott: A Photographic Journey*. Albuquerque: University of New Mexico Press, 1989.

Hurston, Zora Neale. "Diddy-Wah-Diddy." In *Food of a Younger Land*, edited by Mark Kurlansky, 123–25. New York: Riverhead Books, 2009.

Huse, Andrew T. *The Columbia Restaurant: Celebrating a Century of History, Culture, and Cuisine*. Gainesville, Fla.: University Press of Florida, 2009.

Hutchison, Janet. "Better Homes and Gullah." *Agricultural History* 67, no. 2 (1993).

Ingraham, Joseph Holt, ed. *The Sunny South, or, The Southerner at Home: Embracing Five Years' Experience of a Northern Governess in the Land of the Sugar and the Cotton*. 1860; reprint, New York: Negro Universities Press, 1968.

Ingram, Tammy. *Dixie Highway: Road Building and the Making of the Modern South, 1900–1930*. Chapel Hill: University of North Carolina Press, 2014.

Irwin, Don. "Senators Visit Poor in Rural Mississippi." *Los Angeles Times*, April 12, 1967, 11.

———. "U.S. Will Probe Food Program in Mississippi: Agriculture Dept. Aides Sent to Look into Charge." *Los Angeles Times*, April 13, 1967, 11.

Jabbour, Alan, and Karen Singer Jabbour. *Decoration Day in the Mountains: Traditions of Cemetery Decoration in the Southern Appalachians*. Chapel Hill: University of North Carolina Press, 2010.

Jacobs, Emma S. "Pioneering in Home Economics among the Negroes of Tidewater Virginia." *Journal of Home Economics* 21, no. 2 (1929): 85–91.

Jacobs, Harriet A. *Incidents in the Life of a Slave Girl, Written by Herself*. 1861; reprint, Cambridge, Mass.: Harvard University Press, 1987.

Jacoway, Elizabeth. *Yankee Missionaries in the South: The Penn School Experiment*. Baton Rouge: Louisiana State University Press, 1980.

Johnson, Charles, Edwin R. Embree, and W. W. Alexander. *The Collapse of Cotton*

Tenancy: Summary of Field Studies and Statistical Surveys, 1933–35. Chapel Hill: University of North Carolina Press, 1935.
Johnson, Joan Marie. *Southern Ladies, New Women: Race, Region, and Clubwomen in South Carolina, 1890–1930*. Gainesville: University Press of Florida, 2004.
Jones, Allen. "Improving Rural Life for Blacks: The Tuskegee Negro Farmers' Conference, 1892–1915." *Agricultural History* 65, no. 2 (1991): 105–14.
Jones, Jacqueline. *Labor of Love, Labor of Sorrow: Black Women, Work, and the Family, from Slavery to the Present*. New York: Vintage Books, 1985.
Jones, James A. *Bad Blood: The Tuskegee Syphilis Experiment*. New York: Free Press, 1972.
Jones, Lu Ann. *Mama Learned Us to Work: Farm Women in the New South*. Chapel Hill: University of North Carolina Press, 2002.
Joyner, Charles. *Down by the Riverside: A South Carolina Slave Community*. 1984; reprint, Urbana: University of Illinois Press, 2009.
———. *In Shared Traditions: Southern History and Folk Culture*. Urbana: University of Illinois Press, 1999.
———. "A Single Southern Culture: Cultural Interaction in the Old South." In *Black and White Cultural Interaction in the Antebellum South*, edited by Ted Ownby, 3–22. Jackson: University Press of Mississippi, 1993.
Kahn, Charlotte. *Old Southern Tea Room, Vicksburg, Mississippi: A Collection of Favorite Old Recipes*. Edited by Mary McKay. Vicksburg, Miss.: Mary McKay, 1960.
Kaminsky, Peter. *Pig Perfect: Encounters with Remarkable Swine and Some Great Ways to Cook Them*. New York: Hyperion, 2005.
Kamp, David. *The United States of Arugula: How We Became a Gourmet Nation*. New York: Broadway Books, 2006.
Katz, Sandor Ellix. *The Art of Fermentation*. White River Junction, Vt.: Chelsea Green, 2012.
———. *The Revolution Will Not Be Microwaved: Inside America's Underground Food Movements*. White River Junction, Vt.: Chelsea Green, 2006.
———. *Wild Fermentation: The Flavor, Nutrition, and Craft of Live-Culture Foods*. White River Junction, Vt.: Chelsea Green, 2003.
Kayal, Michele. "Hugh Acheson Talks Kimchi Collards and Southern Stories." *American Food Roots*, November 11, 2013. http://www.americanfoodroots.com.
Kelley, Steve. "Dean Smith Challenged Chapel Hill's Old Prejudices." *Seattle Times*, March 29, 1997. http://community.seattletimes.nwsource.com/archive/?date=19970329&slug=2531241.
Kellogg, Paul. Introduction to *School Acres: An Adventure in Rural Education*, by Rosa B. Cooley, xiii. New Haven: Yale University Press, 1930.
Kemble, Frances Anne. *Journal of a Residence on a Georgian Plantation in 1838–1839*. Facsimile of first edition, edited by John A. Scott. Athens: University of Georgia Press, 1984.
Kenan, Randall. "Michael Twitty: The Antebellum Chef." *Garden and Gun*, December/January 2014. http://gardenandgun.com/article/michael-twitty-antebellum-chef.
Kennard, Lucretia. "Personal Notes." *Southern Workman* 36, no. 1 (1907): 60.
Kennedy, Robert F. Introductory Comment to *Hunger, USA: A Report by the Citizens' Board of Inquiry into Hunger and Malnutrition in the United States*. Boston: Beacon Press, 1968.

Kennedy, Samuel Merlin "Scoop." *Dining in New Orleans: A Gourmet's Guide.* New Orleans: Borman House, 1945.

Kennedy, Stetson. *Jim Crow Guide to the U.S.A.* London: Lawrence and Wishart, 1959.

Kennedy, V. Lynn. *Born Southern: Childbirth, Motherhood, and Social Networks in the Old South.* Baltimore: Johns Hopkins University Press, 2009.

Kephart, Horace. *Our Southern Highlanders.* Knoxville: University of Tennessee Press, 1913.

Kierner, Cynthia. *Beyond the Household: Women's Place in the Early South, 1700–1835.* Ithaca: Cornell University Press, 1998.

King, Wayne. Afterword in *The Free Men*, by John Ehle. 1965; reprint, Lewisville, N.C.: Press 53, 2007.

———. "Restaurateur Maddox and Passing Scene." *New York Times*, February 16, 1975, 61.

King, Wilma, ed. *A Northern Woman in the Plantation South: Letters of Tryphena Blanche Holder Fox, 1856–1876.* Columbia: University of South Carolina Press, 1993.

Kirby, Jack Temple. *Rural Worlds Lost: The American South, 1920–1960.* Baton Rouge: Louisiana State University Press, 1987.

Kirk, J. S., et al., eds. *Emergency Relief in North Carolina: A Record of the Development and the Activities of the North Carolina Emergency Relief Administration, 1932–1935.* Raleigh, N.C.: Edwards and Broughton, 1936.

Knipple, Paul and Angela. *The World in a Skillet: A Food Lover's Tour of the New American South.* Chapel Hill: University of North Carolina Press, 2012.

Korn, Bertram Wallace. *The Early Jews of New Orleans.* Waltham, Mass.: American Jewish Historical Society, 1969.

Korstad, Robert R., and James L. Leloudis. *To Right These Wrongs: The North Carolina Fund and the Battle to End Poverty and Inequality in 1960s America.* Chapel Hill: University of North Carolina Press, 2010.

Kotz, Nick. *Let Them Eat Promises: The Politics of Hunger in America.* Englewood Cliffs, N.J.: Prentice-Hall, 1969.

Kraut, Alan M. *Goldberger's War: The Life and Work of a Public Health Crusader.* New York: Hill and Wang, 2003.

Kuepper, Lina. *Quisisana Hygienic Cook Book.* Asheville: French Broad Press, 1899.

Kuhn, Clifford M. "'It Was a Long Way from Perfect, but It Was Working': The Canning and Home Production Initiatives in Greene County, Georgia, 1940–1942." *Agricultural History* 86, no. 2 (2012): 68–90.

Kurlansky, Mark. *The Food of a Younger Land.* New York: Riverhead Books, 2009.

———. *Salt: A World History.* New York: Penguin, 2003.

Lafayette, Bernard. "Movement Food." In *Cornbread Nation 4: The Best of Southern Food Writing*, edited by Dale Volberg Reed and John Shelton Reed, 245–51. Athens: University of Georgia Press, 2008.

Lam, Francis, ed. *Cornbread Nation 7: The Best of Southern Food Writing.* Athens: University of Georgia Press, 2014.

Land, Mary. *Louisiana Cookery.* 1954; reprint, Jackson: University Press of Mississippi, 2005.

———. *New Orleans Cuisine.* Cranbury, N.J.: A. S. Barnes, 1969.

Lange, Dorothea, and Paul S. Taylor. *An American Exodus: A Record of Human Erosion.* New York: Reynal and Hitchcock, 1939.

Langman, Larry, and David Ebner. *Hollywood's Image of the South: A Century of Southern Films*. Westport, Conn.: Greenwood Press, 2001.
Latshaw, Beth A. "Food for Thought: Race, Region, Identity, and Foodways in the American South. *Southern Cultures* 15, no. 4 (2009): 106–28.
Lauterer, Jock. "Mrs. Roxie, Oxford, 1960s." "A Thousand Words," *Carrboro Citizen* 2, no. 48 (February 12, 2009): 10.
———. "Picketing the Dairy Bar, 1963." "A Thousand Words," *Carrboro Citizen* 5, no. 45 (January 19, 2012): 8.
Lawson, John. *A New Voyage to Carolina*. 1709; reprint, Chapel Hill: University of North Carolina Press, 1984.
Lears, T. J. Jackson. *Fables of Abundance: A Cultural History of Advertising in America*. New York: Basic Books, 1994.
Leathem, Karen Trahan. "Mary Land: When I Was Big Enough to Tote a Gun, I Did." In *Louisiana Women: Their Lives and Times*, edited by Janet Allured and Judith F. Gentry, 270–85. Athens: University of Georgia Press, 2009.
———. "Two Women and Their Cookbooks: Lena Richard and Mary Land." In *An Exhibition Guide*, edited by Susan Tucker. Exhibit organized by the Newcomb Archives, Newcomb College Center for Research on Women, Tulane University, New Orleans, La., November 2–December 21, 2001.
Lebsock, Suzanne. *The Free Women of Petersburg: Status and Culture in a Southern Town, 1784–1860*. New York: W. W. Norton, 1984.
Lee, Chana Kai. *For Freedom's Sake: The Life of Fannie Lou Hamer*. Urbana: University of Illinois Press, 1999.
Lee, Matt, and Ted Lee. *The Lee Bros. Charleston Kitchen*. New York: Clarkson Potter, 2013.
———. *The Lee Bros. Southern Cookbook*. New York: W. W. Norton, 2006.
Lemann, Nicholas. *The Promised Land: The Great Black Migration and How It Changed America*. New York: Alfred A. Knopf, 1991.
Lenski, Lois. *Cotton in My Sack*. Philadelphia: J. B. Lippincott, 1949.
———. *Journey into Childhood: The Autobiography of Lois Lenski*. Philadelphia: J. B. Lippincott, 1972.
"Lester Maddox Shuts Cafeteria." *New York Times*, February 8, 1965, 18.
Levenstein, Harvey. *Revolution at the Table: The Transformation of the American Diet*. New York: Oxford University Press, 1988.
Levine, Larry. *Black Culture and Black Consciousness: Afro-American Folk Thought from Slavery to Freedom*. New York: Oxford University Press, 1977.
Levine, Susan. *School Lunch Politics: The Surprising History of America's Favorite Welfare Program*. Princeton: Princeton University Press, 2008.
Lewis, Anthony. "Bench Unanimous: Ruling Clears the Way for Enforcing Law on Full Scale Supreme Court." *New York Times*, December 15, 1964, 1.
———. "Justice Suspends Rights-Law Curb: Black Stays Georgia Ruling Limiting Section of Act." *New York Times*, September 24, 1964, 41.
Lewis, Courtney. "The Case of the Wild Onions: The Impact of Ramps on Cherokee Rights." *Southern Cultures* 18, no. 2 (2012): 104–17.
Lewis, Edna. *The Taste of Country Cooking*. New York: Alfred A. Knopf, 1983.
———. "What Is Southern?" *Gourmet Magazine* 68, no. 1 (January 2008): 24–30.
Lewis, Edna, and Scott Peacock. *The Gift of Southern Cooking*. New York: Alfred A. Knopf, 2003.
Lindsey, Donal F. *Indians at Hampton Institute, 1877–1923*. Urbana: University of Illinois Press, 1994.

Link, Donald, with Paula Disbrowe. *Real Cajun: Rustic Home Cooking from Donald Link's Louisiana.* New York: Clarkson Potter, 2009.

Link, William A. *The Paradox of Southern Progressivism, 1880–1930.* Chapel Hill: University of North Carolina Press, 1992.

Liptak, Adam. "Justices Void Oversight of States, Issue at Heart of Voting Rights Act." *New York Times*, June 25, 2013, A1.

Litwack, Leon F. *Been in the Storm So Long: The Aftermath of Slavery.* New York: Vintage Books, 1979.

———. *Trouble in Mind: Black Southerners in the Age of Jim Crow.* New York: Vintage Books, 1998.

"Live-at-Home." *Time Magazine*, July 7, 1930, 19–20.

Loewald, Klaus G., Beverly Starika, and Paul S. Taylor. "John Martin Bolzius Answers a Questionnaire on Carolina and Georgia: Part II." *William and Mary Quarterly* 15, no. 2 (1958): 228–52.

Loftus, Joseph A. "Johnson Is Asked to Rush Food Aid: 9 Senators Cite Mississippi Hunger and Malnutrition." *New York Times*, April 30, 1967, 51.

Long, Lucy. *Regional American Food Culture.* Santa Barbara, Calif.: Greenwood Press, 2009.

Loughborough, Mary Webster. "By a Lady." *My Cave Life in Vicksburg with Letters of Trial and Travel.* 1864; reprint, Vicksburg, Miss.: Vicksburg and Warren County Historical Society, 2003.

"Louisville and Nashville Railroad." *Railway Journal* 21 (November 1915): 15.

Lumpkin, Katharine Du Pre. *The Making of a Southerner.* 1946; reprint, Athens: University of Georgia Press, 1991.

Lundy, Ronni, ed. *Cornbread Nation 3: Foods of the Mountain South.* Chapel Hill: University of North Carolina Press, 2005.

———. *Shuck Beans, Stack Cakes, and Honest Fried Chicken: The Heart and Soul of Southern Country Kitchens.* New York: Atlantic Monthly Press, 1994.

Lustig, Lillie S., Claire Sondheim, and Sarah Rensel, eds. *The Southern Cook Book of Fine Old Recipes.* Reading, Pa.: Culinary Arts Press, 1935.

Lyford, Carrie Alberta. *A Book of Recipes for the Cooking School.* Hampton, Va.: Press of the Hampton Normal and Agricultural Institute, 1921.

Lytle, Andrew Nelson. "The Hind Tit." In *I'll Take My Stand: The South and the Agrarian Tradition*, edited by Louis D. Rubin Jr., 201–45. 1930; 75th anniversary edition, Baton Rouge: Louisiana State University Press, 2006.

"Maddox Holds Gun, Bars 3 Negroes." *Atlanta Constitution*, July 4, 1964, A1, A10.

Magee, Celia. "The Open Road Wasn't Quite Open to All." *New York Times*, August 22, 2010, C1.

Malone, Bobbie S. "Lois as Storycatcher." In *Lois Lenski: Storycatcher.* Forthcoming.

Maloney, C. J. *Back to the Land: Arthurdale, FDR's New Deal, and the Costs of Economic Planning.* Hoboken, N.J.: John Wiley, 2011.

Manring, M. M. *Slave in a Box: The Strange Career of Aunt Jemima.* Charlottesville: University of Virginia Press, 1998.

"Many Doors Open Quietly to Negroes." *Atlanta Constitution*, July 4, 1964, 2.

Marcum, Homer. "Speak Your Piece: We Don't Need a War on Poverty, Just Good Schools." *Daily Yonder*, July 22, 2007. http://www.dailyyonder.com/speak-your-piece-we-dont-need-war-poverty-just-good-schools.

Martin, Ann Smart. "Frontier Boys and Country Cousins: The Context for Choice in Eighteenth-Century Consumerism." In *Historical Archaeology and the Study of American Culture*, edited by Lu An De Cunzo and Bernard L. Herman, 78. Wilmington, Del.: Winterthur, 1997.

Martin, C. Brenden. "To Keep the Spirit of Mountain Culture Alive: Tourism and Historical Memory in the Southern Highlands." In *Where These Memories Grow: History, Memory, and Southern Identity*, edited by W. Fitzhugh Brundage, 249–69. Chapel Hill: University of North Carolina Press, 2000.

Martin, David G. *The Vicksburg Campaign: April 1862–July 1863*. Cambridge, Mass.: De Capo Press, 1990.

Martin, Josephine W., ed. *"Dear Sister": Letters Written on Hilton Head Island, 1867*. Beaufort, S.C.: Beaufort Book Company, 1977.

Martin, Thomas H. *Atlanta and Its Builders*. Vol. 2. Boston: Century Memorial, 1902.

Massey, Mary Elizabeth. *Ersatz in the Confederacy: Shortages and Substitutes on the Southern Homefront*. 1952; reprint, Columbia: University of South Carolina Press, 1993.

Matthews, Glenna. *Just a Housewife: The Rise and Fall of Domesticity in America*. New York: Oxford University Press, 1987.

Mays, Benjamin E., and Leslie W. Dunbar. Foreword to *Hunger, USA: A Report by the Citizens' Board of Inquiry into Hunger and Malnutrition in the United States*. Boston: Beacon Press, 1968.

McCandless, Amy Thompson. *The Past in the Present: Women's Higher Education in the Twentieth-Century American South*. Tuscaloosa: University of Alabama Press, 1999.

McCleary, Ann E. "'Seizing the Opportunity': Home Demonstration Curb Markets in Virginia." In *Work, Family, and Faith: Rural Southern Women in the Twentieth Century*, edited by Rebecca Sharpless and Melissa Walker, 97–134. Columbia: University of Missouri Press, 2006.

McCulloch-Williams, Martha. *Dishes and Beverages of the Old South*. New York: McBride, Nast, 1913.

McCurry, Stephanie. *Masters of Small Worlds: Yeoman Households, Gender Relations, and the Political Culture of the Antebellum South Carolina Lowcountry*. New York: Oxford University Press, 1995.

McDermott, Nancie. *Southern Cakes*. San Francisco: Chronicle Books, 2007.

———. *Southern Pies*. San Francisco: Chronicle Books, 2010.

McElya, Micki. *Clinging to Mammy: The Faithful Slave in Twentieth-Century America*. Cambridge, Mass.: Harvard University Press, 2007.

McGill, Ralph. "What's Wrong with Southern Cooking?" *Saturday Evening Post*, March 26, 1949, 38–39, 102–3, 105.

McGovern, George. Foreword to *Let Them Eat Promises: The Politics of Hunger in America*, by Nick Kotz, viii. Englewood Cliffs, N.J.: Prentice-Hall, 1969.

McGreger, April. *Sweet Potatoes: A Savor the South Cookbook*. Chapel Hill: University of North Carolina Press, 2014.

McInnis, Maurie D. *The Politics of Taste in Antebellum Charleston*. Chapel Hill: University of North Carolina Press, 2005.

———. "Raphaelle Peale's Still Life with Oranges: Status, Ritual, and the Illusion of Mastery." In *Material Culture in Anglo-America: Regional Identity and Urbanity in the Tidewater, Lowcountry, and Caribbean*, edited by David Shields, 310–27. Columbia: University of South Carolina Press, 2009.

McKay, Mary. *Old Southern Tea Room, Vicksburg, Mississippi: A Collection of Favorite Old Recipes*. Vicksburg, Miss.: Mary McKay, 1960.

McKimmon, Jane Simpson. *When We're Green We Grow*. Chapel Hill: University of North Carolina Press, 1945.

McLeod, Stephen, ed. *Dining with the Washingtons: Historic Recipes, Entertaining, and Hospitality from Mount Vernon*. Chapel Hill: University of North Carolina Press, 2011.

McMinn, Suzanne. *Chickens in the Road: An Adventure in Ordinary Splendor*. New York: HarperOne, 2013.

McPherson, James. *Abolitionist Legacy*. Princeton, N.J.: Princeton University Press, 1975.

———. *Battle Cry of Freedom: The Civil War Era*. New York: Oxford University Press, 1988.

McPherson, Tara. *Reconstructing Dixie: Race, Gender, and Nostalgia in the Imagined South*. Durham, N.C.: Duke University Press, 2003.

McRee, Patsie. *The Kitchen and the Cotton Patch*. Atlanta: Cullom and Ghertner, 1948.

McWilliams, James. *Just Food: Where Locavores Get It Wrong and How We Can Truly Eat Responsibly*. New York: Little, Brown, 2009.

———. *A Revolution in Eating: How the Quest for Food Shaped America*. New York: Columbia University Press, 2005.

Mellon, James., ed. *Bullwhip Days: The Slaves Remember, an Oral History*. New York: Grove, 2002.

Mendelson, Anne. "Cookbooks and Manuscripts, from World War I to World War II." In *The Oxford Encyclopedia of Food and Drink in America*, edited by Andrew F. Smith, 299–301. New York: Oxford University Press, 2004.

Merrens, H. Roy, ed. *The Colonial South Carolina Scene: Contemporary Views, 1697–1774*. Columbia: University of South Carolina Press, 1977.

Miller, Adrian. *Soul Food: The Surprising Story of an American Cuisine, One Plate at a Time*. Chapel Hill: University of North Carolina Press, 2013.

Miller, Bryan. "Craig Claiborne, 79, Times Food Editor and Critic, Is Dead." *New York Times*, January 24, 2000. http://www.nytimes.com/2000/01/24/nyregion/craig-claiborne-79-times-food-editor-and-critic-is-dead.html?pagewanted=all&src=pm.

Miller, Nathan. "Poverty Hearing Results in Clash: Mississippians Deny Report State Starves Negro." *Baltimore Sun*, July 12, 1967, A1.

Miller, Timothy. *The 60s Communes: Hippies and Beyond*. Syracuse, N.Y.: Syracuse University Press, 1999.

Milliken, Matthew E. "Civil Rights History Marked." *Durham Herald-Sun*, June 23, 2008.

Milliones, Peter. "Negroes in South Test Rights Act; Resistance Light: A Steak House in Virginia and a Pool in Georgia Are Integrated Peacefully." *New York Times*, July 4, 1964, 1.

Mills, Kay. *This Little Light of Mine: The Life of Fannie Lou Hamer*. Lexington: University Press of Kentucky, 2007.

Mims, Mrs. M. H., ed. *Edgefield Guest Book: A Handbook for Hostesses*. Edgefield, S.C.: Library League, D. A. Thompkins Memorial Library, Advertiser Print, 1953.

Minges, Patrick, ed. *Far More Terrible for Women: Personal Accounts of Women in Slavery*. Winston-Salem, N.C.: John F. Blair, 2006.

Minor, Wilson F. "They Ate Their Way to Freedom." *Times-Picayune New Orleans Statesman Magazine*, January 9, 1949, 8.

Mintz, Sidney W. *Tasting Food, Tasting Freedom: Excursions into Eating, Culture, and the Past.* Boston: Beacon Press, 1996.
Mintz, Sidney W., and Richard Price. *The Birth of African-American Culture: An Anthropological Perspective.* 1972; reprint, New York: Beacon Press, 1992.
Mitchell, Jerry. "The Last Days of Ben Chester White." *Jackson Clarion-Ledger,* February 23, 2003.
Mitchell, Margaret. *Gone with the Wind.* 1936; reprint, New York: Scribner, 2011.
Mitchell, William Frank. *African American Food Culture.* Westport, Conn.: Greenwood Press, 2009.
Miyuki, Kita. "Seeking Justice: The Civil Rights Movement, Black Nationalism, and Jews at Brandeis University." *Nanzan Review of American Studies* 31 (2009): 101–20.
Moncure, Blanche Elbert. *Emma Jane's Souvenir Cook Book and Some Old Virginia Recipes.* Williamsburg, Va.: Blanche Elbert Moncure, 1937.
Moody, Anne. *Coming of Age in Mississippi.* New York: Dell, 1968.
Mooney, Barbara Burlison. "The Comfortable Tasty Framed Cottage: An African American Architectural Iconography." *Journal of the Society of Architectural Historians* 61, no. 1 (2002): 48–67.
Moore, Ronnie M. *Whistling in the Wind: The Autobiography of the Rev. A. J. McKnight, S.S.Sp.* Opelousas, La.: Southern Development Foundation, 1994.
Moose, Debbie. *Buttermilk: A Savor the South Cookbook.* Chapel Hill: University of North Carolina Press, 2012.
———. *Southern Holidays: A Savor the South Cookbook.* Chapel Hill: University of North Carolina Press, 2014.
Mora, Giles, and Beverly W. Brannan. *FSA: The American Vision.* New York: Abrams, 2006.
Morgan, Edmund Sears. *Virginians at Home: Family Life in the Eighteenth Century.* Williamsburg, Va.: Colonial Williamsburg Foundation, 1952.
Morgan, Jo-Ann. "Mammy the Huckster: Selling the Old South for the New Century." *American Art* 9, no. 1 (1995): 86–109.
Morgan, Philip D. *Slave Counterpoint: Black Culture in the Eighteenth-Century Chesapeake and Lowcountry.* Chapel Hill: University of North Carolina Press, 1998.
Morris, Christopher. *Becoming Southern: The Evolution of a Way of Life, Warren County and Vicksburg, Mississippi, 1770–1860.* New York: Oxford University Press, 1995.
Morris, Robin. "Organizing Breadmakers: Kathryn Dunaway and the Georgia STOP ERA Campaign." In *Entering the Fray: Gender, Politics, and Culture in the New South,* edited by Jonathan Daniel Wells and Sheila R. Phipps, 161–83. Columbia: University of Missouri Press, 2010.
Moskin, Julia. "Can the Jewish Deli Be Reformed?" *New York Times,* April 13, 2010, D1. http://www.nytimes.com/2010/04/14/dining/14deli.html?pagewanted=all.
———. "Southern Farmers Vanquish the Cliches." *New York Times,* December 27, 2011. http://www.nytimes.com/2011/12/28/dining/southern-farmers-vanquish-the-cliches.html?pagewanted=1&_r=1&emc=eta1.
Moye, J. Todd. "Discovering What's Already There: Mississippi Women and Civil Rights Movements." In *Mississippi Women: Their Histories, Their Lives,* edited by Elizabeth Anne Payne, Martha H. Swain, and Marjorie Julian Spruill, 2:249–68. Athens: University of Georgia Press, 2010.
"Mrs. Linnie M. Blanton Obituary." *Baltimore Afro-American,* August 21, 1965, 19.

Muhlenfeld, Elisabeth Showalter. "Mary Boykin Chesnut." In *South Carolina Women: Their Lives and Times*, edited by Marjorie Julian Spruill, Valinda W. Littlefield, and Joan Marie Johnson, 233–54. Athens: University of Georgia Press, 2010.

Murray, Pauli. *Proud Shoes: The Story of an American Family*. Boston: Beacon Press, 1999.

Myers, Robert Manson. *The Children of Pride*. 1972; reprint, New Haven: Yale University Press, 1984.

Neal, Bill. *Bill Neal's Southern Cooking*. Chapel Hill: University of North Carolina Press, 1989.

———. *Biscuits, Spoonbread, and Sweet Potato Pie*. Chapel Hill: University of North Carolina Press, 2003.

Neal, Moreton. "The Birth of La Residence." *Chapel Hill Magazine*, September/October 2013, 44.

———. Foreword to *Chefs of the Triangle: Their Lives, Recipes, and Restaurants*, by Ann Prospero, ix–x. Winston-Salem, N.C.: John F. Blair, 2009.

———. *Remembering Bill Neal: Favorite Recipes from a Life in Cooking*. Chapel Hill: University of North Carolina Press, 2004.

Nelson, Davia, and Nikki Silva. "The Kitchen of a Civil Rights Hero." On *The Kitchen Sisters*, National Public Radio, July 4, 2005. http://www.npr.org/templates/story/story.php?storyId=4728761.

Nembhard, Jessica Gordon. *Collective Courage: A History of African American Cooperative Economic Thought and Practice*. University Park, Pa.: Penn State University Press, 2014.

Nestle, Marion. *Food Politics: How the Food Industry Influences Nutrition and Health*. Berkeley: University of California Press, 2002.

Neverdon-Morton, Cynthia. *Afro-American Women of the South and the Advancement of the Race, 1895–1925*. Knoxville: University of Tennessee Press, 1989.

"News from the Field." *Journal of Home Economics* 12, no. 6 (1920): 285.

Niman, Nicolette Hahn. *Righteous Pork Chop: Finding a Life and Good Food beyond Factory Farms*. New York: HarperCollins Publishers, 2009.

Noblitt, Philip T. *A Mansion in the Mountains: The Story of Moses and Bertha Cone and Their Blowing Rock Manor*. Boone, N.C.: Parkway, 1996.

Noonan, William T. "Railways Improve Agricultural Interests." *Railway Journal* 21 (1915): 4.

Norris, Michelle. "'Still Hungry in America': A Return to Mississippi." NPR, June 22, 2005. http://www.npr.org/templates/story/story.php?storyId=5495641.

Nystrom, Justin. "Segregation's Last Stand: Lester Maddox and the Transformation of Atlanta." *Atlanta History* 45 (2001): 35–51.

O'Brien, M. J. *We Shall Not Be Moved: The Jackson Woolworth's Sit-In and the Movement It Inspired*. Jackson: University Press of Mississippi, 2014.

Odum, Howard W. "New Sources of Vitality for the People." *Journal of the American Dietetic Association* 14 (1938): 417–23.

———. *Southern Regions of the United States*. Chapel Hill: University of North Carolina Press, 1936.

———. *The Way of the South: Toward the Regional Balance of America*. New York: Macmillan, 1947.

Ohles, John F. "Isabel Bevier." In *Biographical Dictionary of American Educators*. Westport, Conn.: Greenwood Press, 1978.

Olmsted, Frederick Law. "A Journey in the Seaboard Slave States." In *The Slave States*, edited by Harvey Wish, 39–125. 1856; reprint, New York: G. P. Putnam's Sons, 1959.

Olson, Lynne. *Freedom's Daughters: A Juneteenth Story*. New York: Scribner, 2001.

O'Neill, Molly, ed. *American Food Writing: An Anthology with Classic Recipes*. New York: Literary Classics of the United States, 2007.

———. *One Big Table: A Portrait of American Cooking*. New York: Simon and Schuster, 2010.

Opie, Frederick Douglass. *Hog and Hominy: Soul Food from Africa to America*. New York: Columbia University Press, 2008.

———. "Molasses-Colored Glasses: WPA and Sundry Sources on Molasses and Southern Foodways." *Southern Cultures* 14, no. 1 (2008): 81–96.

"Orah Belle Sherman, Hostess at Paschal's." *Atlanta Journal-Constitution*, January 19, 2004, 6D.

"Our Southern Highlands." Southern Highlands Issue. *House and Garden* (June 1942): 19, 24, 35, 44–49.

Ownby, Ted. *American Dreams in Mississippi: Consumers, Poverty, and Culture, 1830–1998*. Chapel Hill: University of North Carolina Press, 1999.

———. "Gladys Presley, Dorothy Dickins, and the Limits of Female Agrarianism in Twentieth-Century Mississippi." In *Mississippi Women: Their Histories, Their Lives*, edited by Elizabeth Anne Payne, Martha H. Swain, and Marjorie Julian Spruill, 2:211–33. Athens: University of Georgia Press, 2010.

———, ed. *Black and White Cultural Interaction in the Antebellum South*. Jackson: University Press of Mississippi, 1993.

Paddleford, Clementine. "Cook from New Orleans Shows Northerners 'Tricks of Trade.'" *New York Herald Tribune*, July 8, 1939, 7.

———. "Food Flashes." *Gourmet Magazine*, July 1948. http://www.gourmet.com/magazine/1940s/1948/07/paddlefordfoodflashes.

———. *The Great American Cookbook: A Revised Edition of the Classic Cookbook, How America Eats*, compiled by Kelly Alexander. New York: Rizzoli International Publications, 2011.

———. *How America Eats*. New York: Charles Scribner's Sons, 1960.

———. "Secret Dishes from Old Charleston." *Milwaukee Journal, This Week Magazine*, May 20, 1951, 10–11, 27.

Palermo, Joseph A. *Robert F. Kennedy and the Death of American Idealism*. New York: Pearson Longman, 2007.

Parker, Idella, with Mary Keating. *Idella: Marjorie Rawlings' "Perfect Maid."* Gainesville: University Press of Florida, 1992.

Parker, Karen L. "I Raised My Hand." In *27 Views of Chapel Hill: A Southern University Town in Prose and Poetry*, 179–84. Hillsborough, N.C.: Eno, 2011.

Paschal, James Vaughn, as told to Mae Armster Kendall. *Paschal: Living the Dream, an Inspirational Memoir*. New York: iUniverse, 2006.

"Paschal's Restaurant Founder Dies at 88." *Atlanta Journal-Constitution*, Dec. 3, 2008, 1C.

Percy, George. *A True Relation of the Proceedings and Occurrences of Moment Which Have Happened in Virginia from the Time Sir Thomas Gates Shipwrecked upon the Bermudes Anno 1609 until My Departure out of the Country Which Was in Anno Domini 1612*. London, 1624.

Perdue, Charles L., Jr., ed. *Pigsfoot Jelly and Persimmon Beer: Foodways from the Virginia Writers' Project*. Santa Fe: Ancient City Press, 1992.

Perdue, Charles L., Jr., Thomas E. Barden, and Robert K. Phillips, eds. *Weevils in the Wheat: Interviews with Virginia Ex-Slaves*. Charlottesville: University Press of Virginia, 1976.

Perdue, Theda. *Cherokee Women: Gender and Culture Change, 1700–1835*. Lincoln: University of Nebraska Press, 1998.

———. *Race and the Atlanta Cotton States Exposition of 1895*. Athens: University of Georgia Press, 2010.

Peterkin, Julia. *Green Thursday*. Foreword by Charles Joyner. 1924; reprint, Athens: University of Georgia Press, 1998.

Peterson, Franklynn. "Sunflowers Don't Grow in Sunflower County." *Sepia*, February 1970, 17.

Pharr, Suzanne. "From Distaff to Huckleberry Farm: Report from Arkansas." *Distaff* 1, no. 10 (1973): 4.

The Picayune's Creole Cook Book. 1900; reprint, Mineola, N.Y.: Dover, 2002.

Pinckney, Charles Cotesworth, and J. H. Easterby. "Charles Cotesworth Pinckney's Plantation Diary, April 6–December 15, 1818." *South Carolina Historical and Genealogical Magazine* 14, no. 4 (1940): 136–38.

Pinckney, Eliza Lucas. *The Letterbook of Eliza Lucas Pinckney, 1739–1762*. Edited by Elise Pinckney and Marvin R. Zahniser. Columbia: University of South Carolina Press, 1997.

Plaag, Eric W. "'There Is an Abundance of Those Which Are Genuine': Northern Travelers and Souvenirs of the Antebellum South." In *Dixie Emporium: Tourism*, edited by Anthony J. Stanonis, 24–49. Athens: University of Georgia Press, 2008.

Platt, June. "Good Old Southern Dishes." *House and Garden* 72, no. 5 (1937): 82–83.

———. "Recipes of the Lowcountry." *House and Garden* 75 (March 1939): 48, 81, 89.

"Police Jail 13 Rights Aides." *Washington Post*, October 25, 1964, A3.

Pollan, Michael. *Cooked: A Natural History of Transformation*. New York: Penguin, 2013.

———. *In Defense of Food: An Eater's Manifesto*. New York: Penguin, 2008.

———. *The Omnivore's Dilemma: A Natural History of Four Meals*. New York: Penguin, 2006.

Popkin, Barry. *The World Is Fat*. New York: Penguin, 2010.

Post, Isabelle. "Dyspepsia in Dixie: The Truth about Southern Cookery." *American Mercury*, January 1939, 30–34.

Powdermaker, Hortense. *After Freedom: A Cultural Study in the Deep South*. New York: Viking, 1939.

Powell, Lawrence N. *The Accidental City: Improvising New Orleans*. Cambridge, Mass.: Harvard University Press, 2012.

———. "Lyle Saxon and the WPA Guide to New Orleans." *Southern Spaces*, July 20, 2009. http://www.southernspaces.org/2009/lyle-saxon-and-wpa-guide-new-orleans.

Prenshaw, Peggy Whitman, ed. Special issue, "The Texts of Southern Food." *Southern Quarterly* 30, nos. 2–3 (1992).

Pretlow, Mary D. *Old Southern Receipts*. New York: Robert M. McBride, 1930.

Probyn, Elsbeth. *Carnal Appetites: FoodSexIdentities*. New York: Routledge, 2000.

Prucha, Paul. "Protest by Petition: Jeremiah Evarts and the Cherokee Indians." *Proceedings of the Massachusetts Historical Society*, 3d ser., 97 (1985): 42–58.

Pryor, Sara Agnes Rice. *Reminiscences of Peace and War.* New York: Macmillan, 1905.
"Public History Project Chronicles Life at Moses Cone Estate." *High Country Press,* December 22, 2011. http://www.highcountrypress.com/weekly/2011/12-22-11/public-history-project-chronicles.html.
Purvis, Kathleen. *Bourbon: A Savor the South Cookbook.* Chapel Hill: University of North Carolina Press, 2013.
———. *Pecans: A Savor the South Cookbook.* Chapel Hill: University of North Carolina Press, 2012.
Quatrano, Anne Stiles. *Summerland: Recipes for Celebrating with Southern Hospitality.* New York: Rizzoli, 2013.
The Rambler, or, A tour through Virginia, Tennessee, Alabama, Mississippi, and Louisiana; Describing the Climate, the Manners, Customs, and Religion, of the Inhabitants, Interspersed with Geographical and Political Sketches, by a Citizen of Maryland. Annapolis: J. Green, 1828.
Randolph, Mary. *The Virginia House-Wife.* 1824; reprint, with Historical Notes and Commentaries by Karen Hess, Columbia: University of South Carolina Press, 1984.
Raper, Arthur F. "Good Gardens and 'Precious' Cookers." In *Tenants of the Almighty,* by Arthur F. Raper, 233–38. New York: Macmillan, 1943.
Ratliff, Bob. "Dorothy Dickins: Nutrition Pioneer." *Mississippi Landmarks* 1, no. 2 (2005). http://www.dafvm.msstate.edu/landmarks/05/spring/14_15.pdf.
Rawick, George P., ed. *The American Slave: Georgia Narratives: Part 2.* Ser. 1, vol. 4. Westport, Conn.: Greenwood Press, 1978.
———. *The American Slave: Texas Narratives: Part 9.* Ser. 2, vol. 10. Westport, Conn.: Greenwood Press, 1979.
Reed, John Shelton. *Dixie Bohemia: A French Quarter Circle in the 1920s.* Baton Rouge: Louisiana State University Press, 2012.
Reed, John Shelton, and Dale Volberg Reed. *Holy Smoke: The Big Book of North Carolina Barbecue.* Chapel Hill: University of North Carolina Press, 2008.
———, eds. *Cornbread Nation 4: The Best of Southern Food Writing.* Athens: University of Georgia Press, 2008.
Reed, John Shelton, and Daniel Joseph Singal, eds. *Regionalism and the South: Selected Papers of Rupert Vance.* Chapel Hill: University of North Carolina Press, 1982.
Reichl, Ruth. "Pride of the South." Letter from the editor, *Gourmet Magazine,* January 2008, 18.
Reusing, Andrea. *Cooking in the Moment: A Year of Seasonal Recipes.* New York: Clarkson Potter, 2011.
Richard, Lena. *New Orleans Cook Book.* 1940; reprint, Gretna, La.: Pelican, 1998.
Rieff, Lynn. "Revitalizing Southern Homes: Rural Women, the Professionalization of Home Demonstration Work, and the Limits of Reform, 1917–1945." In *Work, Family, and Faith: Rural Southern Women in the Twentieth Century,* edited by Rebecca Sharpless and Melissa Walker, 134–65. Columbia: University of Missouri Press, 2006.
"Rights Act Tested in N. Carolina." *New York Amsterdam News,* November 21, 1964, 24.
Risen, Clay. *The Bill of the Century: The Epic Battle for the Civil Rights Act.* New York: Bloomsbury Press, 2014.

Roahen, Sara. *Gumbo Tales: Finding My Place at the New Orleans Table*. New York: W. W. Norton, 2008.
Roahen, Sara, and John T. Edge, eds. *The Southern Foodways Alliance Community Cookbook*. Athens: University of Georgia Press, 2010.
Robbins, Gerald. "Rossa B. Cooley and Penn School: Social Dynamo in a Negro Rural Subculture, 1901–1930." *Journal of Negro Education* 33, no. 1 (1964): 43–51.
Roberts, Blain. *Pageants, Parlors, and Pretty Women: Race and Beauty in the Twentieth-Century South*. Chapel Hill: University of North Carolina Press, 2014.
Robertson, Ben. *Red Hills and Cotton: An Upcountry Memory*. 1942; reprint, Columbia: University of South Carolina Press, 1991.
Robison, Sallie Ann, with Gregory Wrenn Smith. *Gullah Home Cooking the Daufuskie Way*. Chapel Hill: University of North Carolina Press, 2003.
Romines, Ann. *The Home Plot: Women, Writing, and Domestic Ritual*. Amherst: University of Massachusetts Press, 1992.
———. "Reading the Cakes: Delta Wedding and Texts of Southern Women's Culture." *Mississippi Quarterly* 50 (Fall 1977): 608–11.
Rose, Willie Lee. *Rehearsal for Reconstruction: The Port Royal Experiment*. Athens: University of Georgia Press, 1964.
Rosengarten, Dale. "Missions and Markets: Sea Island Basketry and the Sweetgrass Revolution." In *Grass Roots: African Origins of an American Art*, edited by Dale Rosengarten, Theodore Rosengarten, and Endi Schildkrout, 128–45. New York: Museum for African Art, 2008.
Rosengarten, Theodore. *Tombee: Portrait of a Cotton Planter with the Journal of Thomas B. Chaplin (1822–1890)*. New York: McGraw-Hill, 1987.
Rubin, Miriam. *Tomatoes: A Savor the South Cookbook*. Chapel Hill: University of North Carolina Press, 2013.
Rugaber, Walter. "In the Delta, Poverty Is a Way of Life: The Delta: Hunger and Unemployment Stalk Rural Negroes." *New York Times*, July 31, 1967, 1.
Russell, Malinda. *A Domestic Cook Book: Containing a Careful Selection of Useful Receipts for the Kitchen*. 1866; reprint, Ann Arbor, Mich.: William L. Clements Library, 2007.
Rutledge, Sarah. *The Carolina Housewife: A Facsimile of the 1847 Edition, with an Introduction and a Preliminary Checklist of South Carolina Cookbooks Published before 1935, by Anna Wells Rutledge*. Columbia: University of South Carolina Press, 1979.
St. George, Robert Blair, ed. *Material Life in America, 1600–1860*. Boston: Northeastern University Press, 1988.
Sanders, Dori. *Dori Sanders' Country Cooking: Recipes and Stories from the Family Farm Stand*. Chapel Hill: Algonquin Books, 1995.
Sanders, Lynn Moss. *Howard W. Odum's Folklore Odyssey: Transformation to Tolerance through African American Folk Studies*. Athens: University of Georgia Press, 2003.
Sauceman, Fred W., ed. *Cornbread Nation 5: The Best of Southern Food Writing*. Athens: University of Georgia Press, 2010.
Saxon, Lyle, and Edward P. Dreyer, eds. *The WPA Guide to New Orleans*. 1938; reprint, New York: Pantheon, 1983.
Schmitt, Edward R. *President of the Other America: Robert Kennedy and the Politics of Poverty*. Amherst: University of Massachusetts Press, 2010.

Schulz, Constance B. *The Digital Editions of Eliza Lucas Pinckney and Harriott Pinckney Horry, 1739–1830*. Center for Digital Humanities, University of South Carolina, 2010. http://src6.cas.sc.edu/poelp/.

———. "Eliza Lucas Pinckney and Harriott Pinckney Horry: A South Carolina Revolutionary-Era Mother and Daughter." In *Carolina Women: Their Lives and Times*, vol. 1, edited by Marjorie Julian Spruill, Valinda W. Littlefield, and Joan Marie Johnson, 79–108. Athens: University of Georgia Press, 2009.

Scott, Anne Firor. "The Ever Widening Circle: The Diffusion of Feminist Values from the Troy Female Seminary, 1822–1872." *History of Education Quarterly* 19, no. 1 (Spring 1979): 3–25.

———. *Making the Invisible Woman Visible*. Urbana: University of Illinois Press, 1984.

———. *The Southern Lady: From Pedestal to Politics, 1830–1930*. Chicago: University of Chicago Press, 1970.

Scott, John A. *Journal of a Residence on a Georgian Plantation in 1838–1839: Frances Anne Kemble*. Athens: University of Georgia Press, 1984.

Scott, Natalie V. *200 Years of New Orleans Cooking*. New York: J. Cape and H. Smith, 1931.

Scott, Natalie V., and Caroline Merrick Jones. *Gourmet's Guide to New Orleans*. New Orleans: Scott and Jones, 1955.

Scott, Roy V. *Eugene Beverly Ferris and Agricultural Science in the Lower South*. Oxford: Center for the Study of Southern Culture, University of Mississippi, 1991.

Seiler, Cotton. *Republic of Drivers: A Cultural History of Automobility in America*. Chicago: University of Chicago Press, 2008.

Severo, Richard. "Lester Maddox, Whites-Only Restaurateur and Georgia Governor, Dies at 87." *New York Times*, June 25, 2003. http://www.nytimes.com/2003/06/25/obituaries/25CND-MADD.html?pagewanted=all.

Severson, Kim. "Blood and Water." In *Cornbread Nation 6: The Best of Southern Food Writing*, edited by Brett Anderson. Athens: University of Georgia Press, 2012.

———. "Sorghum Speaks with a Sweet Drawl." *New York Times*, December 27, 2011, D9.

———. *Spoon Fed: How Eight Cooks Saved My Life*. New York: Riverhead Books, 2010.

Shapiro, Henry D. *Appalachia on Our Mind: The Southern Mountains and Mountaineers in the American Consciousness, 1870–1920*. Chapel Hill: University of North Carolina Press, 1978.

Shapiro, Laura. *Perfection Salad: Women and Cooking at the Turn of the Century*. New York: Modern Library, 2001.

Shapiro, Rabbi Merrill. "St. Augustine to Commemorate Rabbis' Civil Rights Role." *The Rambler: Southern Jewish Historical Society Newsletter* 18, no. 1 (Winter 2014): 7.

Sharpless, Rebecca. *Cooking in Other Women's Kitchens: Domestic Workers in the South, 1865–1960*. Chapel Hill: University of North Carolina Press, 2010.

———. "Neither Friends nor Peers: Idella Parker, Marjorie Kinnan Rawlings, and the Limits of Gender Solidarity at Cross Creek." *Journal of Southern History* 78, no. 2 (2012): 327–60.

———. "'She Ought to Have Taken Those Cakes': Southern Women and Rural Food Supplies." *Southern Cultures* 18, no. 2 (2012): 45–58.

Sharpless, Rebecca, and Melissa Walker, eds. *Work, Family, and Faith: Rural Southern Women in the Twentieth Century*. Columbia: University of Missouri Press, 2006.

Shields, David S. *American Heritage Vegetables: Growing and Cooking pre-1900 American Garden Vegetables*, Center for Digital Humanities, University of South Carolina. http://lichen.csd.sc.edu/vegetable/index.php.

———. "Charleston Gold: A Direct Descendant of Carolina Gold." *The Rice Paper*, February 2011, Carolina Gold Rice Foundation. http://www.carolinagoldrice foundation.org/papers/ricepaper.5.1.2011.pdf.

———. "Prospecting for Oil." In *The Larder: Food Studies Methods from the American South*, edited by John T. Edge, Elizabeth Engelhardt, and Ted Ownby, 56–75. Athens: University of Georgia Press, 2013.

———. *Southern Provisions: The Creation and Revival of a Cuisine*. Chicago: University of Chicago Press, forthcoming 2015.

———, ed. *Material Culture in Anglo-America: Regional Identity and Urbanity in the Tidewater, Lowcountry, and Caribbean*. Columbia: University of South Carolina Press, 2009.

Shipp, Bill. "U.S. Responding Well to Rights Law, Says a Pleased President: Georgians Following Through." *Atlanta Constitution*, July 4, 1964.

Short, Bob. *Everything Is Pickrick: The Life of Lester Maddox*. Macon, Ga.: Mercer University Press, 1999.

Shurtleff, William, and Akiko Aoyagi. *History of Erewhon: Natural Food Pioneer in the United States, 1966–2011*. Lafayette, Calif.: Soyinfo Center, 2011.

Sifton, Sam. "Is There Life after 30?" *New York Times Magazine*, October 20, 2013, MM72.

———. "Sweet Home Cooking Alabama." *New York Times*, October 18, 2013. http://www.nytimes.com/2013/10/20/magazine/sweet-home-cooking-alabama .html.

Silva, Nikki, and Davia Nelson. *Hidden Kitchens*. Emmaus, Pa.: Rodale, 2005.

Silver, Ward, and Mike Grossman. "Comment: Food Day." *Great Speckled Bird* 8, no. 16 (April 17, 1975): 1, backpage.

Sims, Elizabeth, with Chef Brian Sonoskus. *Tupelo Honey Café: New Southern Flavors from the Blue Ridge Mountains*. Kansas City, Mo.: Andrews McMeel Publishing, 2014.

———. *Tupelo Honey Café: Spirited Recipes from Asheville's New South Kitchen*. Kansas City, Mo.: Andrews McMeel Publishing, 2011.

Smart-Grosvenor, Vertamae. *Vibration Cooking or the Travel Notes of a Geechee Girl*. New York: Ballantine Books, 1970.

Smedes, Susan Dabney. *Memorials of a Southern Planter*. Baltimore: Cushings and Bailey, 1888.

Smith, Andrew F. *Eating History: 30 Turning Points in the Making of American Cuisine*. New York: Columbia University Press, 2009.

———. *Peanuts: The Illustrious History of the Goober Pea*. Urbana: University of Illinois Press, 2002.

———. *Starving the South: How the North Won the Civil War*. New York: St. Martin's, 2011.

Smith, Bill. "The Cooks Who Giggle." *Gravy: A Food Newsletter from the Southern Foodways Alliance* 36 (2010): 2–4.

———. *Seasoned in the South: Recipes from Crook's Corner and from Home*. Chapel Hill: Algonquin Books, 2005.

Smith, Bruce D., with contributions by C. Wesley Cowan and Michael P. Hoffman. *Rivers of Change: Essays on Early Agriculture in Eastern North America.* Tuscaloosa: University of Alabama Press, 1992.
Smith, Fred C. *Trouble in Goshen: Plain Folk, Roosevelt, Jesus, and Marx in the Great Depression South*. Jackson: University Press of Mississippi, 2014.
Smith, John. *The Generall Historie of Virginia, New England, and the Summer Isles*. London, 1624; reprint, Chapel Hill: University Library, University of North Carolina, 2006.
Smith, Shawn Michelle. "Spectacles of Whiteness." In *Photography on the Color Line: W. E. B. Du Bois, Race, and Visual Culture*, 113–45. Durham, N.C.: Duke University Press, 2004.
Sohn, Mark. "Sorghum." In *The New Encyclopedia of Southern Culture: Foodways*, edited by John T. Edge, 263–64. Chapel Hill: University of North Carolina Press, 2007.
Sokol, Jason. *There Goes My Everything: White Southerners in the Age of Civil Rights, 1945–1975*. New York: Vintage Books, 2006.
Southall, Ashley. "Senate Approves Payment of Black Farmers' Claims." *New York Times*, November 19, 2010, A12.
"Southerners Gloomily Agree Segregation Is Lost Cause." *Chicago Daily Defender*, December 16, 1964, 12.
"South from Williamsburg." *House and Garden* 72, no. 5 (1937).
Sparks, Elizabeth Hedgecock. *North Carolina and Old Salem Cookery*. Kingsport, Tenn.: Kingsport Press, 1955.
Spirn, Anne Whiston. *Daring to Look: Dorothea Lange's Photographs and Reports from the Field.* Chicago: University of Chicago Press, 2008.
Spruill, Julia Cherry. *Women's Life and Work in the Southern Colonies.* Introduction by Anne Firor Scott. 1938; reprint, New York: W. W. Norton, 1998.
Spruill, Marjorie Julian, Valinda W. Littlefield, and Joan Marie Johnson, eds. *South Carolina Women: Their Lives and Times*. Vol. 2. Athens: University of Georgia Press, 2010.
Stanonis, Anthony J. *Creating the Big Easy: New Orleans and the Emergence of Modern Tourism, 1918–1945*. Athens: University of Georgia Press, 2006.
———, ed. *Dixie Emporium: Tourism, Foodways, and Consumer Culture in the American South*. Athens: University of Georgia Press, 2008.
Staples, Brent. "John Hope Franklin." *New York Times*, Opinion Pages, March 29, 2009, A28.
Stark, Betsy, and Lewis Kilgore. "Dorothy Dickins and Home Economics Research at Mississippi State University." Mississippi State: Mississippi Agricultural and Forestry Station, 1974.
Starnes, Richard D. *Creating the Land of the Sky: Tourism and Society in Western North Carolina.* Tuscaloosa: University of Alabama Press, 2005.
———. "Tourism, Landscape, and History in the Great Smoky Mountains National Park." In *Destination Dixie: Tourism and Southern History*, edited by Karen L. Cox, 267–84. Gainesville: University Press of Florida, 2012.
Starr, Frederick. Foreword to *New Orleans Cuisine: Fourteen Signature Dishes and Their Histories*, edited by Susan Tucker, ix. Jackson: University Press of Mississippi, 2009.
———, ed. *Inventing New Orleans: Writings of Lafcadio Hearn*. Jackson: University Press of Mississippi, 2001.
Steingarten, Jeffrey. "Fresh Prince." *Vogue*, July 2012, 114.

Steponaitis, Vincas P. *The Natchez District in the Old, Old South*. Chapel Hill: Research Laboratories of Archaeology, 1998.

Stern, Julia A. *Mary Chesnut's Civil War Epic*. Chicago: University of Chicago Press, 2010.

Stieff, Frederick Phillip. *Eat, Drink, and Be Merry in Maryland: An Anthology from a Great Tradition*. New York: G. P. Putnam's, 1932.

Stitt, Frank. *Frank Stitt's Southern Table: Recipes and Gracious Traditions from Highlands Bar and Grill*. New York: Artisan, 2004.

Stockett, Kathryn. *The Help*. New York: G. P. Putnam's, 2009.

Stoddart, Jess. *Challenge and Change in Appalachia: The Story of Hindman Settlement School*. Lexington: University Press of Kentucky, 2002.

———, ed. *The Quare Women's Journals: May Stone and Katherine Pettit's Summers in the Kentucky Mountains and the Founding of the Hindman Settlement School*. Ashland, Ky.: Jesse Stuart Foundation, 1997.

Streater, Kristin L. "'She-Rebels' on the Supply Line: Gender Conventions in Civil War Kentucky." In *Occupied Women: Gender, Military Occupation, and the American Civil War*, edited by LeeAnn Whites and Alecia P. Long, 88–102. Baton Rouge: Louisiana State University Press, 2009.

Stryker, Roy Emerson, and Nancy Wood. *In This Proud Land: America, 1935–1943, as Seen in the FSA Photographs*. New York: Galahad Books, 1973.

"Students Aid Hungry South." *Vassar Miscellany News* 48 (February 19, 1964): 1.

Swanson, Drew. *Remaking Wormsloe Plantation: The Environmental History of a Lowcountry Landscape*. Athens: University of Georgia Press, 2012.

Tartan, Beth. "Cookbooks." In *The New Encyclopedia of Southern Culture: Foodways*, edited by John T. Edge, 41–45. Chapel Hill: University of North Carolina Press, 2007.

Tavernise, Sabrina. "Obesity Rate for Young Children Plummets 43% in a Decade." *New York Times*, February 25, 2014, A1.

Taylor, Joe Gray. *Eating, Drinking, and Visiting in the South: An Informal History*. 1982; reprint, Baton Rouge: Louisiana State University Press, 2008.

Taylor, Joe Gray, and John T. Edge. "Southern Food." In *The New Encyclopedia of Southern Culture: Foodways*, edited by John T. Edge, 1–14. Chapel Hill: University of North Carolina Press, 2007.

Taylor, John Martin. *Hoppin' John's Lowcountry Cooking: Recipes and Ruminations from Charleston and the Carolina Coastal Plain*. 1992; reprint, Chapel Hill: University of North Carolina Press, 2012.

Terrill, Tom E., and Jerrold Hirsch, eds. *Such as Us: Southern Voices of the Thirties*. Chapel Hill: University of North Carolina Press, 1978.

Theophano, Janet. *Eat My Words: Reading Women's Lives through the Cookbooks They Wrote*. New York: Palgrave, 2002.

Thompson, Charles D., Jr. *Spirits of Just Men: Mountaineers, Liquor Bosses, and Lawmen in the Moonshine Capital of the World*. Urbana: University of Illinois Press, 2011.

Thompson, Charles L. "Standing Up by Sitting Down." In *27 Views of Chapel Hill: A Southern University Town in Prose and Poetry*, 170–78. Hillsborough, N.C.: Eno, 2011.

Thompson, Evan. *Robert Kennedy: His Life*. New York: Simon and Schuster, 2000.

Thompson, Holland. *From the Cotton Field to the Cotton Mill: A Study of the Industrial Transition in North Carolina*. Freeport, N.Y.: Books for Libraries Press, 1906.

———. *The New South: A Chronicle of Social and Industrial Evolution.* New Haven: Yale University Press, 1919.
Tillery, Carolyn Quick. *A Taste of Freedom: A Cookbook with Recipes and Remembrances from the Hampton Institute.* New York: Kensington, 2002.
Tindall, George. *The Emergence of the New South, 1913–1945.* Baton Rouge: Louisiana State University Press, 1967.
———. "The Significance of Howard W. Odum to Southern History: A Preliminary Estimate." *Journal of Southern History* 24, no. 3 (1958): 285–307.
Tipton-Martin, Toni. "Bluegrass and Black Magic." Introduction to *The Blue Grass Cook Book*, by Minnie C. Fox, v–xxxiii. 1904; reprint, Louisville: University Press of Kentucky, 2005.
———. *The Jemima Code.* Austin: University of Texas Press, forthcoming 2015.
Titus, Mary. "'Groaning Tables' and 'Spit in the Kettles': Food and Race in the Nineteenth-Century South." Special issue, "The Texts of Southern Food," edited by Peggy Whitman Prenshaw. *Southern Quarterly* 30, nos. 2–3 (1992): 13–21.
Tolbert, Lisa C. "The Aristocracy of the Market Basket: Self-Service Food Shopping in the New South." In *Food Chains: From Farmyard to Shopping Cart*, edited by Warren Belasco and Roger Horowitz, 179–95. Philadelphia: University of Pennsylvania Press, 2009.
———. "Doggeries, Jungles, and Piggly Wigglies: Southerners and the Social Landscape of Food Shopping, 1840–1940." http://www.uncg.edu/his/docs/tolbert-index.html.
Tompkins, Kyla Wazana. *Racial Indigestion: Eating Bodies in the 19th Century.* New York: New York University Press, 2012.
Toten, John R. *Thacher-Thatcher Genealogy.* New York: New York Genealogical and Biographical Society, 1910.
Towns, Gail H. "A Piece of History: Clark Atlanta University Buys Historic Paschal's Hotel-Restaurant." *Diverse Issues in Higher Education*, June 17, 2007. http://diverseeducation.com/article/7538/.
Trillin, Calvin. *Feeding a Yen: Savoring Local Specialties, from Kansas City to Cuzco.* New York: Random House, 2003.
Tucker, Susan. *Telling Memories among Southern Women: Domestic Workers and Their Employers in the Segregated South.* Baton Rouge: Louisiana State University Press, 2002.
———, ed. *New Orleans Cuisine: Fourteen Signature Dishes and Their Histories.* Jackson: University Press of Mississippi, 2009.
Tullos, Allen. *Habits of Industry: White Culture and the Transformation of the Carolina Piedmont.* Chapel Hill: University of North Carolina Press, 1989.
Turner, Jeffrey A. *Sitting In and Speaking Out: Student Movements in the American South, 1960–1970.* Athens: University of Georgia Press, 2010.
Turner, Katherine Leonard. *How the Other Half Ate: A History of Working-Class Meals at the Turn of the Century.* Berkeley: University of California Press, 2014.
Turner, Patricia A. *Ceramic Uncles and Celluloid Mammies: Black Images and Their Influence on Culture.* Charlottesville: University of Virginia Press, 2002.
Turner, Sarah E. McNulty. "Hop's Bar-B-Q: A Window on to Southern History and Culture." Honor's thesis, University of North Carolina at Chapel Hill, 2008.
Tyree, Marion Cabell. *Housekeeping in Old Virginia.* Louisville, Ky.: John P. Morton, 1879.
Tyson, Timothy. *Blood Done Sign My Name: A True Story.* New York: Broadway, 2005.

Upton, Dell. "White and Black Landscapes in Eighteenth-Century Virginia." In *Material Life in America, 1600–1860*, edited by Robert Blair St. George, 357–69. Boston: Northeastern University Press, 1988.

"U.S. Court Limits Rights Act Clause: Upsets Discrimination Ban on Restaurants Not in Interstate Commerce." *New York Times*, September 18, 1964, 1.

U.S. Senate. Subcommittee of the Committee on Agriculture and Forestry. *Hearings on Food Stamp Appropriations Authorization*. Washington, D.C.: Government Printing Office, 1967.

Valentine, Vikki. "Q & A: The Causes behind Hunger in America." "Hunger in America" Series, NPR, November 22, 2005. http://www.npr.org/2005/11/22/5021812/q-a-the-causes-behind-hunger-in-america.

van Beuren, Alexe, and Dixie Grimes. *The B.T.C. Old-Fashioned Grocery Cookbook: Recipes and Stories from a Southern Revival*. New York: Clarkson Potter, 2014.

Vance, Rupert B. "Cotton Culture and Social Life and Institutions of the South." In *Regionalism and the South: Selected Papers of Rupert Vance*, edited by John Shelton Reed and Daniel Joseph Singal, 19–27. Chapel Hill: University of North Carolina Press, 1982.

———. *Human Factors in Cotton Culture: A Study in the Social Geography of the American South*. Chapel Hill: University of North Carolina Press, 1929.

———. *Human Geography of the South: A Study in Regional Resources and Human Adequacy*. Chapel Hill: University of North Carolina Press, 1932.

Vaughn, Kate Brew. *Culinary Echoes from Dixie*. Cincinnati: McDonald, 1914.

Veit, Helen Zoe. *Modern Food, Moral Food: Self-Control, Science, and the Rise of Modern American Eating in the Early Twentieth Century*. Chapel Hill: University of North Carolina Press, 2013.

———, ed. *Food in the Civil War Era: The North*. East Lansing: Michigan State University Press, 2014.

Vella, Christina. "Dorothy Dix." In *Louisiana Women: Their Lives and Times*, edited by Janet Allured and Judith F. Gentry, 195–214. Athens: University of Georgia Press, 2009.

Veteto, James R., and Edward M. Maclin, eds. *The Slaw and the Slow Cooked: Culture and Barbecue in the Mid-South*. Nashville: Vanderbilt University Press, 2011.

Vlach, John M. *Back of the Big House: The Architecture of Plantation Slavery*. Chapel Hill: University of North Carolina Press, 1993.

———. *By the Work of Their Hands: Studies in Afro-American Folklife*. Charlottesville: University of Virginia Press, 1991.

Waddington, Chris. "Parades, Bars, Bantering Locals, and a Life of Scholarship Shaped Lawrence Powell's Acclaimed New Orleans History." *New Orleans Times-Picayune*, April 15, 2012. http://www.nola.com/books/index.ssf/2012/04/parades_bars_bantering_locals.html.

Wade, Nicholas. "Girl's Bones Bear Sign of Cannibalism by Starving Virginia Colonists." *New York Times*, May 1, 2013, A11.

Walker, Daisy B. *Good Things to Eat at Tapoco Lodge*. Tapoco, N.C.: Tapoco Lodge, 1937.

Walker, Judy. "Local Historian Digs Up Long-Lost Info on *The Picayune's Creole Cook Book*." *New Orleans Times-Picayune*, October 20, 2011. http://blog.nola.com/food_impact/print.html?entry=/2011/10/local_historian_digs_up_long-l.html.

Walker, Melissa. *All We Knew Was to Farm: Rural Women in the Upcountry South, 1919–1941*. Baltimore: Johns Hopkins University Press, 2000.
Wallace, Emily. "Eugenia Duke Made Her Name Selling Sandwiches, Not Mayonnaise." Paper presented at the symposium of the Southern Foodways Alliance, Oxford, Miss., October 4–6, 2013.
———. "It Was There for Work: Pimento Cheese in the Carolina Piedmont." Master's thesis, University of North Carolina at Chapel Hill, 2010.
———. "Pimento Cheese in the North Carolina Piedmont: From Home to Work and Back Again." *Gravy* 39 (2011): 13–16.
Wallace-Sanders, Kimberly. *Mammy: A Century of Race, Gender, and Southern Memory*. Ann Arbor: University of Michigan Press, 2008.
———. "Southern Memory, Southern Monuments, and the Subversive Black Mammy." *Southern Spaces*, June 15, 2009. http://www.southernspaces.org/2009/southern-memory-southern-monuments-and-subversive-black-mammy.
Wallach, Jennifer Jensen. *How America Eats: A Social History of U.S. Food and Culture*. New York: Rowman & Littlefield, 2013.
Walter, Eugene. *The Happy Table of Eugene Walter: Southern Spirits in Food and Drink*. Edited by Donald Goodman and Thomas Head. Chapel Hill: University of North Carolina Press, 2011.
———. "The Southland I Remember." In *American Cooking: Southern Style*, 8–19. New York: Time-Life Books, 1971.
Warner, Ann Bradford. "Harriet Jacobs's Modest Proposals: Revising Southern Hospitality." Special issue, "The Texts of Southern Food," edited by Peggy Whitman Prenshaw. *Southern Quarterly* 30, nos. 2–3 (1992): 22–28.
Warnes, Andrew. *Savage Barbecue: Race, Culture, and the Invention of America's First Food*. Athens: University of Georgia Press, 2008.
Warren, Reverend Ebenezer. Introduction to *Mrs. Hill's Southern Practical Cookery and Receipt Book*, by Annabella P. Hill. Facsimile of *Mrs. Hill's New Southern Cook Book*, 1872, with Damon L. Fowler. Columbia: University of South Carolina Press, 1995.
Washington, Booker T. *Up from Slavery: An Autobiography*. 1901; facsimile of the first edition, with an introduction by William L. Andrews, New York: Oxford University Press, 2000.
Waters, Alice. Foreword to *The Taste of Country Cooking*, by Edna Lewis, xi–xiii. 30th Anniversary Edition. New York: Alfred A. Knopf, 2006.
Watson, Harry L. "Front Porch." Special issue, "*The Help*," *Southern Cultures* 20, no. 1 (Spring 2014): 1–6.
Webb, Clive. *Fight against Fear: Southern Jews and Black Civil Rights*. Athens: University of Georgia Press, 2001.
Weigl, Andrea. "From Two Chefs, Many." *Raleigh News and Observer*, April 28, 2010. http://www.newsobserver.com/2010/04/28/456362/from-two-chefs-many.html.
———. *Pickles and Preserves: A Savor the South Cookbook*. Chapel Hill: University of North Carolina Press, 2014.
"Welcome to Old Virginia." Virginia Conservation Commission, Richmond. Advertisement in *House and Garden* 72, no. 5 (November 1937): 32E.
Welty, Eudora. "Mississippi Food." In *The Food of a Younger Land*, edited by Mark Kurlansky, 101–9. New York: Riverhead Books, 2009.
Whayne, Jeannie. *Delta Empire: Lee Wilson and the Transformation of*

Agriculture in the New South. Baton Rouge: Louisiana State University Press, 2011.

———. *A New Plantation South: Land, Labor, and Federal Favor in Twentieth-Century Arkansas*. Charlottesville: University of Virginia Press, 1996.

Whayne, Jeannie, and Willard B. Gatewood, eds. *The Arkansas Delta: Land of Paradox*. Fayetteville: University of Arkansas Press, 1993.

Whisnant, Anne Mitchell. *Super-Scenic Motorway: A Blue Ridge Parkway History*. Chapel Hill: University of North Carolina Press, 2006.

Whisnant, David E. *All That Is Native and Fine: The Politics of Culture in an American Region*. Chapel Hill: University of North Carolina Press, 1983.

White, Deborah Gray. *Ar'n't I a Woman: Female Slaves in the Plantation South*. 1985; reprint, New York: W. W. Norton, 1999.

White, Robert. "Travel Writing." In *The New Encyclopedia of Southern Culture: Literature*, edited by M. Thomas Inge, 159–62. Chapel Hill: University of North Carolina Press, 2008.

Whitehouse, Anne. "Memorial to an Uncivil Era: A Personal Journey to Alabama's New Birmingham Civil Rights Institute." *Los Angeles Times*, April 11, 1993, 3.

Whites, LeeAnn, and Alecia P. Long, eds. *Occupied Women: Gender, Military Occupation, and the American Civil War*. Baton Rouge: Louisiana State University Press, 2009.

Whitfield, Stephen J. "Is It True What They Sing about Dixie?" *Southern Cultures* 8, no. 2 (2002): 9–37.

Whiting, Sam. "Carol Ruth Silver: Freedom Rider 50 Years Later." *San Francisco Chronicle*, April 14, 2011. http://www.sfgate.com/cgi-bin/article.cgi?f=/c/a/2011/04/13/DDHA1IENJF.DTL.

Wilcox, Estelle Woods. *The Dixie Cook-Book*. Atlanta: L. A. Clarkson, 1885.

Wiley, Peter. "The Politics of Food: The Terrible Ten." In *Great Speckled Bird* 8, no. 16 (April 17, 1975): 8–9.

Wilkerson, Isabel. *The Warmth of Other Suns: The Epic Story of America's Great Migration*. New York: Vintage, 2011.

Willard, Pat. *America Eats: On the Road with the WPA*. New York: Bloomsbury USA, 2008.

Williams, Ben Ames, ed. *A Diary from Dixie, Mary Boykin Chestnut*. Cambridge, Mass.: Harvard University Press, 1980.

Williams-Forson, Psyche. *Building Houses Out of Chicken Legs: Black Women, Food, and Power*. Chapel Hill: University of North Carolina Press, 2006.

Williamson, Joel. *The Crucible of Race: Black-White Relations in the American South since Emancipation*. New York: Oxford University Press, 1984.

Willigen, John Van, and Anne Van Willigen. *Food and Everyday Life on Kentucky Family Farms, 1920–1950*. Lexington: University Press of Kentucky, 2006.

Willis, Alfred. "Williamsburg." In *The Grove Encyclopedia of American Art*. Vol. 1. Edited by Joan Marter. New York: Oxford University Press, 2011.

Willis, Virginia. *Basic to Brilliant, Y'all: 150 Refined Southern Recipes and Ways to Dress Them Up for Company*. Berkeley, Calif.: Ten Speed Press, 2011.

———. *Okra: A Savor the South Cookbook*. Chapel Hill: University of North Carolina Press, 2014.

"Will Marry in London: Miss Stiles to Wed L. C. Wellington, Attaché of American Embassy." *New York Times*, December 31, 1915. http://query.nytimes.com/mem/archive-free/pdf?res=F00C11F93D5E11738DDDAE0894D9405B878DF1D3.

Wilson, Charles Reagan. "Cornbread." In *The New Encyclopedia of Southern*

Culture: Foodways, edited by John T. Edge, 152–54. Chapel Hill: University of North Carolina Press, 2007.

Wilson, Charles Reagan, and William R. Ferris, eds. *Encyclopedia of Southern Culture*. Chapel Hill: University of North Carolina Press, 1982.

Wilson, Mrs. Henry Lumpkin, Chair, Committee on Agriculture and Horticulture, Board of Women Managers, Cotton States and International Exposition. *Tested Recipe Cook Book*. Atlanta: Foote and Davies, 1895.

Windsor, Wallace. *Some Favorite Southern Recipes of the Duchess of Windsor, and an Introduction by Mrs. Franklin Delano Roosevelt*. New York: Charles Scribner's, 1942.

Witt, Doris. *Black Hunger: Food and the Politics of U.S. Identity*. New York: Oxford University Press, 1999.

Wolf, Bonny. *Talking with My Mouth Full: Crab Cakes, Bundt Cakes, and Other Kitchen Stories*. New York: St. Martin's, 2006.

Wolff, Alexander. "Fanfare for an Uncommon Man." *Sports Illustrated*, December 22, 1997. http://sportsillustrated.cnn.com/vault/article/magazine/MAG1011686/1/index.htm.

"Women's Institutes in North Carolina." *Journal of Home Economics* 1, no. 2 (1909): 161–63.

Wood, Peter H. *Black Majority: Negroes in Colonial South Carolina from 1670 through the Stono Rebellion*. New York: W. W. Norton, 1974.

Woodward, C. Vann. *Origins of the New South, 1877–1913*. 1951; reprint, Baton Rouge: Louisiana State University Press, 1971.

———. Review of *The American Slave: A Composite Autobiography*, by George P. Rawick. *American Historical Review* 79, no. 2 (1974): 474–75.

———, ed. *Mary Chesnut's Civil War*. New Haven: Yale University Press, 1981.

Wray, Esther. *Old-Time Recipes from the Nu-Wray Inn*. Burnsville, N.C.: R. T. Wray, n.d. (c. 1940s).

Wright, Anna. Interviewed by Mary Hicks, Wendell, N.C., August 17, 1937, WPA Slave Narrative Project, North Carolina Narratives, vol. 11, pt. 2, LOC, 423–24.

Wykle, Helen. "Fred Seely's Women: Early Entrepreneurship and Male Mentoring." Special Collections, D. H. Ramsey Library, University of North Carolina at Asheville. http://toto.lib.unca.edu/findingaids/mss/biltmore_industries/seely_women/default_seely_women.htm.

Yellin, Jean Fagin. *Harriet Jacobs: A Life*. New York: Basic Civitas Books, 2004.

Yentsch, Anne. *A Chesapeake Family and Their Slaves: A Study in Historical Archaeology*. New York: Cambridge University Press, 1994.

———. "Excavating the South's African American Food History." In *African American Foodways: Explorations of History and Culture*, edited by Anne Bower, 59–98. Urbana: University of Illinois Press, 2007.

Young, Andrew. Foreword to *Paschal: Living the Dream, an Inspirational Memoir*, by James Vaughn Paschal, xvii–xviii. New York: iUniverse, 2006.

Young, Ashley. "The Case of Lena Richard: Race, Ethnicity, and Cooking in New Orleans." Paper presented at the Duke University Graduate Student History Conference, "(Un)Bound Worlds: Rethinking Boundaries and Borders," Durham, March 16, 2012.

Yuhl, Stephanie E. *A Golden Haze of Memory: The Making of Historic Charleston*. Chapel Hill: University of North Carolina Press, 2005.

Zimmer, Anne Carter. *The Robert E. Lee Family Cooking and Housekeeping Book*. Chapel Hill: University of North Carolina Press, 1997.

Zimmerman, Steve. "Food in Films: A Star Is Born." *Gastronomica* (Spring 2009): 25–34.

Zinneman, Fred. *The Old South*. Directed by Fred Zinneman. Los Angeles: MGM Studios, 1940.

Zogry, Kenneth Joel. *The University's Living Room: A History of the Carolina Inn*. Raleigh, N.C.: Barefoot Press, 1999.

Index